BREWER'S
BRITISH
ROYALTY

David Williamson

CASSELL

For Rebecca

This edition first published in the UK 1996 by
Cassell
Wellington House
125 Strand
London
WC2R 0BB

Distributed in the United States by
Sterling Publishing Co. Inc.
387 Park Avenue South
New York, NY 10016
USA

British Library Cataloguing-in-Publication Data
A catalogue record for this book is available from the British Library

ISBN 0-304-34427-3

Typeset in Great Britain by Gem Graphics, Trenance, Cornwall
Printed and bound by in Great Britain by Mackays of Chatham Ltd

Contents

Introduction

THE AIM OF THIS BOOK is to provide a handy reference tool for readers of history and biography. It covers all aspects of British royalty from the ancient Britons to the present day. It has been specifically designed to cover the lesser known figures in rather more detail than is usually to be found, as well as the better known, for whom a wealth of material is generally available. For the entries on the various kings and queens I have drawn very heavily on my book *Kings and Queens of Britain*, recasting, expanding and updating where necessary.

While every care has been taken to ensure the accuracy of the thousands of facts contained in this book, it is inevitable that some errors will have crept in and that there may be some omissions. I shall be pleased to hear from any readers who spot such errors and omissions, so that these can be rectified in any future edition.

It remains for me to thank those who in one way or another have helped in the production of this work. First of all, Pamela Milne, who has struggled with my untidy and, I am sure, sometimes almost indecipherable manuscript and come up with an impeccable rendering on the word processor. Robert Horley has laid out the genealogical tables contained in the appendices with admirable clarity. Dr Morris Bierbrier very kindly made his hitherto unpublished study on royal bastards available to me. Others who have given help and encouragement have been Arthur Addington, Robert Golden, Charles Kidd and Brian North Lee.

DAVID WILLIAMSON

A note on the arrangement of the dictionary

Articles are arranged alphabetically on a word by word basis. Where there are articles on historical figures who share the same name, alphabetical order is determined, in the first instance, by any words or numbers that may follow the main name. Thus, for example, the article on 'Mary I' is followed by one on 'Mary II' and then by pieces on 'Mary Adelaide of Cambridge' and 'Mary of Gueldres'. Where words follow a comma, these are treated as being of secondary importance, although they are still arranged in alphabetical order. This means that 'Mary, Princess' comes before 'Mary, Princess Royal', which in turn comes before 'Mary, Queen of Scots'. The full sequence of 'Mary' articles consequently runs: 'Mary, Princess' ... 'Mary, Princess Royal' ... 'Mary, Queen of Scots' ... 'Mary I' ... 'Mary II' ... 'Mary Adelaide of Cambridge' ... 'Mary of Gueldres', and so on. People who share precisely the same name and title are listed chronologically and are numbered. For example, 'Isabella of France[1]', the wife of Edward II, is distinguished throughout the text from 'Isabella of France[2]', the wife of Richard II. Articles on particular dukedoms and earldoms tend to list title-holders in chronological order; it is always explicitly stated in the text when this is the case.

Cross-references are indicated by the use of SMALL CAPITALS. Readers are also advised to refer to the genealogical tables at the back of the dictionary.

A

Abdication The renunciation of a throne may be a voluntary act or a forced one. In the latter case it is more properly described as a 'deposition'. Several Saxon kings resigned their thrones voluntarily in order to make pilgrimages to Rome (*see* CAEDWALLA; INE). The first forced deposition of an English king after the Norman Conquest was that of RICHARD II on 29 September 1399. JAMES II, having fled the country following the landing (on 5 November) of his son-in-law William of Orange (WILLIAM III) on 11 December 1688 was on 28 January 1689 declared by Parliament to have abdicated thereby. EDWARD VIII abdicated on 10 December 1936 (*see* ABDICATION CRISIS).

In Scotland CONSTANTINE II abdicated in 942 to become Abbot of St Andrews. On 10 July 1296 John BALLIOL was forced to abdicate at Brechin, and his son Edward BALLIOL, a puppet king set up by England, finally surrendered all his claims to EDWARD III on 20 January 1356. MARY, QUEEN OF SCOTS was forced to abdicate in favour of her son JAMES VI on 24 July 1567.

In Wales OWAIN CYFEILIOG, Prince of Southern Powys, abdicated in favour of his son GWENWYNWYN in 1195 and retired to the monastery of Strata Marcella.

Abdication Crisis The constitutional crisis that culminated in December 1936 in the abdication of EDWARD VIII after he had been king for less than a year. When Edward VIII succeeded his father GEORGE V on 20 January 1936, he was a 41-year-old bachelor and had, since their first meeting on 10 January 1931, maintained a close relationship with Mrs Ernest A. Simpson, an American who had already married and divorced one husband and was now married to a second. As Prince of Wales Edward had enjoyed tremendous popularity but had also acquired the reputation of being a playboy. His father strongly disapproved of many of his activities and had expressed his feelings in his customary bluff and forthright manner:

After I am dead, the boy will ruin himself in 12 months.

I pray to God that my eldest son will never marry and have children, and that nothing will come between Bertie and Lilibet and the Throne.

In August 1936 Mrs Simpson accompanied the king and a few close friends on a Mediterranean cruise on the yacht *Nahlin*, which he had chartered. The following month the king gave a house-party for Mrs Simpson and some of her US friends at Balmoral, where she acted as hostess and even occupied the bedroom formerly used by the king's mother. On 27 October 1936 Mrs Simpson obtained a decree nisi of divorce on the grounds of her husband's adultery and this was set to be made absolute on 27 April 1937, just 15 days before the date fixed for the king's coronation.

The US press had already made much of the 'king's affair' but the British press so far had maintained a dignified silence, which they could not be expected to do for much longer. Edward was so infatuated and so certain of his personal popularity that he felt confident of being able to marry Mrs Simpson and make her queen, over-riding objections from the conservative establishment. The crisis derived from the fact that the government and leaders of the Church of England were convinced that neither the country nor the Commonwealth would accept a queen who had already been twice divorced. Queen Mary pleaded with her son to put his duty to his country first and to give up Mrs Simpson, but Edward was adamant that the marriage would take place as soon as Mrs Simpson was free. He reckoned, however, without his prime minister, Stanley Baldwin, his mother and other members of the royal family, the Archbishop of Canterbury, Cosmo Gordon Lang, and his own private secretary, Alexander Hardinge, all of whom were violently opposed to any such course of action. The necessity to choose between Mrs Simpson and the throne was impressed upon Edward. When Mrs Simpson began to appreciate the dilemma in which she was placing the king, she wavered and suggested in a letter that they break off their relationship:

> ... if I hurt you to this extent isn't it best for me to steal quietly away ... I can't help but feel you will have trouble in the House of Commons etc. and may be forced to go. I can't put you in that position ...

On 16 November 1936, however, the king informed Baldwin of his intention to marry Mrs Simpson as soon as she was free and that if it proved impossible for him to do so as king, he was prepared to abdicate. The story broke in the national press on 3 December and two days later Edward informed Baldwin of his decision to abdicate in favour of his brother the Duke of York. Attempts made by Winston Churchill and Lord Beaverbrook to persuade the king to retain the throne and to rally the country behind him fell on deaf ears (Beaverbrook reluctantly conceded, 'Our cock won't fight'). Baldwin reluctantly accepted the king's decision, wishing him happiness in his married life (upon which Edward, and then Baldwin himself, burst into tears). The instrument of abdication was signed at FORT BELVEDERE on 10 December and witnessed by the king's three brothers. It became law the following day when Parliament passed the Abdication Act. Fortified by a whisky and soda, Edward broadcast a dramatic farewell speech to the nation from WINDSOR CASTLE on 11 December. The following day he sailed away into exile on the destroyer *Fury*, while the same day the Duke of York was proclaimed king as GEORGE VI.

In later years, Edward consoled himself that at least his sacrifice had improved his chances of a lastingly happy marriage, confiding to other married friends, 'I do have a slight advantage over you. It helps in a pinch to be able to remind your bride that you gave up a throne for her.'

Accession Council An extraordinary meeting of the PRIVY COUNCIL, which is held as soon as possible after the accession of a new sovereign, so that he or she may take an oath to maintain the settlement of the Church of England, etc.

Accolade The ceremony by which the honour of knighthood is conferred. The candidate kneels before the sovereign (or person delegated to act for the sovereign), who taps him lightly on both shoulders with a drawn sword. Contrary to popular belief this takes place in silence, the words 'Arise, Sir X' not being used.

Act of Settlement On 12 June 1701 the fifth Parliament of WILLIAM III passed the Act of Settlement, whereby the succession to the crown was settled after Princess (later Queen) ANNE on SOPHIA, ELECTRESS OF HANOVER, the youngest daughter of ELIZABETH, QUEEN OF BOHEMIA, eldest daughter of JAMES I. Sophia was the nearest Protestant heir and the Act excluded all more senior descendants of CHARLES I and James I, they being Roman Catholics. The Electress Sophia did not live to become queen, dying shortly before Anne, who was succeeded by Sophia's son as GEORGE I.

Ada, Countess of Huntingdon (d.1178) The daughter of William de Warenne, 2nd Earl of Surrey, and Isabelle, daughter of Hugues the Great, Count of Vermandois, who married HENRY OF SCOTLAND, EARL OF HUNTINGDON, only surviving son and heir of DAVID I, in 1139. She had three sons (MALCOLM IV, WILLIAM 'THE LION' and David, Earl of Huntingdon), and three daughters (ADA OF SCOTLAND, COUNTESS OF HOLLAND, Margaret, Duchess of Brittany and Matilda, who died young in 1152). Her husband died before his father on 12 June 1152 and was buried in Kelso Abbey. Ada lived to see two of her sons become king and died in 1178 shortly after founding the nunnery of Haddington.

Ada of Scotland, Countess of Holland (d. after 1204) The eldest daughter of HENRY OF SCOTLAND, EARL OF HUNTINGDON, and ADA, COUNTESS OF HUNTINGDON, who married Floris III, Count of Holland, in 1161 and had four sons and four daughters. Her husband died at Antioch while taking part in the Third Crusade on 1 August 1190. Ada died on 11 January in a year after 1204. Her great-great-grandson, Floris V, Count of Holland (d.1296), was one of the 13 competitors for the crown of Scotland in 1291 (*see* SCOTTISH SUCCESSION).

Adda, King of Bernicia (d.*c*.568) The second son of IDA, founder of the kingdom of BERNICIA, who succeeded his elder brother GLAPPA in about 560 and reigned until about 568, when he was succeeded by his next brother Ethelric. No personal details of these early rulers are known.

Adela, Countess of Blois and Chartres (*c*.1062–1138) One of the six or so daughters of WILLIAM I and MATILDA OF FLANDERS, Adela was born in Normandy about 1062 and was married at Chartres in about 1081 to Stephen, Count of Blois and Chartres, eldest son of Thibaut III, Count of Blois and Champagne, and of Alix, daughter of Raoul III, Count of Crépy and Valois. Her husband joined the First Crusade and was killed at Ramleh on 19 May 1102. Adela acted as regent of the counties of Blois and Chartres during his absence and throughout the minority of her son Count Thibaut IV and proved herself a strong and capable ruler. She had five sons and several daughters. Her third son, STEPHEN, succeeded his uncle HENRY I as king of England, while her fourth son, Henry of Blois, became Bishop of Winchester. Adela became a nun in the Cluniac Priory of Marcigny-sur-Loire in about 1122 and died there on 8 March 1138. She was buried in the church of the Holy Trinity at Caen near her mother Queen Matilda.

Adelaide, Queen (1792–1849) The consort of WILLIAM IV, who was born Princess Adelaide Louisa Theresa Caroline Amelia of Saxe-Meiningen at Meiningen on 13 August 1792, the elder daughter and first child of Georg I, reigning Duke of Saxe-Meiningen, and Princess Louise Eleonore of Hohenlohe-Langenburg. Her father died when she was 11 and she, her younger sister Ida and her younger brother Bernhard, who succeeded as reigning duke, were brought up carefully by their capable mother, receiving a sound education. When the death of Princess CHARLOTTE OF WALES, made it necessary for the ageing bachelor sons of GEORGE III to seek brides, negotiations were begun for Adelaide's marriage to the Duke of Clarence, largely at the instigation of Queen CHARLOTTE. On 19 April 1818 the betrothal was announced in Meiningen, and a couple of months later Adelaide and her mother set out for England. They landed at Deal to a meagre reception and proceeded via Canterbury to London, where they arrived on the evening of 4 July 1818 and were lodged at Grillon's Hotel, where at a late hour the same evening they received unexpected visits from the Prince Regent and the prospective bridegroom, whom Adelaide now saw for the first time.

The wedding took place at KEW PALACE in the presence of the ailing Queen Charlotte and was a double ceremony, the Duke and Duchess of Kent, who had been married on the Continent, being remarried by the Anglican rite at the same time. The ceremony took place on the afternoon of 13 July 1818 and Adelaide wore silver tissue, Brussels lace and diamonds. A two-hour dinner followed, and the Duke and Duchess of Clarence and her mother returned to the duke's apartments in ST JAMES'S PALACE, where the wedding night was spent. Within a few weeks of their marriage, the duke's precarious financial position compelled the couple to take up residence in Hanover. It was there that Adelaide's first child was born prematurely on 29 March 1819, as a result of the mother having contracted pleurisy (her chest was always weak). The baby, a girl, was baptized Charlotte Augusta Louisa (*see* CHARLOTTE OF CLARENCE) and died the same day.

In spite of the great disparity in age and temperament, the Clarences' marriage was a happy one from the outset and was destined to remain so. By the late summer Adelaide was again pregnant and the couple decided to return to England for the birth. A round of family visits *en route* proved too much, however, and the Duchess suffered a miscarriage at Dunkirk in early September. After their return the couple resided partly at St James's and partly at Bushy Park, the official residence of the duke as Ranger of Bushy Park. Here Adelaide embarked on a scheme of redecorating and refurnishing and proved a kind stepmother to the six children of William and Mrs JORDAN who still remained at home. She also exerted a very good influence on her husband, curtailing his immoderate eating and drinking habits and his flamboyantly eccentric behaviour.

On 10 December 1820 Adelaide's second child was born at St James's Palace. Although premature, the baby princess was large and apparently healthy. Christened Elizabeth Georgiana Adelaide (*see* ELIZABETH GEORGIANA ADELAIDE OF CLARENCE), she lived for three months before dying of strangulated hernia (then an inoperable condition) on 4 March 1821. Adelaide wrote to her widowed sister-in-law the Duchess of Kent: 'My children are dead, but your child lives, and she is mine too.' Adelaide's fourth and last pregnancy ended when she miscarried male twins at Bushy Park on 23 April 1822. Thereafter, her maternal instincts found an outlet in the close and loving relationships she established and maintained throughout her life with her stepchildren and stepgrandchildren, with her sister Ida's children Prince Edward and Princess Louise of Saxe-Weimar, and with William's nieces and nephews, the future Queen VICTORIA and the Cambridge children.

In 1824 the Duke of Clarence asked his brother the king to provide him with better London accommodation and the result was the building of CLARENCE HOUSE, adjoining

St James's Palace. The death of the Duke of York in January 1827 made William the heir presumptive to the throne and the occasion was marked by Parliament voting an increase of £3000 to his annual allowance and a separate allowance of £6000 to Adelaide. At the same time the office of Lord High Admiral of England was revived in the sailor duke's favour, with an official residence at the Admiralty. However, his eccentric behaviour, culminating in his leading the Fleet to sea without informing the Admiralty or the king, led to his enforced resignation and the abolition of the office in 1828. The Clarences returned to Bushy Park and it was there on the morning of 26 June 1830 that they received the news of GEORGE IV's death at Windsor and William's accession to the throne. It was still early and the new king, who had been up and walking in the garden, returned to bed saying characteristically that he had 'never yet been in bed with a Queen!' The dramatic change in her status and all it entailed was not welcome to Adelaide, but the way in which she carried out her new duties drew admiration from all sides. Her task was a hard one as the king had no idea of etiquette and she often had to cover his many gaffes.

The state of the economy led to a drastic cutting down of the coronation ceremonial. It had been customary in previous reigns for the Queen Consort's crown to be set with hired jewels, but Adelaide disliked the idea of this and supplied her own jewels for her crown, paying for their setting. The coronation took place at WESTMINSTER ABBEY on 8 September 1831. For several years the queen went through a period of personal unpopularity occasioned by her Tory sympathies at a time when there was a Whig government and the unjustified belief that she interfered in politics during the agitation surrounding the passing of the Reform Bill. She also had to contend with the scurrilous rumour that her Lord Chamberlain, Earl Howe, was her lover. On one occasion when she was falsely reported to be pregnant, Lord Alvanley was said to have suggested the singing of the psalm 'Oh Lord *how* wonderful are Thy works' and the gossip was eagerly circulated by Whig ladies opposed to the queen's Tory sympathies.

William IV died at WINDSOR CASTLE on 20 June 1837 with his head on the queen's shoulder. She had nursed him devotedly for three weeks and, according to her sister-in-law Princess ELIZABETH, LANDGRAVINE OF HESSE-HOMBURG, 'for twelve days literally never took off her clothes'. Queen Victoria granted Adelaide's request to be allowed to stay at Windsor Castle until after the king's funeral and told her to take whatever she wished from the castle. All Adelaide chose were the silver cup from which she had fed the king during his last illness and the picture by Hayter of the FitzClarence family grouped round a bust of William with Mrs Jordan's portrait in the background, which Adelaide gave to her stepson Lord Augustus FITZCLARENCE.

Adelaide now became QUEEN DOWAGER, the first to bear that title since CATHERINE OF BRAGANZA. She received Marlborough House as her official residence and an income of £100,000 a year, of which it has been estimated she gave £20,000 annually to charitable works. She now resumed the simple lifestyle which she had always preferred. Her health was not good and she spent the first winter of her widowhood at St Leonards, accompanied by her sister-in-law Princess AUGUSTA. The following year she was advised to spend the winter in a warmer climate and sailed to Malta, where she founded the Anglican Cathedral of St Paul at Valletta at a cost of £10,000, laying the foundation stone on 20 March 1839. Adelaide was now immensely popular with the people as well as with the royal family and was present at Queen Victoria's wedding and at the christening of her goddaughter the Princess Royal, who received her second name in the Queen Dowager's honour. However, her health continued to be very precarious and she lost the use of one lung. In spite of this she spent much time travelling about the country visiting friends and was one of the first members of the royal family to use the railway.

In 1847 Adelaide again wintered abroad, sailing to Madeira and not returning to England until April 1848. She took a lease of Bentley Priory, near Stanmore, Middlesex, from the Marquess of Abercorn for three years and it was there that she died on 2 December 1849. She was buried after a simple funeral in accordance with her wishes in the Royal Tomb House beneath St George's Chapel, Windsor.

Queen Adelaide's gentle personality and general sweetness of character render her one of the most attractive queen consorts to have occupied the throne. Her contemporaries considered her plain, but her portraits seem to belie this. She was well educated, speaking and writing English, French and German fluently and was also an accomplished artist, illustrating her diaries and letters with charming sketches. The capital city of South Australia was named in Queen Adelaide's honour in 1836.

Adeliza of Louvain, Queen of England (*c.*1105–51) The second wife of HENRY I is variously named Adeliza, Adelicia or Alice by different authorities. She was the daughter of Godfrey the Bearded, Duke of Lower Lorraine, and his first wife Ida, daughter of Otto II, Count of Chiny, and was born at Louvain about 1105.

After losing his only legitimate son WILLIAM 'THE ATHELING' in the wreck of the White Ship in 1120, Henry I determined on marrying again in the hope of begetting a male heir. His choice fell on Adeliza, a contemporary of his daughter Matilda (*see* MATILDA, 'LADY OF THE ENGLISH', EMPRESS), and the marriage took place at Windsor on 29 January 1122. The new queen's coronation at WESTMINSTER ABBEY on 3 February following gave rise to an amusing incident. The king, robed and wearing his crown, had taken his seat on the throne to await his consort's crowning when the aged Archbishop of Canterbury, Ralph d'Escures, verging on senility, flew into a rage and, thinking that his right to place the crown on the sovereign's head had been infringed, snatched or knocked it off and was only pacified when allowed to replace it himself. Adeliza's coronation then proceeded without further incident.

Henry's hopes of further issue were not fulfilled and he died on 1 December 1135, leaving Adeliza his widow, still aged only about 30. She had received the Castle and Honour of Arundel as her dower and on her second marriage in 1138 conveyed these to William d'Aubigny, a man of roughly her own age, who thereby became Earl of Arundel. The QUEEN DOWAGER and her husband supported her stepdaughter Matilda's claim to the throne in opposition to STEPHEN. Adeliza's second marriage was as fruitful as her first had been barren. After bearing four sons and three daughters, however, she decided to retire to the convent of Afflighem in Flanders in 1150. She died there a year later and was buried on 23 April 1151. Her husband survived her for many years, dying at Waverley Abbey, Surrey, on 12 October 1176.

Adolphus *see* CAMBRIDGE.

Aedh, King of Scots (d.878) Aedh, nicknamed Whitefoot, was the second son of KENNETH I and succeeded his brother CONSTANTINE I in 877. In the following year he was killed at Strathallan by Giric, Regent

of Strathclyde. He left two sons, CONSTANTINE II, who succeeded as king of Scots in 900, and Donald, who was elected king of Strathclyde as DYFNWAL V in 908.

Aella, King of Deira (d.588) The first recorded king of DEIRA succeeded to power following the death of IDA in 559 or 560 according to the ANGLO-SAXON CHRONICLE, which states that he was the son of Yffi and derives his descent from WODEN through 10 generations. He was a pagan and nothing is known of his exploits. The Chronicle states that he reigned for 30 years, but places his death in 588, when he was succeeded by Ethelric, a son of Ida. Aella was the father of at least three children: EDWIN; a child who became the grandparent of St Hilda, Abbess of Whitby; and Acha, who married Ethelfrith, King of BERNICIA.

Aella, King of Sussex (*fl.*477–514) The founder of the kingdom of the South Saxons, who is recorded in the ANGLO-SAXON CHRONICLE as having come to Britain with his three sons, Cymen, Wlencing and CISSA, and three ships in 477 and to have landed at a place called Cymenesora, which has been identified as the Owers to the south of Selsey Bill. They 'there slew many Welsh [i.e. British] and drove some to flight into the wood which is called Andredesleag [Sussex Weald].' Further fighting is recorded in 485, and in 491 Aella and his son Cissa 'besieged Andredescester [the Roman fort of Anderida, Pevensey], and slew all the inhabitants.' Aella evidently carved out a very powerful kingdom for himself and is recorded as the first BRETWALDA or 'Ruler of Britain'. His son Cissa succeeded him as king of Sussex in about 514. It seems odd that the pedigree of such a doughty warrior king is nowhere recorded and also that the succession of the kings of Sussex has been lost, there being only a few fragmentary references to later kings until its final absorption by WESSEX.

Aescwine, King of Essex (d.587) According to Henry of Huntingdon, Aescwine was the first king of the East Saxons (Essex). He was the son of OFFA, KING OF ESSEX and eighth in descent from WODEN. He is credited with a remarkable reign of 60 years from 527 to 587, but nothing is recorded of his deeds or the establishment of his kingdom. He was succeeded by his son SLEDDA.

Aescwine, King of Wessex (d.676) Aescwine was the son and successor of CENFUS, KING OF WESSEX. The ANGLO-SAXON CHRONICLE records that he 'succeeded to the kingdom of

Wessex' in 674, but gives him no further mention. After a reign of about two years he was succeeded in 676 by his kinsman CENTWINE.

Affie The family nickname by which Queen Victoria's second son Alfred Ernest Albert, Duke of EDINBURGH was known.

Agatha[1] (c.1025–after 1066) The wife of Edward the Exile and mother of EDGAR ATHELING, who has been identified by Szabolcs de Vajay, the distinguished Hungarian historian, as the daughter of Liudolf, Margrave of West Friesland (c.1008–38) and his wife Gertrudis, who was probably daughter of Hugo IV of Egisheim, Count of Lower Alsace. Liudolf's mother, Gisela of Swabia, married three times and his father was her first husband Bruno, Count of Brunswick. Her second husband was Ernst of Babenberg, Duke of Swabia, and her third Conrad II the Salian, German king and Holy Roman Emperor, by whom she became the mother of the Emperor Heinrich III. This explains why Agatha is always referred to as a niece of the German Emperor 'Henry'.

Edward the Exile and his brother Edmund were living at the court of Yaroslav the Great, Prince of Kiev, when the German King Heinrich negotiated a match with his half-niece Agatha in an attempt to form an English-German-Russian alliance to combat Scandinavian attempts at expansion. Agatha journeyed to Russia and her marriage to Edward took place there in 1043 or early in 1044. Shortly thereafter the brothers, taking Agatha with them, joined another exile, Prince Andrew of Hungary, in his successful expedition to regain his kingdom. It seems likely that Edmund perished in the enterprise, but Edward and Agatha settled down in Hungary and it was there that their three children, Margaret (see MARGARET, ST, QUEEN OF SCOTS), Christina and EDGAR ATHELING were born between 1046 and 1056. In 1054 the childless EDWARD THE CONFESSOR decided to recall his half-nephew to England and despatched an embassy to that effect. After several delays the party finally arrived in England in 1056, but unfortunately Edward fell ill and died the following year, leaving Agatha his widow with three young children. Because of his tender years Edgar Atheling was not considered as a serious candidate for the English throne on the death of Edward the Confessor in 1066 and soon after the Norman Conquest Agatha and her children sought refuge in Scotland at the court of MALCOLM III. The king was a widower and in 1069 Agatha's elder daughter Margaret became his second wife. Agatha probably died in Scotland.

Agatha[2] One of the elder daughters of WILLIAM I THE CONQUEROR and MATILDA OF FLANDERS, who is said to have been betrothed to HAROLD II, who was over 30 years her senior. In the event she never married and probably died young.

Agincourt, Battle of Decisive battle fought at the village of Agincourt in northern France on St Crispin's Day, 25 October 1415. With an army of about 9000 men, HENRY V defeated a French army of about 60,000, thereby obtaining the kingdom of France. The French losses are said to have numbered 10,000 and the English about 1600. Henry credited his great victory to God's grace, denying before the battle that he must wish he had more men: '... I would not, even if I could, have a single man more than I do. For these I have here with me are God's people, whom He deigns to let me have at this time.' When the tide of battle threatened to run against the English, however, he decided not to rely wholly upon divine providence and ordered all prisoners to be put to death at once to prevent them rejoining the foe (a less than glorious incident that Shakespeare omitted in his depiction of the battle in his play *Henry V*).

Aidan, King of Dalriada (d.608) The son of GABRAN, king of DALRIADA and Lleian (who was probably the heiress of Manau Guotodin), he succeeded his cousin CONALL I as king of Dalriada in 574 and reigned until his death in 608, when he was succeeded by his son EOCHAID I.

Albany, Dukes of The holders of this title, which is derived from the parts of Scotland situated north of the Firths of Clyde and Forth, are here dealt with chronologically:

1. **Robert Stewart, Duke of Albany** (c.1339/40–1420) The third son of ROBERT II, KING OF SCOTS and his first wife Elizabeth Mure, who became virtual ruler of Scotland for some 32 years. By a dispensation dated 8 September 1361 he became the fourth husband of Margaret, Countess of Menteith in her own right, thereby becoming Earl of Menteith *jure uxoris*. By an indenture (30 March 1371) made at Perth with his sister-in-law Isobel, Countess of Fife (widow of his elder brother Walter), he also obtained the Earldom of Fife and was styled Earl of Fife and Menteith.

He was appointed custodian of Stirling Castle in 1373 and served as Great Chamberlain of Scotland from 1383 to 1407, during which period he led two successful raids into England. On 1 December 1388, his father Robert II being very aged and his elder brother the Earl of Carrick, later ROBERT III, being unable to take any active part in government through bodily infirmity, Robert was recognized as Guardian of the Realm by Parliament and remained in power until superseded when his nephew David (see ROTHESAY, DAVID STEWART, DUKE OF), son and heir of Robert III, was appointed King's Lieutenant on 27 January 1398/9. On 28 April 1398 David and Robert were created Dukes of Rothesay and Albany respectively, being the first two dukes created in Scotland. The Duke of Rothesay, having offended his father by some youthful escapade, was by the king's order arrested and delivered to his uncle for safe-keeping. He was confined in Falkland Castle and died there on 27 March 1402, probably from dysentery, although it was alleged his uncle had him starved to death. However, Albany was acquitted of that charge by Parliament on 16 May 1402. He assumed the office of King's Lieutenant and on the death of Robert III in 1406 was appointed regent of Scotland, his nephew JAMES I, KING OF SCOTS being a prisoner in England (Albany evidently made little attempt to secure his release). In 1417 Albany invaded England and attacked Berwick, but was repelled by the Dukes of Bedford and Exeter.

Albany's first wife, the Countess of Menteith, died in or before 1380, and he married secondly, by a dispensation dated 4 May 1380, Muriel, daughter of Sir William Keith, Marischal of Scotland and Margaret Fraser. She bore him three sons and several daughters.

The Duke of Albany died at Stirling Castle on 3 September 1420 at the then very great age of 80. He was buried in Dunfermline Abbey. His widow died shortly before Whitsunday (1 June) 1449. Albany was succeeded by his only son by his first wife, Murdoch Stewart (see below).

2. **Murdoch Stewart, 2nd Duke of Albany** (c.1362–1425) The son and successor of Robert Stewart, Duke of Albany (see above) and for many years Regent of Scotland. Appointed Justiciar North of the Forth on 2 April 1389, Murdoch Stewart was captured by the English after the Scottish defeat at Homildon Hill on 14 September

1402 and detained until 1415, when he was released in exchange for the Earl of Northumberland. In 1420 he succeeded his father both as Duke of Albany and as Regent and in 1424 successfully negotiated the release of his cousin JAMES I. However, the king 'was not slow in commencing the work of vengeance on the race by whom he had been long supplanted', and in a Parliament held at Perth on 25 March 1425 orders were issued for Albany's arrest. The Parliament adjourned to Stirling and at a trial held on 24 May 1425, Albany, his sons Walter and Alexander and his father-in-law the Earl of Lennox were found guilty and immediately beheaded on Castle Hill, Stirling. The Duke was buried in Blackfriars Church, Stirling, all his honours being forfeited on account of his attainder.

He had married (the settlement dated at Inchmurrin 17 February 1391/2) Isobel, eldest daughter and co-heiress of Duncan, Earl of Lennox (who shared his son-in-law's fate) and Helen Campbell. She survived all her children and died at Inchmurrin Castle, Loch Lomond, in 1458 or 1459. They had four sons (Robert, Master of Fife, who died unmarried shortly before July 1421; Sir Walter, Keeper of Dunbarton Castle, executed with his father, leaving no legitimate issue; Sir Alexander, executed with his father; and Sir James, who fled to England and thence to Ireland, where he died in 1451, leaving no legitimate issue) and one daughter (Isobel, who married Sir Walter Buchanan of that Ilk).

3. **Alexander Stewart, Duke of Albany** (c.1454–85) The second son of JAMES II, KING OF SCOTS, who was styled Lord of Annandale and Earl of March in an Act of Parliament dated 4 August 1455 and between that date and 3 July 1458 was created Duke of Albany. In 1479 his brother JAMES III had him and his other brother John (see MAR, JOHN STEWART, EARL OF) arrested on suspicion of conspiracy and imprisoned in Edinburgh Castle. Mar died in prison, but Albany managed to escape and make his way to France, where he was well received by Louis XI. In 1482 he went to England and made a treasonable agreement with EDWARD IV to assist him in invading Scotland and promising to surrender the town of Berwick and other border lands to England in return for being placed on the Scots throne, claiming the title Alexander IV. He joined the invasion, but soon became reconciled with his brother James III, was made Lieutenant-General of the Realm by Parliament

in December 1482 and was created Earl of Mar and Garioch in January 1482/3. He then changed sides again, surrendered Dunbar Castle to the English and joined the English forces over the border. For this he was attainted by Parliament on 27 June 1483.

Albany invaded Scotland with the Earl of Douglas and an English army, but suffered a total defeat at Lochmaben on 22 July 1483, making a narrow escape to France again. There he is said to have been accidentally killed by the splintering of a lance at a tournament in Paris in 1485. He was buried in the church of the Celestins there.

He had married first, Catherine, eldest daughter of William Sinclair, Earl of Orkney and Caithness, and his first wife Elizabeth, Dowager Countess of Buchan, daughter of Archibald Douglas, 4th Earl of Douglas. This marriage was dissolved on the ground of propinquity on 2 March 1477/8. They had three sons and one daughter. The eldest son, Alexander Stewart, was declared illegitimate by Act of Parliament on 13 November 1516. He became Bishop of Moray in 1527 and died in 1534. Alexander, Duke of Albany married secondly in France (the contract dated 16 January 1478/9) Anne, daughter of Bertrand de la Tour, Count of Boulogne and Auvergne, and Louise de la Tremoïlle, and by her had an only son John (*see below*). Anne married secondly (the contract dated 15 February 1486/7) Louis, Comte de la Chambre, by whom she had further issue, and died at La Rochette in Savoy on 13 October 1512, being buried in the Carmelite Monastery there.

4. **John Stewart, 2nd Duke of Albany** (*c*.1484–1536) The son of Alexander Stewart, Duke of Albany (*see above*), and a grandson of JAMES III, KING OF SCOTS, who was appointed Regent of Scotland during the minority of JAMES V. There is no Act of Parliament or other record in existence referring to his restoration to his father's forfeited dukedom, but it is thought that this probably occurred in 1505, the year in which he came of age and married. He arrived from France on 16 May 1515 and was proclaimed regent on 15 July following. By an Act of Parliament dated 13 November 1516 he was declared to be the only legitimate son of his father and heir to the throne after the king. His regency of eight years is described as 'efficient though spasmodic' by one authority and as 'profuse, weak and inefficient' by another. In the course of it he

spent several long absences in France, where he finally returned in 1523 on losing the governorship of Scotland and was appointed Governor of Bourbonnais, Auvergne, Forez and Beaujolais. In 1533 he escorted Catherine de'Medici from Florence to France to marry the Dauphin (later Henri II). He died at the Château de Mirefleur in Auvergne on 2 June 1536 and was buried in the chapel of Vic-le-Comte.

He had married (the contract dated 13 July 1505), his cousin Anne de la Tour, Countess of Boulogne and Auvergne, daughter of his maternal uncle Jean de la Tour, Count of Boulogne and Auvergne and Jeanne, daughter of Jean de Bourbon, Count of Vendôme. The Duchess of Albany, who was under 10 years of age at the time of her marriage, died without issue at the Château de St Saturin in June 1524. As Albany left no legitimate issue the dukedom became extinct on his death.

5. **Arthur (or Robert) Stewart, Duke of Albany** (1541–41) The second son of JAMES V and his second wife MARY OF GUISE, who was born at Falkland Castle on 24 April 1541 and styled Duke of Albany from birth. There are conflicting accounts as to whether his name was Arthur or Robert. He died eight days after his baptism and was buried at Holyrood.

6. **Henry Stewart, Duke of Albany** (1545–67) Title granted on 20 July 1565 to Henry Stewart, Lord DARNLEY, nine days before his marriage to MARY, QUEEN OF SCOTS. On his death on 10 February 1567 he was succeeded by his only son, James Stewart (*see below*).

7. **James Stewart (or Stuart), Duke of Rothesay and Albany** (1566–1625) The son of MARY, QUEEN OF SCOTS, who succeeded his mother as JAMES VI on 24 July 1567, when the Dukedom of Albany merged in the Crown.

8. **Charles Stewart (or Stuart), Duke of Albany** (1600–49) The second son of James VI (*see* JAMES I, KING OF ENGLAND), who was born at DUNFERMLINE on 19 November 1600 and created Lord Ardmannoch, Earl of Ross, Marquess of Ormond and Duke of Albany at his baptism on 23 December 1600. He was subsequently Duke of Cornwall, Duke of Rothesay, etc., Earl of Chester and Prince of Wales, and succeeded his father as CHARLES I on 27 March 1625, when the Dukedom of Albany and all his other honours merged in the Crown.

9. **James Stewart** (or **Stuart**), **Duke of Albany** (1633–1701) The third (but second surviving) son of CHARLES I, who was created Duke of Albany by his brother CHARLES II on 31 December 1660. He succeeded his brother as JAMES II on 6 February 1685, when the dukedom of Albany and all his other honours merged in the Crown.

10. *See* YORK for the creations of 1717, 1760 and 1784, when the title was combined with the dukedom of York.

11. **Charlotte Stuart, Duchess of Albany** (1753–89) The natural daughter of Prince Charles Edward STUART, titular Prince of Wales, generally known as the 'Young Pretender', and Clementina Maria Sophia WALKINSHAW, who was born at Liège and baptized there on 29 October 1753 as daughter of 'the noble seigneur William Johnston and the noble dame Charlotte Pitt'. Her first seven years were spent with her parents in France and Switzerland, but in July 1760 Clementina left the prince and took her daughter to Paris, where they passed the next 24 years as pensionnaires in various convents, living on the charity first of Charles's father and then of his brother, Cardinal YORK. During this period Charlotte maintained a desultory correspondence with her father, who divided his time between Rome and Florence, signing her letters by her childhood nickname of 'Pouponne'.

Towards the end of the 1770s Charlotte formed a liaison with Prince Ferdinand de Rohan, Archbishop of Bordeaux and later of Cambrai, a brother of the Cardinal de Rohan involved in the infamous diamond necklace scandal (he was duped by Jeanne, Countess de la Motte, into parting with a huge sum for an expensive necklace, thinking he could thus court the favour of Marie Antoinette – but the money disappeared and he was disgraced). Three children resulted from this relationship, Charlotte Maximilienne Amélie, born in 1780 or 1781, Victoire Adélaïde, born in 1782 or 1783, and Charles Edward Auguste Maximilien, later known as Count ROEHENSTART, born in 1784. In her later letters to her mother Charlotte always refers to Rohan as her *ami* and to the children as her *amies*.

On 30 March 1783 Prince Charles Edward executed an Act of Legitimization in Charlotte's favour and, as *de jure* sovereign, created her Duchess of Albany. A further Act of Legitimization and recognition of Charlotte's title was enacted at Paris by King Louis XVI of France on 7 September 1784. She was also granted the much-coveted privilege to sit on a *tabouret* (stool) in the presence of the French queen. The ageing and lonely Prince Charles Edward now desired to have his daughter at his side to solace his declining years and accordingly she left Paris a few months after the birth of her son and arrived in Florence on 4 October 1784. On St Andrew's Day, 30 November 1784, her father invested her with the Order of the THISTLE. Charlotte remained her father's close companion for the rest of his life, first in Florence and then in Rome, where she enjoyed a full social life.

A description of Charlotte as she appeared in 1786 is somewhat unflattering: 'a tall robust woman of a very dark complexion and coarse-grained skin with more masculine boldness than feminine modesty or elegance, but easy and unassuming in her manners and amply possessed of that volubility of tongue and that spirit of coquetry for which the women of the country where she was educated have at all times been particularly distinguished.' Charlotte's day-to-day life is chronicled in her letters to her mother, now in the Bodleian Library in Oxford. She was with her father when he died on 30 January 1788.

Charlotte's own health was now failing – she suffered from cancer of the liver – and her letters to her mother became more and more taken up with her symptoms. She was staying with her friend the Marchesa Giulia Lambertini-Bovio in Bologna when she died on 17 November 1789 at the age of 36. She was buried in the church of San Biagio there and a marble slab with a Latin inscription was placed over her grave. The church was destroyed by French troops in 1797 and it is not known whether Charlotte's coffin was among those later reburied in the Certosa. Her uncle Cardinal York, the Jacobite HENRY IX, took it upon himself to announce the death of his *reale nipote* (royal niece) to the courts of Europe. Her mother survived until 1802.

12. **Louise, Countess of Albany** (1752–1824) Princess Louise Maximilienne Caroline Emmanuele of Stolberg-Gedern was born at Mons on 20 September 1752 and baptized there on the same day. Her father was Colonel Prince Gustav Adolf of Stolberg-Gedern, a serving officer in the Imperial Army, and her mother Princess Elisabeth Philippine Claude de Hornes, second daughter and coheiress of Maximilien Emmanuel, Prince de Hornes, and Lady Charlotte Bruce, daughter of the 2nd Earl of Ailesbury. Louise was

only five years old when her father was killed at the battle of Leuthen on 5 December 1757, leaving his widow with four young daughters, of whom she was the eldest. The Empress Maria Theresa interested herself in the welfare of the fatherless girls of her faithful officer and was instrumental in obtaining the reception of Louise and her next sister Caroline Auguste as lady canonesses of the noble chapter of St Wandru at Mons in 1767. This was a very convenient method of providing impoverished young noblewomen with a livelihood, which they were free to leave at any time on an offer of marriage.

It was the younger sister who first found a husband in the person of the Marquis de la Jamaique, son and heir of the Duke of Berwick, head of the house of FitzJames, which owed its origin to the liaison of JAMES II with Arabella Churchill. The marriage took place in October 1771 and the event prompted the bridegroom's uncle the Duke of FitzJames to suggest Louise as a bride for Prince Charles Edward STUART, the Jacobite CHARLES III, who at the age of 51 was some 30 years older than his proposed bride. The negotiations proved successful and Louise and her mother travelled in secret to Paris, where the marriage by proxy took place on 28 March 1772. They continued their journey to Italy and met the prince at the house of Cardinal Marefoschi in Macerata on Good Friday, 14 April 1772. So eager was the bridegroom that he insisted on the marriage being solemnized immediately in spite of the day – a fact that Louise was later to say should have been an omen of the misery to come. On Easter Sunday the couple left for Rome to take up residence in the palace of the Santi Apostoli, but to Charles's chagrin he was denied many of the honours and privileges of a sovereign in exile which had been enjoyed by his father. In Rome Louise met her brother-in-law Cardinal YORK, who presented her with some magnificent wedding presents and duly recorded in his diary that he 'was pleased with her great charm of manner and her intellectual attainments, for which the excellent education given by her parents was responsible'.

In spite of the great disparity in age the marriage appeared to be going well at first. Charles continued to wrangle with the Papal Court for full recognition of his and his wife's royal titles, while she became a popular hostess and won the name of 'Queen of Hearts' from a young Swiss writer, Carl Victor Bonstetten, who described her as 'of medium height; fair with deep blue eyes; nose tip-tilted; and a lovely white English complexion'. In 1774 Pope Clement XIV refused Charles's request to be granted a royal tribune in St Peter's for the forthcoming Jubilee celebrations and in a fit of pique the prince uprooted himself with his wife and household and left Rome. They spent some months in the neighbourhood of Pisa and it was later rumoured, although quite without any foundation, that Louise had given birth to a son near Lucca in the summer of 1774 (see SOBIESKI-STUART). By the end of the year the couple settled in Florence, where Prince Corsini placed a villa at their disposal, and since the Grand Duke of Tuscany refused to recognize their claims they now assumed the title of Count and Countess of Albany.

Charles, a bitterly disappointed man, now began to eat and drink immoderately and to become jealous of his young wife's popularity, often humiliating her in public. In 1777 he bought a house and garden in Florence that were to become the Palazzo Stuart (now the Palazzo San Clemente) and moved in with his household. It was here that Louise first met the poet, Count Vittorio Alfieri (1749–1803), who soon became her lover. Charles became highly suspicious and in a drunken rage physically attacked his wife on 30 November 1780. Her screams brought servants to her aid and she was rescued from him. A few days later Louise contrived with the connivance of the Grand Duchess of Tuscany to take refuge in a convent, from which she refused to return to her husband. At the end of December, at the invitation of Pope Pius VI, Louise moved back to Rome and took up residence in the Ursuline convent on the Via Vittoria in the rooms once occupied by her mother-in-law Queen Clementina. She was adept at playing the injured innocent and received much sympathy and support from Cardinal York. After several years of attempting to persuade her to return, Charles finally agreed to a legal separation and signed and sealed a document to that effect at Florence on 3 April 1784.

Louise left Rome to take a cure at Baden in Switzerland and thence proceeded to a friend's property at Martinsburg, near Colmar, where she was reunited with Alfieri on 17 August 1784. Two months later the couple returned to Italy separately, she to Bologna and he to Pisa. The following April the Countess went to Paris to visit her sister the Duchess of Berwick and in September again joined Alfieri at Martinsburg. The scandal of their relationship reached the ears of Cardinal York at last in 1786 and brought an end to the fairly cordial relationship that Louise had hitherto enjoyed with him. When Prince Charles Edward died in 1788, Louise and Alfieri were living in Paris, where they remained, in spite of the Revolution, until 1791, when they decided to visit England. They spent three months in London and Louise, as Princess of Stolberg-Gedern, was presented to GEORGE III and Queen CHARLOTTE by her kinswoman the Countess of Ailesbury. Horace Walpole, who saw Louise a few days later, wrote: 'Madame d'Albany ... has not a rag of royalty about her. She has good eyes and teeth, but I think can have had no more beauty than remains, except youth. She is civil and easy, but German and ordinary.'

Louise and Alfieri returned to Paris via the Netherlands, but were obliged to leave France by the progress of the French Revolution and finally settled in Florence in November 1792. They were to remain there for the rest of their lives, the Countess presiding over a brilliant salon much frequented by English visitors. They became friends and patrons of the young French painter François-Xavier-Pascal Fabre (1766–1837), who was to be designated as Louise's heir. Alfieri died on 8 October 1803. He was buried in the church of Santa Croce, where Louise commissioned Antonio Canova to design his monument. The Countess continued to preside over her salon and adorn Florentine society until her own death on 29 January 1824 at the age of 71, 'to the grief of the City which she had selected for her residence' according to the *Gazzetta di Firenze*. She was buried in Santa Croce and her monument there, erected by Fabre and designed by Percier, bears the royal Stuart arms and those of Stolberg-Gedern surmounted by a royal crown and supported by the lion and unicorn. Louise was survived by her three sisters and also by her mother, who died a nonagenarian at Frankfort in 1826.

13. **Prince Leopold, Duke of Albany** (1853–84) Leopold George Duncan Albert, the eighth child and fourth and youngest son of Queen VICTORIA, was born at BUCKINGHAM PALACE on 7 April 1853. At the queen's request, chloroform was administered to her at his birth, setting a precedent and giving official approval to the relief of pain by anaesthesia, the ethics of which had been disputed by some sections of the Church (the queen described it as 'soothing, quiet-

ing and delightful beyond measure'). Almost from the start the little prince was described as 'very delicate' and it soon became apparent that he was a haemophiliac, suffering from a bleeding disease transmitted through a defective gene (*see* HAEMOPHILIA). In spite, or perhaps because of this, he was the least favourite child of his mother, who described him in one of her letters as 'a very common looking child, though amusing'. His delicate state of health curtailed many activities throughout his childhood and youth.

Prince Leopold was not in England when his father died, since it had been felt that his delicate health would benefit from wintering in the south of France. He had accordingly left for Cannes in the charge of Lieutenant-General Sir Edward Bowater, one of his mother's grooms-in-waiting. Sir Edward, a Waterloo veteran, was much too old for the task and fell ill and died soon after their arrival. However, it was decided that Prince Leopold should remain in Cannes throughout the winter. He was educated by private tutors and later attended Christ Church, Oxford, receiving an honourary DCL on 30 May 1876. He was elected FSA the same year. Prince Leopold was the recipient of several honours: KG 1869; KT 1871; PC 1874; GCSI 1877 and GCMG 1880. On 24 May 1881 he was created Baron Arklow, Earl of Clarence and Duke of Albany, and in 1882 was appointed Colonel in the Army and Honorary Colonel of the 3rd Seaforth Highlanders.

Prince Leopold was the most cultured and intellectual of the queen's sons and the only one to inherit his father's artistic tastes. He was elected President of the Royal Society of Literature in 1878 and Vice-President of the Society of Arts the following year. His marriage was carefully contrived by his mother and his eldest sister the Crown Princess of Prussia, the chosen bride being Princess Helena Frederica Augusta of Waldeck and Pyrmont, the third daughter of Georg Viktor, Prince of Waldeck and Pyrmont and his first wife Princess Helene Wilhelmine Henriette Pauline Marianne of Nassau. Her elder sister Emma had become the second wife of the elderly Willem III of the Netherlands in 1879 and the mother of the future Queen Wilhelmina in the following year.

The marriage of Prince Leopold took place at St George's Chapel, Windsor, on 27 April 1882. The newly married couple were given Claremont House, near Esher, as a residence but also spent much time with the queen. Their first child, Princess Alice (*see* ATHLONE, PRINCESS ALICE, COUNTESS OF), was born at WINDSOR CASTLE on 25 February 1883. Early in 1884 the Duchess of Albany was expecting her second child when her husband was advised once again on health grounds to winter at Cannes. Because of her condition she did not accompany him. In March, Prince Leopold stumbled and fell on a staircase, injuring his knee and setting up an internal haemorrhage. He appeared to be recovering when he suffered a cerebral haemorrhage and died suddenly on 28 March 1884, aged 30. He was buried in the ALBERT MEMORIAL CHAPEL at St George's Chapel, Windsor, where his mother erected an ornate tomb with a recumbent effigy. Four months after his death his widow gave birth to a son, who succeeded to his father's dukedom and other titles at birth and was later destined to succeed his uncle Alfred as the last reigning Duke of Saxe-Coburg and Gotha. The Duchess of Albany devoted the rest of her life to bringing up her children and took a keen interest in charitable work, particularly with the Deptford Mission in London's dockland. She died while on holiday at Hinterriss in the Tyrol on 1 September 1922 and at her own request was buried there.

14. **Prince Charles Edward, 2nd Duke of Albany** (1884–1954) The only son of Prince Leopold, Duke of Albany (*see above*) and Princess Helen of Waldeck and Pyrmont, who was born posthumously at Claremont House, Esher, on 19 July 1884 and baptized Leopold Charles Edward George Albert. He succeeded as 2nd Duke of Albany etc. at birth and was educated at Eton. In 1899, following the death of his cousin, Hereditary Prince Alfred of Saxe-Coburg and Gotha, he became heir presumptive to his uncle the reigning Duke Alfred (*see* EDINBURGH, PRINCE ALFRED, DUKE OF), his uncle Prince Arthur (*see* CONNAUGHT, PRINCE ARTHUR, DUKE OF) having renounced his rights of succession to the duchy. On Duke Alfred's death on 30 July 1900, Charles Edward became the reigning duke under the regency of Prince Ernst of Hohenlohe-Langenburg. He was sent to complete his education at the University of Bonn and took over the government of the duchy on his 21st birthday 19 July 1905. He had been created a KG in 1902 and was also the recipient of the Orders of the Black Eagle of Prussia, the Elephant of Denmark, the Seraphim of Sweden, St Hubert of Bavaria, St Cyril and St Methodius of Bulgaria, and others.

On 11 October 1905 he was married at Glücksburg to Victoria Adelheid Helene Luise Marie Friederike, eldest daughter of Friedrich Ferdinand, Duke of Schleswig-Holstein-Sonderburg-Glücksburg, and they had three sons and two daughters. As a German ruler, Charles Edward took up arms against his native country in the First World War and was therefore struck off the roll of the Order of the GARTER in 1915, deprived of his peerages by the Titles Deprivation Act of 8 November 1917 and removed from the Roll of Peers by Order in Council on 28 March 1919. He abdicated the throne of Saxe-Coburg and Gotha on 14 November 1918, and died at Coburg on 6 March 1954. His widow (who was known in the family as 'Dick') died on 3 October 1970. The right to petition for restoration of the Dukedom of Albany and other British peerages is now vested in Charles Edward's great-grandson, Prince Hubertus Richard Ernst Leopold, who was born on 8 December 1961.

Albert, Prince Consort (1819–61) The adored husband of Queen VICTORIA, who was born Prince Francis Charles Augustus Albert Emmanuel of Saxe-Coburg and Gotha at Schloss Rosenau, near Coburg, on 26 August 1819. He was the second son of the reigning Duke Ernest I of Saxe-Coburg and Gotha (1784–1844) and his first wife Princess Louise of Saxe-Gotha (1800–31). His parents were of completely different temperaments and drifted apart soon after Albert's birth. Duke Ernest was a notorious womanizer and his young wife, too, sought consolation elsewhere. The result was a formal separation in 1824, followed by a divorce in 1826. Louise then married Baron Alexander von Hanstein, but it was not until after her death in August 1831 that Duke Ernest remarried. His second wife was his own niece, Duchess Marie of Württemberg (1799–1860), by whom he had no children.

Albert and his elder brother Ernest were thus deprived of a mother's love at an early age, but their grandmother, the Dowager Duchess of Saxe-Saalfeld-Coburg, and stepgrandmother, the Dowager Duchess of Saxe-Gotha, both lavished affection on them and in 1823 they acquired a greatly caring tutor in the person of 'Rath' (or Councillor) Florschütz. The two princes grew up together at Rosenau, but developed very differently, Ernest becoming a womanizer like their father, while Albert was far more serious minded with a genuine interest in the arts and sciences. He was the better looking of the two and was said to bear a very strong resemblance to his mother. The Coburg family had strong ties with England since the boys' uncle Prince LEOPOLD had married Princess CHARLOTTE OF WALES, the only daughter of the Prince Regent (GEORGE IV), who died in childbirth a year after their marriage, while their aunt VICTORIA had married Prince Edward, Duke of KENT, and become the mother of the future Queen Victoria in May 1819.

Plans for the eventual marriage of Albert and Victoria were laid very early in their childhood, their grandmother the Dowager Duchess of Saxe-Coburg first hinting at it in letters to her daughter the Duchess of Kent in 1821 and the idea then being taken up and fostered by their uncle Leopold, who became the first king of the Belgians in 1831. The cousins met for the first time when their father took Ernest and Albert on a visit to England in 1836. Victoria confided to 'Uncle Leopold' in a letter about Albert 'how delighted I am with him, and [how] much I like him in every way. He possesses every quality that could be desired to make me perfectly happy.' Albert, on the other hand, reported laconically that they 'were much pleased with each other'. The two young princes completed their studies under private tutors in Brussels and then at Bonn University, also touring in Italy, Switzerland and Austria. They left Bonn in 1838 and Ernest then joined the Saxon army in Dresden, while Albert embarked on a much fuller tour of Italy, during which he was accompanied by Baron Stockmar and Lieutenant Francis Seymour, who at King Leopold's request was seconded from the British army. It was during this lengthy sojourn in Italy that Albert developed and cultivated his lifelong interest in Italian art and architecture.

In October 1839, Ernest and Albert, again reunited, set out once more for England, arriving at WINDSOR CASTLE on the 10th, ahead of their luggage, so that they were unable to join the household at dinner for want of evening clothes. Five days later Victoria sent for Albert to come and see her privately and formally asked him to marry her. With some perception, Albert wrote to his stepmother 'my future position will have its dark sides, and the sky will not always be blue and unclouded'.

Queen Victoria announced her engagement to the PRIVY COUNCIL on 23 November 1839, when Greville, the Clerk to the Council, recorded that 'her hands trembled so excessively that I wonder she was able to read the paper which she held'. Albert was granted the style of Royal Highness by Letters Patent on 6 February, the day of his arrival in England, and the marriage took place at the Chapel Royal, ST JAMES'S PALACE, on 10 February 1840, both the bride and the bridegroom, who had barely recovered from seasickness after a rough crossing four days previously, wearing the collar of the Order of the GARTER (with which Albert had been invested at Coburg by a special Garter Mission in January). The couple left for their honeymoon at Windsor at four o'clock in the afternoon, arriving after nightfall at a town brightly illuminated. The ecstatic bride wrote to King Leopold that Albert 'is an angel ... To look in those dear eyes, and that dear sunny face, is enough to make me adore him', but the Duchess of Bedford, who was in attendance, reported that while the queen was 'excessively in love' Albert was 'not a bit with her' and gave the impression 'of not being happy'.

The queen and her husband it has been said 'came to understand each other slowly'. Soon after their marriage Albert wrote to a friend in Germany: 'I am only the husband and not the master in the house.' Gradually this position was to alter and Albert's influence on the queen grew stronger, until eventually they worked every morning with their desks side by side and she began to defer to him on every issue.

Towards the end of 1843 the royal couple, by now the parents of three children, began to feel the need to acquire a residence which could be their very own. The Prime Minister, Sir Robert Peel, was consulted and suggested they consider a home on the Isle of Wight. Queen Victoria had happy memories of the island from two childhood visits and received the idea with enthusiasm. Prince Albert had also been very taken with the island in the course of a cruise the pair had made that summer and, ever one for drawing associations, found that its seascapes reminded him of those around Naples. After prolonged negotiations, the Osborne estate on the northern side of the island was acquired from Lady Isabella Blackford, at first at a rental of £1000 per annum and then by outright purchase at an agreed sum of £27,814.18s.5d. The estate was augmented by the leasehold purchase of more land from Winchester College for £18,000 and annual rent charges of

£113.16s.0d. to the College and 13s.4d. to the Bishop of Winchester. Albert was now able to give full rein to his architectural flair. With the aid of the master-builder Thomas Cubitt he oversaw the construction of an elegant Italianate palace overlooking the Solent (*see* OSBORNE HOUSE).

A few years later another private royal residence was acquired, BALMORAL CASTLE on Deeside, where Prince Albert was able to exercise his architectural talents once again in the building of a new castle in Scottish baronial style. Osborne and Balmoral were to become and to remain Queen Victoria's favourite abodes for the rest of her long life.

Prince Albert had become President of the Society of Arts in 1843 and in 1850 became Chairman of the Royal Commission appointed to plan the Great Exhibition of international manufactures and arts, which took place in 1851 in the Crystal Palace designed by Joseph Paxton and erected in Hyde Park. It was to be the greatest achievement of the prince's life and was opened by Queen Victoria on 1 May 1851, remaining open until 15 October and making a surplus profit of £180,000 to be expended on Albert's next project, the creation of the South Kensington museums, institutions and colleges of music and art, which occupied most of his time and attention for the rest of his life. He also took a keen interest in agricultural matters, commissioning the design of the Home Farm at Windsor, where his prize-winning Windsor pigs were bred.

On 26 June 1857 Albert was created Prince Consort by Letters Patent, an honour that conferred a legal status that he had hitherto lacked and that gave him official precedence immediately after his wife. In January 1858 he gave away his eldest and favourite daughter VICTORIA, PRINCESS ROYAL, when she married Prince Frederick William of Prussia and a year later travelled to Potsdam to visit her after the birth of her first child.

The strain of life with Queen Victoria and the care spent in bringing up a large family took its toll on Albert, and at 40 he had lost much of his hair and had the appearance of a much older man. 'Papa works too hard, [and] wears himself out by all he does,' the queen wrote to her daughter. The death of Victoria's mother the Duchess of Kent in March 1861 added to Albert's burdens, since she had appointed him her sole executor and her affairs needed much putting in order.

In November Albert travelled to Cambridge in very inclement weather to visit his son the Prince of Wales (*see* EDWARD VII), who had recently been involved in an entanglement with an actress. On his return he set about re-drafting a despatch to the British Minister in Washington concerning the high-handed behaviour of the Federal Government in taking Confederate officers from a British ship. The original draft had been so badly worded that it practically constituted a declaration of war. Exhausted by his efforts, the prince went down with a 'low fever', a term synonymous with typhoid. His mind rambled and he was racked with rheumatic pains. After several days of suffering the end came at 10.45 pm on 14 December 1861. The prince died in the same room at Windsor Castle in which George IV and WILLIAM IV had both died. The queen immediately gave way to an extravagant display of grief and many feared she would go mad, as GEORGE III had done. At the moment of Albert's death, in the words of Lytton Strachey: 'She shrieked – one long wild shriek that rang through the horror-stricken Castle – and understood that she had lost him for ever.' She confided to a friend that she considered suicide, but relented and adopted 'Still Endure' as her motto. She never appeared out of mourning for the rest of her life. Albert's funeral took place at St George's Chapel, Windsor, on the morning of Monday, 23 December 1861. His coffin was at first deposited in the vault beneath the chapel but was transferred to the Royal Mausoleum that Queen Victoria had constructed in the grounds of FROGMORE HOUSE on 18 March 1862. She was to join him there almost 40 years later.

Although the cause of Albert's death is generally attributed to typhoid, the severe 'rheumatic' pains that he had suffered for many years have led to speculation that he may have suffered from cancer or some other wasting disease.

Albert Edward, Prince of Wales *see* EDWARD VII.

Albert Memorial The great Gothic memorial to ALBERT, PRINCE CONSORT erected to his memory by Queen VICTORIA in Hyde Park, London (close to another memorial to Albert, the Royal Albert Hall). Designed by George Gilbert Scott, the memorial cost £120,000. William Gladstone protested at the amount required for the construction of the memorial and the project was consequently delayed, thus intensifying Victoria's dislike for her prime minister. Loved or loathed by successive generations, according to changing tastes, the monument fell into a serious state of disrepair and extensive restoration was begun in the 1990s.

Albert Memorial Chapel A chapel at the east end of St George's Chapel, WINDSOR, restored by Queen VICTORIA. It contains ALBERT's tomb effigy (although he is not buried there) and the tombs of Prince Leopold, Duke of ALBANY, and Prince Albert Victor, Duke of CLARENCE.

Albert Victor, Duke of Clarence *see* CLARENCE, ALBERT VICTOR, DUKE OF.

Albestroff, Countess of The title used by Clementina WALKINSHAW, the mistress of Prince Charles Edward STUART ('Bonnie Prince Charlie') and mother of Charlotte, Duchess of ALBANY. Accounts vary as to whether it was a genuine title of the Holy Roman Empire (no record of such a creation having been discovered) or merely an assumed *nom de guerre*.

Albion The archaic name for Britain, derived from Latin and referring to the white cliffs of the south coast. To the French 'perfidious Albion' has long been a derogatory term.

Alchfrith (*fl.c.*654–64) The son of OSWY, KING OF NORTHUMBRIA and his first wife Riemmelth, who was associate king with his father in DEIRA and fought and defeated the Mercians with him in 655. He later sided with the Roman as opposed to the Celtic church. He married Cyneburg, daughter of PENDA, KING OF MERCIA, and died before his father, leaving a son OSRIC, who later reigned as king of Northumbria.

Aldfrith, King of Northumbria (d.704) The illegitimate son of OSWY, KING OF NORTH-UMBRIA and his mistress Fina, who succeeded his half-brother EGFRITH, KING OF NORTHUMBRIA in 685. He is noted for his learning and piety and for his championship of the Celtic church. He married Cuthburga, sister of INE, KING OF WESSEX, and died in 704, when he was succeeded by his son OSRED I.

Aldwulf, King of East Anglia (d.713) The son of King ETHELHERE and Hereswith of DEIRA, who separated from his father and became a nun in or before 650, was probably still a child when his father was killed in November 654. The throne of EAST ANGLIA therefore passed to his uncle ETHELWOLD, on whose death Aldwulf succeeded in 663 or 664. According to BEDE Aldwulf could remember seeing (when a boy) the heathen temple in which his predecessors REDWALD and EARPWALD had offered human sacrifices before East Anglia accepted Christianity. The name of Aldwulf's wife has not been preserved, but he had several children: Elric, who is probably identical with his successor ALFWOLD; and three daughters who became abbesses.

Alexander, Prince of Scotland (1264–84) The elder son of ALEXANDER III and MAR-GARET OF ENGLAND, who was born at Jedburgh on 21 January 1264. He was married at Roxburgh on 15 November 1282 to Marguerite, daughter of Guy de Dampierre, Count of Flanders. There were no children and he died before his father at Lindores Abbey in Fife on 28 January 1284, being buried at DUNFERMLINE. His widow married secondly, about 1290, Renaud I, Count of Gueldres, and died in 1330.

Alexander I (the Fierce), King of Scots (*c.*1077–1124) The eighth son of MALCOLM III and the fifth by his second wife St MAR-GARET, who succeeded his brother EDGAR as king of Scots in January 1107. He gained his epithet 'the Fierce' through his defeat of the men of Moray and Mearns about 1115 and founded a church at Scone in thanksgiving for the victory. Towards the end of his reign he entered into a dispute concerning the investiture of the see of St Andrews, maintaining that this lay with the Pope or Archbishop of Canterbury rather than with the Archbishop of York, but died before the matter was resolved.

Alexander married Sibylla, natural daughter of HENRY I, KING OF ENGLAND by Sibylla Corbet. There was no issue of the marriage and she predeceased him. Alex-ander himself died at Stirling on 23 April 1124 and was buried in DUNFERMLINE Abbey. He left a natural son, Malcolm, who made two ineffectual attempts to gain the throne from DAVID I, Alexander's brother and successor.

Alexander II (the Peaceful), King of Scots (1198–1249) The only son of WILLIAM 'THE LION', KING OF SCOTS and his wife ERMEN-GARDE DE BEAUMONT, who was born at Haddington on 24 August 1198. He was knighted by JOHN, KING OF ENGLAND in 1212 and succeeded his father on 4 December 1214, being crowned at Scone two days later by William Malvoisine, Bishop of St Andrews. He took the side of the Barons against King John and besieged Norham Castle in Northumberland in 1215. Reciprocal invasions of the two kingdoms were finally resolved when a treaty with HENRY III was concluded in 1219. Two years later Alexander was married at York to Henry's sister Joan (*see* JOAN, QUEEN OF SCOTS[1]). Alexander continued his warlike campaigns, reducing Argyle and Caithness in 1222 and putting down insurrections in 1224 and 1228. Captured rebels in Caithness were punished by having a hand and a foot cut off. In 1230 he successfully repulsed an attempted Norse invasion. Queen Joan died childless in 1238, and on 15 May 1239 Alexander concluded a second marriage at Roxburgh to Marie de Coucy, who bore him his only son and eventual successor, ALEXANDER III. A further dispute with England was ended by the Treaty of Newcastle in 1244. In 1249 Alexander mounted a campaign to wrest the Hebrides from Norway, but he was taken ill with fever and died on the island of Kerrera in the Firth of Lorne on 8 July 1249. He was buried in Melrose Abbey. In addition to his son and successor, Alexander left a natural daughter, Marjorie, who married Alan Durward and had a daughter Ermengarde, whose son Nicholas de Soules was one of the competitors for the crown in 1291 (*see* SCOTTISH SUCCESSION).

Alexander III, King of Scots (1241–86) The only son of ALEXANDER II and his second wife Marie de Coucy, who was born at Roxburgh on 4 September 1241 and succeeded his father at the age of seven in July 1249. In spite of his tender years he was crowned at SCONE by David de Bernham, Bishop of St Andrews, on 13 July 1249. Alexander was knighted at York by HENRY III, KING OF ENGLAND on 25 December 1251 and the following day was married to that monarch's eldest daughter MARGARET OF ENGLAND, his senior by a year. The chief power in the land during Alexander's minority was Walter Comyn, Earl of Menteith, but in 1255 Henry III, as overlord, replaced him by 15 nobles of his choice. Comyn regained power in 1257 but died the next year, when a new regency of two parties of nobility held sway until Alexander took over the reins of government. In 1261 he resumed and successfully completed his father's conquest of the Hebrides. In 1264 he aided his father-in-law Henry III in his struggle against the barons. Queen Margaret died in 1275 and Alexander was married for a second time at Jedburgh on 14 October 1285, to YOLANDE OF DREUX. On a stormy night, 19 March 1286, Alexander was riding between Burntisland and Kinghorn in Fife when he was killed in a fall from

his horse. He was buried in DUNFERMLINE Abbey. Alexander had two sons and one daughter by his first wife, but no children by his second.

Alexandra, Queen (1844–1925) The consort of EDWARD VII, who was born at the Yellow Palace, Copenhagen, on 1 December 1844 as Princess Alexandra Caroline Mary Charlotte Louisa Julia of Schleswig-Holstein-Sonderburg-Glücksburg. She bore that long and unwieldy title until her father was designated heir to the Danish throne in 1853, eventually becoming Christian IX of Denmark in 1863, eight months after his eldest daughter had become Princess of Wales. Alexandra's mother was Princess Louise Wilhelmina Frederica Caroline Augusta Julia of Hesse-Cassel.

Alexandra was brought up very simply in Copenhagen, sharing an attic bedroom with her sister Dagmar (known in the family as 'Minnie' and later to become, under the name of Maria Feodorovna, the consort of Emperor Alexander III of Russia and mother of the Emperor Nicholas II), where they made and mended many of their own clothes. As girls they often dressed alike and could almost have been taken for twins.

The early tendencies towards profligacy demonstrated by the future Edward VII as Prince of Wales caused his parents to consider an early marriage advisable and Princess Alexandra was the candidate favoured by the Prince Consort, ALBERT. Unfortunately, he did not live to see the marriage take place. The prospective bride and her parents duly arrived in England and the marriage took place in St George's Chapel, WINDSOR, on 10 March 1863. The widowed Queen VICTORIA witnessed the ceremony from the Royal Closet, the small latticed gallery on the north side of the sanctuary.

The new Princess of Wales, hailed as the 'Sea-King's Daughter from over the sea', was described as one of Britain's most beautiful queens, but was also criticized as one of the most superficial and self-centred. Queen Victoria, while aware of her son's failings, once confided that she was 'not worth the price we paid for her', though she later conceded that 'her lot is not an easy one'. Edward himself found his wife sexually frigid and continued to form sexual liaisons outside the marriage and to pursue an active social life without her – indeed, when she was in labour with their third child he went to Windsor races and it took three telegrams before he reluctantly returned home to be by her side. Alexandra forced herself to accept her husband's infidelities without protest over the years and it was generally agreed that for all his profligacy, Edward loved her more than any of his mistresses. When Edward was dying she even went to the extent of summoning his last mistress, Mrs KEPPEL, so that she might say goodbye to him. When he finally died, Alexandra was deeply distressed, but restored her humour with the laconic remark: 'Now at least I know where he is.' Outside the royal family, she was widely popular on account of her beauty and elegance, although she was greatly handicapped by progressive deafness (an hereditary defect). She also had a limp as a result of complications following her first pregnancy and this came to be copied by fashionable ladies (the so-called 'Alexandra glide').

Alexandra proved a violently possessive mother, demanding the complete devotion of her children, who were brought up always to address her as 'Motherdear'. The effect on her eldest son, Prince Albert Victor (known as 'Eddy'), later Duke of CLARENCE, was disastrous. He was of limited intellect, almost ineducable, and when he reached young manhood his dandyism earned him the nickname of 'Prince Collar and Cuffs'. His death from pneumonia caused his mother inexpressible grief, but relief to those who were aware of his shortcomings. His betrothed, Princess MARY OF TECK, was passed on as fiancée to his younger brother George, a far more stable character, and was to become in fullness of time the stately Queen Mary.

Alexandra's three daughters were all considered excessively plain in contrast to their mother. She was as possessive with them as with their brothers, but the eldest and the youngest managed to escape into marriage, the middle one, VICTORIA, becoming her mother's constant companion and living out a spinsterly existence until Alexandra's death at last enabled her to set up her own establishment for the last 10 years of her life.

Both as princess and as queen, Alexandra was notoriously unpunctual – to such an extent that the king had to tell her she would not be crowned if she was not ready in time on their coronation day. As queen mother she caused consternation by trying to insist that she should take precedence over her daughter-in-law the queen consort. In this she was encouraged by her sister Minnie, now the Dowager Empress Maria Feodorovna of Russia, who assured her (accurately, as it happened) that this was the protocol of the Russian court. GEORGE V had to be quite firm with 'Motherdear' for once.

Queen Alexandra was the first queen consort since the Middle Ages to be made a Lady of the Order of the GARTER. GEORGE III had contemplated conferring it on Queen CHARLOTTE, but for some reason had never done so. Now its conferment on Alexandra created a precedent which has been followed ever since.

Towards the end of her life the queen became almost completely deaf and suffered from mild senile dementia. She resided chiefly at SANDRINGHAM HOUSE, Norfolk, which Edward VII had purchased as Prince of Wales, and in her drives about the countryside (the faithful Princess Victoria always in attendance) would graciously wave and bow to the cows in the fields.

Queen Alexandra died at Sandringham House on 20 November 1925, 11 days short of her 81st birthday. She had attained a greater age than any previous queen consort with the possible exception of ELEANOR OF AQUITAINE. Her body was brought to London and the impressive cortège passed through the streets in a snowstorm, recorded forever on archive film. She was buried in St George's Chapel, Windsor, her coffin resting on the floor of the ALBERT MEMORIAL CHAPEL near the tomb of her beloved son Eddy until the tomb she was to share with Edward VII on the south side of the sanctuary had been made ready.

Alexandra of Kent, Princess (1936–) The only daughter and second child of Prince George, Duke of KENT (fourth son of GEORGE V) and Princess Marina of Greece and Denmark, who was born at 3 Belgrave Square, London, on Christmas Day 1936 and was baptized Alexandra Helen Elizabeth Olga Christabel. She was educated at Heathfield School and in Paris and also took a short nursing course at the Great Ormond Street Hospital for Sick Children. Appointed Dame Grand Cross of the ROYAL VICTORIAN ORDER in 1960, she has also been the recipient of many foreign orders. She is Colonel-in-Chief of several regiments and is president or patron of several charitable organizations, including the ALEXANDRA ROSE DAY and Queen Alexandra's Royal Naval Nursing Service. She has been Chancellor of the University of Lancaster since 1964 and of the University of Mauritius since 1974, and holds a number of honorary degrees.

Princess Alexandra married at WESTMINSTER ABBEY on 24 April 1963, the Hon.

Angus James Bruce Ogilvy, second son of the 12th Earl of Airlie. The ceremony was attended by 2000 guests and witnessed by a television audience of some 200 million people. Princess ANNE served as her chief bridesmaid. Ogilvy was invested Knight Commander of the Royal Victorian Order in 1989. Their son James Robert Bruce Ogilvy was born on 29 February 1964 and was married on 30 July 1988 to Julia Caroline Rawlinson, by whom he has a daughter Flora Alexandra, born on 15 December 1994. Their daughter Marina Victoria Alexandra Ogilvy was born on 31 July 1966 and was married on 2 February 1990 to a photographer, Paul Julian Mowat, by whom she has two children, Zenouska May, born on 26 May 1990, and Christian Alexander, born on 4 June 1993. The announcement that Marina Ogilvy was pregnant by Paul Mowatt prior to any plans for marriage threatened a rift with her parents, but they were later reconciled and the couple married before the baby was born.

Alexandra Rose Day The charity founded by Queen ALEXANDRA in 1912. Each year on the third Tuesday in June, it raises funds for the elderly, sick, disabled and young by, among other things, the sale of artificial pink briar roses.

Alfonso, Earl of Chester (1273–84) The third son and ninth child of EDWARD I and his first wife ELEANOR OF CASTILE, who was born at Bayonne in Gascony on 24 November 1273 and baptized by the Bishop of Exeter, receiving his name in honour of his half-uncle and godfather King Alfonso X of Castile. Since his two elder brothers were already dead, he held the position of heir apparent to the throne throughout his short life. He was brought to London in June 1274. In 1284 he is said to have been designated Earl of Chester. He died aged 10 at WINDSOR CASTLE on 19 August 1284 and was buried in WESTMINSTER ABBEY near the shrine of EDWARD THE CONFESSOR on 26 or 28 August 1284. It is interesting to speculate that had Alfonso lived to inherit the throne, England might have had a number of kings bearing his name.

Alfred, Atheling (c.1003–37) The eighth son of ETHELRED II THE UNREADY and the elder by his second wife EMMA OF NORMANDY. Exiled to Normandy while still very young, he imprudently returned to England after the death of his stepfather King CANUTE, but was captured and blinded at the order of his stepbrother HAROLD I HAREFOOT. He

died soon afterwards at Ely on 5 February 1037. According to the ANGLO-SAXON CHRONICLE his followers were treated with similar harshness:

> Some of them were sold for money, some cruelly murdered,
> Some of them were put in chains, and some of them were blinded,
> Some were mutilated and some were scalped ...

Alfred, Prince (1780–2) The ninth and youngest son (and 14th child) of GEORGE III and Queen CHARLOTTE, who was born at Windsor Castle on 22 September 1780. He was handicapped and delicate from birth, perhaps a 'blue baby', and died at Windsor on 20 August 1782, one month short of his second birthday. Prince Alfred was buried in the royal vault at Westminster Abbey, but transferred to the new Royal Tomb House at St George's Chapel, Windsor, soon after his father's burial there in 1820.

Alfred the Great, King of the West Saxons (849?–899) The youngest son of King ETHELWULF and his first wife OSBURGA, who was born at the royal manor of Wantage in Berkshire (now relocated in Oxfordshire) in 849, according to his biographer Asser, the Welsh-born Bishop of Sherborne. As he is elsewhere stated to have been 23 years old at his accession in April 871, however, a date of 847 or 848 seems more likely and would accord better with known events in his later life.

Alfred's great love of learning is said to have been inculcated by his mother, who showed her sons a beautifully illuminated book of poetry and promised to give it to the first one to learn to read it. In spite of his youth, Alfred was allegedly the winner (though he was in fact illiterate until his late thirties). His mother apparently died soon after (there is no evidence to show that she was divorced or repudiated as is sometimes stated) and Alfred accompanied his widowed father on a pilgrimage to Rome. There they were well received by Pope Leo IV who administered the rite of confirmation to Alfred, an act magnified by Asser to being a consecration to future kingship, which could hardly have been intended since Alfred had three elder brothers living. The father and son stayed in Rome for a year and on their return journey stopped at the court of their distant kinsman Charles the Bald, King of the Franks, who gave Ethelwulf his young daughter JUDITH as his second wife.

After Ethelwulf's death in 858, his three

elder sons reigned in turn. The last of these, ETHELRED I, spent his whole reign resisting Danish invaders, in which he was ably assisted by his only surviving brother Alfred. In April 871 Ethelred was mortally wounded at Merton and died of his injuries. His sons were considered too young to reign and Alfred succeeded to the throne of a country largely overrun by Danish invaders. A month after his accession he won a victory at Wilton and followed it up with a number of other successful skirmishes in the south of England, but within two years the Danes had most of MERCIA and NORTHUMBRIA in their grasp. Alfred's brother-in-law, King BURHRED of Mercia, was driven out and went to Rome, where he died. After winning a sea battle in 875, Alfred concluded an uneasy and shortlived peace treaty with the invaders in 876. Further incursions into Devon soon followed, and 'the host', as the ANGLO-SAXON CHRONICLE terms the invaders, took refuge in Exeter where more peace negotiations took place. They withdrew to Mercia in the autumn of 877.

Alfred retired with his army into the island of Athelney, an inaccessible marshy area of Somerset. To this period belongs the story of Alfred disguising himself as a wandering harpist and entering the Danish camp to gain vital knowledge of the enemy. Also attributed to this time is the story of the king taking refuge in a swineherd's hut and being soundly berated by the swineherd's wife for burning the cakes she had set him to watch. The story of the burnt cakes does not appear in Asser's writings on the king and it may be that the tale is an invention dating to some 100 years after Alfred died. The story is told in an anonymous poem:

> Where lying on the hearth to bake
> By chance the cake did burn:
> 'What! Canst thou not, thou lout,' quoth she,
> 'Take pains the same to turn?
> But serve me such another trick,
> I'll thwack thee on the snout.'
> Which made the patient king, good man,
> Of her to stand in doubt?

Alfred left Athelney in May 878 and led his army into Wiltshire, being joined by large contingents from Somerset, Wiltshire and Hampshire. He met the Danes at Ethandune (Edington) and gained a resounding victory, driving the enemy back into their stronghold at Chippenham. The peace terms were settled a few weeks later, the Danes agreeing to withdraw from WESSEX and return into EAST ANGLIA, MERCIA and NORTHUMBRIA, which were ceded to

them and became known as the DANELAW. Their leader, Guthrum, accepted Christianity and Alfred stood sponsor at his baptism, giving him the name of Athelstan.

Over the next few years Alfred consolidated his kingdom, reorganizing the army, building a navy (and thus earning the nickname 'Father of the English Navy'), strengthening the defences, encouraging learning and religion and codifying laws. Alfred was a polymath and could turn his hand to most things, including the translation of classical texts and the invention of a candle-clock. At the age of 38 he studied Latin and copies of his translation of *Pastoralis* (by Pope Gregory the Great) were despatched to every bishop in the kingdom, together with a beautifully made *aestel* (or pointer), an example of which, known as 'King Alfred's Jewel', survives in Oxford's Ashmolean Museum. He also commissioned the ambitious historical record known as the Anglo-Saxon Chronicle. For the better government of the realm he called together a great council of bishops, ealdormen and thanes to meet twice a year, the first embryo parliament. Officials working on his behalf were required to be able to read, or else risked losing their jobs.

According to Asser, who wrote that the king was 'harassed, nay, rather disturbed, day and night, with illnesses unknown to all the physicians in the island', Alfred was afflicted with a mysterious illness that attacked him periodically causing him great pain and mental anguish. The late Sir Iain Moncreiffe of that Ilk suggested that this might be an early reference to the 'royal malady', PORPHYRIA. Others have speculated that he suffered from chronic haemorrhoids, epilepsy or venereal disease.

Alfred married in 868, EALHSWITH, daughter of Ethelred Mucil, Ealdorman of the Gaini (a Mercian tribal group), and his wife Eadburh (Eadburga), a descendant of the royal house of Mercia. Alfred was taken ill on the day of the marriage, but recovered and in due course his wife bore him a large family, of whom two sons and three daughters survived infancy. Alfred died on 26 October 899 and was buried in the New Minster (later Hyde Abbey) at Winchester. His widow survived until 902.

Alfred Ernest Albert, Prince, Duke of Edinburgh *see* EDINBURGH, PRINCE ALFRED, DUKE OF.

Alfwold, King of East Anglia (d.749) Stated by Florence of Worcester and William of Malmesbury to have been a son of King

ETHELHERE and Hereswith of DEIRA, which is extremely unlikely as Hereswith took the veil in or before 650, which would make Alfwold a centenarian. It is equally unlikely that he was the son of Ethelhere by a second wife, and the most likely probability is that he was a son of King ALDWULF, whom he succeeded in 713. Nothing is known of his reign. He died in 749, leaving no clear successor.

Alice, Princess, Countess of Athlone (1883–1981) The only daughter of Prince Leopold, Duke of ALBANY, and Princess Helen of Waldeck and Pyrmont, who was born at WINDSOR CASTLE on 25 February 1883 at 6.30 in the evening. She was baptized Alice Mary Victoria Augusta Pauline in the private chapel at Windsor Castle on Easter Monday, 26 March 1883, her godparents being her grandmother Queen VICTORIA, the German Empress Augusta (for whom Princess BEATRICE[2] stood proxy), her grandmother the Princess of Waldeck and Pyrmont, her aunt the German Crown Princess (for whom the Princess of Wales stood proxy), the Duchess of Cambridge (for whom the Duchess of Teck stood proxy), her aunt the Hereditary Princess of Bentheim (for whom Princess Christian stood proxy), and her four uncles, the Prince of Wales, the King of the Netherlands (represented by proxy), the Grand Duke of Hesse (for whom the Duke of Edinburgh stood proxy), and Prince Wilhelm of Württemberg (for whom the Duke of Teck stood proxy).

Princess Alice of Albany, as she was styled, was left fatherless less than a month after completing her first year and she and her posthumously born brother Charles Edward, who succeeded as 2nd Duke of Albany at birth, were brought up by their widowed mother in the pleasant atmosphere of Claremont House, near Esher, Surrey, which had been assigned to their parents on their marriage. Their life was punctuated by visits to their many foreign relations and to the south of France, where Alice was confirmed in the English Church of St George at Cannes, which had been built as a memorial to her father, on 9 April 1898. The same year she received the Order of VICTORIA AND ALBERT (VA) from her grandmother. The succession of her brother to the duchy of Saxe-Coburg and Gotha in 1900 led to more time being spent abroad.

Princesss Alice attended the coronation of her uncle EDWARD VII in 1902 and in November 1903 became engaged to Prince Alexander Augustus Frederick William Alfred George of TECK, the youngest son of the Duke and Duchess of Teck. The marriage took place at St George's Chapel, Windsor on 10 February 1904, and the honeymoon was spent at Brocket Hall, near Hatfield. Three children were born of the marriage: May Helen Emma (1906–94), who became Lady May Cambridge after her father's renunciation of his German titles in 1917 and is better known by her married name as Lady May Abel Smith; Rupert Alexander George Augustus (1907–28), known as Viscount Trematon after 1917, who inherited the taint of HAEMOPHILIA and died as the result of a motor accident in France; and Maurice Francis George, who died at Schloss Reinhardsbrunn, near Coburg, on 14 September 1910, aged nearly six months. All three children were born at Claremont House.

During the First World War Princess Alice served as Chairman of the Soldiers', Sailors' and Airmen's Families Association and the War Pensions Fund, as well as helping in the Forestry Corps Canteen in Windsor Great Park and the Hayes Munition Canteen. She was the first president of the Women's Section of the British Legion 1918–23, and President of the National Children's Adoption Association, the Deptford Fund (succeeding her mother in 1922), the King Edward VII District Nursing Association (also in South Africa 1924–30), the Royal School of Needlework (until 1975), the Royal Victoria League for Commonwealth Friendship (1931–71), and the Queen's Institute of District Nursing (1957–68).

When Princess Alice's husband renounced his German titles in 1917 and was created Earl of Athlone, she became known as HRH Princess Alice, Countess of Athlone. She became one of the most widely travelled members of the royal family, visiting Colombo, Malaya, Singapore, Siam (where her husband represented GEORGE V at the coronation of King Vajiralongkorn), South Africa, Rhodesia, Uganda, Egypt, Palestine, Saudi Arabia, the West Indies, Canada and USA. Lord Athlone served as Governor-General, Commander-in-Chief and High Commissioner of the Union of South Africa 1924–30 and Princess Alice founded the Princess Alice Orthopaedic Hospital at Musenburg, near Cape Town, in 1930. From 1940 to 1946 Lord Athlone was Governor-General and Commander-in-Chief of the Dominion of Canada. In 1940 Princess Alice became Commandant-in-Chief of the Women's Transport Service (FANY). She was Chancellor of the University of the West Indies 1950–71 and visited the West Indies each year she held that office (except 1957). Princess Alice was appointed Dame Grand Cross of the Order of the British Empire (GBE) in the coronation honours of 1937 and Dame Grand Cross of the ROYAL VICTORIAN ORDER (GCVO) in 1948. She was also a Dame Grand Cross of the Order of St John of Jerusalem and the recipient of many foreign orders, including the French Légion d'honneur and the Portuguese Order of Christ.

Lord Athlone died at KENSINGTON PALACE on 16 January 1957. In 1966 Princess Alice published a volume of discreet memoirs entitled *For My Grandchildren.* As the oldest surviving member of the royal family she was frequently consulted on matters of protocol. At the marriage of Princess ANNE in 1973 she refused a place in the carriage procession to WESTMINSTER ABBEY, saying it was not fitting for a princess of her rank, and travelled by motor-car instead. Princess Alice became a familiar sight in Kensington, where she resided in an apartment in the Palace, walking to and from St Mary Abbots Church on Sundays and frequenting local shops. She also enjoyed riding on public omnibuses. In 1977 she received Queen ELIZABETH II's Silver Jubilee Medal and wore it with pride on the balcony of BUCKINGHAM PALACE.

Princess Alice died peacefully in her sleep at Kensington Palace on 3 January 1981. At almost 98, she was the longest living member of the British royal family to date. She was buried in the royal burial ground at Frogmore after a funeral service in St George's Chapel, Windsor.

Alice Maud Mary, Princess, Grand Duchess of Hesse (1843–78) The second daughter and third child of Queen VICTORIA and Prince ALBERT, who was born at BUCKINGHAM PALACE at five minutes past four on the morning of Tuesday, 25 April 1843. Prince Albert, reporting the event to his brother, wrote that the queen: 'suffered much, but for only a short time, and ... feels as well as can be expected. The little child is said to be very pretty, so experts say.' The little princess was baptized in the private chapel at Buckingham Palace on 2 June 1843 by the Archbishop of Canterbury, her godparents being Princess SOPHIA MATILDA OF GLOUCESTER, Queen Victoria's half-sister the Princess of Hohenlohe-Langenburg (for

whom the Duchess of Kent stood proxy), the King of Hanover (*see* CUMBERLAND, ERNEST AUGUSTUS, DUKE OF) (for whom the Duke of Cambridge stood proxy) and Prince Albert's brother Ernest (for whom the Hereditary Grand Duke of Mecklenburg-Strelitz stood proxy). The Queen, writing to King Leopold of the Belgians, commented on the baby's names as follows: 'Our little baby ... is to be called Alice, an old English name, and the other names are to be Maud (another old English name, and the same as Matilda) and Mary, as she was born on Aunt Gloucester's birthday.'

Princess Alice grew up in the fast-growing family of brothers and sisters and took part in all their activities, particularly excelling in amateur theatricals. Her engagement to Prince Ludwig (or Louis, as he was generally called) of Hesse, her senior by almost six years, was announced to Parliament on 3 May 1861 and she was voted a dowry of £30,000 and an income of £6000 per annum. The death of the prince consort in December 1861 delayed the marriage and Princess Alice 'was a real support to her broken-hearted mother' in the early days of the queen's widowhood. The marriage finally took place with subdued ceremony on 1 July 1862, the dining room of OSBORNE HOUSE being converted into a chapel for the occasion.

Princess Alice's married life was a happy one, but not without its troubles. The war between Austria and Prussia in 1866 and the Franco-Prussian War of 1870–1, in both of which her husband served, were a sore trial. On 13 June 1877, Ludwig succeeded his uncle as reigning Grand Duke of Hesse and Alice became Grand Duchess. They had had seven children, two sons and five daughters. The younger son, Friedrich (or Fritz), inherited the taint of HAEMOPHILIA and died tragically in May 1873 at the age of two and a half as the result of a fall from a window while playing with his brother. In November 1878 the Grand Ducal family was attacked with diphtheria. The Grand Duchess nursed her children devotedly as they suffered in turn and all recovered except the youngest daughter Marie (or May, as she was known in the family), who died on 16 November at the age of four and a half. Her sorrowing mother, worn out by her exertions, sickened with diphtheria herself on the 7 December and died in the Grand Ducal Palace at Darmstadt at 8.30 in the morning of Saturday, 14 December 1878, the same day and the same date on which her father had died 17 years previously. She was buried in the Grand Ducal Mausoleum at Rosenhohe, near Darmstadt, on 18 December 1878.

Princess Alice was described as the most attractive of Victoria's daughters, both in appearance and character. Her husband, Grand Duke Ludwig IV, survived until 13 March 1892, when he died at Darmstadt following a stroke. He was buried with her. His second and morganatic marriage to a lady of somewhat dubious reputation was nipped in the bud by Victoria, who insisted on it being dissolved only two months after it had taken place. Princess Alice's only surviving son, Ernst Ludwig (1868–1937), succeeded his father as Grand Duke and abdicated in November 1918. Of her surviving daughters, Victoria Alberta (1863–1950) married Prince Louis of Battenberg, later 1st Marquess of Milford Haven, and became the grandmother of Prince Philip, Duke of EDINBURGH; Elisabeth (1864–1918) married Grand Duke Serge Alexandrovitch of Russia, who was assassinated at Moscow in 1905, and herself fell a victim to the Bolsheviks in 1918 (she is now regarded as a saint by the Russian Orthodox Church); Irene (1866–1953) married her first cousin Prince Heinrich of Prussia; and Alix (1872–1918) became the tragic Empress Alexandra Feodorovna of Russia following her marriage to Emperor Nicholas II, perishing with him and their children at Ekaterinburg in July 1918.

Alla The nickname by which Mrs Clara Knight, the childhood nurse of ELIZABETH II and Princess MARGARET, COUNTESS OF SNOWDON was known to her charges.

Allectus, Roman Emperor in Britain (*c*.250–96) The chief minister of CARAUSIUS, whom he murdered in 293, usurping the throne. He was a man of obscure origin and little ability and was easily defeated by Constantius, who recovered the province for Rome, Allectus being killed in battle in Hampshire during the process. Coins dating from his reign are numerous.

Alpin, King of Kintyre (d.834) The son of EOCHAID IV the Poisonous, King of DALRIADA, and his wife Fergusa, daughter of his uncle and predecessor Fergus, King of Dalriada by the sister and heiress of CINIATH II and ALPIN II, Kings of the Picts. Alpin's reign in Kintyre was brief, lasting only from March to August 834, when he was killed in battle with the Picts in Galloway. His sons, KENNETH I and DONALD I, reigned successively as King of Scots, the former uniting the Scots and the Picts into one kingdom.

Alpin I, King of the Picts (*fl*.726–41) The son of EOCHAID II, King of Knapdale, by the sister and heiress of TARRAIN, KING OF THE PICTS, he deposed his kinsman King DRUST VI and seized the throne in 726, being himself deposed two years later by his father's cousin NECHTAN III. He seems to have reappeared as a sub-king (*regulus*) in DALRIADA under his grand-nephew OENGUS II between 736 and 741.

Alpin II, King of the Picts (reigned 775–80) The son of Feradach (or Wrad) by a sister of ALPIN I, he succeeded his brother King CINIATH II in 775 and was himself succeeded five years later by his nephew DRUST VII.

Ambrosius (*fl.c*.493) Legendary British leader who resisted the Saxon invaders. BEDE, following GILDAS, speaks of him as Ambrosius Aurelianus, 'a man of good character and the sole survivor of Roman race from the catastrophe. Among the slain had been his own parents, who were of royal birth and title. Under his leadership the Britons took up arms, challenged their conquerors to battle, and with God's help inflicted a defeat on them.' GEOFFREY OF MONMOUTH calls him Aurelius Ambrosius and greatly embellished his story. In Welsh tradition he is known as *Emrys Wledig* (Ruler). Gildas speaks of his descendants as having become degenerate.

Amelia, Princess (1711–86) The second daughter of GEORGE II and Queen CAROLINE, who was born at Herrenhausen in Hanover on 10 June 1711 and baptized Amelia Sophia Eleanor (Amalie Sophie Eleonore in German). Following the succession of her grandfather GEORGE I to the British throne, she accompanied her mother and sisters to England and took up residence in ST JAMES'S PALACE. When her parents were ordered to leave there following their quarrel with the king in 1717, the princesses remained in their grandfather's care, although frequently visited by their parents.

Amelia, usually known as Emily in England, was seriously considered as a possible bride for her cousin Crown Prince Frederick of Prussia (later famous as Frederick the Great), but the negotiations were broken off and in the event Amelia never married. She suffered from delicate health in her teens and was advised to take the waters at Bath, a place which she frequently visited in later life and where she was able to indulge one of her favourite passions, card-playing. After the death of her mother Queen Caroline in 1737, the princess became a constant companion to her widowed father. When George II suffered his fatal seizure at KENSINGTON PALACE on the morning of 25 October 1760, almost his last coherent words to his valet were 'send for Amelia'. She hastened to his side and thinking him still alive put her head close to his to hear what he had to say to her (she being very deaf) and for some moments did not realize he was already dead.

Horace Walpole recorded that after the king's death Princess Amelia 'lived with great dignity, but ... forbore going to Court on account of increased deafness. She was short-sighted as well as deaf, yet had so much quickness and conception that she seemed to hear and see more readily than others. She was an excellent mistress to her servants, steady to her favourites, and nobly generous and charitable.' Lord Harvey, on the other hand, stated that she was 'lively, false, and a great liar, did many ill offices to people and no good ones, and for want of prudence said as many shocking things to their faces, as, for want of good-nature or truth, she said disagreeable ones behind their backs. She had as many enemies as acquaintances, for nobody knew [her] without disliking her.'

Princess Amelia had a great interest in horses and dogs and was greatly attached to her only surviving brother the Duke of Cumberland (*see* CUMBERLAND, PRINCE WILLIAM AUGUSTUS, DUKE OF). After her retirement from court she divided her time between Gunnersbury House, near Ealing, and her London house in Cavendish Square, where she died on 31 October 1786, the last surviving child of her parents. She was buried in the royal vault in King Henry VII's Chapel at WESTMINSTER ABBEY.

Amelia, Princess of Great Britain (1783–1810) The sixth daughter and 15th and youngest child of GEORGE III and Queen CHARLOTTE, who was born at Royal Lodge, WINDSOR, at a quarter to one in the morning of 7 August 1783. She was baptized by the Archbishop of Canterbury in the Great Council Chamber at ST JAMES'S PALACE on 18 September 1783, her godparents being her eldest brother the Prince of Wales and her two eldest sisters, the Princess Royal and Princess AUGUSTA. The princess soon became her father's favourite child, and Fanny Burney penned a delightful picture of her on her third birthday walking on the terrace at Windsor 'in a robe-coat covered with fine muslin, a dressed close cap, white gloves and a fan ... alone and first, highly delighted with the parade, and turning from side to side to see everybody as she passed.'

Unfortunately, Princess Amelia was always delicate and she suffered several grave illnesses. She was, however, vivacious and talented and noted for her sweetness of temper. Her malady was of a tubercular nature and sea-bathing at Weymouth was recommended, but to no avail. Princess Amelia died at Augusta Lodge, Windsor, on 2 November 1810 and was buried in St George's Chapel on 14 November. The death of his favourite child precipitated George III's final loss of reason and resulted in him having to be confined in a straitjacket.

The princess's name was linked romantically with that of Captain (later General) the Hon. Charles FitzRoy (1762–1831), second son of the 1st Baron Southampton, and there was a strong rumour that they were secretly married, although no evidence has ever been produced to confirm the fact.

Amesbury Abbey ELFRIDA, widow of King EDGAR, is said to have founded Amesbury Abbey in Wiltshire in 980 in expiation for her role in the murder of her stepson King EDWARD THE MARTYR. However, it may have been a re-foundation as Queen GUINEVERE is said to have retired to a priory at Amesbury after the death of King ARTHUR. ELEANOR OF PROVENCE, widow of HENRY III, became a nun at Amesbury as did several other members of the royal family. The Abbey was rebuilt in the 19th century and is now a private retirement and nursing home.

Ampulla The item of regalia that contains the holy oil used for the ANOINTING of the sovereign in the CORONATION ceremony. It takes the form of an eagle made of gold, the head of which unscrews to allow it to be filled with the oil, which is then poured through the beak into the anointing spoon. The ampulla and spoon are the only two items in the regalia that escaped destruction under the COMMONWEALTH. The ampulla is of late 14th-century workmanship and was first used at the coronation of HENRY IV in 1399. The spoon, of silver gilt, is of earlier date, being late 12th-century in style. It is presumed that both items were kept apart from the rest of the regalia, probably with the WESTMINSTER ABBEY plate, and so escaped the Parliamentary Commissioners. They were both embellished for the coronation of CHARLES II, the ampulla being realistically engraved to represent an eagle's feathers and the spoon being chased in 17th-century style.

Anarawd ap Gruffydd, Prince of Deheubarth (d.1143) The eldest son of GRUFFYDD AP RHYS I, PRINCE OF DEHEUBARTH by an unknown mother, who succeeded his father in 1137. In 1138 he and others attacked Cardigan Castle, which was held by the Normans, but a truce put an end to the campaign. Two years later Anarawd joined with OWAIN GWYNEDD, KING OF GWYNEDD and his brother CADWALADR in an appeal to Bernard, Bishop of St Davids for support against the appointment of Meurig to the see of Bangor. Anarawd married Margaret, or Margred, the daughter of Cadwaladr, but was treacherously set upon and killed by his father-in-law's followers in 1143. He left an only son, Einion, who was murdered by one of his own men in 1163, leaving three sons, Anarawd (d.1198), Madog (d.1193) and Hywel (d.1193), with whom the descendants of Anarawd ap Gruffydd appear to have died out.

Anarawd ap Rhodri, King of Gwynedd (d.916) The eldest son of RHODRI MAWR, KING OF ALL WALES and his wife Angharad, daughter of Meurig ap Dyfnwallon, King of Seisyllwg, who succeeded his father in Anglesey and part of Gwynedd in 878, the rest of his father's dominions falling to his brother Cadell. He avenged his father's death in a battle with the Mercians fought on the banks of the Conwy in 881. He then sought an alliance with the Danish Kingdom of York and then with ALFRED THE GREAT, whom he acknowledged as his overlord and from whom he received many favours and tokens of friendship. The name of Anarawd's wife is not recorded. He died in 916, leaving two sons, IDWAL FOEL, his successor, and Elise (d.942), whose daughter Prawst was the mother of LLYWELYN AP SEISYLL.

Ancient Ceremonies see CORONATION; CRAMP RINGS; KING'S EVIL; MAUNDY MONEY.

Andrew, Prince see YORK, ANDREW, DUKE OF.

Angharad ferch Maredudd (fl.999–1030) The only daughter and heiress of MAREDUDD AB OWAIN, KING OF DEHEUBARTH AND GWYNEDD, who was married while still a child to LLYWELYN AP SEISYLL, who succeeded his father-in-law and made himself ruler or overlord of all Wales. He died in 1023 and was succeeded by his and Angharad's only son, GRUFFYDD AP LLYWELYN. Angharad, who must have been in her late thirties, then married Cynfyn ap Gwerstan, 'a noble of Powys', and had two more sons, BLEDDYN AP CYNFYN and Rhiwallon.

Angharad ferch Owain (d.1162) The daughter of Owain ab Edwin (d.1105), who married GRUFFYDD AP CYNAN, KING OF GWYNEDD about 1095 and became the mother of three sons and five daughters. The eulogistic biography of her husband describes her as a paragon of beauty and virtue. On his death in 1137 Gruffydd left her two pieces of land and the profits of the port of Abermenai in addition to half of his goods as prescribed by Welsh law. She survived him many years, dying at what must have been a very great age in 1162.

Anglo-Saxon Chronicle The chronological record of events in Britain from early times to the reign of King STEPHEN. It was written in Anglo-Saxon English at the instigation of ALFRED THE GREAT and is one of the most important historical sources for the period it covers. There are several versions.

Anglo-Saxons The blanket name given to the invaders and settlers from Scandinavia and northern Germany who came to Britain after the Roman occupation and established kingdoms throughout the land (see HEPTARCHY). The Anglo-Saxon period ended with the Norman Conquest in 1066.

Anjou, House of The counts of Anjou, an area in northern France, claimed descent from Tortulf the Woodman, a legendary figure. Early in the 11th century Ermengarde, the heiress of Anjou, conveyed the territory to her husband Geoffrey II of Château-Landon, Count of Gatinais. Their great-grandson GEOFFREY PLANTAGENET was selected by HENRY I to be the second husband of his daughter Matilda (see MATILDA, 'LADY OF THE ENGLISH', EMPRESS), widow of the Emperor Henry V. Their son eventually became King HENRY II, the first king of the House of Anjou, later and better known as the House of PLANTAGENET.

Anna, King of East Anglia (d.654) The son of Eni, brother of King REDWALD, who seems to have followed his kinsman Ecgric to the throne in about 635, though the date of his accession is doubtful. BEDE calls Anna 'an excellent man of royal stock' and says that he 'and his nobles' richly endowed the monastery at Burgh Castle, near Yarmouth. He married Saewara, apparently a widow and the mother of a daughter named Saethryth, who became Abbess of Faremoutier-en-Brie. Anna's daughters were: Sexburh, who married Earconbert, King of Kent; ETHELDREDA, who married first Tondberht, Ealdorman of the South Gyrwas, and secondly EGFRITH, KING OF NORTHUMBRIA; Ethelburga, who succeeded her half-sister as Abbess of Faremoutier-en-Brie; and Wihtburh (Wihtburga), a nun at Ely. Anna was killed in battle with the pagan PENDA, KING OF MERCIA in 654 and was succeeded by his brother ETHELHERE. *See also* EAST ANGLIA.

Annabella Drummond, Queen of Scots (d.1401) The consort of King ROBERT III, who was the daughter of Sir John Drummond of Stobhall (ancestor of the Earls of Perth) and his wife Mary Montfichet. Her aunt, Margaret Drummond, had been the second wife of DAVID II and was probably instrumental in arranging the marriage of her niece to that king's half-grand-nephew John, Earl of Carrick, the marriage dispensation being dated 13 March 1366. Annabella's husband succeeded his father ROBERT II in 1390 and assumed the style of Robert III. The royal pair were crowned at Scone on 14 August 1390. Queen Annabella had three sons and four daughters. Very little of her personal life has been recorded. She died at Scone 'in harvest' 1401, and was buried at DUNFERMLINE Abbey. King Robert survived her until 1406.

Anne, Princess (1637–40) The third daughter and sixth child of CHARLES I and Queen HENRIETTA MARIA, who was born at ST JAMES'S PALACE at midnight on 17 March 1637 and named after Anne of Austria, Queen of France, her mother's sister-in-law. She lived for only three years and eight months, but was evidently an advanced and precocious child since it is reported that when she lay dying one of her attendants told her to pray, whereupon she declared: 'I am not able to say my long prayer [meaning the Lord's Prayer] but I will say my short one. Lighten mine eyes, O Lord, lest I sleep the sleep of death.' She died on 5 November 1640 at RICHMOND PALACE, 'of a suffocating catarrh, with inflammatory disposition of the lungs accompanied with continual fever' according to her post mortem report, and was buried in WESTMINSTER ABBEY.

Anne, Princess Royal (1709–59) The eldest daughter and second child of GEORGE II and

CAROLINE OF ANSBACH, who was born at Herrenhausen on 22 October/2 November 1709 and named after Queen ANNE, to whom her great-grandmother the Electress SOPHIA OF HANOVER was then heiress-presumptive. After her grandfather had succeeded to the British throne in 1714 she accompanied her parents and two younger sisters to England. After her father's accession in 1727 she was styled Princess Royal. Like others of her family, Princess Anne was a great admirer of Handel, who was her singing-master for a time.

In 1733 the princess was betrothed to William IV, Prince of Orange-Nassau (1711–51), and their marriage took place in the French Chapel, St James's, in March 1734. The bride was attired in 'virgin robes of silver tissue, having a train six yards long which was supported by ten Dukes' and Earls' daughters, all of whom were attired in robes of silver tissue'. Parliament granted the princess £80,000 and £5000 a year for life. The newly married couple returned to The Hague, and the Prince of Orange having been elected Stadhouder of the several provinces of the Netherlands was proclaimed Stadhouder of the United Provinces, Captain and Admiral-General of the Union on 4 May 1747, these offices being further declared to be hereditary in his family in both male and female lines. Princess Anne had five, or according to some authorities six children: a doubtful son stillborn in December 1734; stillborn or shortlived daughters in 1736 and 1739; Wilhelmina Caroline (later Princess of Nassau-Weilburg) on 28 February 1743; Anne Marie on 15 November 1746 (dying on 29 December following); and William Batavus on 8 March 1748.

The Prince of Orange died at The Hague on 22 October 1751 and was succeeded as Stadhouder by his son William V. Princess Anne was sworn in as regent and acted as such until her death at The Hague on 12 January 1759, upon which she was buried with her husband in the Nieuwe Kerke at Delft. A rather unflattering description of the princess states: 'Her figure was unshapely, and even at an early age was inclined to stoutness. In disposition she was haughty and ambitious.'

Anne (Elizabeth Alice Louise), Princess Royal (1950–) The only daughter and second child of ELIZABETH II and Prince Philip, Duke of EDINBURGH, who was born at CLARENCE HOUSE, St James's, on 15 August 1950. She was the first baby to be born at

Clarence House since it was refurbished by John Nash in 1825 and on her birth automatically succeeded to various honours, including immediate membership of the Automobile Association (its one millionth member). She was educated at Benenden School in Kent and after leaving school devoted her attention to her career as a top rider in three-day events, winning the Individual European Three-Day event in 1971 and the Combined Championship at Hickstead in 1973. In 1976 she participated as one of the British riding team at the Olympic Games in Montreal (though she was concussed in a fall from her horse and the team failed to win any medals). She was voted BBC Television Sports Personality of the Year and Sportswoman of the Year by the national press in 1971.

This passion for horses and horse-riding was inevitably much lampooned by the press, with whom Princess Anne as a young woman had a fairly turbulent relationship. In 1977 the princess commented drily that 'When I appear in public people expect me to neigh, grind my teeth, paw the ground and swish my tail – none of which is easy.' She appreciated the humour had at her expense, however, and joked that when she asked for the sugar some people liked to offer sugar lumps to her on the flat of their palm, as though feeding a horse. On most occasions she managed to maintain her composure in the face of intense public interest in her activities. Attending a show-jumping event at Hickstead a fellow-spectator, evidently unaware of the princess's identity, ventured to ask her, 'Has anyone ever told you that you look like Princess Anne?' Anne demurred, replying, 'I think I'm a bit better-looking than she is.'

The need to protect members of the royal family when going about their public duties was impressed on everybody on 20 March 1974, when a deranged gunman named Ian Ball attempted to kidnap Princess Anne as she drove down the Mall. The man fired six shots, wounding one of the royal bodyguards, the chauffeur, a policeman and a reporter, but the princess escaped unscathed with the exception of a ripped dress. Mindful of his daughter's strength of character, Prince Philip observed of the incident, 'If the man had succeeded in abducting Anne, she'd have given him the hell of a time while in captivity.'

Princess Anne was married at WESTMINSTER ABBEY on 14 November 1973 to Lieutenant (later Captain) Mark Anthony Peter Phillips, the only son of Major Peter William Garside Phillips, MC, late of the 1st King's Dragoon Guards, and his wife Anne Patricia Tiarks. The princess had hoped for a quiet wedding, but in the event the ceremony was staged at Westminster Abbey before a television audience of some 500 million (at Anne's insistence, however, the film crews were forbidden to broadcast the moment when Phillips placed the wedding ring on his new wife's finger). Living from 1976 in Gatcombe Manor, Gloucestershire, the former home of the politician 'Rab' Butler, the couple had two children, Peter Mark Andrew Phillips (born on 15 November 1977) and Zara Anne Elizabeth Phillips (born on 15 May 1981). When the press greeted news of the choice of the name Zara with surprise, as it was not a 'royal' name, Anne responded by saying, 'She is not royal, the Queen just happens to be her grandmother.' In 1989 four 'tender and affectionate' letters to the princess from a former equerry of the queen, Commander Timothy James Hamilton Laurence, RN, were stolen and leaked to the press, intensifying speculation that the Princess's marriage was about to split. After a period of separation the marriage was dissolved in April 1992 and the princess was eventually married to Laurence, younger son of Commander Guy Stewart Laurence, RN, and his wife Barbara Alison Symons, at Crathie Church near Balmoral, on 12 December 1992.

Princess Anne was appointed a Dame Grand Cross of the ROYAL VICTORIAN ORDER (GCVO) in 1974 and was declared Princess Royal on 13 June 1987, largely in recognition of her selfless work on numerous overseas trips, chiefly in connection with the Save the Children Fund, of which she has been a very active and indefatigable President since 1970. She was appointed a Lady of the Order of the GARTER (LG) in 1994. Applauded for her charity work and her dignified demeanour in public after the ructions of her youth, she nonetheless caused some controversy in 1988 when she called the Aids epidemic a 'classic own goal' scored by mankind against itself – a remark that instantly aroused the condemnation of Aids workers.

Anne, Queen (1665–1714) The second daughter and fourth child of James, Duke of York (*see* JAMES II) and his first wife Anne HYDE, who was born at ST JAMES'S PALACE on 6 February 1665, 'at thirty-nine minutes past eleven of the clock at night' as recorded by Francis Sandford in his *Genealogical*

History of the Kings of England. Her god-parents were her elder sister Mary (*see* MARY II), then nearly three years old, the Duchess of Monmouth and Gilbert Sheldon, Archbishop of Canterbury. Anne and Mary were the only two of their parents' eight children to survive infancy and they were brought up together in the Protestant faith of the Church of England from which neither ever swerved. Anne was only six years old when she lost her mother in January 1671. A little over two and a half years later she acquired a stepmother only six years older than herself (*see* MARY OF MODENA). 'I have brought you a new playmate,' said their father when presenting his new wife to his daughters. The three girls got on well and in January 1675 Mary and Anne were godmothers to their half-sister CATHERINE LAURA, who died at the age of nine months.

Anne was described as a heavy child, taking after her mother's family, the Hydes, and unlike her sister Mary, who was a typical Stuart. Both suffered from weak eyes, a result it is now believed of congenital syphilis. Throughout her life Anne was to be noted for her sweet and melodious voice. Her sister Mary was married to their first cousin William, Prince of Orange (*see* WILLIAM III) and in the following year Anne and her stepmother visited her in Holland. This visit and one to Brussels two years later were to be Anne's only sorties into continental Europe.

At the age of 17 Anne became the focus of a considerable scandal, after a courtier, John Sheffield, Lord Mulgrave, was suspected of attempting to seduce her, on the basis of certain leaked letters. The accusations were almost certainly baseless, but Mulgrave was exiled from court and the decision was made to find Anne a husband without delay. In December 1680 the English court had been visited by George Louis, Hereditary Prince of Hanover (*see* GEORGE I) with a view to a possible union, but the couple appear to have formed an antipathy to each other and George had returned to Hanover in March 1681. A more successful suitor now appeared in the form of Prince GEORGE OF DENMARK and Anne's marriage to him duly took place in the Chapel Royal, St James's, at 10 o'clock at night on 28 July 1683. After her marriage Anne was known at court as the Princess of Denmark. Her marriage was happy, but her appalling record of maternity, 18 pregnancies in 16 years producing only five living children, the longest-lived of whom was the engaging Duke of Gloucester (*see* GLOUCESTER, WILLIAM HENRY, DUKE

OF[1]), was to be the great tragedy of Anne's life (*see* QUEEN ANNE'S CHILDREN).

Her father's accession to the throne in 1685 greatly increased Anne's importance. She and her husband attended his coronation on St George's Day 1685 and on 22 May accompanied her stepmother Queen Mary Beatrice to his first state opening of Parliament.

In 1688 it was announced that the queen was pregnant. Eight previous pregnancies, all before James's accession, had resulted in the births of shortlived children or had ended with miscarriages. This time a son was born on 10 June and rumours at once began to circulate that he was a supposititious child. Mary, from Holland, submitted a long questionnaire to Anne seeking the fullest details of their stepmother's pregnancy and delivery. Most of Anne's answers were evasive and non-committal and it seems fairly certain that in her own mind she had no doubt that the child was her half-brother. With the accession of William and Mary in 1689 Anne became heiress-presumptive to the throne (she disliked William and referred to him as 'Caliban' when in private). Queen Mary died in 1694 and in the summer of 1700 Anne lost her only surviving child, the Duke of Gloucester (possibly as a result of hydrocephalus).

The death of William III on 8 March 1702 brought Anne to the throne. When Bishop Burnet arrived with the news of her accession she was at a loss for words and fell back on the usual English opening gambit of the weather. Looking out of the window she remarked, 'It is a fine day'. 'The finest day that ever dawned for England, ma'am,' the courtly Bishop responded.

Anne's health was always precarious and at her coronation on St George's Day 1702 she was suffering so badly from gout that she had to be carried in a chair, unable to stand on her two feet. The devout wish expressed by the Archbishop of York in his sermon at the ceremony that she would 'leave a numerous posterity to rule these kingdoms' was judged unfortunate. Her husband, who had been created Duke of Cumberland by William and Mary soon after their accession, and had been made Lord High Admiral of England by Anne after she was dissuaded from bestowing greater honours upon him, paid homage to her. He was the first husband of a reigning queen to do so, and the ceremony was not to be repeated until Prince Philip, Duke of EDINBURGH paid homage to Queen ELIZABETH II in 1953.

Anne was kindly and warmhearted but

not very bright. The public liked the fact that unlike other monarchs she had uncultivated tastes and eschewed literature and music and other elevated pursuits in favour of gambling and stag-hunting in Windsor Forest. She was also superstitious and reintroduced the tradition of the 'royal touch', believing that she could cure sufferers from scrofula by her touch – among those upon whom she bestowed her touch was the young Dr Johnson (who nonetheless reported no significant improvement in his condition).

Anne never felt happy about supporting William and Mary against her father and taking the place of her half-brother, and worked hard behind the scenes to try to secure his succession after her. When her Parliament proved so unruly that little business could be settled, she took to attending the chamber of the House of Lords in person in the forlorn hope that her ameliorating presence might help calm tempers. She formed an intense (perhaps slightly lesbian) attachment for the masculine-minded Sarah Churchill, Lady Marlborough, whose husband's victories abroad in the course of the War of the Spanish Succession were to be the glory of her reign. Sarah had gained a great ascendancy over Anne while she was still princess, and in letters the two were in the habit of addressing each other as 'Mrs Freeman' (Sarah) and 'Mrs Morley' (Anne) to avoid the formality that would otherwise have been inevitable.

On 6 March 1707 the Act of Union between England and Scotland was passed and Great Britain officially came into being. Anne's title was changed from 'Queen of England, Scotland, France and Ireland' to 'Queen of Great Britain, France and Ireland'. The following year she lost her husband Prince George, who died at KENSINGTON PALACE on 28 October at the age of 55.

In 1711 the Duchess of Marlborough (as she had become) was dismissed as Keeper of the Queen's Privy Purse, her place in Anne's affections having been usurped by her first cousin Abigail Masham, whom she herself had introduced to the queen. Lady Masham remained in the royal favour until the queen's death.

Anne was a High Church Protestant with a great interest in religious affairs. She established QUEEN ANNE'S BOUNTY to increase the stipends of the poorer clergy, and several London churches were built at her insistence, including St John's, Smith Square, the architecture of which is said to have been suggested by the queen's kicked-over footstool.

Anne's health was not helped by her addiction to brandy (her popular nickname was 'Brandy Nan') and it was obvious that she was not going to live very long. Towards the end of her life she became vague and confused, and her ministers, in need of her decisions upon matters of state, learned that there was 'no other remedy but to let Her Majesty take her own time which never failed to be the very longest that the nature of the thing would suffer her to defer it'. She was seriously ill in December 1713 and continued in very indifferent health until 30 July 1714, when she suffered a stroke at Kensington Palace. A second stroke caused her death on 1 August, aged 49. Her burial took place at WESTMINSTER ABBEY. She had become so stout that her massive coffin was almost square.

The saying 'Queen Anne is dead', signifying stale news, is said to have arisen from the fact that her death was never officially announced and that word of it was passed round from mouth to mouth, the first reports of the event having been relayed as early as two days before her demise, so that when the death was finally confirmed it was already stale news. It was, incidentally, Queen Anne that the 'pussycat, pussycat' of the famous nursery rhyme travelled to London to see.

Anne Boleyn (*c*.1500/1–36) The second of the six wives of HENRY VIII, Anne Boleyn was born either at Blickling Hall in Norfolk or at Hever Castle in Kent, probably in late May or early June of 1500 or 1501. Her parents were Sir Thomas Boleyn, later created Earl of Wiltshire and Earl of Ormonde, and Lady Elizabeth Howard, daughter of Thomas Howard, 2nd Duke of Norfolk. Anne's early years were spent between Blickling and Hever. In 1512 her father was appointed ambassador to the court of Archduchess Margaret of Austria, Regent of the Netherlands in Brussels, and he took his three children, Mary, Anne and George with him. On his return to England the following year he left Anne to complete her education as a maid of honour to the Archduchess, a post which she filled with satisfaction until the autumn of 1514, when she joined her sister Mary at the French court as a member of the household of Henry VIII's sister Mary (*see* MARY, PRINCESS, QUEEN OF FRANCE AND DUCHESS OF SUFFOLK), the young wife of King Louis XII of France. Louis died in 1515 and Mary

Boleyn returned to England with his widow, but Anne stayed on and joined the household of Louis' daughter Queen Claude, wife of his successor François I. Here she acquired the polished manners of the French court. In 1521, her father recalled her and she was appointed a maid of honour to Queen CATHERINE OF ARAGON.

Anne's portraits confirm contemporary descriptions of her. She had a rather pointed face with fine eyes and a long, slender neck, and possessed an abundance of long, dark hair. She was marred, however, by a blemish on one hand resembling a rudimentary sixth finger and her enemies were later to point to this as a sign of her being a witch.

Returned to the English court, Anne's vivacity and acquired French *chic* soon brought her an admiring circle of young men, including the poet Sir Thomas Wyatt, who was her cousin. The king, too, began to pay her attention, transferring his affections from her elder sister Mary, who had been his mistress both before and after her marriage to William Carey. Anne kept Henry at bay for several years, flirting coquettishly and entering into an amorous correspondence with him. It does not appear that she became his mistress until 1527 or later. In September 1532 she was created Marchioness of Pembroke and it was when she became pregnant in December 1532 that the matter of the divorce from Catherine assumed paramount importance for Henry.

In her own and Henry's eyes, Anne became queen from the moment of their secret marriage at Whitehall or Westminster on 25 January 1533, but the marriage was not declared valid until 28 May. Anne was crowned on Whit Sunday, 1 June. Her progress through the City, although staged with all the customary magnificence, met with a sullen silence from many of the crowd. Anne was the last queen consort to be accorded a separate coronation. She was six months pregnant and the coronation banquet proved something of an ordeal, two of her ladies having to sit under the table at her feet with a suitable receptacle in order that she might relieve herself frequently as she felt the need.

On 7 September Anne's child was born at GREENWICH PALACE. To Henry's chagrin it was a girl. He was so disappointed that he could not bring himself to attend the christening. The letters which had been prepared to announce the birth to foreign courts had not left enough room for the word 'Princess' to be written in full, so certain had Henry been of a male heir. Henry's passion for Anne began to wane from the moment of his daughter Elizabeth's birth (*see* ELIZABETH I). She was to find herself supplanted by another even as she had supplanted Catherine. Among her ladies-in-waiting was the scheming JANE SEYMOUR, who went out of her way to attract the king's attention from 1534 onwards.

Anne was pregnant again when the king had a bad fall from his horse in January 1536 and lay unconscious for two hours. The shock brought on a premature labour and she miscarried a male child. The loss of this possible heir sealed Anne's fate. Henry determined to rid himself of her and set up a commission to enquire into her conduct and find some fault in her. Anne had undoubtedly indulged in lighthearted flirtations both before and after her marriage, but there is no real evidence that she was guilty of the charges brought against her of adultery with Henry Norris and an incestuous relationship with her own brother George, Viscount Rochford.

On 1 May 1536 Anne presided over the jousts at Greenwich; the next day she was arrested and taken to the Tower. She and Rochford were tried on 15 May and inevitably found guilty and condemned to death. Two days later, as if this was not enough, an ecclesiastical court, convened at Lambeth under Cranmer, declared Anne's marriage to the king to have been null and void *ab initio* on account of the affinity created between them by his former relationship with her sister Mary.

Anne faced death bravely, even finding the courage to say of Henry that 'a gentler nor a more merciful prince was there never; and to me he was ever a good, a gentle and sovereign Lord'. She further conceded that 'The king has been very good to me. He promoted me from a simple maid to be a marchioness. Then he raised me to be a queen. Now he will raise me to be a martyr.' She was beheaded on Tower Green on 19 May 1536 by a headsman brought from Calais, who in the conventional French manner used a sword rather than an axe. Such was Anne's composure, that the executioner was much moved and asked another person present to distract her attention so that he might deliver the fatal blow before she could be aware of it. Her body was unceremoniously bundled into an oak chest and buried in the Chapel of St Peter-ad-Vincula in the Tower, where it still remains. It was rumoured that her heart was stolen and hidden in a church near Thetford, Suffolk.

Anne's headless ghost is said to haunt Blickling Hall to this day, being seen on the anniversary of her death arriving in a coach steered by a similarly headless coachman. On the day following the execution Henry announced his betrothal to Jane Seymour; their marriage took place just 11 days later.

Anne Nevill (1456–85) The younger daughter and co-heiress of Richard Nevill, 1st Earl of Warwick (the great 'king-maker') and Lady Anne Beauchamp, who was born at Warwick Castle on 11 June 1456. Her first marriage at Amboise in France in August 1470 to Edward, Prince of Wales, the only son of HENRY VI, was made in anticipation of the success of her father's expedition to restore Henry to the throne, and Anne was with Queen MARGARET OF ANJOU at Tewkesbury when her father and husband were both slain. The consummation of the marriage was not to have taken place until the restoration had been fully effected, so Anne remained a virgin bride. Anne's elder sister Isabel had married EDWARD IV's brother George, Duke of CLARENCE, in 1469, and Anne's hand was now sought by Edward's youngest brother, Richard, Duke of Gloucester. The marriage took place at Westminster on 12 July 1472, and at the end of the following year Anne's only child, Edward, was born at Middleham Castle, one of Richard's northern possessions. The marriage led to a dissension between the brothers over the Warwick inheritance, ending in Clarence's death in the TOWER OF LONDON in 1478 (earlier he had tried to keep Richard away from Anne by disguising her as a scullery maid in a friend's house).

Anne's husband was proclaimed king, as RICHARD III, on 26 June 1483 and he and Anne were crowned together at WESTMINSTER ABBEY 10 days later. The Rous Roll has an engaging full-length picture of them both, robed and crowned. Anne has long, flowing fair hair and a serene and happy expression that belies the stories of Richard's ill-treatment and neglect. He did have some bastards, but they were almost certainly born before his marriage.

Anne's health was never good (she may have been consumptive) and that of her son was even worse. He spent much of his life in the north and died at his birthplace on 9 April 1484. His beautiful little tomb with his effigy, though badly damaged, may still be seen in Sheriff Hutton Church. The queen survived her child by less than a year, dying in the Palace of Westminster on 16 March 1485. She was buried in West-

minster Abbey, where she had no monument until a few years ago when the Richard III Society commissioned a handsome wall plaque with her arms enamelled in colour to be affixed near her burial site.

Anne remains a shadowy figure and it seems fairly obvious that she was a negative personality, placid and uncomplaining while great events passed by leaving little mark on her life.

Anne of Bohemia (1366–94) The first queen of RICHARD II, who was born at Prague on 11 May 1366, the daughter of Charles IV, Holy Roman Emperor and King of Bohemia, by his fourth wife Elizabeth of Pomerania. With such parentage, she was a brilliant match for the young king, even though she brought no dowry. Richard's tutor Sir Simon Burley was sent to negotiate the marriage and to escort the bride to England. She landed at Dover in December 1381 and was met at Canterbury by the king's uncle Thomas (*see* GLOUCESTER, THOMAS OF WOODSTOCK, DUKE OF) and at Blackheath by the Mayor and citizens of London. The marriage was solemnized in the new chapel of St Stephen at Westminster on 20 January 1382, and the queen's coronation in WESTMINSTER ABBEY followed two days later.

Contemporary chroniclers speak of Anne's beauty, but her only known likeness, her tomb effigy at Westminster Abbey, gives the impression of a plump, expressionless young woman. She brought a large retinue with her to England and the expenses of her household aggravated the struggle between Richard and Parliament. She pleaded unsuccessfully for the life of Sir Simon Burley, who had escorted her to England, and after his execution retired with the king to Bristol for a time. In 1392 the queen acted as a successful mediator between Richard and the citizens of London and staged a spectacular royal progress through the city with him, mounted and wearing their crowns. Anne is credited with having introduced the side-saddle into England.

At Whitsuntide 1394 Anne was struck down by plague and died at SHEEN PALACE on 7 June 1394 after an illness of a few hours, in the presence of her inconsolable husband. The funeral procession wound its way from Sheen to Westminster lit by flambeaux and torches made from wax imported from Flanders, which provided, so Froissart tells us, an 'illumination so great that nothing was seen like it before'. The distraught

Richard was enraged when the Earl of Arundel arrived late for the funeral and struck him down with his sceptre; after the funeral he ordered Sheen Palace to be razed to the ground because of its unhappy associations for him.

Anne of Cleves (1515–57) The fourth of the six wives of HENRY VIII, who was born at Düsseldorf on 22 September 1515, the second daughter of John III, Duke of Cleves and his wife Marie, daughter and heiress of William III, Duke of Jülich and Berg. She received a very limited education, being unable to read or write in any language but her own Dutch dialect, and was completely unaccomplished in musical pursuits, a fact hardly likely to recommend her to the music-loving King Henry.

The quest for a fourth bride for Henry began within a week of JANE SEYMOUR's death. Cromwell pressed for an alliance with a foreign royal house and English ambassadors on the continent were instructed to look for likely candidates. It was in 1538 that the suggestion was first made that Henry should marry a daughter of the Duke of Cleves, who had become one of the most ardent and powerful supporters of the Protestant Reformation. Henry sent for portraits of his two younger daughters, Anne and Amelia, and when they were not forthcoming despatched Hans Holbein to paint them. He had been assured that Anne surpassed the Duchess of Milan in looks 'as the golden sun excelleth the silver moon', and he found her portrait (a version of which is now in the Louvre in Paris) pleasing in spite of the 'monstrous habit and apparel', which his ambassadors complained had prevented them from seeing the sisters properly.

Duke William of Cleves, who succeeded his father in February 1539, sent an emissary to England to negotiate the marriage treaty and it was concluded on 6 October 1539. Anne landed at Deal on 27 December, proceeding to Rochester on 1 January 1540. The eager bridegroom rushed to Rochester to take a look at her unbeknown. What he saw did not please him. He found her 'nothing so well as she had [been] spoken of' and referred to her as 'the Flanders mare'. Had he been able to back out of the marriage at this stage he would have done so, but he was now obliged to go through with it. The union was solemnized at Greenwich on 6 January.

Although Henry slept at Anne's side, the marriage was never consummated and the couple are said to have spent the night hours playing cards together. It took Henry but a short while to think of grounds for an annulment: his own lack of consent, witnessed by his failure to consummate the marriage, and Anne's pre-contract to the son of the Duke of Lorraine. On these grounds Convocation pronounced the marriage null and void on 9 July 1540. It was to be the shortest of Henry's six marriages, having lasted just six months.

Anne, who had been sent to RICHMOND PALACE for 'her health, open air and pleasure', raised no objection to the divorce proceedings. She elected to stay in England (to return to her brother's court, as he wished her to do, would have been an insufferable humiliation). Henry showed his appreciation of her ready compliance by giving her two houses, a household in keeping with her rank, and an annual income of £500 (the equivalent of about £50,000 today).

It is difficult, when looking at Anne's portrait, to see why Henry took such great exception to her as her face is distinctly pleasant. One can only conclude that she was a dull, unaccomplished young woman without conversation or wit and the very opposite of what Henry sought and found most attractive in women.

Once divorced, Henry remained on good terms with Anne and they became good friends. He referred to her as his 'beloved sister', visited her frequently and exchanged presents with her at the New Year. After CATHERINE HOWARD's execution there were even rumours that Henry and Anne were about to remarry. She also proved a good friend to her stepchildren, Mary, Elizabeth and Edward (*see* MARY I, ELIZABETH I and EDWARD VI), and was to share a litter with Elizabeth in Mary's coronation procession.

Anne died at the house Henry had given her in Chelsea on 17 July 1557. She had not completed her 42nd year and had been ill since early spring. Cancer has been suggested as the cause of her death. She was buried with considerable pomp and ceremony on the north side of the sacrarium in WESTMINSTER ABBEY, where the top of her plain but handsome table tomb has since been used for displays of the Abbey plate on the occasions of coronations and royal weddings.

Anne of Denmark (1574–1619) The consort of James VI and I (*see* JAMES I, KING OF ENGLAND), who was born at Skanderborg Castle in Jutland on 14 October 1574, second daughter of Frederik II, King of Denmark and Norway, and his wife Sophia, daughter of Ulrich III, Duke of Mecklenburg-Güstrow.

The negotiations for James's mariage to Anne were commenced in 1585, but were successfully blocked by ELIZABETH I, who held James's mother in captivity in England. It was only after the execution of MARY, QUEEN OF SCOTS in 1587 that James's advisers decided that the marriage should be concluded, and it took a surprising number of ceremonies to do so. A proxy marriage at Kronborg on 20 August 1589 was followed by James's arrival in Oslo, Norway, where the second ceremony took place with the bride and bridegroom in person on 23 November 1589. A round of feasting and visits followed and for good measure there was another ceremony at Kronborg on 21 January 1590. The couple were still in no hurry to return to Scotland and did not land at Leith until 1 May 1590. Anne's coronation in the chapel at Holyroodhouse followed on 17 May.

In the course of the next 12 years five children were born, of whom three survived infancy. When the news of James's accession to the English throne arrived, Anne was again pregnant and he set out for England without her. In May 1603 she was delivered of a stillborn son at Stirling and as soon as she had recovered she set out to join James in England and was crowned with him at WESTMINSTER ABBEY on 25 July. Her two youngest children were born in England and both died in infancy. Their memorials in Westminster Abbey have a strangely touching beauty.

Anne's portraits show a rather plain, masculine-looking woman. Her interests lay in court masques (the equivalent of amateur theatricals), in which she personally appeared, and in building, which ran her into debt. The Queen's House at Greenwich was created for her and is an exquisite example of Jacobean architecture.

The queen also enjoyed travelling about the country and made a spectacular visit to Bath in 1613. She and James led more or less separate lives and ended up with little or no interest in each other. One cause of difference between them was her late conversion to Catholicism and her increasing reliance upon the advice of the priests she kept in close attendance upon her. She died (of dropsy) at HAMPTON COURT PALACE on 4 March 1619 and was buried in the royal vault in Westminster Abbey.

Anointing The central act of the CORONA-

TION rite is the anointing of the sovereign with holy oil. It is based on the biblical precedent of the anointing of the kings of Israel and was adopted by the Eastern Roman and Byzantine emperors and the Frankish kings. The first reference to the practice in England is in the ANGLO-SAXON CHRONICLE, where it is recorded under the year 787 that OFFA, KING OF MERCIA caused his son and heir EGFRITH to be 'consecrated king'. The rite was incorporated into the elaborate coronation order devised by Dunstan, Archbishop of Canterbury for King EDGAR in 973, on which all succeeding coronations have been based. Sovereigns are anointed on the head, breast and hands, but queen consorts are anointed on the head only.

Pope John XXII granted the right to receive anointing and coronation to Scottish sovereigns on 13 June 1329 and the first to do so was DAVID II on 24 November 1331, although most of his predecessors had received some form of crowning or 'consecration'.

Annus horribilis The Latin phrase (meaning 'year of horrors'), first coined by Sir Edward Ford and used by ELIZABETH II in a speech she made at Guildhall referring to the year 1992, which had seen the matrimonial troubles of her three married children and the destruction of a large portion of WINDSOR CASTLE by fire. The phrase is an antithesis of the better known *annus mirabilis* (year of wonders).

Appleton House The Norfolk house, near SANDRINGHAM HOUSE, once occupied by Princess MAUD and her husband Prince Carl of Denmark (later Haakon VII of Norway). It was the birthplace on 2 July 1903 of their only child, the future Olav V of Norway (1903–91).

Ard Rí The title of the 'high-kings' of Ireland. Francis John Byrne in his book *Irish Kings and High-Kings* (1973) states that 'it has no precise significance, and does not necessarily imply sovereignty of Ireland'. A list of the high-kings will be found in Appendix XXXIII.

Argyll, Princess Louise, Duchess of *see* LOUISE, PRINCESS, DUCHESS OF ARGYLL.

Arthgal, King of Strathclyde (d.872) The elder son of King DYFNWAL III, who was King of Strathclyde by 870, in which year Olaf the White, the Norse King of Dublin, and Ivar Beinlaus sailed up the Firth of Clyde, defeated Arthgal and occupied the country for a year. In 872 Arthgal was murdered by CONSTANTINE II, KING OF SCOTS, whose sister was married to Arthgal's son and successor Run.

Arthur, Duke of Brittany (1187–1203) The posthumous son of GEOFFREY, DUKE OF BRITTANY (*jure uxoris*), and his wife Constance, daughter and heiress of Conan IV, Duke of Brittany, who was born at Nantes on the night of 29/30 April 1187. His father having been the fourth son of HENRY II, Arthur became heir-presumptive to his uncle RICHARD I in July 1189 and was officially so declared in 1190. On the king's death in 1199, however, the throne was seized by Richard's youngest brother JOHN. Arthur had the support of King Philip Augustus of France, to whose daughter Marie he was betrothed, but on 1 August 1202 he was captured by John at Mirebeau, north-west of Poitiers, and imprisoned at Rouen, where he was murdered on 3 April 1203 (probably on John's orders or, allegedly, by the hand of John himself, while drunk). His body was thrown into the Seine but was caught up in a fisherman's nets and was secretly buried in the church of Nôtre Dame de Pré at Bec.

Arthur, Duke of Connaught, Prince *see* CONNAUGHT, PRINCE ARTHUR, DUKE OF.

Arthur, King (d.542?) British folk-hero who, although not completely legendary, is surrounded by myths and fables. From his name (*Artorius* in Latin) it has been conjectured that he came from a Romano-British family. The late eighth-century historian NENNIUS is the first to mention him as a war leader of the Britons who defeated the Saxons in 12 battles. GEOFFREY OF MONMOUTH elaborated Arthur's story in his *Historia Regum Britanniae* written about 1136. He tells of Arthur's birth in Cornwall, his court at Caerleon-on-Usk, his defeat of the Saxons, then of the Picts and Scots, his conquest of Ireland and Iceland, his subjugation of Gaul, and his plans to conquer the whole of Europe, which were frustrated when he had to return to put down a rebellion in Britain, ending in his victory at Camlann when he was 'mortally wounded and was carried off to the Isle of Avalon, so that his wounds might be attended to'. This is ascribed to the year 542.

Subsequent writers, including Wace, Chrétien de Troyes and Thomas Malory, have further elaborated the Arthurian legend, telling of his three queens all named GUINEVERE and of his court with the Company of the Round Table, which was to inspire medieval chivalry. The story of the 'once and future king' was also developed, nurturing the belief that Arthur would come again to save his country. The Isle of Avalon to which Arthur is said to have been carried has been identified with Glastonbury, and his supposed tomb there was opened in the reign of HENRY II in 1172, when it appears that some monkish deception was practised in the faking of artefacts to ensure royal patronage of the abbey. The remains found were accompanied by a lead cross inlaid with stone and bearing the Latin inscription *Hic jacet sepultus inclytus rex Arturus cum Genevera uxore sua secunda in insula Avalonia* (Here lie buried the noble King Arthur with Guinevere his second wife in the island of Avalon). The skeletons of a man and woman were re-buried but again disinterred for the inspection of EDWARD I and ELEANOR OF CASTILE. Thereafter they remained in peace until the dissolution of the abbey under HENRY VIII, when the tomb and its contents were destroyed. Carbondating has established that the 'Round Table' preserved in Winchester dates only from the time of Edward I (the table was altered in the reign of HENRY VII).

In recent years the historian Geoffrey Ashe, who has devoted a lifetime to Arthurian studies, has identified Arthur with Riothamus or Rigotamos, who is named in continental sources as a British king who led an army into Gaul. Another historian, the late John Morris, in his serious study *The Age of Arthur* dates the period of Arthur's life somewhat earlier than the traditional date, bringing him into prominence from about 475 and placing his death at Camlann about 515.

Arthur, Prince, Duke of Connaught *see* CONNAUGHT, PRINCE ARTHUR, DUKE OF.

Arthur, Prince of Wales (1486–1502) The eldest son and heir apparent of HENRY VII and ELIZABETH OF YORK, who was born prematurely at St Swithin's Priory, Winchester, on 20 September 1486. He succeeded as Duke of Cornwall at birth and was named Arthur to emphasise the vaunted British lineage of his father. His baptism took place in Winchester Cathedral on 24 September 1486, his godparents being his father's stepfather the Earl of Derby, Lord Maltravers, and his maternal grandmother Queen ELIZABETH WOODVILLE. Prince Arthur was created Prince of Wales and Earl of Chester on 29 November 1489 and installed as a Knight of the Garter on 8 May 1491.

Negotiations for the young prince's marriage to the Infanta CATHERINE OF ARAGON, daughter of the Spanish sovereigns Ferdinand and Isabella, began as early as 1487 or 1488 and were successfully concluded with their betrothal in 1497. Arthur took part in a proxy marriage at Bewdley Palace, Worcestershire, on 19 May 1499 but the bride did not arrive in England until 2 October 1501. She was almost a year older than Arthur and from all accounts she was also very beautiful. He professed himself delighted with her and the marriage was solemnized at St Paul's Cathedral on 14 November 1501. It is almost certain that the marriage was never consummated (Arthur was small and undeveloped and probably sexually immature). The question was to become of vital importance when HENRY VIII was seeking the annulment of his marriage to Catherine.

In December 1501 the Prince and Princess of Wales took up residence in Ludlow Castle. The cold and damp of the Welsh marches had an adverse effect on Arthur's delicate health (he was probably tubercular) and he contracted 'the sweating sickness', from which he died on 2 April 1502. His body remained at Ludlow Castle for three weeks, when it was removed to the parish church and thence conveyed by ox-cart via Bewdley to Worcester, where it was interred in the cathedral.

Arthur of Connaught, Prince (1883–1938) The only son of Prince Arthur, Duke of CONNAUGHT and Princess Louise Margaret of Prussia, who was born at WINDSOR CASTLE on 13 January 1883 and baptized in the private chapel there on 16 February 1883, receiving the names Arthur Frederick Patrick Albert.

Prince Arthur was educated privately and in 1890 joined the 7th Hussars, being promoted to Lieutenant in January 1903. He was appointed Captain of the 2nd Dragoons (Scots Greys) in April 1907, having already been appointed a personal ADC to his uncle EDWARD VII. Created a Knight of the GARTER on 15 July 1902, he was head of the mission to invest the Emperor Mutsuhito of Japan with the Garter at Tokyo in February 1906. He was called to the Bar at Gray's Inn and made a Bencher thereof in June 1907. In 1911–12 he served as one of the four COUNSELLORS OF STATE during GEORGE V's absence in India. In the latter year he also represented the king at the funeral of the emperor of Japan.

Prince Arthur reached the rank of Colonel in 1922, having served in the First World War as ADC to the commander-in-chief of the British Expeditionary Force from 1914 to 1916 and also with the Canadian Corps from 1917 to 1918, being mentioned in despatches twice and receiving the Order of the BATH and the French and Belgian Croix de Guerre with palms. He served as Governor-General and Commander-in-Chief of the Union of South Africa from 1920 to 1924.

On 15 October 1913 Arthur was married at the Chapel Royal, ST JAMES'S PALACE, to his first cousin once removed, Princess Alexandra, Duchess of Fife (*see below*) and they had one son, Alastair Arthur, who succeeded his grandfather as 2nd Duke of Connaught. Prince Arthur fell ill with cancer and died in a nursing home in Belgrave Square, London, on 12 September 1938, aged 55 (survived by his father). His funeral took place at St George's Chapel, Windsor, and he was buried at Frogmore.

Arthur of Connaught, Princess (1891–1959) The wife of Prince ARTHUR OF CONNAUGHT, who was born Lady Alexandra Victoria Alberta Edwina Louise Duff at East Sheen Lodge, near Richmond, on Whit Sunday, 17 May 1891. She was the elder daughter of Alexander William George Duff, 1st Duke of Fife, and his wife Princess Louise Victoria Alexandra Dagmar of Wales (*see* LOUISE, PRINCESS ROYAL, DUCHESS OF FIFE), eldest daughter of Albert Edward, Prince of Wales, later EDWARD VII. Lady Alexandra, known in the family as Alix, was baptized in the Chapel Royal, ST JAMES'S PALACE, on 29 June 1891, her godparents including her great-grandmother Queen VICTORIA.

On 9 November 1905, Lady Alexandra's mother was declared PRINCESS ROYAL by Royal Warrant and at the same time her two daughters were granted the title of Princess with the style of 'Highness' and precedence immediately after all members of the royal family with the style of 'Royal Highness'. This unusual procedure was done at Edward VII's command, despite objections raised by the COLLEGE OF ARMS and some grumbling from the Prince of Wales (*see* GEORGE V).

In December 1911 the Duke of Fife with the Princess Royal and their two daughters set sail for Egypt and the Sudan, where they planned to winter, as in the three preceding years, for the benefit of the Princess Royal's health. They travelled on the P&O liner *Delhi*, which unfortunately went aground in heavy seas off Morocco. The royal party, successfully rescued, continued their journey to Khartoum and Cairo, but the duke caught a chill and died of pneumonia at Assouan (Aswan), on 29 January 1912. Princess Alix wrote: 'It seems to be generally thought that my father died as the result of the shipwreck, but this was not so.' On her father's death Princess Alix succeeded as Duchess of Fife and Countess of Macduff in her own right.

On 15 October 1913 Princess Alix was married at the Chapel Royal, St James's Palace, to her first cousin once removed, Prince Arthur of Connaught. Their only child, Alastair Arthur, was born in Mount Street, London, on 9 August 1914. He was styled Prince Alastair Arthur of Connaught until 1917, when, in accordance with George V's decrees regarding the titles of the royal family, his royal styles were dropped and he was styled His Highness Alastair Arthur, Earl of Macduff, using his mother's second title as a courtesy one. In due time he was to succeed his maternal grandfather as 2nd Duke of Connaught.

Princess Arthur was a fully trained nurse and for many years ran her own private nursing home in London, taking part in operations and in all nursing duties. She possessed a robust sense of humour and delighted in risqué jokes.

Prince Arthur of Connaught died on 12 September 1938. His only child, Alastair Arthur, 2nd Duke of Connaught in succession to his grandfather, caught a chill while on active service at Government House, Ottawa, and died there on 26 April 1943. He was unmarried. Princess Arthur was severely crippled by arthritis in later life, but acted as a COUNSELLOR OF STATE during GEORGE VI's absences abroad in 1939, 1943 and 1944. She died at her house in Avenue Road, St John's Wood, London, on 26 February 1959 and was cremated at Golders Green Crematorium, her ashes being deposited in the chapel at Mar Lodge, Braemar, Aberdeenshire. She was succeeded in the dukedom of Fife and earldom of Macduff by her nephew Lord Carnegie, the only son of her sister Maud, who had predeceased her in 1945.

Asclepiodotus (*fl.* late 3rd century) A prefect of the Roman Caesar Constantius, who took part in the overthrow of ALLECTUS in 296. GEOFFREY OF MONMOUTH elaborated his story, making him 'Duke of Cornwall' and 'King of the Britons' after the fall of Allectus. He attributes the martyrdom of St Alban to his reign and finally states that Asclepiodotus was killed 'in a pitched battle' with 'Coel, Duke of Kaelcolim, that is to say Colchester', who led a rebellion against him and replaced him as king.

Atheling The general designation for a prince of the royal blood in Anglo-Saxon England.

Athelstan, King of England (*c.*895–939) The eldest son of EDWARD THE ELDER and his first wife Ecgwynn (or Egwina), who succeeded his father in July 925 and was crowned by Wulfstan, Archbishop of Canterbury, at Kingston-on-Thames on 5 September 925. The first ruler of all England, he approached his grandfather ALFRED THE GREAT in stature and forged a strong foreign policy through the marriages of his sister and his many half-sisters to powerful continental rulers.

In 927 he drove out the Danish King Guthfrith and received the submission of CONSTANTINE II, KING OF SCOTS and Eugenius, an under-king in North Wales, at Dacre Castle in Cumbria. In 933 he invaded Scotland 'with a land and naval force, and harried much of the country'. Four years later, in 937, he won a great victory over the Danes at Brunanburh 'and there slew five kings and eight jarls'. Thereafter Athelstan's rule or overlordship was acknowledged throughout Britain. Among other laws laid down during his reign was a decree forbidding trade on Sundays and another dictating that perjurers should be buried in unconsecrated ground. Shortly before his death he sent an English fleet to Flanders to assist his nephew, Louis of France, the first military involvement of English forces on the continent.

Athelstan never married and died at Gloucester on 27 October 939, being succeeded by his half-brother EDMUND I. He was buried at Malmesbury Abbey, which he had founded and endowed.

Athlone, Princess Alice, Countess of *see* ALICE, PRINCESS, COUNTESS OF ATHLONE.

Augusta, Princess, Duchess of Brunswick (1737–1813) The eldest child of FREDERICK LOUIS, PRINCE OF WALES and Princess Augusta of Saxe-Gotha (*see* AUGUSTA, PRINCESS OF WALES), who was born at ST JAMES'S PALACE on 31 July 1737. Lord Hervey, who saw her when a few hours old, described her as 'a little rat of a girl, about the bigness of a good large toothpick case', while her grandmother Queen Caroline (*see* CAROLINE OF ANSBACH) felt reassured that 'this poor little ugly she-mouse' could only be her son's and not some 'chairman's brat' smuggled in as she would have supposed had the baby been 'a brave, large, fat, jolly boy'. At her baptism by the Archbishop of Canterbury on 29 August 1737, the baby was named Augusta after her mother, and her godparents were her grandparents the king and queen and the Dowager Duchess of Saxe-Gotha, all represented by proxies.

As a child Augusta took part with her brothers and sisters in the amateur theatricals that were a favourite pastime of the royal family. She lost her father in March 1751, and when her grandfather the king came to Leicester House on a visit of condolence she approached to kiss his hand, but he refused the homage and took her in his arms in a loving embrace, an uncharacteristic gesture for him.

In 1763 Princess Augusta was betrothed to her second cousin, Charles William Ferdinand, Hereditary Prince of Brunswick-Wolfenbüttel, her senior by nearly two years. A description of her at this time states: 'Her manners were lively and engaging, her complexion beautiful. In childhood her loveliness had been remarkable, but before she attained womanhood its bloom had passed away.' The marriage took place in the Great Council Room of St James's Palace at 7 o'clock in the evening of 16 January 1764. Before leaving England for Brunswick the newly married couple ordered £1000 to be distributed for the relief of poor prisoners for debt. The princess's dower was £80,000 and £5000 a year, plus the addition of £3000 from Hanover.

Augusta's husband succeeded his father as reigning Duke of Brunswick in March 1780. By that time the couple had had a family of four sons and three daughters, of whom the youngest died in infancy. Although Augusta had reported to her brother GEORGE III that her husband was 'monstrously fond' of her, the marriage did not prove an outstandingly happy one. The duke found the duchess dull and preferred to spend his time with his mistress, Luise von Hertefeld, who often joined forces with the duchess to thwart the duke when he showed signs of taking another mistress. Augusta whiled away her time in playing cards, a favourite diversion of the Hanoverian family.

In 1795 Augusta's second daughter, Caroline (see CAROLINE OF BRUNSWICK), was sought in marriage by her cousin George, Prince of Wales (see GEORGE IV), and Lord Malmesbury was sent to Brunswick to pursue the negotiations. He was greatly impressed by the duchess although he found her 'now a great deal too large, and her dress made her appear more so, being a thick buff-coloured satin chemise, with long sleeves, entirely lined, as she told me, with fleecy hosiery'.

Brunswick suffered in the Napoleonic Wars. The duke, although over 70, set out to lead his troops in support of Prussia. He was mortally wounded at the battle of Jena and died a few weeks later at Altona on 10 November 1806. Brunswick was occupied by the French and the widowed and nearly penniless duchess managed to escape into Sweden, where her brother George III despatched the frigate *Clyde* to bring her to England. She arrived on 7 July 1807 and joined her daughter the Princess of Wales at Blackheath. She was later received at Windsor and there was a touching reunion with her brother the king, although not quite such a cordial one with Queen CHARLOTTE, with whom she had never got on. Augusta had adopted white mourning for her husband and found speaking English unfamiliar to her after so many years spent in Germany. George III provided her with a pension, and in 1810 she moved from Blackheath to a house in Hanover Square, rented from Lord Palmerston. She was now very infirm and had to be carried about, spending most of her time in one room. Her last years were considerably brightened by the close friendship and affection that grew between her and her granddaughter Princess CHARLOTTE, who on first meeting her had 'told her that she was the merriest old woman she ever saw', much to the duchess's delighted amusement. Princess Augusta died in Hanover Square on 23 March 1813 and was buried at St George's Chapel, Windsor, on the 31st of the same month.

Augusta, Princess of Wales (1719–72) The wife of FREDERICK LOUIS, PRINCE OF WALES and mother of GEORGE III. The sixth and youngest daughter and youngest but one of 19 children of Friedrich II, reigning Duke of Saxe-Gotha-Altenburg, and his wife Princess Magdalene Auguste of Anhalt-Zerbst, she was born at Gotha on 30 November 1719.

When GEORGE II and Queen Caroline (see CAROLINE OF ANSBACH) decided that their estranged eldest son the Prince of Wales should marry in 1735, there were few suitable Protestant princesses of the right age available and the field was narrowed down to the 28-year-old Princess Charlotte

Amelia of Denmark, who was reported to be 'ugly, crooked and a dwarf', and Princess Augusta of Saxe-Gotha, who was sent to Herrenhausen in order that her prospective father-in-law might make an inspection. He expressed himself satisfied with her and Lord De La Warr was despatched to Gotha to make a formal demand for the princess's hand from her brother Duke Friedrich III and to escort her to England.

On 25 April 1736 Augusta, still very young for her age at 16, landed at Greenwich, clutching a doll. No member of the royal family was sent to receive her apart from her future husband, and a few days later on 8 May 1736 she made a laborious progress to ST JAMES'S PALACE by coach, barge and sedan chair, arriving an hour later than the appointed time to be received by the king and queen, both fuming with impatience. Augusta mollified them by prostrating herself before them so that they raised her to her feet and embraced her warmly. That night she dined with the prince and his siblings in his apartments. Frederick's attempt to insist that he and Augusta alone should be seated in armchairs and served on bended knee was thwarted by his sisters, who demanded that chairs be brought before they would enter the dining-room and ordered their own servants to serve them. The dinner was followed at 9 o'clock by the wedding ceremony in the Chapel Royal at St James's. Augusta was led to the altar by William Augustus, Duke of CUMBERLAND, 'wearing a crown of one bar, as Princess of Wales, set all over with diamonds; her robe likewise, as Princess of Wales, being of crimson velvet, turned back with several rows of ermine, and having her train supported by four ladies, all of whom were in virgin habits of silver ... and adorned with diamonds not less in value than from twenty to thirty thousand pounds each'.

In spite of having had dinner before the ceremony, supper was served afterwards and the prince made himself conspicuous by consuming glass after glass of jelly while grinning and winking at his servants, much to the annoyance of his mother. The ritual of 'bedding' the bride and bridegroom followed and the pair were at last left alone.

The early married life of the Prince and Princess of Wales was greatly restricted by the orders of the king and queen, which forbade them to set up their own household. Augusta spoke only German and a little French, but a Mr Wettstein was appointed to coach her in English and to perfect her French and she soon became fluent in both languages. She was lonely, however, and her old governess was brought over to keep her company. The princess also had scruples about receiving communion following the Anglican rite, having been brought up as a Lutheran, and only acquiesced when the queen threatened to annul the marriage and send her home. She continued to play with her dolls, however, and had to be dissuaded from doing so at an open window to the amusement of passers-by.

In spite of Frederick's infidelities, the couple got on well together. Augusta became pregnant towards the end of 1736, but the news was not confirmed to the queen until 5 July 1737, only weeks before the baby was due. The king and queen demanded to be present at the birth, but the rebellious Frederick was determined to prevent this. When Augusta's labour began, shortly after dining formally with the king and queen at Hampton Court on 31 July 1737, Frederick at once ordered a coach to take them back to St James's. The luckless Augusta had to endure the bumpy journey late at night and on arrival had to be carried into the palace, where nothing was ready. No sheets could be found and tablecloths were substituted. The baby, a little girl to be named after her mother, was born at 10.45 pm. The queen was awoken at 1.30 am and at once called for her 'nightgown', upon which her lady-in-waiting responded: 'Your nightgown, Madam, and your coaches too. The princess is at St James's.' The royal party arrived at St James's at 4 am; Frederick received his mother politely and the queen for once forebore to upbraid him.

Queen Caroline died four months later on 20 November 1737 and thereafter Frederick and Augusta were able to lead less circumscribed lives. Apart from his transient affairs with other women, Frederick was a good husband and a good father to their growing family, which by 1751 numbered eight. Frederick fell ill in March that year and died on the 31st, leaving Augusta a widow at 32, pregnant with her ninth child. The baby, CAROLINE MATILDA, was born on 21 July 1751.

Augusta's widowhood was spent bringing up her children and occupying herself in improving the gardens at Kew, which became an absorbing interest encouraged by John Stuart, 3rd Earl of Bute (1713–92), who was widely believed to be her lover and was to become prime minister in the reign of her son George III.

Augusta was often styled 'Dowager Princess of Wales', but as there was no actual Princess of Wales at any time during her lifetime it was an incorrect designation. She saw her son become king in 1760 and had by then become something of a matriarch, frequently admonishing him: 'George, be a king!' The princess died of cancer of the throat at her London residence, CARLTON HOUSE, on 8 February 1772, and was buried in the royal vault at WESTMINSTER ABBEY.

Augusta of Cambridge, Princess, Grand Duchess of Mecklenburg-Strelitz (1822–1916)

The elder daughter and second child of Prince Adolphus, Duke of CAMBRIDGE (seventh son of GEORGE III) and his wife Princess Augusta of Hesse-Cassel, who was born at the Palace of Montbrillant, near Hanover, on 19 July 1822. At her baptism on 16 August following she received the names Augusta Caroline Charlotte Elizabeth Mary Sophia Louisa. Her father had been governor-general of the Kingdom of Hanover since 1816 and assumed the title of Viceroy after the accession of his brother WILLIAM IV in 1830. When William died in 1837 Hanover passed to his next male heir, the Duke of Cumberland (see CUMBERLAND, PRINCE ERNEST AUGUSTUS, DUKE OF), and the Cambridge family returned to England, to Cambridge House, Piccadilly. On 28 June 1843 Princess Augusta was married in the private chapel at BUCKINGHAM PALACE to her first cousin (their mothers being sisters) Frederick William, Hereditary Grand Duke of Mecklenburg-Strelitz, who was born at Neustrelitz on 17 October 1819.

Princess Augusta's first child, a son, was born on 13 January 1845 but lived only a few hours. Her second and last child, George Adolphus Frederick Augustus Victor Ernest Adalbert Gustavus William Wellington, was born on 22 July 1848. In due time he was to succeed his father and become reigning Grand Duke Adolphus Frederick V of Mecklenburg-Strelitz.

In 1860 Augusta's husband succeeded his father as reigning Grand Duke and she became Grand Duchess. She had always enjoyed great popularity in England, frequently to the annoyance of her cousin Queen VICTORIA and in later life was to recall jealous scenes at 'a small Ball' when the Russian Tsarevitch Alexander 'was more attentive to me than to her'. Having no daughter of her own, Princess Augusta became extremely fond of her niece Princess May of Teck (later Queen MARY) and expressed her forthright views on almost every subject in the correspondence they

maintained until the end of the Grand Duchess's long life.

Princess Augusta was a frequent visitor to London and in 1887 took part in Queen Victoria's Golden Jubilee celebrations. There is a rather charming account of her from the pen of Queen Liliuokalani of Hawaii, who (as Crown Princess) accompanied her sister-in-law Queen Kapiolani to the Jubilee:

> There was a little lady who made her appearance [in Westminster Abbey] accompanied by her husband, who was blind; she seated him on a bench back of that we occupied; then she proceeded to adjust his necktie, she pulled down his coat and smoothed it out, and arranged other parts of his uniform to suit her own taste. Finally, when his appearance seemed to her satisfactory, she left him, and coming towards us took a seat directly between Queen Kapiolani and myself. This lady was none other than the Grand Duchess of Mecklenburg-Strelitz ... While we were awaiting the opening ceremonies, the grand duchess turned to me and said, 'Parlez vous Français?' Upon my response in the negative, she addressed to me a similar question, only this time asking if I spoke English; to which I replied, 'Yes, a little.' Then, much to my amusement, she motioned to the princesses opposite to us that her companion understood English, and we were very soon in a most agreeable and animated conversation on the topics of the day.

When EDWARD VII succeeded to the throne in 1901, Grand Duchess Augusta was almost the only person alive who could remember the court of William IV and Queen ADELAIDE and was able to give invaluable advice on points of ceremonial. In 1904 the Grand Duchess lost both her brother the Duke of Cambridge and her husband the Grand Duke, who died on 29 May when his wife was on a visit to England.

The Grand Duchess was 92 when the First World War broke out. Her only son had died two months earlier and the reigning Grand Duke was now her grandson, Adolphus Frederick VI, known to her as 'Fred'. He was devoted to his grandmother and shared her views on many things, both of them being very distressed by the war. Augusta was able to maintain her correspondence with May through the good offices of the Crown Princess of Sweden (see MARGARET OF CONNAUGHT, PRINCESS). She fell ill in November 1916 and, knowing herself to be dying, sent a message to GEORGE V: 'Tell the king that it is a stout old English heart which is ceasing to beat.' She died at Neustrelitz in the morning of 5 December 1916, her last word being her niece's name, 'May'.

Augusta Sophia, Princess (1768–1840) The second daughter and sixth child of GEORGE III and Queen CHARLOTTE, who was born at Buckingham House (now BUCKINGHAM PALACE) at 8.30 in the evening of 8 November 1768. She was baptized by the Archbishop of Canterbury in the Great Council Room at ST JAMES'S PALACE on 7 December 1768, her godparents being her aunts the Hereditary Princess of Brunswick and the Queen of Denmark (both represented by proxies) and her mother's brother, Prince Charles of Mecklenburg-Strelitz, then on a visit to England.

Princess Augusta was brought up with her sisters Charlotte (*see* CHARLOTTE, PRINCESS ROYAL) and Elizabeth (*see* ELIZABETH, PRINCESS, LANDGRAVINE OF HESSE-HOMBURG) under a strict governess, Madame de Lafitte. She grew up to be the most attractive of George III's daughters, as contemporary accounts and her portraits testify. In 1790 there was an offer for her hand from Duke Friedrich Eugen of Württemberg, but her father refused it, thinking it unfitting that Augusta should be married before her elder sister and in actual fact the same suitor did marry the Princess Royal some years later. Most of Princess Augusta's life was passed in attendance on her mother, who when she died in 1818 left her FROGMORE HOUSE, near Windsor. From 1812 the princess had an income of £13,000 voted by Parliament.

Augusta Sophia was the favourite sister of the Prince Regent (GEORGE IV), and after he became king she went on a visit to the continent to see her sisters the Queen of Württemberg and the Landgravine of Hesse-Homburg. The princess was an accomplished musician and composed songs, marches and waltzes. There was a strong rumour, which has never been confirmed, that she was privately married to General Sir Brent Spencer (1760–1828) with the connivance of George IV.

Princess Augusta's London residence was CLARENCE HOUSE, St James's, and it was there that she died on 22 September 1840, after a long illness. Her niece Queen VICTORIA wrote to the king of the Belgians of the death of 'good excellent Aunt Augusta' as follows: 'I regret her very, very sincerely, though for herself we are all most thankful for the release of such unexampled sufferings, borne with such unexampled patience. Almost the last thing she said when she was still conscious, the day before she died, was to Mr More (the apothecary), who wrote me every morning a Report: "Have you written to my darling?" Is this not touching?'

Princess Augusta's body was taken to lie in state at Frogmore House, and thence conveyed to St George's Chapel, Windsor, for burial on 2 October 1840. The princess was noted for her acts of charity, including the establishment at Windsor of an annuity of £300 for the benefit of poor soldiers' wives and children.

Augustus, Prince, Duke of Sussex *see* SUSSEX, AUGUSTUS FREDERICK, DUKE OF.

Aunt Heap, The A humorous allusion to KENSINGTON PALACE coined by Edward, Prince of Wales (later EDWARD VIII). It was a reference to the considerable number of his aunts and great-aunts who occupied apartments there. More recently it has been taken up by CHARLES, PRINCE OF WALES.

Aurum Reginae 'Queen-gold', the right of the QUEEN CONSORT to every tenth mark paid to the king in taxes by the citizens of London in medieval times. Its extraction was often a contentious matter.

Australia, Order of An order instituted by ELIZABETH II in 1975 as an award for citizens of the Commonwealth of Australia. The queen is Sovereign of the Order, which has a General Division and a Military Division and is divided into five classes: AK or AD (Knight or Dame), with precedence after the Order of Merit; AC (Companion), with precedence after Knight/Dame Grand Cross of the Order of the British Empire; AO (Officer), with precedence after Knight Bachelor; AM (Member), with precedence after the Distinguished Service Order; and OAM (Order of Australia Medal), with precedence after the Royal Red Cross (2nd class).

B

Baldred, King of Kent (*fl*.825) The last independent king of Kent. Nothing is known of Baldred beyond an entry in the ANGLO-SAXON CHRONICLE, which states that in 825 EGBERT, KING OF WESSEX 'sent his son Ethelwulf ... and Ealhstan, his bishop, and Wulfheard, his ealdorman, to Kent with a great force, and they drove King Baldred north over Thames, and the Kentishmen submitted to him'.

Baldwin of Blois (*c*.1126–35) The eldest son of King STEPHEN and MATILDA OF BOULOGNE, who was born about 1126 and named after his great-uncle Baldwin, King of Jerusalem. He died at the age of about nine in 1135 before his father's accession to the throne on 2 December that year and was buried in the church of the Holy Trinity at Aldgate.

Balliol, Edward (*c*.1282–1370) The elder son of John BALLIOL, the puppet king of Scotland, and Isabella de Warrenne, who invaded Scotland with English support in August 1332 and was crowned king at Scone on 24 September 1332. He was forced to fly to England in December 1332, but was restored with English aid the following year, formally acknowledging EDWARD III as his overlord in November 1333. Another flight in 1334 and another restoration in 1335 were followed by his final retirement to England in 1338. He surrendered all claim to the crown of Scotland to Edward III in exchange for a pension on 20 January 1356.

Edward Balliol contracted a marriage on 23 October 1295 with Isabel, the three-year-old daughter of Charles, Count of Valois (son of King Philippe III of France). The marriage was never proceeded with and Isabel later married Jean III, Duke of Brittany, and died in 1309. Edward's second attempt at matrimony was essayed many years later with Margaret, daughter of Philip, Prince of Tarentum, and his first wife Thamar, daughter of Nicephorus Angelus. This marriage, too, was never consummated, and after its annulment Margaret married Francesco del Balzo,

Duke of Andria. According to some accounts Edward Balliol died at Bailleul in 1363 or 1364; others state that he died at Wheatley, near Doncaster, after 20 May 1370. At either date he had achieved an age far greater than usual for those times. He was probably buried at Beauvale Priory, Nottinghamshire.

Balliol, John (1249–1314) The fourth and youngest son of John Balliol (d.1268), the founder of Balliol College, Oxford, and his wife DEVORGUILLA, LADY OF GALLOWAY, through whom he was a great-great-great-grandson of DAVID I, KING OF SCOTS. In 1290 the death of MARGARET, QUEEN OF SCOTS ('The Maid of Norway') left no clear heir to the Scottish throne and 13 competitors laid claim thereto, agreeing to submit their claims to the arbitration of EDWARD I of England. Their names were entered in the Great Roll of Scotland on 3 August 1291 (*see* SCOTTISH SUCCESSION) and John Balliol's was the eleventh entered. Although his claim was a fairly slender one, he had the advantage that he was married (the marriage having taken place some time before 7 February 1281) to Isabella, daughter of John de Warrenne, 3rd Earl of Surrey, by his wife Alice de Lusignan, a half-first cousin by marriage to the English king. Edward pronounced at Berwick in Balliol's favour on 17 November 1292 and he was crowned at SCONE on 30 November. He adopted the style of King of Scotland (*Rex Scotiae*) rather than that of King of Scots (*Rex Scotorum*), which had always been used hitherto and was to be revived again after Balliol's reign.

Balliol acknowledged the overlordship of Edward I but later attempted to assert his independence, for which he was forced to abdicate at Brechin on 10 July 1296, after the royal arms had been stripped from his tunic, earning him the nickname of 'Toom Tabard', or 'Empty Coat'. He was held prisoner in England for three years and then released and allowed to go to France, where he settled on his ancestral lands at Bailleul-en-Gouffern in Normandy. He died there in April 1313 according to some accounts, or at Hélicourt towards the end of 1314 according to others. He was probably buried in the church of St Waast at Bailleul. John Balliol left two sons, Edward Balliol (*see above*) and Henry Balliol, who was killed at Annan on 16 December 1332.

Balmoral Castle The Scottish home of the royal family on Deeside, Grampian, which was acquired by Queen VICTORIA and Prince ALBERT from the Duff family trustees in 1852. The Queen described it as 'a pretty little castle in the old Scotch style'. The money for its purchase (30,000 guineas) came from a legacy left to the queen by an eccentric old miser, John Camden Neild, so that the castle and its lands were a private possession and not crown property. Prince Albert at once set about building a new castle in Scottish Baronial style and it was ready for occupation by September 1855. To Victoria the house, with its 14 water-closets (always items of high priority on her agenda) was 'charming; the rooms delightful; the furniture, papers, everything perfection'. The queen and the prince embarked enthusiastically on Highland life and spent a large part of every summer and autumn at Balmoral. Victoria continued to visit it in her widowhood, although slightly less frequently (she had a statue raised in Albert's memory at the spot where he had shot his last stag). She published a book, *A Journal of Our Life in the Highlands*, and a sequel, *More Leaves from Our Life in the Highlands*, inspired by Balmoral, and towards the end of her reign the atmosphere there became so stiff and formal that the word 'Balmorality' was coined to describe it.

EDWARD VII and Queen ALEXANDRA spent only about one month every year at Balmoral, but GEORGE V, GEORGE VI and ELIZABETH II revived the practice of staying there for at least two months every autumn. Not all appreciated the baronial splendour of the building, however. Queen Alexandra described Victoria's taste in wallpapers as 'rather sad and very doubtful' and removed some of the tartan furnishings her mother-in-law had favoured, while the Labour politician Jim Thomas, who stayed at Balmoral as a guest of George V, with whom he was a great favourite, described it as 'a bloody dull 'ouse'.

Baptisms Royal baptisms in Britain have never been occasions for great public display or ceremonial. Royal children are usually baptized by the Archbishop of Canterbury in the silver-gilt lily font which is kept with the royal regalia in the TOWER OF LONDON.

Bath, The Most Honourable Order of the In England, the most senior order of chivalry after the Order of the GARTER. The Order of the Bath derives its name from the ritual bath (symbolizing purity) which formed part of the initiation ceremony of knights in the Middle Ages. HENRY IV is said to have created 17 knights of the Bath on the eve of his coronation in 1399, and the ceremony of their investiture was described by Froissart. However, the real founder of the order was GEORGE I, who, drawing on the ancient tradition, in 1725 founded a new military order to be called the Order of the Bath. The order was enlarged in 1815 and again in 1847, when a civil branch was established. In 1973 it was extended to include ladies. There are three classes of the order: Knights and Dames Grand Cross (GCB), limited to 120; Knights and Dames Commanders (KCB or DCB), limited to 355; and Companions (CB), limited to 1870. The chapel of the order, where the banners of Knights and Dames Grand Cross are hung, is Henry VII's Chapel in Westminster Abbey.

Battenberg German princely family, which owes its origin to the morganatic marriage of Prince Alexander of Hesse (1823–88) to the Polish-born Countess Julie von Hauke (1825–95), who was created successively Countess and Princess of Battenberg. They had four sons and one daughter. The eldest son, Louis (1854–1921), married his first cousin once removed Princess Victoria of Hesse (1863–1950), whose mother was Queen VICTORIA's second daughter Alice (*see* ALICE MAUD MARY, PRINCESS, GRAND DUCHESS OF HESSE). Prince Louis became a naturalized British subject and entered the Royal Navy, rising to the rank of Admiral. He was appointed First Sea Lord in 1912, but was forced to resign in October 1914 when anti-German prejudice ran high. In 1917 he renounced his German styles and titles and assumed the surname MOUNT-BATTEN, being created Marquess of Milford Haven.

The second Battenberg son, Alexander (1857–93), was elected sovereign Prince of Bulgaria in 1879, but was forced to abdicate in 1886. The third son, Henry (1858–96), married Victoria's youngest daughter Princess BEATRICE². Their surviving sons also assumed the surname of Mountbatten in

1917, the elder being created Marquess of Carisbrooke.

It is an irony of history that a family considered ineligible to succeed to the grand duchy of Hesse produced a sovereign prince, queens of Spain and Sweden, and a viceroy of India (Earl MOUNTBATTEN OF BURMA, younger son of the 1st Marquess of Milford Haven).

Bayeux Tapestry The name by which the long strip of embroidery depicting the history of the Norman Conquest of England is generally known, although it is, of course, not a tapestry at all since tapestries are woven. Long believed to have been the work of WILLIAM I THE CONQUEROR's queen MATILDA OF FLANDERS, the Bayeux Tapestry is now believed to have been commissioned by the Conqueror's half-brother, ODO, BISHOP OF BAYEUX. The work is of coarse bleached linen material over 230 feet long and about 20 inches in depth. Eight coloured wools were used in the embroidery. It has been suggested that the tapestry was made in England, possibly at Canterbury, and was first displayed at the dedication of Bayeux Cathedral in 1077. It is mentioned in an inventory of the possessions of Bayeux Cathedral in 1476 but lay forgotten until the 18th century when French scholars began to take an interest in it. Napoleon had it taken to Paris and exhibited in 1803, but returned it to Bayeux the following year. Its condition had greatly deteriorated by the mid-19th century and a certain amount of restoration work has been carried out on several occasions.

Baynard's Castle A grim fortress on the south bank of the Thames, no longer extant, once famous for its royal connections. Built by the Norman knight Ralph Baynard during the reign of WILLIAM I, the castle later passed to Robert Fitzwalter but was demolished when HENRY I's interest in Fitzwalter's daughter Matilda was opposed by both Matilda and her father (Matilda was later murdered in the TOWER OF LONDON by means of a poisoned poached egg). EDWARD IV was residing at the rebuilt castle when he was proclaimed king in 1461 and it was also allegedly here that Richard of Gloucester accepted the crown as RICHARD III. The castle was rebuilt by HENRY VII in 1487 and was later home to CATHERINE OF ARAGON, ANNE BOLEYN and ANNE OF CLEVES. Lady Jane Grey (see Queen JANE) was proclaimed queen while at Baynard's Castle, and the building also played host to ELIZABETH I and other monarchs before its final destruction

in the Great Fire of 1666 shortly after a visit by CHARLES II. The sole surviving tower was pulled down in 1720. The site is now marked by a street and a public house, both bearing the castle's name.

Beatrice, Countess of Richmond (1242–75) The second daughter and third child of HENRY III and ELEANOR OF PROVENCE, who was born at Bordeaux on 25 June 1242 and named after her maternal grandmother Beatrice of Savoy, Countess of Provence. She was married at St Denis on 22 January 1260 to John, Earl of Richmond, the son and heir of John I, Duke of Brittany, and they had four sons and three daughters. The Countess of Richmond died in London while on a visit to her brother EDWARD I on 24 March 1275 and was buried in the church of the Grey Friars at Newgate, her heart being buried at Fontevraud. Her husband succeeded his father as Duke of Brittany in 1286. He died at Lyons on 18 November 1305, having been fatally injured by the collapse of a wall while attending the coronation of Pope Clement V.

Beatrice, Princess[1] Alleged shortlived daughter of EDWARD I, for whose existence there is no surviving contemporary source (see ELEANOR OF CASTILE).

Beatrice, Princess[2] (1857–1944) The fifth daughter and ninth and youngest child of Queen VICTORIA and Prince ALBERT, who was born at BUCKINGHAM PALACE on 14 April 1857 at a quarter to two in the afternoon. She was baptized Beatrice Mary Victoria Feodore in the private chapel of Buckingham Palace on 16 June following, her godparents being her grandmother, the Duchess of Kent (see VICTORIA, DUCHESS OF KENT); her eldest sister, the Princess Royal; and the latter's fiancé, Prince Frederick William of Prussia. Her mother duly reported the event to her uncle Leopold: 'The christening of little Beatrice is just over – and was very brilliant and nice. We had the luncheon in the fine ball-room, which looked very handsome. The Archduke Maximilian (who is here since Sunday evening) led me to the chapel, and at the luncheon I sat between him and Fritz.' The Archduke was in due time to become uncle Leopold's son-in-law and the ill-fated Emperor of Mexico.

The death of her father the Prince Consort in 1861 when she was only four resulted in Princess Beatrice becoming a great solace to her grief-stricken mother, who hoped she would always have her about her to act as her companion and secretary. The princess seemed doomed to a life of spinsterhood, but at the age of 28 she fell in love with Prince Henry Maurice of BATTEN-BERG, her junior by almost one and a half years. Victoria received the news very badly at first and mother and daughter were not on speaking terms for a time, but after Beatrice and Henry expressed their willingness to make their home with the queen and to forego having a separate establishment of their own all was well, and the marriage took place on 23 July 1885 at Whippingham Church, Isle of Wight, the queen herself giving her daughter away. The 10 brides-maids were all princesses and nieces of the bride. The short honeymoon was spent at Quarr Abbey and at the end of the month the bridal couple returned to the queen's side at OSBORNE HOUSE. Prince Henry was granted the qualification of 'Royal Highness' and invested with the Order of the GARTER on his wedding day and naturalized as a British subject by Act of Parliament on 6 August 1885.

Princess Beatrice's first pregnancy ended in a miscarriage, but on 23 November 1886 she gave birth to a son, Alexander Albert, at WINDSOR CASTLE. He was followed by Victoria Eugenie Julia Ena, born at Balmoral on 24 October 1887, Leopold Arthur Louis, born at Windsor Castle on 21 May 1889, and Maurice Victor Donald, born at Balmoral on 3 October 1891.

In November 1895 Prince Henry volunteered for service in the Ashanti expedition and was appointed for special duty by the War Office. His contingent arrived in Africa on Christmas Day and by 10 January 1896 it was reported that the prince 'had a slight attack of fever' and had been sent back to base. A week later he embarked on the cruiser *Blonde* to sail for Madeira, but on 20 January he suffered a relapse and died at sea. The apocryphal lines attributed to the Poet Laureate Alfred Austen (1835–1913) refer to Prince Henry's last illness:

> Across the sea the electric message came:
> 'He is no better; he is much the same.'

Prince Henry's body was returned to England and interred in the Battenberg Chapel at Whippingham Parish Church, where he had been married. His monument was sculpted by his sister-in-law Princess LOUISE.

On 12 June 1896 Princess Beatrice was appointed Governor and Captain of the Isle of Wight and Governor of Carisbrooke Castle, duties which she undertook consci-

entiously for the remainder of her long life. Her only daughter, Princess Victoria Eugenie of Battenberg, was married to King Alfonso XIII of Spain on 31 May 1906, an event that caused many raised eyebrows in European royal circles because of the morganatic status of the bride's father.

Princess Beatrice's three sons all served in the First World War, the youngest, Prince Maurice, being killed in action during the retreat from Mons on 27 October 1914. In 1917 her two surviving sons relinquished their German styles and titles and anglicized their name to MOUNTBATTEN. Alexander was created Marquess of Carisbrooke and Leopold was granted the rank and precedence of a younger son of a marquess, becoming Lord Leopold Mountbatten. He died unmarried at KENSINGTON PALACE on 23 April 1922.

In later life Princess Beatrice became very infirm with arthritis and was confined to a wheelchair. She translated and edited the memoirs of her great-grandmother Duchess Augusta of Saxe-Coburg-Saalfeld, which were published as *In Napoleonic Times*. Princess Beatrice was the last survivor of Queen Victoria's children. She died at Brantridge Park, Balcombe, Sussex, on 26 October 1944, aged 87. Her funeral took place at St George's Chapel, Windsor, and after reposing for a short time in the Royal Tomb House, her coffin was taken to the Isle of Wight and laid beside that of her husband at Whippingham.

Beatrice of York, Princess (1988–) The elder daughter of Prince Andrew, Duke of YORK (second son of ELIZABETH II) and of the Duchess of York, *née* Sarah Margaret FERGUSON, who was born at the Portland Hospital, London, on 8 August 1988. She was baptized Beatrice Elizabeth Mary at the Chapel Royal, ST JAMES'S PALACE, on 20 December 1988. Her mother's decision to leave the baby Beatrice at home with her husband in October 1988, in order to tour Australia, proved unpopular with the press and marked a significant stage in the deterioration of the public image of 'Fergie' (though she explained in her defence that she had been concerned that such an arduous tour would have affected her baby's health).

Beauclerc Sobriquet, meaning 'Fine scholar', attached to the name of HENRY I (though not by his contemporaries). In the form Beauclerk it was adopted by CHARLES II as a surname for his two natural sons by Nell GWYNNE and has continued ever since as the family name of the Dukes of St Albans, who descend from the elder son.

Beaufort Surname adopted by the legitimated offspring of John of Gaunt, Duke of LANCASTER by his mistress and later third wife, Catherine Swynford. It was derived from Beaufort Castle in Champagne, their birthplace.

Bedchamber Crisis A political crisis that arose in 1841 when Queen VICTORIA objected to the dismissal of her Whig ladies-in-waiting in favour of Tory replacements, as custom demanded on a change of government. It led to a dispute between the queen and the incoming Tory prime minister, Sir Robert Peel. Faced with the queen's intransigence on the issue, Peel refused to accept the post of prime minister and Melbourne was temporarily reinstated, despite the fact that Peel had the support of the House of Commons. In standing her ground before Peel, Victoria complimented herself 'I never saw a man so frightened'. She reassured Lord Melbourne, meanwhile, with the words 'The Queen of England will not submit to such trickery'. A compromise was eventually reached whereby the queen relinquished the right to appoint the Lord Steward, the Lord Chamberlain, the Master of the Horse, Lords-in-Waiting, Grooms-in-Waiting and Equerries, but retained the right to appoint her Mistress of the Robes and Ladies of the Bedchamber, regardless of their political allegiance. Peel duly acquiesced to become prime minister.

Bedchamber Plot The name sometimes used by anti-Jacobites in reference to the alleged smuggling of a supposititious child hidden in a warming-pan into the queen's bed in 1688 (*see* JAMES II; MARY OF MODENA).

Bede, The Venerable (673–735) The author of *A History of the English Church and People*, one of the most valuable sources for the early history of Anglo-Saxon England, was born in Northumbria in 673 and at the age of seven was sent to school at the new monastery of St Peter at Wearmouth under Abbot Benedict Biscop. When the new sister-foundation of St Paul at Jarrow was founded in 682, Bede was transferred there and placed in the care of Abbot Ceolfrid. He spent the rest of his life in the two monasteries, becoming a monk and a priest, and probably never journeyed further than Lindisfarne and York.

Apart from an assiduous devotion to his religious duties, Bede applied himself to writing, and apart from his famous *History* was the author of the *Lives of the Abbots of Wearmouth and Jarrow* and of many translations from, and commentaries on, the scriptures, as well as hymns, a martyrology, and treatises on orthography and poetry. At the time of his death he was working on a translation of St John's Gospel and extracts from the writings of St Isidore of Seville. He dictated the last sentence while lying on the floor of his cell at Jarrow and died on 25 May 735. He was formally recognized as a 'Doctor of the Church' by Pope Leo XIII in 1899.

Bedford, George, Duke of (1477–9) The third and youngest son of EDWARD IV and ELIZABETH WOODVILLE, who was born at WINDSOR CASTLE in March 1477. He was designated Duke of Bedford and is so styled on his tombstone, but was never formally so created. He died at Windsor Castle in March 1479 and was buried in St George's Chapel there.

Bedford, John, Duke of (1389–1435) The third surviving son of HENRY IV and his first wife Mary de Bohun, who was born on 20 June 1389. In 1403 he was appointed Warden of the East Marches and Captain of Berwick, an office that he filled until 1414. On 10 September 1403 he was made Constable of England and was confirmed in that office for life in 1410. He was joint ambassador to Scotland in 1411 and on 16 May 1414 his brother HENRY V created him Earl of Kendal and Duke of Bedford for life. These honours were later surrendered and regranted to him and the heirs male of his body on 8 July 1433. He was further created Earl of Richmond on 24 November 1414.

When Henry V left on his French expedition in 1415, Bedford was appointed Guardian of the Realm, filling the same position again in 1417 and 1421. After Henry V's death Bedford was appointed Regent of France and Protector of the Kingdom of England. On 17 August 1424 he commanded the English and Burgundian forces at the battle of Verneuil, in which 7000 French and 2500 Scots were said to have been killed. Bedford saw his nephew HENRY VI crowned as King of France at Paris on 7 September 1432.

The Duke of Bedford was twice married. His first wife, whom he married at Troyes in June 1423, was Anne, daughter of John, Duke of Burgundy, and his wife Margaret of Bavaria. She died at the Hôtel de Bourgogne, Paris, on 14 November 1432, after giving birth to a child that did not survive.

The Duke married secondly at Therouenne on 20 April 1433, Jacquette, daughter of Pierre de Luxembourg, Count of St Pol, and his wife Marguerite, daughter of Francisco del Balzo, Duke of Andria. He died at Joyeux Repos, his residence in Rouen, on 15 September 1435 and was buried at Rouen. His widow, by whom he had no issue, married about a year later Sir Richard Woodville, later created Earl Rivers, and had numerous children, including ELIZABETH WOODVILLE, the consort of EDWARD IV. She died on 30 May 1472.

Beefeaters The popular name by which the Queen's Bodyguard of the Yeomen of the Guard have been known since some time in the mid-17th century. The nickname is popularly believed to refer to the myth that they owe their physical stamina to the consumption of vast quantities of roast beef.

Beohrtric, King of Wessex (d.802) Successor to the throne of Wessex after King CYNEWULF was killed in 786 and ruler for some 16 years. Beohrtric's origins are unknown beyond the statement in the ANGLO-SAXON CHRONICLE that 'his direct paternal ancestry goes back to Cerdic'. In 789 he married EADBURH, daughter of OFFA, KING OF MERCIA. Tradition depicts Eadburh as a powerful and domineering woman and the inadvertent poisoner of her husband, who at a banquet drank from a cup she had prepared for one of his confidential advisers of whom she was jealous. On her husband's death she fled to France, where she is said to have been the abbess of a convent for a few years (until her conduct led to her expulsion) and died a beggar in the streets of Pavia *en route* for Rome, where she hoped to expiate her crime. Her deed is said to have so horrified her countrymen that it was decreed that no future royal consort should be honoured as *regina*, but merely bear the designation of *hlafdig* (lady) or *cwen* (companion), whence the word queen. Beohrtric was buried at Wareham. He had no children and the throne passed to Egbert (*see* EGBERT, KING OF WESSEX).

Beohrtwulf, King of Mercia (d.852) Of unknown origin, Beohrtwulf became king of MERCIA in succession to Wiglaf in 840. His wife Saethryth attested his charters, and he had two sons, Beohrtfrith and Beohrtric. He died or was driven out of Mercia in the thirteenth year of his reign and was succeeded by BURHRED.

Beonna, King of East Anglia (*fl.*749) A shadowy figure, who is said to have divided the kingdom of EAST ANGLIA with the even more shadowy figures Hun and Alberht after the death of King ALFWOLD in 749. According to Florence of Worcester, Beonna was still reigning in 758. His coins are known.

Beonred, King of Mercia (d.757) Of unknown origin, Beonred established himself as king of MERCIA on the murder of King ETHELBALD, but was himself killed the same year by OFFA, who succeeded him.

Beornwulf, King of Mercia (d.825) Of unknown origin, Beornwulf succeeded CEOL-WULF I as king of MERCIA in 823. He was defeated by EGBERT, KING OF WESSEX at the battle of Ellendun, near Wroughton in Wiltshire, in 825 and was killed by the East Angles later in the same year.

Berengaria (1276–8) One of the many daughters of EDWARD I and his first wife ELEANOR OF CASTILE, Berengaria was born at the royal manor of Kempton, Middlesex, on 1 May 1276. She was living on 6 June 1277, when the king gave £6.13.4 to her wet-nurse, but was dead by 27 June 1278, when the same amount was given to the woman who had been her nurse. She was probably buried in WESTMINSTER ABBEY.

Berengaria of Navarre, Queen of England (*c.*1163–after 1230) The consort of RICHARD I, who was the daughter of Sancho VI the Wise, King of Navarre, and his wife Beatrice (or Sanchia), daughter of Alfonso VII, King of Castile. She was born at her father's capital city of Pamplona in about 1163. Richard and Berengaria first met when little more than children at a tournament held at her father's court in Pamplona. Here Richard formed a strong romantic attachment (Agnes Strickland calls it 'an ardent friendship') with Berengaria's brother Sancho. Urged to marry soon after his accession by his mother and others, Richard's thoughts turned to the sister of his beloved friend, whom she may have resembled, and his mother was charged with demanding her hand on his behalf and escorting her to join him at whatever point he might have reached on the Crusade.

Queen Eleanor (*see* ELEANOR OF AQUITAINE) escorted Berengaria as far as Messina, where she handed her over to her daughter, the Queen of Sicily (*see* JOAN, QUEEN OF SICILY), who accompanied her the rest of the way to Cyprus. Here they joined Richard and the marriage and coronation of Berengaria were celebrated at Limasol on 12 May 1191. Berengaria accompanied Richard throughout the Crusade and was always treated courteously by him, but it is doubtful if the marriage was ever consummated.

When Richard's party left the Holy Land to return to Europe the ladies sailed on a different ship from the king. Whereas he was shipwrecked, they landed safely at Naples and proceeded to Rome. After a year in Rome, the Pope gave them a safe-conduct to travel to Marseilles. Here the widowed Queen of Sicily met Raymond de St Gilles, Count of Toulouse; they fell in love and were married shortly afterwards in Poitou.

Richard returned to his Angevin possessions in 1195 but made no attempt to rejoin his queen until exhorted to do so by a monk who railed against his irregular life. A reunion was effected and the royal couple spent the Christmas of 1196 together at Poitiers. On Richard's death Berengaria had the revenues of the tin mines in Devon and Cornwall, the county of Bigorre and the city of Le Mans settled on her as dower, and it was in Le Mans that she settled in widowhood. She founded the Abbey of L'Épau there and retired to it on its completion in 1230, dying, it is believed, soon afterwards. The abbey in which she was buried fell into ruin, and in the 17th century Berengaria's mutilated effigy was found lying with her bones beneath a pile of wheat. It was carefully restored and provides the only known likeness of this almost unknown queen – the only English queen who never set foot in England.

Bermondsey Abbey Cluniac monastery founded at Bermondsey on the south bank of the Thames in 1082 and raised to the status of an abbey in 1399. It was a favourite retreat for ladies of the royal family and the queens CATHERINE OF FRANCE and ELIZABETH WOODVILLE died there in 1437 and 1492 respectively.

Bernicia One of the kingdoms of the Anglo-Saxon HEPTARCHY, stretching from the Tyne northwards to the Forth, and having its capital at Bamburgh. It was united to its southern neighbour DEIRA to form the kingdom of NORTHUMBRIA in about 605.

Bertha, Queen of Kent (d. before 616) Merovingian princess, who was the daughter of Caribert I, King of Paris, and his wife Ingoberg. She married the pagan ETHELBERT I, KING OF KENT and was allowed to bring her chaplain to Kent with her and practise her religion. It was through her influence that Ethelbert agreed to receive St

Augustine's mission sent to England by Pope Gregory I, which resulted in his conversion to Christianity. Bertha died before her husband and was buried in the porch of the church of St Martin at Canterbury. She had two children, EADBALD, who succeeded his father as king of Kent, and ETHELBURGA, who married EDWIN, KING OF NORTHUMBRIA.

Bertie Popular nickname of EDWARD VII and GEORGE VI by which both were known to their immediate families.

Black Prince The name by which EDWARD OF WOODSTOCK, PRINCE OF WALES (1330–76) has become best known to history, although it was never used by his contemporaries. It may have arisen from the fact that the copper-gilt effigy on his tomb in Canterbury Cathedral soon became tarnished and quite blackened, giving the erroneous impression that he wore black armour. The effigy was cleaned some years ago and that impression is now dispelled.

Bladud, King of Britain The legendary founder of Bath, son and successor of King Rud Hud Hudibras. According to a legend not recorded by GEOFFREY OF MONMOUTH, he was a leper and was banished from his father's court to tend swine. One day he found his charges wallowing in hot mud and going in to retrieve them discovered his leprosy cured. After he became king he 'built the town of Kaerbadum, which is now called Bath, and ... constructed the hot baths there which are so suited to the needs of mortal men'. Later Bladud 'constructed a pair of wings for himself and tried to fly through the upper air. He came down ... and was dashed into countless fragments'. Geoffrey says Bladud reigned for 20 years (881–861BC as chronologists have worked out from Geoffrey's narrative). He was succeeded by his son Leir, who was the model for Shakespeare's King Lear.

Blanche Alleged daughter of EDWARD I and his first wife ELEANOR OF CASTILE, for whose existence there is no contemporary evidence.

Blanche of Lancaster, Electress Palatine of the Rhine (1392–1409) The elder daughter of HENRY IV and his first wife Mary de Bohun, who was born at Peterborough Castle in the spring of 1392. She was married at Cologne on 6 July 1402 to Ludwig III, Elector Palatine of the Rhine and Duke of Bavaria, and died of the plague on 22 May 1409, being buried at Neustadt in Alsace.

She had one son. The Elector Ludwig III remarried and died at Heidelberg on 29 December 1436.

Blanche of the Tower (1342) The third daughter and eighth child of EDWARD III and PHILIPPA OF HAINAULT, who was born in the TOWER OF LONDON in March 1342 and died soon after her birth.

Bleddyn ap Cynfyn, King of Gwynedd and Powys (c.1025–75) Welsh king, who was the son of Cynfyn ap Gwerstan, 'a noble of Powys', by his wife ANGHARAD FERCH MAREDUDD, widow of LLYWELYN AP SEISYLL, KING OF DEHEUBARTH AND GWYNEDD, and daughter and heiress of MAREDUDD AB OWAIN AP HYWEL DDA. Bleddyn was probably born about 1025, since his mother's first husband died in 1023. On the death of their half-brother GRUFFYDD AP LLYWELYN in 1063, Bleddyn and his brother Rhiwallon succeeded to Gwynedd and Powys as joint rulers and acknowledged the overlordship of EDWARD THE CONFESSOR.

After the Norman Conquest the brothers allied themselves with the Mercians against WILLIAM I and ravaged Herefordshire. Their power was challenged by their half-nephews Maredudd and Idwal, the sons of Gruffydd, and at the battle of Mechain fought in 1070, the nephews and Rhiwallon were killed and Bleddyn was left as sole ruler. He continued the struggle with the Normans, but in 1075 was treacherously killed at Powys Castle by RHYS AB OWAIN AB EDWIN, KING OF DEHEUBARTH and the nobles of Ystrad Tywi. Three years later his death was avenged by his cousin TRAHAEARN AP CARADOG, who inflicted an overwhelming defeat on Rhys at Goodwick.

The *Brut y Tywysogion* (Chronicle of the Princes) extols Bleddyn as: 'the most beloved and the most merciful of all kings and who wrought good to all and who did harm to no one. He was gentle towards his kinsmen and generous towards the poor and merciful towards pilgrims and orphans and widows. And he was a defence for the weak and the strength of the learned and the honour of the churches and the foundation and comfort of the lands and generous towards all; terrible in war, beloved and meek in peace and a defence for all.'

Bleddyn had several wives and their order is uncertain. By an unknown wife he had two sons, Madog and Rhirid, who were both killed in 1088. By Haer, daughter of Cillin ap y Blaidd Rhudd and the widow of Cynfyn

Hirdref, he had a son MAREDUDD AP BLEDDYN, who reigned as prince of Powys jointly with his brothers and died in 1132. By the daughter of Brochwell ap Moelyn, of Twrcelyn, Anglesey, he had Cadwgan, Llywarch and two daughters. Another wife is said to have been Morien, daughter of Idnerth ap Cadwgan ab Elstan Glodrydd, who became the mother of Iorwerth and Llywelyn (or Rhiwallon). There were also two or more daughters whose mother is not known. The descendants of Bleddyn constitute the genealogical group of families that is known as the Third Royal Tribe of Wales.

Blood, Colonel Thomas (c.1628–80) Irish-born adventurer, the son of Thomas Blood, of Sarney, County Meath, and the scion of a well-known Irish family, who is renowned for his daring exploit to steal the crown jewels from the TOWER OF LONDON on 9 May 1671. Already wanted by the authorities on charges of kidnapping the Duke of Ormonde, Blood was a former soldier in the Parliamentarian army and had been implicated in various plots and intrigues since the Restoration, working allegedly at the behest of such luminaries as the Duke of Buckingham. Legend has it that when he was apprehended in the environs of the Tower he was carrying the crown of England under his cloak. He was imprisoned but was unexpectedly pardoned by CHARLES II on 8 August 1671 and subsequently became a favourite at court, being granted a pension of £500 a year. This magnanimity led some to suppose that the king was privy to the attempted theft or had previously employed Blood to spy on the nonconformists. Colonel Blood died on 28 August 1680.

Bloody Mary Unenviable sobriquet applied to MARY I with reference to her severe persecution of Protestants, some 300 of whom were executed during her reign. In modern times it has become the name of a popular drink composed of tomato juice laced with vodka.

Bluff King Hal Nickname applied to HENRY VIII.

Blunt, Alfred Walter Frank (1879–1957) Bishop of Bradford from 1931 to 1955, who in 1936 preached a sermon in which he expressed the hope that EDWARD VIII might pay greater attention to religious observances. The sermon, which was reported first by the *Yorkshire Post* and later by the national papers, is held to have been one of the factors leading to public awareness of the situation that ended with the king's abdication (*see* ABDICATION CRISIS).

Boadicea, Queen of the Iceni *see* BOUDICCA.

Bobo The nickname by which Miss Margaret Macdonald, nursery maid and later dresser to ELIZABETH II, was known to her charge.

Boleyn, Anne *see* ANNE BOLEYN.

Bolingbroke, Henry *see* HENRY IV.

Bonnie Prince Charlie The designation by which the Young Pretender, Prince Charles Edward STUART, was known to his adherents and admirers.

Boscobel House The seat of the Penderel family in Shropshire, where CHARLES II took refuge after his defeat at the battle of Worcester in 1651. He spent a day there (6 September) hiding in an oak tree in the grounds with Major Carlis, another refugee. From their vantage point, supplied with bread, cheese and small beer, they were able to see Cromwell's soldiers searching the woods for them in vain. Charles delighted in telling the story of his escape from Worcester to his courtiers in later life and proposed founding an Order of Knights of the Royal Oak, but the project came to nothing (*see* OAK-APPLE DAY).

Bosham Small seaside town by a creek in Chichester harbour, Sussex, which is reputed to be the place where King CANUTE commanded the tide to turn in order to refute the foolish flattery of his fawning courtiers. It was long believed that the church contained the tomb of a young daughter of Canute, but archaeological research has revealed that this is not so. Bosham is depicted in the BAYEUX TAPESTRY, where Harold (*see* HAROLD II) is shown entering the church to pray before starting his fateful voyage to Normandy.

Bosworth Field, Battle of Battle fought at Bosworth in Leicestershire on 22 August 1485 between RICHARD III and Henry Tudor (*see* HENRY VII), in which Richard was defeated and killed, thus bringing the Wars of the ROSES to an end. Richard, betrayed by his own commanders who hesitated to come to his support until it was clear which way the battle was turning, died in a desperate attempt to fight his way through to Henry himself (he managed to slay Henry's standard-bearer but his horse was killed under him and he was cut down before he could get any further). His crest crown rolled off his helmet when he fell and was reputedly retrieved from a hawthorn bush

by the Earl of Richmond, who placed it on the head of his stepson Henry.

Bothwell, James Hepburn, Earl of *see* MARY, QUEEN OF SCOTS.

Boudicca, Queen of the Iceni (d.AD62) Famous warrior queen, the wife of PRASUTAGUS, KING OF THE ICENI (the Celtic tribe occupying Suffolk and Norfolk), who became a 'client king' of the Romans. On his death in AD60 Rome appointed her joint heir of his kingdom with his two daughters. The unfortunate girls were raped by some Roman officers, and their mother, on violently protesting at this outrage, was jeered at and flogged. This goaded her into gathering her tribesmen together and heading an armed rebellion against the newly established Roman rule. The Roman governor, Suetonius Paulinus, was absent in Anglesey and Boudicca was able to capture Camulodunum (Colchester) and Londinium, killing, it is said, 80,000 Romans and their allies in the process. Prior to her attack on Camulodunum the inhabitants were reputedly terrified by various supernatural portents of disaster, including spectral bodies left by the ebb tide, a blood-red sea and strange unearthly shrieks. Only the return of Suetonius turned the tide. The Britons were defeated with great slaughter at Mancetter in Warwickshire and the queen ended her life by taking poison. The site of her grave is said to lie beneath platform eight at King's Cross Station, although a tumulus in Parliament Hill Fields is also claimed as her burial place. Boudicca's revolt was the last against Roman rule in southern Britain, which had been firmly established in the course of 19 years and was to last for over three centuries.

Boudicca is best remembered by the popular form of her name, Boadicea (the Roman rendering of Boudicca or Boudica). Tacitus described her fierce, ruddy countenance, her flowing red hair, her harsh voice and her red cloak, and reported the heroic speech she made to her tribesmen while standing in her chariot flanked by her daughters, and she is thus depicted in the well-known sculpture on the Victoria Embankment at Westminster.

Bowes-Lyon The family name of the earls of Strathmore and Kinghorne, from whom Queen ELIZABETH THE QUEEN MOTHER is descended. The founder of the family, Sir John Lyon, married a daughter of ROBERT II and their grandson Patrick was created Lord Glamis in 1445. The 9th Lord Glamis, also a

Patrick, was created Earl of Kinghorne in 1606. His grandson, the third Earl, obtained a charter in 1677 providing that he and his heirs 'should in all future ages be styled Earls of Strathmore and Kinghorne, Viscounts Lyon, Barons Glamis, Tannadyce, Sidlaw and Strathdichtie'. The 9th Earl married a Durham heiress, Mary Eleanor Bowes, and assumed her surname. Their sons, the 10th and 11th Earls, and grandson, the 12th Earl, adopted the surname of Lyon-Bowes, but the 13th Earl reversed the order becoming Bowes-Lyon. The 14th Earl was created Earl of Strathmore and Kinghorne in the peerage of the United Kingdom in the coronation honours of his son-in-law GEORGE VI on 1 June 1937. The modern tendency is not to hyphenate the name.

Brandy Nan Disrespectful nickname for Queen ANNE, probably coined by the Jacobites and referring to her supposed liking for strong liquor. The queen's statue outside St Paul's Cathedral inspired the couplet: 'Brandy Nan, left in the lurch; her face to the gin shop, her back to the church.'

Bretwalda Anglo-Saxon title given to the pre-eminent king of the HEPTARCHY. BEDE lists the first seven as AELLA, KING OF SUSSEX, CEAWLIN, KING OF WESSEX, ETHELBERT I, KING OF KENT, REDWALD, KING OF EAST ANGLIA, EDWIN, KING OF NORTHUMBRIA, OSWALD, KING OF NORTHUMBRIA, and OSWY, KING OF NORTHUMBRIA. Later writers add OFFA, KING OF MERCIA, and EGBERT, KING OF WESSEX to this number.

Brian Boru, High King of Ireland (926–1014) The son of Cennetig, chief of the Dal Cais (d.951), and Babhion of West Connaught, who claimed descent in a direct male line from a king of Munster baptized by St Patrick. Brian's elder brother Mathgamain seized Cashel in 964 and Brian joined him in fighting the Danish invaders, inflicting a great defeat on them in Tipperary in about 968. Mathgamain died in 976 and Brian succeeded as chief of the Dal Cais, but did not win the kingdom of Cashel until two years later when he defeated and killed Maelmuad mac Brain. He later defeated the king of Ossory and was acknowledged as king of Leinster in 984. In 1000 he allied himself with Maelsechnaill mac Domnaill, High King of Ireland, and defeated the Danes at Glenmama, Wicklow. The following year he turned against his ally and took over the High Kingship. In 1004 he granted a charter recognizing the ecclesiastical supremacy of Armagh. During the next

few years he made a triumphal tour of Ireland, receiving hostages from all the tribes.

When the Danish menace increased, Brian re-allied himself with Maelsechnaill and besieged the Danes near Dublin in 1013. At first they were unsuccessful, but a rousing victory at Clontarf on 23 April 1014 put an end to Danish power in Ireland, although the aged Brian was killed in his tent by a Dane following the victory. Maelsechnaill resumed the High Kingship and reigned until his death in 1022. Brian was undoubtedly the most famous king of Ireland, and his descendants continued to reign in Munster and Thomond for many centuries.

Bridget, Princess Supposititious daughter of MARY, QUEEN OF SCOTS. Mary was known to be pregnant by James Bothwell when she was imprisoned at Lochleven Castle and probably miscarried there, but a legend arose that she gave birth to a daughter named Bridget or Bride in February 1568. The child was said to have been secretly sent to France to be brought up, but the ship in which she was travelling was wrecked off the English coast and the baby was rescued by 'Sir Richard Talbot, of Bridgefield' and subsequently married his son 'Sir Humphrey Talbot'. An alternative version of the legend says that the infant arrived safely in France and later became a nun at Soissons.

Brigantes Celtic tribe, which early in the first century AD established a federation in north Yorkshire stretching from the Calder valley over the Pennines to the Tyne. Ptolemy in his description of Britain lists nine Brigantian towns as follows: Vinnovium (Binchester, near Bishop Auckland); Caturactonium (Catterick); Isurium (Aldborough); Olicana (Ilkley); Eboracum (York); Camoludunum (Almondbury, near Huddersfield), which seems to have been the capital; Rigodunum (Ingleborough); Epiacum (probably the hill settlement of Black Rod, near Wigan); and Calatum (which has not been identified). Brigantia was one of the most powerful and prosperous British kingdoms and hoards of gold and silver coins have been found from time to time, often interspersed with Roman coins of varying dates indicating a contact with Roman traders from an early period. The names of Brigantian rulers known from their coins are Volisios, Dumnoverus (or Dumnocoveros), and CARTIMANDUA, thought to represent three generations of rulers ending in Queen Cartimandua. The

Brigantians finally submitted to Rome after the defeat of Cartimandua's ex-husband Venutius by Petilius Cerialis in AD74.

Brighton Pavilion The small Sussex seaside town of Brighton (formerly Brighthelmstone) began its rise to fame and prosperity in 1783 when it was first visited by George, Prince of Wales (later GEORGE IV), who had been recommended a course of sea-bathing to alleviate swollen neck glands. Whether the desired cure was effected is not known, but the prince was so taken with the place that in the following year he sent his German pastry cook, Louis Weltje, to rent a house on the Steine on his behalf. The lease ran out in 1786, and Weltje then rented a nearby farmhouse, rebuilt it as a Palladian mansion to the design of the architect Henry Holland and, having acquired the freehold, let it to his master on a 21-year lease for £1000 a year. The house, renamed the Marine Pavilion, became a favourite residence of the prince over the next 10 years and he installed his unofficial wife Mrs FITZHERBERT in a nearby villa. Weltje had trouble in collecting regular payment of his rent and in about 1797 decided to sell the Marine Pavilion to the prince for £22,000. He was destined to die with the debt still outstanding.

Once in full possession, George embarked on a programme of extension and after he had become regent engaged the architect John ('Beau') Nash to construct a magnificent oriental palace in a blend of Indian and Chinese styles. The result was so astonishing that Sydney Smith on seeing it for the first time commented: 'It is as though St Paul's had gone down to the sea and pupped.' Some guests, however, complained that the building's new-fangled gas lighting and stoves left them with headaches and sore throats. The extravagance involved in the rebuilding also caused dissent among critics of the royal family.

After he became king, George's visits to Brighton became less frequent and he last stayed at the Royal Pavilion in 1827, three years before his death. His successor, WILLIAM IV, was fond of the place and often stayed there, but Queen VICTORIA did not care for it and it is easy to imagine Prince ALBERT's distaste for its vulgar flamboyance. Victoria considered demolishing the whole building, but in 1850 instead sold the Pavilion to Brighton Corporation for £50,000.

After many years of decay and neglect, the Pavilion has now been restored to a semblance of its original magnificence and re-furnished with many of its original furnishings. It is open to the public daily.

Britannia Royal yacht, launched by ELIZABETH II at Clydebank in 1953. Weighing 5862 tonnes (5769 tons), the vessel has a cruising speed of 21 knots and carries a crew of 22 officers and 254 men. Thought to be the 75th royal yacht in Royal Naval service, the *Britannia* has taken members of the royal family on state visits all round the world as well as on honeymoons and holidays. It has also been used for other purposes on occasion, being converted into a hospital ship during the Falklands campaign of 1982, for instance. The *Britannia* is the only vessel in the Navy to be commanded by an Admiral (officially Flag Officer Royal Yachts). In the mid-1990s it was announced that the *Britannia* would shortly be taken out of royal service.

British Empire, The Most Excellent Order of the Order of chivalry founded by GEORGE V in June 1917 and extended and altered on subsequent dates. It was designed to reward important services rendered to the Empire and is awarded to both men and women. It consists of five classes: Knights and Dames Grand Cross (GBE), limited to 27 military and 73 civil; Knights and Dames Commander (KBE or DBE), limited to 215 military and 630 civil; Commanders (CBE), limited to 1660 military and 7300 civil; Officers (OBE), limited to not more than 713 military and 745 civil in any one year; and Members (MBE), limited to not more than 228 military and not more than 1256 civil in any one year. There was also a medal attached to the Order, known as the British Empire Medal (BEM), but this is no longer conferred. The queen is Sovereign of the Order and the present Grand Master is the Duke of EDINBURGH. The chapel of the Order is in the crypt of St Paul's Cathedral.

Brown, John (1826–83) Queen VICTORIA's faithful Highland servant, who was on such intimate terms with her that their relationship became a matter of concern to the royal household, especially when a scurrilous pamphlet entitled *Mrs John Brown* appeared. Sir Frederick Ponsonby, though, in *Recollections of Three Reigns* concluded that if any sexual feeling existed between the queen and Brown 'it was quite unconscious on both sides, and ... their relations up to the last were simply those of employer and devoted retainer'.

Brown had served the royal family as a

ghillie at BALMORAL since the time of the Prince Consort and it was on the advice of Sir Charles Phipps and the queen's physician Dr (later Sir) William Jenner that Brown was summoned to OSBORNE HOUSE in December 1864 for the calming influence he appeared to have on the seriously over-wrought widowed queen. She was soon call-ing him 'the perfection of a servant for he thinks of everything'. From then until his death nearly 20 years later, Brown was sel-dom far from the queen's side and she deferred to him as she had been wont to do with her husband. There was endless gossip and the *Gazette de Lausanne* reported that the queen was secretly married to Brown and was pregnant by him. Other rumours claimed Victoria had become interested in spiritualism and that Brown served as her medium with the dead Albert. Lampoons and cartoons appeared in the British press and the queen referred in her journal to 'those wicked and idle lies about poor, good Brown'.

Brown's autocratic ways rendered him unpopular with fellow servants and his high-handed way with royal equerries often caused embarrassing situations. On one occasion when General Sir John M'Neill was in waiting, Brown was sent by the queen to the equerries' room at Osborne with a message about the ordering of some car-riages. When the General told him to wait outside until the order had been written, Brown took offence and complained to the queen that he had been shouted at as if he was a private soldier. As a result M'Neill received a letter from the queen threatening him with a command in India (she did not speak to him for several years afterwards). Another equerry who fell foul of Brown was General Sir Lyndoch Gardiner. On meet-ing Brown in a corridor he enquired how the queen was and received the reply: 'The queen's verra well. It was only the other day that she said to me "There's that dommed old fool General Gardner coming into wait-ing and I know he'll be putting his bloody nose into everything that doesn't concern him."'

Brown had a great fondness for whisky and was sometimes incapable of taking his place on the box of the queen's carriage. At Balmoral he once fell flat on his face in front of the queen, who immediately stated that she, too, had felt an earth tremor.

After having Brown's pedigree investi-gated and finding that he had a tenuous link with several landed families, the queen insisted that he should be listed as an 'esquire' in the royal household lists. It must be said to Brown's credit, however, that he was in no way ambitious or grasping. He died of erysipelas at WINDSOR CASTLE in March 1883 and was buried in Crathie Churchyard near Balmoral.

On the queen's instructions, when she died a photograph of Brown was secretly placed in her hand as she lay in her coffin.

Bruce, Robert *see* ROBERT I (BRUCE), KING OF SCOTS.

Brude I, King of the Picts (d.584) The son of MAELGWN GWYNEDD, KING OF GWYNEDD and a sister of the Pictish kings DRUST III, GARTNAIT III and CALTRAM, who became king of the Picts in about 554 and was bap-tized by St Columba about 10 years later. He married Peithan, sister of Aneirin, and had a son Wid Feith, the father of BRUDE II. Brude died in 584 and was succeeded by his nephew Gartnait IV. His name is also writ-ten Bridei.

Brude II, King of the Picts (d.642) The son of Wid Feith (a son of BRUDE I) and a sister of King NECHTAN II, who succeeded his brother GARTNAIT V about 637 and died about 642, being succeeded by his brother TALORC IV.

Brude III, King of the Picts (d.693) The son of Beli (or Bile), King of Strathclyde, by a sister of King TALORCAN I, who was sub-king (*regulus*) of Fortrinn from an unknown date until about 672, when he deposed his first cousin DRUST V and became king of the Picts. In May 685 he defeated and killed EGFRITH, KING OF NORTHUMBRIA at Dunnichen. He died about 693 and was suc-ceeded by his nephew TARRAIN.

Brude IV, King of the Picts (d.706) The son of Derile by a sister of BRUDE III, who deposed his cousin King TARRAIN and became king of the Picts about 697, reigning until his death in 706, when he was suc-ceeded by his brother NECHTAN III.

Brude V, King of the Picts (d.763) The son of Urguist, or Fergus, by a sister of BRUDE IV and NECHTAN III, who succeeded his brother OENGUS I as king of the Picts in 761, having previously been sub-king (*regulus*) of Fortrinn since about 729. He died in 763, and was succeeded by CINIATH II.

Brude VI, King of the Picts (d.843) The son of Bargoit by a sister of King CANAUL COEM, who succeeded his brother King Ferat in 842 and died the following year, being suc-ceeded by Ciniath IV.

Brude VII, King of the Picts (*fl*.844–46) Son of Fethal or Wtheil by a daughter of Conall MacAidan, King of Argyll and a sister of CANAUL COEM. He was a brother of TALOR-CAN IV and reigned in opposition to KEN-NETH MACALPIN.

Brunswick, House of Alternative name for the House of HANOVER, occupants of the British throne from 1714 to 1901.

Brutus Legendary first king of the Britons, who was, according to GEOFFREY OF MON-MOUTH, the son of Silvius, son of Ascanius, son of Aeneas the Trojan. After accidentally killing his father in a hunting accident, he was expelled from Italy and after many adventures finally arrived in Britain where he overcame the native giants and founded a kingdom, building his capital city on the banks of the Thames and naming it Troia Nova (New Troy), which became corrupted to Trinovantum. The dates assigned to his reign by a careful study of Geoffrey's narrative are *c*.1109–1081 BC.

Buckingham Palace The London residence of the royal family. Originally the town house of the dukes of Buckingham, the palace was built early in the 18th century on land given to John Sheffield, Duke of Buckingham, by Queen ANNE. In the early 17th century the land had been used by JAMES I for the planting of black mulberry trees, in the hope that he would be able to breed silkworms on them and thus start an English silk industry – the experiment failed, though at least one of the trees survives to this day in a corner of the palace gardens.

GEORGE III bought the palace from Sir Charles Sheffield for £21,000 in 1762, attracted by its spacious garden, and it became known as the Queen's House when Queen CHARLOTTE resided there. The king preferred his homes at Kew and Windsor, however, and on most days, after dinner, he would ride the 20 miles to WINDSOR CASTLE to spend the night there. On GEORGE IV's accession in 1820, he decided to make it his principal London residence and got Parliament to vote £200,000 for 'a repair and improvement of Buckingham Palace'. It was rather contemptuously referred to as 'the King's House in Pimlico'. George spent almost three times the allotted amount on the reconstruction, which included a tri-umphal arch at the entrance to the three-sided courtyard. However, this proved too narrow to allow the easy passage of the state coach and it was later removed to its present site, where it has become well known as Marble Arch.

George IV died before the palace was completed and WILLIAM IV and all succeed-ing sovereigns never felt much affection for the building, with the possible exception of EDWARD VII, who was born and died there and made it the setting for his brilliant courts and balls. GEORGE V and Queen MARY OF TECK would have preferred to return to KENSINGTON PALACE, but decided not to and had the final major alterations made by the addition of the west front of Portland stone designed by Sir Aston Webb in 1913. The balcony of the palace facing down the Mall is used for many public appearances of the royal family on the occasions of coronations, royal weddings, TROOPING THE COLOUR and other events. On 13 September 1940 a stick of bombs fell across Buckingham Palace destroying the chapel (an incident that prompted Queen ELIZA-BETH THE QUEEN MOTHER to remark, 'I'm glad we have been bombed; I feel I can look the East End in the face'). ELIZABETH II had the chapel restored in 1959 and opened as an art gallery to enable the public to see exhibi-tions of treasures from the royal collection. In 1993 the state apartments were opened to the public on an occasional basis to help raise funds for the repairs required after the serious fire at Windsor Castle in 1992. The daily changing of the guard at Buckingham Palace remains tourist attraction.

As the London home of the royal family, public access to Buckingham Palace is strictly limited for fear of infiltration by assassins or other unwelcome intruders. In 1840 security arrangements were over-hauled after a 17-year-old youth called Edmund Jones was discovered 'rolled up under a sofa' upon which Queen Victoria had been sitting some time earlier. Jones, who was motivated purely by curiosity about the royal family, had entered the palace by an open window and had explored more or less unchallenged, catching sight of the queen and sitting upon the throne itself. This was, in fact, the second time he had been caught trespassing in the palace (the first time he was declared insane, but the second time he was set upon a treadmill by way of punishment). Undeterred, Jones actually penetrated the palace a third time, in March 1841: this time he was sent to sea, where he contrived to behave himself (though he jumped ship on two occasions).

On 9 July 1982 security at Buckingham Palace again came under heated discussion when Michael Fagan, a 35-year-old man who suffered from delusions, managed to enter the palace by shinning up a drainpipe and to find his way into Elizabeth II's bedroom, waking her around 7.15 in the morning. The startled queen, finding a distraught young stranger sitting on her bed, attempted to summon assistance by ringing a night alarm button, only to find it was not working, and similarly got no response after pressing her bedside bell. Faced with a range of domestic problems, Fagan had intended to slash his wrists in the queen's presence – but the queen calmly kept him talking about his worries for some 10 minutes before others became aware of his presence and he was promptly removed. The first person to arrive on the scene was her maid, a Yorkshirewoman, who on seeing Fagan exclaimed, 'Bloody 'ell, ma'am, what's he doing here?'

Burhred, King of Mercia (d. after 874) Of unknown origin, Burhred (or Burgred) acceded to the throne of MERCIA after the death or expulsion of King BEORHTWULF in 852. In the following year he sought an alliance with King ETHELWULF to help subdue the Welsh, in which he was successful. The alliance was cemented by Burhred's marriage to Ethelwulf's daughter Ethel-swith at Chippenham, Wiltshire, shortly after Easter (2 April) 853. In 867 the Danish invaders 'went into Mercia to Nottingham, and there took winter-quarters'. Burhred 'and his councillors begged [his brothers-in-law] Ethelred, King of Wessex, and his brother Alfred to help them fight against the host; and then they proceeded with the West Saxon levies into Mercia as far as Nottingham and came upon the host there in the fortification, and besieged it therein, but there was no serious engagement, and the Mercians made peace with the host.' In 869 the Danes withdrew to York, but they moved south again in 871 and after several uneasy treaties with the Mercians drove Burhred into exile in 874, conquering the kingdom and setting up a puppet king, CEOLWULF II. Burhred went to Rome 'and there resided'. The date of his death is unknown, but the ANGLO-SAXON CHRONI-CLE notes that he was buried in 'St Mary's church in "the School of the English"'. His wife Ethelswith, by whom he had no children (or at any rate none surviving), returned to the court of her brother King ALFRED and in 888 was charged with the Ealdorman Beocca to take the alms of the West Saxons to Rome. She died on the journey and was buried at Pavia.

C

Cade, Jack (d.1450) The leader of the Kentish rebellion against HENRY VI in May 1450. Said to have been of Irish origin and to have served in the household of Sir Thomas Dacre in Sussex, Cade (after several discreditable youthful escapades) emerged as leader of the Kentish insurgents roused by the fiscal exactions of Henry VI's officials in May 1450. He organized his forces so well that he was able to defeat the royal army and take London on 2 July. He then assumed the name of Mortimer and claimed kinship with the Duke of York. On 3 July he ordered the arrest of Lord Saye and Sele and his son-in-law William Crowmer, Sheriff of Kent, who were regarded as the chief causes of the oppressive taxation, and they were beheaded the following day after a cursory trial. The city then rose against the insurgents and after a bloody struggle on the night of 5 July, Cade and his followers withdrew to Rochester. A reward was offered for his capture and he was taken prisoner at Heathfield on 11 July, dying the following day from the wounds he received in the struggle. His head was exposed on London Bridge. Henry VI's public image suffered from the episode, during which he had fled from Cade's forces, but his queen, MARGARET OF ANJOU distinguished herself by refusing to desert Greenwich.

Cadfan, King of Gwynedd (d.c.625) Successor of his father Iago ap Beli as King of Gwynedd in 613. Nothing is known of his deeds. His tombstone in the church of Llangadwaladr in Anglesey bears the inscription: *Catamanus rex sapientisimus opinatisimus omnium regum* (King Cadfan the most wise and most renowned of all kings). He was succeeded by his son CADWALLON.

Cadwaladr, King of Gwynedd (d.664) The son of CADWALLON by a sister of PENDA, KING OF MERCIA, who was probably still very young at his father's death in 633 as the throne of Gwynedd was usurped by Cadafael ap Cynfedw, who was defeated and forced to flee after the battle of Winwaed

Field fought with Cadwaladr's uncle Penda in 654. Cadwaladr gained the throne and died of plague in 664 after an uneventful reign of 10 years. He became a great figure in bardic lore.

Cadwallon, King of Gwynedd (d.633) The son of CADFAN, who succeeded his father as king of Gwynedd in about 625. He was a thorn in the flesh of the Saxons of northern England and after forming an alliance with PENDA, KING OF MERCIA, whose sister he married, invaded DEIRA and defeated and killed King EDWIN at the battle of Heathfield (possibly Hatfield, near Doncaster) on 12 October 632. The re-establishment of British rule in the country was within his grasp, but his lack of statesmanship and his intent on plundering and ravaging were his undoing. At the end of 633 he was encamped with his army south of Hexham when he was set upon by OSWALD, KING OF BERNICIA, and killed in the ensuing battle.

Caedwalla, King of Wessex (c.659–89) The son of Coenberht, a *regulus* or sub-king whose death is recorded in 661, and a descendant of King CEAWLIN, who, according to the ANGLO-SAXON CHRONICLE, in 685 'began to contend for the kingdom [of Wessex]', which was then held by his kinsman AESCWINE, whom he overthrew and probably killed. In 686 Caedwalla and his brother Mul 'laid waste Kent and the Isle of Wight'. In the following year Mul and 12 of his men were burnt to death in Kent, and Caedwalla exacted revenge by again laying it to waste. Caedwalla had not been baptized and was probably brought up as a pagan, but after he had reigned two years he apparently underwent a conversion to Christianity and decided to abdicate and go on pilgrimage to Rome. In 688, therefore, he resigned his throne to his kinsman INE and set out. 'Arriving in Rome during the pontificate of Sergius [I]', as recorded by BEDE, 'he was baptized on Holy Saturday before Easter in the year of our Lord 689, and he fell ill and while still wearing his white robes departed this life on the twentieth of April.'

Pope Sergius gave him the baptismal name of Peter and he was buried in St Peter's. Caedwalla appears to have had a wife named Centhryth, but nothing is known about her.

Caernarfon Castle Thirteenth-century castle at Caernarfon, overlooking the Menai Strait in north Wales, which has many royal connections. Founded in 1283 by EDWARD I, the castle was one of the four great strongholds from which English kings wielded military influence over the Welsh. With its nine huge towers and thick walls, the castle was deemed impregnable to attack, although in the event it was briefly overrun in 1294 by the forces of the Welsh rebel Madog ap Llywelyn (subsequently it survived three protracted sieges by Parliament during the Civil War). In 1301, as tradition has it, Caernarfon Castle witnessed the declaration of the future EDWARD II as Prince of Wales. In 1911 the future EDWARD VIII was invested as Prince of Wales there. In 1969 the castle witnessed another magnificent investiture ceremony, when CHARLES, PRINCE OF WALES was similarly honoured by his mother ELIZABETH II.

Caesar EDWARD VII's pet terrier, which was led behind his coffin in his funeral procession through London.

Caltram, King of the Picts (d.541) The son of Girom and the elder sister of GALAM I, KING OF THE PICTS as conjectured by H. Pirie-Gordon of Buthlaw. He succeeded his brother King GARTNAIT III and reigned for about one year.

Cambridge The surname adopted in 1917 by the members of the TECK family, when at GEORGE V's request they renounced their German styles and titles. Adolphus, 2nd Duke and Prince of Teck, was created Marquess of Cambridge and Earl of Eltham on 16 July 1917, and those titles became extinct on the death of his son George, the 2nd Marquess, on 16 April 1981. The family is now represented by his only child, Lady Mary Whitley, née Cambridge.

Cambridge, Earls and Dukes of The royal holders of this honour are here dealt with chronologically.

1. Edmund of Langley, Earl of Cambridge (1344–1402) The fifth son of EDWARD III, who was created Earl of Cambridge on 13 November 1362. He was subsequently created Duke of York on 6 August 1385 (*see* YORK).

2. Richard of Conisburgh, Earl of Cambridge (1376–1415) The second son of Edmund of Langley, Earl of Cambridge (*see above*), who was born at Conisburgh Castle, Yorkshire, in about September 1376 and was a godson of his cousin RICHARD II. He was knighted on 26 July 1406 and from August to December that year served as ambassador to Denmark. On 1 May 1414 he was created Earl of Cambridge in Parliament. He was also appointed Almoner of England and Constable of Brimpsfield Castle. After conspiring to depose HENRY V in favour of his brother-in-law the Earl of March (the heir general of EDWARD III), Richard was attainted and beheaded on Southampton Green on 5 August 1415, being buried in the chapel of God's House at Southampton.

He had married, first (and without parental consent), Anne, daughter of Roger de Mortimer, Earl of March, by his wife Eleanor, daughter of Thomas de Holand, Earl of Kent. She died in September 1411 and the earl married secondly, in about 1414, Maud, daughter of Thomas de Clifford, 4th Baron Clifford, by his wife Elizabeth de Ros, and divorced wife of John Nevill, 6th Baron Latimer. She died on 26 August 1446 and was buried in Roche Abbey, Yorkshire.

3. Richard Plantagenet, Earl of Cambridge (1412–60) The only son of Richard of Conisburgh, Earl of Cambridge (*see above*) by his first wife, Anne de Mortimer, who became 2nd Earl of Cambridge prior to 19 May 1426, when he was restored as Duke of York (*see* YORK).

4. Edward Plantagenet, Earl of Cambridge (1428–83) The son of Richard Plantagenet, Earl of Cambridge (*see above*), who succeeded to his father's honours and was proclaimed king as EDWARD IV on 4 March 1461, when his existing titles merged in the Crown.

5. Henry Stuart (1640–60) The fourth, but third surviving, son of CHARLES I and Queen HENRIETTA MARIA, who was created Earl of Cambridge and Duke of Gloucester (*see* GLOUCESTER, HENRY (STUART), DUKE OF) by his brother CHARLES II on 13 May 1659.

6. Charles Stuart (1660–1) The eldest son of James, Duke of York (later JAMES II), and his first wife Anne HYDE, who was born at Worcester House in the Strand on 22 October 1660 and baptized there on 1 January 1661, his uncle CHARLES II and Queen CATHERINE OF BRAGANZA being among his godparents. He was designated Duke of Cambridge, but died at Whitehall before the patent was passed on 5 May 1661, being buried in WESTMINSTER ABBEY the following day.

7. **James Stuart** (1663–7) The second son of James, Duke of York (later JAMES II), and his first wife Anne HYDE, who was born at ST JAMES'S PALACE on 11 July 1663 and baptized at St Martin-in-the-Fields on 22 July 1663. He was designated Duke of Cambridge from birth and on 23 August 1664 was created Baron of Dauntsey, Wiltshire, and Earl and Duke of Cambridge. On 3 December 1666, at the age of only three, he was knighted at Whitehall and nominated a knight of the GARTER. He fell sick the following April and after rallying for a time died at RICHMOND PALACE on 20 June 1667. Samuel Pepys commented in his diary that the little duke's death was 'a great loss to the nation, having, I think, never an heyre male now of the King's or Duke's to succeed to the Crown'. He was buried in WESTMINSTER ABBEY on 26 June 1667. There is an engaging portrait of the duke by John Michael Wright in the collection of Earl Bathurst.

8. **Edgar Stuart** (1667–71) The fourth son of James, Duke of York (later JAMES II), and his first wife Anne HYDE, who was born at ST JAMES'S PALACE on 14 September 1667. Pepys noted 'the King and Duke of York and the whole Court is mighty joyful at the Duchess of York's being brought to bed this day ... of a son'. The little prince was baptized a day or two after his birth and on 7 October 1667 was created Baron of Dauntsey, Wiltshire, and Earl and Duke of Cambridge as his deceased elder brother James had been. He died at RICHMOND PALACE on 8 June 1671 and was buried in WESTMINSTER ABBEY on 12 June following.

9. **Charles Stuart** (1677) The fifth son of James, Duke of York (later JAMES II), and the first by his second wife MARY OF MODENA, who was born at ST JAMES'S PALACE on 7 November 1677 and baptized the following day, his godparents being his uncle CHARLES II, his half brother-in-law the Prince of Orange (later WILLIAM III) and his infant sister Princess ISABELLA. He was designated Duke of Cambridge but died at St James's Palace before the patent was passed on 12 December 1677, being buried in WESTMINSTER ABBEY the following day.

10. **George Augustus, Electoral Prince of Brunswick and Lüneburg** (1683–1760)

The only son of George Louis, Elector of Hanover (later GEORGE I), who was created Baron of Tewkesbury, Gloucester, Viscount Northallerton, York, Earl of Milford Haven, and Marquess and Duke of Cambridge by his father's second cousin Queen ANNE on 9 November 1706. On his father's accession to the throne on 1 August 1714, he became Duke of Cornwall and on 27 September following was created Prince of Wales and Earl of Chester. On his own accession to the throne as GEORGE II on 11 June 1727 all his honours merged in the Crown.

11. **Adolphus Frederick, Duke of Cambridge** (1774–1850) The seventh son and tenth child of GEORGE III and Queen CHARLOTTE, who was born at Buckingham House (then the Queen's House) on 24 February 1774. He was baptized in the Great Council Chamber of ST JAMES'S PALACE on 24 March 1774, his godparents (all represented by proxies) being his great-uncle Prince Johann Adolf of Saxe-Gotha, his cousin Prince Karl of Hesse-Cassel and his cousin Friederike, Princess of Orange. The prince was educated by private tutors at Kew and later at the University of Göttingen.

Known to his family as 'Dolly', Prince Adolphus became a Colonel in the Hanoverian army in 1793 and was promoted Lieutenant-General in 1798. Transferring to the British army in 1803, he was promoted General in April 1808 (antedated to September 1803) and received his Field Marshal's baton in November 1813. He was appointed Colonel of the Coldstream Guards in 1805 and Colonel-in-Chief of the 60th Foot in 1827, holding both appointments until his death. On 27 November 1801 he had been created Baron of Culloden, Earl of Tipperary in Ireland, and Duke of Cambridge. He was Chancellor of the University of St Andrews from 1811 to 1814.

On 24 October 1816 the duke was appointed Governor-General of the kingdom of Hanover, his title being changed to Viceroy on 22 February 1831. He proved himself an efficient ruler and remained in Hanover until its separation from Great Britain in 1837. After the death of Princess CHARLOTTE OF WALES in 1817, the bachelor sons of George III were obliged to seek brides to provide for the succession. The Duke of Cambridge's choice fell on Princess Augusta Wilhelmina Louisa of Hesse-Cassel, born at Schloss Rumpenheim on 25

July 1797, daughter of Landgrave Friedrich of Hesse-Cassel and Princess Caroline Polyxene of Nassau-Usingen. They were married at Cassel on 7 May 1818 and again on 1 June 1818 at the Queen's House, St James's, in the presence of the ailing Queen Charlotte. The Archbishop of Canterbury had been misinformed as to the time of the wedding and arrived three hours late to perform the ceremony, which otherwise passed off without a hitch. The bride was described as 'a most accomplished and amiable young lady' and her bridegroom, who was her senior by 23 years, was very much in love with her. The marriage was a happy one and produced three children, Prince George, who was to succeed his father as Duke of Cambridge, Princess Augusta (see AUGUSTA OF CAMBRIDGE, PRINCESS, GRAND DUCHESS OF MECKLENBURG-STRELITZ) and Princess MARY ADELAIDE.

The duke, whom Lord Broughton described as 'not a disagreeable man, though he does chatter, and talk very loud', died 'of cramp in the stomach' at Cambridge House, Piccadilly, on 8 July 1850, being buried on the 17 July in the mausoleum he had had constructed at the east end of Kew Parish Church. Queen VICTORIA duly reported his death to her uncle Leopold: 'My poor good Uncle Cambridge breathed his last, without a struggle, at a few minutes before ten, last night.' His widow survived him for many years, dying at St James's Palace on 6 April 1889, aged 91. She was buried with him, but in 1928 their coffins were removed to the Royal Tomb House at Windsor at the instigation of their granddaughter Queen Mary (see MARY OF TECK). Their faithful Chamberlain, Baron Knesebeck, who had shared their resting-place at Kew, was left behind and when Queen Mary's niece the Marchioness of Cambridge ventured to remonstrate with her about this, she received the reply: 'Really, Dorothy, if we all had our servants buried in our graves there would be no room for us!'

12. **George, 2nd Duke of Cambridge** (1819–1904) The only son of Adolphus, Duke of Cambridge (see *above*), Prince George William Frederick Charles was born in Hanover on 26 March 1819. He embarked on a career in the army, rising from Colonel at the age of 18 in 1837 to Field Marshal in 1862 and was appointed Commander-in-Chief by patent in 1887, holding that office until 1895. He succeeded his father in the dukedom in 1850. In the Crimean War he saw active service at the battles of Alma, Balaclava and Inkerman, as well as at the siege of Sebastopol. Like his father he served as Ranger of Hyde, St James's and Richmond Parks and received numerous honours. His time as Commander-in-Chief was characterized by his utter opposition to all army reform. Nevertheless, he was described as 'a bluff, fresh, hale, country gentleman, with something of the vigorous healthy frankness of the English skipper, and something, too, of the Prussian martinet; industrious, punctual, rising early, seeking rest late, fond of life and its pleasures, of good dinners, good cigars, pleasant women, of the opera, and of the play'.

A lighter side of the duke's life was afforded by his highly romantic marriage contracted in contravention of the ROYAL MARRIAGES ACT at St John's Church, Clerkenwell, on 8 January 1847 to a popular actress, Sarah (called Louisa) FAIRBROTHER. She was known after the marriage as Mrs FITZGEORGE, and the duke established her and her children in a house in Queen Street, Mayfair, conveniently near his residence in Piccadilly. He remained devoted to her until her death in January 1890. The duke died at Gloucester House, Piccadilly, on 17 March 1904. After a funeral service in WESTMINSTER ABBEY on 22 March, his body was taken by guncarriage to Kensal Green Cemetery and placed beside that of Mrs Fitzgeorge in the mausoleum which he had constructed for them both.

Canada, Order of Order of Chivalry for Canada founded by ELIZABETH II in 1967. There are three grades: Companion (CG), Officer (OC) and Member (CM). The Cross of Valour, the Star of Courage and the Medal of Bravery are medals attached to the Order.

Canaul Coem, King of the Picts (d.807) The son of Teige by a sister of Kings CINIATH II and ALPIN II, he succeeded his kinsman TALORCAN III on the Pictish throne in 784, but was deposed in 789 by his cousin CONSTANTINE. He reigned as sub-king (*regulus*) in Argyll until defeated and killed by his brother-in-law CONALL III in 807.

Cantium The ancient name of the county of Kent, which according to Julius Caesar was divided into four tribal districts (which he does not name). Ptolemy, in his *Geography*, written *c*.100–150, refers to the Cantii as the most easterly of the British tribes and names their principal cities as Durovernum

(Canterbury), Rutupiae (Richborough) and Londinium (London). No names of independent rulers of the area are known, and Cantium seems to have passed to the rule of the CATUVELLAUNI by the middle of the first century AD.

Canute, King of England (*c*.995–1035) The son of King SWEYN FORKBEARD and his first wife Gunhild, daughter of Mieszko I, Duke of Poland, who was born in Denmark in about 995 and as a youth and young man accompanied his father on his English campaigns. On Sweyn's death at Gainsborough on 3 February 1014 Canute (or Cnut) was chosen as king by the Danish fleet, but at first failed to establish his position. It was only after his victory at Ashingdon in Essex and the conclusion of peace with EDMUND II IRONSIDE that he secured MERCIA and the DANELAW (while Edmund retained the south). On Edmund's death on 30 November 1016 he succeeded to the whole kingdom and was crowned at St Paul's Cathedral, London, on 6 January 1017. Two years later, the death of his elder brother Harald made him king of Denmark also, and he became the ruler of a large Scandinavian empire.

Canute had formed an alliance with Elfgiva, the daughter of Elfhelm, Ealdorman of Northampton, and she had borne him two sons. Early in 1017 he repudiated her (although she was a very able woman and was later to govern Norway with her son Sweyn) and on 2 July 1017 he married EMMA OF NORMANDY, the widow of ETHELRED II. The ANGLO-SAXON CHRONICLE relates that he 'commanded [her] to be brought to him so that she might beome his queen'. Emma was a willing bride, probably excited by the prospect of a vigorous young Danish husband several years her junior after her life with the prosaic Ethelred. She bore Canute a son, HARDICANUTE, and a daughter Gunhild, who (renamed Kunigunde) became the first wife of the Emperor Heinrich III and died in Italy on 18 July 1038. Another alleged daughter is said to have died as a child and to have been buried in Bosham church, West Sussex, where her supposed tomb is still shown, but the story has been disproved.

Canute's reign was a busy one, with much coming and going between England, Denmark and Norway, which he conquered in 1030. To secure his position he had no compunction in adopting the most extreme measures. Shortly after he acceded to the throne he arranged the assassination of Edmund Ironside's brother Eadwig, a potential rival, and would no doubt have also procured the murder of Edmund's infant sons if they had not been spirited away to Hungary, where they were beyond his reach. Another victim was his adviser Eadric Streona, Earl of Mercia, whose treacherous ways were well known and prompted Canute to order his death (as well as those of other confederates) before he, too, was betrayed. By way of contrast, in later life Canute arranged to subsidize entirely at his own expense the tolls of pilgrims on their way to Rome. He also promoted the codification of English law.

Canute is usually remembered in England for the story of his ordering the tide to turn as an object lesson to his flattering courtiers who had told him that even the sea would obey his commands. It did not, of course. According to Henry of Huntingdon, as the waves lapped at Canute's feet, the king leapt up from his throne, which had been placed on the foreshore, and addressed his retainers thus: 'Let all men know how empty and worthless is the power of kings, for there is none worthy of the name, but He whom heaven, earth and sea obey by eternal laws.' From that moment on, he is reputed to have discarded his gold crown as a symbol of his humility, placing it upon a figure of Christ on the cross.

Legend has it that Canute had an uncertain temper, which could flare up into violence. On one occasion he is reputed to have killed one of his housecarls, a deed that he soon came to regret. The court before which he subsequently presented himself declined to pass sentence, but he voluntarily fined himself nine times the man's worth. Another passion was music. When he visited the monks of Ely he composed a song for them to sing as the royal party rowed past:

> Merrily sung the monks in Ely,
> When Cnut the king rowed thereby;
> Rowed knights near the land,
> And hear we these monks sing.

Canute was no more than 40 when he died at Shaftesbury on 12 November 1035. He was taken to Winchester for burial. The painted wooden chests containing the mingled bones of the Saxon and Danish kings buried there may be seen today on top of the choir-screen in Winchester Cathedral.

Caratacus (*fl.c*.AD50) The leader of British opposition to the Roman conquest, who was a son of CUNOBELINUS, king of the CATUVELLAUNI. His mother may have been a Silurian princess. Caratacus led the British resistance for nine years and was finally forced to seek refuge with the BRIGANTES of Yorkshire, only to be betrayed by their Queen CARTIMANDUA, his stepmother, who delivered him in chains to the Romans. He was taken with his wife and children to grace a Roman triumph. On seeing the wonders of Rome, he is said to have remarked: 'It is strange, indeed, that a people who have so many and such rich possessions of their own should envy me and mine. It is strange that the owners of these palaces should desire to drive us from our poor hovels.' Rome treated Caratacus with magnanimity, but it is not known if he was ever allowed to return to Britain.

Carausius, Roman Emperor (d.293) Marcus Aurelius Mausaeus Carausius, of humble Menapian (German) origin, served as a general under the Emperor Maximianus (286–305) and was appointed commander of the fleet stationed at Gesoriacum (Boulogne), charged with clearing the Channel of Frankish and Saxon pirates. As Gibbon put it, 'The integrity of the new admiral corresponded not with his abilities', and he turned pirate himself. Fearing reprisals from Maximianus, he proclaimed himself emperor and sailed to Britain, where he overthrew the governor and took possession in 287. He extended his rule over part of Gaul and maintained his position until 293, when Constantius recaptured Boulogne. Later in the same year Carausius was murdered by the prefect ALLECTUS, who usurped the throne.

The coins of Carausius, struck at London, Rouen and other mints, are very numerous. A shadowy Carausius II appears to have attempted to gain power in Britain about a century later, as can be inferred from the existence of a unique coin.

Carlton House Royal residence in Pall Mall, London, which was substantially rebuilt by GEORGE IV when Prince Regent in the late 18th century. The original Carlton House, close to ST JAMES'S PALACE, was built by Henry Boyle, MP, in 1709 but on George's instructions was completely redesigned from 1791 by the architect Henry Holland at the huge cost of £225,000. A special parliamentary inquiry was set up to enquire into the debts the prince had thus incurred, and as a price for financial assistance from the government he was required to marry Princess CAROLINE OF BRUNSWICK. The house was officially opened in 1811, with members of the 'well-dressed' public being admitted in large groups: such was the

excitement of the crowd, though, a number of people were injured in the rush to get in, with one lady sustaining a broken leg and others being carried away 'apparently dead'. Though admired for its tasteful decoration, the house was little visited by George after he became king and in 1827 he ordered its demolition. Various furnishings and fitments were transferred to other prestigious sites, and the columns of the portico were made use of for the famous portico of the National Gallery in Trafalgar Square.

Caroline, Princess (1713–57) The third daughter and fourth child of GEORGE II and Queen CAROLINE OF ANSBACH, who was born at Herrenhausen on 10 June 1713 and baptized two days later, receiving the names Caroline Elizabeth. She was only 16 months old when she accompanied her mother and two elder sisters to England following the accession of her grandfather GEORGE I. The royal party landed at Margate on 13 October 1714 and proceeded to London, where they arrived on 15 October. The princess grew up in the stuffy atmosphere of her mother's court, passing her time in needlework, cards and gossip. She formed a romantic attachment for Lord Hervey and after his death in 1743 became almost a recluse in ST JAMES'S PALACE, devoting herself to charitable works and seeing nobody apart from her father, her sister Princess AMELIA and her brother William Augustus, Duke of CUMBERLAND. Her health was always delicate and she died at St James's Palace on 28 December 1757, being buried in the royal vault in Henry VII's Chapel at WESTMINSTER ABBEY on 5 January 1758.

Caroline Matilda, Queen of Denmark (1751–75) The fourth and youngest daughter of FREDERICK LOUIS, PRINCE OF WALES and Augusta of Saxe-Gotha, who was born posthumously at Leicester House, London, on 11/22 July 1751 and baptized 10 days later by Dr Hayter, Bishop of Norwich, her godparents being her aunt Princess CAROLINE (represented by proxy), her eldest sister AUGUSTA and her eldest brother George, Prince of Wales (later GEORGE III).

The princess was well educated by her mother, speaking French and German fluently and understanding Latin. At the age of 15 she was described as 'above the middle size, and though well shaped, rather inclined to what the French call *embonpoint*' and possessing 'a most pleasing physiognomy'. It was at this age that she was betrothed to her first cousin King Christian VII of Denmark, and their proxy marriage took place in the Chapel Royal, St James's, on 1 October 1766, the new young queen setting out for Denmark almost immediately thereafter. She arrived at Altona on 18 October and made her state entry into Copenhagen on 8 November, the marriage being solemnized again that evening in the chapel of Christiansborg. Queen Caroline Matilda gave birth to a son, Frederik (later King Frederik VI of Denmark) on 28 January 1768, and to a daughter, Louise Augusta, on 7 July 1771, her only children.

Unfortunately, the queen fell a victim to the machinations of her husband's stepmother, the Queen Dowager Juliana Maria, who coveted the succession of her own son to the Danish throne. Christian VII, although generally agreed to be intelligent and endowed with a pleasing personality, had been subjected to the harsh regime of a brutal governor and also seems to have inherited the terrible 'royal malady' of PORPHYRIA from his Hanoverian mother, his mental capacities being greatly impaired thereby. He neglected his wife shamefully while indulging in 'every form of gaiety and dissipation', including playing leading roles at the court theatre. However, he acquitted himself well on a tour of European courts that he made in 1768. On his return he fell under the influence of his physician, Johann Friedrich Struensee, a German and a radical free thinker, who in 1770 became Master of Requests and Minister of the Royal Cabinet with almost unlimited powers. He was also reputed to be the lover of the queen, who had found her marriage far from satisfactory, and, rumour had it, the father of Princess Louise Augusta. Queen Juliana Maria was not slow to take advantage of the rumours and manoeuvred a court revolution to bring about Struensee's fall and to discredit Caroline Matilda.

Early in the morning of 17 January 1772 following a ball at the Royal Theatre, the king was awakened and induced to sign orders for the immediate arrest of the queen, Struensee and his henchman Brandt. The queen, vigorously protesting her innocence, was conveyed under escort to Kronborg Castle. Struensee, on hearing of her arrest, confessed his relationship with her and the wretched girl (she was still only 20) was compelled to admit to it as well. Struensee was hastily brought to trial and condemned to death, his right hand being severed first and his body broken on the wheel before his final beheading. Brandt suffered the same fate. The marriage of the king and queen was declared dissolved on 6 April 1772 and Caroline Matilda, parted forcibly from her children, was, through the intervention of her brother George III, conveyed by a British warship to his Hanoverian dominions and lodged in the castle at Celle where her great-grandmother SOPHIA DOROTHEA had ended her days.

The queen's dowry was restored to her and she was able to live in comfort, but she felt the separation from her children keenly and three years later succumbed to 'a putrid fever and sore throat', dying at Celle on 10 May 1775, aged 23. She was buried in the parish church there on 13 May 1775. Her former husband, Christian VII, survived her for nearly 33 years, dying at Rendsborg on 13 March 1808 after resigning the regency to his only son Frederik in April 1784.

Caroline of Ansbach, Queen of Great Britain (1683–1737) Wilhelmine Dorothea Caroline, queen of GEORGE II, was the third and youngest daughter of Johann Friedrich, Margrave of Brandenburg-Ansbach, and the first child and only daughter of his second marriage to Eleonore Erdmuthe Louise of Saxe-Eisenach. She was born at Schloss Ansbach on 11 March 1683. Her father died when she was only three and in 1692 her widowed mother married the Elector of Saxony and took her with her to Dresden. There were some plans for her to marry Duke Friedrich II of Saxe-Gotha, whose daughter Augusta (see AUGUSTA, PRINCESS OF WALES) was later to become Caroline's daughter-in-law, but nothing came of them. After her mother's death in September 1696 Caroline became a ward of the King and Queen of Prussia and went to live in Berlin. There she became acquainted with the queen's Hanoverian family, including her mother the Electress SOPHIA.

A grandiose scheme for Caroline's marriage to the future Emperor Charles VI came to naught because of her staunch Protestantism. She returned to Ansbach in 1704. The Electress Sophia had marked her down as a suitable wife for her grandson George Augustus and, the necessary negotiations being satisfactorily concluded, they were married at Herrenhausen on 2 September 1705. The young couple were very well suited and the marriage was happy. In anticipation of being called to the British throne Caroline began to learn English, and was to become fluent in the language although she always preferred to write in French.

When her father-in-law ascended the throne as GEORGE I in 1714, Caroline came with her husband to England and, in the absence of a queen, occupied the position of first lady of the land as Princess of Wales. Four children had been born to her in Hanover and the stillbirth of her fifth child at ST JAMES'S PALACE in November 1716 was attributed by Caroline and her German ladies to the insistence of the English doctors on using instruments contrary to the natural childbirth methods in vogue in Germany. Four more children were to be born in England. Caroline loyally supported her husband in his quarrel with his father, which resulted in their withdrawal from the king's court and the setting up of a separate establishment at Leicester House and Richmond Lodge.

The death of the king in 1727 brought George and Caroline to the throne and, although she remained more German than English in outlook and temperament all her life, she was to play a greater role in affairs of state than any other queen consort since the Middle Ages. She gave her unqualified support to Robert Walpole and was to find a great mentor in all political matters in the person of Lord Hervey, who sat as Whig MP for Bury St Edmunds for eight years and held the office of Vice-Chamberlain of the Household for 10.

Caroline's control of affairs was acknowledged by the witty couplet:

You may strut, dapper George, but 'twill all be in vain,
We know 'tis Queen Caroline, not you, that reign.

The king and queen were crowned together at WESTMINSTER ABBEY on 11 October 1727 and Caroline's dress was so heavily embroidered and encrusted with jewels (mostly hired or borrowed) on that occasion that a pulley system had to be devised to raise and lower her skirt like a curtain to enable her to kneel at the appropriate points of the service.

The queen wisely flattered George's vanity and connived at his affairs, particularly that with her Bedchamber Woman, Mrs Howard, later Countess of Suffolk, with whom she remained on the best possible terms. When, for instance, George showed signs of switching his affections to new (and therefore unpredictable) lovers, Caroline actually went out of her way to encourage the Countess of Suffolk to renew her attentions to her husband in the hope of distracting him. George for his part was well content to allow Caroline to run things and

she acted as regent during his absences in Hanover.

Caroline had sustained an umbilical rupture at the birth of her last child in 1724 and, doubtless fearing the crude medical practices of the day, made light of the matter for many years until the condition became acute in 1737 and surgical intervention of some sort became imperative. There was of course no anaesthetic, and while the surgeons prodded and probed the queen's body she had to beg them to desist for a moment when she was overcome with laughter at the sight of a smouldering wig on the head of a surgeon who had bent over her in too close proximity to a candle. The operation was hopeless: gangrene set in and all hope of saving the queen's life was abandoned. She died at St James's Palace on 1 December 1737.

As Caroline lay dying she begged her weeping husband to marry again after her death. 'Never, never,' he sobbed, 'I shall only have mistresses.' He was true to his word and when he died left instructions that the side boards of their coffins be removed and the two joined together so that their bones might mingle.

The only flaw in Caroline's character seems to have been her complete detestation of her eldest son, whom she was to describe as 'the greatest ass, and the greatest liar' that ever lived. In this matter George and Caroline repeated the pattern of George I's behaviour towards them, continuing a trend which was to last in greater or lesser degree for two centuries.

Caroline of Brunswick, Queen of Great Britain (1768–1821) Caroline Amelia Elizabeth, queen of GEORGE IV, who was the second daughter and third child of Karl II, Duke of Brunswick, and his wife Augusta (see AUGUSTA, PRINCESS, DUCHESS OF BRUNSWICK), the eldest daughter of FREDERICK LOUIS, PRINCE OF WALES, and who was born at Brunswick on 17 May 1768. She grew up a high-spirited, ill-educated young woman in her parents' uncultured court. Her mother, GEORGE III's eldest sister, spent her time 'in knitting, netting, embroidery, and even the homely occupation of knitting stockings' with her ladies at her palace outside Brunswick, while the duke lived happily in the capital, with his mistress Luise von Hertefeld installed in the palace.

Caroline was brought up without religion, as were many princesses of that day, so that she might adopt that of her future husband. She was vivacious, wilful and witty, always seeking to gain attention and raise a laugh with her sallies, which were often cruelly barbed. At the age of 16 she was forbidden to attend a ball on which she had set her heart. She retired to bed, announcing that she was pregnant, and made such a fuss that her parents sent for a midwife, whereupon Caroline jumped up crying: 'Now will you forbid me to go to a ball again?'

Although regarded as unfeminine in many respects and careless of her appearance and personal hygiene, Caroline had an eye for men and was alleged to have had at least one serious affair before her first cousin George, Prince of Wales, asked for her hand in 1794. Their first meeting did not bode well, however – having taken a good look at his intended bride, the Prince of Wales turned aside to one of his attendants with the order, 'Harris, I am not well; pray get me a glass of brandy.' George's then-current mistress, Lady Jersey, became a Lady of the Bedchamber to Caroline, who on learning of the relationship indulged in a number of coarse jokes at her expense. The marriage took place in the Chapel Royal, St James's, on 8 April 1795.

Queen CHARLOTTE was no friend to her new daughter-in-law, whose reputation had preceded her, and almost her only friend at court was her uncle the king. By her own account, Caroline became pregnant on her wedding night when, in her own words, the prince 'passed the greatest part of his bridal night under the grate, where he fell, and where I left him' (she maintained that was the only occasion on which they ever slept together). Queen Charlotte, the mother of 15 children, took the keenest possible interest in the arrangements for the lying-in, supervising every minute detail. Caroline was in labour for nine hours and gave birth to 'an immense girl', as George was to write, at CARLTON HOUSE on the morning of 7 January 1796.

Lady Jersey had become a great thorn in Caroline's flesh. Her poise, elegance and general air of sophistication contrasted with the princess's gaucheness and probably irritated her by making her aware of her shortcomings. An acrimonious correspondence between the prince and princess was at its height when Lady Jersey resigned, temporarily solving the problem. In the long run, however, the situation was little eased, and in August 1797 Caroline left Carlton House and went to live at Blackheath. She rented Montague House and occupied herself by running an orphanage for nine children. She took such an interest in one of these, William Austin, that rumours began

to circulate that he was her own child. This became the subject of a 'Delicate Investigation', which completely cleared the princess, whose spirited remark when asked outright if the boy was hers was 'Prove it, and he shall be your King!'

Caroline was denied any part in the upbringing of her daughter Princess Charlotte (see CHARLOTTE OF WALES, PRINCESS) and was allowed to see her only at infrequent intervals. In 1807 her mother, now a widow, arrived in England as a refugee from Napoleon, who had overrun the Duchy of Brunswick. Caroline let her have Montague House for a time, herself moving into apartments in KENSINGTON PALACE. In 1810 the duchess moved to a house in Hanover Square and Caroline moved back to Blackheath, where she stayed until 1813 when, forced to economize, she moved to Connaught Place, Bayswater. Her way of life was becoming more and more eccentric and her appearance increasingly odd. This contributed to her deliberate exclusion from the celebrations surrounding the visit of the allied sovereigns, at which her daughter shone.

With the Napoleonic wars nearly at an end, Caroline won permission to travel abroad. She then spent several years wandering, visiting Germany, Switzerland, Italy, Tunis and Palestine. When in Milan she engaged as courier one Bartolomeo Pergami, an attractive rogue with pretensions to nobility. Very soon Caroline had appointed him her Chamberlain and accorded him the style of baron, which was attached to a small estate she bought for him in Sicily. It is clear that she was infatuated with him, but whether they actually became lovers is open to doubt. When the question of adultery came up, Caroline teasingly stated that she had only committed adultery once – with Mrs FITZHERBERT's husband.

While in Jerusalem Caroline amused herself by founding an order of chivalry (which she had no right to do). It was called the Order of St Caroline of Jerusalem and the insignia consisted of a red cross inscribed with the motto of the Order of the GARTER, *Honi soit qui mal y pense*, suspended from a lilac and silver ribbon. Pergami was appointed Grand Master of the Order and the rest of her entourage, including William Austin, became Knights. Pergami's appointment, coupled with the rumour that he shared baths with Queen Caroline, led to the devising of a much-repeated contemporary rhyme:

The Grand Master of St Caroline has found
   promotion's path.
He is made both Knight Companion and
   Commander of the Bath.

The travellers eventually returned to
Italy, where Caroline bought the Villa
d'Este on Lake Como and set up house. Her
daughter Charlotte had been forbidden to
write to her by her father but, once married,
she entered into a friendly correspondence
with her mother. The news of Charlotte's
death affected Caroline greatly: 'This is not
only my last hope gone, but what has
England lost?'

On the death of George III in January
1820, Caroline suddenly found herself
queen and determined to return to England
to assert her rights. She was on her way to
Calais when she received a proposition from
her husband offering her £50,000 a year for
life if she would continue to reside abroad.
She indignantly rejected this proposal and
returned to England, receiving an enthusiastic reception from the majority of the people. Her arrival was stage-managed to a
large extent by Sir Matthew Wood, a radical
City Alderman, who saw an opportunity to
further his own interests by supporting the
queen. Caroline landed at Dover on 6 June
and was greeted by a royal salute of 21 guns
from Dover Castle. Her drive to London the
following day was a triumphal progress all
the way.

The Bill of Pains and Penalties to enquire
into Caroline's conduct and deprive her of
her title was introduced in August and
the queen appeared in the House of Lords
for what amounted to, and has come to
be known as, her trial. She was ably
defended by Mr (later Lord) Brougham, her
Attorney-General, and Thomas Denman,
her Solicitor-General. Caroline was treated
with the utmost courtesy throughout the
proceedings, which lasted until 10 November, when the vote following the third reading of the Bill resulted in a majority of only
nine in favour and the Government thought
it prudent to withdraw it.

Scenes of wild rejoicing lasted for three
days and nights, and Caroline returned
to Brandenburg House, Hammersmith,
loaned to her by the Margravine of Ansbach
(formerly Lady Craven). On 29 November
she attended a public thanksgiving service at
St Paul's Cathedral, escorted by 150 horse-
men, and was received at Temple Bar by the
Lord Mayor and Sheriffs. Her disgruntled
husband meanwhile sulked in Brighton.

George's coronation was set for 19 July
1821, but no provision was made for the
queen's coronation or for her participation
in the ceremony. Undeterred, she drove to
the abbey and demanded admittance, only
to find her way barred at every entrance
until she gave up in despair and drove back
to Hammersmith. She still had enough
spirit to write to the king demanding that he
should agree to her being crowned 'next
Monday', and having done so set off for the
theatre at Drury Lane.

Caroline had suffered intermittently
from bowel trouble (probably a form of coli-
tis) for several years and was in the habit of
dosing herself with calomel and laudanum
to ease her pains. She felt unwell while at the
theatre on the coronation evening and in a
day or two had taken to her bed and sent for
her physician Henry Holland, who diagnosed 'acute inflammation of the bowels',
bled her and administered calomel and cas-
tor oil in 'a quantity ... that would have
turned the stomach of a horse'. Caroline rallied to receive Brougham and to sign her
will. Almost her last words to him were: 'I
am going to die, Mr Brougham, but it does
not signify.' The end came on 7 August 1821
after a long night of pain. She died at much
the same time as Napoleon Bonaparte: when
the news of Napoleon's death was brought
to George, who was awaiting news of his
wife's condition, the messenger told him,
'Sir, your bitterest enemy is dead' – to which
the king replied, 'Is she, by God!'

The queen had expressed a wish that she
should not be buried in England, but in
Brunswick. The funeral procession through
London was the scene of a violent conflict
between the Life Guards, who had been
instructed to escort it through the side
streets, and the people, who insisted on it
passing through the main thoroughfares,
and in the end the people had their way.

Later generations knew Queen Caroline
from the popular nursery rhyme:

Queen, Queen Caroline
Washed her hands in turpentine,
Turpentine did make them shine,
Poor Queen Caroline.

Caroline of Gloucester, Princess (1774–5)

The younger daughter and third and youngest child of Prince William Henry[2], Duke of
GLOUCESTER (brother of GEORGE III) and
his wife Maria Walpole, who was born at her
father's residence Gloucester House in the
parish of St George, Hanover Square,
London, on 24 June 1774. She was baptized
Caroline Augusta Maria on 22 July following, her godparents being her mother the
Duchess of Gloucester and her aunt and

uncle the Prince and Princess (later Duke and Duchess) of Brunswick. The death of the little princess at the age of nine months was recorded by her maternal great-uncle Horace Walpole: 'The Duke, who was preparing to go abroad for his health, and to carry the Duchess and his children along with him, had determined the two Princesses should first be inoculated, though the youngest was but nine months old, and was asthmatic and unhealthy, like her father. They were accordingly inoculated, and the smallpox was come out favourably on both, but on the tenth day the youngest Princess had a fit, and died on the eleventh.'

Caroline died on 14 March 1775 and her father sent a message to his brother the king asking for his orders with regard to the child's burial. The king's reply was that he had none to give, thus implying that he would not order the burial to take place in the royal vault at WESTMINSTER ABBEY because of his disapproval of his brother's unequal marriage. The duke then had a new vault constructed in St George's Chapel, Windsor, observing that 'seeing the King did not intend the Duchess and his children should lie in the Royal vault, he would not lie there himself'. The body of Princess Caroline was deposited in the new vault on 23 March 1775.

Cartimandua, Queen of the Brigantes (*fl*.AD43–51) The probable daughter and successor of Dumnocoveros and granddaughter of Volisios (both known from their gold coinage). Cartimandua had several husbands, an early one being CUNOBELINUS, KING OF THE CATUVELLAUNI. After his death in AD43, she married a Brigantian named Venutius, who is mentioned by Tacitus for his prowess in fighting the Roman invaders in AD51, but the queen was pro-Roman and deserted Venutius for her standard-bearer Vellocatus. Her chief claim to infamy, however, is her betrayal of her stepson CARATACUS, the son of Cunobelin, when she delivered him in chains to the Roman commander after he had sought refuge at her court. Her subsequent history is unknown.

Cassi Alternative name for the CATUVELLAUNI.

Cassivellaunus, King of the Catuvellanni (*fl*.55–54BC) The brave leader of the British forces that opposed Julius Caesar. His ancestors had migrated from Gaul in the third or second century BC and settled north of the Thames, establishing their capital at the town now called Wheathampstead, near St Albans in Hertfordshire. According to GEOFFREY OF MONMOUTH, Cassivellaunus was the second son of King Heli, who reigned for 40 years, and succeeded his brother Lud to the exclusion of the latter's two young sons. Cassivellaunus was a warlike king and fought with neighbouring tribes, coming to be regarded as a kind of high king of Britain. He commanded a chariot force and joined with other tribes such as the Atrebates, the Cantii and the TRINOVANTES in operating a 'scorched earth' policy in the face of Caesar's advancing army. He was so successful that Caesar felt Britain was not worth the battle and finally withdrew in September 54BC. Cassivellaunus continued to reign peacefully for several years (six, according to Geoffrey) until his death. He probably died at Verulamium (St Albans), to which he had moved his capital. He was succeeded in turn by his two sons, Androco, whose reign appears to have been short, and TASCIOVANUS, both known from their coinage (Geoffrey of Monmouth calls them Androgeus and Tenvantius and makes them the sons of Lud).

Castlemaine, Barbara Palmer, Countess of *see* CLEVELAND, BARBARA PALMER, DUCHESS OF.

Caswallon The Welsh form of the name of CASSIVELLAUNUS. It was occasionally used by Welsh princely families in later times.

Catherine, Princess[1] (1253–6) The third and youngest daughter of HENRY III and ELEANOR OF PROVENCE, who was born at the Palace of Westminster on St Catherine's Day, 25 November 1253. She was deaf and dumb from birth and died at WINDSOR CASTLE on 3 May 1256, being buried in WESTMINSTER ABBEY near the entrance to St Edmund's Chapel.

Catherine, Princess[2] (1639) The fourth daughter of CHARLES I and Queen HENRIETTA MARIA, who was born at Whitehall on 29 June 1639 and died the same day, half an hour after her baptism. She was buried in WESTMINSTER ABBEY, although there is no record in the register thereof.

Catherine, Princess, Countess of Devon (1479–1527) The sixth daughter of EDWARD IV and ELIZABETH WOODVILLE, who was born at Eltham, Kent, on 14 August 1479. At the age of 16 in or before October 1495 she was married to William Courtenay, Lord Courtenay, who later became an object of jealousy to his wife's brother-in-law HENRY VII and was imprisoned by him from 1503 to 1509 for his alleged participation in the Earl of Suffolk's rebellion. He was attainted in February 1504 and consequently was disabled from inheriting the earldom of Devon on his father's death on 28 May 1509. However, he was received back into favour by his wife's nephew HENRY VIII and bore the Third Sword at the coronation on 24 June 1509. His attainder was reversed by Act of Parliament on 9 May 1511 and the following day he was created Earl of Devon. He did not live to enjoy the honour for very long, dying of pleurisy at Greenwich on 9 June 1511. His widow took a vow of perpetual chastity on 13 July 1511 and died at Tiverton, Devon, on 15 November 1527. She was buried in Tiverton parish church, where a chapel and tomb were erected to her memory by her only surviving son Henry, Marquess of Exeter.

Catherine Howard (c.1520–42) The fifth queen of HENRY VIII, who was a first cousin of his second wife, ANNE BOLEYN, being the daughter of Lord Edmund Howard (a younger son of the 2nd Duke of Norfolk) and his first wife Joyce, daughter of Sir Richard Culpeper, of Oxenheath, Kent. She was born at Lambeth in about 1520. Her mother died when she was still a child and she was brought up at Horsham, Norfolk, and later at Lambeth, by her step-grandmother the Dowager Duchess of Norfolk. She was a highly sexed girl and indulged in torrid affairs with Henry Manox, her music teacher, with Francis Dereham, one of her grandmother's retainers, and with her cousin Thomas Culpeper. Henry met her at the London house of Stephen Gardiner, Bishop of Winchester, and was immediately so smitten by the petite Catherine that he arranged for her to be appointed a maid of honour to ANNE OF CLEVES.

Catherine, well aware of the king's interest, set out to captivate him and was, of course, aided by his distaste for Anne. Her relations encouraged her scheming and the king's intentions were made plain to all by the favours he showered on Catherine. On the day after the annulment of Henry's marriage to Anne, the Council, headed by Gardiner and Catherine's uncle Norfolk, implored the king to marry again 'to the comfort of his realm', and following their advice Henry and Catherine were married in a quiet ceremony at Hampton Court on 28 July 1540.

For a while Henry seemed to regain the vigour of his youth. He rose early, hunted, made royal progresses about the country and lavished lands and jewellery on his bewitching young bride. She, for her part, could have found little joy in a husband who was by now gross and repugnant, and unwisely turned again to her old lovers Dereham and Culpeper. She was aided and abetted by Viscountess Rochford, one of her ladies-in-waiting and the widow of Anne Boleyn's brother, who had suffered death for his supposed incest with her. Lady Rochford smuggled Culpeper into the queen's apartments at every opportunity during the course of a progress to the north that she made with Henry in August and September 1541. An informer told the Council and Cranmer was delegated to tell the king of his wife's infidelities. Henry at first refused to believe any of the accusations against Catherine, but, finally convinced, indulged in an orgy of self-pity and took himself off on a long hunting expedition.

Catherine was placed under guard at Syon House after she had been removed from Hampton Court, following a distressing episode during which she ran through the palace, shrieking her denials, to throw herself at Henry's feet as he heard mass in the Chapel Royal (the gallery through which she passed is known as the Haunted Gallery and her ghost is still reputed to re-enact the scene).

The wretched queen's lovers were brought to trial with several members of the Howard clan, and Dereham and Culpeper were executed. Culpeper was beheaded and Dereham was half-hanged, then cut down and disembowelled before being beheaded and quartered. A bill of attainder against Catherine was introduced into Parliament and received the royal assent (through a commission, appointed to spare Henry's feelings) on 11 February 1542. Henry declared himself too upset by the whole business to hear the 'wicked facts of the case', but then caused some consternation at court by demanding a sword so that he might carry out his wife's execution personally. Two days later Catherine and her accomplice Lady Rochford were beheaded on Tower Green. Henry did not attend the execution. The queen was buried near her cousin Anne Boleyn in the Chapel of St Peter-ad-Vincula.

The sordid affair had made Henry an old man. His disillusionment in Catherine almost broke him, but his usual resilience saved him once again and within a week of her death he was feasting to celebrate the pre-Lenten carnival.

Catherine Laura of York, Princess (1675)

The fifth daughter of James, Duke of York (later JAMES II) and his first child by his second wife MARY OF MODENA, who was born at ST JAMES'S PALACE 'at twenty-four minutes past four o'clock in the afternoon' on 10 January 1675. Her mother, a devout Catholic, had her baptized by her confessor Father Gallis, but her uncle CHARLES II ignored this and had the baby carried to the Chapel Royal and re-baptized by the Anglican rite. She was named Catherine after the queen and Laura after her grandmother the Duchess of Modena. Her godparents were her half-sisters Mary (later MARY II) and Anne (later Queen ANNE), and Charles II's natural son, James, Duke of MONMOUTH. The little princess died of convulsions at St James's Palace on 3 October 1675 and was buried in WESTMINSTER ABBEY two days later.

Catherine of Aragon (1485–1536) The first

queen of HENRY VIII, who was born at Alcala de Henares, near Madrid, on 15 December 1485, the fourth and youngest daughter of Fernando II, king of Aragon (Fernando V as king of Castile) and Isabel I, Queen of Castile, the famous 'Catholic Kings' whose marriage had effectively united Spain into one kingdom. She was only two years old when HENRY VII made overtures to her parents for her hand on behalf of his son ARTHUR, PRINCE OF WALES, her junior by nine months, and the marriage treaty was concluded in 1500.

On her wedding day, 14 November 1501, Catherine was escorted to St Paul's Cathedral by the 10-year-old Duke of York, her future brother-in-law and eventual husband. Immediately after the marriage the young couple took up residence in Ludlow Castle, where Arthur presided over the council of the Marches of Wales. He was an immature 15 and apart from being racked with consumption was very probably infected by syphilis as the result of some youthful escapades. The marriage was almost certainly never consummated in the fullest sense, a matter which was to be of the utmost importance in the future, but Arthur's coarse braggings ('last night I was *in* Spain') indicate that some attempt at intercourse was probably made, perhaps sufficient to infect Catherine with syphilis. Catherine steadfastly maintained that she was still a virgin when she married Henry.

The damp atmosphere of Ludlow Castle swiftly proved fatal to Arthur and he died there on 2 April 1502 nearly five months after his marriage. The young widow, now known as the Dowager Princess of Wales, was almost at once proposed as a bride for Prince Henry and at the beginning of the following year, Henry VII having become a widower, there was even some talk of her marrying her father-in-law. However, the treaty of her marriage to the younger Henry was concluded on 23 June 1503 and papal dispensation for the marriage between sister-in-law and brother-in-law was obtained from Pope Julius II in 1504. Once this had been done, however, Henry VII was in no hurry to complete the marriage and, characteristically, kept Catherine so short of money and the common necessities of life, that she was obliged to apply to her father for the wherewithal to pay the members of her household. Henry VII's motivation in delaying matters was the hope that a better match might turn up for his son, in which case Catherine could quietly be discarded.

Once Henry VII was dead, matters moved swiftly. Henry VIII was ardently in love with his betrothed, a tall blonde girl who matched him well for grace and looks, and the marriage took place at the Grey Friars' Church, Greenwich, on 11 June 1509, being followed two weeks later by the coronation of the young king and queen at WESTMINSTER ABBEY.

Catherine's first child, a daughter, was prematurely stillborn at the end of January 1510, but the following 1 January she gave birth to a living son, Henry. The birth was celebrated with jousts and tournaments, but sadly the baby survived barely two months. A second boy was born in November 1513 and died at once, and a third was stillborn in December 1514. In February 1516, Catherine again became a mother and this time the baby, a girl named Mary (*see* MARY I), though sickly, survived. Two miscarriages followed in 1517 and Catherine's last pregnancy in 1518 ended in the birth of a stillborn daughter.

When Henry left on his French campaign in 1513, Catherine was constituted Governor of the Realm and Captain-General of the Forces and left in charge during his absence. Following the defeat of the Scots at FLODDEN, Catherine sent JAMES IV's bloodstained coat to Henry in Flanders, a grim souvenir of the victory achieved under her regency. In 1520 the queen accompanied Henry to France and was present at the FIELD OF THE CLOTH OF GOLD.

By 1525 Catherine was 40 and the likelihood of further issue seemed remote.

Furthermore, her looks had faded and the king, a vigorous 34, had become infatuated with ANNE BOLEYN (one of several mistresses). Husband and wife ceased to cohabit in 1526, and in the following year the long divorce process began. Henry's suit was for nullity on the grounds of the affinity existing between him and Catherine as the widow of his brother. Catherine had powerful support on the Continent from her nephew the Emperor Charles V, who was influential at Rome, and the Pope refused to concede that the dispensation granted by his predecessor could have been invalid. This stalemate resulted in Henry's breach with Rome and the declaration of a compliant Archbishop Cranmer that the marriage was null and void on 23 May 1533, followed by an Act of Parliament that his marriage to Catherine was null and 'utterly dissolved' in March 1534. Henry hypocritically referred to her as 'so good a lady and loving companion' and expressed regret that he must 'put her away' after living in sin with her for nearly 20 years.

Catherine had her daughter taken from her in 1531 and was removed to Moor Park, Hertfordshire, and thence to Bishop's Hatfield. Following the annulment, she was deprived of the title of queen and again styled Dowager Princess of Wales. She enjoyed great personal popularity and was constantly moved about for fear of an uprising in her favour. She had the hollow satisfaction of knowing that the Pope had pronounced her marriage to be valid on 23 March 1534 and resolutely refused to accept the Act of Succession which bastardized Mary and placed Anne Boleyn's daughter Elizabeth first in line to the throne.

Catherine's spirit remained unbroken to the last. She died at Kimbolton Castle, Huntingdonshire, where she was confined, after an illness of about a month's duration, on 7 January 1536. Poison was rumoured, but the embalmer's account makes it clear that she died of cancer, her heart being described as 'quite black and hideous to look at' with a 'black round body stuck to the outside', an indication of a secondary melanotic sarcoma. The other organs were described as being 'as healthy and normal as possible', so the embalmer evidently did not recognize the primary growth which must have existed. Catherine had just completed her 50th year. She was buried in Peterborough Cathedral, where, in Victorian times, the subscriptions of 'English ladies bearing the name of Catherine' paid for a handsome black marble slab to mark her grave opposite that in which MARY, QUEEN OF SCOTS, lay before her removal to Westminster.

Catherine of Braganza (1638–1705) The consort of CHARLES II, who was the second daughter of Dom João, 8th Duke of Bragança, by his wife Luisa Maria, daughter of Don Juan Manuel Domingo Perez de Guzman, 8th Duke of Medina Sidonia. She was born at Vila Viçosa, near Lisbon, on St Catherine's Day, 25 November 1638, and named Catarina Henriqueta. By the time she was two years old Portugal had thrown off the hated Spanish yoke and her father was proclaimed King of Portugal and the Algarves on 1 December 1640, thus bringing about a great change in his family's status.

Catherine's father first put her forward as a possible bride for the future Charles II in 1645, the proposals being renewed by her mother the Queen Regent after Charles's Restoration in 1660. Rumours that she was barren had already begun to circulate, but the match went ahead as Charles was eager to secure the promised dowry of £300,000 (with Tangier and Bombay thrown in). The marriage contract was signed on 23 June 1661 and Catherine sailed for England the following April, landing at Portsmouth on 13 May. The marriage took place privately there on 21 May and Catherine was conducted to Hampton Court, where Charles, with uncharacteristic insensitivity, compelled her to receive his mistress Lady Castlemaine, causing a great emotional outburst from the new queen. In August the court moved to Whitehall and Pepys reported in his diary on seeing her for the first time, 'though she be not very charming, yet she hath a good, modest, and innocent look, which is pleasing'. Charles himself evidently found his new queen acceptable enough, writing of her: 'her face is not so exact as to be called a beauty though her eyes are excellent good, and not anything in her face that can in the least shock one, on the contrary she hath as much agreeableness in her looks altogether as ever I saw ... In a word I think myself very happy.' To another friend, however, he was heard to remark that he had been provided with a bat rather than a woman.

Sadly the reports of Catherine's barrenness were to be proved true, although she did become pregnant and miscarry more than once. On 9 October 1662 Pepys reported: 'It is believed the Queen is with child, for that the coaches are ordered to ride very easily through the streets.' No more was heard of this, however. On 19 February 1666 Pepys wrote of Catherine that 'it is confessed by all that she miscarried lately; Dr Clerke telling me yesterday at White Hall that he had the membranes and other vessels in his hands which she voided, and were perfect as ever woman's was that bore a child'. Again on 9 May 1668 he reported: 'I ... hear that the Queene hath miscarryed of a perfect child, being gone about ten weeks, which do show that she can conceive, though it be unfortunate that she cannot bring forth.' Nor apparently was this Catherine's last attempt at maternity, for on 19 May 1669 Pepys 'waited upon the King and Queen all dinner-time, in the Queen's lodgings, she being in her white pinner and apron, like a woman with child; and she seemed handsomer plain so, than dressed'. Obviously Catherine was wearing the fashionable maternity dress of the day. There is another reference to her 'being supposed with child' on 26 May, but after that no more.

Catherine chose to live at Somerset House rather than at Whitehall and her chapel there became a fashionable rendezvous for Catholics and others, giving cause for complaint. Probably the music was good and the unaccustomed ceremonial had its appeal. Attempts by the Whigs to implicate the queen in the Popish Plot in 1678 were refuted by Charles.

When Charles was dying Catherine was ill and sent a message begging his forgiveness for not being able to come to him. 'Alas, poor woman', said Charles, 'it is I who should be begging her forgiveness.' After her initial shock at the presentation of Lady Castlemaine, Catherine had maintained a dignified attitude towards Charles's mistresses and had shown many acts of kindness to his illegitimate children.

Catherine continued to reside at Somerset House after Charles's death and in 1688 was present at the birth of JAMES II's son, to whom she stood godmother, later giving evidence as to his legitimacy to the Council. She remained in London after James II fled but, finding she did not get on well with WILLIAM III and MARY II, decided to return to her native Portugal. She made a leisurely journey through France and Spain and arrived in Lisbon in January 1693. In the last year of her life she acted as regent of Portugal for her brother Pedro II, who had grown weary of government. She died of a sudden attack of 'colic' at the Palace of Bemposta in Lisbon on 31 December 1705 and was buried in the monastery of Belém.

Catherine of France (1401–37) The consort of HENRY V, who was born at the Hôtel de St Pol, Paris, on 27 October 1401, the youngest child of the mad King Charles VI of France and his rapacious, nymphomaniac queen, Isabelle of Bavaria. An elder daughter of this couple was ISABELLA OF FRANCE[2], who had already been queen of England as the child bride of RICHARD II.

Catherine's childhood was passed at her birthplace, the Hôtel de St Pol, where she and her sister Michelle lived in a deplorable condition of squalor, dirty and half-starved, while their mother disported herself with her paramour and brother-in-law, the Duke of Orléans. Charles VI's madness is now believed to have been occasioned by PORPHYRIA, 'the royal malady', which also afflicted GEORGE III. In a period of lucidity he became aware of the state of his unfortunate children and, having no other resources, gave their governess a gold cup to sell to provide for their necessities. The king's temporary recovery lasted several years, during which the Duke of Orléans was assassinated by the Duke of Burgundy, Queen Isabelle was imprisoned at Tours, and Catherine was educated in the convent of Poissy, where her sister Marie was a nun.

The first demand for Catherine's hand in marriage was made by Henry V soon after his accession in 1413, but it was not until after the Treaty of Troyes had been signed that the couple were married in St Peter's Church in that town on 2 June 1420. The betrothal ring which Henry gave to his bride was to be used as the coronation ring of succeeding queen consorts, and was presumably broken up with the rest of the old regalia under the Commonwealth in the 17th century. The couple did not return to England for Catherine's coronation until the following February and the ceremony took place at WESTMINSTER ABBEY on the 24th of that month. There is the usual detailed description of the coronation banquet, which included 'dead eels stewed', jelly coloured with columbine flowers and the usual 'subtleties', this time a figure of St Catherine and a tiger looking in a mirror. At the banquet the new queen interceded for the release of JAMES I, KING OF SCOTS, who had been imprisoned in the Tower and elsewhere since 1406, although he had accompanied Henry to France in 1420.

Towards the end of 1421 Catherine gave birth to her first child, the future HENRY VI, at Windsor, and the following May crossed to France to join her husband and effect a reunion with her parents (now reconciled) at Paris. Catherine and her mother were both present at Henry V's deathbed and after only 18 months of marriage she found herself a widow at the age of 20.

Catherine accompanied Henry's body back to England and busied herself with the upbringing of the infant Henry VI. BAYNARD'S CASTLE on the Surrey side of the Thames was assigned to her as a residence in 1424. She had barely settled in when rumours were heard of her intrigue with Owen TUDOR, a handsome young Welsh squire of good family but little fortune. A secret marriage was alleged, although no proof has ever been forthcoming. There were, however, three sons, Edmund, Jasper and Owen.

Catherine accompanied Henry VI to Paris for his French coronation and again visited her mother, now, to quote Agnes Strickland, 'full of years, and it must be added, of dishonours'. The old queen died in 1436 and Catherine only survived her mother a year. In the summer of 1436 she gave birth to a daughter, Margaret, who lived only a few days. This event appears to have alerted the king's guardians to his mother's ménage and she was forced to withdraw to BERMONDSEY ABBEY, her three young sons being taken from her. Although only 35, the queen's spirit broke, she fell into some sort of decline, made her will, and died in the Abbey on 3 January 1437.

Catherine's body was buried in the old Lady Chapel of Westminster Abbey and a tomb was erected by Henry VI. The Latin inscription referred to her only as the widow of Henry V, but when her grandson Henry Tudor had become HENRY VII, he had it replaced by another acknowledging her Tudor marriage. Catherine's mummified body was disinterred when Henry VII was buried and remained above ground in a chest near Henry V's tomb for the best part of three centuries. Here it was shown to the curious for a few pence, and Samuel Pepys recorded in his Diary on 23 February 1669, when he visited the Abbey with his wife and a party of friends: 'I had the upper part of her body in my hands, and I did kiss her mouth, reflecting upon it that I did kiss a Queen, and that this was my birthday, thirty-six years old, that I did first kiss a Queen.'

Catherine of York, Princess (1671) The fourth daughter of James, Duke of York (later JAMES II) and his first wife Anne HYDE, who was born at Whitehall 'at thirty-nine minutes past five o'clock in the evening' on 9 February 1671. Her godparents were the Duchess of Buckingham, the Marchioness of Worcester and her cousin the Prince of Orange (later WILLIAM III). Her mother died when she was only seven weeks old. The little princess died at ST JAMES'S PALACE on 5 December 1671, aged 10 months, and was buried in WESTMINSTER ABBEY on 8 December 1671 without ceremony.

Catherine Parr (c.1512–48) The sixth and last queen of HENRY VIII, who was the daughter of Sir Thomas Parr, of Kendal, Westmorland, by his wife Maud, daughter of Sir Thomas Green, of Green's Norton, Northamptonshire. She was born at Kendal Castle in about 1512. Her father died in 1517, leaving his widow with three young children, and Catherine probably passed much of her childhood with her mother's family in Northamptonshire. When she was about 17 she married Sir Edward Borough (or Burgh), the eldest son of Thomas, 3rd Lord Borough of Gainsborough. There were no children of the marriage and Edward died sometime before April 1533. In the same year his widow became the third wife of John Nevill, 3rd Lord Latimer, a man of 40. The marriage was childless but happy, and Catherine was a good nurse to her ailing husband and an understanding friend to the children of his first marriage, some of whom were but a few years younger than she was.

Lord Latimer died in March 1543, leaving Catherine a widow for the second time at the age of 31. Now, it would seem, she fell in love for the first time in her life with the dashing Thomas Seymour, a brother of the late Queen JANE and therefore Henry VIII's brother-in-law, and it was anticipated that they would marry, when the king intervened and carried off the widow for himself. The marriage, at which Stephen Gardiner officiated, took place quietly at Hampton Court on 12 July 1543.

A contemporary described Catherine Parr as being plainer than ANNE OF CLEVES and by the time he married her Henry, wracked by syphilis and prematurely aged, sought only a nurse and a kindly stepmother for his children, all hopes of a young wife to bring him further heirs having perished on the scaffold with CATHERINE HOWARD. As Lady Latimer, Catherine had proved herself as the third wife of a husband nearly 20 years her senior, loved and esteemed by her stepchildren.

Catherine may be considered the first Protestant Queen of England. She cultivated the friendship of the reformers Coverdale and Latimer and entered into long theological discussions with the king, who still retained his old interest in such matters.

The Christmas of 1543 saw a reunion of the royal family brought about by Catherine's influence. Her three ill-assorted stepchildren, Mary, Elizabeth and Edward (see MARY I, ELIZABETH I and EDWARD VI), came together for the first time and soon developed a genuine affection for their father's kind wife. She was assiduous in her efforts to provide for their education and further their intellectual pursuits and personally chose the tutors for Prince Edward.

In 1544 the war with France was again renewed and Henry departed for Calais, leaving Catherine as Governor of the Realm and Protector during his absence of two months, a duty which she discharged with her customary diligence.

Catherine's religious leanings incited a pro-Roman faction, led by Gardiner and Wriothesley, to bring a charge of heresy against her in 1546, going so far as to draw up a bill against her and persuading the near senile king to sign it. A copy of the bill came into Catherine's hands by accident and in a state of great trepidation she went to throw herself upon Henry's mercy. She pleaded cleverly and eloquently that she had talked theology with the king, to whom she was ever obedient in all matters concerning religion, to ease his infirmity, and elicited the reply: 'And is it even so, sweetheart, and tended your argument to no worse end? Then perfect friends we are now again as ever at any time heretofore.' The next day Henry and Catherine were walking in the gardens of Whitehall when a party arrived to arrest the queen and take her to the Tower. Henry sent them packing forthwith, calling Wriothesley 'Knave, arrant knave, beast and fool!'

Henry's death in January 1547 left Catherine free to renew her friendship with Thomas Seymour, and she secretly married for the fourth and last time in April or May the same year. As an uncle of the new king, Edward VI, Seymour had been created Baron Seymour of Sudeley very soon after his nephew's succession. He was now aged about 39 and had the reputation of being a rogue and a womanizer. Catherine, whose first three marriages had remained childless, found herself pregnant for the first time at the age of 36 in 1548. On 29 August 1548 she was safely delivered of a daughter, but puerperal fever ensued and she died on 5 September. She was buried in the chapel of Sudeley Castle but the coffin was reburied in the Chandos vault in 1817. Her daughter appears to have died young.

Catuvellauni Celtic tribe that migrated to Britain from the area of Châlons-sur-Marne in Gaul and established a powerful kingdom north of the Thames. Its best known rulers, who struck a plentiful coinage in gold, silver and copper, were CASSIVELLAUNUS, his sons Androco and Tehvant or TASCIOVANUS, and the latter's son CUNOBELINUS, on whose death in AD43 the Roman conquest of Britain began.

Ceawlin, King of Wessex (d.593) The son of King CYNRIC, who was first mentioned in the ANGLO-SAXON CHRONICLE as fighting with his father against the Britons at Beranburh (Barbury Castle, Wiltshire) in 556. Four years later, in 560, he succeeded his father as king and reigned for 30 years. BEDE listed him as the second BRETWALDA or acknowledged overlord of the southern English. With his brother Cutha he fought against ETHELBERT I of Kent, who appears to have encroached into Wessex, and drove him back within his boundaries, killing two (presumably Kentish) princes, Oslac (or Oslaf) and Cnebba, at a place called Wibbandun. In 571 they were again fighting the Britons and captured four villages. Cutha died that year, and Ceawlin's son, Cuthwine, took his place at Ceawlin's side, although there seems to be some confusion between the names Cutha and Cuthwine. The Chronicle states that Cutha (sic) was killed fighting the Britons in 584 near Stoke Lyne in Oxfordshire, 'and Ceawlin captured many villages and countless booty, and departed in anger to his own [territories]'. In 591 or 592 Ceawlin 'was expelled' or perhaps compelled to associate his nephew CEOL in the kingdom. He died in 593. His son Cuthwine had died before him (probably the individual killed in 584), but several of his descendants later reigned in Wessex, including EGBERT.

Cecilia, Abbess of Caen (c.1055–1126) A daughter of WILLIAM I and MATILDA OF FLANDERS, who is usually accounted their eldest daughter. Cecilia (or Cecily) was born in Normandy about 1055. She is said to have accompanied her mother to England in 1068 and to have returned to Normandy to enter her novitiate in the Benedictine Convent of the Holy Trinity at Caen in 1074. On Easter

Day, 5 April 1075, she took her solemn vows of profession. On the death of the Abbess Matilda in June 1112, Cecilia was elected as her successor. She held office until her death on 30 July 1126 and was buried in the nun's choir. She was succeeded as Abbess by her great-niece Elizabeth of Blois, daughter of William, Count of Chartres, and granddaughter of ADELA, COUNTESS OF BLOIS.

Cenfus, King of Wessex (d.674?) The son of Cenferth (son of Cuthgils, son of King CEOLWULF), Cenfus replaced Queen SEXBURGA on the throne of Wessex in 673. Florence of Worcester says he reigned for two years, but this seems doubtful. He was succeeded by his son AESCWINE.

Centwine, King of Wessex (d.685) The youngest son of King CYNEGILS and brother of King CENWALH, who succeeded his kinsman King AESCWINE in 676 and was overthrown and probably killed by another kinsman, CAEDWALLA, in 685. He married a sister of Eormenburh, the second wife of EGFRITH, KING OF NORTHUMBRIA, and had a daughter Eadburga or Bugge, an Abbess of Minster in Kent, who died in 751 and is mentioned by the poet Aldhelm.

Cenwalh, King of Wessex (d.672) The son of King CYNEGILS, whom he succeeded in 643. He was married to a sister of PENDA, KING OF MERCIA, but soon after his accession he repudiated her and took another wife. In retaliation Penda expelled him from his kingdom and he took refuge at the court of ANNA, KING OF EAST ANGLIA, where he lived in exile for three years. Although Cenwalh's father had been baptized, he himself had not renounced paganism. Under King Anna's influence, however, he took instruction in the Christian faith and was baptized in 646. After his restoration, Cenwalh gave a large tract of land to his nephew Cuthred, son of his brother Cwichelm, perhaps in compensation for having taken the throne to which Cuthred had a prior right. Cenwalh founded the cathedral at Winchester in 648. According to BEDE he invited 'a bishop from Gaul named Agilbert' to preside as chief bishop, but later 'grew tired of the bishop's foreign speech' and replaced him by the Saxon-speaking Wini. Agilbert returned to Gaul and became Bishop of Paris. Cenwalh grew tired of Wini also and expelled him. Wini sought refuge in Mercia and eventually became Bishop of London. The West Saxons remained without a bishop for several years, during which Cenwalh 'suffered great damage to his kingdom from his enemies'. Seeing this as evidence of divine retribution, he sent messengers to Paris imploring Agilbert to return. This he declined to do, but he sent his nephew Leutherius in his place and he was duly consecrated Bishop of Winchester by Theodore, Archbishop of Canterbury, in 670. Cenwalh died in 672, leaving no issue and was succeeded for one year by his widow SEXBURGA. It is not known if she was the wife for whom he had repudiated Penda's sister.

Ceol, King of Wessex (d.597) A son of Cutha and grandson of CYNRIC, KING OF WESSEX, who was associated in the kingdom with his uncle CEAWLIN in 591 and succeeded him as sole king in 593. He died in 597, leaving a son CYNEGILS, later king, and was succeeded by his brother CEOLWULF.

Ceolred, King of Mercia (d.716) The son of ETHELRED, KING OF MERCIA and his wife Osthryth of Northumbria, who succeeded his cousin COENRED on his resignation in 709. He died in 716, apparently without issue, and was buried at Lichfield. His widow, Werburh, became a nun and is said to have died an abbess at what must have been a very great age in 782.

Ceolwulf, King of Northumbria (d.764) The son of Cuthwine, a descendant of IDA, KING OF BERNICIA, who was appointed to succeed his kinsman OSRIC, KING OF NORTHUMBRIA in 729. In 737 he resigned the throne to his cousin EADBERHT and 'received the Petrine tonsure', or in other words was ordained a secular priest. He became a monk at Lindisfarne and died in 764. He is the king to whom BEDE dedicated his *History*.

Ceolwulf, King of Wessex (d.611) A son of Cutha and grandson of King CYNRIC, who succeeded his brother CEOL, KING OF WESSEX in 597. He spent his whole reign fighting the Angles, the Welsh, the Picts and the Scots and died in 611, when he was succeeded by his nephew CYNEGILS, the son of Ceol. He left a son Cuthgils, the grandfather of King CENFUS.

Ceolwulf I, King of Mercia (d. after 823) The son of Cuthbert, a descendant of Coenwalh, brother of PENDA, KING OF MERCIA, who succeeded his brother King COENWULF in 821 and was driven out of his kingdom two years later. He had a daughter Aelfled (Elfleda), who married Wigmund, son of King WIGLAF, and became the mother of St Wistan and possibly of a daughter Eadburh, the mother-in-law of ALFRED THE GREAT.

Ceolwulf II, King of Mercia (d. before 883?) Of unknown origin, Ceolwulf II was described in the ANGLO-SAXON CHRONICLE as 'a foolish King's thane', who was set up as a puppet king by the Danes in 873 after BURHRED, KING OF MERCIA had been driven out. In the autumn of 877 the Danes settled in East Mercia, leaving West Mercia to Ceolwulf. He had ceased to reign by 883, when Ealdorman Ethelred acknowledged the overlordship of ALFRED THE GREAT.

Cerdic, King of Wessex (d.534) According to the ANGLO-SAXON CHRONICLE, the son of Elesa, son of Esla, son of Gewis, son of Wig, son of Freawine, son of Frithugar, son of Brand, son of Baeldaeg, son of WODEN – though this pedigree seems to incorporate two distinct traditions welded together. Cerdic is said to have come to Britain with his son CYNRIC and five ships in 495, landing at a place called Cerdicesora. They had many fights with the Welsh (signifying the British) over the next few years and in 508 defeated and killed a king named Natanleod and his army of 5000 men. In 514 they were joined by their kinsmen Stuf and Wihtgar and in 519 the Chronicle records that 'Cerdic and Cynric obtained the kingdom of the West Saxons ... And from that day on the princes of the West Saxons have reigned.' In 530 they conquered the Isle of Wight and in 534 Cerdic died 'and his son Cynric continued to reign twenty-six years'.

Charles, Prince of Wales (1948–) The eldest son of ELIZABETH II and Prince Philip, Duke of EDINBURGH, who was born (by forceps delivery) at BUCKINGHAM PALACE, London, on 14 November 1948 and baptized Charles Philip Arthur George. It was, incidentally, the first time a royal baby had been born without witnesses and a government minister being present since the 17th century (Prince Philip played squash as he waited for news of the birth). Charles became a prince of the United Kingdom of Great Britain and Northern Ireland and a Royal Highness from birth following an order to that effect made by his maternal grandfather GEORGE VI. On his mother's accession to the throne in February 1952 he became Duke of Cornwall and Duke of Rothesay, Earl of Carrick, Baron of Renfrew, Lord of the Isles and Great Steward of Scotland. The first royal heir to be taught outside the palace, he was educated at Hill House School, London; Cheam Preparatory School, Hampshire; Gordonstoun, Elgin; Geelong Grammar School, Melbourne, Australia; Trinity College, Cambridge (BA 1970); and the University College of Wales, Aberystwyth.

As a boy, Charles was perceived to be shy, especially in comparison with his more extrovert father. Despite this natural reticence, however, he indulged a passion for drama while at school, and also inadvertently captured the headlines in 1963 when he was caught buying a cherry brandy at a hotel in the Outer Hebrides, though at 14 under age for purchasing alcohol. A taste for physical activity, nurtured at Gordonstoun, expressed itself in such pursuits as riding (especially at polo), skiing, shooting, fishing, flying, parachuting and windsurfing. For his younger siblings Andrew (*see* YORK, ANDREW, DUKE OF) and EDWARD he also wrote a children's story, *The Old Man of Lochnagar*, which became a bestseller when published for charity in 1980.

On 26 July 1958 Prince Charles was created Prince of Wales and Earl of Chester, thereby also becoming a Knight of the GARTER. He was invested as Prince of Wales and Earl of Chester at CAERNARFON CASTLE on 1 July 1969 (in spite of death threats from Welsh nationalists) and took his seat in the House of Lords on 11 February 1970 (his maiden speech, in 1974, called for people to be enabled to make better use of their leisure time). Having won his wings with the RAF in 1971, he was appointed a Knight Grand Cross of the Order of the Bath and Great Master of the Order of the Bath in 1975, a Knight of the THISTLE in 1977, a Privy Councillor in 1977, a Knight of the Order of Australia in 1981, and an Extra Companion of the QUEEN'S SERVICE ORDER OF NEW ZEALAND in 1983. In addition he holds many foreign orders and decorations, honorary degrees and freedoms. As a captain in the Royal Navy, he commanded HMS *Bronington* before retiring from the Service in 1976. He is also Colonel-in-Chief of several regiments. He has represented the queen on many occasions abroad and acted as Counsellor of State during his mother's overseas tours.

Having reached the age of 30 without getting married, Charles was well-established as 'the world's most eligible bachelor' and pressure for him to find a wife intensified. His name had been linked romantically with various names, including Lucia Santa Cruz, Davina Sheffield, Lady Jane Wellesley,

Princess Marie-Astrid of Luxembourg, film actress Susan George and Lady Sarah Spencer. On 29 July 1981 (in defiance of at least two astrologers who said the match was ill-starred) Prince Charles married at St Paul's Cathedral, London, Lady Diana Frances Spencer, third and youngest daughter of (Edward) John Spencer, 8th Earl Spencer, LVO, by his first wife, Frances Ruth Burke Roche, daughter of the 4th Baron Fermoy (see DIANA, PRINCESS OF WALES). Charles had met Diana when she was still a young girl and had been much attracted by her vitality when they met later on, explaining to reporters on their engagement, 'Diana will certainly help to keep me young. I think I shall be exhausted.' A son, William (see WILLIAM OF WALES, PRINCE), was born at St Mary's Hospital, Paddington, on 21 June 1982, and a second son, Prince Henry (Harry) Charles Albert David of Wales, was born at St Mary's Hospital, Paddington, on 15 September 1984.

After a while rumours surfaced that the royal marriage was running into trouble, with much attention being paid to the strains and stresses under which Diana in particular was placed, and to Charles's relationship with the married Camilla Parker Bowles. Charles became the object of increasing criticism, not least on account of such admitted eccentricities as talking to plants to encourage them to grow and also for his public denunciations of certain modes of contemporary architecture (he described the proposed extension to the National Gallery as 'a kind of vast municipal fire station ... like a monstrous carbuncle on the face of a beloved friend'). Such 'interference' in non-royal issues raised hackles in many quarters, though (at least in relation to his views on architecture) Charles showed reluctance to retreat from his stated views, once protesting, 'If people think me square, then I am happy to be thought square'. Comments to the effect that he would not wish to rule over a divided Britain, meanwhile, were enthusiastically repeated by the Labour Party, who interpreted them as a veiled attack upon Conservative Thatcherite policies.

Despite tireless efforts by royal officials to restore the prince's image as a hardworking, conscientious monarch-in-waiting, a tide of anti-royal sentiment gathered strength in the late 1980s and early 1990s, further exacerbated by the marital problems of other members of the royal family. In 1992 the situation was complicated when it was announced that the Prince and Princess of Wales had decided to separate (thereby threatening a constitutional crisis should the prince wish to remarry in the future). Unsuccessful attempts were subsequently made to keep the princess out of the limelight, but the furore continued, with many observers going so far as to question whether the prince had the right qualities to occupy the British throne (adding fuel to the arguments of anti-monarchists). Those sympathetic to the prince, however, pointed out the well-nigh impossible role he was being asked to play and emphasized his undoubted sincerity and unstinting work on behalf of his country. The prince and princess were finally divorced in July 1996. Following prolonged negotiations, a decree nisi of divorce was granted to the prince and princess on 15 July 1996 and made absolute on 28 August following.

Charles I, King of England (1600–49) The second son of JAMES I and ANNE OF DENMARK, who was born at DUNFERMLINE Palace on 19 November 1600. He was a delicate, backward child, still unable to walk or talk at the age of three, and was left behind in the care of nurses and servants when, on his father's accession to the English throne in 1603, his parents went to London with his elder brother and sister. He was finally considered strong enough to make the journey south in July 1604 and proceeded in easy stages in a curtained litter. His parents met him at Northampton and placed him in the excellent hands of Lady Carey, whose husband had carried the news of James's accession to Scotland. She patiently persevered with 'Baby Charles' and gradually he learned both to walk on his rickety legs and to talk with his stammering tongue.

Charles adored his elder brother Henry and longed to emulate him; when Henry died at the age of 18, the 12-year-old Charles felt it keenly. The separation from his sister Elizabeth on her marriage the following year was another blow and Charles now found himself virtually an only child.

Charles had been created Duke of Albany, Marquess of Ormond, Earl of Ross and Baron of Ardmannoch in the peerage of Scotland on 23 December 1603 and Duke of York in the peerage of England on 6 January 1605. He was also made a Knight of the Order of the BATH in 1605 and a Knight of the GARTER in 1611. Shortly before his 16th birthday he was created Prince of Wales and Earl Chester on 4 November 1616, having succeeded as Duke of Cornwall, Duke of Rothesay, etc. on Henry's death in November 1612.

Even as an adult Charles was only four feet seven inches tall, with a mournful face and heavy-lidded eyes. He bore himself with great dignity, however, and James envisaged a marriage alliance for him with the Infanta Maria of Spain. In 1623 Charles was sent to Madrid accompanied by 'Steenie', the Duke of Buckingham, to pay court to her. They travelled incognito via Paris, where Charles had a first sighting of the French king's sister HENRIETTA MARIA, who was eventually to become his bride, as she rehearsed a masque with the queen and other members of the royal family. Charles and Buckingham were well received in Madrid, but the marriage negotiations foundered on the stumbling block of religion (Charles was the first monarch to be brought up in the Church of England), and the travellers returned to England in October.

Charles succeeded his father in March 1625 and two months later was married by proxy to Henrietta Maria of France. The new queen arrived in England in June and the marriage was solemnized at Canterbury on 13 June. Charles was crowned in WEST-MINSTER ABBEY on Candlemas Day, 2 February 1626, but because of the religious difficulties his queen was not crowned with him. As he arrived at the ceremony he was seen to stumble – an ominous sign for the future, according to superstitious witnesses.

Charles encountered the same troubles with Parliament as his father had done, and clashed with its members over a combination of financial, religious and political issues. It was summoned and dissolved three times, and in 1629 the king decided to govern without it, beginning an 11-year period of personal rule. To raise revenue Charles sold monopolies and levied the unpopular 'ship money' from seaports and later from inland towns. After Parliament had finally been summoned again, in 1640, the king proved unable to resist demands for the execution of his adviser Thomas Wentworth, Earl of Strafford (for whose death Charles never forgave himself) and reconciliation of the two sides became impossible. Matters came to a head on 4 January 1642, when Charles committed the unprecedented act of entering the House of Commons with an armed guard and demanding the arrest of five Members of Parliament, who were planning the impeachment of the queen (forewarned the five men had already made their escape).

In the face of public hostility, Charles fled London and CIVIL WAR became inevitable.

Charles raised his standard at Nottingham and the long struggle between Cavaliers and Roundheads began in earnest. The Royalist troops failed to score a decisive victory over the Parliamentarians at the opening battle of Edgehill (23 October 1642), despite the assistance of the dashing Prince RUPERT, Charles's 23-year-old nephew, who had extensive experience of warfare on the continent (but proved impulsive on the field). The tide of war ran largely with the Cavaliers through 1643, with victories at Roundway Down, Wiltshire, and elsewhere, but subsequently the Royalists suffered crippling defeats at the hands of Oliver Cromwell's New Model Army, culminating in disaster at Marston Moor in 1644 and at Naseby in 1645. Charles surrendered to the Scots in 1646, expecting to be well treated, but was promptly handed over to the English and confined. Cromwell was initially against having the king executed, as some of his more radical colleagues demanded, but revelations that Charles had been negotiating for the invasion of England by Irish and other foreign armies, coupled with letters betraying his deep-seated lack of respect for Parliament and his determination to abolish anti-Catholic laws, made further defence of the monarch impossible.

After an imprisonment in Carisbrooke Castle in the Isle of Wight, Charles was brought to trial in WESTMINSTER HALL before a tribunal of 135 judges. Refusing to recognize the capacity of the court to try a king, Charles declined to plead and was found guilty by 68 votes to 67, a majority of only one. It was said that, though at all times he behaved with courteous disdain, the king's chestnut hair went quite grey during the proceedings. A sentence of death was passed and, after bidding farewell to two of his children, on 30 January 1649 Charles walked from ST JAMES'S PALACE, where he was last confined, to Whitehall, where a scaffold had been erected outside Inigo Jones's elegantly proportioned Banqueting House. Charles wore two shirts, for it was a cold day and he was concerned that if he were to tremble from cold people might mistake it for fear. He entered the Banqueting House and stepped onto the scaffold from a first floor window. He was attended by Bishop Juxon, to whom he spoke his last word, 'Remember'. When his head was severed from his body a great groan went up from the assembled crowd and people pressed forward to soak their handkerchiefs in the royal blood.

Later that day Cromwell looked on the king's body as it lay in its coffin at St James's Palace before being taken to Windsor for burial. 'Cruel necessity!' he was heard to utter. There was no state funeral and public mourning was banned. As the king's coffin was carried into St George's Chapel, Windsor, on 7 February 1649, a fall of snow turned the black velvet pall white: Heaven had declared his innocence, his supporters claimed.

Charles was one of England's most artistically cultured kings, and he delighted in collecting works of art and in patronizing artists (he amassed a collection of some 1400 paintings and 400 sculptures). The superb artistry of Van Dyck has made his face almost as familiar as the work of Holbein has made that of Henry VIII (curiously, a famous portrait by Van Dyck shows him carrying two right-handed gauntlets). The famous equestrian statue of Charles now standing in Whitehall was modelled by Le Sueur in 1633 and was supposed to have been melted down by order of Parliament in 1650 – but a certain John Revett had acquired it and hid it away until after the Restoration, making out to anyone who enquired that he had in fact destroyed it and had used the metal to make cutlery. Legend has it that when Charles was presented with a bust by Bernini, the sculpture was ominously spattered across the throat with blood falling from the corpse of a small bird being carried by a hawk high overhead. His favourite reading included Shakespeare, Spenser, Herbert, Tasso and Ariosto, and he also enjoyed masques by Ben Jonson and Inigo Jones.

The coffin of Charles I was opened in 1813, when workmen accidentally broke into the vault containing it. The body of the king was discovered to have been carefully embalmed and much of the original flesh, as well as his beard and hair, was substantially undecayed. Various relics were removed from the coffin and kept in a casket until 1888, when Queen VICTORIA ordered that they be replaced. A vertebra taken from the corpse by one of the workmen had reputedly been turned into a salt cellar.

Charles II, King of England (1630–85) The second but first surviving son of CHARLES I and HENRIETTA MARIA, who was born at ST JAMES'S PALACE on 29 May 1630. He owed his dark and swarthy appearance to his mother's Italian ancestry. Duke of Cornwall

and Duke of Rothesay, etc. from the moment of his birth, he was declared Prince of Wales in 1638, but was never formally created so by patent. His education was confided to the Earl (later Duke) of Newcastle and Dr Brian Duppa, Bishop of Chichester, who was later replaced by Dr John Earle. These wise men did not cram the boy's head full of learning as had been the fashion under the Tudors, but gave him a good grounding of general knowledge and plenty of sensible advice on everyday life. He was tutored in mathematics by Thomas Hobbes.

As a boy of 12, Charles, with his brother James (see JAMES II), accompanied their father at the battle of Edgehill, narrowly escaping capture by the Parliamentarians. He was at his father's side throughout most of the CIVIL WAR, at the age of 15 commanding troops in the West Country. Towards the end of the conflict he escaped to France (1646), later moving to Holland (1648), where his sister Mary was married to the Prince of Orange (see MARY, PRINCESS ROYAL, PRINCESS OF ORANGE). The execution of Charles I in January 1649 made Charles the *de jure* King Charles II, and in 1650 he landed in Scotland, raised an army of 10,000 men and, after being crowned King of Scots at SCONE on 1 January 1651 (in a ceremony that included the recitation of the names of Charles's 100 or more predecessors as ruler), marched into England, only to suffer an overwhelming and final defeat by Cromwell's army at the battle of Worcester. A price of £1000 was put on Charles's head and he became a fugitive for six weeks. In order to conceal his identity from his enemies, Charles's supporters stained his skin with boiled walnut juice and passed him off as a servant by the name of 'Will Jackson'. The romantic story of his hiding in an oak tree belongs to this period (see BOSCOBEL HOUSE).

Eventually Charles made his escape to France on a coal-brig called the *Surprise* and the next eight years were spent in exile in France, Germany and Holland, engaged in plotting and planning and trying to raise money for a future campaign. Cromwell, who had been installed as Lord Protector seated on the Coronation Chair, which was taken from the Abbey to WESTMINSTER HALL for that purpose, died on 3 September 1658 and was succeeded in that office by his son Richard. A new dynasty of hereditary Lord Protectors might have been envisaged, but Richard was not the man his father had been and had no stomach for government. In May 1659 he was compelled to resign by the army, leaving the way open to negotiate Charles's restoration. The prime mover in the matter was General Monck (later Duke of Albemarle), and the outcome was the return of Charles, who entered London on his 30th birthday, 29 May 1660. He was crowned on St George's Day, 23 April 1661, by William Juxon, Archbishop of Canterbury, the prelate who had attended his father on the scaffold. The old regalia had been broken up and sold under the COMMONWEALTH and a completely new set had to be made. It has been used, at least in part, at all subsequent coronations.

Charles proved himself an astute and pragmatic ruler and the Earl of Rochester's famous lampoon that 'he never said a foolish thing and never did a wise one' is largely untrue. (Charles's reply to Rochester was, 'This is very true, for my words are my own, and my actions are those of my ministers.') His foreign policy, however, tended to make him over-reliant on French support, particularly in later years when difficulties with Parliament drove him to seek French financial aid. Thus, for example, Dunkirk was sold to France for £400,000. In 1672 a Dutch fleet sailed up the Medway and fired at British warships at Chatham, greatly damaging the country's prestige abroad, but peace was concluded in 1674.

In 1662 Charles had married the Portuguese Infanta CATHERINE OF BRAGANZA, who brought him a dowry of £300,000 and the naval bases of Tangier and Bombay. There were to be no children of the marriage, but Charles fathered a large progeny – eight sons and five daughters – by his many mistresses (the most famous of whom included Lady Byron; his sister's lady-in-waiting Louise de Kéroualle, later Duchess of PORTSMOUTH; Barbara Villiers, Duchess of CLEVELAND, Hortense Mancini, Cardinal Mazarin's niece; and the actress Nell GWYNNE). Most of these illegitimate offspring were recognized and ennobled by their father, and the present Dukes of Buccleuch, Grafton, Richmond and St Albans derive their origin from sons of Charles. Some women, however, resisted the temptation to take a royal lover – one being Frances Stewart, Duchess of Richmond, who is said to have served as the model for the figure of Britannia depicted on the coinage.

It was Rochester who was responsible for dubbing Charles the 'Merry Monarch', writing of him:

Restless he rolls about from whore to whore,
A merry Monarch, scandalous and poor.

Charles enjoyed his first mistress, Lucy Walter, while in Holland in 1648, and by her fathered James, Duke of MONMOUTH, his favourite child. Such was his reputation for dalliance with the opposite sex that contemporary satirists often depicted him under the name 'Old Rowley', the name of a celebrated stallion known to breed fine foals. Though he was conscious of not behaving as he might towards his lawful wife, Charles was inclined to forgive himself his weakness for beautiful women, explaining to friends that he did not think God would make a man miserable for 'taking a little pleasure'. He did not, however, consider himself especially attractive a proposition to the ladies, exclaiming of his portrait by Lely, 'Odd's fish, I am an ugly fellow!' The diarist John Evelyn, though, noted his 'countenance fierce, his voice greate, proper of person'.

Charles enjoyed walking, sailing, tennis, pall mall, hunting, hawking and riding, and as a jockey himself won the 12–Stone Plate at Newmarket in 1675 (he fed his Arab racehorses on soaked bread and eggs). He was also much interested in art, architecture, dancing and the theatre. Other pleasures including regaling courtiers with tales and anecdotes, many of them from his own life – to the extent that royal officials learned to make themselves scarce as soon as their master launched himself into yet another reminiscence. He was very fond of dogs, especially the liver-and-white 'King Charles' spaniels to which he gave his name. These pets were allowed to go everywhere with him, even to Council meetings. They also slept in his bedchamber, which according to Evelyn in 1683, 'rendred it very offensive, and indeede made the whole Court nasty and stinking'.

Two domestic events overshadowed Charles's reign: the Great Plague of London in 1665, and the Great Fire in 1666, in which Charles himself helped to fight the flames and displayed great personal bravery. Charles was active on other fronts as well. He was a great patron of the arts and sciences and the founder of the Royal Society (he even had his own laboratory in which he could dabble in scientific experiments). At the behest of Nell Gwynne he also founded the Royal Hospital in Chelsea as a home for army pensioners. The Habeas Corpus Act was passed in Charles's reign and Parliamentary government began to develop the party system, Whigs and Tories emerging for the first time.

Like other monarchs before him, Charles consented to touch sufferers from scrofula, the so-called KING'S EVIL, in deference to the old belief that this would cure them. Such was the demand for his healing touch that at one ceremony in March 1684 six or seven people were crushed to death in the press to get tickets. In all, he is estimated to have touched some 90,000 scrofula victims.

On 2 February 1685 Charles, who was 54, suffered an apparent stroke at Whitehall. He rallied and lingered until 6 February, when he died after apologizing for having been 'an unconscionable time a-dying'. The real cause of his death appears to have been uraemia. He was received into the Roman Catholic Church on his deathbed, but was buried in WESTMINSTER ABBEY with Anglican rites. He was the last sovereign to have an effigy carried at his funeral and the full-length wax figure, wearing the oldest known set of GARTER robes in Britain (there is an older set in Denmark), is still displayed in Westminster Abbey and may be said to convey more of the king's character than any other portrait. Among those to leave tributes to Charles as a monarch was Evelyn, who called him 'A Prince of many Virtues, and many greate Imperfections, Debonaire, Easy of accesse, not bloudy or Cruel', and John Dryden, who described him as 'forgiving, humble, bounteous, just and kind'.

Charles III The style by which Prince Charles Edward STUART was known to the Jacobites and their adherents from the death of his father in 1766 until his own death in 1788.

Charles Edward Stuart, Prince *see* STUART, PRINCE CHARLES EDWARD.

Charles James, Duke of Cornwall *see* CORNWALL, CHARLES JAMES STUART, DUKE OF.

Charlotte GEORGE V's pet parrot, which accompanied him everywhere and was allowed to walk on the breakfast table. If she made a mess the king slid the mustard pot over it.

Charlotte, Princess Royal and Queen of Württemberg (1766–1828) The eldest daughter and fourth child of GEORGE III and Queen CHARLOTTE, who was born at Buckingham House, London, on 29 September 1766, 'between six and seven o'clock' in the morning. Her mother referred to her playfully as her 'Michaelmas goose'. She was baptized Charlotte Augusta Matilda by the Archbishop of Canterbury on 27 October 1766, her godparents being her

aunts Princess LOUISA ANNE and CAROLINE MATILDA, QUEEN OF DENMARK and the latter's husband Christian VII of Denmark (the last two being represented by proxies). Princess Charlotte grew up 'imbued with the love of history and a taste for modern languages, by which she became distinguished, and her retentive memory excited the admiration of all who conversed with her'. She was also a talented amateur artist, studying under Benjamin West. On 22 June 1789 she was declared Princess Royal, being the third to bear that title. At this period a courtier described her as possessing 'excessive sensibility, a great sense of injury, and a great sense of her own situation, much timidity, without wanting resolution, she wants presence of mind, from the extreme quickness of her feelings, which show themselves in her perpetual blushes. She has excellent judgment, wonderful memory, and great application.'

In 1791 the princess royal's hand in marriage was sought by Duke Ferdinand of Württemberg, but the suit came to nothing and a few years later she married his elder brother, Duke Friedrich, the widower of her cousin Princess Augusta of Brunswick. The marriage took place in the Chapel Royal, St James's, on 18 May 1797 and seven months later Friedrich succeeded his father as reigning Duke of Württemberg. Princess Charlotte's only child, a daughter, was still-born at Stuttgart on 26 April 1798, but she was an affectionate stepmother to her husband's children.

Duke Friedrich was raised to the dignity of Elector on 25 February 1803 and proclaimed King of Württemberg as Friedrich I on 1 January 1806, acceding to the Confederation of the Rhine on 20 July 1806. The assumption of the royal title and his siding with Napoleon greatly incensed his mother-in-law Queen Charlotte, who was most put out when her daughter, the new Queen of Württemberg, ventured to address her as 'My dearest Mama and Sister'. For many years she refused to concede the new rank to her daughter and her letters to her had to be sent to the Prince Regent for re-direction.

King Friedrich was so enormously fat that card tables had to be specially constructed with a half-circle cut out to accommodate his person. He died at Stuttgart on 30 October 1816 and the following day his widow wrote to her trustee Sir John Coxe Hippisley: 'I believe never was anybody more attached to another than I was to the late King. This affection, which during our union was the happiness of my life, makes me look forward with impatience to the end of my life, when I trust, through the mercy of Providence, to be re-united to my husband in a better world.' As Queen Dowager, Charlotte resided at Schloss Ludwigsburg in the Black Forest. She came to England for the last time in 1827 to visit the surviving members of her family and to seek medical advice for her dropsical condition. Her niece, the future Queen VICTORIA, recorded years later: 'I recollect perfectly well seeing her drive through the Park in the King's carriage with red liveries and 4 horses, in a *Cap* and evening dress, – my Aunt, her sister Princess Augusta, sitting *opposite* to her, also in evening attire, having dined early with the Duke of Sussex at Kensington. She had adopted all the German fashions and spoke broken English ... She was very kind and good-humoured but very large and unwieldy.'

The Queen of Württemberg died at Ludwigsburg on 6 October 1828, 'without a struggle, gently and imperceptibly in the arms of the King, her step-son, and surrounded by affectionate friends and faithful servants'. She was buried in the same vault as her husband in the cathedral at Stuttgart on 12 October 1828.

Charlotte, Queen (1744–1818) The consort of GEORGE III, who was born Princess Sophie Charlotte of Mecklenburg-Strelitz at Mirow on 19 May 1744, the fifth and youngest daughter and eighth of the 10 children of Prince Karl of Mecklenburg-Strelitz (brother of the reigning Duke Adolf Friedrich III), by his wife Elisabeth Albertine, daughter of Ernst Friedrich I, Duke of Saxe-Hildburghausen. Her father died when she was only eight and the death of his brother six months later made Charlotte's brother the reigning duke as Adolf Friedrich IV. The ducal house of Mecklenburg was descended from the Slavonic Niklot, Prince of the Obotrites, who died in 1160 and whose descendants obtained Mecklenburg and other territories in northern Germany from the Holy Roman Emperors.

The story of Charlotte writing to Frederick the Great of Prussia and the publication of the letter first bringing her to the notice of George III has been proved apocryphal. George began to cast around for a suitable bride very soon after his accession and it was after his initial overtures to Lady Sarah Lennox had been set aside that his choice fell on the Mecklenburg princess. It seems highly probable that his mother had a good deal to do with the choice.

Once the marriage had been agreed the princess set out for England. On the voyage she practised playing 'God Save the King!' on her harpsichord while most of her attendants were prostrate with seasickness. The marriage took place at ST JAMES'S PALACE on 8 September 1761 and the coronation followed a fortnight later, the 17-year-old princess being admired for the perfect equanimity with which she responded to her sudden elevation to queen. The only note of disharmony in these early days was the reaction of the public to her upturned nose, which led to taunts of 'Pug! Pug!'. The bewildered Charlotte asked an attendant, the Duchess of Ancaster, what was meant by 'Poog!' and received the tactful reply, 'It means "God bless Your Royal Majesty"'.

George and Charlotte settled down to a comfortable married life and were quite content with each other. George, if not handsome, was tolerably good-looking and had the fresh complexion and blue eyes characteristic of the Hanoverians, while Charlotte's 'monkey face' had a certain appeal, which is apparent in her portraits. The couple produced 15 handsome children, only two of whom died young, and Gainsborough's portraits of them together show them to be a family of which their parents could be justly proud.

The life led by the king and queen was simple in the extreme and almost the only disruptions in their routine were caused by George's attacks of illness, which sorely worried Charlotte. The queen's life was tranquil and uneventful, although she lived through stirring times. She exercised little political influence and was only interested in domestic matters.

When the king finally lapsed into insanity the queen was given the custody of his person but could seldom bring herself to see him. When her husband's condition became apparent, she was devastated, as reported by Fanny Burney: 'My poor Royal mistress! Never can I forget her countenance – pale, ghastly pale she looked ... her whole frame was disordered, yet she was still and quiet.' The death of her granddaughter, Princess Charlotte, a year before her own was a great blow to her, especially as she was staying in Bath when it occurred and received some criticism for not being present. She became immensely stout in her old age, prompting an unkind observer to remark that she looked as if she were carrying all her 15 children at once.

The queen was able to preside at the weddings of her sons at KEW PALACE during the last year of her life, but her health was failing fast and she died on 17 November 1818, seated in a small armchair (still to be seen in Kew Palace) with her hand in that of her son, the Regent. She was buried in the new Royal Tomb House at St George's Chapel, Windsor.

Charlotte Maria of York, Princess (1682) The seventh daughter of James, Duke of York (later JAMES II) and third daughter and fourth child by his second wife MARY OF MODENA, who was born at ST JAMES'S PALACE on 16 August 1682 'at about seven o'clock in the morning'. She was baptized the following day by Henry Compton, Bishop of London, her godparents being the Countesses of Clarendon and Arundel and the Duke of Ormonde. The little princess died of convulsions on 6 October 1682 and was buried two days later in WESTMINSTER ABBEY.

Charlotte of Clarence, Princess (1819) The first child of Prince William Henry, Duke of Clarence (later WILLIAM IV) and his wife Princess ADELAIDE, who was born prematurely at the Fürstenhof in Hanover on 27 March 1819 at ten minutes past seven in the morning. She was baptized Charlotte Augusta Louisa at nine o'clock and died a few hours later, being buried in the royal vault at Hanover.

Charlotte of Wales, Princess (1796–1817) The only daughter of George, Prince of Wales (later Prince Regent and GEORGE IV) by his wife CAROLINE OF BRUNSWICK, who was born at CARLTON HOUSE, London, 'between one and two o'clock on the morning' of 7 January 1796. She was baptized Charlotte Augusta by the Archbishop of Canterbury in the Great Audience Chamber of Carlton House on 11 February 1796, her godparents being her paternal grandparents, the king and queen, and her maternal grandmother, the Duchess of Brunswick (for whom the princess royal stood proxy). The separation of the Prince and Princess of Wales soon after their daughter's birth led to a somewhat disrupted childhood and upbringing, as she spent time first with one parent and then with the other. She developed a dislike for her grandmother Queen CHARLOTTE because of her hostility towards her mother and nicknamed her the 'Merry Wife of Windsor'. Her father on hearing this reprimanded her: 'Don't you know my mother is

the Queen of England?' 'But *you* seem to forget,' his daughter replied, 'that *my* mother is the Princess of Wales.'

Princess Charlotte grew up high-spirited and pleasure-loving and found a devoted companion and governess in the person of Miss Cornelia Knight. Her father began to seek a husband for her and there was no lack of suitors in view of her position as the next heir to the throne. The Prince Regent favoured the suit of the Prince of Orange, who had been educated in England and served under Wellington in the Peninsular War, but Charlotte would have none of him, which was hardly surprising as his looks had earned him the nickname of 'The Young Frog'. Her refusal enraged her father, who dismissed Miss Knight and the rest of her personal attendants in July 1814 and kept Charlotte virtually imprisoned in her own house. She managed to escape, however, and took a hackney coach to her mother's house in Connaught Place, from which she was only persuaded to return by her uncles the Dukes of York and Sussex and others.

Among the many foreign royal personages who visited England in 1814 was Prince LEOPOLD OF SAXE-COBURG. Princess Charlotte met him and it was a case of love at first sight. The Prince Regent favoured his suit and the wedding took place in the Crimson State Room at Carlton House in the evening of 2 May 1816. After a honeymoon spent at Oatlands in Surrey, the country seat of the Duke of York, the young couple took up residence at Claremont House, near Esher, which had been purchased for them. The princess had been voted a dowry of £60,000 and an income of £60,000 a year by Parliament.

Princess Charlotte miscarried twice in the early months of her marriage, but a third pregnancy in 1817 appeared to be going well. However, on the evening of 5 November 1817, after a protracted labour of over 50 hours, she was delivered of a stillborn son at Claremont House. Her treatment following the birth was grossly mismanaged and she died of post-partum haemorrhage and shock at two o'clock in the morning of 6 November 1817. She was buried in the Royal Tomb House at St George's Chapel, Windsor, with her infant at her feet. Princess Charlotte's death occasioned something of a crisis in the royal family and her bachelor uncles were compelled to seek brides to ensure the succession. Prince Leopold was elected first King of the Belgians in 1831 and was to become

Christian, Princess *see* HELENA, PRINCESS.

Cicely, Princess, Viscountess Welles (1469–1507) The third daughter of EDWARD IV and ELIZABETH WOODVILLE, who was born on 20 March 1469 and named after her paternal grandmother, Cicely, Duchess of York. On 26 December 1474 she was affianced to Prince James (later JAMES IV), the son and heir of JAMES III, KING OF SCOTS, and was styled 'the Princess of Scots' for several years. The intended marriage never took place and Cicely did not find a husband until her brother-in-law HENRY VII was on the throne. She was married at Westminster sometime before December 1487 to John, 1st Viscount Welles, the half-brother of Henry VII's mother Margaret, Countess of Richmond (*see* RICHMOND AND DERBY, MARGARET BEAUFORT, COUNTESS OF). They had two daughters, Elizabeth and Anne, who both died young and unmarried. Lord Welles died in London on 9 February 1499 and was buried in WESTMINSTER ABBEY. Princess Cicely married secondly, before January 1504, Thomas Kyme, of the Isle of Wight. There was almost certainly no issue of this marriage, Thomas Kyme's son and daughter (Richard and Margaret) probably stemming from another marriage of his. Princess Cicely died on the Isle of Wight on 24 August 1507 and was buried at Quarr Abbey there.

Ciniath I, King of the Picts (reigned 621–32) The son of Lutrin Luchtren by the elder sister of King NECHTAN I, whom he succeeded. He was succeeded by his cousin GARTNAIT V.

Ciniath II, King of the Picts (reigned 763–75) A son of Feradach (or Wrad) of Lorn by a sister of ALPIN I, KING OF THE PICTS, who succeeded his kinsman King BRUDE V. His successor was his brother ALPIN II.

Ciniath III, King of the Picts *see* KENNETH I MAC ALPIN, KING OF SCOTS.

Cissa, King of Sussex (*fl.*514) Son of AELLA, KING OF SUSSEX, who came to England from Scandinavia with his father and his brothers Cymen and Wlencing and played an active part with them in establishing the kingdom of Sussex, to which he succeeded on his father's death in 514. Nothing is known of his subsequent history.

Civil War, The The name popularly given to the sequence of civil wars that spanned more than two decades, from 1639 to 1660. During the 1630s CHARLES I's autocratic rule, his controversial religious policies and his methods of levying taxes caused considerable discontent in Parliament. His position was undermined by conflicts in Scotland and Ireland, the final split with Parliament arising from the question of who would control an army to suppress a serious rebellion in Ireland. Several years of armed conflict resulted. Charles was finally tried and executed in 1649, kingship was abolished, and a COMMONWEALTH was instituted, under the control of Oliver Cromwell.

Clarence, Dukes of The Dukes of Clarence are here dealt with chronologically.

1. **Lionel of Antwerp, Duke of Clarence** (1338–68) The third but second surviving son of EDWARD III and PHILIPPA OF HAINAULT, who was born at Antwerp on 29 November 1338. When only in his fourth year he was married at the TOWER OF LONDON on 9 September 1342 to Elizabeth de Burgh, daughter of William de Burgh, 3rd Earl of Ulster, and his wife Maud, daughter of Henry, 3rd Earl of LANCASTER. The bride was six years his senior, having been born on 6 July 1332, and the marriage was consummated in 1352 when he was 14 and she 20. Lionel became Earl of Ulster in his wife's right and gained possession of large estates in Ireland and also of the honour of Clare in Suffolk and other estates in right of his wife's grandmother Elizabeth de Clare. For this reason he was created Duke of Clarence in full Parliament on 13 November 1362.

While still a child he was twice made Guardian of England and in 1361 he was nominated a Knight of the GARTER. He served as Chief Governor of Ireland from 1361 to 1364, again from 1364 to 1365 and also for part of 1367. His wife died in Dublin on or about 10 December 1363 and was buried at Clare Priory in Suffolk. They had an only child, PHILIPPA OF CLARENCE. Duke Lionel married secondly at Milan on 28 May 1368, Violante, daughter of Galeazzo II Visconti, Lord of Milan, by his wife Bianca Maria, daughter of Aimone, Count of Savoy. He survived the marriage by only a few months, dying at Alba in Piedmont on 17 October 1368. He was buried first at Pavia, but was later transferred to Clare Priory.

His widow, who was born about 1353, married secondly at Pavia on 2 August 1377,

Ottone Paleologo, Marquis of Montferrat, who was murdered at Langhirano, near Parma, on 16 December 1378. She married thirdly, on 18 April 1381, her first cousin, Lodovico Visconti, Lord of Lodi, and died in 1382. The dukedom of Clarence became extinct on Lionel's death, but the earldom of Ulster and honour of Clare passed to his only daughter and heiress.

2. **Thomas, Duke of Clarence** (1389–1421) The third but second surviving son of HENRY IV by his first wife Mary de Bohun, who was born at Kenilworth, Warwickshire, on 29 September 1389. On 4 October 1399, at the age of 10, he was appointed Seneschal of England with the Earl of Worcester to act as his deputy. Appointments as Chief Governor of Ireland, Lord High Admiral, Member of the Council and Constable of Hawarden Castle, Chester, and Mohaut Castle, Flint, followed over the next 10 years, and on 9 July 1412 he was created Earl of Aumale and Duke of Clarence. He was Lieutenant of Aquitaine 1412–13 and High Steward of Chester in 1415, in which year he presided at the trial for treason of Richard of Conisburgh, Earl of CAMBRIDGE and Henry, Lord Scrope of Masham. He was appointed Constable of the Army in 1417 and Lieutenant General in France and Normandy (1417–21) and was in command at the siege of Rouen that ended in its capture on 19 January 1419. He married by Papal Dispensation dated 10 November 1411, Margaret, widow of his father's half-brother John Beaufort, Marquess of Dorset and Somerset, and daughter of Thomas de Holand, 2nd Earl of Kent. There were no children of the marriage and Duke Thomas was killed at the battle of Baugé in Anjou on 22 March 1421, when the dukedom became extinct. His body was brought back to England and buried in Canterbury Cathedral near that of his father Henry IV. His widow, having expressed the desire 'to lead a celibate life ... putting aside worldly pomps' retired to live near the Augustinian monastery of St Saviour in London and died on 30 December 1439.

3. **George Plantagenet, Duke of Clarence** (1449–78) The sixth but third surviving son of Richard, 3rd Duke of YORK, by his wife Cicely, daughter of Ralph Nevill, Earl of Westmorland, who was born in Dublin Castle on 21 October 1449. On his elder brother's accession to the throne as EDWARD IV in 1461, he was nominated a Knight of the Garter and further created Duke of Clarence on 28 June 1461, the eve of his brother's coronation. In February 1462 Clarence was appointed Chief Governor of Ireland and in September of the same year was granted the honour and lordship of Richmond by letters patent. He married at Calais on 11 July 1469 Isabel, eldest daughter and co-heiress of Richard Nevill, 1st Earl of Warwick and 2nd Earl of Salisbury, by his wife Anne, daughter of Richard Beauchamp, Earl of Warwick. Their first child, a daughter probably named Anne, was born at sea off Calais in April 1470 and died shortly afterwards, being buried at Calais. A second daughter, Margaret, was born at Farley Castle, Somerset, on 14 August 1473, and was followed by two sons, Edward, born at Warwick Castle on 21 February 1475, and Richard, born at Tewkesbury Abbey on 6 October 1476 and died at Warwick Castle on 1 January 1478, being buried at Warwick. The Duchess of Clarence died at Warwick Castle (where she had been born on 5 September 1451) on 22 December 1476 from the effect of having been given 'a venomous drink of ale mixed with poison' by a former servant, Ankarette Twynho, who was tried, convicted and hanged for the crime. The duchess was buried at Tewkesbury Abbey.

Before this event, however, the Duke of Clarence had taken part with his father-in-law the Earl of Warwick in the rebellion against Edward IV and the restoration of HENRY VI, but he changed sides again and supported his brother at the battle of Barnet on 14 April 1471, where Warwick was killed. Clarence received his father-in-law's earldoms of Warwick and Salisbury and on 20 May 1472 was appointed Great Chamberlain of England. He accompanied Edward IV to France in 1474–5 and signed the treaty of peace on 13 August 1475. After the death of his wife he contemplated marrying Mary of Burgundy, but the match was greatly opposed by ELIZABETH WOODVILLE, who pointed out the dangers of an invasion from that quarter. Mistrusted and feared, Clarence rarely presented himself at court and when he did do so carefully avoided eating or drinking anything in case it was poisoned.

After attempting to defend one of his servants accused of predicting Edward's death, Clarence himself was accused of high treason, brought to trial, found guilty, and attainted on 8 February 1478, thereby forfeiting all his honours. He was confined in the TOWER OF LONDON and died there on 18 February 1478, allegedly drowned in a butt of Malmsey wine. His downfall was long attributed to the machinations of his brother Richard, Duke of Gloucester (later RICHARD III), but there is no evidence to support this. He was buried with his wife in Tewkesbury Abbey.

4. **William Henry, Duke of Clarence** (1765–1837) The third son of GEORGE III and Queen CHARLOTTE, who was created Earl of Munster and Duke of Clarence and St Andrews on 20 May 1789. On 26 June 1830 he succeeded to the throne as WILLIAM IV, when all his peerage honours merged in the Crown. He thus became the only one of the five holders of the dukedom of Clarence (consequently considered an unlucky title) to prosper and to avoid an early death.

5. **Albert Victor, Duke of Clarence** (1864–92) The eldest son and first child of Albert Edward, Prince of Wales (later EDWARD VII) and ALEXANDRA OF DENMARK, who was born at FROGMORE HOUSE, near Windsor, at 8.45 pm on 8 January 1864 and baptized in the private chapel at BUCKINGHAM PALACE on 10 March following, receiving the names of Albert Victor Christian Edward. He was always known as Eddy in the family and later as 'Prince Eddy' in the popular press. He was a premature baby, weighing only three and three-quarter pounds at birth, but he soon began to thrive and a year later was joined by a brother, George (later GEORGE V). Being so close in age, the two boys were brought up together and were all but swamped by the intensive mother-love of Princess Alexandra, who brought them up to call her 'Motherdear' and allowed them far more freedom than their grandmother Queen VICTORIA approved. She considered them 'such ill-bred, ill-trained children, that I can't fancy them at all' and 'past all management'. She chose a tutor for them in the person of the Rev. John Neale Dalton, curate of Whippingham, Isle of Wight, who taught them every subject except French. Eddy was backward and remarkable for his laziness and it has been suggested that he may have inherited his mother's deafness in some measure and also perhaps suffered from mild epilepsy.

In November 1877 the two boys joined HMS *Britannia*, where they remained for nearly two years before embarking on a long three-year cruise in HMS *Bacchante*, with Mr Dalton always in attendance. Eddy spent a short time at Trinity College, Cambridge, in 1883. He was appointed a Knight of the GARTER the same year and a Knight of St Patrick in 1887 and was also the recipient of several foreign orders, as well as holding several army appointments (he was an ADC to his grandmother the queen). On 24 May 1890 he was created Earl of Athlone and Duke of Clarence and Avondale. Prince Eddy's apathetic attitude to life and lack of interest in any serious matters were the cause of much anxiety to his family. He was something of a dandy, affecting tightly waisted suits, shirts with high collars (which may have been to help support his head, balanced on a long, slender neck), and a large expanse of cuff, thereby earning himself the nickname of 'Prince Collar and Cuffs'.

Several modern writers have suggested that the Duke of Clarence was a homosexual and a frequenter of the notorious male brothel in Cleveland Street, which figured in a public scandal in the 1880s. A theory has also been put forward that he was the East End murderer 'Jack the Ripper', who butchered a succession of 'unfortunate females' in 1889, but there is no real evidence to support this.

Prince Eddy formed a strong attachment for the statuesque Princess Hélène of France, daughter of the Comte de Paris, pretender to the French throne, and wished to marry her, but the difficulties – particularly the religious difference – were insuperable and any idea of a marriage between them had to be abandoned. In 1891 Eddy became engaged to Princess Victoria MARY OF TECK and the wedding was planned to take place on 27 February 1892. However, the prospective bridegroom caught a cold while out shooting at Sandringham in January, developed pneumonia and died there on 14 January 1892, to the inexpressible grief of his mother and the relief of a great many others. He was buried in the ALBERT MEMORIAL CHAPEL at Windsor. His fiancée married his brother George the following year and in fullness of time was to become the greatly revered Queen Mary.

Clarence House House adjoining ST JAMES'S PALACE, London, which was built by the Prince Regent (later GEORGE IV) at the request of his brother William Henry, Duke of Clarence (later WILLIAM IV), who complained of the inadequacy of the apartments allotted to him in St James's Palace. It has always been used as a royal residence (though it was used as the headquarters of the Red Cross and the St John's Ambulance Brigade during the Second World War) and was the London house of ELIZABETH II from the time of her marriage until her accession to the throne. Princess ANNE was born at

Clarence House in 1950. Since 1952 it has been the London residence of Queen ELIZABETH THE QUEEN MOTHER.

Claudius, Roman Emperor (10BC–AD54) Tiberius Claudius Drusus Nero Germanicus, Emperor of Rome from 41 to 54, was the emperor under whom the Roman conquest of Britain took place in AD43. He named his son Britannicus in honour of the event.

Cleveland, Barbara Palmer, Duchess of (c.1641–1709) Born Barbara Villiers, only daughter and heiress of William Villiers, 2nd Viscount Grandison, by his wife Mary, daughter of Paul Bayning, 1st Viscount Bayning, she became one of the more famous mistresses of CHARLES II. She was only two years old when her father, a royalist officer, died at Oxford on 30 September 1643 of wounds received at the siege of Bristol on 24 July preceding. Barbara was married in London on 14 April 1659 to Roger Palmer, who was created Baron Limerick and Earl of Castlemaine in the peerage of Ireland on 11 December 1661 after his wife had become the mistress of Charles II while still in exile at The Hague in 1659. The newly styled Countess of Castlemaine accompanied Charles back to England on his restoration in May 1660 and maintained a great influence over the king for 10 years. He was almost certainly the father of all her children, with the possible exception of her eldest, Anne.

In August 1662 Charles forced his newly married queen, CATHERINE OF BRAGANZA, to accept Lady Castlemaine as a Lady of the Bedchamber and there was a distressing scene at court when the queen had to receive her new lady-in-waiting. Lady Castlemaine was notorious for her many amours and it was said that 'she had as many lovers as Messalina'. She is said to have been a great beauty, though this is not especially apparent in her portraits. She fell out of favour in 1668 but was recompensed two years later by being created Baroness Nonsuch, Surrey, Countess of Southampton and Duchess of Cleveland, on 3 August 1670. She lived in France for a time, but on returning to England was appointed Ranger of Bushy Park in 1677 and received various grants of land and pensions.

The Duchess of Cleveland was an inveterate gambler and was said by Samuel Pepys to have played £1000 to £1500 at a cast and to have won £15,000 in a single night, only to lose £25,000 the next. Lord Castlemaine died on 28 July 1705, and on 25 November the same year, at the age of 64, his widow married a man many years younger than herself, Robert Feilding, known as 'Beau Feilding' and described as being 'as handsome as any of the early lovers'. However, he already had a wife living and on 23 May 1707 the duchess obtained a decree of nullity of marriage. After a short term of imprisonment Feilding was pardoned by Queen ANNE and went to Scotland with his legal wife. He died in 1712.

The Duchess of Cleveland died of dropsy at her house at Chiswick on 9 October 1709 and was buried in the parish church of St Nicholas there. Her ghost is said to be seen still at the window of her house (now known as Walpole House).

Cnut, King see CANUTE, KING OF ENGLAND.

Coel, King (early 5th century AD) The 'Old King Cole' of the nursery rhyme was Coel the Old, or Coel Hen, a king who reigned in the early fifth century. His name has been Romanized as Caelius Votepacus. According to the genealogies, his wife was named Stradwawl and their daughter Gwawl was the mother or wife of CUNEDDA WLEDIG. Coel's descendants ruled the kingdom of Reged in the western region of Hadrian's Wall for several centuries.

Coenred, King of Mercia (d. after 709) The son of King WULFHERE and Eormengild of Kent, he succeeded to the throne on the abdication of his uncle King ETHELRED in 704. According to BEDE, he 'ruled the kingdom of Mercia with great renown for some while'. When still a young man, however, he grew weary of reigning and in 709 abdicated in favour of his cousin CEOLRED and went to Rome, where he became a monk and died.

Coenwulf, King of Mercia (d.821) The son of Cuthbert, a descendant of PYBBA, he succeeded to the throne of MERCIA in December 796 on the death of his distant kinsman King EGFRITH. He made grants of land in Worcestershire to Bishop Denebeorht between 814 and 820. According to Florence of Worcester (supported by charters), his wife was named Aelthryth and he had at least three children: Cwenthryth, Abbess of Minster in Kent; Burgenhild; and Cenelm, who has become the legendary St Kenelm, said to have been born in 814 and murdered by his ambitious sister Cwenthryth following their father's death in 821, his feast day being observed on 17 July. There is no real evidence for this, and Cenelm probably died before his father, who was succeeded by his brother CEOLWULF.

Cogidubnus, King of the Regni (*fl.*AD50) Possibly a grandson of VERICA, who reigned over the Regni in Sussex, submitted to the Romans soon after their invasion in AD43 and became a 'client king'. He proudly styled himself 'Tiberius Claudius Cogidubnus, Legate of the Emperor in Britain', and as a reward for his subservience was either granted, or allowed to build, the vast and magnificent palace at FISHBOURNE, near Chichester, which has been fully excavated comparatively recently. He had a son, but his subsequent history and that of his family is unknown.

College of Arms The official registry of English, Welsh, Northern Irish and Commonwealth arms and pedigrees, which was incorporated by royal charter of RICHARD III in 1484 and given a house called Coldharbour in the City of London in which the heralds could hold their meetings and store their records. Following the battle of Bosworth in 1485, the College was disbanded and the heralds remained homeless until a new royal charter was granted by MARY I in 1555, together with a house on the site that they still occupy. The College consists of 13 officers of arms, who form part of the royal household and are appointed by letters patent under the Great Seal on the recommendation of the Duke of Norfolk, hereditary Earl Marshal of England. There are three Kings of Arms (Garter, Clarenceux, and Norroy and Ulster), six Heralds (Chester, Lancaster, Richmond, Somerset, Windsor and York) and four Pursuivants (Bluemantle, Portcullis, Rouge Croix and Rouge Dragon). Extraordinary Heralds and Pursuivants are appointed from time to time. The members of the College make proclamations and attend all ceremonial and state occasions wearing their distinctive tabards emblazoned with the royal arms. The equivalent authority in Scotland is the Court of the Lord Lyon.

Comgall, King of Dalriada (d.537) The son of DOMANGART I, whom he succeeded in c.506. He was succeeded by his brother GABRAN, who was succeeded in turn by Comgall's son CONALL I.

Commius, King of the Atrebates (*fl.*57BC onwards) As king of the Celtic Atrebates in Gaul, Commius was defeated there by Caesar in 57BC and with his tribesmen sought refuge in Britain, where he established a kingdom in the south central region with its capital at Silchester. On his death his dominions were divided between his three sons, EPPILLUS receiving north-east Kent, TINCOMMIUS receiving Sussex, and VERICA receiving the main tribal lands in Hampshire.

Commonwealth The name given to the republican form of government that ruled England between 1649 and 1660. Following the defeat and execution of CHARLES I power was exercised by the army and its leader Oliver Cromwell (1599–1658). On 20 April 1653 Cromwell turned out the 'Rump' Parliament and in July set up a new Council of State and a nominated Parliament of 140 members, which became known as the 'Barebone's' or Little Parliament. On 12 December Parliament resigned its powers to Cromwell and on 16 December he was proclaimed LORD PROTECTOR of the Commonwealth of England, Scotland and Ireland. He was installed in WESTMINSTER HALL, the coronation chair being taken there for that purpose, and assumed many of the trappings of kingship. A written constitution, the 'Instrument of Government', was promulgated and Cromwell ruled with a council of 21 and a Parliament of 460 members, which was to be elected triennially, but he was virtually a dictator. His third Parliament (17 September 1656–4 February 1658) established a second house (the Protectorate House of Lords) and petitioned Cromwell to take the title of king, which he refused on 8 May 1657. On 3 September 1658 Cromwell died and was accorded a funeral with royal honours and burial in WESTMINSTER ABBEY. His son, Richard Cromwell (1626–1712), was elected Lord Protector in his place, but had little taste for government and resigned on 25 May 1659, leaving the way open for the restoration of CHARLES II the following year.

Commonwealth Day Holiday, formerly known as Empire Day and celebrated on the anniversary of Queen VICTORIA's birthday (24 May), now observed in many parts of the Commonwealth on the second Monday in March each year.

Commonwealth of Nations An association of sovereign states that are or at some time have been ruled by Britain, created largely out of what was formerly known as the British Empire. The reigning British sovereign is recognized as Head of the Commonwealth.

Companions of Honour, Order of the (CH) Order instituted by GEORGE V on 4 June 1917 and altered on 15 October 1919. It consists of the sovereign and not more than

65 members (exclusive of honorary and additional members) and is conferred on both sexes as a reward for conspicuous national service. It carries no title or precedence, but its members are entitled to place the initials 'CH' after their names immediately after 'GBE'. The badge of the order is an oval medallion in gold with the representation of an oak tree with a shield of the royal arms pendant from one of its branches and a mounted knight in armour, within a circle bearing the motto in gold letters, 'In action faithful and in honour clear'. The whole is ensigned with the imperial crown. Men wear the badge suspended around the neck from a carmine riband with a bordure interlaced with gold; women wear it attached to a similar riband tied in a bow on the left shoulder.

Conall I, King of Dalriada (d.574) The son of COMGALL, he succeeded his uncle GABRAN in 559. He was the king who gave Iona to his cousin St Columba. He died in 574 and was succeeded by his cousin AIDAN.

Conall II Cramdomna, King of Dalriada (d. *c*.659) The son of EOCHAID I, he succeeded his brother DOMNALL BRECC and was succeeded in turn by Domnall's son DOMANGART II. Conall's sons, Maelduin and Domnall Dunn, both reigned later.

Conall III, King of Dalriada (d. after 811) The son of one Aidan, he became king after defeating and killing his brother-in-law CANAUL COEM, King of the Picts, in 807. He was deposed by CONSTANTINE, King of the Picts in 811. By his wife, the sister of Canaul Coem, he had two daughters, who both conveyed the Pictish succession to their sons.

Connaught, Prince Arthur, Duke of (1850–1942) The third son and seventh child of Queen VICTORIA and Prince ALBERT, who was born at BUCKINGHAM PALACE on 1 May 1850 and named Arthur William Patrick Albert at his baptism on 22 June. He received his first name in honour of his godfather, Arthur Wellesley, 1st Duke of Wellington, on whose 81st birthday he was born. The little prince's first birthday coincided with the opening of the Great Exhibition in Hyde Park and was commemorated in Winterhalter's picture *The First of May 1851*, which shows Arthur in his mother's arms being presented with a golden casket by his illustrious godfather, while Prince Albert stands behind holding a plan of the Great Exhibition, and the Crystal Palace, in which it was housed, looms in the background. Arthur was to become his mother's favourite son and, fittingly as the godson of a great soldier, was destined for an army career. He entered the Royal Military Academy at Woolwich in 1866 and was commissioned Lieutenant RE and RA in 1868. He served in Canada with the 1st batallion of The Rifle Brigade from 1869 to 1870, and was promoted Captain in 1871. His accumulation of honours had begun in 1867 with his nomination as KG and was followed by KP (March 1869), KT (May 1869), GCMG (1870) and PC (1871). He also received the Prussian Order of the Black Eagle in 1872 and in the course of his life was to acquire many other foreign orders. On 24 May 1874 he was created Earl of Sussex and Duke of Connaught and Strathearn. In the same year he transferred to the 7th Hussars and from 1875 to 1876 served as assistant adjutant-general in Gibraltar. He was appointed Lt-Col, 1st battalion, The Rifle Brigade in 1879 and was promoted Major-General and Colonel-in-Chief of The Rifle Brigade in 1880. On 13 March 1879 the duke married at St George's Chapel, Windsor, Princess Louise Margaret Alexandra Victoria Agnes, third daughter of Prince Friedrich Karl of Prussia and Princess Maria Anna of Anhalt. The duke commanded a Brigade of Guards in the Egyptian expedition in 1882, for which he received the thanks of Parliament. He was Colonel of the Scots Guards from 1883 to 1904 and Commander-in-Chief at Bombay from 1886 to 1890. He was promoted General in 1893. Prince Arthur was appointed GCIE (1887), GCVO (1896) and GCB (1898, having previously been appointed CB in 1882 and KCB in 1890). He was an Elder Brother of Trinity House in 1898 and a PC (Ireland) in 1900, serving as Commander of the Forces in Ireland from 1900 to 1904. Prince Arthur was present at the deathbed of his mother Queen Victoria at OSBORNE HOUSE in January 1901 and it was he and his elder brother EDWARD VII who lifted her into her coffin. The duke was appointed Great Master of the Order of the Bath in 1901 and received his Field Marshal's baton on 26 June 1902 (the day appointed for the coronation of Edward VII, which was however postponed until 9 August because of the king's illness).

Further appointments held by duke were Inspector-General of the Forces (1904–7), High Commissioner and C-in-C in the Mediterranean (1907–9) and Governor-General of Canada (1911–16). In addition, he opened the Union Parliament in South Africa in 1910. The ill-health of the

Duchess of Connaught brought about their return from Canada and she died at CLARENCE HOUSE, St James's, on 14 March 1917. She had been born at the Marmaorpalais, Potsdam on 25 June 1860 and held the honours of VA, CI, RRC and DJStJ. She had the distinction of being the first member of the royal family to be cremated (at Golders Green) and her ashes were buried in the royal burial ground at Frogmore. The couple had three children: Arthur (see ARTHUR OF CONNAUGHT, PRINCE); Margaret (see MARGARET OF CONNAUGHT, PRINCESS, CROWN PRINCESS OF SWEDEN); and (Victoria) Patricia Helena Elizabeth, born at Buckingham Palace on 17 March 1886, married at Westminster Abbey on 27 February 1919 to Admiral the Hon Sir Alexander Robert Maule Ramsay, GCVO, KCB, DSO, third son of the 13th Earl of Dalhousie, KT. Princess Pat, as she was popularly known (and 'Patsy' to her family), was authorized by Royal Warrant dated 25 February 1919, to relinquish on her marriage the title of Princess and style of 'Royal Highness' and to assume the prefix of Lady with precedence before Marchionesses of England, thus becoming known as Lady Patricia Ramsay. She nevertheless remained a member of the royal family and a princess of the blood royal, wearing the appropriate robes and coronet and walking in the processions at the coronations of 1937 and 1953. Her husband died at their residence, Ribsden Holt, Windlesham, Surrey on 8 October 1972, and she died there on 12 January 1974, both being buried at Frogmore. They had one son.

The Duke of Connaught and his son Prince Arthur renounced their rights of succession to the Duchy of Saxe-Coburg and Gotha in 1899. In 1921 the duke opened the new chambers of the Indian legislature at Delhi. Apart from his military interests, he was also concerned with horticulture and freemasonry. His long and useful life of service to the Crown ended at Bagshot Park, Surrey on 16 January 1942. He was buried at Frogmore. His only son had predeceased him in 1938 and he was succeeded in the dukedom by his grandson Alastair Arthur, who held it for only a little over a year, dying of pneumonia at Government House, Ottawa, Canada on 26 April 1943, when the peerage became extinct.

Constance, Countess of Brittany (c.1066–90) One of the daughters of WILLIAM I THE CONQUEROR and MATILDA OF FLANDERS, who was born in Normandy in about 1066.

In 1086 she was married at Caen to Alan IV, Count of Brittany, and on 13 August 1090 she died without issue, supposedly poisoned by her servants. She was buried at St Melans, near Rhedon, where her tomb was opened in 1672, revealing her bones wrapped in 'some fragments of woollen stuff and skin' and a lead cross on which her epitaph was engraved. Her widower married Ermengarde of Anjou, the paternal great-aunt of HENRY II, and died on 13 October 1119, having had issue by her.

Constance of York, Countess of Gloucester (c.1374–1416) The only daughter of Edmund of Langley, Duke of YORK by his first wife Isabel of Castile, who was born about 1374. At the age of four, on 16 April 1378, she was affianced to Edward, Lord le Despenser, but he died shortly afterwards and she married, before 7 November 1379, his only surviving brother, Thomas, who was created Earl of Gloucester on 29 September 1397. Having joined the conspiracy against Henry of Lancaster (HENRY IV) her husband was attainted and beheaded at Bristol on 13 January 1400. They had one son, Richard (1396–1413), and two daughters, Elizabeth (born c.1398 and died in infancy) and Isabel (1400–39), who married first, Richard Beauchamp, Earl of Worcester, and secondly, Richard Beauchamp, Earl of Warwick, and had issue by both. As a widow, Princess Constance had a liaison with Edmund Holland, Earl of Kent, by whom she had a daughter, Eleanor or Alianore (born at Kenilworth about 1405), who married James Touchet, Lord Audley, and who, in 1430, claimed the title and estates of her father the Earl of Kent, bringing witnesses to prove the marriage of her parents in about 1404. However, on the petition of Edmund's sisters, the Duchesses of Clarence and York, Eleanor was adjudged illegitimate. Constance, who was one of the ladies for whom robes of the Order of the GARTER were provided, died on 28 November 1416 and was buried in Reading Abbey.

Constantine, King of the Picts and Dalriada (d.820) The son of Fergus Mac Eochaid, King of DALRIADA by a sister of the Pictish Kings CINIATH II and ALPIN II, he ruled as a sub-king (regulus) of Fortrinn from an unknown date until 789, when he deposed his cousin CANAUL COEM and seized the Pictish throne, reigning thereafter as King of the Picts and Dalriada. After Iona was sacked by the Norsemen, he moved the ecclesiastical supremacy to

Dunkeld in 802. He died in 820 and was succeeded by his brother OENGUS II.

Constantine I, King of Scots (d.877) The elder son of KENNETH I, who succeeded his uncle DONALD I in 863. His reign was troubled by continual Viking raids, and in 879 he was killed in battle with them at the Black Cove in Angus. He was succeeded by his brother AEDH, KING OF SCOTS and left a son who later became king as DONALD II. Constantine was buried at Iona.

Constantine II, King of Scots (d.952) The elder son of AEDH, KING OF SCOTS, who succeeded his cousin DONALD II in 900. He did much to settle the discipline of the Celtic Church and acknowledged EDWARD THE ELDER as his overlord in 924. Later, however, he fought with Edward's son and successor ATHELSTAN and was defeated by him at Brunanburh, near the Humber, in 937. Constantine abdicated in favour of his kinsman MALCOLM I in 942 and ended his days as Abbot of St Andrews in 952. He had two sons, Cellach, who was killed at Brunanburh, and INDULF, who succeeded Malcolm I as king, and a daughter, who married Olav Sihtricsson (alias Anlaf Cuaran), the Danish King of York (941–3) and later of Dublin (945–9 and 953–81).

Constantine III, King of Scots (d.997) The son of CULEN, KING OF SCOTS, who obtained the throne after the murder of his kinsman KENNETH II at Fetteresso in 995 and after a short and troubled reign was in his turn murdered at Rathinveramon by KENNETH III in 997. He is not known to have left any issue.

Corgi Breed of small, fierce, snappy, Welsh terrier dog, much favoured as pets by ELIZABETH II. The name of the breed is the Welsh word for rascal. Some of the queen's family of corgis have mated with dachshunds owned by other members of the royal family and the resulting offspring are known as dorgis.

Cornwall, Earls and Dukes of The royal holders of these titles are here dealt with chronologically.

1. **Reynold de Dunstanville, Earl of Cornwall** (d.1175) An illegitimate son of HENRY I by Sybilla Corbet, who married Beatrice, daughter and heiress of William FitzRichard, the owner of extensive lands in Cornwall, and was created Earl of Cornwall by his half-sister the Empress MATILDA, 'LADY OF THE ENGLISH', about April 1141, which creation was subsequently recog-

nized by King STEPHEN. Reynold acted as a witness to the agreement between Stephen and the future HENRY II in 1153. He served as Sheriff of Devon from 1173 to 1175 and took the king's side against the rebellious barons in October 1173. He died at Chertsey, Surrey, on 1 July 1175 and was buried in Reading Abbey. He had no legitimate male issue, but left four daughters and co-heiresses, Denise (or Hawise), Maud, Ursula and Sarah. He also had two natural sons by Beatrice de Vannes, Henry and William. The elder, Henry FitzCount (or FitzEarl), was a person of prominence in the reigns of King JOHN and HENRY III. He died in the Crusades in 1222.

2. **Richard, Earl of Cornwall** (1209–72) The younger son of King JOHN and ISABELLA OF ANGOULÊME, who was born at Winchester Castle on 5 January 1209. He was appointed Constable of Wallingford Castle at the age of seven in 1216 and knighted by his brother HENRY III on 2 February 1225, being created Earl of Cornwall in 1227. In 1225 he had also been created Count of Poitou, but he renounced that dignity in 1243. Earl Richard served his brother loyally as Lieutenant of Guienne (1226–7), Chief Commissioner for concluding a treaty with France (1230), Keeper of the Honours of Wallingford (1230–1) and of Knaresborough (1235), and as ambassador to the Emperor Friedrich II (1237) and Pope Innocent IV (1250). He somehow found time to take the Cross in 1236 and was commander in chief of the Crusaders 1240–1, when he concluded a truce with the Sultan of Krak.

From August 1253 to May 1254 he was Joint Guardian (or co-regent) of England with his sister-in-law Queen ELEANOR OF PROVENCE during the king's absence in Gascony, and from May to December 1254 he was sole Guardian. Having amassed vast estates and riches, the Earl of Cornwall was elected King of the Romans by the princes of the Empire at Frankfurt on 13 January 1257 and was crowned at Aachen by Konrad von Hochstaden, Archbishop of Cologne, on 17 May 1257. He was unable to maintain this position and was 'forced to return into England a poorer King than he went out an Earl'. In 1259 he was ambassador to Pope Alexander IV.

A staunch supporter of his brother against the rebellious barons, Richard was taken prisoner with the king at the battle of Lewes on 14 May 1264, but was unconditionally released after the battle of Evesham in 1265.

Richard was married three times, first, at Fawley, near Marlow in Buckinghamshire, on 30 March 1231, to Isabella, widow of Gilbert de Clare, 5th Earl of Hertford and 1st Earl of Gloucester, and third daughter of William Marshal, 1st Earl of Pembroke, by his wife Isabella de Clare. She was born at Pembroke Castle on 9 October 1200 and died of jaundice in childbed at Berkhamsted, Hertfordshire, on 17 January 1240, being buried at Beaulieu Abbey, Hampshire (and her heart at Tewkesbury Abbey). There were four children of this marriage: John, born at Marlow on 2 February 1232 (died there on 22 September 1232, and buried in Reading Abbey); Isabella, born at Marlow on 9 September 1233 (died there on 10 October 1234 and buried in Reading Abbey); Henry (see HENRY OF ALMAYNE); and Nicholas, born and died at Berkhamsted in January 1240, being buried with his mother at Beaulieu.

Earl Richard married secondly at WESTMINSTER ABBEY on 23 November 1243, Sanchia, third daughter and co-heiress of Raymond Berenger V, Count of Provence, and sister of Queen Eleanor. She was born at Aix-en-Provence in about 1225 and was crowned as Queen of the Romans with her husband at Aachen on 17 May 1257. She died at Berkhamsted on 9 November 1261 and was buried at Hayles Abbey, Gloucester, which her husband had founded in 1251 to enshrine a relic of the holy blood, which he had brought back from Palestine. She had two sons: Richard, born at Wallingford in July 1246 (died there the following month and buried at Grove Mill); and Edmund, who succeeded his father as Earl of Cornwall (see below).

The King of the Romans married thirdly at Kaiserslautern on 16 June 1269, Beatrix, second daughter of Dirk (or Dieter) II, Lord of Falkenburg (brother of Engelbert, Archbishop of Cologne), by his second wife, Johanna van Loon. She was born about 1253 and died on 17 October 1277, being buried in the church of the Friars Minor at Oxford. There were no children of this marriage, but Richard had a natural son by Jeanne de Valletort, Richard de Cornwall, who received the manor of Thunnock, Leicestershire, from his half-brother Edmund in 1280 and was the ancestor of the Cornwalls of Burford.

Richard died at Berkhamsted Castle after 'having been bled for ague' on 2 April 1272 and was buried at Hayles Abbey, his heart being buried separately at Rewley Abbey, Oxfordshire, another of his foundations. His widow erected 'a noble pyramis' over his tomb at Hayles, but it was destroyed at the Dissolution. History records Richard as an extremely able man who was always a loyal supporter of his much weaker willed brother Henry III. His achievements included the reform of the coinage.

3. **Edmund of Almayne, 2nd Earl of Cornwall** (1250–1300) The fifth and youngest son of Richard, Earl of Cornwall (see above) and the younger son of his second wife Sanchia of Provence, who was born at Berkhamsted on 26 December 1249. He was invested with his father's earldom and knighted by his uncle HENRY III at Westminster on 13 October 1272. He served as Joint Guardian of the Realm from November 1272 to January 1273 and from April 1279 to 1280, Sheriff of Cornwall 1278–1300, Sole Guardian of the Realm from June 1286 to August 1289, Sheriff of Rutland 1288–1300, and Councillor to the Prince of Wales 1297–8. He married at Ruislip, Middlesex, on 7 October 1272, Margaret, daughter of Richard de Clare, 6th Earl of Hertford and 2nd Earl of Gloucester, by his wife Maud, daughter of John de Lacy, Earl of Lincoln. They were divorced or legally separated in February 1294. Earl Edmund died without issue at Asbridge Abbey, Buckinghamshire (which he had founded in 1283), on 1 October 1300 and was buried near his father in Hayles Abbey. His former wife, who was born in 1249, died in February 1313, and was buried in Chertsey Abbey. The earldom of Cornwall reverted to the Crown.

4. **John of Eltham, Earl of Cornwall** (1316–36) The younger son of EDWARD II and ISABELLA OF FRANCE[1], who was born at Eltham Palace, Kent, on 25 August 1316. He was made Warden of the City and TOWER OF LONDON at the age of 10 in October 1326, and two years later, in October 1328, was created Earl of Cornwall in the Parliament held at Salisbury. He served as Guardian of the Realm from May to June 1329 and again in April 1331. He was Warden of the Northern Marches in 1335 and commander against Scotland in 1336. In October 1334 he had a papal dispensation to marry Maria, daughter of Fernando IV, King of Castile and Leon, but the marriage never took place, probably because of the premature death of the intended bride. He died at Perth on 13 September 1336 and was buried in WESTMINSTER ABBEY.

5. **Edward of Woodstock, Duke of Cornwall** *see* EDWARD OF WOODSTOCK, PRINCE OF WALES.

6. **Richard of Bordeaux, Duke of Cornwall** *see* RICHARD II.

7. **Henry of Monmouth, Duke of Cornwall** *see* HENRY V.

8. **Henry, Duke of Cornwall** *see* HENRY VI.

9. **Edward Plantagenet, Duke of Cornwall** *see* EDWARD V.

10. **Edward Plantagenet, Duke of Cornwall** *see* EDWARD OF MIDDLEHAM, PRINCE OF WALES.

11. **Arthur Tudor, Duke of Cornwall** *see* ARTHUR, PRINCE OF WALES.

12. **Henry Tudor, Duke of Cornwall** *see* HENRY VIII.

13. **Henry Tudor, Duke of Cornwall** (1511) The eldest son of HENRY VIII and CATHERINE OF ARAGON, who was born at RICHMOND PALACE, Surrey, on 1 January 1511 and succeeded as Duke of Cornwall at birth. A great joust was held to celebrate the occasion but the duke died on 22 February 1511 and was buried in WESTMINSTER ABBEY.

14. **Edward Tudor, Duke of Cornwall** *see* EDWARD VI.

15. **Henry Frederick Stuart, Duke of Cornwall** *see* HENRY FREDERICK, PRINCE OF WALES.

16. **Charles Stuart, Duke of Cornwall** *see* CHARLES I.

17. **Charles James Stuart, Duke of Cornwall** (1629) The eldest son of CHARLES I and Queen HENRIETTA MARIA, who was born prematurely at GREENWICH PALACE on 13 May 1629 after his mother had been frightened by a mastiff jumping at her. He became Duke of Cornwall at birth and died the same day, being buried in WESTMINSTER ABBEY as 'Charles, Prince of Wales'.

18. **Charles Stuart, Duke of Cornwall** *see* CHARLES II.

19. **James Francis Edward Stuart, Duke of Cornwall** *see* STUART, PRINCE JAMES FRANCIS EDWARD.

20. **George Augustus, Duke of Cornwall** *see* GEORGE II.

21. **Frederick Louis, Duke of Cornwall** *see* FREDERICK LOUIS, PRINCE OF WALES.

22. **George Augustus Frederick, Duke of Cornwall** *see* GEORGE IV.

23. **Albert Edward, Duke of Cornwall** *see* EDWARD VII.

24. **George Frederick Ernest Albert, Duke of Cornwall** *see* GEORGE V.

25. **Edward Albert Christian George Andrew Patrick David, Duke of Cornwall** *see* EDWARD VIII.

26. **Charles Philip Arthur George, Duke of Cornwall** *see* CHARLES, PRINCE OF WALES.

Coronation The solemn rite or ceremony whereby a sovereign is 'anointed, crowned and consecrated' king or queen. The earliest inaugurations of kings and tribal leaders throughout Europe took the form of the presentation of the ruler elect to a gathering of his people, who were asked to signify their consent by acclamation. This done, he was raised shoulder high on a shield so that all might see him and know him. These two elements, now known as the recognition and the inthronization, still form part of the coronation rite performed today. The custom of anointing the sovereign with chrism and consecrated oil found its way to western Europe about the middle of the eighth century and was borrowed from the prevailing usage in the Eastern Roman or Byzantine Empire. It followed the biblical precedent of Samuel anointing David to be king in place of Saul, who had lost God's favour, and was considered a good means by which to confirm and legitimate a new dynasty.

The first specific reference to such an event in England is recorded in the ANGLOSAXON CHRONICLE under the year 787, where it is stated that OFFA, KING OF MERCIA caused his son and heir EGFRITH to be 'consecrated King'.

The kings of WESSEX were inaugurated at Kingston-upon-Thames, which derived its name from the ancient 'King's stone' at which they were presented to the people. It still stands there, re-sited outside Kingston Guildhall, but how it originally came to Kingston and when it was first used remain matters of mystery. By tradition, ALFRED THE GREAT was acclaimed there in 871, as presumably had been his predecessors for many generations. Alfred's son, EDWARD THE ELDER, was certainly 'consecrated king' there, as were his four immediate successors, but in the reign of EDGAR (959–75) a new and more elaborate rite was devised and initiated by Dunstan, Archbishop of Canterbury. He drew up a coronation 'order' based on that used at the coronations of the Frankish kings, and Edgar and his second wife ELFRIDA were anointed and crowned at Bath Abbey on Whit Sunday, 11 May 973. The ceremonies then used have survived with some additions and modifications to the present day.

The basic rite consists of the recognition, the administration of the oath, the anointing, the vesting with the coronation vestments, the delivery of various items of regalia, culminating with the actual crowning, the inthronization, the homage, the anointing and coronation of the QUEEN CONSORT if there is one, and the reception of holy communion by the newly crowned sovereigns.

Coronations have generally proved sombre, formal affairs – but not all new monarchs treated them as such. GEORGE IV caused offence by 'nodding and winking' at his mistress Lady Conyngham throughout the ceremony.

A list of British coronations can be found in Appendices XXXV–VII.

Coronet The lesser crown or circlet worn by princes and princesses of the blood royal and by peers and peeresses at CORONATIONS. The design varies according to the rank of the person. There are five types of royal coronet: that of the Prince of Wales or Heir Apparent, which consists of a gold circlet, chased as jewelled and surmounted by alternating cross pattées and fleurs-de-lis and closed by a single arch with mond and cross; those of the younger sons and daughters of a sovereign, which are of the same design without the arch; those of the younger children of the Heir Apparent and of the daughters of a sovereign's sons, in which the circlet is surmounted by two cross pattées, four fleurs-de-lis and two strawberry leaves; those of the grandsons through younger sons of a sovereign, in which the circlet is surmounted by cross pattées and strawberry leaves alternately; and those of the grandchildren through daughters of a sovereign, in which the circlet is surmounted by fleurs-de-lis and strawberry leaves alternately.

Counsellors of State In the event of the sovereign's absence abroad it has always been recognized that the royal authority must be delegated to someone empowered to carry on the government of the country. The medieval kings appointed a Guardian of the Realm (*Custos Regni*) to fulfil this function and later the first two Georges appointed a Regent to do so during their frequent absences in Hanover. When GEORGE V visited India for three months in 1911, he appointed Counsellors of State, and following his severe illness in 1928–9, the whole question was examined. The Regency Acts of 1937, 1943 and 1953 provide powers under which, in the absence or incapacity through illness of the sovereign, Counsellors of State may be appointed by Letters Patent 'to prevent delay or difficulty in the despatch of public business'. The Acts specify that the Counsellors shall be the spouse of the sovereign and the next four adults in line of succession to the throne. Queen ELIZABETH THE QUEEN MOTHER is added to this number for her lifetime. A quorum of two or more Counsellors may act jointly in the exercise of the royal functions.

Counsellors of State may not dissolve Parliament or create peerages and grant honours and awards, but they may hold PRIVY COUNCILS, issue commissions for giving the royal assent to Acts of Parliament, approve and sign PROCLAMATIONS, warrants and other documents, and receive the credentials of foreign ambassadors and high commissioners.

Cramp Rings Rings made from gold offered and redeemed at the altar and blessed by the sovereign on Good Friday to be distributed to favoured persons. They were supposed to be efficacious against cramps and agues and particularly valuable for allaying the pains of childbirth.

ANNE BOLEYN was a noteworthy distributor of cramp rings, which were at her disposal long before her marriage to HENRY VIII, thus creating a minor scandal. The blessing and distribution of cramp rings, which was never very well documented, probably ceased with MARY I.

Crawfie The nickname by which Miss Marion Crawford was known to her charges Princess Elizabeth (later ELIZABETH II) and Princess Margaret (*see* MARGARET, PRINCESS, COUNTESS OF SNOWDON), to whom she was appointed governess in 1932. After her retirement from royal service, in 1950 she published a completely innocuous book entitled *The Little Princesses*. In spite of its innocent naiveté, it caused grave offence to her former pupils, who considered the author had betrayed their confidence. After the furore surrounding her book, 'Crawfie' turned to journalism, but caused herself more embarrassment when, in 1955, she described (in advance to meet a magazine's deadlines) the scenes at TROOPING THE COLOUR and at Royal Ascot – unfortunately, Royal Ascot was postponed that year because of a rail strike and there was much amusement when her piece appeared regardless. She remained in oblivion until her death in March 1988.

Crinan, Mormaer of Athole, Abthane of Dule and Lay Abbot of Dunkeld (d.1045) The father of DUNCAN I, KING OF SCOTS, who was the eldest son of Duncan, Lord and Mormaer of Athole, Abthane of Dule and Hereditary Lay Abbot of Dunkeld (who commanded the left wing of the Scottish army at the battle of Luncarty in about 990). Duncan's father, also Duncan, was killed (together with his opponent Dubdon, Mormaer of Athole) at the battle of Duncrub in about 965. Although his exact lineage has not been recorded, it is believed that he was of the kin of St Columba and descended from the Cineal Conaill of the Tyrconell branch of the descendants of NIALL OF THE NINE HOSTAGES. Crinan succeeded to the hereditary honours of his family and married in about 1000 Bethoc, the elder daughter and co-heiress of MALCOLM II, KING OF SCOTS, and their elder son Duncan succeeded his maternal grandfather in November 1034. He was murdered by a rival claimant to the throne, MACBETH, in August 1040. Although of mature years, Crinan took up arms to avenge his son and was killed in battle with Macbeth in 1045, leaving the struggle to be completed by Duncan's son Malcolm (*see* MALCOLM III). Crinan's younger son Maldred, Lord of Allerdale, was the ancestor of the Dunbars, the Nevills and probably the Washingtons.

Cromwell, Oliver and Richard *see* COMMONWEALTH.

Crown of India, Imperial When GEORGE V visited India in 1911 to hold his Coronation Durbar at Delhi, he intended to take the Imperial State Crown with him and wear it when receiving the homage of the Indian princes. However, it was discovered that the law forbade any of the existing crowns to be taken out of the country, so an elegant new crown was made for the occasion (the only one as it happened on which it was ever used). It is now on display with the rest of the regalia in the TOWER OF LONDON. It is of such beauty that it is to be hoped it may one day be re-designated as the Crown of the Commonwealth and used by the sovereign when opening Commonwealth Parliaments.

Crown of India, Imperial Order of the Order for ladies instituted by Queen VICTORIA on 1 January 1878 to commemorate her assumption of the title of Empress of India, and revised on 14 May 1927 and 18 March 1939. It consisted of the sovereign and princesses of the royal family and the wives or other female relatives of Indian princes and other Indian ladies, and of the wives or other female relatives of any of the persons who held the office of Viceroy and Governor-General of India, Governor of Madras, Bombay or Bengal, or of Principal Secretary of State for India, or Commander-in-Chief in India. No appointments to the order have been made since 14 August 1947, when the last King-Emperor, GEORGE VI, conferred it on his daughters. Recipients of the order were entitled to place the initials CI after their names, these being placed immediately before GCVO. The insignia of the order consisted of a badge of the royal and imperial cypher of Queen Victoria (VRI) in diamonds, pearls and turquoises, encircled by a border of pearls and surmounted by the imperial crown jewelled and enamelled in proper colours, attached to a light blue watered-silk ribbon, edged with white and tied with a bow on the left shoulder. The insignia is returnable at death to the Central Chancery of the Orders of Knighthood.

Culen (or **Cuilean**), **King of Scots** (d.971) The eldest son of King INDULF, who succeeded his kinsman King DUBH in 966 or 967 and was killed in battle with another kinsman, Riderch of Strathclyde, in 971. His brother Eochaid was also killed in the same battle. Culen had two sons, CONSTANTINE III and Malcolm, who was a co-benefactor (with Donald MacRuadri of Moray) of the Abbey of Deer around 1000.

Cumberland, Dukes of The royal holders of this dukedom are here dealt with chronologically.

1. **Prince Rupert, Duke of Cumberland** *see* RUPERT OF THE RHINE, PRINCE.

2. **George of Denmark, Duke of Cumberland** *see* GEORGE OF DENMARK, PRINCE.

3. **Prince William Augustus, Duke of Cumberland** (1721–65) The second son of GEORGE II and CAROLINE OF ANSBACH, who was born at Leicester House, London, on 15 April 1721, when his parents were still Prince and Princess of Wales. He became a great favourite with his grandfather GEORGE I and, when the Order of the BATH was reconstituted in 1725, was nominated the first Knight Companion of the order at the age of four. In the following year he was created Baron of Alderney, Viscount Trematon, Earl of Kennington, Marquess of

Berkhamsted and Duke of Cumberland. He was Colonel of the Coldstream Guards 1740–2, of the 1st Foot Guards 1742–57 and of the 15th Dragoons 1746–9, and was promoted to Lieutenant General in 1743. He saw active service at the battle of DETTINGEN, where he served under his father, on 16 June 1743 and was severely wounded in the leg; he was made Knight Banneret on the field by the king.

The duke served as Captain General of the Army from 1745 to 1757, in the course of which time he was in command at the battle of Fontenoy in 1745. His decision to launch a frontal assault on an impreganable position held by the much larger French army resulted in heavy losses and an embarrassing defeat for England and her allies. Subsequently he headed the Hanoverian forces against the Jacobite rising of 1745–6, culminating in the battle of Culloden. His severity in pursuing the rebels after Culloden earned him the unenviable sobriquet of 'Butcher Cumberland' and ensured him lasting infamy in Scottish history. In September 1757 Cumberland concluded the convention of Klosterseven with the French whereby 38,000 Hanoverians laid down their arms. The king considered this so humiliating that the duke was obliged to resign all his military commands and retire into private life.

The Duke of Cumberland was an inveterate gambler and a great follower of the turf. His civilian appointments included the Chancellorship of St Andrews and Dublin Universities and the Rangerships of Windsor Forest and Great Park and Cranborne Chase. In politics, he favoured the Whigs.

The Duke grew immensely stout in middle age and suffered a succession of strokes before dying of the last at his house in Upper Grosvenor Street, London, on 31 October 1765. He was buried in WESTMINSTER ABBEY on 10 November following. As he had never married and left no legitimate issue, all his honours became extinct.

4. **Prince Henry Frederick, Duke of Cumberland** (1745–90) The fourth son and sixth child of FREDERICK LOUIS, PRINCE OF WALES and Augusta of Saxe-Gotha (see AUGUSTA, PRINCESS OF WALES), who was born at Leicester House, London, on 26 October 1745 and baptized there on the 19 November following, the event being recorded in the register of St Anne's, Soho. He was appointed Ranger of Windsor Forest and Great Park in July 1766 in succession to his uncle William Augustus, Duke of

Cumberland (see above) and on 22 October 1766 was created Earl of Dublin and Duke of Cumberland and Strathearn. This was followed by his being sworn a Privy Councillor on 3 December 1766, and nominated and invested a Knight of the GARTER on 21 December 1767. He entered the Royal Navy in 1768 and was promoted to Rear Admiral in 1769, Vice Admiral in 1770, Admiral in 1778 and Admiral of the White in 1782. He was one of the first members of the royal family to become a freemason and served as Grand Master from 1782 until his death. On 26 January 1789 he was elected a Fellow of the Royal Society.

Prince Henry caused some embarrassment to his brother GEORGE III when, in 1770, he was accused of criminal conspiracy by the husband of Lady Grosvenor, with whom he was alleged to have had an affair. The king was obliged to find the huge sum of £13,000 to cover the damages and costs arising from the subsequent divorce case. Further trouble followed the next year when the duke married – on 2 October 1771 at her house in Hertford Street, Mayfair – Anne, widow of Christopher Horton, of Catton Hall, Derbyshire (by whom she had issue, one son who died in infancy), and eldest daughter of Simon Luttrell, 1st Baron Irnham, later 1st Earl of Carhampton, by his wife Maria, daughter of Sir Nicholas Lawes, sometime Governor of Jamaica. This marriage to a commoner incurred the extreme displeasure of the king, who had already been incensed by the marriage of his second brother the Duke of Gloucester (see GLOUCESTER, WILLIAM HENRY, DUKE OF) to the Dowager Countess Waldegrave in 1766. George ranted that such a marriage was 'dishonourable' and warned that 'civil wars would by such measures be again coming in this country'. The two marriages led to the passing of the ROYAL MARRIAGES ACT in 1772, which demanded that in future all royal marriages required the king's consent.

The duke was of very limited intellect and was described by Lady Louisa Stuart as 'an idiot prince'. His wife was noted for her vulgarity and indelicate utterances, and was 'without either beauty, fortune, or respectable connections'. The Duke and Duchess of Cumberland figure in Gainsborough's picture *The Morning Walk*. The duke died 'of an ulcer' at his house in Pall Mall, London, on 18 September 1790 and was buried in WESTMINSTER ABBEY on 28 September following, leaving huge debts. His widow, who was born in London on 24 January 1743, was denied more than a small pension by the king, who desired to emphasize that he did not consider her a member of the royal family, and died at Trieste on 28 December 1808, being buried there. There were no children of the marriage, but in 1820 Mrs Olivia Serres (1772–1834), wife of the marine painter John Thomas Serres (1759–1825) and herself an artist of some merit who had exhibited at the Royal Academy, assumed the style and title of 'HRH Princess Olive of Cumberland', claiming to be the legitimate daughter of Prince Henry Frederick by an earlier and secret marriage to one Olive Wilmot, contracted on 4 March 1767. Her claim, which was supported by many documents, found favour with some members of the royal family for a time, but in 1821 she was arrested for debt and eventually died within the rules of the King's Bench. The elder of her two surviving daughters, Lavinia Janetta Horton Serres (1797–1871), later claimed to have been created Duchess of Lancaster by George III, but was unable to prove her case. She married Antony Thomas Ryves, a portrait painter, and had six children.

5. **Prince Ernest Augustus, Duke of Cumberland and Teviotdale** (1771–1851) The fifth son and eighth child of GEORGE III and Queen CHARLOTTE, who was born at the Queen's House (later BUCKINGHAM PALACE), on 5 June 1771. He was baptized at ST JAMES'S PALACE on 1 July following and received the name Ernest in honour of one of his godfathers, Prince Ernst of Mecklenburg-Strelitz, Queen Charlotte's brother, although the combined names Ernest Augustus were those of both the father and brother of GEORGE I and were therefore not new to the House of Hanover. Prince Ernest was educated at the University of Göttingen and was nominated a Knight of the GARTER with his brothers, Edward, Augustus and Adolphus, on 2 June 1786. He was commissioned Lieutenant in the 9th Hanoverian Hussars in 1790 and became Lieutenant-Colonel in 1793 and Major-General in the Hanoverian Army in February 1794. He served with distinction at Tournai, where he was wounded, and at Nijmegen. Promoted to Lieutenant General in 1799, General in 1808 and Field Marshal on 26 November 1813, he was also Colonel of the 15th Light Dragoons (Hussars 1806) from 1801 to 1827 and of the Royal Horse Guards (The Blues) from 1827 until 1830, when he resigned in a fit of pique because the regiment had been placed under the authority of his elder brother the Duke of York (see YORK,

FREDERICK, DUKE OF) as commander-in-chief. On 24 April 1799 Prince Ernest was created Earl of Armagh and Duke of Cumberland and Teviotdale.

The duke was the least popular of George III's sons, with an unprepossessing appearance heightened by the loss of an eye. He also enjoyed, probably unjustifiably, a very unsavoury reputation, being allegedly involved in the murder of his valet Sallis and also accused of having an incestuous relationship with his sister Princess SOPHIA[2] and being the father of her natural son. In 1815 the duke, greatly to the disapproval of his mother Queen Charlotte, fell in love with his first cousin, Princess Friederike Louise Caroline Sophie Alexandrine, fifth daughter of Karl, Grand Duke of Mecklenburg-Strelitz, by his wife Friederike Caroline Louise, eldest daughter of Prince Georg Wilhelm of Hesse-Darmstadt. Princess Frederica (as she was known in England), who was born at Hanover on 2 March 1778, had already been married twice: first, in 1793, to Prince Ludwig of Prussia, who died in 1796; and secondly, in 1798, to Friedrich Wilhelm, Prince of Solms-Braunfels, from whom she was divorced before his death in April 1814. The Duke of Cumberland and Frederica, who enjoyed a raffish reputation to say the least, married at Neustrelitz on 29 May 1815 and again at CARLTON HOUSE, London, on 29 August 1815. Queen Charlotte declined to be present and refused to receive her new daughter-in-law, even though she was her own niece. On 27 January 1817 the duchess was delivered of a stillborn daughter, but on 27 May 1819 she gave birth to a son George (see below).

On the death of his brother WILLIAM IV on 20 June 1837, the Duke of Cumberland succeeded to the throne of Hanover through the operation of the Salic Law. His unpopularity in England and the relief felt at his departure were expressed by the striking of a satirical medal, which depicted him on a galloping horse with the words 'To Hanover' inscribed above. Once settled in his new kingdom, he set out to become the 'father of his people' and for the first time in his life, at the age of 66, found himself at last gaining some popularity. He did possess a certain rough and ready geniality, which went down well with the Hanoverians, who were glad to have their sovereign present among them after years of rule by viceroys. The king did repeal the liberal constitution, which had been granted in 1833, arousing a certain amount of protest thereby, but he replaced it with another in 1840, which was so well-balanced that Hanover weathered the year of revolutions, 1848, with only a minor disturbance, in which one life was lost. To reward his troops for maintaining order, the king abolished flogging as a military punishment, several decades before it was done away with in Britain, where, as duke, he had been considered 'brutal'. The king and queen assumed a very modest life style. Queen Frederica died at Hanover on 21 June 1841, and the king at Herrenhausen on 18 November 1851. Both were buried at Herrenhausen.

6. **Prince George, 2nd Duke of Cumberland and Teviotdale** (1819–78) The only son of Prince Ernest Augustus, Duke of Cumberland and Teviotdale and later King of Hanover (*see above*) and Princess Frederica of Mecklenburg-Strelitz, who was born at Berlin on 27 May 1819 and baptized George Frederick Alexander Charles Ernest Augustus. An accident with a swinging bunch of keys brought about the loss of his eyesight and he was completely blind by 1835. In 1851 he succeeded his father, becoming King Georg V of Hanover.

In 1866 Hanover voted with Austria in the Diet of the German Confederation and at once received an ultimatum from Bismarck to accept Prussian demands for the reform of the Confederation and maintain unarmed neutrality in the impending war between Austria and Prussia. Hanover rejected this and was invaded by Prussian troops, which occupied the capital. On 27 June 1866, King Georg was present with his troops at Langensalza, where they won a victory but were forced to capitulate the following day. Hanover was annexed to Prussia on 20 September 1866, and the king and royal family went into exile. He addressed a protest to the European powers from Hietzing, near Vienna, on 23 September, but it was disregarded and the rest of his life was spent in exile in Austria and Paris. In 1876 he was appointed a General in the British army.

King Georg had married at Hanover on 18 February 1843, Princess (Alexandrine) Marie Wilhelmine Katharina Charlotte Therese Henriette Louise Pauline Elisabeth Friederike Georgine, eldest daughter of Joseph, Duke of Saxe-Altenburg, by his wife Amalie Therese Luise Wilhelmine Philippine, daughter of Duke Ludwig Friedrich Alexander of Württemberg, and they had one son and two daughters. The king died at 7 rue Presbourg, Paris, on 12 June 1878. A funeral service was held at the Lutheran Church in the rue Chaucat, and his body was then taken to England to be buried in the Royal Tomb House at St George's Chapel, Windsor, on 25 June. Queen Marie, who was born at Hildburghausen on 14 April 1818 and received the first class of the Order of VICTORIA AND ALBERT (VA) from Queen Victoria, died at Schloss Gmunden in Austria on 9 January 1907 and was buried in the mausoleum there.

7. **Prince Ernest Augustus, 3rd Duke of Cumberland and Teviotdale** (1845–1923) The only son of Prince George, 2nd Duke of Cumberland, later King Georg V of Hanover (*see above*), and Princess Marie of Saxe-Altenburg, who was born at Hanover on 21 September 1845 and baptized Ernst August Wilhelm Adolf Georg Friedrich. On his father's accession to the throne he became Crown Prince of Hanover. He entered the Hanoverian army in 1862 and was appointed Colonel of the 42nd Infantry Regiment in the Austrian army in 1866, a Colonel in the British army in 1876, Major-General in 1886, Lieutenant-General in 1892 and General in 1898.

On the death of his father in 1878 Prince Ernest became head of the royal house of Hanover and also succeeded to the British peerages, generally being styled Duke of Cumberland thereafter. In 1884 he succeeded his distant kinsman Duke Wilhelm as Duke of Brunswick and issued a proclamation from Gmunden stating that he thereby took possession of the duchy, but he was impeached from reigning by decree of the Federal Diet on 2 July 1885 and again on 28 February 1907. On 24 October 1913 he renounced his rights to the duchy of Brunswick in favour of his only surviving son, Prince Ernst August, who was allowed to ascend the ducal throne on 1 November 1913 after the Federal Diet annulled the impeachment on 27 October. These events were occasioned by the fact that the young prince had recently married Princess Viktoria Luise of Prussia, the only daughter of the German Emperor Wilhelm II, thus bringing an end to the feud between the two royal houses.

Having taken up arms against Great Britain in the First World War, the Duke of Cumberland was struck off the roll of the Order of the GARTER (to which he had been appointed in 1878) on 13 May 1915 and deprived of his peerages and title of Prince of Great Britain and Ireland by Order in Council on 28 March 1919. He had married at Christiansborg Castle, Copenhagen, on 21 December 1878, Princess Thyra Amelia Caroline Charlotte Anne, third and youngest daughter of King Christian IX of Denmark and Princess Louise of Hesse-Cassel, and sister of Queen ALEXANDRA of Great Britain and the Empress Maria Feodorovna of Russia. The princess, who was born at Copenhagen on 29 September 1853, had a somewhat tarnished reputation, having already borne a child out of wedlock to one of her father's equerries. She and the duke had three sons, of whom the first two, Georg Wilhelm (1880–1912) and Christian (1885–1901), died before them, and three daughters: Marie Louise (1879–1948), who married Prince Max of Baden, sometime Chancellor of the German Empire; Alexandra (1882–1963), who married Grand Duke Friedrich Franz IV of Mecklenburg-Schwerin; and Olga (1884–1958), who died unmarried. The former Duke of Cumberland died at Schloss Gmunden on 14 November 1923 and his widow on 26 February 1933. Both are buried in the mausoleum there.

The right to petition for the restoration of the British peerages is now vested in Prince Ernst August (Prince of Hanover), the great-grandson of the 3rd Duke and *de jure* 6th Duke of Cumberland and Teviotdale. He was born on 26 February 1954 and it is a remarkable fact that the dukedom to which he is heir is the only one of those conferred on the sons of GEORGE III to have male heirs surviving to the present day.

Cunedda Wledig (*fl.c.*400) Romano-British leader who came from Manaw Gododin (on the Firth of Forth) to drive the Irish out of North Wales. Although his name is Celtic, his father Edeyrn (Eternus), grandfather Padarn Beisrudd (Paternus of the Red Robe, believed to indicate an official rank) and great-grandfather Tegid (Tacitus) all bore Roman names and are accepted as historical personages by modern historians. Cunedda's wife (or possibly his mother) is said to have been Gwawl, daughter of King COEL. He was accompanied in his mission by his eight sons, some of whom also bore Roman names – e.g. Rhufon (Romanus), Meriaun (Marianus), etc. – and after whom some districts and counties in North Wales were named. Cunedda established himself in Anglesey and was the ancestor of most of the Welsh ruling dynasties.

Cunobelinus, King of the Catuvellauni (d.43) The son of TASCIOVANUS, whom he succeeded in about AD10, and grandson of CASSIVELLAUNUS. His name in Celtic signifies 'The Hound of Bel', Bel being an important Celtic god. He moved his capital from Verulamium to Camulodunum (the fort of Camulos, the patron god of the Catuvellauni), the modern Colchester, and struck a plentiful coinage in gold and silver, inscribed with his name CVNO and the figure of a horseman. He concluded an alliance with the Roman Emperor Augustus and reigned peacefully until his death in or shortly before AD43, which was followed by the Roman conquest of Britain. Cunobelinus, whose name was rendered as Cymbeline by Shakespeare, was at one time married to CARTIMANDUA, QUEEN OF THE BRIGANTES, but she does not appear to have been the mother of any of his children, the most famous of whom was CARATACUS.

Cuthred, King of Wessex (d.756) Very little is known of this king, who is said to have been of the house of CERDIC, although his descent is nowhere recorded. The ANGLO-SAXON CHRONICLE records that he succeeded King ETHELHEARD in 741 and 'ruled sixteen years'. He made war against King Ethelbald of Mercia, occasionally joining him in fighting the Welsh. His death is recorded as occurring in 756. He had a son, Cynric, who was killed in battle in 748. His successor was SIGEBERHT.

Cynegils, King of Wessex (d.643) The son of King CEOL, who succeeded his uncle King CEOLWULF in 611. In 614 he and his son Cwichelm fought with the Welsh at a place called Beandun 'and slew two thousand and sixty-five [of them]'. In 628 they fought against PENDA, KING OF MERCIA at Cirencester and then concluded peace. A few years after this Pope Honorius I despatched the missionary Bishop Birinus to Britain, and Cynegils and Cwichelm (who appears to have been associated in the kingdom with his father) were converted by his preaching and baptized at Dorchester, Cynegils in 635 and Cwichelm in the following year. Cwichelm died soon after, leaving a son Cuthred, who was baptized also by Birinus in 639. Cynegils died in 643 and was succeeded by his eldest surviving son CENWALH, who lapsed into paganism for a time. His youngest son CENTWINE reigned from 676 to 685. Cynegils also had two daughters, Cyneburh, who married St OSWALD, KING OF NORTHUMBRIA, and St Egelwine (or Ethelwine), who was venerated at Athelney according to William of Malmesbury.

Cynethryth, Queen of Mercia (*fl.*796) The consort of OFFA, KING OF MERCIA, who is said to have been a foreigner, possibly a Frank. She exerted great influence on her husband, and her head even appears on some of his coins, probably to emphasize his imperial aspirations, as the Roman emperors had been in the habit of depicting their wives and other members of their families on the coinage. Tradition represents Cynethryth as a sinister intriguer. She had one son, EGFRITH, who succeeded his father, and several daughters, two of whom later became queens of WESSEX (*see* BEOHRTRIC) and NORTHUMBRIA (*see* ETHELRED I).

Cynewulf, King of Wessex (d.786) Of the lineage of CERDIC, Cynewulf succeeded to the throne of Wessex following the deposition of his kinsman King SIGEBERHT in 757. The ANGLO-SAXON CHRONICLE records that he 'frequently fought great battles against the Welsh'. In 786 he was surprised while visiting his mistress at Merantun (possibly Merton in Surrey) by Cyneheard, the brother of his predecessor, and both men were killed in the fray, together with 84 men. Cynewulf was buried at Winchester and Cyneheard at Axminster, Devon. Cynewulf was succeeded by his kinsman BEOHRTRIC.

Cynric, King of Wessex (d.560) Cynric came to Britain with his father CERDIC and five ships in 495 and fought with him to establish the kingdom of the West Saxons, or WESSEX, in 519 and in the capture of the Isle of Wight in 530. He became sole ruler on his father's death in 534 and gave the Isle of Wight to his two *nefan* Stuf and Wihtgar, probably his maternal nephews. He died in 560 and was succeeded by his son CEAWLIN. If Cynric was no more than 15 when he accompanied Cerdic to Britain, he must have been about 80 years old at his death, a somewhat unlikely age for those days, which lends credence to the account in some versions that makes him the son of Creoda, son of Cerdic. The exploits of Cerdic, Creoda and Cynric have very probably become inextricably mixed.

D

Dafydd I, Prince of Gwynedd (d.1203) The son of OWAIN GWYNEDD, KING OF GWYNEDD by his second wife Christina, daughter of Gronw ab Owain ab Edwin, who was considered illegitimate because his parents were first cousins and had married without obtaining papal dispensation. His father, who changed his title of king to that of prince on acknowledging the overlordship of HENRY II in about 1154, died in November 1170 and was succeeded by his undoubtedly legitimate son, IORWERTH DRWYNDWN, who in turn died after a short reign in about 1174, leaving an infant son Llywelyn (*see* LLYWELYN II). Dafydd then usurped the throne of Gwynedd and reigned for the next 20 years until he was dispossessed by Llywelyn, now grown to manhood. He had strengthened his position in the summer of 1174 by his marriage to Emma, widow of Guy, Sire de Laval, and natural daughter of GEOFFREY PLANTA-GENET, COUNT OF ANJOU, consequently a half-sister of Henry II. They had a son Owain, who died young, and a daughter. In 1198 Dafydd retired to England and died there in about May 1203.

Dafydd II, Prince of Gwynedd (*c*.1208–46) The only legitimate son of LLYWELYN II THE GREAT, by his wife Joan, natural daughter of King JOHN, who was born about 1208. He succeeded his father in April 1240 and did homage for Gwynedd to his maternal half-uncle HENRY III, who knighted him and crowned him as prince at Gloucester on 15 May 1240. In 1230 Dafydd had contracted an advantageous marriage with Isabella, eldest daughter of William de Breos, by his wife Eva, youngest daughter of William Marshal, Earl of Pembroke. There was no issue of the marriage, and the prince died at his manor of Aber on 25 February 1246, being buried with his parents at Aberconwy Abbey. His widow died before February 1248. Dafydd was succeeded by his half-nephew LLYWELYN III.

Dafydd III, Prince of Gwynedd (*c*.1235–83) The youngest son of Gruffydd ap Llywelyn,

Lord of Lleyn, by his wife Senena, who was born about 1235. His father, who was the son of LLYWELYN II THE GREAT by an irregular alliance with Tangwystl, daughter of Llywarch Goch, of Rhos, was held prisoner in England for some years and was killed while attempting to escape from the TOWER OF LONDON on 1 March 1244. Dafydd was a staunch supporter of his brother LLYWELYN III in his long struggle to maintain Welsh independence, and when the latter was killed near Builth on 11 December 1282 he took over as his legitimate successor and leader of the resistance against EDWARD I until June 1283, when he was captured. He was executed at Shrewsbury on 3 October 1283. He had married Elizabeth Ferrers, a kinswoman of the Earls of Derby, and had two sons, Llywelyn (d.1288) and Owain (d.1305), who both died as prisoners in Bristol Castle, and several daughters, who all became nuns.

Dalriada Irish kingdom, which roughly corresponded to the modern county of Antrim. Towards the end of the fifth century AD FERGUS MOR MAC ERC emigrated from Ulster to Scotland with his brothers Loarn and Angus and established the Scottish kingdom of Dalriada in Argyll. He died about 501and his descendants fought frequently with the Picts, who held sway in the northern and eastern regions of the country. The two kingdoms were occasionally united under one ruler as a result of matrimonial alliances and became united permanently in 844 when KENNETH I MAC ALPIN, King of Dalriada, succeeded as King of the Picts also.

Danelaw The name given to the northern, central and eastern parts of Anglo-Saxon England in which Danish rule and custom prevailed after the Danish invasions of the 9th and 10th centuries.

Darlington, Sophia Charlotte, Countess of (1675–1725) Officially the daughter of Franz Ernst, Count von Platen-Haller-mund (1631–1709), sometime first minister to Ernst August, Elector of Hanover, and of his wife Klara Elisabeth (1648–1700), daughter of Georg Philipp von Meysenbug – though her actual father was the Elector Ernst August, as shown by the coat of arms granted to her in England, which included the arms of the house of Brunswick debruised by a bend sinister. Sophia Charlotte, therefore, was the half-sister of GEORGE I, with whom she enjoyed a close and affectionate friendship, so much so that since their relationship was not generally known, she was usually regarded as being his mistress, as her mother had been to his father.

In 1701 Sophia Charlotte married the Hanoverian courtier Johann Adolf, Freiherr von Kielmansegg (1668–1717), who was George I's Vice-Master of the Horse in Hanover. When George I ascended the British throne in 1714, he was accompanied by Sophia Charlotte and her husband, who had been obliged by their many creditors to leave Hanover in disguise. When the long procession of carriages entered London they were greeted by jeers and catcalls from the assembled crowds. Sophia Charlotte, who evidently had a rudimentary command of English, leaned out of her carriage window and shouted: 'Goot people pray desist – we haf come for your goots.' 'Aye, and our chattels, too' was the prompt reply from a cockney wit.

Baron von Kielmansegg died on 15 November 1717 and was buried at St James's, Westminster. His widow was naturalized a British subject and on 11 September 1721 was created Countess of Leinster for life in the peerage of Ireland. This was followed on 6 April 1722 by her creation as Baroness of Brentford and Countess of Darlington for life in the peerage of Great Britain.

The countess was a lady of such ample proportions that she was nicknamed 'the Elephant'. Horace Walpole wrote: 'I remember, as a boy, being terrified at her enormous figure. The fierce black eyes, large and rolling, beneath two lofty arched eyebrows, two acres of cheeks spread with crimson, an ocean of neck that overflowed and was not distinguished from the lower part of her body, and no part restrained by stays.' She was, however, a woman of some taste and culture, and she eventually gained a measure of popularity in English society.

The Countess of Darlington died at her house in St James's on 20 April 1725 and was buried in WESTMINSTER ABBEY on 23 April. She had six children: Franz Ernst (1702–19); Sophie Charlotte Marie

(1703–84), who married Emanuel Scrope, Viscount Howe; Georg Ludwig (1705–85); Karl August (1708–34); Karoline Wilhelmine (1711–31), who married Friedrich von Spörcken; and Ernst August (1714–39). The three surviving sons were, at George I's request, raised to the rank of Counts of the Empire by the Emperor Karl VI in 1723.

Darnley, Henry Stewart, Lord (1545–67) The style by which the second husband of MARY, QUEEN OF SCOTS is generally known, it being his courtesy title as second but eldest surviving son and heir apparent of Matthew Stewart, 4th Earl of Lennox, by his wife Margaret, daughter of Archibald Douglas, 6th Earl of Angus, by his wife Margaret (see MARGARET TUDOR, QUEEN OF SCOTS), widow of JAMES IV and daughter of HENRY VII. He was born at Temple Newsam in Yorkshire on 7 December 1545. When he was barely 14 his mother sent him to complete his education at the French court, where his prowess as a lutenist, combined with his large stature and his excellence in physical exercise, rendered him popular. On the death of François II of France, Darnley was at once proposed as a suitable husband for the widowed Queen Mary. On returning to Britain in 1561, he and his mother were at first confined in London by ELIZABETH I, but in the following year they were released and well received at court. At Queen Mary's request they were allowed to go to Scotland in 1565 and in anticipation of his marriage to the queen, Darnley was created Earl of Rosse and Lord of Ardmannoch on 15 May and Duke of Albany on 20 July. On the eve of the wedding he was granted the title of king by proclamation.

The marriage took place in a private ceremony at HOLYROODHOUSE on 29 July 1565. The young couple had little or no affection for each other, and Darnley soon discovered that his title of king was but a hollow one, he being allowed to exercise no political influence, the real power lying with Mary's half-brother James, Earl of Moray. Mary was greatly influenced by her secretary, the Italian David Riccio, whom Darnley suspected of being her lover. A conspiracy against Riccio was formed and while he was at supper with the queen and her ladies at Holyrood, a band headed by Darnley burst into the room, dragged Riccio from the queen's side and put him to death in an antechamber. Mary, who was pregnant at the time with her and Darnley's only child, the future JAMES I, KING OF ENGLAND who was born on 19 June 1566, never forgave her husband. Darnley betrayed his fellow conspirators, who managed to escape to England, and himself joined the queen on a flight from Holyroodhouse to Dunbar Castle, whence she returned in triumph a week later. At the beginning of June 1566, Mary moved into Edinburgh Castle for the birth of her child. The baby was baptized by the Catholic rite and Darnley, who favoured Protestantism, refused to attend the ceremony on 17 December 1566.

The breach between the queen and her husband was now final, and the possibility of a divorce or annulment was contemplated for a time. However, a band of nobles loyal to the queen determined on a sterner measure. Darnley, who had been ill, returned from Glasgow to Edinburgh and took up residence in a small house at Kirk o' Field beside the city walls. In the early morning of 10 February 1567 the house was wrecked by an explosion of gunpowder and Darnley's naked body covered in stab wounds was found in the garden. It is highly unlikely that Queen Mary had any prior knowledge of the murder plot, but she was believed guilty by her subjects, particularly because Bothwell, whom she subsequently married, was one of the chief conspirators. Darnley, who was a weak character both mentally and morally, was buried in the royal vault at Holyrood.

Darnley, John Stewart, Lord (*c*.1532–63) The natural son of JAMES V, KING OF SCOTS by Catherine (or Elizabeth in some accounts), daughter of Sir John Carmichael, who was born about 1532 and styled Lord John until created a peer. He was appointed Commendator of the Priory of Coldingham in 1541 and was granted letters of legitimation under the Great Seal on 7 February 1551. After receiving a grant of the forfeited lands of Matthew Stewart, Earl of Lennox, he was created Lord Darnley between 21 January 1562 and 7 February 1563. He married at Crichton Castle on 11 January 1562, Jean, daughter of Patrick Hepburn, 3rd Earl of Bothwell, by his wife Agnes, daughter of Henry, 3rd Lord Sinclair. Her brother, the 4th Earl of Bothwell, later became the third husband of MARY, QUEEN OF SCOTS, Darnley's half-sister. Lord Darnley died at Inverness in October or November 1563. His widow married secondly, John Sinclair, Master of Caithness, and thirdly, Archibald Douglas, Rector of Douglas, a Senator of the College of Justice.

Lord Darnley left one legitimate son, Francis Stewart, born about November 1562, who succeeded his father as 2nd Lord Darnley and was created Earl of Bothwell and Lord Hailes on 16 June 1581. Known as 'The Wizard Earl', he was attainted for witchcraft by Act of Parliament on 21 July 1593, being suspected of plotting to gain the throne by securing the death of the king, and all his honours were forfeited. He died in poverty in Naples, where he had eked out a living casting horoscopes and doing conjuring tricks. The exact date of his death is unknown, but it was probably in about 1612.

David I the Saint, King of Scots (*c*.1080–1153) The youngest son of MALCOLM III and St MARGARET, who was born about 1080 and spent many of his early years at the English court. He was appointed ruler of Strathclyde and South Lothian by his brother ALEXANDER I in 1107 and in 1113 or 1114 married Matilda (*see* MATILDA, QUEEN OF SCOTS), widow of Simon de St Liz, and daughter and heiress of Waltheof, Earl of Northampton and Huntingdon, by his wife Judith, daughter of Lambert, Count of Lens, by his wife Adelaide, the sister or half-sister of WILLIAM I THE CONQUEROR. By this marriage he acquired the earldom of Northampton and Honour of Huntingdon *jure uxoris*.

David succeeded Alexander as King of Scots in April 1124 and was crowned at SCONE the following month. On the death of his brother-in-law HENRY I of England in 1135, he supported the claim to the English throne of his niece Matilda (*see* MATILDA, 'LADY OF THE ENGLISH', EMPRESS) against STEPHEN, but was defeated at the battle of the Standard fought at Northallerton on 22 August 1138 after the Archbishop of York had produced a consecrated standard to rally Stephen's forces. An advantageous treaty of peace was concluded at Carlisle, but David later joined Matilda at Winchester where she was acknowledged as 'Lady of the English' in 1041, and continued to support her until she finally relinquished her claim in 1152.

David earned his sobriquet of 'the Saint' from the number of his religious foundations, which included the sees of Brechin, Dunblane, Caithness, Ross and Aberdeen, and from his introduction of the new monastic orders into Scotland, particularly the Cistercians. He also established feudal law in Scotland and was applauded for his fairness (he was reputed to have given up a day's hunting in order to hear a petition from one of his poorest subjects). King David died while at prayer in his chapel at Carlisle on 24 May 1153 and was buried in DUNFERMLINE Abbey. His wife, Queen Matilda, had predeceased him by over 20 years. They had two sons, Malcolm, who died in infancy, and HENRY OF SCOTLAND, EARL OF HUNTINGDON, who died before his father, and two daughters, Claricia and Hodierna, who both died young and unmarried. The death of the young Malcolm was especially tragic, coming at the hands of a deranged Scandinavian priest, whom David had taken into his household out of pity. The priest killed the child by savagely attacking him with his artificial iron hand. The grief-stricken David ordered the murderer to be torn apart by wild horses.

Having extended Scottish territory further south than any of his predecessors, King David was succeeded by his grandson MALCOLM IV.

David II, King of Scots (1324–71) The elder but only surviving son of ROBERT I by his second wife Elizabeth, daughter of Richard de Burgh, 2nd Earl of Ulster, who was born at DUNFERMLINE on 5 March 1324 and styled Earl of Carrick until he succeeded his father at the age of five on 7 June 1329. He had already been married at Berwick on 17 July 1328 to the seven-year-old Joan (*see* JOAN, QUEEN OF SCOTS), younger daughter of EDWARD II, KING OF ENGLAND. The child king and queen were anointed and crowned at SCONE on 24 November 1331, the right to receive anointing having been granted to Robert I and his successors by Pope John XXII on 13 June 1329 (actually six days after that king's death). After his brother-in-law EDWARD III, KING OF ENGLAND invaded Scotland in support of Edward BALLIOL's claim to the throne and defeated the regent Archibald Douglas, King David and his wife sought refuge in France and remained there from 1334 until May 1341, when they returned and the king took up the reins of government. In 1346 he was persuaded by Philippe VI of France to invade England, but was defeated at the battle of Neville's Cross on 17 October 1346 and taken prisoner (he was also wounded by an arrow in the face). He remained in English captivity for 11 years and was freed by the Treaty of Berwick in 1357 on agreeing to pay a large ransom over the next 10 years. Queen Joan, who had faithfully accompanied him in all his exiles and vicissitudes, died at Hertford on 7 September 1362. On or about 20 February 1364 King David married secondly, at Inchmurdach in Fife,

Margaret, widow of Sir John Logie of that Ilk, and daughter of Sir Malcolm Drummond. The marriage was not a success and the king divorced her in March 1370, although the queen persuaded the pope to reverse the decree. King David, who had no children by either marriage, died at Edinburgh Castle on 22 February 1371 and was buried at Holyrood Abbey. He was succeeded by his half-nephew Robert, High Steward of Scotland (*see* ROBERT II).

Dawson of Penn, Bertrand Dawson, 1st Viscount (1864–1945) Physician-in-Ordinary to GEORGE V, whose end he precipitated on his own admission (revealed in 1986, long after his death) by the administration of massive injections of morphia and cocaine into the king's jugular vein. His reputation was such that it gave rise to the jingle:

> Lord Dawson of Penn
> Killed a great many men
> Which is why we all sing
> 'God save our King'.

Lord Dawson's motive in determining the king's end was occasioned by his feeling that it would save the family further grief and that it would be 'more appropriate' for the news of his death to appear in the morning papers rather than in the 'evening journals'. Margot Asquith, widow of George V's first prime minister, was quoted as saying in old age, 'The King told me he would never have died if it had not been for that fool Dawson of Penn.'

Defender of the Faith English rendering of the Latin title *Fidei Defensor* conferred on HENRY VIII by Pope Leo X in 1521 after the king had published his theological work in defence of the seven sacraments (ghost-written for him by Sir Thomas More). In spite of its papal origin, the title has been retained and used as part of their style by every subsequent sovereign whether Catholic or Protestant. In 1995 there was much heated discussion after CHARLES, PRINCE OF WALES let it be known that he would prefer to be styled 'Defender of Faith' in recognition of Britain's religiously diverse population should he ever be crowned king.

Deheubarth The kingdom of South Wales, comprising the kingdoms of Seisyllwg and Dyfed, which came into being on the death of HYWEL DDA, KING OF ALL WALES in 950. It was at first ruled jointly by his three sons, Rhodri (d.953), Edwin (d.954) and Owain (*see* OWAIN AP HYWEL DDA, KING OF

DEHEUBARTH), who became sole king after the deaths of his brothers. His descendants continued to reign as kings until 1093 and thereafter as princes until 1201.

Deira The Anglo-Saxon kingdom in northern Britain that eventually combined with BERNICIA to form the kingdom of NORTHUMBRIA.

Dettingen, Battle of Famous battle fought at Dettingen in Bavaria in June 1743 between the British, Hanoverian and Hessian armies (numbering 52,000) and the French army (numbering 60,000). It was the last occasion on which a British sovereign, GEORGE II, took the field in person at the head of his troops and resulted in the rout of the French with the loss of 3000 men. Handel's *Dettingen Te Deum* was composed to commemorate the victory and first performed on 27 November 1743.

Devorguilla, Lady of Galloway (1214–90) The third and youngest daughter and co-heiress of Alan, Lord of Galloway (d.1234), by his wife Margaret (d.1228), eldest daughter of David, Earl of Huntingdon, who was born in 1214 and married at the age of nine in 1223 to John de Balliol, the founder of Balliol College, Oxford, son of Hugh de Balliol and Cecilia de Fontaines. He died shortly before Pentecost (27 May) 1268. They had four sons, of whom Hugh, Alan and Alexander died without issue, and the youngest, John, became king of Scotland in 1292 when EDWARD I of England arbitrated in his favour (*see* BALLIOL). Devorguilla also had four daughters: Margaret, Lady of Gillesland, who married a man called Multon, but had no issue; Ada, who married William de Lindsay, and had issue; Cecily, who married John de Burgh; and Mary, who married John Comyn of Badenoch, also a competitor for the crown, and had issue. The Lady of Galloway was noted for her piety and religious foundations, among them being the friary in Dundee and Sweetheart Abbey, where she was buried after her death on 28 January 1290.

Diamond Jubilee The 60th anniversary of the accession of Queen VICTORIA, which was celebrated in 1897. The major event was a thanksgiving service held at St Paul's Cathedral. The queen was too infirm to negotiate the cathedral steps and it was therefore decided that her carriage should draw up before the steps on which the robed Archbishop of Canterbury and cathedral clergy would be assembled to conduct a short service. The arrangement greatly out-

raged the queen's cousin, Grand Duchess AUGUSTA OF MECKLENBURG-STRELITZ, who in a letter to her niece May, the future Queen Mary (*see* MARY OF TECK), wrote: 'after 60 years Reign, to thank God in the street!!! who *can* have started such an idea, and how could the Queen adopt it?' *See also* JUBILEES.

Diana, Princess of Wales (1961–) The third and youngest daughter of (Edward) John Spencer, 8th Earl Spencer, LVO, by his first wife, the Hon. Frances Ruth Burke Roche (later the Hon. Mrs Shand Kydd), daughter of the 4th Baron Fermoy, who on 29 July 1981 married CHARLES, PRINCE OF WALES. Born Diana Frances Spencer at Park House, Sandringham, Norfolk, on 1 July 1961, she was educated at Riddlesworth Hall, Norfolk, and at West Heath School, Sevenoaks, Kent, and became Lady Diana Spencer when her father succeeded to the earldom in 1975. She mixed with members of the royal family quite regularly throughout her childhood (her maternal grandmother, Ruth, Lady Fermoy, being a Woman of the Bedchamber to Queen ELIZABETH THE QUEEN MOTHER) but was quietly working as a kindergarten assistant in Pimlico, London, when the revelation of her growing friendship with the heir apparent suddenly made her the focus of intense media interest. Dubbed 'Shy Di' because of her reticence towards eager journalists and photographers, at 19 (12 years Charles's junior) she rapidly became one of the best known faces in the country. It was noted with approval by devoted royalists that, though technically a commoner, she could herself trace lines of ancestry back to HENRY VII and several of the illegitimate offspring of CHARLES II.

The announcement of the couple's engagement (with Charles presenting her with a £28,500 sapphire and diamond ring) was greeted as a cause for national celebration and the actual wedding, in St Paul's Cathedral, was witnessed by a huge international audience on television. Particular attention was paid to her wedding dress, designed by the Emanuels. The couple settled at Highgrove House, Gloucestershire, and in due course the princess gave birth to two sons, Prince William Arthur Philip Louis of Wales, born at St Mary's Hospital, Paddington, on 21 June 1982 (*see* WILLIAM OF WALES, PRINCE), and Prince Henry (Harry) Charles Albert David of Wales, born at St Mary's Hospital, Paddington, on 15 September 1984.

As Princess of Wales, Diana assumed all the royal duties that were expected of her, touring widely with her husband and also on her own and interesting herself in a range of social issues and campaigns, such as Aids charities and the marriage advisory service Relate (of which she became president). She also became something of a fashion icon, her immaculate appearance and dress always exciting comment in the popular press. Her wardrobe for a tour of Australia in 1983 reportedly weighed some three tons.

The strains of her role, coupled with unceasing press attention, soon began to take their toll, however, and in the mid-1980s, despite initial denials, it emerged that the princess was suffering from the eating disorder bulimia (from which her sister Sarah had also suffered). Rumours began to circulate of difficulties in the marriage itself, intensifying media interest in the couple still further. At first, most commentators were inclined to side with the princess, pointing out the unrealistic demands that were being placed upon her without, it often appeared, much support from her husband. Later, though, supporters of the Prince of Wales depicted her as greedy and determined to hold onto her position of influence by any means possible. Revelations of apparent affairs, eventually publicly confessed, further confused the situation.

The announcement, in 1992, that the Prince and Princess of Wales were to separate was widely lamented and questions were asked about the future of the monarchy itself. Protracted negotiations for an acceptable divorce settlement were initiated in 1994, the queen demanding a speedy resolution in order to limit the constitutional implications of the rift, though the atmosphere was soured by constant press coverage and by appearances by both parties on national television, each attempting to enlist public sympathy to defend their interests. As part of the process of reaching a divorce settlement, the princess agreed in 1995 to give up many of her formal duties, though she continued to resist the alleged efforts of the royal household to exclude her from the queen's inner circle. A decree nisi of divorce was finally granted on 15 July 1996 and made absolute on 28 August 1996, when the princess relinquished the style of 'Royal Highness', but at the queen's express wish continued to be regarded as a member of the Royal Family with precedence as before. Much uncertainty inevitably surrounds the role the princess might play in the future.

Dieu et mon droit French motto meaning 'God and my right' first adopted by HENRY V and used by most of his successors to the present day.

Distinguished Service Order (DSO) Order instituted by Queen VICTORIA by Royal Warrant on 6 September 1886 as an award for naval and army officers who perform distinguished service. It ranks after the LVO (*see* ROYAL VICTORIAN ORDER). The insignia is a white enamelled cross with the imperial crown on one side and the royal cipher on the other worn on the left breast suspended from a red ribbon with blue edges.

Domangart I, King of Dalriada (d. *c*.506) The son and successor of FERGUS MOR MAC ERC, he died after a short reign of five or six years. By his wife Fedlim Foltchoem he had several children, of whom COMGALL and GABRAN succeeded him in DALRIADA, while Seadna became the ancestor of subsequent high-kings of Ireland, and Feidilmid Fedlimid of Gartan married Ethne, daughter of Dimma mac Naul and became the father of St Columba.

Domangart II, King of Dalriada (d.673) The son of Domnall Brecc, King of DALRIADA, and an unknown mother, he succeeded his uncle CONALL II in *c*.659. He was the father of EOCHAID II.

Donald I, King of Scots (d.863) The younger son of ALPIN, KING OF KINTYRE, who succeeded his brother KENNETH I in 859 and died in 863, being succeeded by Kenneth's son CONSTANTINE I.

Donald II Dasachtach, King of Scots (d.900) The son of CONSTANTINE I, who deposed his cousin King EOCHAID in 889 and died in 900, being buried at Iona. He was the father of MALCOLM I and was succeeded by CONSTANTINE II, the son of King AEDH.

Donald III (Donalbane), King of Scots (*c*.1033–99) The second son of DUNCAN I, who helped his brother MALCOLM III to regain the throne in 1058. On Malcolm's death in November 1093, Donald was chosen king by the people, but was deposed by his nephew DUNCAN II in May 1094. He regained the throne on Duncan's death in the following November and is said to have shared the government with his nephew Edmund until he was deposed and blinded by another nephew Edgar (*see* EDGAR, KING OF SCOTS) in October 1097. Edmund fled to England and became a monk, dying at

Montacute in Somerset. Donald died at Rescobie, Forfarshire, in 1099. He was buried at Dunkeld and later transferred to Iona. The name of his wife is unknown, but he had one daughter, Bethoc, who married Uhtred of Tynedale and had a daughter Hextilda, who married Richard Comyn and was ancestor of John Comyn, Lord of Badenoch, one of the competitors for the crown in 1291.

Drust The name of nine kings of the Picts, the first four of whom are shadowy, semi-legendary figures. Drust I, for example, is said to have 'reigned 100 years and fought 100 battles; in the 19th year of his reign St Patrick came to Ireland'. This would place his date of accession at about 414 and the Irish Annals record his death in 458.

Drust V, King of the Picts (*fl.*663–72) A son of DOMNALL BRECC, King of DALRIADA (d.643), by the younger sister of Kings GARTNAIT V, BRUDE II and TALORC IV, who succeeded his brother King Gartnait VI in about 663 and reigned until about 672, when he was deposed by his kinsman BRUDE III.

Drust VI, King of the Picts (d.729) The son of a sister of King NECHTAN II, whom he succeeded in about 724. He reigned for about two years and was deposed by ALPIN I. He attempted to regain the throne in 729, but was defeated and killed by OENGUS I.

Drust VII, King of the Picts (*fl.*780–2) The son of a sister of King ALPIN II, whom he succeeded in 780. He reigned for about two years and was succeeded by TALORCAN III.

Drust VIII, King of the Picts (*fl.*820–36) A son of CONSTANTINE I, KING OF THE PICTS (d.820), who reigned from about 834 to 836 as a rival to his kinsman TALORCAN IV.

Drust IX, King of the Picts (*fl.*846–50) The last Pictish king, who was a son of Ferat or Wrad, King of the Picts, and reigned in opposition to KENNETH I MAC ALPIN.

Dubh (or **Duff**), **King of Scots** (d.967) The son of MALCOLM I, who became sub-king of Strathclyde and then succeeded INDULF as king after he was killed by the Danes in 962. His reign witnessed considerable turmoil, and Dubh himself was ultimately kidnapped and murdered at Forres by the men of Moray who supported his rival Indulf's son CULEN, his body being found in a ditch at Kinross, covered with turf. He left two sons, Malcolm, who reigned as king of Strathclyde 973–90, and KENNETH III, who became king in 997.

Duncan I, King of Scots (*c.*1000–40) The elder son of CRINAN, MORMAER OF ATHOLE, ABTHANE OF DULE AND LAY ABBOT OF DUNKELD by Bethoc, daughter of MALCOLM II, who was born about 1000. In 1018 his maternal grandfather secured Strathclyde as an appanage for him. In about 1030 he married Sibylla, the sister of Siward Digre, the powerful Earl of Northumbria, and daughter of Bjorn Bearsson. She was a first cousin of Gytha, the wife of Earl GODWIN and mother of HAROLD II of England and a first cousin once removed of King CANUTE. On the death of his grandfather in November 1034, Duncan succeeded to the Scottish throne and was crowned or inaugurated at SCONE. His title to the throne was disputed by MACBETH, Mormaer of Moray, whose wife Gruoch was a granddaughter of KENNETH III, and Duncan made yearly progresses through the country in an endeavour to strengthen his position and relieve oppression. He was killed in battle with Macbeth at Bothnagowan (now Pitgaveny), near Elgin in Morayshire on 14 August 1040 and was buried at Iona. He left three sons: MALCOLM III and DONALD III, who both reigned later as kings of Scots, and Melmare, who was ancestor of the Robertsons of Struan.

Duncan II, King of Scots (*c.*1060–94) The eldest son of MALCOLM III by his first wife Ingibiorg, who was born about 1060. As a young man he was captured by the Normans and held prisoner in Normandy until 1087, when he was released and knighted by Duke ROBERT. He received Norman support in deposing his uncle DONALD III in May 1094, but enjoyed a reign of six months only, being killed, at the instigation of his half-brother Edmund and his uncle Donald, by Malpeder MacLoen, Mormaer of the Mearns at Mondynes, Kincardineshire, on 12 November 1094. He was buried in DUNFERMLINE Abbey. Duncan married in about 1090, his second cousin, Ethelreda, daughter of Gospatrick, 1st Earl of Dunbar. The date of her death is unknown, but she was also buried at Dunfermline. They had one son, William, who married the heiress of Moray and whose descendants made several unsuccessful attempts to regain the throne.

Dunfermline Scottish town with ancient royal associations. MALCOLM III, KING OF SCOTS established his capital at Dunfermline and built a royal residence there, while his wife St MARGARET founded the Benedictine abbey that superseded Iona as the royal burial place. DAVID I enlarged his mother's church, and in 1210 King WILLIAM THE LION was persuaded not to invade England after receiving divine warning in a dream while he slept beside his great-grandmother's tomb. The abbey attained greater status after Queen Margaret was canonized in 1250. It was burned by EDWARD I but restored by ROBERT I. James VI (*see* JAMES I, KING OF ENGLAND) subsequently constructed a palace around the old abbey guest house and it was here that CHARLES I was born in 1600.

Dyfnwal I, King of Strathclyde (d.694) The son of OWAIN I, who succeeded his brother Gwriad in 658. His name is also rendered as Dumnagual and Domnal Macavin. He allied himself with the Picts and Scots against the Northumbrians and probably regained some territories to the north of the Solway Firth. He died at an advanced age in 694 and was succeeded by his nephew Beli II.

Dyfnwal II, King of Strathclyde (d.760) The son of King Teudur, whom he succeeded in 752. During his reign Strathclyde was invaded by the Northumbrians, who captured Dunbarton, the capital, on 1 August 756. The king was probably taken prisoner and forced to agree to the imposition of Northumbrian overlordship, but his subjects set on the returning invaders and inflicted an overwhelming defeat on them. Dyfnwal died in 760 and was succeeded by his son OWAIN II.

Dyfnwal III, King of Strathclyde (*fl.c.*850) The son and successor of King Riderch II, about whom very little is known. He was the father of ARTHGAL, his successor, and of Giric, who acted as regent for his great-nephew Eochaid.

Dyfnwal IV, King of Strathclyde (d.*c.*908) The son of King Run or of the regent Giric, who succeeded his brother (or cousin) Eochaid on an unknown date and reigned until his death in about 908. He was the last king of Strathclyde of his house.

Dyfnwal V, King of Strathclyde (*fl.*908) The elected successor of King DYFNWAL IV, who was born Donald, younger son of AEDH, KING OF SCOTS. He was dead by 927 when his son OWAIN III was king.

Dyfnwal VI, King of Strathclyde (d.976) The son and successor of King OWAIN III, who abdicated in 973 and became a monk, dying at Rome in 976. He had three sons: Riderch, who killed King CULEN of Alba and his brother Eochaid in 971, and MALCOLM III and OWAIN IV, both successively kings of Strathclyde.

E

Eadbald, King of Kent (d.640) The son of ETHELBERT I, KING OF KENT and presumably of the Merovingian Princess BERTHA, although from his lapse into paganism after his accession it might be inferred that his mother was an earlier wife of Ethelbert. Eadbald succeeded his father in February 616 and at once, in the words of the ANGLO-SAXON CHRONICLE, 'abandoned Christianity and followed heathen custom, having his father's widow to wife'. He was eventually brought to repentance by Archbishop Laurence of Canterbury, repudiated his stepmother and restored Christianity in Kent. Shortly after 618 he married the Merovingian Princess Emma, who was probably a daughter of Chlothacar (Clotaire) II, King of the Franks, and his first wife Adaltrudis. Eadbald died in 640. Mildred, or Miltrude, Abbess of Lyminge was possibly his daughter by his alliance with his stepmother. By Emma he had EORMENRED, who died before his father, EORCENBERHT, his successor, and St EANSWYTHE, for whom her father founded a religious community of nuns at Folkestone over which she presided and where the parish church still enshrines her reputed remains.

Eadberht, King of Northumbria (d.768) The son of Eata, son of Leodwald, who succeeded his first cousin King CEOLWULF on his abdication in 737. His brother Egbert had already been Archbishop of York for about five years. Eadberht abdicated and became a monk in 757. He was succeeded by his son OSWULF, who was murdered the following year. Archbishop Egbert died at York on 19 November 766 and his brother the former King Eadberht on 19 August 768. They were buried together in a sidechapel of York Minster.

Eadberht I, King of Kent (d.748) The son of King WIHTRED by his first wife Cynegyth, who, on his father's death in April 725, succeeded to the kingdom of Kent and reigned jointly with his brother ETHELBERT II and half-brother ALRIC. From about 747 Eadberht's son Eardwulf was also associated in the kingdom. Eadberht died in 748 and thereafter Ethelbert exercised the supreme power.

Eadberht II Praen, King of Kent (d.798?) Presumed son of King ETHELBERT II. According to the ANGLO-SAXON CHRONICLE, 'Eadberht, whose nickname was Praen, took possession of the kingdom of Kent' in 796. Two years later it records that King COENWULF of Mercia 'harried Kent, and seized Eadberht Praen, their king; he led him bound into Mercia (and had his eyes put out and his hands cut off)'. It seems hardly likely that he could have survived such treatment.

Eadburh, Queen of Wessex (d. after 802) A daughter of OFFA, KING OF MERCIA and Queen CYNETHRYTH, who was married in 789 to BEOHTRIC, KING OF WESSEX and is said to have been instrumental in driving his rival EGBERT into exile in France. In 802 she inadvertently poisoned her husband when he drank from a cup she had prepared for another. To expiate her crime she set out on a pilgrimage to Rome and is said to have died begging in the streets of Pavia *en route*. Her deed so horrified the people of Wessex that they decreed that no woman should again be honoured as *regina*, the wives of their kings being styled only consort or companion. The Saxon word for this was *cwen*, whence the English word 'queen' was derived.

Eadred *see* EDRED.

Eadwig *see* EDWY.

Ealdorman Important Anglo-Saxon title that applied to a nobleman who ruled a shire under the king and commanded the levies or bodies of troops called up for the defence of the kingdom. The title was later superseded by that of *eorl*, which has become the modern title of earl, the third rank of the peerage equivalent to the continental count.

Ealhmund, King of Kent (*fl.*786) A scion of the royal house of WESSEX, who, according to the ANGLO-SAXON CHRONICLE, was reigning in Kent in 786. His title to the throne was probably derived from his wife, who it is conjectured was a daughter of ETHELBERT II. He was the father of EGBERT, who became king of Wessex and eventually of most of England.

Ealhswith, Queen of Wessex (d.902) The consort of ALFRED THE GREAT, who was the daughter of Ethelred Mucil, Ealdorman of the Gaini, by his wife Eadburh, a princess of the royal house of MERCIA, conjecturally a daughter of Wigmund (son of King WIGLAF) by his wife Elfleda, daughter of King CEOLWULF I. Apart from several children who died in infancy, Ealhswith was the mother of EDWARD THE ELDER, of Ethelweard (d.922), and of three daughters: ETHELFLEDA, LADY OF THE MERCIANS; Ethelgiva, Abbess of Shaftesbury; and Elfthryth (or Elftrudis), who married Baldwin II, Count of Flanders, and was an ancestor of MATILDA OF FLANDERS. Ealhswith survived Alfred and died in 902. In her widowhood she founded a nunnery at Winchester.

Eanfled, Queen of Northumbria (626–after 685) The daughter of EDWIN, KING OF NORTHUMBRIA by his wife ETHELBURGA OF KENT, who was born on Easter Day (20 April) and baptized by Archbishop Paulinus on Whitsunday Eve (7 June) 626, she being the first Northumbrian to receive baptism. Her father and his court were baptized at Easter the following year. After King Edwin was killed in 633, Paulinus escorted Queen Ethelburga and her surviving children to Kent, where he was made Bishop of Rochester. In about 651 Eanfled's hand in marriage was sought by King OSWY OF NORTHUMBRIA, who sent a priest named Utta to escort her back from Kent. The marriage produced at least four children: EGFRITH, who succeeded his father as king of Northumbria; Elfwine, born about 661 and killed in a battle fought with ETHELRED, KING OF MERCIA near the river Trent in 679; Osthryth, who married the said Ethelred; and Elfleda, born abut 654 who became Abbess of Whitby and died in 713 or 714.

Eanfled, because of her Kentish upbringing, favoured the Roman usage in preference to the Celtic that obtained in the north, and was instrumental in promoting the Synod of Whitby to determine the date of Easter. Some time after the death of King Oswy in 670, Eanfled retired to the abbey of Whitby, where her kinswoman St Hilda was abbess and her daughter Elfleda had, at barely a year old, been 'dedicated ... in perpetual virginity' to God's service by her father in thanksgiving for his victory over

King PENDA OF MERCIA in 655. On St Hilda's death in 680, Eanfled and her daughter became joint-abbesses. Eanfled survived Egfrith, who died in 685, but the date of her death has not been recorded.

Eanfrith, King of Bernicia (d.633/4) The son of King Ethelfrith and his first wife Bebba(b), he succeeded to the throne in 632 or 633 after the defeat of EDWIN and was killed by CADWALLON, King of Gwynedd after a reign of about one year. He had formed an alliance with a Pictish princess, presumed to have been the elder sister of the Pictish kings GARTNAIT V, BRUDE II and TALORC IV, and by her became the father of TALORCAN I and of a daughter who married Beli, or Bile, sub-king of Fortrinn, and carried on the Pictish line of succession.

Eanred, King of Northumbria (d.840/1) The son of King EARDWULF, he acceded to the throne of Northumbria in 809 or 810 and reigned for over 30 years. He acknowledged EGBERT OF WESSEX as his overlord in 827 and died in 840 or 841, when he was succeeded by his son ETHELRED II.

Eanswythe, St (*fl.*640) The daughter of EADBALD, KING OF KENT and his Merovingian wife EMMA, who is said to have determined on a religious life very early and persuaded her father to give her land at Folkestone on which to build a nunnery. The place had no fresh water supply and the prayers of Eanswythe are said to have caused a stream to run uphill to furnish the needs of her community. A small pool on the site is still known as St Eanswythe's Pond. Her supposed remains were discovered in the 19th century and are now enshrined in Folkestone parish church, which is dedicated to St Mary and St Eanswythe. St Eanswythe's feast day is observed on 31 August.

Eardwulf, King of Northumbria (d.*c.*809/ 10) The son of another Eardwulf, whose lineage is unrecorded, he deposed King OSBALD and seized the Northumbrian throne on 14 May 796, according to the ANGLO-SAXON CHRONICLE, which further records that 'he was ... consecrated and enthroned on 26 May in York by Archbishop Eanbald and Aethelberht and Hygebald and Baldwulf'. In 806 'he was driven from his kingdom and replaced by a shadowy ELFWALD II, being restored two years later with the aid of Charlemagne and Pope Leo III. His restoration appears to hve been very brief and he was succeeded by his son EANRED in 809 or 810.

Earpwald, King of East Anglia (d.627/8) A son of King REDWALD, whom he succeeded in about 617. He was persuaded by EDWIN, KING OF NORTHUMBRIA 'to abandon his superstitious idolatry and accept the Faith and Sacraments of Christ with his whole province' in 627. Shortly thereafter 'he was killed by a pagan named Ricbert, and for three years the province relapsed into heathendom'.

East Anglia One of the kingdoms of the Saxon HEPTARCHY. The kings of East Anglia were known as the Wuffings, after WUFFA, whom Roger of Wendover reckoned as the first king (reigning c.571–8). His grandson REDWALD was the fourth BRETWALDA and is almost certainly the king of the Sutton Hoo ship burial. Another notable king was ANNA and the last was St EDMUND, who was barbarously murdered by the Danes in 869.

East Saxons see ESSEX.

Eddy, Prince The name by which Prince Albert Victor, Duke of CLARENCE was generally known to his contemporaries.

Edgar, King of Scots (c.1074–1107) The seventh son of MALCOLM III and the fourth by his second wife St MARGARET, who was born about 1074. He fled to England on his uncle DONALD III's usurpation of the throne in 1093, but returned with English aid and succeeded in deposing Donald and becoming king in his place in October 1097. In the following year he was obliged to surrender to the Norwegian King Magnus Barefoot all the western isles around which Magnus could steer a sailing vessel. Edgar, who was a patron of the Church, died unmarried at Edinburgh Castle on 8 January 1107 and was buried at DUNFERMLINE Abbey.

Edgar Atheling (c.1047–after 1126) The only son of Edward the Exile and his wife AGATHA[1], who was born in Hungary about 1047 and returned to England with his parents and sisters Margaret (see ST MARGARET, QUEEN OF SCOTS) and Christina when recalled by EDWARD THE CONFESSOR in 1057. His father died soon after their return and Edgar was regarded by many as Edward's heir. After the death of HAROLD II at HASTINGS in October 1066, the citizens of London chose Edgar to be king, but he submitted to WILLIAM I THE CONQUEROR and swore an oath of fealty to him. In 1067 he accompanied his mother and sisters to Scotland and spent the rest of his life wandering between Scotland, Flanders and France. He assisted his nephew EDGAR to gain the Scottish throne in 1097 and in 1099 joined the Crusades. He was taken prisoner at Tinchebrai fighting for ROBERT, Duke of Normandy in 1106, but was released later the same year. He never married and died in Scotland after 1126.

Edgar Stuart, Prince, Duke of Cambridge see CAMBRIDGE.

Edgar the Peaceful, King of England (943/4–75) The younger son of EDMUND I by his first wife ELFGIFU, who was born in 943 or 944. He was associated in the government with his brother King EDWY from 957, MERCIA and the DANELAW being under his special supervision. He was only 15 or 16 when his brother's death left him as sole ruler. He was to be the last great king of his dynasty. In all things he was guided by Dunstan, who virtually occupied the position of chief minister of the crown. All the other rulers of Britain submitted to Edgar's overlordship. The North Welsh princes agreed to pay a tribute of 300 wolves' heads for four years running, and the goodwill of KENNETH II, KING OF SCOTS was secured by the cession of Lothian, while a limited autonomy was allowed to the Danes in the north.

Edgar's first marriage took place when he was about 18 in 961. Ethelfleda was the daughter of Ealdorman Ordmaer and it seems logical to suppose that she died in childbirth the following year, leaving one son, Edward. Edgar then formed an attachment for a girl named Wulfthrith, said to have been a nun (probably a lay sister) at Wilton. She bore him a daughter at Kemsing, Kent. The girl, Eadgyth or EDITH, eventually became a nun at Wilton, where she died on 16 September 984, still in her early twenties. She is regarded as an Anglo-Saxon saint. Edgar's second marriage took place in around 964. The lady of his choice was (Elfthrith) ELFRIDA, the widow of his friend Ethelwold, Ealdorman of EAST ANGLIA, and the daughter of Ordgar, Ealdorman of Devon. She was an able woman and was destined to play a prominent part in future events.

Edgar is presumed to have been consecrated king at Kingston in the traditional manner soon after his accession, but in 973 Dunstan conceived the idea of a much grander ceremony based on the imperial coronations of the Holy Roman Emperors. A Coronation Order was carefully drawn up and it has formed the basis of all coronations since, not only in this country but in France and other continental countries, too. On Whit Sunday, 11 May 973 Edgar was solemnly anointed and crowned at Bath Abbey by Dunstan and Oswald, Archbishop of York. His wife Elfrida was also anointed and crowned as no other Saxon queen had been, with the exception of King Ethelwulf's second wife Judith, who had been consecrated queen immediately after her marriage in France in 856. The coronation was followed by a great banquet at which the king and queen presided over separate tables.

The celebrations over, Edgar proceeded to Chester, where he was to receive the homage of six (or eight, according to some accounts) subject kings from Wales, Scotland and the north, who, as a token of their submission, rowed him in state on the River Dee from his palace to the monastery of St John the Baptist and back in a great cavalcade of many boats.

Edgar lived only another two years, dying on 8 July 975, aged 31, and being buried beside his father at Glastonbury Abbey. The ANGLO-SAXON CHRONICLE is fulsome in its praise, but with typical English xenophobia adds that 'he loved evil foreign customs and brought too firmly heathen manners within this land, and attracted hither foreigners and enticed harmful people to this country'.

Edinburgh, Prince Alfred, Duke of (1844–1900) The second son and fourth child of Queen VICTORIA and Prince ALBERT, who was born at WINDSOR CASTLE at ten minutes to eight in the morning on 6 August 1844. He was baptized on 7 September in the private chapel at Windsor, receiving the names of Alfred Ernest Albert, his godparents being Prince George (later 2nd Duke) of CAMBRIDGE, the Prince of Leiningen (Queen Victoria's half-brother) and the Duchess of Saxe-Coburg and Gotha, the last two being represented by the Duke of Wellington and the Duchess of Kent. Within the royal family he was commonly known as 'Affie'.

Prince Alfred entered the Royal Navy in 1858, becoming a Rear Admiral in 1878, Vice Admiral in 1882, Admiral in 1887 and Admiral of the Fleet in 1893. In the course of his service he travelled all over the world and was the first member of the royal family to visit Australia (a triumphal tour marred by a slight injury when he was shot at by a 'deranged Fenian'). He was also Master of Trinity House (1866–94), Superintendent of Naval Reserves (1879–82), Commander

of the Channel Squadron (1883–4), Commander-in-Chief of the Mediterranean Fleet (1886–9), and Commander-in-Chief at Devonport (1890–3). In December 1862 he was elected king of Greece, but declined the throne. He was created Earl of Ulster, Earl of Kent and Duke of Edinburgh on 24 May 1866.

On 23 January 1874 he was married at the Winter Palace in St Petersburg to Grand Duchess Marie Alexandrovna of Russia, daughter of Emperor Alexander II and Empress Marie Alexandrovna, daughter of Grand Duke Ludwig II of Hesse. They were married by both the Orthodox and Anglican rites, the latter ceremony being solemnized by the Dean of Westminster. The couple made their entry into London on 12 March 1874, when, in spite of a heavy snowstorm, they drove through the streets in an open carriage accompanied by the queen and Princess BEATRICE (Victoria refused to attend the wedding, however, disapproving of this link with the Romanovs). On the death of his paternal uncle, Duke Ernst II of Saxe-Coburg and Gotha, on 22 August 1893, the Duke of Edinburgh, in accordance with family treaties and the renunciation (on 19 April 1863) of his elder brother the Prince of Wales (*see* EDWARD VII), succeeded to the ducal throne and he and the duchess with their son Prince Alfred made their state entry into Gotha on 31 January 1894.

Prince Alfred Alexander William Ernest Albert, the only surviving son of the duke and duchess, was born at BUCKINGHAM PALACE on 15 October 1874. On 6 February 1899 he shot himself at Meran in the Austrian Tyrol in circumstances that have never been fully elucidated. He was unmarried and it was a shattering blow to his parents, especially to his father who was already suffering from cancer of the throat, from which he died at Schloss Rosenau in the evening of 10 July 1900. He was buried in the Ducal Mausoleum at Coburg. In addition to Prince Alfred, he and the duchess had had a stillborn son at Eastwell Park on 13 October 1879 and four daughters: Marie Alexandra Victoria, who married Ferdinand I, King of Romania; Victoria Melita (later called Victoria Feodorovna), who married, first, her cousin Grand Duke Ernst Ludwig of Hesse, from whom she was divorced, and, second, Grand Duke Kirill Vladimirovitch of Russia; Alexandra Louise Olga Victoria, who married Prince Ernst of Hohenlohe-Langenburg; and Beatrice Leopoldine Victoria, who married the Infante Alfonso of Bourbon-Orléans.

Duke Alfred was succeeded as reigning Duke of Saxe-Coburg and Gotha by his nephew Prince Charles Edward, Duke of ALBANY. Duchess Marie, who was born at Tsarskoie-Selo on 17 October 1853, died suddenly at a hotel in Zurich, Switzerland, on 25 October 1920, allegedly from shock at receiving a letter addressed to her as 'Frau Coburg'. She was buried with her husband in the Ducal Mausoleum.

Edinburgh, Prince Philip, Duke of (1921–)
The consort of ELIZABETH II, who was born Prince Philip of Greece and Denmark, the only son and fifth and youngest child of Prince Andrew of Greece and Denmark (fourth son of George I, King of the Hellenes) and Princess (Victoria) Alice Elisabeth Julie Marie of Battenberg, elder daughter of Prince Louis of Battenberg, later 1st Marquess of Milford Haven, and Princess Victoria of Hesse, whose mother was Princess Alice (see ALICE, PRINCESS, GRAND DUCHESS OF HESSE), the second daughter of Queen VICTORIA. Prince Philip was born on the dining-room table at Mon Repos, Corfu, on 10 June 1921, and was educated at Cheam School, Salem, Baden, Gordonstoun and the Royal Naval College at Dartmouth. He joined the Royal Navy in 1939 and served in the Second World War with the Mediterranean Fleet (Home Waters) and with the British Pacific Fleet in Southeast Asia and the Pacific, being mentioned in despatches and receiving the Greek War Cross, 1939–45, Atlantic, Africa, Burma (with Pacific rosette) and Italy Stars, the War Medal 1939–45 (with oak leaf) and the French Croix de Guerre (with palme).

Philip first met the future queen, then 13 years old, when she visited Dartmouth Naval College with her family in July 1939. The 18-year-old Philip was invited to dine with the royal family and when the royal yacht departed he was among the many cadets who rowed out in its wake. After all the other oarsmen had given up the chase only Philip's rowing-boat kept going, the young Princess Elizabeth watching with admiration from the yacht through binoculars.

The romance blossomed in the years that followed and the couple's engagement was officially announced on 15 July 1947. On 28 February 1947 Philip renounced his rights to the throne of Greece and was naturalized a British subject, taking the surname MOUNTBATTEN and becoming known as Lieutenant Philip Mountbatten, RN. On 19 November 1947 he was granted the title, style and attribute of Royal Highness and on the following day he was created Baron Greenwich, of Greenwich, Earl of Merioneth and Duke of Edinburgh in the peerage of the United Kingdom and was married at WESTMINSTER ABBEY to Princess Elizabeth.

The newly created Duke of Edinburgh took his seat in the House of Lords on 21 July 1948 and was granted the style and titular dignity of a Prince of the United Kingdom of Great Britain and Northern Ireland on 22 February 1957. His other honours include the KG (1947), KT (1952), OM (1968), GBE (Grand Master and First or Principal Knight Grand Cross, 1953), FRS (1951) and very many foreign orders and decorations. He was given his own naval command, of HMS *Magpie*, in 1950 but retired from the navy a year later to assist his wife in her duties.

Adjusting to life as the queen's consort was not easy for a man used to giving orders and making his own decisions. Particularly galling to him was the announcement made in 1952 that the royal family would use the surname WINDSOR rather than Mountbatten. The duke is said to have responded angrily with the protest, 'An amoeba ... I'm just a bloody amoeba!' The press began to repeat rumours of difficulties arising between the royal couple as a result of this dilemma and concern was expressed when the pair spent four months apart in late 1956 and early 1957. Speculation that the royal marriage was in trouble was intensified when the wife of one of the duke's aides announced she was seeking a divorce, and it was rumoured that Philip was involved. The queen's officials sprang quickly to the couple's defence, however, denying there was any truth in these tales and the announcement that Philip was to be granted the dignity of Prince did much to quash further speculation.

The Duke of Edinburgh is an Admiral of the Fleet, a Field Marshal in the Army, Marshal of the RAF, Captain-General of the Royal Marines and Colonel-in-Chief of many regiments throughout the Commonwealth. He has been the recipient of many honorary degrees and is chairman, president or patron of many charitable foundations and organizations. Of particular note has been his interest in the Duke of Edinburgh's Award Scheme, which he founded in 1956 to encourage young people to take up a range of outdoor activities, and the World Wildlife Fund (now the Worldwide Fund for Nature). He is interested in photography, painting and four-in-hand driving, and as a young man was a keen polo player.

The duke has also never been afraid to speak his mind on matters of national importance. In 1961, for example, he caused some consternation when he told leaders of British industry that it was 'about time that we pulled our fingers out' – critics warned the prince not to interfere in politics and protested at the bluntness of his language – while in 1965 comments he made about the Rhodesian crisis led to a motion reminding him of the obligations of royalty to Parliament being tabled in the House of Commons.

Prince Philip's relations with the media have not always been harmonious. From time to time his exasperation at the tireless interest of the press in the private lives of the royal family has incurred his wrath, and it is clear that he holds a low opinion of journalists. When, for instance, he was shown the monkeys on the Rock of Gibraltar during the course of a visit there, he gestured to the crowds of photographers and pressmen also perched on the rocks and remarked drily, 'Which are the monkeys?'. In retaliation, the press have cast a cold eye over the duke's apparently stern attitude towards his four children, insisting that they excel at sports and other outdoor activities rather than in more academic disciplines. The duke's supporters, however, insist that he is kindhearted and quote as proof of this the story of the five-year-old Philip who, on realizing that during a hand-out of presents to local children a handicapped child had been left out, immediately fetched out his own most precious toys and offered her a choice of any one of them.

Edith, Queen (*c*.1025–75) The consort of King EDWARD THE CONFESSOR, who was the eldest daughter of Earl GODWIN of WESSEX and his wife Gytha, daughter of Thorgils Sprakalegg, a scion of the royal houses of Sweden and Denmark and was born in about 1025. She was brought up in the nunnery at Wilton and is said to have excelled in needlework. On 23 January 1045 she was married to Edward, and her coronation at Winchester followed soon thereafter. It is generally accepted that the marriage was never consummated, the king having taken a vow of celibacy. However, he treated her with great consideration and respect and she was endowed with a great deal of valuable property all over the country. She was also the first queen to receive the AURUM REGINAE. In 1050 Edward had an open quarrel with Earl Godwin, which resulted in the latter being banished for a time with his sons. Queen Edith was accused of infidelity by the Archbishop of Canterbury and was sent for a time to stay with the king's sister in the convent of Wherwell together with her mother-in-law Queen Emma (*see* EMMA OF NORMANDY, QUEEN OF ENGLAND). She returned to court when her father and brothers were received back into favour. Queen Edith was present at the dedication of WALTHAM ABBEY in 1062 and represented her ailing husband at the consecration of WESTMINSTER ABBEY on 28 December 1065. The king died on 5 January following and Edith's brother Harold (*see* HAROLD II) was elected king and duly crowned. The queen dowager lived on quietly at Winchester for the rest of her life and although deprived of some of her dower was treated with great respect by WILLIAM I THE CONQUEROR. She died at St Mary's Abbey, Winchester, on 18 December 1075 and was buried beside her husband at Westminster Abbey.

Edith of Wilton, St (*c*.961–84) The natural daughter of King EDGAR THE PEACEFUL by his liaison with Wulfthrith (or Wulfrida), who was born at Kemsing in about 961. Her mother took Edith (or Eadgyth) while still a small child to the nunnery at Wilton, near Salisbury, where she remained for the rest of her life. It is said that she refused the office of abbess, preferring 'to serve her sisters in the most humble capacities, like Martha herself'. She died at Wilton in 984, aged about 23, and her feast day is observed on 16 September, the day of her death.

Edmund, St, King of East Anglia (841–69/70) Of obscure origin, Edmund was chosen king of EAST ANGLIA at the age of 14 in 855. In 869 a large contingent of Danish invaders occupied Thetford in Norfolk and Edmund led his forces against them. He suffered a defeat and is said to have been taken prisoner at Hoxne in Suffolk. He steadfastly refused to share his kingdom with the pagan invaders or to renounce Christianity and on 20 November 869 or 870 he was tied to a tree by his captors and shot to death with arrows and then beheaded. He was revered as a martyr and his cult quickly spread. His body was interred at Bury St Edmunds, where an abbey was founded in 1020, and his relics were translated to a new shrine there in 1198.

Edmund I the Magnificent, King of England (*c*.921–46) The son of EDWARD THE ELDER by his third wife Eadgifu. He was born about 921 and succeeded his half-brother ATHELSTAN in October 939, being crowned at Kingston-upon-Thames on 16 November 939. He was a warrior king like his predecessors and captured many towns, including the five boroughs of Leicester, Lincoln, Nottingham, Derby and Stamford, from the Danes. He brought NORTHUMBRIA into subjection and ravaged Strathclyde, which he ceded to MALCOLM I, KING OF SCOTS in order to secure him as an ally. His potentially great career was ended by his untimely death. On 26 May 946 he was dining with his thanes at Pucklechurch in Gloucestershire when an outlaw named Liofa was recognized in the hall. The king joined in the struggle to arrest him and was stabbed in the stomach, dying almost immediately. He was buried at Glastonbury Abbey.

Edmund's first wife was St Elfgifu (Elfgiva), who died in 944 and was buried at Shaftesbury, leaving two sons, the future kings EDWY and EDGAR. His second wife was Ethelfleda of Damerham, daughter of Ealdorman Alfgar. She had no children by the king and remarried with Ealdorman Athelstan. She was still living in 975.

Edmund II Ironside, King of England (*c*.993–1016) The third son of ETHELRED II and his first wife Elfgiva, daughter of Ealdorman Thored of Northumbria, who was born in or shortly before 993. His two elder brothers, Athelstan and Egbert, having predeceased their father, Edmund was, on Ethelred's death in April 1016, chosen king by 'all the councillors who were in London and the citizens' and crowned at St Paul's Cathedral. From the start he had to contest the throne with CANUTE, Sweyn's son and heir. After Canute had won the fiercely fought battle of Ashingdon, the two kings met at Alney in Gloucestershire and agreed to divide the kingdom, Edmund (dubbed 'Ironside' for his courage) taking WESSEX and Canute MERCIA. Edmund, however, did not live long to enjoy his share for he died at Oxford on St Andrew's Day, 30 November 1016, and was buried with his grandfather King EDGAR at Glastonbury. A later legend claims he was murdered by the son of one of his arch-rivals, Edric Streona (Grasper), the assassin hiding himself in the king's privy and then stabbing the monarch

twice from beneath when he came to relieve himself, leaving the dagger fixed in the king's bowels. When Edric brought the news of the murder to Canute the outraged king promised to elevate him higher than all other nobles – and had him beheaded and his head displayed on a high pole.

Edmund had married in the summer of 1015 Ealdgith, widow of Sigeferth, son of Earngrim, an Anglo-Scandinavian thane, and left two infant sons, Edmund and Edward, possibly twins, who were sent to far off Hungary for safe-keeping.

Edmund 'Crouchback', Earl of Lancaster *see* LANCASTER, EDMUND 'CROUCHBACK', EARL OF.

Edmund of Langley, Duke of York *see* YORK, EDMUND OF LANGLEY, DUKE OF.

Edred, King of England (*c*.923–55) The youngest son of EDWARD THE ELDER by his third wife Eadgifu, who was born about 923. He succeeded his brother EDMUND I in May 946 since Edmund's sons EDWY and EDGAR were considered too young to reign and was crowned at Kingston-upon-Thames by Oda, Archbishop of Canterbury, on 16 August 946. He continued his brother's work in spite of being afflicted with some congenital defect (possibly PORPHYRIA), for which reason he never married. He died at Frome, Somerset, on 23 November 955 and was buried at Winchester aged about 32.

Edward, Prince (1964–) The third son and fourth and youngest child of ELIZABETH II and Prince Philip, Duke of EDINBURGH, who was born at BUCKINGHAM PALACE on 10 March 1964 and baptized Edward Antony Richard Louis in the private chapel at Windsor Castle on 2 May 1964. He was educated at Gordonstoun, where he was head boy, and at Jesus College, Cambridge, where he studied anthropology and archaeology, and for a short period was house tutor and junior master at Wanganui Collegiate School, New Zealand. He was commissioned as Second Lieutenant in the Royal Marines in 1983, but disliked the life and resigned his commission in 1987 (to the evident displeasure of his father, honorary captain-general of the Royal Marines). Subsequently he devoted himself to a career in theatrical management, initially as a production assistant with Andrew Lloyd Webber's Really Useful Theatre Company (he is also patron of the National Youth Theatre). His other official posts include that of chairman of the Duke of Edinburgh's

Award Special Projects Group. He was appointed a CVO in 1989.

Edward, Duke of Kent *see* KENT, EDWARD, DUKE OF.

Edward, Prince, 2nd Duke of Kent *see* KENT, PRINCE EDWARD, 2ND DUKE OF.

Edward I, King of England (1239–1307) The eldest son of HENRY III and ELEANOR OF PROVENCE, who was born at the Palace of Westminster on 17 June 1239 and was named after the revered EDWARD THE CONFESSOR. Edward inherited none of his father's weaknesses and took far more after his very able uncle Richard of Cornwall. He also possessed his mother's strength of character without her pleasure-loving frivolity. He was further reputed to enjoy the special favour of heaven and to have the protection of the angels. Substance for this belief was provided early on by an incident that occurred when the young Edward suddenly rose from his seat for no apparent reason during a game of chess and walked away from the table – seconds later a huge block of dislodged masonry crashed down where he had been sitting. Later, during his military campaigns, it was said that no weapon could touch him, though they frequently wounded those standing close to him, and he also seemed to be immune from illness. Similarly, he escaped unharmed when his entourage was struck by a lightning bolt in Gascony in 1287, leaving two retainers dead. He could, however, be hot-tempered, and records survive of bills incurred for the repair of a royal coronet flung into the fire by the exasperated Edward and of a fine he had to pay a servant whom he had struck and injured.

The young 'Lord Edward', as he was known, loyally supported his father throughout the civil war of 1264–8 and Simon de Montfort's rebellion. At the age of 15 he journeyed to Spain, where he received the honour of a knighthood from King Alfonso X of Castile and the hand of Alfonso's half-sister the Infanta Leonor, or ELEANOR OF CASTILE, to whom he was married at Las Huelgas in October 1254. She became the love of his life and, like his father before him, he was a faithful husband.

By 1270 peace had been restored to the country and Edward went off on the Crusades, accompanied by Eleanor. When Henry III died in November 1272, Edward was in Sicily making his slow way back. England, he felt, was safe under his mother's regency and he did not hurry, arriving in the summer of 1274 for a spectacular coronation. He and Eleanor were crowned together at WESTMINSTER ABBEY on 19 August.

Edward's encouragement of 'parliaments', which he used to keep in touch with the problems and needs of the country, has led him to be described as the 'Father of the Mother of Parliaments'. Other nicknames included 'the English Justinian', a reference to his skills as a lawgiver, 'the Flower of Chivalry' and 'the best lance in the world'. He was also dubbed 'Longshanks' on account of his great height (a characteristic that was confirmed in 1774 when his tomb was opened, revealing his well-preserved bones). His relentless, but unsuccessful, attempts to assert his overlordship of the Scottish kingdom (resisted by William Wallace and Robert Bruce among others) earned him the grim title of 'Hammer of the Scots', which was to be inscribed on his simple tomb in Westminster. His Welsh campaign was more successful and the country was completely subjugated in two wars, ending with the deaths of LLYWELYN III and DAFYDD III, the last two native princes of Wales (Llywelyn was killed near Builth in 1282 and Dafydd was executed in 1283). A policy of castle building ensured that Wales remained under English rule and the mighty fortresses of Rhuddlan, Conwy, Denbigh, Harlech and Caernarfon still stand. Edward had earlier promised the Welsh he would provide them with a new Prince of Wales, who would not speak a word of English. According to popular legend, he fulfilled his promise in 1284, when he presented the Welsh with his infant son (later EDWARD II) shortly after his birth at CAERNARFON CASTLE.

These successes led to comparisons between Edward and King ARTHUR, a link that the king did much to foster, holding his own 'Round Tables' with feasting and tournaments. Trophies presented to him at the conclusion of his Welsh campaign included a crown reputed to be Arthur's (he was also present when the alleged graves of Arthur and GUINEVERE were opened at Glastonbury in 1278).

When campaigning in Scotland Edward captured and took back to England the Stone of SCONE on which Scottish kings had always been crowned. Edward's reign was one of architectural flowering and many cathedrals and abbey churches were begun or rebuilt, including Exeter, Lichfield and York Minster, while the first scientific attempt at town planning took place at

Winchelsea. It is also from his reign that the earliest records of a monarch touching subjects to heal the KING'S EVIL survive (at least 2000 people presented themselves for Edward's touch in the years 1305–6).

Edward's beloved wife Eleanor died in 1290 and nine years later, on 10 September 1299, at the age of 60, he married at Canterbury the 20-year-old MARGARET OF FRANCE. The marriage was not unhappy, in spite of the great disparity in age, and three more children were born, making Edward the father of more legitimate children than any other English king before or since.

In June 1307 Edward was again campaigning in the north when he was struck down by dysentery. He died at Burgh-on-the-Sands, near Carlisle, on 7 July, having just completed his 68th year. His body was taken back to Westminster for burial near his father and his first wife, adjacent to the Confessor's shrine. One contemporary story had it that the king requested that his body be boiled and his bones carried with English armies until Scotland finally succumbed to English overlordship.

Edward I was the outstanding English king of the Middle Ages. A great soldier and a wise statesman, he initiated constitutional reforms that laid the foundations of parliamentary government. A fulsome elegy was left to posterity by the rhyming chronicler Peter of Langtoft.

> Speak of king Edward and of his memory
> As of the most renowned combatant on steed.
> Since the time of Adam never was any time
> That prince for nobility, or baron for splendour,
> Or merchant for wealth, or clerk for learning,
> By art or by genius could escape death.
> Of chivalry, after king Arthur,
> Was king Edward the flower of Christendom.
> He was so handsome and great, so powerful in arms,
> That of him may one speak as long as the world lasts.
> For he had no equal as a knight in armour
> For vigour and valour, neither present nor future.

Edward II, King of England (1284–1327)

The fourth and youngest son of EDWARD I and his first wife ELEANOR OF CASTILE, who was born at CAERNARFON CASTLE on 25 April 1284 and following the custom of the day was known as Edward of Caernarfon from his birthplace. The apocryphal story of his father presenting the baby on his shield to the people of Wales as a prince who could speak no word of English has often been told. In fact, Edward did not become heir apparent until he was four months old,

when his elder brother ALFONSO, EARL OF CHESTER, died, and he was not created Prince of Wales and Earl of Chester until 7 February 1301.

Edward lost his mother at the age of six and his father did not remarry for another nine years, so Edward lacked parental guidance for most of his childhood. He was a lonely boy and his longing for companions of his own age and sex were probably engendered at this early stage of his life. He also developed a passion for a range of 'unsuitable' rustic pursuits, which were rumoured to include bricklaying, thatching and rowing.

His 'favourites' were badly chosen. The first was Piers Gaveston, a Gascon of good family, who became the prince's inseparable companion and rendered himself odious to the court by the sarcastic and offensive nicknames he applied to its members. Indeed, things got so bad that Edward I banished him shortly before his death. Edward II recalled him immediately after his accession and bestowed the royal Earldom of Cornwall upon him.

Before his father's death Edward had been betrothed to ISABELLA OF FRANCE[1] and in January 1308 he sailed to Boulogne to complete the marriage, leaving Gaveston as Guardian of the Realm, or regent, in his absence. The wedding was celebrated with great splendour on 25 January, and the young couple returned to England early in February. Gaveston came to receive them at Dover and the slobbering display of affection with which Edward greeted him caused great dismay to the new queen and her two uncles who had accompanied them. Further offence was caused at the coronation on 25 February, when the high honour of carrying ST EDWARD'S CROWN was assigned to Gaveston, who, it is said, in purple velvet and pearls, 'was dressed more magnificently than the sovereign himself'. The king's cousins, who had been allotted lesser honours, were so outraged that they could scarcely be prevented from coming to blows with Gaveston in the abbey itself, and they and the rest of the nobility were further incensed when it became apparent later that Gaveston had bungled the arrangements for the coronation banquet, which was badly cooked and not served till after dark.

The feeling against the favourite was such that Edward, who had recently married him off to his niece Margaret (the daughter of JOAN OF ACRE), found it politic to send him to Ireland. He soon found he could not live without him, however, and recalled him the following year. Gaveston regained his old ascendancy over Edward and continued his offensive ways for the next three years until Guy, Earl of Warwick, whom he had nicknamed 'The Black Dog of Arden', kidnapped him in June 1312 and threw him into gaol in Warwick. Gaveston, realizing the gravity of his plight, threw himself on the mercy of the Earl of Warwick and his accomplice the Earl of Lancaster, but to no avail: despite pledges of safe conduct, he was led out of the castle and up to Blacklow Hill, where he was first run through with a sword and then beheaded. Edward hid his feelings by the seemingly callous comment: 'By God, what a fool he was! I could have told him never to get into Warwick's hands.' He did, however, contrive to get hold of Gaveston's body and had it embalmed with aromatic herbs and buried with considerable ceremony at Windsor, the Archbishop of Canterbury presiding (very few nobles attended).

In 1314 Edward took up arms in an attempt to complete his father's Scottish campaign and suffered a complete and ignominious defeat at Bannockburn at the hands of ROBERT BRUCE, who thus finally secured Scottish independence.

A new favourite now arose in the person of Hugh le Despenser, who was appointed the King's Chamberlain in 1313. He and his father, Hugh 'the elder', Earl of Winchester, had both been supporters of Gaveston and gained the royal favour thereby. They now supported the king against the coalition of nobles, the 'Lords Ordainers', which had been constituted in 1310. They also intrigued against the queen and induced Edward to deprive her of her estates in 1324. For her, it was the last straw. She left for France in 1325 and with Roger Mortimer, who became her lover, raised an army in Germany and the Low Countries and returned in 1326. She swept all before her, the Despensers being captured and publicly humiliated while the wretched Edward, deposed in favour of his son, was confined in Berkeley Castle. The end of Sir Hugh le Despenser, at the end of a celebratory banquet in Hereford, was especially barbarous, as recorded in a contemporary history:

> When the feast was over, Sir Hugh ... was brought before the Queen and all the barons and knights in full assembly. A list of all his misdeeds was read out to him, to which he made no reply ... Then he was tied on a tall ladder in full view of all the people both high and low, and a large fire was lit. Then his private parts were cut off, because he was held to be a heretic, and guilty of unnatural practices, even

with the King, whose affections he had alienated from the Queen ... When the other parts of his body had been disposed of, Sir Hugh's head was cut off and sent to London. His body was then divided into quarters, which were sent to the four next largest cities in England.

Edward's end at the hands of his gaolers was equally horrific. He was confined first in a cell over a pit in which lay decaying corpses, in the hope that the stench of these would be enough to kill him – but when it became clear that this would not suffice more direct action was planned. Holinshed describes it thus:

> With heavy feather beds or a table (as some write) being cast upon him they kept him down ... put into his fundament an horn and through the same they thrust up into his body an hot spit or (as others have) through the pipe of a trumpet, a plumber's instrument of iron made very hot, the which passing up into his entrailes and being rolled to and fro burnt the same, but so as no appearance of any wound or hurt outwardlie might be perceived.

The ghostly screams of the dying king were long reputed to be heard ringing through Berkeley Castle.

It is related that Edward once dined with the abbot of Gloucester, who possessed a collection of royal portraits, and asked him if he proposed to add one of himself. The abbot courteously replied that the king's likeness would appear in a more distinguished position than those of his predecessors. His utterance was prophetic, for Edward's body was brought to Gloucester Cathedral for burial and a fine alabaster effigy was raised over his tomb by Edward III. Disgust at the manner of Edward's death caused his tomb to become the centre of a popular cult and the offerings of the pilgrims were sufficient to enable the rebuilding of the choir of the cathedral in Perpendicular style.

Somewhat curious is a lone account written by the papal notary Manuele de Fieschi that suggests Edward II evaded death at Berkeley Castle altogether. According to this version of events, the king was warned of the approach of his murderers and exchanged clothes with his sympathetic gaoler, thus making good his escape with the gaoler after killing the porter at the main gate. The murderers, finding their quarry gone, offered the body of the porter as that of the king in order to cover their failure to secure the royal murder. It seems from this account that Edward then travelled to Ireland and then wandered through Europe, visiting the pope and eventually settling down in a hermitage.

Edward III, King of England (1312–77)
Edward of Windsor, the eldest child of
EDWARD II and ISABELLA OF FRANCE[1], who
was the first English king to have the time of
his birth noted exactly. He was born at
Windsor Castle at 5.40 am on Monday, 13
November 1312 and baptized four days later
in the old chapel of St Edward in Windsor
Castle. The names of seven godfathers are
recorded, but no godmother. A few days
later his father created him Earl of Chester,
but not, for some reason, Prince of Wales.

Edward's proclamation as Keeper of
the Realm and then as king followed the
deposition and brutal murder of his hapless
father (*see above*). A coup (1330) staged at
Nottingham Castle aimed at his mother's
ambitious lover, Roger de Mortimer (who
was tried, then drawn and hanged) allowed
him the freedom to act as king in deed as well
as name. His principal preoccupation during his long reign of 50 years was to be his
claim to the throne of France, which began
the Hundred Years' War. Edward assumed
the title of King of France in 1340, claiming
the crown through his mother, as heir of her
brother Charles IV, who had died in 1328.
The French barons, however, did not recognize the principle of inheritance through the
female line and Charles had been succeeded
by his cousin Philippe VI, the nearest male
heir. Edward did homage to him for his
French fiefs in 1329 and 1331. Some years
later, English commercial interests connected with the wool trade in Flanders precipitated a commercial crisis. Flanders had
passed under French administration in 1328
and it was the powerful Flemish weavers
who persuaded Edward to advance his claim
to France after concluding a commercial
treaty with him in 1338.

Philippe's answer to Edward's pretensions was to declare his French fiefs forfeited and to invade Guienne. Edward, no
less a warrior than his grandfather EDWARD
I, took up arms to defend his title by sea and
land. The great naval battle of Sluys in 1340
gave England control of the Channel, and
this was followed by the land victories of
Crécy (1346) and Poitiers (1356), in which
the superiority of the English longbowmen
over the heavily armoured French cavalry
won the day. Calais was taken after a long
siege in 1347, thus giving the English an
important economic and military base.

The hero of the wars was Edward's eldest
son, EDWARD OF WOODSTOCK, PRINCE OF
WALES, later known as 'The Black Prince',
who came to be regarded as the 'model
of chivalry', but who was in reality bad-
tempered, foul-mouthed and cruel. It
was perhaps a mercy that he died a year
before his father and never lived to become
king.

In the years 1348–50 northern Europe
was ravaged by the Black Death, an outbreak of bubonic plague, which is said to
have halved the population of England and
served greatly to undermine her military
strength. The Treaty of Bretigny in 1360
ended the wars for a time, and Edward
renounced his claim to the French crown.
King Jean II of France, the son and successor of Philippe, was released from prison in
England, where he had been held since his
capture at Poitiers, and allowed to return
home.

In 1369 Edward renewed his claim and
resumed the title of King of France after the
Black Prince had refused to appear at the
court of Charles V (Jean's successor) to
answer complaints brought against him by
the Count of Armagnac. Poitou was recon-
quered but the French regained control of
the Channel, with Castilian aid, at the battle
of La Rochelle (1372) and successfully
blocked English transport. When the Black
Prince died of dysentery in 1376, English
fortunes were at their lowest ebb and all that
remained were the five fortified towns of
Bordeaux, Bayonne, Brest, Calais and
Cherbourg and their coastal lands. France,
however, was in a ruinous state.

At home, Edward III's reign saw many
changes. English replaced French as the
official language of the law courts (and
Chaucer commenced writing his *Canterbury Tales* in English), the office of Justice
of the Peace was created, and Parliament
was divided into two houses. Admirers of
Edward said he inherited a kingdom, but
bequeathed a nation. Thomas Walsingham,
recounting Edward's reign, said of him:

> Indeed this king among all other kings and
> princes of the world had been glorious, gra-
> cious, merciful and magnificent, and was called
> *par excellence* 'Most Gracious' for his pre-emi-
> nent and outstanding grace. His face was more
> like an angel's than a man's, for there was such a
> miraculous light of grace in it, that anyone who
> looked openly into it or dreamed of it at night,
> might hope that comforting delights would
> come to him that very day.

In 1348 Edward founded the Order of the
GARTER, which was to become (and still
remains) one of the leading orders of chivalry in Europe.

Edward was a tall, dignified man of regal
bearing. Though sometimes given to violent outbursts of temper, a PLANTAGENET

characteristic, his charm, generosity, and affinity with the baronial classes helped him to retain his popularity for most of his reign. He was happily married to the plump and somewhat stolid PHILIPPA OF HAINAULT for over 40 years.

After her death in 1369, Edward acquired a rapacious mistress, the late Queen Philippa's lady-in-waiting Alice Perrers – 'that wanton baggage' as a contemporary account describes her – who rendered the declining years of the senile though lecherous king a thorough misery. She and her daughter Isabella were in the habit of sleeping with the king together and it seems highly probable that one or the other of them infected the old man with gonorrhoea. Edward was taken ill in September 1376 and only partially recovered in the following spring when an abscess (the locality of which is not specified) burst and gave him some relief. He was able to attend Parliament, but towards the end of May suffered a stroke and died at SHEEN PALACE, Surrey, on 21 June 1377. His body was left unattended for several hours and Alice Perrers (accused by some of ensnaring the king's affections through witchcraft) is said to have robbed it of its rings and personal jewellery before making herself scarce. She lived comfortably on her ill-gotten gains until her death in 1400.

Edward was buried in WESTMINSTER ABBEY beside Philippa. The wooden head of the effigy carried on the coffin at his funeral in accordance with custom is preserved in the Abbey museum and appears to have been modelled from a death mask, as the mouth shows signs of the characteristic distortion suffered by some stroke victims. The impressive effigy on his tomb was probably derived from the same source, although it is more stylized.

Edward IV, King of England (1442–83) The second son of Richard, 3rd Duke of YORK and Cicely Nevill (an elder brother Henry having died in infancy), who was born at Rouen when his father was acting as Lieutenant and Captain-General of the Duchy of Aquitaine and Chief Commissary, Ambassador and Deputy to treat with France. Edward and his brother Edmund, his junior by one year, were installed at Ludlow Castle, whence they wrote letters to their campaigning father, thanking him for such things as 'our green gowns now late sent unto us to our great comfort', and requesting him to send 'some fine bonnets ... by the next sure messenger, for necessity

so requireth'. They also complained bitterly about their tutor Richard Crofte. Edward grew up a burly, blond giant, over six feet tall, skilled in military arts and with an eye for the ladies, who found him an amusing companion and accomplished dancing partner. In courtly pursuits he was trained by his mother 'The Rose of Raby', also known as 'proud Cis', who through her mother, Joan Beaufort, was a granddaughter of John of Gaunt, Duke of LANCASTER, bringing to her children yet another line of descent from EDWARD III. Of particular value to him as king was his remarkable ability to remember the names and occupations of the thousands of knights and officials who were presented to him – a touch that much promoted the loyalty of his supporters.

As soon as they were old enough, Edward and Edmund took up arms in their family cause (see ROSES, WARS OF THE). Edmund perished with his father at Wakefield in December 1460, but Edward lived to triumph over his enemies and was finally declared king in Parliament on 4 March 1461 and crowned at WESTMINSTER ABBEY on St Peter's Day (29 June) following. Victory at the bloody battle of Towton, near Tadcaster, during a snowstorm on 29 March 1461 cemented his claim to the throne.

Three years later the king married in a somewhat furtive manner. While hunting on May Day 1464, he slipped away to Grafton Regis and was married in the parish church to the widowed Lady Grey, five years his senior. Her maiden name was ELIZABETH WOODVILLE and she had been a maid of honour to MARGARET OF ANJOU. On her father's side she belonged to an obscure enough family, but her mother was Jacquette of Luxembourg, Duchess of Bedford, the widow of HENRY IV's doughty son. Nevertheless, Elizabeth was hardly a suitable match for the king, who did not make his marriage public until the autumn, when he was pressed to seek the hand of a foreign princess. The newly acknowledged queen was brought to London and the ceremonies of her state entry and crowning were observed with more than usual magnificence. In spite of his marriage and the large family Elizabeth bore him, Edward remained a philanderer and was wont to boast of his three concubines, 'one the merriest, the other the wiliest, the third the holiest harlot in the realm'. These mistresses were abandoned without compunction as soon as he tired of him, and it was noted that he would pursue any woman who caught his eye, regardless of whether she were married or unmarried, noble or lowly. His favourite though, was undoubtedly 'Jane' (really Elizabeth) Shore, wife of a London Merchant, who was the 'merriest' of his mistresses. Of her Sir Thomas More wrote, 'For many he had, but her he loved.' He had, however, only two proven bastards, one being Arthur Plantagenet, Viscount LISLE, who was to serve his half-nephew HENRY VIII as Deputy of Calais.

Edward's marriage alienated many of his supporters, including Warwick 'the Kingmaker', who joined the Lancastrians and reopened the civil war, defeating the king near Banbury in 1469. He then went to France to raise more troops and returned to effect the brief 're-adeption' of HENRY VI. Edward was forced to fly to France and his wife and family to take refuge in sanctuary at Westminster. He returned and regained the throne in April 1471. Warwick was defeated and killed at Barnet soon after, while the battle of Tewkesbury and the deaths of Henry VI and his son ended all Lancastrian hopes for the foreseeable future. Edward's brother George, Duke of CLARENCE, had sided with his father-in-law Warwick and was declared a traitor and imprisoned in the Tower. There he is alleged to have been drowned in a butt of malmsey wine on 18 February 1478. How far Edward and his youngest brother, Richard, Duke of Gloucester (see RICHARD III), were implicated in his death is not known.

Although apparently a popular and pleasure-loving king, who grew quite stout through his love of food and drink and took emetics so that he might gorge himself over and over again, Edward possessed all the ruthlessness and strong will of a Renaissance despot. Had he lived longer he might well have become one of the most powerful of English kings. He died at Westminster on 9 April 1483, a few weeks before his 41st birthday, probably of pneumonia following a fishing trip on the Thames though possibly of typhoid fever or even of poison or malaria (very few details of his last illness have been recorded). He was buried in St George's Chapel, Windsor, where his tomb is marked by a simple slab of black marble inscribed with his name in gilt lettering.

Edward V, King of England (1470–83?) The eldest son of EDWARD IV and ELIZABETH WOODVILLE, who was born in sanctuary at Westminster on 4 November 1470 at a moment when his parents' fortunes seemed at their lowest ebb. In a few months, however, all had changed: Edward IV was back in power and able to create his firstborn son Prince of Wales and Earl of Chester, Duke of Cornwall, a Knight of the GARTER, Earl of March and Earl of Pembroke successively. The young prince was placed in the charge of his paternal uncles (see George, Duke of CLARENCE and RICHARD III) and his maternal uncle, Anthony Woodville, Earl Rivers.

When Edward IV died unexpectedly in April 1483, the 12-year-old Edward was at Ludlow and on receipt of the news that he was now king set out for London, being met on the way at Stony Stratford by his uncle Richard of Gloucester who was coming from York. Richard conducted him to London with every sign of loyalty and they were met outside the city by the Lord Mayor and leading citizens, who escorted them to the Tower, which it is alleged the young Edward V never left again.

Some weeks later Robert Stillington, Bishop of Bath and Wells, who had been Chancellor from 1467 to 1475 and was openly hostile to the Woodvilles, caused a sensation when he questioned the validity of Edward IV's marriage. The fact that Edward had been pre-contracted to Lady Eleanor Butler, widow of Sir Thomas Butler, and daughter of John Talbot, 1st Earl of Shrewsbury, and that she was still living at the time of his marriage to Elizabeth was good enough reason in canon law to invalidate any subsequent marriage contracted by him. The bishop's allegation may have had some justification, or may have been a complete fabrication, but it served to induce Parliament to declare Elizabeth Woodville's marriage to Edward invalid and their children bastards. It therefore followed that Edward V was no longer king and he was declared deposed on 25 June 1483, after a reign of only two months. Richard of Gloucester was proclaimed king in his place, as Richard III, the following day.

What ensued is now recognized as one of the greatest unsolved historical mysteries – the fate of the 'Princes in the Tower'. Tudor propaganda, engineered by HENRY VII, insists that Edward and his brother Richard were smothered in their sleep by Sir James Tyrrell (whose surname is curiously reminiscent of that of the alleged slayer of WILLIAM II), who was later induced by torture to confess the deed and was beheaded in 1502. It seems strange, however, that no search for the princes' bodies was made at that time and it was not until 1674, during the reign of CHARLES II, that the bones of two children were found beneath a staircase in the Tower and solemnly deposited in an urn in WESTMINSTER ABBEY. These pathetic remains were medically examined in 1933 by Professor William Wright. He concluded that they came from the skeletons of two boys aged approximately 12 and nine or 10, their heights being four feet nine and a half inches and four feet six and a half inches respectively. It proved impossible to establish that these were beyond dispute the princes – and added little to the debate as to who was responsible for their deaths – Richard III or Henry VII. As long as the boys lived they provided rivals to both. There are many who believe that Richard had the princes moved to Middleham Castle in Yorkshire and that they were still alive there at the time of the battle of Bosworth, and that it was Henry who consequently ordered their deaths rather than Richard, the more conventional suspect. The argument was reopened in 1987, when various experts contributed their views in the light of modern scientific analysis. It was suggested that the bones discovered in 1674 were indeed those of the princes and that the likely date of their deaths was some time soon after Easter 1484 (when the first rumours of their murders were heard). This conclusion appears to place the blame firmly with Richard, as Henry did not gain control of the Tower until 1485, but defenders of Richard continue to challenge the basis upon which such a conclusion is reached, emphasizing the unreliability of contemporary documentation.

Little is known for certain about the character and potential of Edward V, the 'Boy King' who was never crowned. It seems, though, that he did well in his lessons and behaved in an appropriately dignified manner. As a consequence of Victorian romanticization of the episode in art and print, to most people his name only conjures up a sentimental vision of two pale fair-haired little boys in black velvet, looking wistful and pensive in the grim surroundings of a room in the Tower.

Edward VI, King of England (1537–53) The only son of HENRY VIII by his third wife JANE SEYMOUR, who was born at HAMPTON COURT PALACE on 12 October 1537. The birth of a seemingly healthy son brought Henry VIII to a state of felicity only slightly clouded by the death of the mother two weeks later. The motherless child was con-

fided to the care of nurses and as he grew older was tutored by four of the greatest scholars of the kingdom, carefully chosen by his stepmother CATHERINE PARR. These were Sir John Cheke, Professor of Greek at Cambridge; Richard Cox, Headmaster of Eton; Sir Anthony Cooke, a politician; and Roger Ascham, another Cambridge classical scholar and educationist. These men imparted not only a sound knowledge of Greek, Latin and French, but also the tenets of the Protestant Reformation that had swept Germany and the Netherlands. For relaxation Edward played the lute and studied the stars. It is astounding that a young boy could have assimilated so much knowledge and Edward must have been something of a prodigy. Deprived of the company of children of his own age, he was surrounded by scholarly men and took on the character of a scholarly, rather humourless, man in a child's body.

Edward could have known no family life until Catherine Parr gathered the king's children together for the first time at Christmas 1543, when he was six years old. His half-sisters Mary (*see* MARY I) and Elizabeth (*see* ELIZABETH I) became genuinely fond of him, and Elizabeth, who was only four years older, shared his tutors. Henry must have been sadly disappointed to see his son growing up a sickly, pale boy, so different from what he himself had been.

On the 10-year-old Edward's succession to the throne in January 1547 his maternal uncle Lord Hertford became Protector of the Realm and was created Duke of Somerset. Edward had imbibed the Protestant leanings of his stepmother, and John Knox, Ridley, Latimer and Hooper, all zealous reformers, were appointed as court chaplains, while Archbishop Cranmer was authorized to compile the first English Prayer Book, which appeared in 1548.

Edward was forced to agree to the execution of his uncle Thomas Seymour (who had married the Queen Dowager Catherine Parr) for alleged high treason early in 1549. The attractive, swashbuckling Thomas was his favourite uncle and the incident may well have embittered him towards his other uncle, the Protector, as he was to view the latter's fall and subsequent execution with a show of indifference. Somerset was replaced as Protector by John Dudley, Earl of Warwick, who was at once created Duke of Northumberland.

Edward's love of learning induced him to found numerous grammar-schools, which bore his name. He also gave the old palace of

Bridewell to the corporation of London to provide a workhouse, and converted the Grey Friars' monastery into Christ's Hospital. He received instructions in political matters from his Clerk of the Council, William Thomas, who drew up a series of discourses for his use.

So much learning forced into a delicate boy was bound to have an adverse effect. In 1552 Edward supposedly suffered from measles and then from smallpox, both doubtful diagnoses. Early in the following year it became apparent that he was suffering from pulmonary tuberculosis. In addition to the normal symptoms of that disease, 'eruptions came out over his skin, his hair fell off, and then his nails, and afterwards the joints of his toes and fingers'. All this indicates that his condition was complicated by congenital syphilis, Henry's legacy to his children. The boy king, still only 15, died at GREENWICH PALACE after great suffering on 6 July 1553. He was buried near the tomb of his grandfather HENRY VII in WESTMINSTER ABBEY, but has no memorial.

Many have dismissed Edward VI as a precocious, Protestant prig. This was probably accurate to some extent, but he also appears to have been quick-minded and intelligent.

Edward VII, King of Great Britain (1841–1910) The eldest son and second child of Queen VICTORIA and Prince ALBERT, who was born at BUCKINGHAM PALACE at 12 minutes before 11 am on 9 November 1841. His mother described him in a letter to her uncle Leopold, King of the Belgians (*see* LEOPOLD OF SAXE-COBURG), as 'a wonderfully strong and large child, with very large dark blue eyes, a finely formed but somewhat large nose, and a pretty little mouth'. He was born Duke of Cornwall and Duke of Rothesay, etc., and was created Prince of Wales and Earl of Chester on 8 December 1841. On 25 January 1842 he was baptized by the names of Albert Edward at St George's Chapel, Windsor, his godparents being King Friedrich Wilhelm IV of Prussia (who conferred the Order of the Black Eagle on him), the Duke of Cambridge (*see* CAMBRIDGE, ADOLPHUS FREDERICK, DUKE OF), Duke Ferdinand of Saxe-Coburg, the Duchess of Saxe-Coburg and Gotha, the Dowager Duchess of Saxe-Gotha, and Princess SOPHIA. Always known in the family as 'Bertie', the Prince of Wales was further created Earl of Dublin on 17 January 1850.

It seems scarcely credible that Queen Victoria's eldest son was an unwanted child.

The young queen had strongly resented a second pregnancy coming so soon after the birth of the Princess Royal and curtailing her activities, especially dancing, for which she had a passion. This resentment was to mar the relationship between mother and son for the rest of her life. In a milder form it was a continuation of the feud waged by the first three Georges against their sons and heirs. Prince Albert devised a careful plan for his son's education, but it soon became evident that he was not a brilliant scholar and was also lacking in diligence. He was denied the companionship of any children of his own age apart from his brothers and sisters, and the tutors chosen by his father were for the most part gravely austere and humourless. It was a sad environment for a high-spirited, affectionate boy, but he managed not to be crushed by it and later developed a marked taste for uproarious practical jokes (though friends were not encouraged to try any on him).

The prince had inherited the strong sexuality of his Georgian great-uncles, as well as that of his paternal grandfather and uncle, and his parents soon became well aware of this. Victoria was to attribute the Prince Consort's untimely death in part to a journey he made to Oxford to sort out some of Albert Edward's early sexual adventures at a time when he was in a weakened state of health. This further exacerbated the uneasy relations between mother and son. When someone remarked to the queen that her son must be a source of comfort to her, she retorted, 'Comfort! Why, I caught him smoking a fortnight after his dear father died!' She later lamented to a friend, 'Oh! that boy – much as I pity him I never can or shall look at him without a shudder as you can imagine.'

Bertie's sister Princess Friedrich Wilhelm of Prussia played a large part in finding a bride for him when the time came. The choice fell on Princess ALEXANDRA OF DENMARK, who, as Queen Victoria and her new family were soon to discover, was 'sadly deaf'. Nonetheless, Bertie and 'Alix' were married at St George's Chapel, Windsor, on 10 March 1863, with the recently widowed queen mournfully gazing down upon them from the Royal Closet, the small latticed gallery on the north side of the sanctuary. Six children were born in fairly quick succession and then marital relations probably ceased, although the couple remained on friendly, even deeply affectionate, terms for the rest of their lives together.

Bertie found satisfaction in the society of

warmer-natured ladies, his many mistresses including the actress Lily Langtry (the so-called 'Jersey Lily') and society beauties Frances 'Daisy' Brooke and Mrs Alice KEPPEL. He was a *bon viveur* in every sense, loving good food, good wine, good clothes, good cigars and good company. His mother excluded him completely from any participation in affairs of state so that he had all the time in the world to indulge his sybaritic tastes. He was especially noted for his sartorial knowledge, often advising dignitaries upon the correct form of dress for formal occasions. When a friend proposed wearing a tail coat to an art exhibition, the prince exclaimed, 'I thought everyone must know that a short jacket is always worn with a silk hat at a private view in the morning'. The short Norfolk jackets he wore quickly became a standard form of dress, and the fact that he liked to leave the last button of his waistcoat undone, to accomodate his expanding waistline, meant that soon everyone was leaving the button undone as a dictate of fashion.

Many happy times were spent in Europe visiting fashionable resorts. At the Café de Paris in Monte Carlo the Prince of Wales was credited with naming 'crêpes suzette'. The inventor of the dish begged leave to name it after His Royal Highness, who pooh-poohed the idea with an expansive wave of the royal cigar, saying, 'No, no, don't name it after me. Name it after that pretty girl over there instead.'

The Prince of Wales also visited Canada and India, where his mother would have loved to go had such a journey been more feasible in her youth. He shot tigers from the backs of elephants and was fêted by the maharajas, most of whom probably recognized a kindred spirit. Another passion was gambling and playing baccarat – and this weakness caused further problems in 1891, when he was summoned as a witness in a court case arising out of charges of cheating against one of his fellow baccarat players, Sir William Gordon-Cumming.

In 1871 the nation was thrown into a state of consternation when it was learnt that the Prince of Wales was seriously ill with typhoid. The royal family gathered in attendance at his bed at Sandringham and regular bulletins of changes in his condition were posted on street corners until, at length, he recovered. The Archbishop of Canterbury even sent a special prayer for the prince by telegraph.

The old queen's death in January 1901 brought Bertie to the throne at last, in his 60th year, and he chose to reign as Edward VII. It had been a long apprenticeship: as prince he had once admitted, 'I don't mind praying to the eternal Father, but I must be the only man in the country afflicted with an eternal mother'. The coronation was arranged for 26 June 1902 and London filled with visitors from all over the world, including many of the maharajas with whom the king had gone tiger hunting in India. A day or two before the date the king was struck down with an illness diagnosed as acute appendicitis and an emergency operation was performed at Buckingham Palace. It was entirely successful and the king's recovery was so rapid that the coronation was held, with slightly curtailed ceremonial, on 9 August 1902. Most of the souvenir china prepared for the event carried the June date, but some items have the postponement date added and these have now become much sought after.

Edward was an able linguist and well informed on foreign affairs. He was enthusiastically pro-French, and supported the gradual rapprochement between France and Britain which culminated in the conclusion of the Entente Cordiale in 1904. His efforts won him the name 'Edward the Peacemaker'.

'King Teddy', or 'Tum-Tum', enjoyed immense popularity with all classes and his ebullience and bonhomie came as a welcome relief after the rather drab years of the latter half of his mother's reign. The years of self-indulgent good living, however, had inevitably undermined his health and he was a martyr to chronic bronchitis. His death at Buckingham Palace came peacefully and quite suddenly after a short illness on 6 May 1910, not long after he had returned from an enjoyable stay at Biarritz. The nation grieved sincerely. Many realized that the king's influence had contributed significantly to the maintenance of peace in Europe and that it would now be only a matter of time before that peace was broken. He was buried at St George's Chapel, Windsor, on 20 May 1910.

Edward VIII, King of Great Britain (1894–1972) The first son and eldest child of George, Duke of York (later GEORGE V) and Victoria MARY OF TECK (later Queen Mary), who was born at White Lodge, Richmond Park, Surrey, at 10 pm on 23 June 1894. He was baptized by the Archbishop of Canterbury, using water that his father himself had brought from the river Jordan, in the drawing room at White Lodge on 16 July

1894, receiving the names of Edward Albert Christian George Andrew Patrick David, the last four names being those of the patron saints of England, Scotland, Ireland and Wales. In his family he was always known as David. He had an impressive array of god-parents, his two grandfathers, the Prince of Wales and the Duke of TECK, the Duke of Cambridge (see CAMBRIDGE, GEORGE, 2ND DUKE OF), the Emperor Nikolai II of Russia, the kings of Denmark and Württemberg, and the Duke of Saxe-Coburg and Gotha, his great-grandmother Queen VICTORIA, his two grandmothers, the Princess of Wales and the Duchess of Teck, and the queens of Denmark and of the Hellenes.

At his birth the prince occupied the unique position of being the third male heir in direct line to the throne. On his father's accession in May 1910 he became Duke of Cornwall and Duke of Rothesay, Earl of Carrick, Baron of Renfrew, Lord of the Isles and Great Steward of Scotland, and on 2 June 1910 he was created Prince of Wales and Earl of Chester, thereby becoming a Knight of the GARTER. He took his seat in the House of Lords on 19 Feburary 1918.

Edward's good looks and boyish charm were to be his undoing. He was wilful and irresponsible and as he grew up it became obvious that he was almost as much addicted to worldly pleasure as his grandfather EDWARD VII had been. Things might have been improved had David been allowed to see active service in the front line in the First World War, a thing he very much wished to do but which was categorically forbidden by his father, in spite of David pointing out that as he had four younger brothers his life could be risked. The sense of frustration he felt was to be recalled throughout his life. David chafed at all royal ceremonial and protocol. At the sensitive age of 17, while still attending the Royal Naval College, he was made to dress up in what he considered a ridiculous fancy dress and take part in a cer-emony, largely devised by Lloyd George, formally to invest him as Prince of Wales at CAERNARFON CASTLE on 13 July 1911.

In the twenties and thirties the prince made several successful overseas tours, where his charm stood him in good stead. He had a great following at home and abroad, being considered something of an arbiter of fashion, admired for his style of dress and ease of manner. He showed no sign of wanting to marry and settle down, however, much to his father's annoyance, and it soon became obvious that his taste,

like that of an earlier Prince of Wales (GEORGE IV), was for mature married ladies, although whereas 'Prinny' had liked them to be well-rounded, David preferred them to have thin, boyish figures in the prevailing fashion. A succession of ladies occupied his attention, but by the mid-1930s it became evident in court circles that his affections had been permanently engaged by the American Mrs Wallis Simpson, who resided in London with her businessman husband Ernest Simpson. Having first met the heir-apparent at a country house party at Melton Mowbray in January 1931, the Simpsons became frequent guests at David's house FORT BELVEDERE, near Windsor, and Wallis acted as his hostess in spite of the presence of her complacent hus-band.

Matters were swiftly coming to a head when George V died on 20 January 1936 and David found himself King Edward VIII. He was now completely besotted with Wallis and with almost incredible naïvety was convinced that once she was freed of her marriage he would be able to marry her and make her his queen. For the sovereign head of the Church of England to marry a twice divorced woman was unthinkable to the Establishment, and the king's insistence on going ahead with his plans in spite of all advice provoked a government crisis (see ABDICATION CRISIS). Compromise was impossible and, after a reign of nearly 11 months, the king abdicated on 10 December 1936 in favour of his brother the Duke of York. The first English monarch to abdicate since RICHARD II in 1399, he left the country after making a touching farewell broadcast (the words of which were drafted for him by Winston Churchill):

At long last I am able to say a few words of my own. I have never wanted to withhold any-thing, but until now it has been not constitu-tionally possible for me to speak. A few hours ago I discharged my last duty as King and Emperor, and now that I have been succeeded by my brother, the Duke of York, my first words must be to declare my allegiance to him. This I do with all my heart. You all know the reasons which have impelled me to renounce the Throne. But I want you to understand that in making up my mind I did not forget the country or the Empire which as Prince of Wales, and lately as King, I have for twenty-five years tried to serve. But you must believe me when I tell you that I have found it impos-sible to carry the heavy burden of respon-sibility and to discharge my duties as King as I would wish to do without the help and support of the woman I love. And I want you to know that the decision I have made has been mine and mine alone. This was a thing I had to judge entirely for myself. The other person most nearly concerned has tried up to the last to persuade me to take a different course. I have made this, the most serious decision of my life, upon a single thought of what would in the end be best for all. The decision has been made less difficult to me by the sure knowledge that my Brother, with his long training in the public affairs of this country and with his fine qualities, will be able to take my place forthwith, without interruption or injury to the life and progress of the Empire. And he has one matchless blessing, enjoyed by so many of you and not bestowed on me – a happy home with his wife and children. During these hard days I have been comforted by my Mother and by my Family. The Ministers of the Crown, and in particular Mr Baldwin, the Prime-Minister, have always treated me with full consideration. There has never been any constitutional difference between me and them and between me and Parliament. Bred in the constitutional tradition by my Father, I should never have allowed any such issue to arise. Ever since I was Prince of Wales, and later on when I occupied the Throne, I have been treated with the greatest kindness by all classes, wherever I have lived or journeyed throughout the Empire. For that I am very grateful. I now quit altogether public affairs, and I lay down my burden. It may be some time before I return to my native land, but I shall always follow the fortunes of the British race and Empire with profound interest, and if at any time in the future I can be found of service to His Majesty in a private station I shall not fail. And now we all have a new King. I wish him, and you, his people, happiness and prosperity with all my heart. God bless you all. God Save the King.

Wallis's divorce from Ernest Simpson was later made final and on 3 June 1937 she and the former king were married in France. On 8 March David had been created Duke of Windsor by his brother and successor GEORGE VI and on 27 May had received 'reconferment' of the qualification of Royal Highness by Letters Patent, which expressly stated that this style was reserved to him alone and could not extend to any wife or children he might acquire. The legality of this was extremely doubtful. As the son of a sovereign, David was naturally entitled to the qualification, which should have reverted to him automatically on his renunciation of the throne, while the limitation imposed by the new Letters Patent was completely unconstitutional. David was to chafe for the rest of his life at this injustice, but out of deference to his brother never made an open issue of it, although within his own household the Duchess was always addressed as 'Royal Highness'.

Apart from a short wartime tour of duty as Governor and Commander-in-Chief of the Bahamas from 1940 to 1945, the rest of

David's life was lived out in the obscurity of a self-imposed exile in France, participating with his wife in an endless social round, which from time to time he clearly found unfulfilling – though he virtually never voiced regrets at the action he had taken. He produced a volume of memoirs, *A King's Story*, and two other books of royal reminiscence, while his wife produced her version under the title *The Heart Has its Reasons*. He once spoke of his experience of the Abdication: 'People can say what they like for it or against it, I don't care; but one thing is certain: I acted in good faith. And I was treated bloody shabbily.'

Tired, old and ill, the duke was dying of cancer at his residence in the Bois de Boulogne when he was cheered by a visit from his beloved niece ELIZABETH II with her husband and eldest son, and was able to muster up the last vestiges of his strength to receive them. He died within a matter of days thereafter on 28 May 1972. His body was flown back to Britain and lay in state in St George's Chapel, Windsor, where thousands flocked to pay their respects to their one-time monarch before he was taken to the royal burial ground at Frogmore, where he rests beneath a simple memorial. His widow lived on for nearly 14 years in an increasing state of senile dementia until on 24 April 1986 she, too, died in the Paris home they had shared. Her body was flown to England and buried beside that of her husband at Frogmore.

Edward Augustus, Prince, Duke of York and Albany *see* YORK, PRINCE EDWARD AUGUSTUS, DUKE OF.

Edward of Angoulême (1365–72) The elder son of EDWARD OF WOODSTOCK, PRINCE OF WALES and Joan, Countess of Kent (*see* JOAN, PRINCESS OF WALES), who was born at Angoulême on 27 January 1365. He died at Bordeaux in January 1371/2 and was buried in the church of the Austin Friars in London.

Edward of Middleham, Prince of Wales (1475/6–84) The only child of RICHARD III and ANNE NEVILL, who was born at Middleham Castle in Yorkshire in 1475 or early 1476. He was created Earl of Salisbury by his uncle EDWARD IV on 15 February 1478 and on his father's proclamation as king he became Duke of Cornwall on 26 June 1483. On 19 July he was created Lord Lieutenant of Ireland for three years and on 24 August he was created Prince of Wales and Earl of Chester. On the latter date he joined his parents at Pontefract where they had arrived in the course of a great royal progress of the kingdom. He accompanied them to York, where his ceremonial investiture as Prince of Wales took place on 8 September in great splendour. The royal party returned to Pontefract later in the month and some two weeks later the king returned south and Edward, probably accompanied by his mother, returned to Middleham. By a writ dated 9 December 1483 he was summoned to a Parliament to be held on 23 January following, but there is no evidence that he ever attended and he probably remained at Middleham.

The fact that Edward was a delicate child appears to have been the reason for his continuing to stay in the north. His household expenses include 13s 4d for a primer covered in black satin, 20d each for the making of gowns of green cloth, and five shillings for a feather. The prince's parents were again on a progress to the north and had reached Nottingham when news reached them that their son had died at Middleham Castle after a short illness early in April 1484. The *Chronicle of Croyland* reported that 'you might have seen his father and mother in a state almost bordering on madness, by reason of their sudden grief'. The little prince was buried in the parish church of Sheriff Hutton, some 10 miles northeast of York. His beautiful alabaster tomb with his recumbent effigy has been carefully reconstructed.

Edward of Norfolk, Prince (*c*.1319–*c*.1332)
The only son and heir apparent of THOMAS OF BROTHERTON, EARL OF NORFOLK and Earl Marshal of England (fifth son of EDWARD I) and his first wife Alice, daughter of Sir Roger de Hales, Coroner of Norfolk, who was born about 1319. He was only about eight years old when he was married at Hereford in May or June 1328 to Beatrice, seventh daughter of Roger Mortimer, 1st Earl of March and his wife Joan de Geneville. Edward died before his father in about 1332, aged about 13. His burial place appears to be unknown. His widow was married in about 1334 to Thomas de Braose, 1st Baron de Braose, the brother of her first husband's stepmother. By him she had three sons and three daughters. He died in June 1361 and she survived him until 16 October 1383.

Edward of Woodstock, Prince of Wales (1330–76) The eldest son of EDWARD III and PHILIPPA OF HAINAULT, who was born at Woodstock, Oxfordshire, on 15 June 1330.

He was created Earl of Chester by Charter on 18 May 1333 and Duke of Cornwall in Parliament on 3 March 1337, this being the first creation of a dukedom in England. On 12 May 1343 he was further created Prince of Wales in Parliament and invested with a coronet.

Edward, remembered by posterity as the BLACK PRINCE, embarked early on a military career, accompanying his father to France, where he was knighted on 12 July 1346 and fought bravely at Crécy on 26 August the same year. When the prince found himself in the midst of the conflict at Crécy other knights implored his father to recall him, but the king demurred, instructing 'let the boy win his spurs'. The story that he adopted the device of three ostrich feathers and the motto *Ich dien* (I serve) from the arms of the blind King John of Bohemia, who was killed at Crécy, is almost certainly apocryphal. He was a founder knight of the Order of the GARTER in 1348 and distinguished himself by winning the great victory of Poitiers on 19 September 1356 and taking prisoner Jean II, King of France. He was Lieutenant of the Duchy of Aquitaine from 1355 to 1372 and was created Prince of Aquitaine by Charter on 19 July 1362.

Edward came to be regarded as the 'model of chivalry', but he was in reality bad-tempered, foul-mouthed, ruthless and cruel, and it might be regarded as a mercy that he died before his father and never lived to become king. A particularly shameful episode took place in 1370 when, having sacked the city of Limoges, he ordered the razing of all the buildings and the murder of most of the population.

He married at Windsor on 10 October 1361 his father's first cousin, Joan, Countess of Kent, known as 'The Fair Maid of Kent' (*see* JOAN, PRINCESS OF WALES), a lady whose previous marital exploits had endowed her with a somewhat dubious reputation. She bore him two sons, EDWARD OF ANGOULÊME and Richard of Bordeaux (*see* RICHARD II). The prince also had an acknowledged natural son Edward (*fl*.1349) and was probably also the father of Sir Roger Clarendon (d.1402) and Sir John Sounder.

The French wars were renewed in 1369, when Edward III reasserted his claim to the French throne, but in spite of the reconquest of Poitou proved indecisive. Edward died of dysentery at Westminster on 8 June 1376 and was buried in Canterbury Cathedral near the shrine of St Thomas à Becket.

Edward the Confessor, King of England

(*c*.1004–66) The youngest son of ETHELRED II and his second wife EMMA OF NORMANDY, who was born at Islip, Oxfordshire, about 1004. He spent his early years in Normandy, returning to England after his half-brother HARDICANUTE became king in 1040. On Hardicanute's death in June 1042, Edward's peaceful succession to the throne was largely engineered by GODWIN, EARL OF WESSEX, who had become the most powerful man in the land under King CANUTE, a kinswoman of whom he had married.

Edward was crowned at Winchester Cathedral on Easter Sunday, 3 April 1043, probably with more ceremonial than had been seen since King EDGAR's coronation at Bath in 973. On 23 January 1045 Edward was married to Earl Godwin's daughter EDITH. Although he always treated her with the greatest consideration and respect (except for a short period when Godwin and his family were out of favour and he deprived her of her property and sent her to live with his sister in the convent at Wherwell), it was to be a marriage in name only, all Edward's inclinations being directed towards the religious life. The temporary break with the Godwin family in 1051, incidentally, had far-reaching consequences, for it was this development that prompted Edward to promise the throne to William, Duke of Normandy (*see* WILLIAM I THE CONQUEROR), thus precipitating the Norman Conquest that followed his own death.

Edward's greatest achievement was the foundation of WESTMINSTER ABBEY, which he built and endowed to expiate the breaking of a vow to make a pilgrimage to Rome. Matters of government were left in the hands of his brother-in-law Harold, Godwin's able son. Westminster Abbey was consecrated on Holy Innocents' Day, 28 December 1065. Edward, now over 60, was ill with 'fever' and probably too ill to attend, although some accounts say he was carried there on a litter. It was the culmination of his life's work and he was ready to die. The end came a few days later on 5 January 1066 and the king was buried the following day in his new foundation. He was canonized by Pope Alexander III in 1161 and his body was solemnly transferred to a new shrine on Henry III's rebuilding of the abbey. It still rests there today. Legend has it that on his deathbed Edward was cunningly deceived by his brother-in-law Harold Godwinsson, Earl of Wessex (*see* HAROLD II), into bestowing his blessing upon his claims as his successor as king.

Queen Edith lived on quietly at Winchester until 18 December 1075. William I the Conqueror had her interred beside Edward at Westminster 'with great ceremony'.

Edward the Confessor was the first English monarch to be credited with the power of healing by the 'royal touch'.

Edward the Elder, King of England

(*c*.871/2–925) The elder surviving son of ALFRED THE GREAT and EALHSWITH, who was probably born in 871 or 872 and succeeded his father in October 899. His succession was at once contested by his cousin Ethelwold, a son of ETHELRED I, who seized Wimborne. Edward pursued him, but he escaped to the north and induced the DANELAW to receive him as king. He made harrying raids into MERCIA until he was defeated and killed in 909.

Edward was crowned by Plegmund, Archbishop of Canterbury, on 8 June 900 at Kingston-upon-Thames, where the ancient coronation stone of the Saxon kings (which gave the town its name) may still be seen. In the course of his reign he annexed the Danelaw south of the Humber and was acknowledged as overlord by the Danish king of York, the king of Scots, the king of the Strathclyde Britons and others.

Edward was married three times and had a large family. His first wife, Ecgwynn (Egwina), is sometimes described as a concubine 'of humble origin', but there is no real reason to suppose this, even though her antecedents have not been recorded. At any rate, her son ATHELSTAN was always regarded as Edward's heir and as a child a great favourite of his grandfather Alfred. Edward's second wife was ELFLEDA, daughter of Ealdorman Ethelhelm. By her he had two sons, the elder of whom died very soon after his father, the younger being drowned in the English Channel in 933. There were also six daughters. Edward's third and last wife was Eadgifu, daughter of Ealdorman Sigehelm of Kent. She bore him two sons, EDMUND and EDRED, successively kings, and two daughters. Edward's many daughters either made grand marriages with continental royalty or became nuns.

The king died at Farndon-on-Dee in Mercia on 17 July 925 and was buried at Winchester. His widow Queen Eadgifu lived on for many years and died in the reign of her grandson King EDGAR on 25 August 968.

Edward the Martyr, King of England

(*c*.962–79) The eldest son of King EDGAR

and the only child of his first wife Ethelfleda, daughter of Ealdorman Ordmaer,
who was born about 962 and succeeded his
father at the age of 13 in July 975, being
crowned at Kingston-upon-Thames by
Dunstan, Archbishop of Canterbury. His
stepmother Queen ELFRIDA felt that her son
Ethelred (see ETHELRED II) should have succeeded, as the son of parents who had both
been crowned, and there was a certain
amount of sympathy and support for this
view throughout the country.

In March 979 Edward, who must have
been an ingenuous young man, set out to
visit his stepmother and half-brother at
Corfe Castle, Dorset, where they resided.
Elfrida, in the best tradition of wicked stepmothers, saw her chance. The young king
was intercepted by her henchmen and was
hacked to death on 18 March. He was buried
at Wareham 'with no royal honours', but
very soon miracles began to be attributed to
his intercession and in 980 his body was
reinterred 'with great ceremony' at Shaftesbury.

In 1931 an archaeological dig in the ruins
of Shaftesbury Abbey unearthed bones
believed to be those of Edward. A medical
examination made in 1970 found evidence
to support the accounts of Edward's death,
which tell of his being knifed in the back and
then dragged along the ground by his bolt-
ing horse with his foot caught in a stirrup.
The Anglican and Roman Catholic
Churches having both declined to accept
the relics for reinterment, the bones were
offered to the Russian Orthodox Church in
Exile, who determined to enshrine the
remains in their chapel at Brookwood
Cemetery, Surrey. This was done on 15
September 1984, but a High Court ruling
ordered the bones to be returned to the custody of the Midland Bank in Croydon
immediately after the ceremony, and there
they remain. Local opinion in Shaftesbury
felt that the bones should be returned to the
town, in part because the Orthodox arrangement seems particularly inappropriate for
the final resting place of an English king.
As a correspondent wrote in The Times of
27 September 1984: 'No Saxon can have
deserved that fate.'

Edwin, King of Northumbria (c.585–633)
The son of AELLA, KING OF DEIRA, who was
born about 585 and as a child of about three,
on his father's death and the occupation of
DEIRA by Ethelric of BERNICIA, was taken to
refuge at the court of King Ceorl of MERCIA,
where he grew up. He subsequently married

Ceorl's daughter Cwenburga, who bore him
two sons, Osfrith and Eadfrith.

In 617, with the aid of REDWALD, KING OF
EAST ANGLIA, he defeated and killed
Ethelric's son and successor Ethelfrith,
whereupon Edwin became king of Deira.
He subsequently annexed Bernicia and by
later conquests brought 'all Britain except
Kent alone' under his rule or overlordship,
being reckoned by Bede and others as the
fifth BRETWALDA. Cwenburga having died
or been repudiated, Edwin sent an embassy
to EADBALD, KING OF KENT to ask for the
hand of his sister ETHELBURGA in marriage.
However, Edwin was a pagan and 'received
the reply that it was not permissible for a
Christian maiden to be given in marriage to
a heathen husband, lest the Christian Faith
and Sacraments be profaned by her association with a king who was wholly ignorant of
the worship of the true God'. Edwin gave
assurances that he would permit Ethelburga
and her attendants complete freedom to
practise their religion and on these being
received the princess and her entourage set
out for Northumbria. She brought with her
as her chaplain Paulinus, who was consecrated bishop by Archbishop Justus of
Canterbury on 21 July 625.

The following Easter, Edwin narrowly
escaped assassination at the hands of an
emissary of King Cwichelm of WESSEX and
on the same night the queen was safely
delivered of a daughter EANFLED. Bishop
Paulinus seized the opportunity to tell
Edwin that it was Christ who had given
the queen a safe and painless delivery
in response to his prayers. The king
was impressed and promised that if he was
victorious in his revenge campaign against
Wessex 'he would renounce his idols and
serve Christ'. The expedition was successful and Edwin abandoned idol-worship
immediately and undertook a course of
instruction from Paulinus. He 'was by
nature a wise and prudent man, and often sat
alone in silent converse with himself for long
periods, turning over in his inmost heart
what he should do and which religion he
should follow'. His long deliberation on the
matter of his conversion was encouraged by
a letter from Pope Boniface V urging him to
accept the faith and sending him 'a tunic
with a golden ornament, and a cloak from
Ancyra'. The pope also wrote to the queen,
urging her to support her husband with her
prayers and example and sending her 'a silver mirror, together with a gold and ivory
comb'. Edwin's conversion was finally
brought about by his remembrance of a

vision that he had while in exile at the court of King Redwald. In 627 Edwin announced his decision to accept Christianity to his council, the members of which were unanimous in their agreement. The pagan high priest Coifi, in a dramatic gesture, profaned the temple and its idols with his own hand.

Edwin and his court were baptized by Paulinus at York on Easter Day, 12 April 627, in a hastily constructed wooden church, which the king later replaced with one of stone. Paulinus was appointed the first Archbishop of York and received the pallium from Pope Honorius I.

In 633 Edwin had to face a rebellion against his rule led by CADWALLON, KING OF GWYNEDD and PENDA, KING OF MERCIA. A fierce battle was fought at Hatfield Chase, near Doncaster, on 14 October 633. Edwin and his eldest son Osfrith were both killed and Northumbria was laid waste. Paulinus escorted Queen Ethelburga and her children to exile in Kent, where he became Bishop of Rochester and ended his days in 644.

Edwy, King of England (*c*.941–59) The elder son of EDMUND I and his first wife Elfgifu (or Elfgiva), who was born about 941. He was only five years old when his father was killed in May 946 and since the accession of such a young child was not considered feasible the throne passed to his uncle EDRED. On Edred's death in November 955, the 14-year-old Edwy succeeded him and was crowned at Kingston-upon-Thames by Oda, Archbishop of Canterbury, probably in the January following.

The young king had fallen passionately in love with a young kinswoman Elfgifu, whose mother Ethelgifu was probably his mother's sister. Marriage with such a close relation was within the prohibited degrees of kindred and affinity, but the couple contrived to wed secretly. Growing weary with the long ceremonial of his coronation banquet, Edwy absented himself and retired to his private apartments. Archbishop Oda, noticing his absence, sent Dunstan, Abbot of Glastonbury, to enquire after the king and request him to return to his duty. Dunstan found Edwy relaxing in the company of his young wife and her mother. His horror and fury at this knew no bounds – he physically attacked the two women, dragging the king from their arms and forcing him to return to the banquet.

Edwy made a valiant attempt to stand by his wife, ordering Dunstan into exile, but finally the marriage was annulled by

Archbishop Oda in 958, the ANGLO-SAXON CHRONICLE making a bare mention of the fact. Elfgifu died in suspicious circumstances at Gloucester in September 959 and the king also died there on 1 October. Oda's hostility must be accounted largely responsible for these two untimely deaths. On his own death in 961 he was succeeded as Archbishop of Canterbury by Dunstan, whose influence reached its height during the reign of Edwy's brother and successor EDGAR.

Egbert, King of Wessex (*c*.770/5–839) The son of EALHMUND, KING OF KENT, a scion of the royal house of Wessex, and probably of a Kentish princess, perhaps a daughter of ETHELBERT II, who was born about 770/5. As a young man, Egbert must have evinced aspirations that led OFFA, KING OF MERCIA and his son-in-law BEOHRTRIC, KING OF WESSEX to expel him from England in 789. He took refuge at the Frankish court of Charlemagne, and it was there apparently that he met and married his wife, Raedburh (more euphoniously written as Redburga), who is described as a daughter of the sister-in-law (*sororia*) of Charlemagne. At the period of Egbert's stay at the Frankish court, Charlemagne's wife (his third or fourth) was Fastrada, a daughter of Radulf, Count in eastern France. Raedburh's mother, therefore, may have been another daughter of Count Radulf.

Egbert returned to England and seems to have succeeded to the throne peacefully, the ANGLO-SAXON CHRONICLE recording in 802 that 'King Beohrtric passed away ... and Egbert succeeded to the Kingdom of Wessex'. The Chronicle has nothing more to say of him for over 20 years, then in 825 he fought a battle at Ellendun, near Wroughton in Wiltshire, with BEORNWULF, KING OF MERCIA in which he 'was victorious, and great slaughter was made there'. Following this victory, Egbert sent his son Ethelwulf into Kent 'with a great force, and they drove King Baldred north over Thames, and the Kentishmen submitted to him, and the men of Surrey and Sussex and Essex ... And the same year the King of the East Angles and the court turned to King Egbert as their protector and guardian against the fear of Mercian aggression; and ... the East Angles slew Beornwulf, King of the Mercians'.

Two more shadowy kings reigned in Mercia in quick succession, then in 829 Egbert 'conquered Mercia and all that was south of the Humber', thereby becoming acknowledged as the eighth BRETWALDA or

'Ruler of Britain'. He also made incursions into Northumbria and Wales, both of which submitted to him and paid tribute.

His final years were spent dealing with Danish invaders in the south and west, who allied themselves with the Cornish. The doughty old warrior put them to flight at Hingston Down. Egbert must have been well into his sixties when he died in the second half of 839 after a reign of 'thirty-seven years and seven months'. He was buried at Winchester.

Egbert was succeeded as king of Wessex by his elder son ETHELWULF. His younger son, Athelstan, who has sometimes mistakenly been named as a son of Ethelwulf, succeeded as sub-king in Kent, Essex, Sussex and Surrey, and is mentioned in 851 as successfully repelling a fleet of Danish invaders at Sandwich in Kent and capturing nine of their ships.

Egbert I, King of Kent (d.673) The son of King EORCENBERHT and his wife SEX-BURGA, who succeeded to the throne of Kent on his father's death in July 664. It was during Egbert's reign that Theodore of Tarsus was appointed Archbishop of Canterbury. Egbert died on 4 July 673 and was succeeded by his brother HLOTHERE. Egbert's sons EDRIC and WIHTRED both reigned subsequently.

Egbert I, King of Northumbria (d.873) Puppet king who was set up by the Danes in the region north of the Tyne in 867. He was driven out in 872 and died the following year.

Egbert II, King of Kent (d.c.780) Probably a son of ETHELBERT II, who began to reign about 765. Charters granted by him bear the dates 765, 778 and 779. He appears to have reigned as a dependent of OFFA OF MERCIA.

Egbert II, King of Northumbria (d.878?) Puppet king who was set up by the Danes in the region north of the Tyne in 876. He is said to have reigned two years and is the last recorded English king of Northumbria.

Egfrith, King of Mercia (d.796) The only son of King OFFA and Queen CYNETHRYTH, who was, at his father's instigation, 'consecrated king' during his father's lifetime in 787. Offa, who had succeeded a distant kinsman, doubtless thought to consolidate his position by having his son anointed and crowned during his own lifetime, a practice borrowed from the Frankish kings and derived ultimately from the Roman Empire. It was all of little avail, however, for when Egfrith suc-

ceeded his father on 29 July 796, his reign lasted for only 141 days. He died childless and probably unmarried on 17 December 796 and was succeeded by a distant kinsman COENWULF.

Egfrith, King of Northumbria (c.645–85) The son of King OSWY and his second wife EANFLED, daughter of King EDWIN, who was born about 645 and succeeded his father in February 670. He annexed the province of Lindsey in Lincolnshire and was much given to ecclesiastical disputes. Egfrith had been married at the age of 15 in 660 to ETHELDREDA, a daughter of ANNA, KING OF EAST ANGLIA and the widow of Tondbert, Ealdorman of the South Gyrwas. BEDE records that: 'Although she lived with him for twelve years, she preserved the glory of perpetual virginity.' Egfrith enlisted the aid of Bishop Wilfrid to 'persuade the queen to consummate the marriage', but it was to no avail, and eventually the king allowed her to retire to the Abbey of Coldingham, where she took the veil. She later founded the Abbey of Ely, becoming its first abbess, 'the virgin mother of many virgins vowed to God', as Bede puts it. She died in 679. Egfrith's second wife was Eormenburg. He had no children and on 20 May 685 was killed while leading an expedition north of the Firth of Forth. He was succeeded by his half-brother ALDFRITH.

Eleanor, Princess[1] (1184–1241) The first child and elder daughter of GEOFFREY, DUKE OF BRITTANY *jure uxoris* (the fourth son of HENRY II), by his wife Constance, daughter and heiress of Conan IV, Duke of Brittany, who was born in 1184. Her father was killed in a tournament at Paris in August 1186 and her mother subsequently remarried twice. At the age of nine Eleanor was betrothed to Friedrich, the son of Leopold VI, Duke of Austria, who was holding her uncle RICHARD I captive and who made the betrothal a condition for his release. In 1194 she went to Vienna with Baldwin of Bethune, one of the hostages for the payment of Richard's ransom, but Duke Leopold died suddenly and his son having 'no great inclination' for the Damsel of Bretagne, as she was known, she was allowed to return to England.

In 1203 Eleanor became *de jure* Duchess of Brittany on the death of her brother Arthur and by strict primogeniture, which was not adhered to in those days, should also have been sovereign of England instead of her uncle King JOHN. She was kept in captivity for the rest of her life and never allowed to marry. Apart from restrictions on her movements, her captivity was not onerous. 'Robes' were provided for her, as were two ladies-in-waiting in 1230, and she was given money for alms and linen for her 'work'. She was also granted the manor of Swaffham and a supply of venison from the royal forests. In 1236 Eleanor was at Gloucester Castle, but she was later removed to Bristol Castle, where she died on 10 August 1241, probably of natural causes and not starved to death as legend would have it. She was buried in St James's Priory Church, Bristol, but later removed to the Convent of Amesbury, Wiltshire.

Eleanor, Princess[2] (1306–11) The nineteenth child and eleventh and youngest daughter of EDWARD I and the only daughter by his second wife MARGARET OF FRANCE, who was born at Winchester on 4 May 1306. At a very tender age she was betrothed to Robert of Franche Comté, the only son and heir of Othon IV, Count of Burgundy. However, she died at Amesbury in 1311. She was buried either at Beaulieu Abbey in Hampshire, or, as seems more likely, in WESTMINSTER ABBEY. Her intended bridegroom died in 1316.

Eleanor, Princess, Countess of Bar (1269–98) The fourth, but eldest surviving daughter and sixth child of EDWARD I and ELEANOR OF CASTILE, who was born at WINDSOR CASTLE on or about 18 June 1269, the day on which her grandfather HENRY III gave a sum of money to the yeoman who brought him news of her birth. In 1293 Henri III, Count of Bar, came to England to seek her hand in marriage and was favourably received by her father. The couple were married at Bristol by the Archbishop of Dublin on 20 September 1293. They returned to Count Henri's dominions the following May, when a safe conduct was issued for the suite in attendance on 'the king's daughter, gone abroad'. Eleanor's only son, Edouard, who later succeeded his father, was born in 1295. She also had a daughter, Jeanne (or Joan), who later married John de Warenne, 8th Earl of Surrey, whose repeated attempts to have the marriage dissolved were unsuccessful. One of his grounds for seeking annulment was the fact that before his marriage 'he had had carnal knowledge of Mary, sister of Eleanor, Joan's mother'. The Countess of Bar has also had another daughter attributed to her, Eleanor, said to have married Llywelyn ab Owain, Lord of South Wales, but this is an invention of later genealogists seeking to

boost the claim of the TUDORS to the throne. Princess Eleanor, Countess of Bar, appears to have died at Ghent on 29 August 1298. Her body is said to have been brought back to England and buried in WESTMINSTER ABBEY. Count Henri survived her and died in about September or October 1302 (news of his death was brought to Edward I on 13 October). He was buried in Naples Cathedral, so presumably died there.

Eleanor, Princess, Countess of Pembroke and Leicester (1215–75) The third daughter and fifth and youngest child of King JOHN and ISABELLA OF ANGOULÊME, who was born in 1215. At the age of nine she was married on 23 April 1224 to William Marshall, 2nd Earl of Pembroke, who died on 15 April 1231 and was buried in the New Temple Church, London, where his effigy may still be seen. The princess remained a widow for seven years and then married secondly, in the king's private chapel at Westminster on 7 January 1239, Simon de Montfort, 2nd Earl of Leicester, the famous statesman and soldier who was killed at the battle of Evesham on 4 August 1265 and buried in Evesham Abbey. By this marriage Eleanor had five sons and one daughter. The eldest son, Henry, was killed with his father, and the other sons were forced to seek refuge abroad. The daughter, ELEANOR, PRINCESS OF WALES, became the wife of LLYWELYN III, PRINCE OF WALES. After her husband's death Eleanor retired to France. She died a nun at the Abbey of Montargis on 13 April 1275 and was buried there.

Eleanor, Princess, Duchess of Gueldres (1318–55) The elder daughter and third child of EDWARD II and ISABELLA OF FRANCE[1], who was born at Woodstock on 18 June 1318. She was married at Nijmegen in May 1332 to Rainald II, Count (later Duke) of Gueldres, Vicar-General of the Empire under the Emperor Ludwig of Bavaria. She was his second wife and according to Sandford her dowry was £15,000. Duke Rainald died at Arnhem on 12 October 1343 and Eleanor died at Deventer on 22 April 1355 and was buried there. She left two sons.

Eleanor, Princess of Wales (1252–82) The only daughter of Simon de Montfort, Earl of Leicester, and his wife ELEANOR, COUNTESS OF PEMBROKE AND LEICESTER, youngest daughter of King JOHN, who was born at Kenilworth about Michaelmas (29 September) 1252. After her father and eldest brother had been killed at the battle of

Evesham in August 1265, she accompanied her mother to France and remained with her until her death at Montargis in April 1275. She then returned to England and lived at the court of her cousin EDWARD I. She was married at Worcester on 13 October 1278 to LLYWELYN III, PRINCE OF WALES, the marriage being attended by Edward I of England and ALEXANDER III, KING OF SCOTS. The princess died in childbirth on 21 June 1282 and was buried at Llanfaes. Her only child, Gwenllian, born on 19 June 1282, became a nun at Sempringham and died there on 7 June 1337. She was not, as later alleged, an ancestor of the TUDORS.

Eleanor, Queen of Castile (1162–1214) The second daughter of HENRY II and ELEANOR OF AQUITAINE, who was born at Domfront, Normandy, on 13 October 1162. She was married at Tarragona in September 1179 to Alfonso VIII, King of Castile, who had succeeded his father Sancho III in August 1158 (at the age of three). It appears to have been a happy marriage and four sons and eight daughters were born over a period of 15 or 16 years. Alfonso died at Burgos on 6 October 1214 and the queen, stricken with grief, survived him for 25 days only, dying at Burgos on 31 October 1214. Both were buried in the monastery of Las Huelgas, near Burgos, where their fourth daughter, Constance, was abbess.

Eleanor Crosses The name given to the series of 12 crosses erected by EDWARD I at the places where the funeral cortège of his beloved first wife ELEANOR OF CASTILE halted overnight during its progress from Harby, Lincolnshire, to Westminster. Of the original 12 crosses erected at Lincoln, Grantham, Stamford, Geddington, Northampton, Stony Stratford, Woburn, Dunstable, St Albans, Waltham, West Cheap and Charing Cross, the only surviving ones are at Geddington, Northampton and Waltham Cross (though part of the Lincoln cross can also be seen and a replica now stands in the courtyard of Charing Cross Station in London). The rest were destroyed by order of the Long Parliament in 1643. Some were more elaborate than others: the Waltham Cross, for example, cost just £95, while that erected at Charing Cross cost the king no less than £650.

Eleanor of Aquitaine (c.1122–1204) The consort of HENRY II, who was the elder daughter of William X, Duke of Aquitaine, and his wife Aënor, daughter of Amaury I, Vicomte de Châtellerault. She was born at Bordeaux or Belin in about 1122 and her name is said to have been invented by adding the prefix of Ali- to that of her mother (Alienor signifying 'another Aënor'). This seems rather fanciful, however, since the name was not unknown before Eleanor's time and the Spanish equivalent, Leonor, had been frequently used in the Iberian peninsula for some centuries. In April 1137 she succeeded her father as sovereign duchess of Aquitaine and in July or August of that year was married at Bordeaux to Louis VII, King of France. She bore him two daughters, Marie and Alix, but the couple were quite incompatible. Her levity of conduct when she accompanied him to Palestine on a Crusade, where she is said to have had an affair with Saladin among others, led Louis on their return to seek an annulment on the grounds of consanguinity. The marriage was annulled on 11 March 1152.

Given her freedom, Eleanor lost no time in seducing the young Duke of Normandy and Count of Anjou, who probably saw her merely as a means of adding Aquitaine to his growing dominions and annoying his enemy the king of France. When they married at Bordeaux on 18 May 1152, Eleanor was about 30 years old and Henry just 19. A large family of five sons and three daughters was born over the next 15 years. Henry's flagrant infidelities were perhaps only to be expected from the still vigorous husband of an ageing wife, and Eleanor herself had never been noted for chasteness of conduct.

When Henry succeeded to the English throne in 1154, as Henry II, Eleanor accompanied him to England and her coronation took place at Worcester Cathedral on 25 December 1158, her advanced stage of pregnancy having prevented her coronation with the king in December 1154. After the ceremony she was moved to remark, with reference to her earlier divorce, that 'I am queen of England by the wrath of God'.

The romantic story of Henry's love for 'The Fair Rosamund', whom he installed in a bower (the 'site' of which is still pointed out in Kent), where she was discovered by Eleanor and put to death, can safely be consigned to legend. As their children grew up, though, the couple undoubtedly grew further apart and Eleanor took a delight in backing first one son and then another against his father (Henry once caught her disguised as a man, about to join their rebellious sons at the French court).

After Henry's death in 1189 Eleanor continued to lead a spritely life ill-befitting her years, and she again visited the eastern Mediterranean when she escorted BEREN-GARIA OF NAVARRE on part of the journey to marry her son RICHARD I. Eleanor lived to see her favourite son JOHN ascend the throne, and when she died at Fontevraud on 31 March or 1 April 1204 she was about 82, an age that no other queen consort was to attain or exceed for over 700 years. She was buried in the abbey church at Fontevraud, where her monumental effigy is still preserved.

Eleanor of Castile (1241–90) The first consort of EDWARD I, who was the daughter of (Saint) Fernando III, King of Castile and Leon, and his second wife Jeanne de Dammartin, in her own right Countess of Ponthieu. She was born in Castile towards the end of 1241 as recent meticulous research has shown. She was, therefore, about 13 years old when married to the 15-year-old Edward of Westminster at Las Huelgas in October 1254.

Edward and Eleanor were to remain inseparable throughout their married life. In 1270 she accompanied him on a Crusade, in the course of which she is said to have sucked the poison from Edward's wounded arm after an assassination attempt with a poisoned dagger (more prosaic sources, though, say that the distraught queen was ordered out of the sickroom by the surgeon). Two of Eleanor's children were born in the Holy Land, the younger being JOAN OF ACRE (so called from her birthplace).

Edward's accession to the throne in November 1272 brought him and Eleanor back to England and they were crowned together at WESTMINSTER ABBEY on 19 August 1274, the first king and queen since the conquest to take part in a double ceremony.

The names and number of Eleanor's children have been the cause of much confusion and controversy. John Carmi Parsons (the researcher who established Eleanor's year of birth) lists them as follows:

1. A daughter, born on 29 May in a year before 1287. She was either stillborn or died very young and was buried in the Dominican Priory at Bordeaux. The indications are that she was the first child and born prematurely in 1255.
2. Katherine, born probably in 1261 or 1262 and died on 5 September 1264, being buried in Westminster Abbey.
3. Joan, born in January 1265 and died shortly before 7 September 1265, being buried in Westminster Abbey.
4. John, born at Windsor on 13 or 14 July 1266 and died at Wallingford on 3 August 1271, being buried in Westminster Abbey.
5. Henry, born shortly before 6 May 1268 and died at Guildford between 14 and 17 October 1274, being buried in Westminster Abbey.
6. ELEANOR, COUNTESS OF BAR, born at Windsor about 18 June 1269.
7. A daughter, born at Acre in Palestine in 1271 and died there in infancy.
8. JOAN OF ACRE, born at Acre in 1272.
9. ALFONSO, born at Bayonne, Gascony, on 23 or 24 November 1273. Confusion over his foreign name has led some historians to credit Edward and Eleanor with a daughter Alice.
10. MARGARET, DUCHESS OF BRABANT, born at Windsor probably on 15 March 1275.
11. BERENGARIA, born at Kempton, Middlesex, on 1 May 1276 and dead by 27 June 1278.
12. A daughter, born at Westminster on or shortly after 3 January 1278 and died at birth.
13. Mary, later a nun at Amesbury, born at Woodstock on 11 or 12 March 1279.
14. Possibly a son, born in 1280 or 1281 and died in infancy.
15. ELIZABETH, COUNTESS OF HOLLAND AND HEREFORD, born at Rhuddlan in Wales about 7 August 1282.
16. Edward, later EDWARD II, born at Caernarfon on 25 April 1284.

In 1290 news of the death of Queen MARGARET OF SCOTLAND, 'The Maid of Norway', sent Edward hastening north, leaving the queen to follow at a more leisurely pace. She had reached Lincolnshire when she fell ill with a fever and was lodged at Harby, near Lincoln, in the house of one Master Weston. She grew worse and messengers were sent to recall the king, but before he arrived Eleanor had died. Edward's grief was expressed by the erection of 12 ELEANOR CROSSES at the places where the queen's body rested overnight on its journey to London. Eleanor lies at the feet of her father-in-law HENRY III and her effigy manages to convey something of the serenity and beauty which so captivated her husband.

It is said, incidentally, that to English ears Eleanor's Spanish title of Infanta of Castile sounded so strange that it beame corrupted in speech to 'Elephant and Castle', giving rise to the district of south London and the many inn signs of that name.

Eleanor of Provence (c.1223–91) The consort of HENRY III, who was the second of the four beautiful daughters of Raymond Berenger V, Count of Provence, by his wife Beatrice, daughter of Tommaso I, Count of Savoy. She was born at Aix-en-Provence about 1223 and brought up at her father's court, renowned for its patronage of the troubadors. All the count's daughters made brilliant marriages: Marguerite to St Louis IX, King of France; Eleanor to Henry III; Sanchia to Henry's brother Richard, Earl of CORNWALL, King of the Romans; and Beatrice to Charles of Anjou, King of Naples.

Henry III had first negotiated for the hand of Joan, Countess of Ponthieu, whose daughter ELEANOR OF CASTILE was later to become the wife of his son Edward (*see* EDWARD I). However, having heard from his brother Richard of the beauty and vivacity of the Provençal ladies, he cancelled his suit and made proposals for the hand of Eleanor, which were finally accepted after some haggling about her dower. This was necessarily limited because Henry's mother was still alive and in full possession of her jointure, which could be dowered to Eleanor only in reversion.

Eleanor journeyed through France, visiting the court of her sister Queen Marguerite on the way, landed at Dover, and proceeded to Canterbury where she was married to the king by Edmund Rich on 4 January 1236. Sixteen days later she was crowned at WESTMINSTER ABBEY. Henry spared no expense in having the Palace of Westminster refurbished for his young queen, installing refinements of plumbing, window-glazing and a standard of comfort hitherto unknown in England. Instructions remain for chambers in the Palace to 'be painted a good green colour, like a curtain'. The queen's coronation was an occasion of great display and a large equestrian procession escorted the sovereigns from the Tower to Westminster in a splendid cavalcade.

Henry was a loving and faithful husband and the couple's married life remained a completely happy one. However, the queen's popularity suffered when her Savoyard uncles visited England and were generously entertained, the king extracting money for that purpose from the Jews with threats of expulsion. The marriage of the queen's sister Sanchia to the king's brother Richard was another occasion of great display, for which the Jews were again obliged to furnish funds.

On the death of Edmund Rich in 1240, Eleanor procured the Archbishopric of Canterbury for her uncle, Boniface of Savoy, writing to the pope herself to assure the nomination. Boniface's attempts to institute a visitation of the province of Canterbury were strongly resented, and there was an unseemly brawl when he visited St Bartholomew's Priory in the diocese of London and was told by the monks that they would accept a visitation only from their own bishop. Boniface lost his temper, personally assaulted the sub-prior, and encouraged his attendants to beat the monks savagely. The king refused to listen to the monks' complaint and the people of London chased Boniface into Lambeth Palace, where he was forced to lie low until they had calmed down.

The queen's extravagances continued to excite the hostility of Londoners for many years and, even after she received the reversion of the dower lands on the death of ISABELLA OF ANGOULÊME in 1240, she and Henry still found it necessary to raise funds by every possible means. In 1252, when Henry went to France to deal with a revolt in Gascony, Eleanor was constituted joint-regent with her brother-in-law Richard. She attempted to extract the payment of AURUM REGINAE (queen-gold), a right to every tenth mark paid to the king for various purposes, from her old enemies the citizens of London, and had the sheriffs committed to prison on their refusal to pay.

In the words of Agnes Strickland, Eleanor 'loved power well, but pleasure better', and in 1254 she accompanied her son Edward to Spain in order to take part in the festivities planned to celebrate his marriage to the Infanta of Castile. On the way back, Henry, Eleanor and the young couple were invited to stay at the French court by Eleanor's sister and brother-in-law. After a long and pleasant sojourn the king and queen finally returned to England in January 1255 after an absence of nearly a year.

Throughout the civil war against Simon de Montfort and the barons Eleanor was active in support of her husband and son, raising money on her jewellery to aid their cause. 'This noble virago,' as Matthew of Westminster termed her, was in France when the victory of Evesham was won and rejoined her husband and son as soon as a favourable wind would allow.

On Henry III's death Eleanor exercised the regency until her son Edward returned. She had the sorrow of losing her daughters, the Queen of Scots and the Countess of Richmond, who both died in 1275. In 1280 she retired to the Benedictine convent of Amesbury, where she intended to take the veil – not, however, until the pope had given her permission to retain her dower. This being finally granted, she was professed a nun and assumed the religious habit on 7 July 1284.

Eleanor continued to take an interest in

the affairs of her widely dispersed family and lived on at Amesbury until her death after a short illness on 24 June 1291, with her son the king at her bedside. She was buried in the convent church at Amesbury, her heart being buried in the church of the Friars Minor (Minories) in London. Eleanor was not a very sympathetic character, being strong-willed, avaricious and pleasure-loving, but she was a loyal wife and mother, and her religious vocation appears to have been genuine.

Elfgifu or **Elfgiva** The name of several Anglo-Saxon queens and princesses, notice of whom will be found under the entries of their respective husbands or fathers, there being insufficient material in most cases to warrant separate entries.

Elfleda (d. before 920) The second wife of EDWARD THE ELDER (to whom she bore eight children), who was the daughter of Ealdorman Ethelhelm. She had two sons: Elfward, who died at Oxford very soon after his father on 2 August 925 and was buried at Winchester; and Edwin, who was drowned in the English Channel in 933 and buried at St Bertin's Abbey, St Omer. Elfleda also had six daughters: Eadfled, a nun at Wilton; Eadgifu (Ogive), who married first, probably in 918, as his second wife Charles III the Simple, King of France (died 7 October 929), and had one son, and secondly, Herbert (or Heribert), Count of Meaux and of Troyes, and had further issue, dying after 951 and being buried in the church of St Médard at Soissons; Ethelhild, a nun at Wilton; Eadhild, who married in 926, as his first wife, Hugues the Great, Duke of France and Count of Paris, and died without issue before 938; Eadgyth (Edith), who married in 930, as his first wife, Otto I, Holy Roman Emperor and Duke of Saxony, and died on 26 January 946 or 947, leaving issue; and Elfgifu (Adiva), who married 'some king not far from the Jupiter Mountains' (i.e. the Alps), who has been identified on numismatic evidence as possibly being Boleslav II, Duke of Bohemia, although there are chronological difficulties attached to this identification.

Elfrida, Queen of England (c.945–1000) The second wife of King EDGAR, who was the daughter of Ordgar, Ealdorman of Devon, and was born about 945. Edgar is said to have fallen in love with her when she was a young girl, but her father had arranged a marriage for her with Ethelwold, Ealdorman of EAST ANGLIA, Edgar's foster-brother. Edgar's first wife Ethelfled died within a year of their marriage and Ethelwold's death following soon thereafter, caused suspicion to fall on the king and Elfrida. They were married in around 964, and on 11 May 973 Elfrida was crowned with Edgar at Bath, the first Anglo-Saxon queen to be acknowledged as such since Judith, the Frankish second wife of King ETHELWULF. The couple had two sons, Edmund, who died young in 971 and was buried at Romsey Abbey, and Ethelred (see ETHELRED II), later to become king.

Edgar died in July 975, and his widow and her son took up their residence at Corfe Castle, Dorset. In March 979 they were visited there by Elfrida's stepson and Ethelred's half-brother King EDWARD THE MARTYR, who was on a hunting expedition. The queen, in the best tradition of wicked stepmothers, handed the king a stirrup cup and as he drank from it signalled to one of her servants to stab him in the back. His horse bolted and he was dragged across the ground with one foot caught in a stirrup, dying of his injuries soon afterwards. Elfrida thus achieved her ambition of seeing her son become king but was thwarted by St Dunstan of any hopes she might have had of becoming regent. Apparently overtaken by remorse, she founded the Benedictine priory of Wherwell in Hampshire to spend the rest of her life in prayer and contemplation as a nun. She died there on 17 November 1000.

Elfrida's story has been greatly embellished by the accretion of later legend, which relates that the fame of her great beauty having reached Edgar's ears, he sent his foster-brother to see her and report on it to him. Ethelwold fell in love with her himself, told the king she was not without blemish and married her. When Edgar and later Elfrida discovered this deception they connived to do away with Ethelwold and he was despatched on a mission where he was waylaid and murdered, in some versions by the king himself, on the spot where Elfrida later built the priory of Wherwell in expiation. Ethelwold and Elfrida are said to have had a son, Edgar, to whom the king stood godfather, and the spiritual relationship created thereby is said to have been the chief cause of Dunstan's objection to their marriage.

Elizabeth, Princess[1] (1492–5) The second daughter and fourth child of HENRY VII and ELIZABETH OF YORK, who was born on 2 July 1492, probably at the Palace of Westminster. She appears to have suffered some wasting disease as her death was attributed to 'atrophy'. She died at Eltham in Kent on 14 September 1495 and was buried in WESTMINSTER ABBEY near the shrine of EDWARD THE CONFESSOR. Of her 'small altar-tomb of black marble' with her effigy 'of copper gilt (since stolen away)' there is now no trace.

Elizabeth, Princess[2] *see* ELIZABETH I, QUEEN OF ENGLAND.

Elizabeth, Princess[3] (1635–50) The second daughter and fifth child of CHARLES I and HENRIETTA MARIA, who was born at ST JAMES'S PALACE on 29 December 1635. From the age of seven onwards she and her brother Henry (*see* GLOUCESTER, HENRY, DUKE OF) were held prisoners of the Parliamentarians. The princess spent her captivity in studying languages and theology. The two children were allowed to take leave of their father before his execution in January 1649 and Elizabeth wrote a touching account of the occasion. Her father gave her a Bible, telling her it had 'been his constant companion and greatest comfort through all his sorrows, and he hoped it would be hers'. After their father's death the children were imprisoned in Carisbrooke Castle, Isle of Wight, and there Elizabeth died, probably of consumption, in the afternoon of Sunday, 8 September 1650 with her head resting on her father's Bible. She was buried in St Thomas's Church, Newport, on 24 September.

More than two centuries later, Queen VICTORIA had a handsome monument erected to her memory, 'a token of respect for her virtues and sympathy for her misfortunes'. A rubbing of the princess's coffin lid is displayed at Carisbrooke Castle.

Elizabeth, Princess[4] *see* ELIZABETH II, QUEEN OF GREAT BRITAIN.

Elizabeth, Princess, Countess of Holland, Hereford and Essex (1282–1316) The youngest daughter of EDWARD I and his first wife ELEANOR OF CASTILE, who was born at Rhuddlan Castle in Wales on or about 7 August 1282. She was married first, at Ipswich on 8 January 1297, to John I, Count of Holland and Zeeland. According to Sandford, her dower was £8000 per annum. There were no children of this marriage and the count died at Haarlem on 10 November 1299. His widow returned to England and married secondly, at Westminster on 14 November 1302, Humphrey de Bohun, 4th Earl of Hereford and Essex and Constable of England. This marriage produced six sons

and four daughters. Elizabeth died at Quendon, Essex, on 5 May 1316 in childbirth with her last child, Isabel, who did not survive. She was buried at Walden Priory on 23 May. Her husband survived her and was killed at Boroughbridge on 16 March 1322. He was buried in the church of the Friars Preachers at York, although by his will he had requested to be buried at Walden near his wife.

Elizabeth, Princess, Landgravine of Hesse-Homburg (1770–1840) The third daughter and seventh child of GEORGE III and Queen CHARLOTTE, who was born at the Queen's House, St James's (now BUCKINGHAM PALACE) on 22 May 1770, between eight and nine o'clock in the morning. She was baptized by the Archbishop of Canterbury in the Great Council Chamber of ST JAMES'S PALACE on 17 June following, her godparents being her father's cousins the Crown Princess of Sweden and the Princess of Nassau-Weilburg and the Hereditary Prince of Hesse-Cassel (all represented by proxies).

Princess Elizabeth grew up to be in many ways the most attractive of her parents' daughters. She was good-humoured, highspirited, intelligent and a gifted artist and musician. She suffered much illness in her youth, but was always inclined to be stout. Her health is said to have improved when she took up riding. In 1805 the princess was given a cottage at Old Windsor, 'where she would sometimes in summer give little fêtes'. She founded a society at Windsor to provide marriage portions for poor but virtuous girls in 1808.

After the death of Princess AMELIA in 1810 had precipitated George III's final lapse into dementia, Princess Elizabeth became a close companion to her mother Queen Charlotte, often acting as her secretary. She accompanied her on a visit to Bath in 1817, where they received the news of the death of Princess CHARLOTTE OF WALES and at once returned to Windsor. The following year a late romance blossomed for the princess and she accepted the hand of the Hereditary Prince Friedrich Joseph Ludwig Karl August of Hesse-Homburg, who was her senior by almost a year, having been born at Homburg on 30 July 1769. He was very stout like his bride and of unprepossessing appearance, but they were 'delighted' with each other according to a contemporary. The marriage took place at the Queen's House on 7 April 1818 and Elizabeth, although nearly 48, was decked out like a young bride. The couple passed the first few days of their honeymoon at the Regent's Cottage, Windsor, and then at Brighton, whence they set out for Frankfurt, via Calais and Brussels.

In 1820 Princess Elizabeth's husband succeeded his father as reigning Landgrave of Hesse-Homburg. His dominions, an English diarist noted contemptuously, 'are in extent about the size of Windsor Park, and he has about 32 soldiers; but he is a Prince'. The Landgravine superintended the planting and laying out of an English garden in the grounds of the old Schloss at Homburg. Always generously proportioned, she grew even stouter with age, and in 1823 a visitor reported 'that when one had once made a journey round the Princess, one had had walking enough for one day; also it was said that the Princess had great difficulty in finding a shawl that reached as far as her shoulders – that it should cover any part of her chest was not expected from a shawl'. Princess Elizabeth's brothers and sisters referred to her affectionately as 'Betty Humbug'.

Her husband died at Homburg on 2 April 1829 and the widowed Landgravine took up residence in Hanover. She visited England for the last time in 1831 and died at Frankfurt-am-Main on 10 January 1840. She was buried in the mausoleum of the landgraves at Homburg. In England the deep court mourning occasioned by her death was temporarily suspended for a few days to allow the festivities surrounding the celebration of the marriage of her niece Queen VICTORIA.

Elizabeth, Princess, Queen of Bohemia (1596–1662) The eldest daughter and second child of JAMES I, KING OF ENGLAND and ANNE OF DENMARK, who was born at DUNFERMLINE (not at Falkland Palace as often stated) on 19 August 1596 and baptized in the Chapel Royal at Holyrood on 28 December 1596, the City of Edinburgh, represented by the Provost and Bailies, standing sponsor.

Following her father's accession to the English throne in 1603, Elizabeth accompanied her mother and brother Henry (*see* HENRY, PRINCE OF WALES) to London. Part of the intention of the GUNPOWDER PLOT in 1605, had it succeeded in its objective of killing the king, was to seize the person of Princess Elizabeth and proclaim her queen as Elizabeth II. She had been staying at Combe Abbey, but her attendants, getting wind of the plot, had the foresight to

remove her to Coventry for safety. Elizabeth experienced great sorrow at the death of her brother Henry, Prince of Wales in November 1612. She was not allowed to see him for fear of 'contagion' and his last words are said to have been, 'Where is my dear sister?'

In February 1613, the princess was married in the Chapel Royal at Whitehall to Friedrich V, Elector Palatine of the Rhine. In August 1619 he was elected king of Bohemia and crowned at Prague on 4 November 1619. Elizabeth, who was in a very advanced state of pregnancy, was crowned there two days later (6 November) and scandalized the Calvinist clergy who officiated by her insistence on being anointed as her father and mother had been at their coronation. The couple's reign in Bohemia was very short lived, however, and they were soon forced to fly from Prague, becoming known as the 'Winter King and Queen'. In January 1621 Friedrich was placed under the ban of the Empire at the Diet held at Regensburg and forced to give up the Palatinate also. The couple and their growing family sought refuge at The Hague where the last eight of their 13 children were born. Friedrich died at Mainz on 29 November 1632, aged 36, and was buried first in the Dom-Kirche at Frankenthal and later removed to Sedan.

Elizabeth's charm earned her the nickname of 'Queen of Hearts' and she was much extolled by the poets and writers of the day. She raised a small army on behalf of her eldest surviving son, Karl Ludwig, to whom the dignity of Elector Palatine was finally restored in 1648, but he showed his gratitude by allowing her to remain dependent on Dutch generosity. She found a champion in the person of William Craven, 1st Baron Craven of Hampsted Marshal (later 1st and last Earl of Craven), who contributed a great deal to her finances. He was rumoured to be her lover and even her husband, but there appears to be no foundation for such a belief. On the restoration of her nephew CHARLES II, Elizabeth returned to England and was granted a pension of £10,000 a year by Parliament. Samuel Pepys recorded going to see her at The Hague on 17 May 1660, while preparing for the Restoration. 'She seems a very debonaire, but plain lady', was his comment.

On her return to England, Lord Craven placed his house in Drury Lane at her disposal and she resided there until within five days of her death, when she removed to Leicester House on the north side of the present Leicester Square. She fell ill with bronchitis and died there in the evening of 12 February 1662. She was buried beside her brother Henry, Prince of Wales, in Henry VII's Chapel at WESTMINSTER ABBEY. Most of her jewellery was bequeathed to her favourite son Prince RUPERT. Her youngest daughter, Sophia (see SOPHIA, ELECTRESS OF HANOVER), was the mother of GEORGE I.

Elizabeth I, Queen of England (1533–1603)

The only daughter of HENRY VIII and his second wife ANNE BOLEYN, who was born at GREENWICH PALACE between three and four o'clock in the afternoon on Sunday 7 September 1533. The birth was a bitter disappointment to her father, who had anticipated the birth of a son to such an extent that the documents that had been prepared for despatch to foreign courts to announce the event allowed no room for the word 'princess' to be written instead of 'prince' and only one final 's' could be squeezed in. Nevertheless, Henry had his daughter proclaimed heiress-presumptive to the crown, displacing her elder half-sister Mary (later MARY I), and she was christened with great pomp in the Grey Friars' Church at Greenwich. The Bishop of London officiated and the godparents were Thomas Cranmer, Archbishop of Canterbury, the Dowager Duchess of Norfolk and the Marchioness of Dorset. Fortunately, the baby was a strong, healthy child.

Anne Boleyn's disgrace and execution led to Elizabeth being declared illegitimate by Act of Parliament and deprived of her place in the succession before she was three years old. For some years she was kept away from court, and was provided with 'neither gown, nor kirtle, nor petticoat, nor no manner of linen'. A later Act reinstated her and the kindness of her stepmother CATHERINE PARR brought her back to court, where she shared the tutors of her half-brother Edward (later EDWARD VI), becoming proficient in Latin, French, Italian (in which she was coached by Castiglione) and some Greek. She also had some leanings towards the Protestant faith, although she was by no means committed at this time.

In July 1553 Elizabeth entered London at Mary's side and attended her coronation in October in the company of her one-time stepmother ANNE OF CLEVES. In the following year she refused to take part in Sir Thomas Wyatt's rebellion but was nevertheless, at the instigation of Stephen Gardiner, imprisoned in the TOWER OF LONDON. As she landed at the Tower's Traitor's Gate, she announced firmly, 'Here lands as true a subject, being prisoner, as ever landed at these stairs.' She was later removed to Woodstock and thence to HATFIELD HOUSE, Hertfordshire. It was there that she received the news of Mary's death and her own accession, by tradition while sitting reading under a tree in the grounds of Hatfield House (although it seems unlikely that she would have been thus engaged in the middle of an English November). 'This is the Lord's doing and it is marvellous in our eyes' was the scriptural quotation with which she greeted the news.

Elizabeth's entry into London occasioned great popular rejoicing. Like her father, she loved display and magnificence of dress and soon proved she could stir the people by her rhetoric and proud, masterful manner. She took up residence at RICHMOND PALACE, the fittings of which included one of the first working water closets in England.

Elizabeth's coronation took place at WESTMINSTER ABBEY on 15 January 1559 (a date settled on after Elizabeth consulted Dr John Dee, the famous astrologer, for the most propitious date for the event). The see of Canterbury had been vacant since the death of Cardinal Pole, and the only bishop who could be found to perform the ceremony was Owen Oglethorpe, Bishop of Carlisle. At her anointing the queen complained that the oil used was 'grease and smelled ill' and expressed further displeasure when the bishop elevated the host at the consecration (she withdrew to a private pew while this rite was enacted). One highlight of the festivities was the burning of a wicker effigy of the Pope, stuffed with cats. Elizabeth had decided to re-establish the Protestant faith, and set about doing so with dogged resolution. Successive popes were to thunder against her to no avail, and it was quite useless for Pius V to excommunicate her in 1570 and declare her subjects absolved of their allegiance to her. Pope Sixtus V, indeed, was so impressed with Elizabeth's firmness of purpose he exclaimed: 'What a valiant woman … it is a pity that Elizabeth and I cannot marry: our children would have ruled the whole world.'

Elizabeth's reign is now recalled as a golden age in English history. It was not without its moments of controversy, however, with repeated clashes with Spain and dissension within her own court. One deed that was felt to reflect especially poorly upon her was the execution of her cousin MARY, QUEEN OF SCOTS in 1587 after 18 years' captivity in England. In Elizabeth's defence, however, it is impossible to deny that Mary did represent a threat and was the hope of the Catholic party that intrigued on her behalf (intrigues that culminated in the Babington Plot of 1586 to kill Elizabeth and put Mary on the throne). Certainly, Elizabeth took no pleasure in ordering the execution, and when news of the queen's death reached London 'her countenance changed, her words faltered, and with excessive sorrow she was in a manner astonished, in so much as she gave herself over to grief, putting herself into mourning weeds and shedding abundance of tears'.

Drake's defeat of the Spanish Armada in the following year was the crowning glory of Elizabeth's reign and consolidated her reputation as a strong monarch – as emphasized by herself in one of her most famous addresses in 1588:

I know I have but the body of a weak and feeble woman; but I have the heart and stomach of a King, and a King of England too.

This victory was made possible by the maritime experience of England's seamen, who had been encouraged by their queen to seek new wealth overseas. The Elizabethan Age was one of adventure and discovery, Hawkins, Drake, Raleigh and the Gilberts all extending England's possessions in the Americas. The colony of Virginia was founded and named after the 'Virgin Queen' and the East India Company also had its beginnings. By way of contrast, Elizabeth herself never ventured over the Channel, and, indeed, never visited Ireland, Wales or Scotland (though she toured extensively with her court on costly progresses through England). It was a flourishing age for literature, too, and produced Shakespeare, Spenser, Sidney, Bacon, Marlowe and many others.

Elizabeth was vain of her appearance and loved to dress richly with many jewels about her person. She refused to admit to ageing and in later life wore a huge red wig and employed many cosmetics. She loved dancing and the company of young men, who flattered her ego and dubbed her 'Gloriana'. Elizabeth shrewdly saw quite early on that her strength lay in her single state and she cleverly played her many suitors from home and abroad (among them the French heir the Duke of Alençon, Henry of Navarre and PHILIP II of Spain) until she was well past middle age. One device employed with the dwarfish Duke of Alençon (whom Elizabeth called her 'little frog') was to accept his proposal of marriage and then to stipulate marriage conditions that were certain to be refused, thus preventing any loss of face on either side. Fostering the image of the semi-divine Virgin Queen, she repeatedly declared the English people to be her only spouse. She was heard to joke, 'I should call the wedding-ring the yoke-ring'.

Elizabeth called Parliament only 13 times in 44 years, but she was well served by her advisers the Cecils, Sir Nicholas Bacon and Francis Walsingham and was a loyal mistress to those who served her loyally (though courtiers found her mean with her money later in life). Some found her distinctly masculine in her behaviour, as noted in the *Dictionary of National Biography*: 'She swore, she spat upon a courtier's coat when it did not please her taste, she beat her gentlewomen soundly, she kissed whom she pleased, she gave Essex a good stinging blow on the face, she called the members of her privy council by all sorts of nicknames.'

Her greatest weakness was her fondness for such unworthy, albeit handsome, favourites as Robert Dudley, Earl of Leicester and Robert Devereux, 2nd Earl of Essex, which provoked much scandalous speculation. When, for instance, Dudley's wife Amy Robsart died in 1560, apparently after falling downstairs, the gossips were even heard to suggest she had been murdered so that Dudley would be free to marry the queen. Others claimed that Elizabeth had borne Dudley a child (though such scandalmongers risked having their ears cut off for spreading such rumours if brought before the authorities). It was said that Elizabeth had given Essex, meanwhile, a ring, which she told him to send to her if he ever needed her forgiveness for any wrong – when he was subsequently placed under sentence of death he is reputed to have sent the ring to her, confident of a pardon, but it was intercepted by an enemy, and he was executed. (Legend has it that for the rest of her life the heartbroken queen would burst into tears whenever his name was mentioned.) Another favourite was Sir Walter Raleigh, their relationship developing after the young Raleigh, hoping for advancement, scratched on a window-pane at court, 'Fain would I climb, but that I fear to fall' – to which the queen appended the celebrated rejoinder, 'If thy heart fail thee, climb then not at all.'

Elizabeth enjoyed generally good health, although she had black teeth (a consequence of her fondness for sugar) and had to powder her face white after contracting near-fatal smallpox in 1562 (she attempted to reduce the resultant scarring by wiping her own urine on her skin). She recovered and lived another 41 years, determined to conceal from the world the fact that she was ageing (she had all the mirrors in her palace removed so that she would not have to look at her own reflection). In the middle of January 1603, Elizabeth, who at 69 had attained a greater age than that reached by any of her predecessors, was suffering from a cold when she removed from Whitehall to Richmond Palace. She recovered, but fell ill again at the end of February with severe tonsilitis, which was relieved when a small abscess broke. She had no appetite, however, and complained of bad dreams. On 18 March she became very ill again, but refused to take to her bed, lying instead on a heap of pillows piled on the floor. When Cecil urged her to go to bed she showed a last flash of her great spirit in her reply, 'Little man, little man, "must" is not a word to use to princes'. Elizabeth died at three o'clock in the morning on Wednesday 24 March 1603. A messenger at once set out for Scotland to convey the news of his accession to the new king, JAMES I.

Elizabeth was buried in Westminster Abbey in the same vault as her half-sister Mary I. The tomb erected above it bears Elizabeth's effigy only, but the following epitaph was inscribed by order of James I: *Regno Consortes et Urna, Hic obdormimus Elizabetha et Maria Sorores In Spe Resurrectionis* (Consorts both in Throne and Grave, here rest we two sisters, Elizabeth and Mary, in hope of our resurrection).

Elizabeth II, Queen of Great Britain

(1926–) The elder daughter of GEORGE VI and Queen ELIZABETH THE QUEEN MOTHER, who was born at 17 Bruton Street, London W1 (the London residence of her maternal grandparents the Earl and Countess of Strathmore), at 2.40 am on 21 April 1926, and baptized Elizabeth Alexandra Mary. At the time of her birth her parents were Duke and Duchess of York and she became third in line of succession to the throne. She received a private education, under the guidance of her governess Marion Crawford (*see* CRAWFIE), but, though intelligent and able, made few pretensions to being an intellectual and preferred such pursuits as riding and amateur drama. On her father's accession on the abdication of his brother EDWARD VIII in December 1936 (*see* ABDICATION CRISIS), she became heiress presumptive to the throne at the age of 10,

moving with her family to their new home, BUCKINGHAM PALACE. She attended her parents' coronation in the following May.

The greater part of the war years were spent at WINDSOR CASTLE with her younger sister Princess Margaret (*see* MARGARET, PRINCESS, COUNTESS OF SNOWDON), her father refusing her permission to contribute to the war effort by training as a nurse, because of her youth. However, towards the end of the conflict she was permitted to join the ATS (Auxiliary Territorial Service) and learned how to drive various kinds of heavy transport. On the last day of her ATS course, her father admonished her for being unable to restart the engine of a stalled vehicle (only to reveal that he had removed the distributor to tease her). When VE Day arrived in 1945, the princesses were allowed to mingle (largely unrecognized) with the celebrating crowds outside Buckingham Palace, and Elizabeth herself later recalled knocking off a policeman's helmet during the general rejoicing.

Among her first acts as a counsellor of state (which she became in 1944) were the signing of several Acts of Parliament and the granting of a reprieve for a murderer. In 1947 the princesses accompanied their parents on a South African tour, in the course of which Princess Elizabeth celebrated her 21st birthday at Cape Town, where she made a moving broadcast to the Commonwealth in which she pledged her whole life to its service.

Soon after the royal family's return to England, the princess's engagement to Lieutenant Philip Mountbatten, RN, was announced. He had been born Prince Philip of Greece and Denmark, but had spent almost all his life in England under the guardianship of his maternal uncles, the 2nd Marquess of Milford Haven and Lord Louis Mountbatten (later Earl MOUNTBATTEN OF BURMA). On naturalization as a British subject he had chosen to take their surname, which their father had adopted in 1917 as an anglicization of the German BATTENBERG. The young couple were third cousins, both being great-great-grandchildren of Queen VICTORIA, and their wedding at WESTMINSTER ABBEY on 20 November 1947 was the first occasion to see a relaxation of the wartime austerity still prevailing. The bridegroom received the title of Duke of EDINBURGH on his wedding day and the qualification of Royal Highness, which he had relinquished on his naturalization. In due course, the couple had four children, CHARLES, PRINCE OF WALES, ANNE,

PRINCESS ROYAL, Andrew, Duke of YORK and Prince EDWARD.

George VI marked the 600th anniversary of the founding of the Order of the GARTER on St George's Day 23 April 1948 by conferring it on his elder daughter, who thus joined her mother and grandmother, and Queen Wilhelmina of the Netherlands, as a Lady of the Order, an honour unprecedented since the Middle Ages, when robes of the Order used to be provided for most of the ladies of the royal family.

Princess Elizabeth was recalled from Kenya, where she was about to start a world tour, in February 1952, when the death of her father brought her to the throne as Elizabeth II, aged 25 (the same age at which her predecessor ELIZABETH I acceded). The news was brought to her as she sat in a wild fig tree near Treetops Hotel watching elephants and other animals at a waterhole (she could thus claim to be the only monarch to accede to the English throne while up a tree). She was crowned at Westminster Abbey on 2 June 1953 before a huge television audience, having insisted against the advice of her Cabinet that the event be televised so that as many of her people as possible could participate. Highlights of the ceremony included views of her riding in the splendid golden coronation coach. The oil with which she was anointed was specially formulated according to the ingredients of that used as far back as the coronation of CHARLES I.

During the course of her lengthy reign, the queen has set about presenting herself as everything a monarch should be in the 20th century, winning praise for her dignified acceptance of her duties and responsibilities and making efforts to communicate with her subjects on a regular basis (hence her popular broadcast Christmas messages, first televised in 1957), while never reducing the mystique of royalty by becoming too familiar. As head of the Commonwealth she has undertaken strenuous tours all over the world with unflagging enthusiasm. A visit to Australia and New Zealand in 1970 was especially successful for its introduction of the 'royal walkabout', in which the queen adopted a new approach to the crowds who turned up to see her, actually pausing now and then to exchange a few words with her admirers and accept flowers and small presents, despite the obvious security risks.

Considered politically astute, she has impressed all the prime ministers with whom she has come into contact, from Winston Churchill – who found her as a child to have 'an air of authority and reflectiveness astonishing in an infant' – to Harold Wilson (though her relations with Margaret Thatcher were reportedly somewhat strained). Labour prime minister James Callaghan, though, observed that 'What one gets is friendliness but not friendship'.

The royal couple celebrated their silver wedding in 1972, an occasion made memorable by a speech at Guildhall in which the queen explained that for once she would not be using the royal 'we': 'I think everyone will concede that today, of all occasions, I should begin my speech with "My husband and I"'. The phrase 'my husband and I' had already become something of a royal catchphrase.

The occasion of the Queen's Silver Jubilee in 1977 saw many spontaneous demonstrations of loyalty and affection from all classes and ages, with huge crowds lining the processional route from Buckingham Palace to St Paul's Cathedral and many thousands attending street parties and other celebrations. Similar enthusiasm, on a somewhat reduced scale, was to mark the celebration of her 60th birthday in April 1986. In 1981, however, she was the object of more hostile attention, when a disenchanted 17-year-old youth, Marcus Sergeant, fired six blank shots at her while she was riding her horse Burmese to Trooping the Colour. Though riding sidesaddle, the queen successfully kept her seat and the youth was quickly arrested. Similarly unwelcome was the intrusion of 35-year-old Michael Fagan on 9 July 1982, when he successfully infiltrated the security system at Buckingham Palace and actually confronted the startled queen in her bedroom (she managed to keep him talking until help arrived).

The accumulation of problems that gathered around the royal family in the late 1980s and 1990s, especially the marriage difficulties of the Prince of Wales and his siblings, the disastrous fire at Windsor Castle and repeated invasions of privacy by the world's press, have proved a challenge to the monarchy and have sometimes threatened the high public standing of the institution, in spite of the esteem in which Elizabeth herself continues almost universally to be held (*see* ANNUS HORRIBILIS). In an attempt to mollify some critics, the queen – said to be the richest woman in the world – agreed, among other measures, to pay income tax and urged her eldest son to reach a speedy resolution of his marital difficulties, so that any damage done to the image of the royal family might be limited.

Tributes to the queen's remarkable success as monarch for well over 40 years have been many and various. Among the more informal, but nonetheless sincere, of these was a song that proved a considerable hit around the time of the coronation:

> Everybody's mad about ya
> Where would Britannia be without ya?
> Sailing in the yacht Britannia
> Nowhere in the world would ban ya.
> Queenie Baby, I'm not foolin',
> Only you could do the ruling,
> In your own sweet royal way.

Elizabeth Caroline of Wales, Princess (1740–59) The second daughter and fourth child of FREDERICK LOUIS, PRINCE OF WALES and Augusta of Saxe-Gotha (*see* AUGUSTA, PRINCESS OF WALES), who was born at Norfolk House, St James's Square, London, at seven o'clock in the morning on 30 December 1740. She was baptized there by the Bishop of Oxford on 24 January 1741and her godparents (all represented by proxies) were the Margrave of Brandenburg-Ansbach, Queen Sophia Magdalena of Denmark, and Louise Dorothea, Duchess of Saxe-Gotha.

The princess was extremely delicate and backward and at the age of eight was still unable to read. However, she took part in amateur theatricals with her brothers and sisters, learning her words parrot fashion, and Horace Walpole, who saw the performance, said that 'she could not stand alone, but was forced to lean against the side scene'. Even so, she acted 'better than either of her brothers or sisters'. The play performed was *Cato* and the princess took the part of Lucia. As she grew older, Princess Elizabeth Caroline developed intellectually, but unfortunately her bodily deformity did not improve. She died at Kew 'of violent inflammation' after an illness of two days on 4 September 1759, aged only 18. Her private burial in the royal vault in Henry VII's Chapel at WESTMINSTER ABBEY took place 10 days later.

Elizabeth Georgiana Adelaide of Clarence, Princess (1820–1) The younger daughter of Prince William Henry, Duke of Clarence (later WILLIAM IV) and the Duchess (later Queen ADELAIDE), who was born at ST JAMES'S PALACE at five past five o'clock in the afternoon of 10 December 1820. She was privately baptized by the Bishop of London the following evening, receiving her first name in accordance with the wish of her uncle GEORGE IV. The baby princess, although premature, appeared to be a strong and healthy child, but on 1 March 1821 she became feverish and she died in a convulsive fit in the early hours of 4 March 1821. Her parents were present and the Duchess of Clarence fainted in her husband's arms. The cause of death was a strangulated hernia, a condition then inoperable. The princess was buried in the Royal Tomb House in St George's Chapel, Windsor, on 10 March, her funeral being conducted with considerable ceremony for such a young child. Throughout her short life she occupied the position of third in line to the throne. A beautiful statue of the little princess sleeping, sculpted by Scoular, became her mother's most treasured possession. It is now at WINDSOR CASTLE.

Elizabeth of Lancaster, Princess, Countess of Pembroke and Duchess of Exeter (1363–1425) The second daughter of John of Gaunt, Duke of LANCASTER and his first wife Blanche of Lancaster, who was born shortly before 21 February 1363, on which date one of her father's servants was rewarded for bringing the news of her birth to her grandfather EDWARD III. On St George's Day, 23 April, 1379 the princess received robes as a Lady Companion of the Order of the Garter.

On or about 24 June 1380 she was married at Kenilworth to John Hastings, 3rd Earl of Pembroke. He was still a child, being her junior by about 10 years. Although the princess amused herself for a while by lavishing expensive presents on her boy husband at her father's expense, she soon grew tired of him and went to Spain with her father, the unconsummated marriage being dissolved in the summer of 1383. Elizabeth then fell in love with Sir John Holland, the half-brother of RICHARD II, and, having become pregnant by him, they were hurriedly married near Plymouth on 24 June 1386 just before accompanying her father on another expedition to Spain. On 2 June 1388 Holland was created Earl of Huntingdon by his half-brother the king and on 29 September 1397 he was created Duke of Exeter.

Having opposed the usurpation of his brother-in-law HENRY IV in 1399, the duke was taken prisoner and summarily beheaded at Pleshey Castle, Essex, on 9 January 1400. His head was set up on London Bridge and his body buried in the Collegiate Church at Pleshey. He was declared a traitor by Parliament and all his peerage honours were forfeited, but his widow, being the sister of the reigning king, received a grant of 1000 marks a year for her maintenance and various other grants from his forfeited goods.

Princess Elizabeth had three sons and two daughters. Her second son, John, was restored to his father's lands and eventually received a new creation of the dukedom of Exeter in 1444. Princess Elizabeth in her late thirties found consolation in a third marriage with Sir John Cornwall, which took place before 12 December 1400. He is said to have fallen in love with her at a tournament held at York in July that year. She died on her husband's estate at Burford, Shropshire, on 24 November 1425 and was buried in Burford Church. Her husband, who was created Baron Fanhope in 1432 and Baron Milbroke c.1441, died at Ampthill, Bedfordshire, on 10 or 11 December 1443 and was buried in Blackfriars Church, London.

Elizabeth of York, Queen of England

(1466–1503) The consort of HENRY VII, who was the eldest daughter of EDWARD IV and ELIZABETH WOODVILLE and was born at the Palace of Westminster on 11 February 1466. She was baptized in WESTMINSTER ABBEY 'with much solemnity', her godparents being her grandmothers the Duchesses of York and Bedford and the Earl of Warwick.

Elizabeth was one of history's pawns from the day of her birth, which took place when the 'sun of York' was very much in the ascendant; her father Edward IV had secured the throne and her mother Elizabeth Woodville had been crowned queen. Her governess at this time was her future mother-in-law Margaret Beaufort (see RICHMOND AND DERBY, MARGARET BEAUFORT, COUNTESS OF). When she was four years old she accompanied her mother and sister into sanctuary at Westminster during the short-lived restoration of HENRY VI.

By the time of her father's death in 1483, Elizabeth had already been promised in marriage three times, first to Henry, Earl of Richmond (her eventual bridegroom), then to the son of Henry VI, and lastly to the Dauphin Charles, son of Louis XI. The negotiations for the last match were abruptly broken off on Edward's death. Thereafter, Elizabeth's mother and the Countess of Richmond came to a private agreement that she should be betrothed to her first suitor, her cousin Henry Tudor, then still exiled in Brittany. RICHARD III's plans to marry Elizabeth were abruptly abandoned in 1484 when his supporters in the north indicated that they would withdraw their assistance to his cause if he contemplated such an 'incestuous' match.

Henry's victory at Bosworth paved the way for the conclusion of the secret agreement made between the Queen Dowager Elizabeth Woodville and the Countess of Richmond, and Elizabeth's marriage to Henry took place at the Palace of Westminster on 18 January 1486. As she became pregnant almost immediately, her coronation was deferred until 25 November 1487.

If Henry was not a particularly good husband, he was at least a faithful one, a rare thing in those times. Cold and unloving by nature, only one illegitimate child has been attributed to him (falsely as it has now been proved). Elizabeth bore him seven children, but their begetting would almost certainly be considered a matter of duty on the part of both parents. There is, however, one rather touching account of the king and queen comforting each other after they received the news of the death of their eldest son Prince ARTHUR that shows them in a more human light. Elizabeth appears to have taken every change of fortune placidly, never demurring for an instant when first one marriage then another was proposed for her by her father. In her final acceptance of Henry VII she again acquiesced willingly, probably for the sake of her mother and sisters, who were well nigh destitute. As queen she led a dull existence, albeit a comfortable and often splendid one.

No contemporary portraits of Elizabeth have survived. Her tomb effigy depicts a figure of serenely calm majesty, but the carved wooden funeral effigy (partially restored) and the portrait in the National Portrait Gallery (probably a late 16th-century copy of a contemporary original) both give the impression of a stolid, plump-cheeked, pouting woman, listless and cow-eyed. Her whole life was in fact dominated by women of stronger character: her mother, of whom in later life she does not seem to have been particularly fond; her formidable grandmother 'proud Cis', the old Duchess of York, and her mother's sworn enemy (see YORK, RICHARD PLANTAGENET, 3RD DUKE OF); and most of all her mother-in-law, the energetic, forthright, bluestocking Countess of Richmond and Derby, with whom she got on remarkably well.

Elizabeth's health was tolerably good for the period. Three of her seven children died in childhood; nine days after the birth of her last baby she died in the TOWER OF LONDON, on 11 February 1503 (her birthday), probably of puerperal fever. If Henry had not been a demonstratively loving husband, he mourned her sincerely and only contemplated remarriage as a political expedient some years after her death. His own breakdown in health was to prevent these plans from ever coming to fruition. Elizabeth was buried in Henry VII's Chapel in Westminster Abbey.

Elizabeth the Queen Mother, Queen (1900–) The consort of GEORGE VI and mother of ELIZABETH II, who was born in London on 4 August 1900, the fourth and youngest daughter and ninth of the 10 children of Claude George BOWES-LYON, Lord Glamis (who succeeded his father as 14th Earl of Strathmore and Kinghorne in February 1904) and his wife Nina Cecilia Cavendish-Bentinck, of the family of the Dukes of Portland. Her father registered her birth as having taken place at St Paul's Walden Bury, near Hitchin in Hertfordshire, but there is no doubt that her birth actually took place in London, although the exact location and the circumstances by which Lady Glamis happened to be in London in early August have never been elucidated. The baby was baptized at St Paul's Walden on 23 September 1900 and received the names of Elizabeth Angela Marguerite. She bore the courtesy prefix of 'Hon' until her father's accession to the peerage, when she exchanged it for 'Lady'.

Lady Elizabeth Bowes-Lyon was brought up at the family seat in Scotland, Glamis Castle, and was educated privately. She first came into the public eye when she acted as a bridesmaid at the wedding of Princess Mary (*see* MARY, PRINCESS ROYAL, COUNTESS OF HAREWOOD) to Viscount Lascelles in 1922. The first meeting with her future husband Bertie (Prince Albert, Duke of York (*see* GEORGE VI)) took place as early as 1905 at a children's party – legend has it that the young Elizabeth offered Albert the crystallized cherries from the top of a cake – but they did not meet again until 1920, by which time Elizabeth was considered the most eligible debutante of her generation, charming, witty and attractive. Her sense of humour delighted her friends – once, when she ran out of money, she sent the following telegram to her father: 'S.O.S. L.S.D. R.S.V.P. ELIZABETH.' She refused Bertie's first proposal of marriage, made in 1921, but he continued to press his suit and the news of their engagement was finally announced on 5 January 1923, the wedding taking place at WESTMINSTER ABBEY on 26 April 1923.

The marriage was to be an extremely happy one and his wife's support and encouragement were undoubtedly crucial in enabling Bertie, as George VI, to take on the burdens of kingship thrust upon him by the abdication of his elder brother EDWARD VIII in December 1936. During the ABDICATION CRISIS itself Elizabeth sided with the Establishment against Wallis Simpson, thus opening a rift that was only mended towards the end of the duchess's life. Recalling their first meeting many years later, Mrs Simpson observed that she left 'with a distinct impression that while the Duke of York was sold on the American station wagon, the Duchess was not sold on David's other American interest'. Acquaintances reported how in latter years the Duchess of Windsor scowled with anger whenever she spoke of the Queen Mother.

Queen Elizabeth was crowned with her husband at Westminster Abbey on 12 May 1937. She had been appointed a Dame Grand Cross of the Order of the BRITISH EMPIRE (GBE) in 1927 and a member of the Imperial Order of the CROWN OF INDIA (CI) in 1931, and received many more honours after her husband's accession, including the Order of the GARTER. As queen she did much to restore the standing of the monarchy after the abdication, and presented a united front with her husband and their daughters, Princess Elizabeth and Princess Margaret (*see* MARGARET, PRINCESS, COUNTESS OF SNOWDON), during the years of the Second World War. It was suggested during the Blitz that she would be wise to take the princesses to a place of safety outside the capital or even the country, but she only replied, 'The children will not leave unless I do. I shall not leave unless their father does, and the king will not leave the country in any circumstances whatever.' The family stayed, and Elizabeth herself arranged to have instruction in shooting. She won the hearts of many Londoners when she surveyed the damage done by bombing to BUCKINGHAM PALACE, dismissing the calamity with the words, 'I'm glad we have been bombed; I feel I can look the East End in the face.' In 1947, during a visit to South Africa, she demonstrated the same ability to say the right thing and to win over those she met when she was accosted by an old Afrikaner, who explained how he resented the influence of Westminster in his country – to which the queen calmly agreed, 'I understand perfectly. We feel very much the same in Scotland.'

After the death of George VI in February 1952 she assumed the style of Queen Elizabeth the Queen Mother and devoted herself to supporting her daughter, the new queen, fulfilling countless official engagements and conducting exhausting overseas tours to huge acclaim. As a tireless matriarch of the royal family, her popularity has gone from strength to strength, matching her longevity. Her birthday on the 4 August every year has become something of a national event, with the Queen Mother herself always endeavouring to make a public appearance, health allowing. Well into her nineties, Queen Elizabeth continues to undertake a busy schedule of public engagements, as well as pursuing her lifelong interest in racing (her horse Devon Loch, ridden by Dick Francis, nearly won the Grand National in 1956, but collapsed within yards of the finish).

Elizabeth Woodville, Queen of England

(c.1437–92) The consort of EDWARD IV, who was the eldest daughter of Richard Woodville, later 1st Earl Rivers, and his wife Jacquette of Luxembourg, the widow of John Duke of BEDFORD, the fourth son of HENRY IV. She was born on her father's estate at Grafton Regis, Northamptonshire, in about 1437 and as a young girl became, probably through her mother's grand court connections, a MAID OF HONOUR to MARGARET OF ANJOU, who appears to have held her in some affection.

A marriage was arranged for Elizabeth with Sir John Grey, sometimes styled 2nd Baron Grey of Groby. Two sons were born before Grey was killed at the second battle of St Albans on 17 February 1461. Edward IV is said to have fallen in love with Lady Grey's cool, blonde beauty when she presented a petition for the restoration of her husband's forfeited lands. He paid ardent suit to her, but she steadfastly refused to become his mistress, saying 'that she did account herself too base to be his wife, so she did think herself too good to be his harlot'. She remained steadfast in her resistance to his advances even when, so legend claims, he held a dagger to her throat. The king's passion was so great, however, that he persuaded her into a secret marriage at Grafton Regis on 1 May 1464 and declared her to be his queen some months later. Elizabeth was crowned at WESTMINSTER ABBEY on 26 May 1465 with considerable pomp.

The sudden arrival of this stately but aloof unknown caused much resentment at court, notably with the king's brother Richard, Duke of Gloucester (later RICHARD III), who heartily disliked his new sister-in-law and showed it at every opportunity. It was even suggested that she had used witchcraft to ensnare the king's affections. The advancement of the Woodville family also caused grave offence. As a Lancastrian, Elizabeth's father had been created Baron Rivers and a Knight of the GARTER by HENRY VI in 1448. He was now advanced to an earldom by his new son-in-law and also made Lord High Constable of England. Brilliant marriages were arranged for Elizabeth's sisters, Margaret becoming Countess of Arundel, Anne becoming Countess of Kent, Jacquetta becoming Lady Strange of Knokyn, Mary becoming Countess of Huntingdon, and Catherine becoming Duchess of Buckingham, while Elizabeth's elder son, Thomas Grey, was created Marquess of Dorset.

Elizabeth bore Edward a large family of three sons and seven daughters. During Edward IV's flight and the 're-adeption' of Henry VI she took refuge in sanctuary at Westminster with her mother and children and it was there that she gave birth to Edward, Prince of Wales (later EDWARD V).

The death of Edward IV in April 1483 forced his queen to again seek refuge in sanctuary with her younger children, fearing the enmity of her brother-in-law Richard of Gloucester and that of Buckingham. After the youthful Edward V had been lodged in the TOWER OF LONDON, Elizabeth was persuaded by Cardinal Bourchier to allow her younger son Richard Plantagenet, Duke of YORK, to leave sanctuary to join his brother, who was lonely without a companion. She did so reluctantly and was never to see him again.

In 1484 Parliament declared Elizabeth's marriage to Edward IV to have been invalid on the grounds of his having been previously contracted to marry Lady Eleanor Butler, who was still living when he married Lady Grey. This, of course, automatically bastardized all Elizabeth's children by Edward IV and upheld Richard III's title to the throne. Richard III eventually persuaded his sister-in-law to leave sanctuary with her daughters on a promise of providing for them, which, to his credit, he did; Elizabeth and her daughters are even reputed to have graced his court with their presence, the girls joining in the dancing.

After HENRY VII's accession and marriage to her eldest daughter, Elizabeth was reinstated as QUEEN DOWAGER in 1486, but in the following year her lands were forfeited for her alleged perfidy in attending Richard's court in 1484 and she was obliged to retire in reduced circumstances to BERMONDSEY ABBEY, where she died on 8 June 1492, aged about 55. She was buried with Edward in St George's Chapel, Windsor.

Edward was infatuated with Elizabeth, yet she appears to have been cold and aloof. Her daughters were not fond of her and cared little that she spent the greater part of her widowhood within the grim walls of Bermondsey Abbey. Although assiduous in her advancement of her brothers and sisters and her sons from her first marriage, her royal children seemed to mean less to her and she was apparently unconcerned about the fate of Edward V and his brother, thus adding to the mystery surrounding this most enigmatic of queens.

Emma, Queen of Kent (*c*.603–after 640) The consort of EADBALD, KING OF KENT, who was a Merovingian princess, the daughter of Chlothachar (Clotaire) II, King of the Franks (d.629) and his first wife Adaltrudis, a lady of unknown origin. In or shortly after 618 she was married to Eadbald, who had repudiated his first wife (name unknown) whom he had married in defiance of the Church, she being his stepmother. If Eadbald was the son of Queen Bertha, he and his Merovingian wife would have been distant kin. Emma became the mother of two sons, EORMENRED and EORCENBERHT (who succeeded his father), and a daughter, St EANSWYTHE. The date of Emma's death is unknown, but it seems probable that she survived Eadbald.

Emma of Anjou, Princess of North Wales (*fl*.1170) The natural daughter of GEOFFREY PLANTAGENET, Count of Anjou, by an unknown mother and consequently the half-sister of HENRY II, who was married first, to Guy, Sire de Laval, who died in or soon after 1170. She was married secondly, in the summer of 1174, to DAFYDD I, PRINCE OF GWYNEDD, by whom she had a son Owain, who was killed with his father (dispossessed by his nephew LLYWELYN II in 1194) at Aberconwy about May 1203; and a daughter Angharad, who married Griffith ap Cadwgan, son of Cadwgan ap Bleddyn, Prince of Powys, and had issue. It is not known if Emma survived her husband.

Emma of Normandy, Queen of England (*c*.985–1052) The only woman to be the consort of two kings of England, ETHELRED II and CANUTE. Born in Normandy about 985, she was the eldest daughter of Richard I, Duke of Normandy, by his mistress Gunnor, who later became his second wife. She is alleged to have grown up a beauty designated the 'Pearl of Normandy'. Ethelred II, having become a widower, sent an embassy to Normandy to ask for Emma's hand in marriage. It met with a favourable reception and Emma and her entourage sailed to England during Lent 1002. The exact date of the marriage has not been recorded, but it might be assumed that it took place at Eastertide in early April.

The new queen assumed the popular English name of Elfgifu or Elfgiva, which had been that of Ethelred's first wife. In the course of the next few years she gave birth to two sons, Alfred (*see* ALFRED, ATHELING) and the future King EDWARD THE CONFESSOR, and one daughter, Godgifu. As the Danish invaders under SWEYN encroached into southern England, Emma and her children were sent to the Isle of Wight for safety. King Ethelred joined them there in 1013 and in August sent the queen and children to Normandy for their further protection, later following them. The death of Sweyn in February 1014 brought about Ethelred's recall to England, accompanied by Emma and their children. After Ethelred's death in April 1016, Emma remained in London and was there when it was besieged by Canute, who demanded the sum of £15,000 for the queen's ransom. However, the Londoners held out, the Danes were forced to retire, and Emma's stepson EDMUND IRONSIDE, who had managed to escape, returned in triumph.

On the conclusion of peace and the division of the kingdom, Emma again retired to Normandy with her children. After Canute had gained the whole kingdom in 1017, he deemed it expedient to marry Ethelred's widow and sent to Normandy for her 'to be brought to him so that she might become his queen'. The astute Emma readily assented and the marriage took place in London on 2 July 1017. By her second marriage Emma became the mother of a son HARDICANUTE and of a daughter Gunhild, who, under the name of Kunigunde, became the wife of the Holy Roman Emperor Heinrich III. Another daughter, who is said to have died in childhood and been buried in the church at Bosham in Sussex, is spurious.

After Canute's death in November 1035, Emma took up residence at Winchester, but was forced to go into exile again by her stepson HAROLD HAREFOOT. She sought refuge in Flanders, where she was well received by Count Baldwin V, who assigned her the Castle of Bruges as a residence, together with an adequate pension. It is interesting to speculate that during her stay there she may well have met Baldwin's little daughter Matilda (see MATILDA OF FLANDERS), later to become the wife of WILLIAM I THE CONQUEROR. Matters improved in 1040 after Harold Harefoot died and Emma's son Hardicanute became king of England. Emma was able to return to her favourite residence in Winchester. On Hardicanute's sudden death in June 1042, Emma was instrumental in smoothing the succession for her surviving son by Ethelred, Edward the Confessor, who came over from Normandy and was crowned at Winchester Cathedral on Easter Sunday, 3 April 1043, his mother being present.

A few years later Emma fell out of favour with her son and he confiscated her land and goods 'because she had been too tight-fisted with him', forcing her to take refuge in the convent at Wherwell. Here much graver charges were brought against her, to the effect that she had been implicated in the murder of her eldest son, Alfred, and had also attempted to poison Edward. A trial by ordeal was ordered and Emma was required to walk barefoot over nine red-hot ploughshares (if she did so unscathed she would be deemed innocent). Emma spent the night before the trial in prayer at the shrine of St Swithun. In the morning she trod on each of the ploughshares and came through 'not even sensible that she had touched them'. The king, her son, was overcome with remorse at having doubted his mother and, bathed in tears, lay on the ground beside his chair to beg her forgiveness and demanded that she beat him with a wand. All the queen's former rights and properties were immediately restored to her. Emma died in St Mary's Convent at Winchester on 6 March 1052, aged about 66 or 67. She was buried there, but her tomb was destroyed in the reign of King STEPHEN. Her remains were preserved and her bones are among those contained in the mortuary chests reposing on the choir-screen in Winchester Cathedral, placed there by Bishop Fox in 1525. Queen Emma was a great benefactor of the Church, particularly in conjunction with her second husband Canute.

Eochaid I Buide ('the Yellow-haired'), King of Dalriada (d.630) The son of King AIDAN, whom he succeeded in 606. He died

in 630 and was succeeded by CONNAD CERR, the son of CONALL I. His sons DONALD II and CONALL II both reigned later.

Eochaid II ('Crooked-nose'), King of Dalriada (d.697) The son of DOMANGART II, he succeeded to the throne in 696 and was killed the following year. He had at least two wives, by one of whom, the sister of TARRAIN, King of the Picts, he was father of ALPIN I, King of the Picts, and of two daughters who conveyed the Pictish succession through their offspring. By a non-Pictish wife he was the father of EOCHAID III.

Eochaid III, King of Dalriada (d.733) The son of King EOCHAID II, the date of the commencement of his reign is uncertain. He has been identified with the legendary 'King Achaius', the alleged founder of the Order of the THISTLE. He died in 733, leaving two sons, Aed Find and Fergus, who both reigned later.

Eochaid IV ('the Poisonous'), King of Dalriada (fl.781 onwards) The son of Aed Find, he succeeded his uncle and father-in-law Fergus as King of DALRIADA in 781. The length of his reign is unknown. By his wife Fergusa he was the father of ALPIN, who reigned briefly in Kintyre and was the father of KENNETH I, who finally united the Picts and Scots in one kingdom.

Eorcenberht, King of Kent (c.620–64) The younger son of EADBALD, KING OF KENT and his Merovingian wife EMMA, who succeeded his father in 640, his elder brother EORMENRED being passed over for some reason. BEDE speaks very highly of Eorcenberht (whose name is also spelt Earconbert), saying that he 'ruled most nobly for over twenty-four years and some months' and 'was the first of the English kings to give orders for the complete abandonment and destruction of idols throughout his realm, and for the observance of the Lenten fast, enforcing his decrees by suitable penalties for disobedience'. Eorcenberht married SEXBURGA, the eldest daughter of ANNA, KING OF EAST ANGLIA, and she bore him two sons, EGBERT and HLOTHERE, successively kings of Kent, and two daughters, Eorcongota, 'a nun of outstanding virtue' at Faremoûtier-en-Brie, and Eormengild, who married WULFHERE, KING OF MERCIA. Eorcenberht died on 14 July 664, the same day as Deusdedit, 6th Archbishop of Canterbury, as Bede notes. His widow Queen Sexburga took the veil and founded a large convent in Sheppey. She later returned to her native East Anglia and succeeded her sister ETHELDREDA as abbess of Ely.

Eormenred, Kentish Prince (*fl*.640) The elder son of EADBALD, KING OF KENT and his Merovingian wife EMMA, who was passed over on his father's death, the succession going to his younger brother EORCENBERHT. The reason for this is not clear, but it does not seem to have been a cause of any dissension. Perhaps Eormenred had a delicate constitution. He was married to a lady named Oslava and had two sons, Ethelred and Ethelbert, who were murdered by one Thunor early in the reign of EGBERT I, and a daughter Ermenburga or Domneva, who married Merwald, ruler of the Magonsaetan in Herefordshire and Shropshire, and who became the mother of St Mildburga, St Mildred, St Mildgytha and a son Meresin, who died young.

Eormenric, King of Kent (d.560) The son of King Octa of Kent, whom he succeeded in about 540. Nothing is known of him apart from the fact that he was the father of ETHELBERT I and of a daughter, Ricula, who married SLEDDA, KING OF ESSEX. That he died in 560 or thereabouts may be deduced from the length of reign assigned to his son Ethelbert.

Epatticus (*fl.c.*AD10) Celtic ruler of southern Britain, who was the son of TASCIOVANUS and a brother of CUNOBELINUS. He succeeded to part of his father's dominions and struck a coinage in his own name.

Eppillus (*fl.* 1st century BC) Celtic ruler, son of COMMIUS, KING OF THE ATREBATES, who came to Britain from Gaul with his father and brothers after their territory had been conquered by Caesar. On his father's death he received north-east Kent as his portion.

Equerry An officer in the royal household, originally charged with the care of horses. The duties of a modern equerry are to act as a gentleman-in-waiting.

Ermengarde de Beaumont, Queen of Scots (d.1234) The consort of WILLIAM THE LION, who was the daughter of Richard, Vicomte de Beaumont. Her mother's name is unknown, but her father was son of Roscelin, Vicomte de Beaumont, by his wife Constance, a natural daughter of HENRY I. Ermengarde was married to William the Lion at Woodstock, Oxfordshire, on 5 September 1186 and had one son and three daughters. She became a widow in December 1214 and died on 11 February 1234, being buried in Balmerino Abbey, Fife.

Essex Kingdom of the Saxon HEPTARCHY, which was founded about 527 by AESCWINE, according to Henry of Huntingdon, or by his son SLEDDA, according to William of Malmesbury. The kingdom was annexed to WESSEX in 825.

Ethelbald, King of England (d.860) The eldest son of King ETHELWULF and presumably of his first wife OSBURGA, who became ruler of WESSEX in 855 when his father left on his journey to Rome and the Frankish court and succeeded to Kent, Sussex and Essex on his father's death in January 858. He had fallen in love with his stepmother Judith, the daughter of Charles the Bald, King of the West Franks, and married her in defiance of the Church later in 858 or in 859, but was forced to repudiate her. He died in the summer of 860 and was buried in Sherborne Abbey.

Ethelbert, King of England (d.865) The second son of King ETHELWULF and presumably of OSBURGA, who reigned as sub-king in Kent, Essex, Sussex and Surrey during the reign of his brother ETHELBALD, whom he succeeded in WESSEX in 860. He died in 865, or possibly 866, apparently unmarried, and was buried in Sherborne Abbey.

Ethelbert, King of the East Angles (d.794) The son of King ETHELRED and his wife Leofrun, who succeeded his father on an unknown date. He was invited by King OFFA and Queen CYNETHRYTH of MERCIA to visit them in Hereford with the object of marrying their daughter Elfleda, but it was a ruse thought up by the evil queen, who had designs on the East Anglian kingdom, and Ethelbert was murdered at Sutton Walls, Herefordshire, on 20 May 794. The nature of his death caused him to be regarded as a martyr and his body was enshrined in a Hereford church, which received rich endowments from Offa in expiation of the crime. Hereford Cathedral is dedicated to St Mary and St Ethelbert.

Ethelbert I, King of Kent (d.616) The son of EORMENRIC, KING OF KENT, whom he succeeded in about 560. One account dates his birth to 552, but it is extremely improbable that he succeeded at the age of eight. He may have had an earlier pagan wife, or wives, but soon after 590 he married the Merovingian princess BERTHA, daughter of Caribert I, King of Paris, and as a Christian she was allowed to bring her chaplain to Kent with her and to practise her religion.

Meanwhile, Pope Gregory the Great had seen some fair-haired, blue-eyed children for sale in the slave market at Rome and enquiring whence they came was told that they were Angles. *Non Angli, sed Angeli* (Not Angles, but Angels), was the pope's comment and he resolved forthwith that the nation of these beautiful children should receive the light of the Gospel. This story is not recounted by BEDE and may well be apocryphal, but Gregory despatched the monk Augustine to England. Ethelbert already knew something of Christianity from his wife and agreed to receive Augustine's mission and hear what they had to say (though he insisted that they met in the open, as he feared – in accordance with ancient superstition – that if they met indoors they would be able to deceive him with magic). He proved an easy convert and granted Augustine a residence in the royal city of Canterbury, of which Augustine became the first archbishop after visiting France for consecration by the Archbishop of Arles.

Queen Bertha, who had two children, EADBALD and ETHELBURGA, died early in the seventh century and Ethelbert married again, but his new wife's name has not been recorded. He died on 24 February 616 and was buried with Bertha 'in Saint Martin's Porch in the Church of the Blessed Apostles Peter and Paul' at Canterbury. He was accounted the third BRETWALDA, or over-lord of all England south of the Humber. Other achievements of his reign included the introduction of a legal code based on Roman law.

Ethelbert II, King of Kent (d.762) The son of King WIHTRED and his first wife Cynegyth, who succeeded his father in 725 and reigned jointly with his brother EAD-BERHT until the latter's death in 748. Thereafter he may have reigned in conjunc-tion with his half-brother ALRIC and his nephew EARDWULF, the son of Eadbert, but there is much confusion. Most accounts agree that Ethelbert died in 762.

Ethelburga of Kent, Queen of North-umbria (*c.*595–647) The daughter of ETHELBERT I, KING OF KENT and his Mero-vingian wife BERTHA, daughter of Caribert I, King of Paris, who was born about 595, possibly at the royal manor of Lyminge. She bore the childhood nickname of Tatta or Tate and was probably taught by St Paulinus, who was later to accompany her

north and become the first Archbishop of York. Surprisingly for those days, Ethel-burga remained unmarried until the age of about 30, when her hand was sought by the widowed EDWIN, KING OF NORTHUMBRIA, who guaranteed her freedom to practise the Christian religion. Paulinus was conse-crated a bishop by Archbishop Justus of Canterbury on 21 July 625 in order to accompany her to Northumbria and solem-nize her marriage to the pagan Edwin and the ceremony probably took place in York at the end of July or beginning of August.

Ethelburga's first child, EANFLED, was born on Easter Day, 20 April 626. The birth was probably premature and brought on by the fright the queen received from the attempted assassination of Edwin earlier in the day. These events took place at the royal residence on the banks of the Derwent. Paulinus was not slow in telling the king that it was Christ who had given the queen a safe and painless delivery in response to his prayers. This pleased Edwin, who allowed Paulinus to baptize his baby daughter on the feast of Pentecost and vowed that he too would become a Christian if granted victory over his enemy King CWICHELM of WESSEX, who had sent the would-be assassin. He was eventually baptized in the hastily con-structed wooden church of St Peter at York on Easter Day, 12 April 627. In the next few years Queen Ethelburga gave birth to three more children, a son Ethelhun and a daughter Ethelthryth, who both died in infancy soon after their baptisms, and a son Wuscfrea, who survived.

After the defeat and death of Edwin at Hatfield, near Doncaster, on 12 October 633, Ethelburga, accompanied by her chil-dren Eanfled and Wuscfrea and Edwin's grandson Yffi, returned by sea to Kent, escorted by Paulinus and one of Edwin's warriors named Bassus. They were well received by her brother King Eadbald, and Paulinus was given the bishopric of Rochester, which happened to be vacant. The two young princes, Wuscfrea and Yffi, were sent overseas to be brought up at the court of Ethelburga's kinsman King Dagobert I, but unfortunately both died there while still young. Eadbald gave his sis-ter the manor of Lyminge and she founded the church and two religious houses (one for men and one for women) there, herself becoming prioress of the new foundation. She died there in 647 and was buried on the north side of the church. Her body was removed to Canterbury by Archbishop Lanfranc in 1085 and eventually came to rest in St Augustine's Monastery, being lost when it was desecrated after the Reformation. The site of her original tomb at Lyminge was excavated in 1859. A well known as St Ethelburga's Well may still be seen at Lyminge, where, more mundanely, her name is also preserved by the Ethelburga Tea-rooms.

Etheldreda of East Anglia, Queen of Northumbria (*c*.630–718) A daughter of ANNA, KING OF EAST ANGLIA and his wife Saewara. Etheldreda (or Aethelthryth) was born at Exning in about 630 and was first married to Tondberht, Ealdorman of the South Gyrwas, who died shortly afterwards, before the marriage was consummated. She was then married in about 660 to EGFRITH, KING OF NORTHUMBRIA and, says BEDE, 'although she lived with him for twelve years, she preserved the glory of perpetual virginity'. Egfrith, quite naturally, grew tired of the platonic relationship imposed upon him by his strong-minded queen and did everything in his power to get St Wilfrid to persuade her to consummate the marriage, but it was to no avail, a separation was effected and Etheldreda took the veil.

Etheldreda lived for a time at Coldingham, where St Wilfrid's aunt Ebba was abbess, and then went to Ely and founded a double monastery there on the site where Ely Cathedral now stands. She presided there as abbess, 'the virgin mother of many virgins vowed to God', as Bede puts it, until her death in 679, which was caused by a 'large tumour under the jaw'. Her feast day is observed on 23 June, doubtless the day of her death. She was buried in a wooden coffin within the precincts of the abbey, but 16 years after her death her sister Sexburga, who had succeeded her as abbess, had her body exhumed and reburied in a white marble sarcophagus, probably of Roman origin, which had been discovered at Grantchester, near Cambridge. When her body was removed from its original coffin it was found to be incorrupt and the wound under the chin, where her tumour had been opened and drained, had healed into a faint scar. The feast of her translation is observed on the 17 October. She is popularly known as St Audrey and the English word 'tawdry' owes its origin to the cheap and shoddy goods that used to be sold at St Audrey's Fair.

Ethelfleda, Lady of the Mercians (*c*.870–918) The eldest daughter and first child of ALFRED THE GREAT and his wife EALHSWITH, who was born about 870. She was married in or soon after 886 to her father's loyal lieutenant Ethelred, Ealdorman of Mercia, and resided with him in London, which Alfred had consigned to his care. Ethelfleda was one of the most remarkable women of her time and seems to have inherited many of her father's great qualities. Her husband died in 911 and was buried at Gloucester and Ethelfleda took over the administration of Mercia with the exception of London and Oxford, which passed to the direct rule of her brother EDWARD THE ELDER. She ably assisted in the struggle against the Danes, building fortresses at many sites, including Bridgnorth, Tamworth and Stafford. In 916 she sent an army into Wales and stormed Brecknock, taking prisoner Queen Angharad (*see* ANGHARAD FERCH MAREDUDD) and 33 others. In the summer of the following year she captured Derby and the surrounding region, and early in 918 'she secured possession of the borough of Leicester by peaceful means; and the majority of the Danish forces that owed allegiance to it became subject to her'. She was entering into negotiations to effect a similar arrangement with York when she died suddenly at Tamworth on 12 June 918. She was buried at Gloucester 'in the east chapel of St Peter's Church'. She left an only child, a daughter named Elfwynn, who evidently lacked her mother's ability as she was deprived of power by her uncle King Edward and taken to WESSEX in December 919. Her subsequent history is unknown.

Ethelheard, King of Wessex (d.740) A descendant of CERDIC, whose parentage has otherwise not been recorded. His sister Ethelburga was the wife of King INE, on whose abdication in 726, Ethelheard succeeded to the throne of Wessex. His succession was contested by his kinsman Oswald, a descendant of CEAWLIN, KING OF WESSEX, but Ethelheard's arms prevailed and Oswald died in 730. Ethelheard's queen, Frithugyth, went to Rome with Bishop Forthhere of Sherborne in 737. Ethelheard died in 740 and was succeeded by his kinsman (in one account his brother) CUTHRED.

Ethelhere, King of East Anglia (d.654) The son of Eni, who succeeded his brother King ANNA in 653 or 654 and was killed in battle fighting as an ally of PENDA, KING OF MERCIA against OSWY, KING OF NORTHUMBRIA on 15 November 654. He married Hereswith, sister of Hilda, Abbess of Whitby, and had two sons, Aldwulf and Alfwold, both of whom reigned later in EAST ANGLIA. He was succeeded by his brother ETHELWOLD.

Ethelred, King of Mercia (d.716) A son of PENDA, KING OF MERCIA and his wife Cynewise, who succeeded his brother WULFHERE in 675. In 676 he ravaged Kent. He was married to Osthryth or Osthryd, daughter of OSWY, KING OF NORTHUMBRIA, a lady of great piety who, with her husband, richly endowed Bardney Abbey in Lincolnshire, to which the body of her uncle St OSWALD was translated. In 697, however, the queen was murdered by some disaffected Mercian nobles. Six years later, in 704, King Ethelred abdicated and became a monk, being succeeded by his nephew COENRED, the son of Wulfhere. He abdicated in his turn in 709 and went to Rome, being succeeded by Ethelred's son CEOLRED. Ethelred and his son both died in 716. Ethelred was buried at Bardney.

Ethelred I, King of England (d.871) The third son of King ETHELWULF and his first wife OSBURGA, who succeeded his brother King ETHELBERT in 865. The whole of his reign was spent fighting the Danish invaders, in which he was ably assisted by his younger brother ALFRED. Some time after Easter (15 April) 871, Ethelred was wounded at Merton and died of his injuries soon afterwards. He was buried in Wimborne Minster, where the site of his grave is marked by a brass, made centuries later, representing a crowned king in ermine-trimmed robes. Ethelred was married to a lady named Wulfthryth and had two sons, Ethelhelm and Ethelwold, who were both children at the time of his death and too young to rule, so the succession passed to Alfred. Ethelhelm, on doubtful authority, has been identified with the man of that name who became Bishop of Wells in 909 and Archbishop of Canterbury in 914 and died on 8 January 923. Ethelwold rebelled against his cousin EDWARD THE ELDER in an attempt to gain the throne, but was finally defeated and killed in 904.

Ethelred I, King of Northumbria (763–96) The son of King ETHELWALD MOLL and his wife Ethelthryth, who was made King of Northumbria when only about 11 years old after the deposition of King Alchred at Eastertide (early April) 774. He was deposed and sent into exile by Elfwald, the son of King OSWULF in 778 or 779, but restored to the throne in 790 on the deposition of OSRED II. The name of his first wife is unrecorded, but on 29 September 792 he

married Elfleda, one of the daughters of OFFA, KING OF MERCIA. He 'was killed by his own court' on 18 April 796 and was succeeded by EARDWULF.

Ethelred II the Unready, King of England (*c*.968–1016) The younger son of King EDGAR and his second wife ELFRIDA, who was born about 968. The infant Ethelred was baptized by St Dunstan, but urinated in the font as he was held over it, prompting Dunstan to interpret this as a bad omen for the country. Ethelred was undoubtedly entirely innocent of any implication in the murder of his half-brother, EDWARD THE MARTYR, at Corfe Castle in March 979, being no more than 10 or 11 years old at the time, but history has continued to associate him with the crime. When Dunstan crowned him at Kingston on 14 April 979 he may well have taken the opportunity of repeating the predictions he had made at Ethelred's baptism, warning that calamities would befall the nation in expiation for the death of Edward (as he was to do many times before his death in 988).

Ethelred has gone down in history as 'the Unready' and it is an apt sobriquet (although an incorrect rendering of the original 'Redeless', which signified lacking in counsel). Coastal raids by pirates continued through most of the reign, and in 986 the king himself laid waste the diocese of Rochester to gratify his own cupidity. A pestilence among cattle (possibly foot and mouth disease) made its first appearance in England in that year. In 994 the Norwegian King Olaf Tryggvesson (called Anlaf by the ANGLO-SAXON CHRONICLE) and SWEYN FORKBEARD of Denmark sailed up the Thames with 94 ships and besieged London until the king and his council bought them off for £16,000 (thus instituting a policy of paying regular protection money – 'Danegeld' – to the Danes). Olaf visited Ethelred at Andover and there was an exchange of gifts and mutual assurances of non-aggression.

In 1002, on St Brice's Day (13 November), Ethelred ordered the murder of all Danes living in England. Following this atrocity, Sweyn of Denmark (who had lost his own sister in the massacre) renewed his attack in 1004, sacking and burning Norwich, but the following year there was a great famine throughout the country, forcing the Danish invaders to withdraw temporarily. They were back again very soon, however, and in the course of the next few years the whole of England came under

their rule. In 1013 Sweyn was acknowledged as king and Ethelred fled, first to the
Isle of Wight, then to Normandy. Sweyn's
death early in 1014 brought about Ethelred's recall and he reigned uneasily until his
death in London on St George's Day, 23
April 1016, 'after a life of much hardship
and many difficulties', says the Chronicle.
He was buried in St Paul's Cathedral.

Ethelred was first married about 985 to
Elfgiva, daughter of Ealdorman Thored of
Northumbria. She bore him a large family
of sons and daughters, some of whom were
to die before their father. After Elfgiva's
death Ethelred married again, in 1002, this
time choosing a bride from the continent.
She was EMMA OF NORMANDY, the eldest
daughter of Richard I, Duke of Normandy,
and the marriage was to have far-reaching
repercussions, realized in the Norman
Conquest of 1066. The new queen assumed
the popular English name of Elfgiva (the
same as that of Ethelred's first wife) and
gave Ethelred two more sons and a daughter. After his death she married CANUTE.

Ethelred II, King of Northumbria (d.*c*.850)
The son of King EANRED, whom he succeeded in 840 or 841. He was deposed for a
time in 844 by one Redwulf, but was restored after he was killed and reigned until
his death in 849 or 850.

Ethelswith of Wessex, Queen of Mercia
(d.888 or 889) The only daughter of King
ETHELWULF and his first wife OSBURGA,
who was married at Chippenham in Wiltshire soon after Easter (2 April) 853 to her
father's ally BURHRED, KING OF MERCIA.
After he was driven out by the Danes and
went to Rome in 874, Ethelswith, who had
no children, or at any rate none surviving,
joined the court of her brother ALFRED THE
GREAT. In 888 she was deputed with
Ealdorman Beocca to take the alms of the
West Saxons to Rome. She died on the journey and was buried at Pavia.

Ethelwald Moll, King of Northumbria (d.
after 765) Of unknown origin, Ethelwald
Moll acceded to the throne of Northumbria
on 5 August 758 after the murder of King
OSWULF. According to one account he married on 1 November 762 a lady named
Ethelthryth, and they had a son ETHELRED,
who later became king. Ethelwald Moll
either abdicated or was deposed on 30
October 765. The date of his death is
unknown.

Ethelwalh, King of Sussex (d.680/5) Presumably a descendant of AELLA and CISSA

(although the intervening generations and
names of the rulers of Sussex have not been
recorded), who was reigning as king of
Sussex by 674, when he was baptized in
MERCIA 'under the influence of King
WULFHERE, who was present at his baptism
and became his godfather at the font'. Wulfhere gave his godson the Isle of Wight and
the province of the Meanwaras in the eastern part of Hampshire. St Wilfrid preached
the gospel in Sussex and made many conversions, receiving from the king land at Selsey
on which he built a monastery. Ethelwalh's
queen, Eaba, was already a Christian, being
the daughter of Eanfrid, brother of Aenheri,
both rulers of the Hwiccas. Between 680 and
685 Sussex was invaded by CAEDWALLA,
KING OF WESSEX, who killed Ethelwalh and
set about 'wasting the province with slaugh-
tering and plunder'. He was driven out by
two of Ethelwalh's ealdormen, Berthun and
Andhun.

Ethelwulf, King of England (*c*.795–858) The
elder son of King EGBERT and his Frankish
wife Raedburh, who was probably born
about 795. He was appointed sub-king in
Kent, Essex, Sussex and Surrey in 825, so
was presumably well versed in government.
On succeeding his father in the larger kingdom in 839, the sub-kingship was taken
over by Athelstan, his younger brother.
Ethelwulf spent the greater part of his reign
dealing with the Danish marauders whose
raids on England were made in increasing
numbers.

His first wife, whom he probably married
in about 830, was OSBURGA (or Osburh),
daughter of Ealdorman Oslac of Hampshire, the royal cup-bearer, a descendant of
CERDIC's nephew Wihtgar, who had settled
in the Isle of Wight. She bore him at least
four sons and one daughter, ETHELSWITH,
who was married in 853 to her father's ally
BURHRED, KING OF MERCIA. Osburga seems
to have died soon after this event and the
sorrowing Ethelwulf resigned his kingdom
to his son ETHELBALD and went on a pilgrimage to Rome, taking with him his
youngest son (the future ALFRED THE
GREAT), a boy of some eight years old, who
had already reportedly been to Rome three
years before.

Ethelwulf and his son were well received
by Pope Leo IV, who administered the rite
of confirmation to Alfred, an act mistakenly
taken by Asser, King Alfred's biographer,
to be a consecration to future kingship,
which was hardly foreseeable as Alfred had
three elder brothers living. Ethelwulf and

Alfred stayed in Rome for a year and on the return journey stopped at the court of Charles the Bald, King of the Franks and Charlemagne's grandson. Charles had a daughter Judith, who could not have been more than 12 or 13, and he gave her in marriage to Ethelwulf, the wedding being solemnized at Verberie-sur-Oise on 1 October 856. Ethelwulf returned home 'in good health' but died over a year later on 13 January 858. He was buried first at Steyning in Sussex, but was later removed to Winchester.

Eugénie of York, Princess (1990–) The younger daughter of Prince Andrew, Duke of YORK, and his wife Sarah FERGUSON, who was born at the Portland Hospital, London, on 23 March 1990 and was baptized Eugénie Victoria Helena at the church of St Mary Magdalene, Sandringham on 23 December 1990. At the time of her birth she was sixth in line to the throne.

Euphemia de Ross, Queen of Scots (d.1387) The daughter of Hugh de Ross, 4th Earl of Ross (killed at the battle of Halidon Hill on 19 July 1333), by his second wife, Margaret, daughter of Sir David Graham of Montrose. Her parents were granted a dispensation to marry and legitimation of past and future offspring on 29 November 1329, so Euphemia may have been born before or after that date. She was married to John Randolph, 3rd Earl of Moray, who was killed at the battle of Neville's Cross on 17 October 1346, leaving her a childless widow. She married secondly, by dispensation granted by Pope Innocent VI at Avignon dated 2 May 1355, as his second wife, Robert Stuart, Earl of Strathearn, who succeeded to the throne as ROBERT II on 22 February 1371. Queen Euphemia was crowned at SCONE by Alexander de Kyninmund II, Bishop of Aberdeen, in 1372. She had two sons, David and Walter, and two daughters, Egidia and Katherine (also called Jean and Elizabeth), but very little is known about her personally. She died in 1387, but the exact date and her place of burial appear to be unrecorded.

Eustace IV, Count of Boulogne (c.1126–53) The second, but first surviving, son of King STEPHEN and MATILDA OF BOULOGNE, who was born in about 1126 and was invested with his mother's county of Boulogne in 1147. He had been married at Paris in February 1140 to Constance, the only daughter of Louis VI, King of France, and his second wife Adelaide of Savoy. It was hoped that the marriage would bring Normandy into Eustace's possession, but it was not to be. As he grew older an unpleasant character was revealed. The ANGLO-SAXON CHRONICLE speaks of him as 'an evil man' who 'robbed the lands and laid heavy taxes upon them'. He brought his wife to England and more or less imprisoned her in Canterbury Castle. 'She was a good woman, but enjoyed little happiness with him.' He died without issue 'of fever' or 'in a fit of madness' at Bury St Edmunds (or at Canterbury, according to some authorities) on 10 or 11 August 1153 and was buried at Faversham Abbey. His widow married in 1154 Raymond V, Count of Toulouse, and died at Rheims on 16 August 1176. She had three sons and two daughters by her second marriage and her eldest son, Count Raymond VI, later married (as his third or fourth wife) Joan (see JOAN, QUEEN OF SICILY), daughter of HENRY II.

F

Fair Maid of Kent Sobriquet applied to JOAN, PRINCESS OF WALES, the wife of EDWARD OF WOODSTOCK, PRINCE OF WALES, himself dubbed 'The Black Prince', and the mother of RICHARD II.

Fairbrother, Louisa *see* FITZGEORGE, MRS.

Fergus Mor Mac Erc, King of Dalriada (d.*c*.501) The son of Erc, son of Eochaid, who reigned in the Irish kingdom of DAL-RIADA (Dal Riata), roughly corresponding to the modern county of Antrim. Towards the end of the fifth century, accompanied by his brothers Loarn and Angus, he left Ulster and went to Scotland, where he established the Scottish kingdom of Dalriada in Argyll in about 490. The brothers are credited with building the first fortress on the volcanic outcrop of Dunadd, which became their capital. Fergus is said to have brought the famous 'stone of destiny' with him from Ireland, and it was kept at Dunadd until moved to Dunstaffnage and thence to SCONE. Fergus was killed about 501 and succeeded by his son DOMANGART I.

Ferguson, Sarah Margaret, Duchess of York (1959–) The second daughter of Major Ronald Ivor Ferguson, of Dummer House, Dummer, Basingstoke, Hampshire, and his first wife Susan Mary (later Mrs Hector Barrantes), daughter of FitzHerbert Wright, who married Prince Andrew, Duke of YORK at WESTMINSTER ABBEY on 23 July 1986. Born at 27 Welbeck Street, London, on 15 October 1959, 'Fergie' (as she came to be known in the popular press) came into the spotlight when her engagement to the prince was announced on 19 March 1986. Until then her main connection with the royal family had been through her father's work as manager of the Prince of Wales's polo team; she got to know the prince better after a lunch arranged by DIANA, PRINCESS OF WALES at WINDSOR CASTLE during Ascot week. With her vivacity, red hair and lively personality, she rapidly established herself as a favourite with the media, who confidently expected her to bring a new energy and informality to royal circles. The wedding itself was watched by an estimated television audience of 800 million.

The duchess gave birth to her first child, Princess Beatrice Elizabeth Mary (*see* BEATRICE OF YORK, PRINCESS), on 8 August 1988, and a second, Princess Eugénie Victoria Helena (*see* EUGÉNIE OF YORK, PRINCESS), on 23 March 1990. Relations between the duchess and the press had, however, deteriorated somewhat by then, not least over public criticism voiced when the new mother left her first baby behind in the UK when she made an official tour of Australia in October 1988. Her glamorous lifestyle, 'unroyal' brashness and alleged extravagance fuelled further press attacks, and it soon became evident that the marriage itself was in trouble (hard evidence of this being supplied in the form of photographs of the duchess with various 'close friends'). An amicable separation between the duke and duchess was announced in March 1992 and the couple were granted a decree nisi on 17 April 1996, followed by a decree absolute on 30 May 1996. It emerged that the duchess faced severe financial problems – when it became clear that the Palace was reluctant to help with these, plans were made to alleviate them through the marketing of her fictional children's character 'Budgie the Helicopter'. The Duchess lost the style or attribute of 'Royal Highness' on her divorce.

Field of the Cloth of Gold Name given to the famous meeting that took place between HENRY VIII and François I of France near Calais in June 1529. It was so called because of the splendour of the occasion, the two kings vying to outdo each other in magnificent display. Cardinal Wolsey played a prominent part in the proceedings, which led to a treaty between England and France.

Fifteen, The The designation by which the Jacobite rising of 1715 is usually known.

Fishbourne The site in Sussex of a great Roman palace, which is believed to have been built for the client king of the Regni,

COGIDUBNUS. It has been excavated this century and is open to the public.

FitzClarence The surname assumed by the 10 illegitimate children of Prince William Henry, Duke of Clarence (later WILLIAM IV) and the actress Dorothea JORDAN. After his accession to the throne the king created the eldest son Baron Tewkesbury, Viscount FitzClarence and Earl of Munster in the peerage of the United Kingdom on 4 June 1831. On 24 May 1831 the king had granted to all the surviving younger sons and daughters, with the exception of the Countess of Erroll and Viscountess Falkland, who had already attained higher rank through their marriages, the title and precedence of the younger sons and daughters of a marquess.

1. **George Augustus Frederick FitzClarence, 1st Earl of Munster** (1794–1842) The first of WILLIAM IV's illegitimate children by Dorothea JORDAN, who was born in Somerset Street, Portman Square, London, on 29 January 1794. He married at St George's, Hanover Square, London, on 18 October 1819, Mary Wyndham Fox, natural daughter of George Wyndham, 2nd Earl of Egremont, by Elizabeth Fox. She was probably the Mary, daughter of Elizabeth Fox, who was born on 29 August 1792 and baptized at St Martin-in-the-Fields, Westminster, on 23 September 1792. The earl committed suicide in Upper Belgrave Street, London, on 20 March 1842. His wife died in Portland Place, London, on 3 December 1842 and was buried with her husband in Hampton Church, Middlesex. The present (7th) Earl of Munster is their great-great-grandson, but as he only has daughters and there are no surviving male line collaterals, it appears he will be the last of the line.

2. **Lady Sophia FitzClarence** (1795–1837) The second of WILLIAM IV's illegitimate children by Dorothea JORDAN, who was born in Somerset Street, Portman Square, on 4 March 1795. She died in childbirth in London on 10 April 1837, having married at St George's, Hanover Square, on 13 August 1825, Philip Charles Sidney, 1st Baron De L'Isle and Dudley (created 1835), who died on 4 March 1851. The 2nd Viscount De L'Isle (also 7th Baron De L'Isle and Dudley) is their great-great-grandson.

3. **Henry Edward FitzClarence** (1797–1817) The third of WILLIAM IV's illegitimate children by Dorothea JORDAN, who was born at Richmond, Surrey, on 8 March 1797. He died at Darwar, India, on 3 September 1817.

4. **Lady Mary FitzClarence** (1798–1864) The fourth of WILLIAM IV's illegitimate children by Dorothea JORDAN, who was born at Bushy House, Bushy Park, Middlesex, on 19 December 1798. She died in Addison Road, London, on 13 July 1864, having married at St George's, Hanover Square, on 19 June 1824, Charles Richard Fox, natural son of Henry Richard Fox, 3rd Baron Holland and Elizabeth Vassall (whom his father later married). Her husband died on 13 April 1873. They had no issue.

5. **Lord Frederick FitzClarence** (1799–1876) The fifth of WILLIAM IV's illegitimate children by Dorothea JORDAN, who was born at Bushy House on 9 December 1799. He died at Poorundhur, near Poona, India, on 30 November 1854, having married at Kent House, Knightsbridge, London, on 19 May 1821, Lady Augusta Boyle, daughter of George Boyle, 4th Earl of Glasgow, who died on 28 July 1876. They had one daughter, who died unmarried.

6. **Elizabeth FitzClarence** (1801–46) The sixth of WILLIAM IV's illegitimate children by Dorothea JORDAN, who was born at Bushy House on 17 January 1801. She died in Edinburgh on 16 January 1856, having married at St George's, Hanover Square, London, on 4 December 1820, William George Hay, 18th Earl of Erroll, who died 19 April 1846. The present (24th) Earl of Erroll is their descendant, and their second daughter, Lady Agnes Georgiana Elizabeth Hay, married the 5th Earl of Fife and was the mother of the 1st Duke of Fife, who married LOUISE, PRINCESS ROYAL, the eldest daughter of EDWARD VII.

7. **Lord Adolphus FitzClarence** (1802–56) The seventh of WILLIAM IV's illegitimate children by Dorothea JORDAN, who was born at Bushy House on 17 February 1802. He died unmarried at Newburgh Park, Easingwold, Yorkshire, on 17 May 1856.

8. **Lady Augusta FitzClarence** (1803–65) The eighth of WILLIAM IV's illegitimate children by Dorothea JORDAN, who was born at Bushy House on 3 November 1803. She married, first, at HAMPTON COURT PALACE on 5 July 1827, the Hon. John Erskine Kennedy-Erskine of Dun, younger son of Archibald Kennedy, 12th Earl of Cassillis, later 1st Marquess of Ailsa, who died at Pisa, Italy, on 6 March 1831. Lady

Augusta married secondly, at WINDSOR CASTLE on 24 August 1836, Lord John Frederick Gordon, later Halyburton, son of George Gordon, 9th Marquess of Huntly, who died on 29 September 1878. Lady Augusta had issue by her first marriage. She died at Halyburton House, Cupar-Angus, Perthshire, on 8 December 1865.

9. **Rev. Lord Augustus FitzClarence** (1805–54) The ninth of WILLIAM IV's illegitimate children by Dorothea JORDAN, who was born at Bushy House on 1 March 1805. He became Rector of Mapledurham, Oxfordshire, and was married at Kensington, London, on 2 January 1845, to Sarah Elizabeth Catherine Gordon, daughter of Lord Henry Gordon, fourth son of the 9th Marquess of Huntly, who died in London on 23 March 1901. They had issue. He died at Mapledurham on 14 June 1854.

10. **Amelia FitzClarence** (1807–58) The tenth and last of WILLIAM IV's illegitimate children by Dorothea JORDAN, who was born at Bushy House on 21 March 1807. She was married at the Royal Pavilion, Brighton, on 27 December 1830, to Lucius Bentinck Cary, 10th Viscount Falkland, who died at Montpellier, France, on 12 March 1884. They had one son who died before his father without issue. She died in London on 2 July 1858.

FitzGeorge, Mrs Pseudonym assumed by the actress Sarah (known as Louisa) FAIRBROTHER after her clandestine marriage to Prince George (later 2nd Duke) of CAMBRIDGE. She was born in London on 31 October 1815. No record of her baptism has been found, but the baptisms of several of her siblings, children of Robert and Mary Fairbrother, took place at St Giles-in-the-Fields. In 1832 she embarked on an acting career at the Theatre Royal, Drury Lane, in spite of parental opposition and made a name for herself as a pantomime actress. In 1839 she gave birth to a son, later known as Charles Manners Sutton Fairbrother, whose father was probably Charles John Manners-Sutton, 2nd Viscount Canterbury (1812–69).

Louisa and Prince George of Cambridge, as he then was, first met on 10 February 1840, the day of Queen VICTORIA's wedding. The fact was recorded in the prince's diary many years later. On 22 March 1841 she gave birth to a daughter, Louisa Catherine, who, although never openly acknowledged as such, was probably the daughter of Prince George, as she married

under the name of FitzGeorge and was present at the Duke of Cambridge's deathbed in 1904. Two sons, George William Adolphus FitzGeorge, born on 27 August 1843, and Adolphus Augustus Frederick FitzGeorge, born on 30 January 1846, were undoubtedly by the prince, and on 8 January 1847 he and Louisa went through a form of marriage in contravention of the ROYAL MARRIAGES ACT at St John's Church, Clerkenwell, giving many false and deliberately misleading details in the register. Louisa's last child, Augustus Charles Frederick FitzGeorge, was born five months later on 12 June 1847.

Louisa assumed the name 'Mrs FitzGeorge' and was provided with a house at 6 Queen Street, Mayfair, conveniently close to Gloucester House, Piccadilly, where her husband resided. The irregular marriage appears to have been extremely happy for both parties, as the duke's diaries and letters testify. As her companion at Queen Street, Louisa had her sister (probably her twin) Georgiana Elizabeth Browne, whose death in 1886 at the age of 70, was a great blow both to Louisa and the duke. Louisa herself died at Queen Street on 12 January 1890 and was buried on 16 January in the mausoleum which the Duke of Cambridge had built for them at Kensal Green Cemetery. Until a few years ago it was possible to peer through the broken glass in the doors of the mausoleum and see the vast lead coffins of the duke and Louisa resting on ledges opposite each other.

Louisa's son, Charles Manners-Sutton Fairbrother, a colonel in the 19th Hussars, died at 19 Pall Mall on 14 March 1901 and was also buried in the mausoleum. He never married. Louisa Catherine FitzGeorge was married at St George's, Hanover Square, on 7 May 1859 to Captain (later Major-General) Francis Fisher Hamilton. She had no children and died his widow on 13 June 1919. The two elder FitzGeorge sons both married and left issue. The second had a distinguished naval career and the youngest entered the army, retiring as a colonel in the 11th Hussars in 1900. Both were appointed KCVO.

Fitzherbert, Mary Anne (1756–1837) The ill-used and blameless first wife of George, Prince of Wales (later GEORGE IV). 'Mrs Fitzherbert', who was always known as Maria rather than Mary Anne, was the eldest child of Walter Smythe, of Brambridge, Hampshire (a son of Sir John Smythe, 3rd Baronet), by his wife Mary, daughter of John Errington, of Red Rice,

Andover, Hampshire, who both belonged to old Catholic recusant families. She was probably born in the Red Room at Tong Castle, Shropshire, on 26 July 1756, although there is an unsubstantiated family tradition that her mother fell into labour after leaving Tong by coach for London and sought shelter at Hatton Hall Farm, Shifnal, where her daughter was born.

Maria married first in 1775, Edward Weld, of Lulworth Castle, Dorset, a childless widower some 15 years older than herself. He was killed by a fall from his horse in the same year and she married secondly, in 1778, Thomas Fitzherbert, of Norbury, Derbyshire, and Swynnerton, Staffordshire, who was born on 30 August 1746 and died on 7 May 1781. The sole issue of the marriage was a son, who died in infancy. Widowed for a second time, Maria moved to London, where she soon attracted the attention of George, Prince of Wales. As a Roman Catholic of strict principles she refused to become his mistress. The prince maintained his campaign though – in 1784 he even (apparently) stabbed himself in order to impress her with the vehemence of his passion. 'Deprived almost of consciousness' by her alarm at the incident, she allowed him to put a ring on her finger and was finally persuaded to go through a form of marriage (in contravention of the ROYAL MARRIAGES ACT) in the drawing-room of her own house in Park Street, Mayfair, on 15 December 1785. The ceremony was performed by an Anglican clergyman, the Rev. Robert Burt, for an agreed fee of £500 and a promise of preferment. It was witnessed by Maria's brother, John Smythe, and her uncle, Henry Errington, and the prince himself wrote out the certificate. Such a marriage was recognized as valid by the Roman Catholic Church in the case of marriage of a Catholic to a Protestant.

The marriage was kept a close secret for a considerable time and only guessed at by most of their intimates. Maria was no great beauty, but she possessed a stately manner and a keen intelligence and was able to exercise a restraining influence on the prince. They loved each other deeply. In April 1786 it was revealed that the prince's debts amounted to the sum of £269,878.6s.7d. and his father the king refused to come to the rescue until he had 'reason to expect that the attempt to relieve him may be effectual, instead of probably only serving to involve him still deeper'. The prince then made the wily move of closing up CARLTON HOUSE, and dismissing his servants, pawning his

jewellery and selling off his carriages, horses and racing stud. He then retired to Brighton accompanied by Maria and lay low until the ruse worked and the king agreed to settle his debts and arranged that he should receive an extra £10,000 a year from the Civil List.

Inevitably, however, the prince began to run up more debts and in a few years these amounted to £400,000. The only solution was for him to marry and he was obliged to part from Maria and marry, this time legally though ecclesiastically bigamously, his cousin Princess CAROLINE OF BRUNSWICK, a marriage that turned out disastrously. At the wedding the prince instructed his brother, 'William, tell Mrs Fitzherbert she is the only woman I shall ever love'. After this marriage had broken up, the prince implored Mrs Fitzherbert to return to him, which she did after consulting Rome as to the propriety of her so doing and being reassured that her marriage was a valid one in the eyes of her church. They remained together until the establishment of the regency in 1811. The prince gave a great fête at Carlton House to celebrate this event, and Mrs Fitzherbert, after receiving her invitation, wrote to him to ask at which table he wished her to sit. He replied that she might sit where she liked, but not at his table, which was reserved for persons of high rank only. Naturally hurt by this, Mrs Fitzherbert told him that their relationship entitled her to take the first place at his table, but being too dignified to press the claim she decided to absent herself from the occasion. Her place was taken by the regent's new mistress, Lady Hertford.

Mrs Fitzherbert retired to her house on the Steyne at Brighton, where she lived quietly for the rest of her life. On the death of George IV in 1830 she was visited by his brother and successor WILLIAM IV, who treated her with great kindness and wanted to create her a duchess after she had shown him her marriage lines. This she refused, but she accepted his wish that she should dress her servants in the royal livery colours of red and gold. The king also continued her allowance of £6000 a year. She became a visitor to the Royal Pavilion and received many kindnesses from Queen ADELAIDE. She died at her Brighton house at 7 pm on 27 March 1837 and was buried in the Roman Catholic Church of St John the Baptist at Brighton, where her effigy depicts her wearing her three wedding rings.

FitzRoy Surname frequently assumed by the illegitimate offspring of English kings.

'Fitzroy' is Norman French for 'son of the king' (from *fils du roi*). In the Middle Ages, before surnames became established, it was quite common for sons to be designated by reference to their fathers, thus creating such names as FitzWilliam, FitzHugh and FitzHerbert. Because of the adoption of the usage for royal bastards, as noted above, it has become popularly supposed that a prefix 'Fitz' always denotes illegitimate descent, but this is not so.

The name FitzRoy has sometimes been applied to some of the many natural sons of HENRY I, but it is doubtful if it was ever done so by their contemporaries. In later times it was used by Henry FitzRoy, Duke of RICH-MOND, natural son of HENRY VIII, and CHARLES II gave the name to his children by Barbara Villiers, Duchess of CLEVELAND.

Flodden, Battle of Battle fought on Friday, 9 September 1513 between JAMES IV, KING OF SCOTS and an English army under the Earl of Surrey. The Scots were encamped on Flodden Hill, between Cold-stream and Wooler in Northumberland, but after Surrey crossed the Till and cut off communications with Scotland, they were forced to attack. The left side of the Scots army under Huntly and Home drove back the English right, but the Scots right, under Lennox and Argyll, was routed by the English bowmen. Night fell and at dawn the Scots retreated, leaving between 8000 and 10,000 dead and wounded. James IV was among the dead, as also were his natural son the Archbishop of St Andrews, one bishop, two abbots, 12 earls, 13 barons and 50 clan chiefs. The English losses exceeded 6000, and the victory so dearly bought impeded Surrey's northern advance.

Fort Belvedere The house assigned to Edward, Prince of Wales (later EDWARD VIII) by his father GEORGE V in 1930. 'It was a castellated conglomeration,' to quote the duke's own words, '... situated on Crown land bordering the Great Park near Sunningdale. When I went to my father to ask whether I might live there, he was sur-prised. "What could you possibly want that queer old place for? Those damn week-ends, I suppose." But then he smiled, "Well, if you want it, you can have it."' The Fort was originally built in the 18th century by William Augustus, Duke of CUMBERLAND, the son of GEORGE II. It was enlarged and embellished by Wyatville on the orders of GEORGE IV and took on the aspect of a pseudo-Gothic castle. It underwent further modifiction in 1912, and after the Prince of

Wales acquired it he spent much time and effort in improving the house and gardens and passed a great deal of his time there in entertaining his many friends at 'those damn week-ends', as his father had fore-seen. It remained his favourite residence, even after his accession to the throne in January 1936, and it was there that he signed his Instrument of Abdication on the morn-ing of Thursday, 10 December 1936 (*see* ABDICATION CRISIS).

Forty-five, The The designation by which the Jacobite rising of 1745–6 is generally known. The Scottish noblemen who sup-ported the pretenders are spoken of as hav-ing been 'out in the Fifteen', or 'out in the Forty-five'.

Fotheringay Castle Castle in Northampton-shire on the banks of the river Nene, which in 1587 was the scene of the execution of MARY, QUEEN OF SCOTS. The castle be-longed to the Dukes of York and the future RICHARD III was born there in 1452. In the following century it was the scene of Mary's final imprisonment, trial and execution. JAMES I ordered the castle to be ruined after he came to the throne, and after further damage during the CIVIL WAR only one lump of masonry now remains, surrounded by an iron railing bearing plaques to commem-orate the two chief royal events of the cas-tle's history.

Frederick, Prince, Duke of York *see* YORK, PRINCE FREDERICK, DUKE OF.

Frederick Louis, Prince of Wales (1707–51) The eldest son and heir apparent of GEORGE II and CAROLINE OF ANSBACH, who was born at Hanover on 31 January 1707. At the time of his birth, his great-grandmother, the Electress SOPHIA OF HANOVER, was heiress presumptive to the throne of Great Britain and Prince Frederick became fourth in line after his grandfather (later GEORGE I) and father. Very little is known of his childhood and his unprepossessing personal appear-ance (sallow with heavy features) may have been the origin of the dislike with which his parents regarded him almost from his birth. When his grandfather ascended the British throne in 1714, Frederick was left behind in Hanover and his education was left to 'com-mon school-masters of the city'. However, they did a good job, as he grew up to be accomplished and a fluent linguist.

Frederick was created a Knight of the GARTER in 1717 and from that year onwards was styled Duke of Gloucester, though never formally so created. It was not until

26 July 1726 that his grandfather created him Baron Snowdon, Viscount Launceston, Earl of Eltham, Marquess of Ely and Duke of Edinburgh. On his father's accession to the throne in June 1727, Frederick became Duke of Cornwall and Duke of Rothesay. The following year his father summoned him to London, where he was met with no official reception and was even obliged to take a hackney carriage to ST JAMES'S PALACE. He had not seen his parents or siblings for 14 years and there was very little love lost between them. However, the prince, who was something of a dandy, made a good impression on London society. This did not please his mother, who commented: 'My God, popularity always makes me sick, but Fretz's [her nickname for him] popularity makes me vomit.'

The king was quite reluctant at first to create his son Prince of Wales and Earl of Chester, but finally yielded to government pressure and did so on 8 January 1729. His allowance was very meagre and he was allowed no independent household of his own. Frederick, with nothing to occupy his time, became a wild young man about town, roaming at night with a gang of young aristocrats whose chief amusement consisted in breaking the windows of some of the titled residents of London. Drinking, gambling and whoring were among their other occupations. In 1730 the prince borrowed the wherewithal to buy Kew House, also known as the White House, situated near Richmond Lodge, one of the royal residences. It was to remain his favourite residence all his life and to become that of his widow.

For a short while Frederick became friendly with his mother's vice-chamberlain Lord Hervey, a witty, two-faced character who would vilify his mother and sisters to the prince and vice-versa. They finally fell out when Hervey presumed too much in his relationship with the prince. Oddly enough, Frederick acquired a mistress who had also made free of her favours with Hervey and with the Earl of Harrington. She was one of the queen's maids of honour, the Hon. Anne Vane (nicknamed 'Vanella'), eldest daughter of Gilbert Vane, 2nd Baron Barnard and his wife Mary Randyll. She was described by a contemporary as 'a fat and ill-shaped dwarf, who has nothing good to recommend her'. Frederick acknowledged her two children as his, although contemporaries asserted that either Hervey or Harrington was the real father. The children were Cornwall FitzFrederick, who was born in Soho Square, London, on 4 June 1732 and died on 23 February 1736, being buried in WESTMINSTER ABBEY on 26 February, and Anne FitzFrederick, who was born and died in London on 21/22 April 1733.

Anne Vane was eventually replaced in the prince's affections by Lady Archibald Hamilton, 'a middle-aged woman of no particular beauty, with 10 children and an elderly husband'. She was pensioned off and went to live in Bath, where she died very soon after on 27 March 1736. The question of Frederick's marriage was now mooted and the chosen bride was Princess Augusta of Saxe-Gotha (*see* AUGUSTA, PRINCESS OF WALES), who duly arrived in England and was married to the prince at the Chapel Royal, St James's Palace, on 8 May 1736. Relations between Frederick and his parents became even worse following the flight of the Prince and Princess of Wales from Hampton Court to St James's when the birth of their first child was imminent, in order to prevent the grandparents being present at the birth. The king ordered them to leave St James's Palace, and in September 1737 they moved to Kew. The queen paid a formal visit to her son and daughter-in-law before they left St James's, but her reception was so chilly that on her return she declared to the king 'I hope to God I shall never see him again'. Her hope was fulfilled as she died two months later without any reconciliation having taken place.

In 1734 Frederick had purchased CARLTON HOUSE in Pall Mall with a borrowed £6000, but not content with that as a London residence, he now rented Norfolk House in St James's Square and this was to be the birthplace of his next three children, the future GEORGE III, Edward Augustus, Duke of YORK, and Princess ELIZABETH CAROLINE. In 1742 he rented Leicester House, which his parents had also done in their time, and also rented Cliveden as an additional country residence. His five youngest children (the last born posthumously) were all born at Leicester House. Frederick was a devoted husband and father in spite of the many minor amours to which he was prone in the true Hanoverian manner. Horace Walpole said: 'His chief passion was women, but like the rest of his race, beauty was not a necessary ingredient.'

Much to the king's annoyance, the Prince and Princess of Wales appeared in public together, visiting Bath and Bristol and gaining a great measure of popularity. Frederick was a man of culture and taste as well as being a keen sportsman, playing cricket, rounders and nine-pins. He was fond, too, of amateur theatricals, in which he and his children would take part. He looked forward to his eventual accession to the throne and, through the influence of Viscount Bolingbroke, was determined to be 'a patriot king'. He took great delight in opposing the government at every opportunity and lending his support to the opposition. After the Jacobite rising of 1745, Frederick favoured a policy of leniency towards the rebels rather than that of severity sponsored by his father and brother. He visited Flora Macdonald when she was under house arrest in London, and she was so charmed by him that she said she would have done as much for him as she had done for Prince Charles Edward, had he been in the same predicament.

Frederick's health began to fail early in 1751. On 5 March he caught a chill while gardening at Kew, but went to attend the king in the House of Lords, where he became very over-heated. He returned to Kew and thence returned to Carlton House, where he imprudently sat at an open window. The next day he was feverish and was bled and blistered following the medical treatment of the day. He appeared to recover, but a relapse occurred a few days later. Drastic purging and bleeding was again applied and the prince again rallied, but on the evening of the 20 March 1751 (31 March new style), he was seized with a fit of coughing after partaking of a light supper and died quite suddenly. An autopsy attributed his death to an imposthume (abcess) in the breast, which had suddenly burst. It was popularly believed that this had been caused by a blow from a cricket ball the previous summer. A ruptured aneurysm would appear to be the most likely cause of the prince's death.

Frederick's father received the news of his son's death while playing cards with his mistress the Countess of Yarmouth. He did not interrupt his game and later remarked, 'I have lost my eldest son, but I am glad'. Frederick was buried in the royal vault in Henry VII's Chapel in Westminster Abbey on 13 April 1751. He is often remembered by a frequently quoted epitaph by an anonymous lampoonist:

> Here lies poor Fred, who was alive and is dead;
> Had it been his father, I had much rather;
> Had it been his brother, still better than another;
> Had it been his sister, nobody would have missed her;

> Had it been the whole generation, so much better for the nation.
> But since it is Fred, who was alive and is dead,
> There is no more to be said.

Frederick William, Prince (1750–65) The fifth and youngest son and eighth child of FREDERICK LOUIS, PRINCE OF WALES and Augusta of Saxe-Gotha (*see* AUGUSTA, PRINCESS OF WALES), who was born at Leicester House on 13 May 1750 and baptized there in June, his godparents being his eldest brother Prince George (later GEORGE III), his uncle Prince Wilhelm of Saxe-Gotha (represented by Lord North as proxy) and his eldest sister Princess Augusta (*see* AUGUSTA, PRINCESS, DUCHESS OF BRUNSWICK). The prince died at Leicester House at the age of 15 on 29 December 1765 and was buried in WESTMINSTER ABBEY on 4 January 1766.

Freemasonry The Grand Lodge of England was convened in 1717 and the first member of the royal family to join the craft was FREDERICK LOUIS, PRINCE OF WALES in 1737. Three of his sons later became masons, as did six of the sons of GEORGE III. The future EDWARD VII became a mason in 1868, as did his brother Arthur, Duke of CONNAUGHT in 1874 and his son Albert Victor, Duke of CLARENCE in 1885. The future kings EDWARD VIII and GEORGE VI entered in 1919, to be joined by their brother George, Duke of KENT in 1928. Prince Edward, Duke of Kent, son of the last, became a mason in 1963 and was elected Grand Master in 1967. Prince Philip, Duke of EDINBURGH is also a mason, having joined in 1952.

Frogmore House Former royal residence about a mile south of WINDSOR CASTLE. The estate of over 300 acres between the Home and Great Parks was acquired for the crown by HENRY VIII. A new house was built there in 1680 for CHARLES II's architect Thomas May. In 1709 the estate was leased to the Duke of Northumberland, one of Charles II's natural sons by the Duchess of CLEVELAND. It later passed through several hands and was finally purchased by Queen CHARLOTTE in 1792. The queen had the house considerably altered and landscaped the park. The alterations were carried out by George Wyatt.

On Queen Charlotte's death in 1818 the house passed to her daughter Princess Augusta (*see* AUGUSTA SOPHIA, PRINCESS), and on her death in 1841, Queen VICTORIA offered it to her mother the Duchess of Kent, who carried out a programme of modernization and redecoration. She died there in March 1861 and was buried in a circular mausoleum in the grounds. Victoria loved the house and spent much time there. When she died she was laid to rest alongside Prince ALBERT in the mausoleum nearby (which Albert had designed). Thereafter the house was occupied by various members of the royal family, including GEORGE V and Queen MARY OF TECK when Prince and Princess of Wales. The Duke and Duchess of York (later GEORGE VI and ELIZABETH THE QUEEN MOTHER) spent part of their honeymoon at Frogmore in 1923. Queen Mary took a great interest in the house and, in her own words, arranged it as 'a "family" souvenir museum as well as a museum of "bygones" and of interesting odds and ends'.

The house fell into a state of disrepair and extensive restoration work has been carried out in recent years. The house and part of the gardens were opened to the public for the first time in 1990.

G

Gabran, King of Dalriada (d.559) A son of DOMANGART I, who succeeded his brother COMGALL as King of DALRIADA in 537. His wife, Ingenach or Lleian, was the daughter and heiress of Brychan, Lord of Manau Guotodin, and they had two sons, AIDAN, later King of Dalriada, and Aed, who married a Pictish princess and was the father of GARTNAIT IV, King of the Picts. Gabran was killed, it is believed, by BRUDE I, KING OF THE PICTS in about 559. He was succeeded by his nephew CONALL I, the son of Comgall.

Galam I, King of the Picts (*fl*.498–513) The son of Geraint, King of Strathclyde, by a sister of DRUST II, King of the Picts, whom he succeeded in about 498 after abdicating the throne of Strathclyde. Originally known as Caw or Caunus, he was deposed by his nephews DRUST III and DRUST IV in about 513 and went to live at Twrcelyn in Anglesey, where several of his children were revered as Celtic saints.

Galam II, King of the Picts (d.580) The (conjectured) son of the elder sister of DRUST III, GARTNAIT III and CALTRAM, who reigned as king of the Picts from about 552 until about 555, when he abdicated. He died about 580.

Garter, Most Noble Order of the The premier order of chivalry in England, which was founded by EDWARD III in about August 1348. How the order came to be founded is the subject of legend (*see* JOAN, PRINCESS OF WALES). The Order consists of the sovereign and 24 Knights (or Ladies) Companions. The Prince of Wales is a constituent part of the original institution and extra knights and ladies (foreign sovereigns, etc.) may be admitted by special statutes. The insignia of the order are: (1) a garter of dark blue velvet, edged with gold, bearing the motto *Honi soit qui mal y pense* in gold letters, with a buckle and pendant of gold, worn below the left knee, or in the case of ladies on the left arm; (2) a mantle of dark blue velvet lined with white taffeta, having a representation of the garter encircling the cross of St George on an escutcheon argent embroidered on the left shoulder; (3) a hood of crimson velvet; (4) a surcoat of crimson velvet, lined with white taffeta (now no longer worn); (5) a hat of black velvet, lined with white taffeta, and having a plume of ostrich feathers fastened thereto by a band of diamonds; (6) a collar of gold consisting of 24 pieces in the form of a garter surrounding a Tudor rose, connected by 24 knots of chased gold; (7) the 'George', an enamelled figure of St George on horseback slaying the dragon, worn suspended from the collar; (8) the 'Lesser George' or badge of gold worn pendent from a four-inch blue ribbon over the left shoulder; (9) the 'Star' of 8 points of silver with the cross of St George encircled with the garter.

St George is the patron saint of the Order and nominations to it, which are in the gift of the sovereign alone, are usually made on St George's Day, 23 April. The Queen's Royal Free Chapel of St George in WINDSOR CASTLE is the chapel of the Order and the banners of the knights are hung over their stalls in the choir. The arms of past knights of the Order are enamelled on plates fastened to the backs of the stalls and present a fascinating display of heraldry. The annual service of the Order is held on the second or third Monday in June, known as Garter Day.

In the Middle Ages it was customary for robes of the Order to be provided for ladies of the royal family and the recipients are often referred to as 'Lady Companions of the Order of the Garter'. This custom lapsed with the Tudors and, although subsequent queens regnant wore the insignia as sovereigns of the Order, no ladies were admitted to it until EDWARD VII appointed Queen ALEXANDRA in 1901. In 1990, ELIZABETH II decreed that both sexes were eligible to be ordinary knights (KG) and ladies (LG) of the Order.

Gartnait The name of several kings of the Picts. Gartnait III, who reigned about 533–40, was the son of one Girom by the elder sister of GALAM I and succeeded his brother DRUST III. Gartnait IV reigned about 584–94 and was the son of Aed (son of GABRAN I, KING OF DALRIADA) by Domelch, sister of BRUDE I, whom he succeeded. Gartnait V was a son of Wid Feith (son of BRUDE I) by a sister of King NECHTAN and succeeded his cousin CINIATH in about 631 or 632. He was succeeded by his brother BRUDE II in about 635. Gartnait VI, who reigned about 657–63 was a son of Donald I, King of DALRIADA, by a younger sister of Gartnait IV and succeeded his cousin TALORCAN I. He was succeeded by his brother DRUST VI.

Gaunt, John of see LANCASTER, JOHN OF GAUNT, DUKE OF.

Geoffrey, Duke of Brittany (1158–86) The fourth son and fifth child of HENRY II and ELEANOR OF AQUITAINE, who was born on 23 September 1158. While still a child he was betrothed to Constance, the only daughter and heiress of Conan IV, Duke of Brittany, and his wife Margaret, sister of MALCOLM IV and WILLIAM THE LION, successive kings of Scots. Together they were invested as Duke and Duchess of Brittany at Rennes in 1169, but the marriage was not consummated until 1181 or 1182. A daughter ELEANOR[1] was born in 1184. The duchess was pregnant with her second child when Geoffrey was killed while taking part in a tournament at Paris on 19 August 1186, being flung from his horse and trampled to death. He was buried in Notre-Dame Cathedral. His son Arthur (see ARTHUR, DUKE OF BRITTANY) was born posthumously in April 1187.

Geoffrey of Monmouth (d.1155) The author of the fabulous *Historia Regum Britanniae* (History of the Kings of Britain), which he claimed to have translated into Latin from 'a certain very ancient book written in the British language', which Walter, Archdeacon of Oxford had acquired in Brittany and presented to him. Geoffrey was a cleric of Welsh origin who was elected Bishop of St Asaph in 1151 and probably died in 1155. His work purports to tell of the wanderings of BRUTUS the Trojan, the great-grandson of Aeneas, forced to leave Italy after accidentally killing his father and eventually, after many adventures, coming to Albion, which he renamed Britain from his own name, after driving out the aboriginal giants. The story continues with the fabulous deeds of Brutus's descendants and successors from about 1100BC until the coming of the Romans, when fact begins to blend with fiction. The main portion of the book is concerned with the exploits of King ARTHUR. Lewis Thorpe's introduction to his translation of Geoffrey's *History* points out that it might 'be said to bear the same relationship to the story of the early British inhabitants of our own island as do the 17 historical books in the Old Testament, from Genesis to Esther, to the early history of the Israelites in Palestine'. A list of Geoffrey's fabulous rulers will be found in Appendix I.

Geoffrey Plantagenet, Count of Anjou and Maine (1113–51) The ancestor of the PLANTAGENET kings of England, who was the eldest son of Fulk V, Count of Anjou, later King of Jerusalem, by his first wife Eremburge, Countess of Maine, only daughter and heiress of Hélie I, Count of Maine. Geoffrey was born on 24 August 1113 and was married at Le Mans on 22 May 1127 to MATILDA, LADY OF THE ENGLISH, the childless widow of Emperor Heinrich V, and only surviving legitimate child of HENRY I, who chose him as his daughter's husband in the hope that he would father a long line of kings, which in fact he did. The bride was some 10 years older than her groom and entered into the marriage with some reluctance, but it turned out well. The king knighted his new son-in-law and hung around his neck a shield charged with golden 'lioncels'.

In 1129, on leaving for the Holy Land to marry Queen Melesende of Jerusalem, Geoffrey's father resigned the counties of Anjou and Maine to him. As Count of Anjou, Geoffrey is reckoned as Geoffrey V. Three sons were born of his marriage to Matilda: Henry, who became HENRY II, in 1133; Geoffrey Martel, Count of Nantes, in 1134; and William in 1136. Geoffrey also had three natural children, whose mother may have been the wife of the Sire d'Osteilli: Hamelin, Earl of Surrey (d.1202); Emma (see EMMA OF ANJOU, PRINCESS OF NORTH WALES), who married DAFYDD I, PRINCE OF GWYNEDD; and Marie, Abbess of Shaftesbury (who died in September 1216).

Geoffrey died at Château-du-Loir on 7 September 1151 and was buried in Le Mans Cathedral, where his tomb was marked by an enamel plaque (now in Le Mans Museum) depicting him bearing the shield that his father-in-law had hung around his neck on knighting him. It covers his body from neck to toe and shows a blue field and an indeterminate number of 'lioncels' in gold. Two generations later the same arms (azure, six lions rampant or, three, two and one) were borne by Geoffrey's grandson, William Longespée, Earl of Salisbury, an illegitimate son of Henry II and are to be seen depicted on his tomb in Salisbury Cathedral, the first known example of true heraldry in western Europe.

George, Duke of Bedford *see* BEDFORD, GEORGE, DUKE OF.

George, Duke of Cambridge *see* CAMBRIDGE, GEORGE, 2ND DUKE OF.

George, Duke of Clarence *see* CLARENCE, GEORGE PLANTAGENET, DUKE OF.

George, Duke of Kent *see* KENT, GEORGE, DUKE OF.

George I, King of Great Britain (1660–1727) The first Hanoverian king of England (*see* HANOVER, HOUSE OF), who was the eldest child of Ernst August, Duke of Brunswick-Lüneburg and first Elector of Hanover, by his wife Sophia (*see* SOPHIA, ELECTRESS OF HANOVER), fifth and youngest daughter of Friedrich V, Elector Palatine and sometime King of Bohemia, by his wife Elizabeth (*see* ELIZABETH, PRINCESS, QUEEN OF BOHEMIA), eldest daughter of JAMES I. He was born at the Leineschloss, Hanover, on 28 May (7 June new style) 1660, the eve of the day on which his mother's first cousin CHARLES II was restored to the English throne, which he himself was to ascend 54 years later, a possibility so remote then that it must have been entirely uncontemplated when he was born. He was christened George Louis and his mother was to describe him as 'beautiful as an angel'. Sturdy, strong and healthy he was to remain all his life, although his heavy features and slightly disagreeable expression, apparent in all his portraits, do not give the impression of a handsome man.

The law of primogeniture had not been established in the Duchy of Brunswick-Lüneburg, and George's father was the youngest of four brothers between whom complicated exchanges of various portions of their inheritance were continually taking place. Ernst August first achieved ruling status a year after his eldest son's birth when he became Prince-Bishop of Osnabrück, an office that had been secularized in 1648, since when Catholic and Protestant 'bishops' alternated. In 1679, by a rearrangement following the death of one of his elder brothers, he became Duke of Brunswick-Lüneburg-Calenberg, and finally, in 1692,

acquired the much coveted title of Elector from the Emperor, being known thereafter as Elector of Hanover.

George Louis had five younger brothers and one sister. Their loving mother, whose own childhood had been unhappy, took great care with their education and in providing a happy home atmosphere. George displayed an early bent for a military career and campaigned in the Dutch and Turkish wars. In 1680 he paid his first visit to his future kingdom, where it was suggested he might become a suitor for the hand of his second cousin Princess Anne (later Queen ANNE). The couple developed a mutual antipathy, however, and Anne's later opposition to the Hanoverian succession has been attributed in part to her memories of an unhappy encounter when George made it plain that she held no attractions for him.

On his return to Hanover, the question of George's marriage was settled by his father, who betrothed him to his cousin SOPHIA DOROTHEA OF CELLE, the only surviving daughter and heiress of Duke Georg Wilhelm of Brunswick-Lüneburg-Celle. The marriage took place at Celle on 22 November 1682 and was reasonably happy at first, but after the birth of two children the affections of both husband and wife became engaged elsewhere. George fell in love with one of his mother's ladies-in-waiting, Melusine von der Schulenburg (later to be ennobled in England as the Duchess of Kendal (*see* KENDAL, EHRENGARD MELUSINE VON DER SCHULENBURG, DUCHESS OF)), who bore him three daughters, never publicly acknowledged as such. Sophia Dorothea, for her part, fell in love with Count Philipp Christoph von Königsmarck, a young officer in the Hanoverian army. Königsmarck disappeared under mysterious circumstances (his strangled body was reportedly discovered under the floor of the Electoral Princess's dressing-room during alterations to the palace in Hanover many years later). A tribunal of jurists and Lutheran Church officials hastily convened at Hanover on 28 December 1694 declared the marriage dissolved on the grounds of the wife's refusal to cohabit with her husband. The right to remarry was reserved to George alone and, although there is no proof, it seems highly likely that he did contract a secret marriage with Melusine, whom Robert Walpole later described as being 'as much Queen of England as anyone ever was'.

The Elector Ernst August died at Herrenhausen on 23 January 1698 and

George Louis succeeded him as Elector of Hanover. Three years later the ACT OF SETTLEMENT made his mother heiress presumptive to the throne of Great Britain, and George Louis received the Order of the GARTER. In 1705 he was naturalized by Act of Parliament. The old Electress Sophia, who said it was her ambition to have the words 'Queen of Great Britain and Ireland' inscribed on her tombstone, was within two months of its achievement when she died in June 1714. George Louis became heir presumptive in her place and on 1 August 1714 the death of Queen Anne made him king.

George lost no time in repairing to England and made his state entry into London on 20 September 1714. He was accompanied by Melusine von der Schulenburg, who was soon to be nicknamed 'the Maypole' because of her tall, thin appearance. The amply proportioned Sophie Charlotte, Baroness von Kielmansegg, later to be created Countess of DARLINGTON, was also prominent at court. She was nicknamed 'the Elephant' and was popularly believed to be another of George's mistresses but was, in fact, his illegitimate half-sister.

It has often been stated that George knew no English, but the researches of a recent biographer have shown that he did have a limited knowledge of the language. He opened his first Parliament with an English sentence (which might, of course, have been learned by heart): 'My Lords and Gentlemen, I have ordered my Lord Chancellor to declare to you in my name the causes of calling this Parliament.' A memorandum of 1723, annotated in English by the king's own hand, is in the Public Record Office, and there is evidence that he often used English words and phrases and sometimes whole sentences in his conversation, although his preferred language was French, which was the language of polite society throughout Europe at the time. George's coronation service at WESTMINSTER ABBEY on 20 October 1714 was largely conducted in Latin in order to overcome the language difficulties.

In 1715 the Jacobite rising in Scotland in favour of the Stuart claimant 'James III and VIII' was soon put down and several of its leaders were executed. The new king was tolerated rather than popular, and the Whigs, with a view to strengthening his support, introduced septennial Parliaments. George himself presided over cabinet meetings throughout his reign, the Prince of Wales acting as interpreter where necessary until the rift between father and son in 1717

(see GEORGE II). Relations between the two subsequently deteriorated to such an extent that there is evidence that loyal courtiers approached the king with the idea of kidnapping the prince and transporting him to the plantations.

George frequently visited his German dominions, where he was happiest, and in 1719 these were increased by the cession of the secularized bishoprics of Bremen and Verden. George set out for Hanover for the last time on 3 June 1727. He embarked on his yacht at Greenwich and sailed for Holland, landing at Schoonhaven on 18 June. His coach was waiting for him and, although he had been seasick, he set out on the road at once. The next evening he reached Delden, where he had supper and afterwards unwisely gorged himself on melons (or in some accounts strawberries and oranges). In the morning he set out early after breakfasting on a cup of chocolate. A violent attack of diarrhoea forced a halt, and when the king returned to his coach it was noticed that his face was distorted and his right hand hung limply at his side. He fainted almost immediately and a surgeon was fetched from another coach. George recovered consciousness on being bled and at once demanded that the journey should continue, crying out 'Osnabrück, Osnabrück!' in slurred tones. He soon lost consciousness again, but it was decided to complete the journey. The party reached Osnabrück late in the evening and George rallied sufficiently to be able to raise his hat with his left hand as a sign of greeting before being carried from his coach to his bed, where he again lapsed into unconsciousness. Death came at 1.30 am on 22 June 1727. In modern terms, George died of a cerebral haemorrhage, precipitated by the stomach upset. He had left a request that his body was not to be opened or embalmed, and on George II's instructions he was buried in the Leineschloss Church at Hanover near his mother the Electress Sophia. The church was severely damaged during the Second World War, and in 1957 George's sarcophagus and that of his mother were moved to the mausoleum in the grounds of Herrenhausen, where they still repose.

George I was plain and simple in his tastes and appearance. The general impression is of a dull, rather humourless man and an uninspiring monarch, but it is said that he could be lighthearted and amusing with his intimates. His family relations were marred by the quarrel with his son and daughter-in-law. He had little interest in intellectual pursuits, but he appreciated music, especially opera, and was the patron of Handel.

George II, King of Great Britain (1683–1760) The only son of GEORGE I and SOPHIA DOROTHEA OF CELLE, who was born at Herrenhausen in Hanover on 30 October 1683 and named George Augustus. Deprived of their mother's care when George Augustus was 11 and his sister SOPHIA DOROTHEA (later Queen of Prussia) seven, the children were brought up with loving kindness by their grandmother, the Electress Sophia, and in the charge of her *Oberhofmeisterin* (Mistress of the Robes), Frau von Harling, who had similarly looked after their father. His grandmother was careful to engage English tutors for her grandchildren and great-grandchildren as soon as she had been declared heiress presumptive by the ACT OF SETTLEMENT in 1701. George Augustus learned to speak English fluently but he never lost his guttural accent and must have seemed very foreign to his English subjects. However, he was a courteous and courtly man, although hasty tempered, and these qualities were greatly appreciated by his ministers.

George was naturalized a British subject in 1705 and the following year received the Order of the GARTER and was created Baron Tewkesbury, Viscount Northallerton, Earl of Milford Haven, and Duke and Marquess of Cambridge on 9 November 1706. He was married at Herrenhausen on 22 August (1 September new style) 1705 to Princess CAROLINE OF ANSBACH, a marriage that was to prove a happy one in spite of George's occasional wanderings elsewhere. George became Duke of Cornwall and Rothesay on his father's accession in August 1714 and was created Prince of Wales and Earl of Chester on 22 September 1714, two days after the state entry into London. The Prince and Princess of Wales took part in George I's coronation, George Augustus wearing MARY OF MODENA's crown adapted for his use by the removal of one of the arches.

For the first three years of the new reign the Prince of Wales attended cabinet and Privy Council meetings, acting as his father's interpreter where necessary, but in 1717 a rift occurred between the king and the Prince and Princess of Wales, who withdrew themselves from court early in 1718. The quarrel was precipitated by a disagreement over the choice of godparents for the prince and princess's shortlived son George William, and soon grew out of proportion.

The selection of the Duke of Newcastle as a godfather especially infuriated the prince, who at the font accosted the duke with the words, 'Rascal, I find you out'. The startled duke, confused by the prince's German accent, believed the prince had threatened him with the words 'I fight you' and fled to the king for protection. The prince was subsequently placed under virtual arrest and the cabinet was summoned to discuss the matter. As a result, the prince and princess were exiled from ST JAMES'S PALACE and moved into Leicester House, Leicester Square, which became their chief residence until their succession. Their children were kept at St James's. Relations between the two rival courts thus established remained uneasy for the rest of George I's reign.

'Dat is vun big lie!' So bawled George Augustus in his heavily accented English when the news that his father was dead and that he had ascended the throne was first brought to him. After years of being at loggerheads with his disagreeable father, the disagreeable son could not believe that he was free of parental oppression at last. Strangely enough, the bad relations that had existed between him and his father were to be repeated in the next generation, as George and his son Frederick (*see* FREDERICK LOUIS, PRINCE OF WALES) were equally antagonistic towards each other. The new king and queen were crowned at WESTMINSTER ABBEY by William Wake, Archbishop of Canterbury, on 11 October 1727, George pledging himself to the country with the proud reassurance, 'I have not a drop of blood in my veins which is not English' (despite the fact that as Prince of Wales he is supposed to have questioned English manners, horses and cooking).

George II's reign was a time of great prosperity for the country both at home and abroad. Peace with Spain was concluded in 1729, but infractions of the Treaty of Seville and encroachments on foreign trade led to war being declared again in 1739. Admiral Vernon was sent with a squadron to the West Indies and demolished Portobello but failed to take Cartagena. In 1743 George himself took the field, the last British monarch to do so, and led his army on the continent, where the French were beaten in the battle of DETTINGEN. In the Jacobite rising of 1745, 'Bonnie Prince Charlie' (*see* STUART, CHARLES EDWARD), a more forceful and attractive character than his father 'The Old Pretender' (*see* STUART, JAMES FRANCIS EDWARD), marched as far south as Derby. This rebellion was put down with great severity by George's son, William Augustus, the Duke of CUMBERLAND, who thereby earned himself the unenviable nickname 'Butcher' Cumberland. The continental war was ended by the Treaty of Aix-la-Chapelle in 1748. War with France broke out again in 1755 and did not go well until William Pitt (later Earl of Chatham) took over the administration and concluded treaties with Prussia. A series of victories in 1759 destroyed French power in the East Indies and led to the conquest of Canada and the capture of Guadaloupe and Senegal. The British Empire was beginning to take shape. George took personal delight in these successes and when critics suggested General Wolfe, the hero of Quebec, was mad, the king sprang to his defence with the words, 'Then I wish he would bite some other of my generals!'

By now the House of Hanover had gained a measure of popularity and support, and the earliest version of what was to become the national anthem, 'God Save Great George Our King', was first heard when George attended a gala performance at a London theatre to celebrate one of Britain's victories. Less calculated to excite public approval was a move by George's ministers to reduce consumption of gin – a proposal that led to mobs attacking the royal coach with the cry of 'No gin! No king!'. George's frequent absences from England, on visits to Hanover, were also frowned upon, and at one point a notice was placed by wags on the gates of St James's Palace, giving notice of a reward for anyone who could locate the monarch: 'Lost or strayed out of this house, a man who has left a wife and six children on the parish' – the reward offered amounted to four shillings and sixpence, 'nobody judging him to deserve a crown [five shillings]'. History, however, agrees that George's reign was a time of considerable advance in many spheres, and is inclined on the whole to reject Walter Savage Landor's hostile assessment of the king:

George the First was always reckoned
Vile, but viler George the Second.

George lost his queen in 1737 and his eldest son, Frederick, Prince of Wales, in 1751. Caroline's death saddened him, and he promised her that he would not marry again, despite her suggestions that he should do so – though he rather spoiled the effect by adding that from then on he would only keep mistresses. On 25 October 1760 he rose as usual at KENSINGTON PALACE and breakfasted on the inevitable cup of chocolate.

After enquiring about the direction of the wind, being anxious for the arrival of his overseas mail, he entered his water-closet. A few minutes later his valet heard a crash and found the king lying on the floor. He was lifted on to his bed and asked 'in a faint voice' for his favourite daughter, Princess AMELIA, but before she reached him he was dead. A post-mortem revealed the cause of death as a ruptured aneurysm of the aorta. He was buried in Westminster Abbey.

George II was a small man of delicate build and majestic carriage. He was inordinately proud of his 'fine foot', which was given due prominence in the coronation portrait from the studio of Charles Jervas now in the National Portrait Gallery. He had the protuberant blue eyes and pink and white complexion characteristic of the House of Hanover. Like his father, he had little interest in the arts and deprecated all 'boets and bainters', but he had a taste for music and continued the royal patronage of Handel. Indeed, he is said to have been so moved on hearing the 'Hallelujah Chorus' in *Messiah* that he spontaneously rose to his feet, starting the custom that has been observed ever since whenever that great work is performed.

George II acknowledged no bastard children, but it is generally believed that he was the father of Johann Ludwig, Graf von Wallmoden-Gimborn, born in Hanover on 27 April 1736, whose mother Amalie Sophie Marianne von Wendt, later created Countess of Yarmouth (1704–65), wife of Gottlieb Adam von Wallmoden-Gimborn, became the king's mistress (as supported by his own correspondence) in the summer of 1735. Johann Ludwig died in 1811 and there are many descendants.

George III, King of Great Britain (1738–1820) The eldest son and second child of FREDERICK LOUIS, PRINCE OF WALES and Augusta of Saxe-Gotha (*see* AUGUSTA, PRINCESS OF WALES), who was born at Norfolk House, St James's Square, London, on 4 June 1738 and named George William Frederick. At the time of his birth his parents were estranged from his grandfather GEORGE II and were to remain so until the Prince of Wales's death in 1751, when George succeeded him in the dukedom of Edinburgh and other peerages that had been created in 1726. George II called on his widowed daughter-in-law to express his condolences and told his grandsons that 'they must be brave boys, obedient to their mother, and deserve the fortune to which they were born'. On 20 April 1751, a month after his father's death, George was created Prince of Wales and Earl of Chester. His education was entrusted to Lord Harcourt and the Bishop of Norwich, though his mother was also to play a big part in the formation of his mind and character. It was she who, when George misbehaved, admonished him with the words, 'George, be a king!'.

George succeeded his grandfather George II in October 1760 at a time when the country was enjoying a high peak of prosperity. An early event of the reign was the appointment of the Earl of Bute, a favourite of the king's mother, as prime minister. George III declared at his first opening of Parliament that he 'gloried in the name of Briton', referring to his birth as the first British-born monarch since ANNE. In spite of his German antecedents he was the epitome of everything considered British and a living example of the triumph of environment over heredity. The young king possessed the strong sex drive common to many of the House of Hanover, but he also had strong moral principles, which inhibited him from finding relief with a mistress, so he was determined to marry as soon as possible. His interest was aroused by Lady Sarah Lennox, but realizing the unsuitabilty of the match he set his sights elsewhere and finally decided on an obscure German princess, Charlotte of Mecklenburg-Strelitz (see CHARLOTTE, QUEEN). It was to prove an excellent choice and in due course he fathered 15 children by her. The princess arrived in time to marry the king at ST JAMES'S PALACE on 8 September 1761 and be crowned with him at WESTMINSTER ABBEY two weeks later on 22 September. This was to be the last coronation of a British sovereign who also claimed to be king of France and, in accordance with an established custom, two actors were hired to impersonate the Dukes of Normandy and Aquitaine at the ceremony. An eye-witness was much amused by the jaunty way in which these two gentlemen clapped on their caps of maintenance at the moment when the king was crowned and the peers donned their coronets. On leaving the Abbey a large jewel fell from its setting in George's crown and the superstitious were later to point to this as an omen foretelling the loss of the American colonies.

George was a man of very simple habits and tastes and he and Queen Charlotte adopted a lifestyle far more akin to that of the rising middle class than to that of the nobility and gentry. This way of life has been largely maintained by the royal family ever since, with one or two notable exceptions. Their preferred residences were Kew or Windsor, and in 1762 George bought Buckingham House in St James's Park for £21,000 from Sir Charles Sheffield. Buckingham House, sometimes referred to as the Queen's House, was to become BUCKINGHAM PALACE.

Early in 1764 the king suffered the first attack of an illness now believed to have been PORPHYRIA, the 'royal malady' (though suspicion has also fallen on lead poisoning through the drinking vessels he used). On recovering from this attack he proposed that Parliament should legislate an act enabling him to appoint the queen, or some other member of the royal family, guardian to the heir apparent and regent of the kingdom if the necessity arose. The bill was passed but met with a considerable amount of opposition, leading to a change of ministry.

The king was anxious to break the power of the Whig oligarchy that had ruled the country under the first two Georges and created his own party of 'King's Friends'. Through them he was able to manipulate affairs and effected frequent changes of ministry. He finally appointed his own minister, Lord North, in 1770.

The marriages of two of the king's brothers to ladies he considered entirely unsuitable led to the passing of the ROYAL MARRIAGES ACT in 1772. This provided that no descendant of George II under the age of 25 (with the exception of the descendants of princesses married into foreign families) might contract matrimony without first obtaining the consent of the sovereign in council. Over the age of 25, those wishing to marry without obtaining this consent were obliged to give notice of their intention to do so to the Privy Council. They would then be free to marry after a year had elapsed provided no objection had been raised by either House of Parliament. The Act was to give rise to some strange situations affecting George's sons and grandsons.

The American War of Independence was a great blow to the king and in 1788 he suffered a second attack of porphyria. This time it was more serious and he was badly deranged from October to the following February. Fanny Burney has left a graphic account of some of his delusions, and on one memorable occasion she was chased by him at Windsor. A characteristic of the illness was that the king would become extremely agitated, uttering staccato shouts of 'What!

What! What!'. On one famous occasion (possibly apocryphal) he was found in deep conversation with an oak tree in Windsor Great Park believing it to be the King of Prussia. He made a full recovery, however, and on St George's Day 1790 went in state with the queen and royal family to St Paul's to return thanks for his deliverance.

The French Revolution was a further cause for concern, and in the 1790s there were several attempts on the king's life. On 15 May 1798 he was attending a review in Hyde Park when a gentleman standing by him was wounded by a musket-ball, whether by accident or by design there is no knowing. The incident caused the king's attendants to try to dissuade him from visiting the Drury Lane Theatre that evening. He refused to listen to them and, accompanied by the queen and some of their daughters, went to the theatre. A moment after he had entered the royal box a man in the pit (later identified as James Hadfield) fired at him but a person near the would-be assassin was able to deflect his aim so that the bullet missed the king and lodged in the roof of the box. George remained quite calm and turned to the queen and princesses who were just entering the box, saying 'Keep back, keep back; they are firing squibs for diversion, and perhaps there may be more'. The loyalty of the audience at this display of firmness was shown by prolonged cheering and the singing of 'God Save the King!' three times, with the addition of an impromptu verse hastily penned by Sheridan:

> From every latent foe,
> From the assassin's blow,
> God Save the King!
> O'er him thine arm extend,
> For Britain's sake defend,
> Our father, prince and friend;
> God Save the King!

The would-be assassin was indicted for high treason but found to be of unsound mind and committed to Bedlam.

The last 10 years of George's active reign were dominated by the Napoleonic wars in Europe and the threat of invasion. The king entered the 50th year of his reign on 25 October 1809 and a jubilee was held. His eyesight had virtually given out by 1805 and the death of his youngest daughter Princess AMELIA from consumption at the end of 1810 precipitated his last attack of insanity. This time there was to be no recovery. He alarmed officials with his claims that he could talk with the angels. The Regency Act was passed and on 11 February 1811 the Prince of Wales (*see* GEORGE IV) was proclaimed Prince Regent of the United Kingdom. George passed the last years of his life at Windsor, blind, deaf and mad. His beard was allowed to grow and the patriarchal figure was sometimes to be glimpsed staring with sightless eyes from a window of the Castle. He was unaware of the death of the queen in November 1818 and under the care of his second son, the Duke of York, lived on until 29 January 1820, when he died of senile decay, having lived longer than any previous sovereign. He was buried in the new Royal Tomb House, which he had himself had constructed at Windsor.

By the time of his death George had established himself as one of the more popular Hanoverian kings, admired for the respectability of his private life and for his piety and sympathized with for his lengthy illness. He had inherited the family love of music and was also a patron of the arts and sciences, his books forming the nucleus of the future British Library. He had, however, a healthy contempt for Shakespeare ('Was there ever such *stuff* as this Shakespeare, Miss Burney? Only one must not say so, what! what!'). He took a keen interest in agriculture and his creation of model farms at Windsor earned him the humble nickname 'Farmer George', which he greatly relished.

George IV, King of Great Britain (1762–1830) The eldest child of GEORGE III and Queen CHARLOTTE, who was born at ST JAMES'S PALACE on 12 August 1762 and baptized there by the Archbishop of Canterbury on 8 September 1762, receiving the names of George Augustus Frederick. His godparents were his great-uncle William Augustus, Duke of CUMBERLAND, his uncle the Duke of Mecklenburg-Strelitz (for whom the Duke of Devonshire stood proxy) and his grandmother AUGUSTA, PRINCESS OF WALES. He succeeded as Duke of Cornwall, Duke of Rothesay, etc. at birth and was created Prince of Wales and Earl of Chester five days later on 17 August 1762.

Like all his parents' children he was endowed with outstanding good looks, fair hair, blue eyes and a pink and white complexion, although a tendency to corpulence was to become more pronounced in later life, aided by indulgence in food and drink and lack of exercise. George was very close to his next brother Frederick, and the two boys shared an upbringing and education in the privacy of KEW PALACE. George learned easily and acquired a good grounding in literature and science. As he grew up, his good looks, high spirits and agreeable manners were to earn him considerable popularity and make him the darling of the fashionable world, among whom he was familiarly known as 'Prinny'.

Up to his 18th year the prince met few people apart from his family circle and his tutors, but he then began to associate with the Whig nobility. He also possessed the strong sex drive of the Hanoverians and developed a penchant for amply proportioned ladies somewhat older than himself. His first mistress was the actress Mrs Robinson, whom he first saw as Perdita in Shakespeare's *The Winter's Tale* in 1778, when she was 20 and he 16. She was very beautiful, as her protraits by Reynolds, Gainsborough, Romney and other artists testify, but George soon deserted her and embarked on a series of love affairs.

On coming of age in 1783, George set up his own establishment at CARLTON HOUSE, was voted £30,000 by Parliament to pay his debts, and received an annual allowance of £50,000 from his father. About this time he fell in love with a respectable Roman Catholic widow of 27, Mary Anne (or Maria) Fitzherbert (*see* FITZHERBERT, MRS). George's passion knew no bounds, but the only way he could get her was by marriage. Consequently, on 21 December 1785, having impressed his beloved by stabbing himself (or at least pretending to) to show his love for her, a ceremony was performed at the lady's house in London. The marriage was null and void in law as it contravened the terms of the ROYAL MARRIAGES ACT. Had it not been illegal, George, as the husband of a Roman Catholic, would have lost his position as heir to the throne under the terms of the ACT OF SETTLEMENT. Rumours of the prince's marriage were soon all over London, and he took the step of getting his friend Charles James Fox to deny it in the House of Commons.

The lavish redecorating of Carlton House had again involved George in debts, this time amounting to more than £250,000, and he applied to the king, who refused help. George accordingly sold off his racehorses, dismissed many of his servants and announced his intention of living in retirement until he had liquidated his debt. The good impression this created paid off. The king agreed to add £10,000 per annum to his son's income out of the civil list and Parliament voted a further £161,000 to satisfy his creditors and £20,000 for the completion of Carlton House. George's immediate reaction was to plunge into a new round of extravagance (new projects included the construction of BRIGHTON PAVILION).

George III's first prolonged attack of madness in 1788 brought the question of the Prince of Wales's possible regency to the fore, and pressures were put on him to marry. He had temporarily deserted Mrs Fizherbert for the Countess of Jersey, 'the worst and most dangerous of profligate women', as she was to be described in an anonymous letter sent to the Duchess of Brunswick. She was the most mature of his mistresses to date, nine years his senior and already a grandmother at 41. In 1794 George's creditors were pressing again and the conditional promise of a settlement, together with an increase of income, led him to announce that he was ready to marry his cousin Princess CAROLINE OF BRUNSWICK. The Earl of Malmesbury was despatched to Brunswick to negotiate with the ducal family and escort the princess back to England. They arrived on 5 April 1795, but the first meeting between George and Caroline was disastrous. George took one look at his proposed bride, ordered a glass of brandy and then promptly left the room. 'Mon dieu!', said Caroline, 'Is the Prince always like that? I find him very fat, and nothing like as handsome as his portrait.' Nevertheless the marriage took place at the Chapel Royal, St James's, on 8 April 1795. George only got through the ceremony by being drunk – in fact he was so far gone that at one stage he rose from his knees and began to wander about, having to be led back to his place by the king. He spent his wedding-night lying insensible in the grate, as Caroline was to relate later, but he had managed to consummate the marriage and from that one act of intercourse (they never slept together again, if the princess is to be believed) Caroline conceived and bore Princess Charlotte (*see* CHARLOTTE OF WALES, PRINCESS) nine months later.

The Princess of Wales had been obliged to accept Lady Jersey as a Lady of the Bedchamber and was soon to learn of the circumstances that had led to her unhappy marriage. After Princess Charlotte's birth George sent her proposals for a separation, to which she readily acceded. In 1804 there was a dispute over the custody of Princess Charlotte, which was settled by the king undertaking her guardianship. George now returned to Mrs Fitzherbert, but continued to be distracted by other mature ladies from time to time.

The threat of invasion by Napoleon led

George, then only the colonel of a regiment of dragoons while the Duke of York was Commander-in-Chief and some of his other brothers were generals, to demand to be given a higher position in the army – but the ministry coolly declined his request. The deterioration in the king's mental health, however, led to new proposals for a regency and, after negotiations with the Whigs, George was persuaded by his current mistress, Lady Hertford, to agree to a restricted regency, being proclaimed Prince Regent of the United Kingdom on 5 February 1811. The Regency saw the final defeat of Napoleon and gave George a chance to indulge his love of display by lavishly entertaining the Emperor of Russia, the King of Prussia and other allied sovereigns when they visited England in the course of their triumphant victory progress.

George's only daughter, Princess Charlotte, was married in May 1816 to Prince Leopold of Saxe-Coburg-Saalfeld (*see* LEOPOLD OF SAXE-COBURG, PRINCE). The young couple were blissfully happy and were given Claremont House near Esher in Surrey as a residence. The mismanagement of Charlotte's third unsuccessful pregnancy by the princess's physician (who subsequently committed suicide) led to the birth of a stillborn son and her death from haemorrhage and shock the following morning. His daughter's death plunged George into a paroxysm of grief and meant that there were now no legitimate heirs to the throne in the second generation. George's unmarried brothers, the Dukes of Clarence, Kent, and Cambridge, hastily sought brides to provide for the succession.

Meanwhile, the unrest felt throughout the country in the aftermath of the Napoleonic wars caused serious rioting in the large manufacturing towns. In London a few desperate men, later to be known as the Cato Street Conspirators, were tried and executed for plotting to assassinate the Regent and leading members of the administration.

The death of George III on 29 January 1820 brought the regent to the throne as George IV. Almost his first concern was to find a way to prevent his estranged wife, who had been living abroad for some years, from returning to England to take up her position as queen. Failing in this, he forced his ministers to introduce a Bill of Pains and Penalties to deprive her of the title of queen and effectively dissolve the marriage. The so-called 'trial of Queen Caroline' followed in the House of Lords, ending with the Bill being dropped after its third reading on 10 November 1820.

George spent much time planning the details of his coronation. As a result, it was probably the most magnificent ever staged in this country, and it was the last at which the sovereign proceeded on foot from WEST-MINSTER HALL to the abbey and then back again for the banquet. The ceremony was marred by the pathetic attempts of Queen Caroline to gain entrance to the abbey, no provision having been made for her to be crowned or even to witness the spectacle. She died a few weeks later.

In August 1821 the king visited Ireland; in September he went to Hanover; and in 1822 he went to Scotland, the first Hanoverian monarch to set foot there. The event was largely stage-managed by Sir Walter Scott and was a great success. George wore a kilt over pink tights and displayed the graciousness and affability for which he was never at a loss. The reign was to see many changes of ministry, and the most important event towards its end was the Catholic Emancipation Act, which was passed in April 1829 after George had done his best to block it.

The king suffered from gout in his later years and divided his time between Brighton and Windsor, living very quietly with his last mistress, Lady Conyngham. His final illness began in January 1830 with a severe cough, and although there was a slight improvement in March, respiratory trouble persisted, complicated by pain in the urinary tract and faintness. He rode in Windsor Great Park for the last time on 12 April and thereafter attacks of biliousness and difficulty in breathing became increasingly frequent. At 3.15 on the morning of 26 June he died peacefully, murmuring 'This is death' to his attendants. He was buried in the Royal Tomb House at St George's Chapel, Windsor.

George IV had many redeeming qualities. He was naturally kind and generous and his life was marked by many acts of private benevolence. He encouraged literature and art and was the patron of public institutions for charitable objects and the advancement of science. Possessed of a lively imagination, he was often to indulge in flights of fancy. A good instance is the way in which he was able to delude himself that he had actually been present and led a charge at the battle of Waterloo. On one occasion, perceiving that his listeners appeared to doubt his word, he called to the Duke of Wellington for confirmation: 'Is that not so, Duke?' The wily duke tactfully replied, 'I have often heard Your Majesty say so.'

George did not openly acknowledge any bastard offspring, but he did privately own to and provide for two natural sons. The first was George Seymour Crole, whose mother was Elizabeth Fox *alias* Crole (died on 15 February 1840). He was born in London on 23 August 1799 and had a not undistinguished army career before dying unmarried at Chatham on 13 June 1863. The other was William Francis, born to a Mrs Davies in 1806. It is possible that the king also fathered several other children, in particular Georgina Augusta Frederica Seymour, who was born in London on 30 March 1782 and baptized at St Marylebone on 30 July following as 'daughter of the Prince of Wales'. Her mother was Grace Dalrymple, wife of Sir John Elliott. This daughter later married Lord Charles Bentinck, a son of the 3rd Duke of Portland. She died in London on 10 December 1813 and her only daughter died unmarried.

George V, King of Great Britain (1865–1936)

The second son of Albert Edward, Prince of Wales (later EDWARD VII) and ALEXANDRA OF DENMARK, who was born at Marlborough House, London, on 3 June 1865 and baptized George Frederick Ernest Albert in the private chapel at WINDSOR CASTLE on 7 July following, his godparents being King George V of Hanover, the Crown Prince (later King Frederik VIII) of Denmark, the Duke of Saxe-Coburg and Gotha (all represented by proxies), the Duke of Cambridge, the Prince of Leiningen, his grandmother the Queen of Denmark (for whom Queen VICTORIA stood proxy), his aunt Princess Alice and his great-grand-aunt the Duchess of Cambridge (both also represented by proxies).

As the second son of the heir apparent, George was able to embark on a naval career, his prospects of succeeding to the throne being considered remote. He was therefore able to see more of life at an ordinary level than many princes, and the rough and ready manners of the quarterdeck were to remain with him to a large extent throughout his life. In this he resembled WILLIAM IV, though without that king's eccentricity. His brusque heartiness was to endear him to his subjects, so that by the end of his reign he had become one of the best loved and respected of all English monarchs. He was very touched by the warmth of the reception accorded to him by the crowds when he drove through the streets of London on the occasion of his Silver Jubilee in 1935, recording in his diary 'They must love me for myself alone.'

George grew up a devoted son to both his parents and a devoted brother to his brother and sisters. He had a simple, straightforward mind and was completely incapable of deviousness in any form. His relations with his father were particularly good, unlike those that had persisted between the sovereigns and the heir apparent since the time of GEORGE I. This is surprising since no two men could have been more different in temperament, outlook and general lifestyle than George and his father. Unfortunately, the same cordial relations were not to extend into the next generation, and George and his eldest son grew increasingly irritated with each other, although their differences never reached the proportions of those that had obtained in the 18th century.

On 14 January 1892 the unexpected death of George's elder brother the Duke of Clarence (*see* CLARENCE, ALBERT VICTOR, DUKE OF) placed him second in line to the throne and on 24 May the same year his grandmother Queen Victoria created him Baron Killarney, Earl of Inverness and Duke of York. His engagement to Princess Victoria MARY OF TECK, the fiancée of his late brother, was announced on 3 May 1893 and they were married at the Chapel Royal, ST JAMES'S PALACE, 'at half-past twelve o'clock' on 6 July 1893. George had found a wife who was ideally suited to him. He remained entirely faithful to her, although he and his sister Princess VICTORIA, both notoriously philistine, were often to scoff at May's artistic pretensions. The king, who once said that his favourite opera was *La Bohème* 'because it is the shortest', was interested in little other than sailing, racing, stamp-collecting and shooting (led by George, royal shooting parties were known to account for as many as 10,000 birds in just four days). Another weakness was his parrot, CHARLOTTE, who was allowed to roam unrestrained on the dining-table at breakfast at Sandringham. Lord Tweedsmuir related an amusing story recounted to him by his father, the novelist John Buchan, who was received in audience by the king on being appointed Governor-General of Canada in 1935. In the course of conversation the king remarked how much he enjoyed reading Buchan's books. After making appropriately gratified noises the author was passed on to Queen Mary who also said how much she enjoyed his books, but added 'the king only reads the most dreadful rubbish'.

At about the same time that the engagement to Princess May was announced, some English papers carried a story that the prince was, in fact, already married – either to an American woman or in Malta to the daughter of a British naval officer. A case for libel was instituted by the Palace and the originator of the story was in due course sentenced to a year in prison, the prince's reputation restored.

The death of Queen Victoria in January 1901 brought George's father to the throne as Edward VII and George himself became Duke of Cornwall and Duke of Rothesey, etc. He was styled Duke of Cornwall and York until his creation as Prince of Wales and Earl of Chester on 9 November 1901. On Edward's death on 6 May 1910, George ascended the throne and he and Queen Mary were crowned at WESTMINSTER ABBEY on 22 June 1911. Later in the year they travelled to India to hold the great Delhi Durbar, a triumph of Empire, when as King-Emperor and Queen-Empress they received the homage of the Indian princes and showed themselves in imperial splendour to their Indian subjects. It was a unique occasion, and it must have seemed then that the British Empire was one not only on which the sun never set, but on which the sun never would set. Three years later the world was plunged into the First World War, which was to bring about the biggest change in the old order of things since the Napoleonic wars a century before. Britain weathered the storm and the Empire survived, although it was clear that the days of colonialism were now numbered. It is doubtful if George V ever accepted this, however, and among the last words attributed to him as he lay dying at Sandringham was the question, 'How is the Empire?'

During the war, George went out of his way to prove himself an able leader, visiting the front and supporting the propaganda effort. In 1917, in response to anti-German feeling, the king decreed that henceforth the royal family would take the surname Windsor, rather than Saxe-Coburg or Wettin as it had done previously. After the war, he continued to impress his people with his sense of duty towards the constitution and the country, despite the difficulties posed by failing health.

George V died of a severe bronchial infection at his favourite residence, SANDRING-HAM HOUSE, Norfolk, on 20 January 1936 (see DAWSON OF PENN, BERTRAND DAWSON,

1ST VISCOUNT). One version of his last hours insists that his last utterance was the prosaic though characteristic 'Bugger Bognor!', allegedly uttered in response to the suggestion by Queen Mary that the king would recover his health at Bognor again, as he had done after being gravely ill with septicaemia in 1928. Like 'How is the Empire?', these 'last words' are now considered apocryphal, and it seems most likely that his last coherent utterance was an apology for his inability to concentrate when called upon to sign the deed appointing COUNSELLORS OF STATE to act for him during his illness. He was buried at St George's Chapel, Windsor, where his tomb and that of Queen Mary are the last to bear sculptured recumbent effigies of the occupants in the medieval manner.

George V was the first king to make use of wireless to broadcast a message to his people and established the custom of an annual Christmas message, since continued by his successors. It is also interesting to note that he revived the custom of distributing the Royal MAUNDY MONEY in person on the Thursday before Easter, a function that had long been delegated to the Lord High Almoner. The king's interest in the matter was stimulated by his cousin Princess Marie Louise, who had formed the habit of attending the service at Westminster Abbey and felt it would be appropriate for the sovereign to resume this pleasant custom, whereby gifts of money are distributed to as many men and women as the years of the sovereign's age.

George VI, King of Great Britain (1895–1952) The second son of George, Duke of York (later GEORGE V) and Princess Victoria Mary of Teck (later Queen MARY), who was born at York Cottage, Sandringham, Norfolk, at 3.40 am on 14 December 1895. It was the anniversary of the death of his great-grandfather the Prince Consort in 1861, and Queen VICTORIA received the news of the birth with mixed feelings, her son the Prince of Wales (later EDWARD VII) writing to the baby's father to report that 'Grandmama was rather distressed that this happy event should have taken place on a darkly sad anniversary for us, but I think – as well as most of us in the family here – that it will "break the spell" of this unlucky date'. The child was baptized by the Bishop of Norwich at St Mary's Church, Sandringham, on 17 February 1896, receiving the names of Albert Frederick Arthur George. To his family he was always to be known as Bertie.

Bertie grew up, as his father had done, without any specific training for the throne, which it seemed unlikely he would ever occupy. Following the tradition for second sons in the royal family, he entered the Royal Navy as a midshipman in 1913 (despite the fact that he suffered from sea-sickness and would rather have gone to Oxford, like Edward). Unlike his elder brother, he was allowed to see active service during the First World War with the Grand Fleet and distinguished himself at the battle of Jutland in 1916 (while with HMS *Collingwood*), being mentioned in despatches. He was promoted Lieutenant in 1918 and Commander in 1920, finishing the war with the Royal Naval Air Service. His health was always delicate, however, and apart from a speech impediment which he fought hard to overcome, he had a severe attack of appendicitis, necessitating an operation in August 1914. This was followed by recurring attacks of gastric trouble for several years, eventually diagnosed as a duodenal ulcer, which was successfully operated on in November 1917. His active naval career came to an end, and on 3 June 1920 he was created Baron Killarney, Earl of Inverness and Duke of York, the same titles that his father had received in 1892. He wrote ingenuously to his father, 'I must ... thank you again ever so very much for having made me Duke of York. I'm very proud to bear the name you did for many years and I hope I shall live up to it in every way'. The young prince had already been created a Knight of the GARTER in 1916 and was later granted many more honours.

In the early 1920s Bertie started the Duke of York's Camps, a scheme for bringing together public schoolboys and working-class boys in seaside summer holiday camps. They were a great success, being held annually until 1939. The duke himself attended the camps and enjoyed participating in the nightly sing-songs around the camp fire. Another pleasure was playing tennis, and, having won the RAF tennis doubles championship in 1920, he made a one and only appearance in the doubles at Wimbledon (he went out in the first round).

At about this time, the duke began to develop his friendship with Lady Elizabeth Bowes-Lyon (*see* ELIZABETH THE QUEEN MOTHER) who, as a Girl Guide District Commissioner, had become a close friend of his sister Princess Mary, at whose wedding in 1922 she was a bridesmaid. The engagement of the Duke of York and Lady Elizabeth was announced in January 1923

and the wedding took place at WESTMINSTER ABBEY on 26 April. The romance fired the popular imagination from the start. King George and Queen Mary were delighted with their new daughter-in-law and with the two little granddaughters who appeared on the scene in the course of the next seven years.

It seemed that the Duke and Duchess of York were destined to fulfil a supporting role in the royal family far into the foreseeable future, but the abdication of EDWARD VIII in December 1936 (*see* ABDICATION CRISIS) suddenly called them (initially reluctantly) to the throne. The prince greeted the news of his brother's decision to abdicate with dismay, as shown in a letter to Lord Louis MOUNTBATTEN:

> Dickie, this is absolutely terrible. I never wanted this to happen; I'm quite unprepared for it. David has been trained for this all his life. I've never even seen a State Paper. I'm only a Naval Officer, it's the only thing I know about.

Mountbatten assured the prince that there could be no better training for a future monarch than a naval career and Bertie resigned himself to his fate, choosing to reign as George VI, using his last Christian name. Under expert tutelage he also set about countering his debilitating stammer, with some success (though he never entirely conquered it).

The new king and queen and their daughters were tremendously popular, and the country soon recovered from the blow of the abdication. The coronation took place at Westminster Abbey on 12 May 1937, the day already appointed for that of Edward VIII (in whose name many coronation souvenirs had already been made and marketed), and for the first time for many centuries it was attended by the Queen Mother. The two little princesses were also a novel sight in their miniature robes and coronets.

Within a few years the country was plunged into the Second World War. The example of the king and queen, who refused to leave London throughout the bombing or to send their children to a safe area, did much for public morale. BUCKINGHAM PALACE received a stick of six bombs in September 1940 while the royal family were in residence and the royal couple themselves had a narrow escape. In 1945 the king nursed hopes of being present at the D-Day landings, as did Winston Churchill, but advisers persuaded both men that their presence would prove a hindrance.

The years succeeding the war were busy

ones, including a strenuous tour of South Africa and the Festival of Britain in 1951. King George's never very robust health began to give cause for anxiety, and some months after he and the queen celebrated their silver wedding in 1948 he underwent an operation for a circulatory obstruction in the leg arteries. Three years later he fell ill again, and in September 1951 part of his left lung was removed and found to be cancerous (though the king himself was told that he was merely suffering from a 'bronchial blockage'). He made a partial recovery and in January 1952 felt so much better that his daughter Princess Elizabeth, the heiress presumptive, was able to set off on a projected world tour without any qualms. On 5 February 1952 the king spent a happy day out shooting on the Sandringham estate, but some time after midnight that night he died peacefully in his sleep, aged 56. He was buried at St George's Chapel, Windsor, where a new chantry chapel was constructed off the north choir aisle and dedicated on 31 March 1969.

Few monarchs have been as greatly loved as George VI, a shy, retiring man who never wanted to be king but who shouldered the burdens of sovereignty with characteristic courage and dignity.

George of Denmark, Prince (1653–1708) The consort of Queen ANNE, who was the third and youngest son and sixth child of Frederik III, King of Denmark and Norway, by his wife Sophie Amalie, daughter of Georg, Duke of Brunswick-Lüneburg, and was born at Copenhagen on 2 April 1653. As a prince of Denmark he was invested with the Danish Order of the Elephant. His early life appears to have passed uneventfully and he was already in his 30th year when he was put forward as a husband for his second cousin Anne, the second daughter of James, Duke of York (later JAMES II). It is believed that Louis XIV of France had a hand in the matchmaking, being desirous of gaining Danish support for his policies in northern Europe.

George, a solid, dull, phlegmatic young man, journeyed to England and the marriage was solemnized at the Chapel Royal, St James's, on the evening of 28 July 1683. CHARLES II admonished his new nephew: 'Walk with me, hunt with my brother and do justice to my niece.' George certainly strove to fulfil the last of these injunctions, as testified by Anne's many pregnancies (see QUEEN ANNE'S CHILDREN). He was naturalized in England on 20 September 1683, invested as

a Knight of the GARTER in 1684 and, after acting as chief mourner at the funeral of Charles II, was sworn in as a Privy Councillor in 1685. In 1688 he deserted his father-in-law and sided with his wife's brother-in-law William of Orange (later WILLIAM III). He was sworn in as a Privy Councillor to the new joint sovereigns in 1689 and was subsequently created Baron Ockingham (or Wokingham), Earl of Kendal and Duke of Cumberland (though he was never called or referred to by his peerage title). He was appointed Chief Commissioner of Greenwich Hospital in 1695.

George took a keen fatherly interest in the upbringing of his only child to survive infancy, William Henry[1], Duke of GLOUCESTER, on one occasion administering corporal punishment after the boy used some mildly profane language, and shared in the general grief when the child died in 1700. On the death of William III, whereby George's wife succeeded to the throne, he was again appointed to fulfil the role of chief mourner at the funeral of a sovereign. Anne contemplated making him king consort, but was dissuaded and instead he was appointed Generalissimo of all the Forces, Constable of WINDSOR CASTLE, Lord High Admiral, Lord Warden of the Cinque Ports and Captain General of the Honourable Artillery Company. At Anne's coronation on 23 April 1702, George paid her homage, the first occasion on which the husband of a reigning queen had done so.

Prince George played no part whatsoever in politics and was entirely devoid of ambition, being interested solely in eating and drinking. He adored his wife and when he died, at KENSINGTON PALACE on 28 October 1708, she grieved deeply for him. He was buried in WESTMINSTER ABBEY on 13 November 1708.

History remembers Prince George as a man of considerable denseness. His response to almost everything that was said to him was *Est il possible?*: when his father-in-law James II heard that George had joined the Prince of Orange he was moved to remark, 'What, is *est il possible?* gone too?'. Much earlier, Charles II had said of George, 'I have tried him drunk and I have tried him sober, and drunk or sober, there is nothing in him.'

George William, Prince (1717–18) The third son and sixth child of George, Prince of Wales (later GEORGE II) and CAROLINE OF ANSBACH, who was born at ST JAMES'S

PALACE on 2 November (13 November new style) 1717. A dispute between his parents and his grandfather GEORGE I regarding the choice of his godparents led to the prince's parents being expelled from St James's Palace by the king. The baptism took place on 28 November and was registered at St Martin-in-the-Fields. The king got his way, for he and the Duke of Newcastle were godfathers, whereas the parents had wanted George I's brother Ernst August to be godfather with the king. The little prince lived for only four months, dying at KENSINGTON PALACE on 6 February (17 February new style) 1718. He was buried at WESTMINSTER ABBEY on 12 February with considerable pomp for such a young child.

Gervase of Blois, Abbot of Westminster (c.1115/20–60) A natural son of King STEPHEN by a Norman girl named Dameta, who was appointed Abbot of Westminster in 1137. He resigned his office in 1157 and died in 1160.

Gildas, St (c.500–c.570) The author of the diatribe entitled *De Excidio et Conquestu Britanniae* (Concerning the Ruin and Conquest of Britain), who belonged to a Romano-British family from Strathclyde. He is said to have studied at the monastic school established by St Illtyd at Llantwit Major in Glamorgan. His famous work was a savage denunciation of the five contemporary British rulers of Britain, all of whom had transgressed the strong Christian principles held by him. He exhorted them to amend their ways before it was too late and cited scripture to make his points. He is said to have spent some time as a hermit on an island in the Bristol Channel, to have visited Ireland and to have spent his last days in Brittany, where he died on the isle of Houat. His feast day is observed on 29 January. The authenticity of his work has been questioned by recent scholars, who believe part of it to be a later forgery. There has also been some confusion with a younger Gildas who belonged to the royal house of Strathclyde.

Glappa, King of Bernicia (d.560?) This very shadowy figure appears to have been the eldest son of IDA, KING OF BERNICIA and his wife Bearnoch. He succeeded his father in 559 and appears to have reigned for one year only, being succeeded by his brother ADDA.

Glorious Revolution, The The sequence of events that led to JAMES II's replacement on the throne by WILLIAM III and MARY II, precipitated by James's Catholic policies.

Gloucester, Earls and Dukes of The royal holders of this title are here dealt with chronologically.

1. **Robert de Caen, alias FitzRoy, Earl of Gloucester** (c.1090–1147) The natural son of HENRY I, probably by Sibylla, daughter of Roger Corbet, burgess of Caen, who was born at Caen in Normandy in about 1090. He witnessed his father's charters from about April 1113 and fought in the battle of Brémulé on 20 August 1119 when Henry I defeated Louis VI of France. He was created Earl of Gloucester between June and September 1122. In 1126 he was given the custody of his uncle ROBERT, DUKE OF NORMANDY, held prisoner at Bristol and later at Cardiff. He recognized his half-sister the Empress Matilda (*see* MATILDA, 'LADY OF THE ENGLISH', EMPRESS) as his father's heir in 1127 and was later to become one of her most staunch supporters and her commander-in-chief in the long struggle with STEPHEN. His father had arranged a marriage for him with his ward Mabel, daughter and heiress of Robert FitzHamon and his wife Sibyl, daughter of Roger de Montgomery, Earl of Shrewsbury, and they had a large family of at least six sons and one daughter. The Earl of Gloucester died of fever at Bristol, his chief residence, on 31 October 1147, and was buried in the Priory of St James there, which he had founded. His widow died in 1157. The earldom of Gloucester passed to Robert's eldest son, William FitzRobert, and on his death without surviving male issue on 23 November 1183, it fell into abeyance between his three daughters and co-heiresses, the youngest of whom, Isabella (*see* ISABELLA OF GLOUCESTER), received it on her marriage to John, Count of Mortain (later King JOHN).

2. **Thomas of Woodstock, Duke of Gloucester** (1355–97) The sixth son and twelfth and youngest child of EDWARD III and PHILIPPA OF HAINAULT, who was born at Woodstock on 7 January 1355. Thomas was only six months old when he was appointed a Guardian of the Kingdom in July 1355 during his father's absences in France until May 1360. In 1358 he and some of his siblings were placed in their mother's keeping, and she received £200 a year for their maintenance.

Thomas was appointed Constable of England on 10 June 1376 and summoned to Parliament as such on 1 December following. He was knighted on 23 April 1377. On the accession of his nephew RICHARD II he was reappointed Constable of England on

22 June 1377 and carried the sceptre and the crown at the king's coronation, on which day he was created Earl of Buckingham. He took an active part with his brother Edmund in the successful actions against the French and Spanish fleets in 1377 and 1378. On 23 April 1380 he was nominated a Knight of the GARTER and, following his wife's coming of age later in the year, became Earl of Essex in her right.

The next few years were occupied by military campaigns in France and Scotland and in putting down the Peasants' Revolt. On 6 August 1385 he was created Duke of Gloucester. Subsequently he fell out with his nephew the king because of his opposition to Richard's favourites, Michael de la Pole, Earl of Suffolk, and Robert de Vere, Duke of Ireland. He totally defeated the latter at a battle in Oxfordshire on 20 December 1387 and returned to London to receive a triumphal reception from the citizens, who gained possession of the Tower and seized the king, who was forced to accept his uncle's demands. Some of the favourites were impeached and executed, and Gloucester remained all powerful until May 1389, when the king began to regain a measure of power and by recalling another uncle, John of Gaunt, Duke of LANCASTER, was able to end Gloucester's domination of affairs.

The duke, probably feeling frustrated by his exclusion from government, set out for Prussia in September 1391 to visit the Teutonic Knights and seek adventure with them, but he was driven back by adverse winds and forced to land at Tynemouth, whence he returned to his estates at Pleshey in Essex. After a short tenure as Lieutenant of Ireland from April to July 1392, the duke again busied himself with the affairs of Londoners and interceded for them with the king. In the following year he went to France with his brother the Duke of Lancaster to sue for peace, and in 1394 went to Ireland with the king.

The duke and duchess attended the king's wedding to Princess ISABELLA OF FRANCE[2] at Calais on 4 November 1396, in spite of his disapproval of the match. His unpopularity at his nephew's court was increasing and in 1397 he retired to Pleshey pleading ill-health. Here he conspired with others to depose the king. He was betrayed by Mowbray, the Earl Marshal, and on 10 July 1397 Richard set out for Pleshey at the head of a considerable force. His uncle met him in the courtyard with all due honour and was persuaded to return with him to London.

On the journey the king had him arrested at Stratford and taken to Calais, where he was kept under arrest by the Earl of Nottingham, Captain of Calais. A justice of the common pleas, Sir William Rickhill, was sent to obtain the duke's confession, which he did on 8 September. That night or the following the duke was smothered under a feather bed. When Parliament met later in the month an order was sent to the Earl Marshal to produce his prisoner for trial on the charge of high treason, but a reply was received on 24 September that the duke was dead. His confession was read to Parliament and he was declared guilty of treason and his estates and goods were forfeited to the crown, a forfeiture that was reversed in the first Parliament of HENRY IV. The duke's body was returned to England and buried in the Chapel of St Edmund the King and St Thomas of Canterbury in WESTMINSTER ABBEY, whence Henry IV had it removed to a site nearer the Confessor's shrine in 1399.

The duke had married before 24 August 1376, Eleanor, the eldest daughter and co-heiress of Humphrey de Bohun, 7th Earl of Hereford, and his wife Joan, daughter of Richard FitzAlan, 8th Earl of Arundel. She was born in May 1366 and after the deaths of her husband and only son became a nun at Barking Abbey, Essex. She died either there or at the Minoresses Convent in Aldgate on 3 October 1399, and was buried in St Edmund's Chapel at Westminster Abbey. They had one son, Humphrey, who was born about April 1382 and kept in confinement at Westminster after his father's death until April 1399, when Richard II took him to Ireland and imprisoned him in Trim Castle. He was released in August by Henry IV, but died of plague at Chester while on his return journey on 2 September 1399. He was buried at Walden Priory, Essex. The Duke and Duchess of Gloucester also had four daughters: Anne, born in April 1383, who married first, Thomas Stafford, 3rd Earl of Stafford, secondly, his brother Edmund, the 5th Earl, by whom she had issue, and thirdly, Sir William Bourchier, by whom she also had issue (she died on 16 October 1438); Joan, who was born in 1384 and died unmarried on 16 August 1400, being buried at Walden Priory; Isabel, who was born on 12 March 1386, professed a nun of the Order of St Clare at the Minoresses Convent in Aldgate on 23 April 1399, and died in about April 1402; and Philippa, who was born in about 1389 and died in 1399.

Thomas, Duke of Gloucester, resembled his eldest brother, EDWARD OF WOOD-

STOCK, PRINCE OF WALES, in character, being, according to Froissart, 'obstinate in his opinions' and 'proud and presuming in manner'. Elsewhere it is also stated that his manners were 'severe and rough'. However, he was much loved by the Londoners who admired his bravery and his business acumen. His wife, too, appears to have been devoted to him and it was reported that 'in prudence, modesty and holiness, she surpassed all the women of her day'.

3. **Humphrey, Duke of Gloucester** (1390–1447) The fifth and youngest son of Henry, Earl of Derby (later HENRY IV) and his first wife Mary de Bohun, who was born on 3 October 1390, his father being absent in Prussia at the time. Humphrey was knighted by his father on the eve of his coronation 12 October 1399 and nominated a Knight of the Garter the following year. He was granted several manors and at the tender age of 12 years and nine months fought at the battle of Shrewsbury on 21 July 1403. He is said to have been educated at Balliol College, Oxford, which seems likely as he developed a great love of learning and became a passionate collector of books and manuscripts, many of which he presented to the university, forming the nucleus of the Bodleian Library.

He was appointed Lord Great Chamberlain of England by his brother HENRY V on 7 May 1413 and at the Parliament held at Leicester on 16 May 1414 he was created Earl of Pembroke and Duke of Gloucester. In 1415 he accompanied Henry V to France and fought at AGINCOURT, where he was wounded in the groin and rescued by his brother after his men had fled, leaving him surrounded by the enemy. On 27 November 1415 he was appointed Constable of Dover Castle and Lord Warden of the Cinque Ports (offices confirmed for life on 23 June 1416) and on 28 December 1415 he was granted the reversion of the lordship of the Isle of Wight and governorship of Carisbrooke Castle after the death of the then holder, Philippa, Duchess of York, which did not take place until 1431. Other appointments and grants followed, and in 1416 Humphrey surrendered himself as a hostage to guarantee the safety of the Duke of Burgundy during the delicate peace negotiations being conducted by the Emperor Sigismund.

In July 1417 he again accompanied Henry V to France and played an active part in the ensuing military campaign. He was appointed Lieutenant of the Marshes of Normandy in June 1418 and Governor of Rouen the following January. A commissioner to treat for peace and the king's marriage to CATHERINE OF FRANCE in June 1419, he was appointed Keeper of the Realm and the king's deputy on 30 December 1419. He was present at the king's marriage in June 1420 and acted as 'overseer' at the coronation of Queen Catherine on 21 February 1421. In May 1422 he was appointed Regent of England and after Henry V's death in August 1422 was further appointed 'Protector and Defender of the Realm and Church of England' on 5 December 1422, during his brother the Duke of Bedford's absence in France. He continued to play an important part in public affairs in both England and France for the rest of his life and earned himself the name 'Good Duke Humphrey'.

He was not fortunate in his marital ventures. He married, first, before 7 March 1423, Jacqueline, Countess of Holland, Zealand and Hainault, only daughter and heiress of Willem VI, Count of Holland, and his wife Marguerite, daughter of Philippe le Hardi, Duke of Burgundy. She had previously married Jean of France, Dauphin of Viennois (son of King Charles VI), who died in 1417, and then Jean IV, Duke of Brabant, who treated her so harshly that she fled from him and took refuge in England, where she married Humphrey after obtaining an annulment of her previous marriage from the Antipope Benedict XIII. This annulment was not recognized as valid by Pope Martin V and he declared the marriage to the Duke of Gloucester null and void on 9 January 1428. The Duke of Brabant had died in the meanwhile in 1426, but Humphrey and Jacqueline did not remarry, although they appear to have remained on friendly terms. She returned to her dominions in Holland and married fourthly in July 1432, Floris van Borselen, Count of Ostrevant and Governor of Holland and Zeeland. She died at Teilingen on 8 October 1436 and was buried at The Hague.

Duke Humphrey married secondly, in 1428, Eleanor, daughter of Reginald de Cobham, 2nd Baron Cobham of Sterborough, and his first wife Eleanor, daughter of Sir Thomas Colepepper. Robes of the Order of the Garter were provided for her in 1432 and later, but in October 1441 she was tried and convicted of treason, having conspired with Master Thomas Southwell, a canon of St Stephen's Chapel at Westminster, Master John Hum, her own chaplain, Master Roger Bolyngbroke, 'a man expert in necromancy', and Margery Jourdemayne, known as the witch of Eye (near Winchester) to make a wax image of the king, 'the which image they dealt so with, that by their devilish incantations and sorcery they intended to bring out of life, little and little, the king's person, as they little and little consumed that image'. On her conviction, Eleanor's marriage to the duke was annulled and she was condemned to perpetual imprisonment after doing public penance in London. She was imprisoned first at Chester Castle and then transferred to Kenilworth, where she lived in considerable comfort with a household of 12 persons. In 1446 she was moved to Peel Castle, Isle of Man. After her former husband's death she was assigned no dower and her final place of imprisonment was Beaumaris Castle, Anglesey, where she died on 7 July 1452. She was buried at Beaumaris.

Duke Humphrey died at Bury St Edmunds on 23 February 1447, probably from natural causes, although there was some suspicion of foul play. He was buried in the tomb that he had prepared for himself in St Albans Abbey, of which he was a benefactor. He left no legitimate issue, but had two natural children, a son Arthur, who was condemned and executed for treason soon after his father's death, and a daughter Antigone, who married first, Henry Grey, Earl of Tankerville, by whom she had issue, and secondly Jean d'Amancier.

4. **Richard, Duke of Gloucester** see RICHARD III.

5. **Henry (Stuart), Duke of Gloucester** (1640–60) The fourth and youngest son and eighth child of CHARLES I and Queen HENRIETTA MARIA, who was born at Oatlands, Surrey, on 8 July and baptized there on 22 July 1640. He is said by one authority to have been created Earl of Cambridge and Duke of Gloucester on 13 May 1644. With his sister Princess Elizabeth (see ELIZABETH, PRINCESS, QUEEN OF BOHEMIA) he fell into the hands of the Parliamentarians and they were confined at Carisbrooke Castle, where they were the only two of the king's children allowed to take leave of their father before he was taken to London for his trial and execution. After Princess Elizabeth's death in September 1650, Henry was released and allowed to join his brother the exiled CHARLES II at The Hague. He was there nominated a Knight of the GARTER in 1653. Other authorities date his creation as Earl of Cambridge and Duke of Gloucester to 1659, and following the Restoration,

although no patent was every produced, he took his seat in the House of Lords on 31 May 1660. He was appointed Ranger of Hyde Park in July 1660. The young prince did not live long to enjoy his return to his native land. He fell ill with smallpox and died at Whitehall on 13 September 1660, 'by the great negligence of the doctors' as Samuel Pepys recorded. John Evelyn also recorded the sad event in his diary, describing the duke as 'a prince of extraordinary hopes'. He was buried in WESTMINSTER ABBEY on 21 September 1660. Several elegies on his death were printed, one being entitled 'Some Teares dropt on the Herse of the incomparable Prince Henry, Duke of Gloucester'.

6. **William Henry, Duke of Gloucester**[1] (1689–1700) The first son and third living child of Prince GEORGE OF DENMARK and his wife Princess (later Queen) ANNE, who was born at Hampton Court at five o'clock in the morning on 24 July 1689, and baptized there by the Bishop of London three days later, when his uncle and principal godfather WILLIAM III declared him to be Duke of Gloucester. His other godparents were his uncle King Christian V of Denmark (for whom the Earl of Dorset was proxy) and the Marchioness of Halifax.

The prince, though delicate from the first, was the only one of his parents' children to survive early infancy. He showed promise of great intelligence and his daily life was minutely chronicled by his personal body-servant and page Jenkin Lewis, a young Welshman, in his *Memoirs of Prince William Henry, Duke of Gloucester*. Gloucester was tall and well-made for his age but had an over-large head and it is believed that he suffered from hydrocephalus (water on the brain). He was lively and high-spirited and displayed a great interest in military matters. He was also given to fits of bad temper and on occasion used bad language, which he had probably picked up from servants or companions. His father birched him once for refusing to walk upstairs unaided and another time for refusing to take his medicine, both punishments achieving the desired result.

Gloucester was nominated and invested as a Knight of the GARTER on 6 January 1696 and there is a charming portrait of him in his Garter robes. At the age of eight, the duke was given his own household at ST JAMES'S PALACE and provided with an entourage of about 100 people, including the Earl (later 1st Duke) of Marlborough as 'governor' and

Bishop Burnet as head tutor. To maintain this household he received a yearly grant of £15,000 from the king, a sum which his mother considered very inadequate. On 24 July 1700 Gloucester's 11th birthday was celebrated at Windsor with a banquet and ball that left the boy exhausted. The following day he complained of a headache, sore throat and nausea and later became feverish. The usual treatments of the day, blood-letting and blistering, were applied, but to no avail. The prince became delirious and after several days of suffering died on 30 July 1700. His body was conveyed to Westminster in his own state coach and after lying in state in his lodgings in the Palace of Westminster was buried in Henry VII's Chapel at WESTMINSTER ABBEY in the evening of 7 August 1700. Three months later his uncle William III wrote to Marlborough referring to Glou-cester's death as 'so great a loss to me as well as to all England, that it pierces my heart'.

7. **William Henry, Duke of Gloucester**[2] (1743–1805) The third son and fifth child of FREDERICK LOUIS, PRINCE OF WALES and Augusta of Saxe-Gotha (see AUGUSTA, PRINCESS OF WALES), who was born at Leicester House, London, on 14 November (25 November new style) 1743, and bap-tized on 25 November, his godparents being his uncles, William Augustus, Duke of CUMBERLAND and the Prince of Orange (represented by proxy) and his aunt Princess AMELIA. He was nominated and invested as a Knight of the GARTER on 27 May and installed on 22 September 1762. On 19 November 1764 his brother GEORGE III created him Earl of Connaught and Duke of Gloucester and Edinburgh and he took his seat in the House of Lords on 10 January 1765. He had been appointed a Privy Councillor on 19 December 1764.

The duke embarked on a military career and was promoted Major-General in 1767, Lieutenant-General in 1770, General in 1772 and Field Marshal in 1793. He was Colonel of the 13th Foot 1766–7, of the 3rd Foot Guards 1767–70, and of the 1st Foot Guards 1770–1805. In addition to his mili-tary appointments he was also Ranger of Hampton Court, Keeper of Windsor Forest and Cranborne Chase, and Warden of the New Forest.

The Duke of Gloucester married pri-vately at her house in Pall Mall, London, on 6 September 1766, Maria, widow of James Waldegrave, 2nd Earl Waldegrave (by

whom she had three daughters), and natural daughter of the Hon. Sir Edward Walpole, by Dorothy Clement. She was his senior by seven years, having been born at her father's house in Westminster on 3 July and bap-tized at St James's, Westminster, on 10 July 1736. The marriage was made public in 1772 and caused grave offence to George III, who appointed a committee consisting of the Archbishop of Canterbury, the Bishop of London, and the Lord Chancellor to enquire into its validity, since the duchess's chaplain, who had performed the ceremony, was dead. The committee found in favour of its validity, and this marriage and that of the Duke of Cumberland in 1771 were the occasion of the passing of the ROYAL MARRIAGES ACT at the king's insti-gation.

The marriage proved a happy one and three children were born, Princess SOPHIA MATILDA, Princess CAROLINE AUGUSTA MARIA, and Prince William Frederick, who succeeded his father as 2nd Duke of Gloucester of this creation (see below). The duchess's uncle, Horace Walpole, wrote of the duke that he had 'more good nature than good humour, and more good sense than commonly appeared; for though he never said a silly thing, he had none of the graces of conversation, nor an ingratiating manner, but he had a just sense of honour, and strict veracity, and no insincerity'. He adds that he was 'a very fond and indulgent father'. The duke's shyness made him eschew society and he took no interest in politics, seldom voting in the House of Lords. He died at Gloucester House, Grosvenor Street, London, on 25 August, and was buried in the Gloucester vault at St George's Chapel, Windsor, on 4 September 1805. His widow died at Oxford Lodge, Brompton, on 22 August and was buried with him on 31 August 1807.

In addition to his three legitimate chil-dren, the Duke of Gloucester had a natural daughter by Lady Almeria Carpenter (born on 20 February 1752 and died in London on 13 September 1809), daughter of George Carpenter, 1st Earl of Tyrconnell and his wife Frances Clifton. This daughter, known as Louisa Maria La Coast, was born on 6 January 1782 and baptized at Leatherhead, Surrey, as the daughter of Farley Edsir, the duke's steward and tenant of a dairy farm at Hampton Court. She was married at Norwich on 29 December 1803 to the Hon. Godfrey Macdonald (later Bosville and Bosville-Macdonald), later 3rd Baron Macdonald of Slate, and died at Bossall,

Yorkshire, on 10 February 1835, having had issue born both before and after her marriage.

8. **William Frederick, 2nd Duke of Gloucester** (1776–1834) The only son of William Henry, Duke of Gloucester (*see above*), who was born at the Palazzo Teodoli in Rome on 15 January 1776. From his birth until his succession to the dukedom he was styled Prince William of Gloucester. He was educated at Trinity College, Cambridge, and, like his father, made the army his career. He served in Flanders from 1794 to 1799, being promoted to Major-General in 1795 and Lieutenant-General in 1799. While serving he was nominated a Knight of the GARTER on 16 July 1794 and was invested in Flanders by his cousin the Duke of York (*see* YORK, FREDERICK, DUKE OF), but he was not installed until 29 May 1801. He was promoted to full General in 1808 and received his Field Marshal's baton in 1816, and was Colonel of the 6th Foot 1795–1806 and of the 3rd Foot Guards 1806–34.

In politics the duke sided with the Whig opposition and was a supporter of the Anti-slavery Society. He voted against the prosecution of Queen Caroline (*see* CAROLINE OF BRUNSWICK) and for Catholic Emancipation, but was violently opposed to the Reform Bill. His nickname 'Silly Billy' does not appear to have been wholly justified.

The duke remained a bachelor until the age of 40, when he married at the Queen's House (now BUCKINGHAM PALACE), St James's Park, on 22 July 1816, his first cousin, Princess Mary (*see* MARY, PRINCESS, DUCHESS OF GLOUCESTER), the fourth daughter of GEORGE III. On the occasion of his marriage he was granted the style of Royal Highness, having previously held that of Highness only, as the great-grandson of a sovereign. There were to be no children of the marriage, but it remained a happy one until the duke's death after two weeks' illness at Bagshot Park, Surrey, on 30 November 1834, when all his titles became extinct. He was buried in the Gloucester vault at St George's Chapel, Windsor, on 11 December 1834. His unostentatious life style resulted in his leaving a fortune of over £90,000, his widow being the chief beneficiary.

9. **Henry, Duke of Gloucester** (1900–74) The third son and fourth child of George, Duke of York (later GEORGE V) and Princess Victoria Mary of Teck (later Queen MARY), who was born at York Cottage, Sandringham, on 31 March 1900 and named Henry William Frederick Albert. He was educated at Eton, the Royal Military College at Sandhurst and Trinity College, Cambridge. He was nominated a Knight of the GARTER in 1921 and on 31 March 1928 (his 28th birthday) was created Baron Culloden, Earl of Ulster and Duke of Gloucester. He was appointed to the PRIVY COUNCIL in 1925.

Prince Henry followed an army career and was promoted to Captain in 1927, Brevet Major in 1934, Major in 1935, Major-General in 1937, Lieutenant-General in 1941, General in 1944 and Field Marshal in 1955. He was also Colonel-in-Chief of many regiments, an honorary Commodore RNR and a Marshal of the RAF. The duke was Governor General of Australia from 1945 to 1947 and Lord High Commissioner to the General Assembly of the Church of Scotland in 1949 and 1963. Among the duke's many civil appointments his chairmanship of King George's Jubilee Trust from 1936 was especially significant.

The duke was married at BUCKINGHAM PALACE on 6 November 1935 to Lady Alice Christabel Montagu-Douglas-Scott, the third daughter of the 7th Duke of Buccleuch and (9th Duke of) Queensberry by his wife Lady Margaret Alice Bridgeman, second daughter of the 4th Earl of Bradford. The marriage was celebrated quietly because of the recent death of the bride's father. The duke and duchess made their country home at Barnwell Manor, Peterborough, where they took a great interest in practical farming. They had two sons. The elder, Prince William Henry Andrew Frederick, was born at Barnet, Hertfordshire, on 18 December 1941 and educated at Eton, Magdalene College, Cambridge, and Stanford University, California. He grew up to be a young man of great promise and many interests, but unfortunately was killed in a flying accident while taking part in the Goodyear Air Race near Wolverhampton on 28 August 1972. He was buried at the royal burial ground at Frogmore on 2 September 1972. The royal pair's younger son, Prince Richard, succeeded his father as 2nd Duke of Gloucester (*see below*).

Prince Henry was incapacitated for the last few years of his life following a stroke. He died at Barnwell Manor on 10 June 1974 and was buried at Frogmore. His widow, now known as Princess Alice, Duchess of Gloucester, was the first lady to be appointed a Dame Grand Cross of the Most Honourable Order of the BATH (GCB) in

1975. Born in London on Christmas Day, 25 December 1901, she celebrated her 94th birthday on Christmas Day 1995.

10. **Richard, 2nd Duke of Gloucester** (1944–) The younger son of Henry, Duke of Gloucester (*see above*), who was born at Northampton on 26 August 1944 and baptized Richard Alexander Walter George. He was styled Prince Richard of Gloucester until he succeeded to the dukedom. He was educated at Eton and at Magdalene College, Cambridge, where he graduated in 1966, and gained a Diploma of Architecture in 1969. He was appointed GCVO in 1974, and has been Grand Prior of the Venerable Order of St John of Jerusalem since 1975.

Prince Richard married at Barnwell parish church on 8 July 1972, Birgitte Eva van Deurs, younger daughter of Asger Preben Wissing Henriksen, of Odense, Denmark, and his former wife Vivian (later Mrs Marx-Nielsen), daughter of Waldemar Oswald van Deurs, of Copenhagen, whose name his granddaughter assumed. The untimely death of Prince William in August 1972 made Prince Richard heir to his father's dukedom, to which he succeeded in 1974.

Although Colonel-in-Chief of the Gloucester Regiment since 1975, his interests have always been civilian ones, particularly architecture and housing. He has published several books, including *On Public View* and *The Face of London*. The Duchess of Gloucester, who was born at Odense on the Island of Funen, Denmark, on 20 June 1946, undertakes a full programme of royal duties. She was appointed GCVO in 1989. The duke and duchess have three children: Alexander Patrick Gregers Richard, Earl of Ulster, who was born at St Mary's Hospital, Paddington, London, on 24 October 1974; Lady Davina Elizabeth Alice Benedikte Windsor, who was born at St Mary's Hospital, Paddington, on 19 November 1977; and Lady Rose Victoria Birgitte Louise Windsor, who was also born there on 1 March 1980.

God is my help Motto of Prince Philip, Duke of EDINBURGH.

Godwin, Earl of Wessex (d.1053) Son of Wulfnoth, Thegn of Sussex, who emerged as a powerful statesman and became the father of a queen and a king. Godwin was probably born in southern England towards the end of the tenth century. In recent times ingenious attempts have been made to trace his descent in the direct male line from ETHELRED I, the elder brother and immediate predecessor of ALFRED THE GREAT, but these remain unconvincing, and it is quite inconceivable that had such a descent existed it would not have been brought forward to boost his son HAROLD II's claim to the throne on the death of EDWARD THE CONFESSOR.

Godwin's rise to prominence at the beginning of CANUTE's reign was probably bolstered by his marriage in about 1018 to the king's kinswoman Gytha, daughter of Thorgils Sprakalegg, whose mother Thyra was a sister of Canute's father SWEYN. At about the same time Gytha's brother Ulf married Canute's half-sister Estrid, or Margaret, by whom he was destined to become the ancestor of future kings of Denmark. Godwin accompanied Canute to Denmark in 1019 and gave valiant service in his campaign against the Swedes. On their return to England he was rewarded with large grants of land and was appointed Ealdorman (usually rendered as Earl) of Wessex. His avarice added greatly to his fortune, and his powers of oratory ensured the growth of his influential position at court.

On Canute's death in 1035, Godwin at first supported the claim of HARDICANUTE to the crown, but found it expedient to change sides and support HAROLD HARE-FOOT. In 1037 he was strongly suspected of being implicated in the death of the Atheling ALFRED, and on the succession of Hardicanute in 1040 he was obliged to clear himself of the charge by solemn oath. Godwin's greatest exercise of power began with the reign of Edward the Confessor. In January 1045 he married his daughter Edith (*see* EDITH, QUEEN) to the king and obtained large estates for his two eldest sons, Sweyn and Harold. He greatly opposed the growing influence of Norman favourites at court and the appointment of Robert of Jumièges as Bishop of London and later Archbishop of Canterbury. The archbishop revived the old charge against Godwin of the murder of the king's brother Alfred, and as a result the whole family was banished in 1051. Godwin and his wife, accompanied by their sons, Sweyn, Tostig and Gurth, went to Bruges and two other sons, Harold and Leofwine, sought refuge in Ireland. Queen Edith was sent to the convent at Wherwell, where the king's sister was abbess.

In June 1052 Godwin assembled a small fleet of ships and set sail from Bruges. He reached Dungeness, where he received word that the king's men had put out from Sandwich. He put to sea again and returned to Bruges, while the royal fleet, unable to ascertain his whereabouts, sailed to London. When Godwin heard of this he set sail again and made for the Isle of Wight, where he landed and, after exacting a tribute from the inhabitants, lay offshore until he was joined by his son Harold and a fleet of nine ships from Ireland. They proceeded along the coast, collecting ships and men as they went, and landed at Sandwich 'with an overwhelming host'. The news reached the king, who sent for reinforcements. Before they had arrived, Godwin and his men had reached Southwark and he deployed his ships along the south bank of the Thames facing the royal ships on the north bank. The prospect of a civil war was abhorrent to both sides and a truce was agreed to discuss the situation. The result was a complete pardon and restoration to favour of Godwin and his sons and the return of Queen Edith to court.

The ANGLO-SAXON CHRONICLE reports that Godwin 'was taken ill soon after he landed and afterwards recovered, but he made far too few amends regarding the church property which he had taken from many holy places'. The illness was probably a stroke, for the next year Godwin, with his sons Harold and Tostig, was spending Easter with the king at Winchester when 'on the second day of Easter he sat at table with the king, he suddenly sank down against the footstool, speechless and helpless; he was carried into the king's chamber and it was thought it would pass off, but it was not to be; yet he lingered on like this, unable to speak and helpless, until the Thursday [15 April], and then gave up his life'. According to Henry of Huntingdon, things happened rather differently: on sitting to dine with the king, Godwin denied that he had ever harboured traitorous designs upon the monarch and added 'may this morsel of bread choke me, if even in thought I have ever been false to you'. The bread immediately lodged in his throat, leading to his death. He was buried in the Old Minster at Winchester.

Godwin's wife Gytha lived on for many years, surviving the reign of her son Harold and the Norman Conquest. She died at St Omer in or soon after 1069. They had a large family of at least 10 children: (1) Sweyn, born about 1020, who after going into exile at Bruges went on pilgrimage to Jerusalem and died at Constantinople on his return journey on 29 September 1052; (2) Harold II; (3) Tostig, Ealdorman of Kent and Northumberland; (4) Gurth, Ealdorman of

Mercia, who was killed at HASTINGS on 14 October 1066; (5) Leofwine, also killed at Hastings; (6) Queen Edith; (7) Wulfnoth, who died at Salisbury after 1087; (8) Edgar, who died a monk at Reims after 1066; (9) Gunhild, who died at Bruges in 1087; and (10) Aelfgifu.

Golden Jubilee *see* JUBILEES.

Good Queen Bess Affectionate contemporary allusion to Queen ELIZABETH I.

Greenwich Palace Although the site of Greenwich Palace on the south bank of the Thames between Deptford and Woolwich had royal connections since Saxon times, the first castle was built there by Humphrey, Duke of GLOUCESTER, who named it Bella Court, with the purpose of guarding London from invaders approaching up river or along the Dover road. It was seized by Queen MARGARET OF ANJOU after the duke's death in 1447, and she renamed it Placentia (the pleasant place). It was a favourite residence of HENRY VII and all the Tudor monarchs. HENRY VIII, MARY I and ELIZABETH I were all born there, and EDWARD VI died there. In 1615 JAMES I commissioned Inigo Jones to build the Queen's House for ANNE OF DENMARK on the site of the gatehouse to the Tudor palace, where, according to legend, Sir Walter Raleigh spread his cloak in the mud for Elizabeth I to step across. Queen's House was unfinished when Anne of Denmark died in 1619 and was completed by CHARLES I for HENRIETTA MARIA in 1635. It was a favourite residence until the outbreak of the CIVIL WAR in 1642, and the queen again lived there on her brief visit to London after the Restoration. CHARLES II had the old Tudor palace pulled down and began the building of a new palace in 1665 but ran out of funds and it remained for William and Mary to commission Sir Christopher Wren to build the magnificent hospital for wounded and aged sailors on the site. It took 50 years to complete. The Royal Hospital for Seamen, as it was called, became the Royal Naval College in 1873.

It was at Greenwich that Elizabeth I knighted Sir Francis Drake on the deck of the *Golden Hind* on 4 April 1581 after his return from his circumnavigation of the globe; and also at Greenwich where ELIZABETH II knighted Sir Francis Chichester in 1967 on his return from his solo voyage round the world in *Gipsy Moth IV*. The Queen's House has recently been carefully restored to give a semblance of its original splendours, but not without a measure of criticism from those purists who deplore a 'pastiche'. The fate of Wren's magnificent buildings, including the painted hall, decorated by Thornhill, and the chapel, was in the balance after the Royal Naval College gave them up until it was announced in 1996 that it was to become a university.

Grey, Lady Jane see JANE, QUEEN OF ENGLAND.

Groom of the Stole Euphemistic rendering of the title of that member of the royal household who was responsible for the ordering of the royal chamberpot or close stool. The office is now obsolete.

Gruffydd ap Cynan, King of Gwynedd (c.1055–1137) The son of Cynan ab Iago (who had been forced to seek refuge in Ireland) by his wife Ragnhildr, daughter of Olaf, son of Sitric of the Silken Beard, Norse king of Dublin, who was born in Dublin in about 1055. In 1075 he left Ireland with the intention of regaining his paternal inheritance and landed at Abermenai. He met with some measure of success, but because of the resentment felt towards the Norsemen in his army by the native Welsh, was eventually defeated by TRAHAEARN AP CARADOG and compelled to return to Ireland. He came back again in 1081 and joined forces with RHYS AP TEWDWR. They fought a battle with Trahaearn at Mynydd Carn, where they defeated and killed him, and Gruffydd thereupon became king of Gwynedd. Shortly afterwards, however, through the treachery of one of his own men, Meirion Goch, he was captured by the Normans at Rug, near Corwen, and held prisoner by them in England for 12 years or more. Released by 1094, he played a prominent part in the resistance to Norman power during the next few years, but in 1098 was driven into Anglesey and thence forced again to seek refuge in Ireland. He returned the following year and was allowed to rule Anglesey with Norman consent. In the course of the next few years he was able to regain Gwynedd uwch Conwy, and he reigned peacefully for the rest of his long life. Blind and decrepit, he died in 1137 and was buried in Bangor Cathedral.

He had married, in about 1095, the very able Angharad (see ANGHARAD FERCH OWAIN), daughter of Owain ab Edwin, of the royal line of DEHEUBARTH. She survived until 1162, when she must have attained a very great age for those days. Their children were: (1) Cadwallon, who was killed in battle with the men of Powys near Llangollen in 1132; (2) OWAIN GWYNEDD, who succeeded his father; (3) Cadwaladr, who married Alice, daughter of Richard FitzGilbert de Clare, 1st Earl of Hereford, and died on 29 February 1172; (4) Gwenllian, who married shortly after 1116, GRUFFYDD AP RHYS, PRINCE OF DEHEUBARTH; (5) Marared; (6) Rainillt; (7) Susanna, who married MADOG AP MAREDUDD, KING OF POWYS; and (8) Annest. Gruffydd also had a natural daughter, Gwenllian, born in about 1080, who married in 1098, Cadwgan ap Bleddyn, Prince of Powys.

Gruffydd ap Llywelyn, King of Wales (d.1063) The son of LLYWELYN AP SEISYLL, KING OF DEHEUBARTH AND GWYNEDD, and Angharad (see ANGHARAD FERCH MAREDUDD), daughter and heiress of MAREDUDD AB OWAIN, KING OF DEHEUBARTH, who was probably still only a child when his father died in 1023 and is said to have spent his youth in indolence. He became king of Gwynedd and Powys after IAGO AB IDWAL FOEL had been killed by his own men in 1039 and immediately began campaigning against the English, gaining a victory at Rhyd-y-groes in the Severn valley that made him a national hero. He then turned his attention to reconquering Deheubarth, the throne of which had been usurped since his father's death. After a long struggle against Hywel ab Edwin, he finally defeated and killed him in a battle fought at the mouth of the Towy in 1044. He then had to contend with GRUFFYDD AP RHYDDERCH, who managed to hold power in Deheubarth until he, too, was defeated and slain in 1055, when Gruffydd ap Llywelyn became the undisputed master of all Wales.

Gruffydd allied himself with Earl Aelfgar of Mercia to attack the Saxons and Normans of Hereford and drove them out, setting fire to the town. Earl Harold (later HAROLD II) was sent against him to avenge the incident, but only managed to rebuild the town and conclude peace with Aelfgar. On 16 June 1056 Bishop Leofgar of Hereford led an army against Gruffydd and was defeated by him in a battle fought in the Machawy valley. Shortly afterwards, an agreement was negotiated through the mediation of Harold, Earl Leofric of Mercia and Earl Ealdred of Worcester, and Gruffydd accepted EDWARD THE CONFESSOR as his overlord. It was probably in the same year that Gruffydd married Ealdgyth, the daughter of his old ally Aelfgar, whom he helped to regain his lands.

Gruffydd was not allowed to end his reign

in peace. After Aelfgar's death in 1062, Harold made a surprise raid on Gruffydd's court at Rhuddlan, but he managed to escape. He was killed 'through the treachery of his own men' in 1063 and was eulogized by the *Brut y Tywysogion* as having been 'the head and shield and defender of the Britons'. He left two young sons, Maredudd and Idwal, both of whom died in 1070, and a daughter, Nest, who married Osbern FitzRichard, Lord of Richard's Castle and Byton, and had issue. Gruffydd's widow, Ealdgyth, maried Earl Harold in 1065.

Gruffydd ap Rhydderch, King of Deheubarth (d.1055) The son of RHYD-DERCH AB IESTYN (who usurped the throne of DEHEUBARTH from 1023 until his death in 1033), who emerged as the leader of the resistance against GRUFFYDD AP LLYWELYN in 1045 and successfully maintained independence for 10 years, defying the Danish invaders. He was finally overcome and killed by Gruffydd ap Llywelyn in 1055. He left two sons, Caradog (who died in 1081) and Ieuan Gwent, and his descendants enjoyed semi-independence in part of Glamorgan until about 1270.

Gruffydd ap Rhys I, Prince of Deheubarth (*c.*1090–1137) The son of RHYS AP TEWDWR, the last king of DEHEUBARTH, and his wife Gwladus, daughter of Rhiwallon ap Cynfyn, who was born in about 1090 and was only about three years old when his father was killed in 1093. He was taken to Ireland, where he grew to manhood, and returned to Wales in 1113. After several years of ineffective resistance to Norman rule, he finally achieved an agreement with HENRY I and received land in the commote of Caeo. He lived there fairly quietly, except for another brief exile in Ireland in 1127, until Henry's death in 1135, when he took a prominent part in the general revolt against the Normans and succeeded in establishing himself as reigning prince of Deheubarth, consolidating his position at the battle of Crug Mawr in 1136. He did not live long to enjoy it, however, as he died in the following year 1137.

By an early wife or concubine he had two sons, Anarawd and Cadell, who succeeded him in turn, and two daughters, Gwladus (who married Caradog ap Iestyn of Morgannwg, and had issue, and subsequently Seisyll ap Dyfnwal) and Nest, who married Ifor Bach. Shortly after 1116, Gruffydd married Gwenllian, daughter of GRUFFYDD AP CYNAN, KING OF GWYNEDD. She was as redoubtable a warrior as her hus-

band and was killed while leading her men in an attack on the Norman castle of Kidwelly in 1136. The two sons she bore, Maredudd (*see* MAREDUDD AP GRUFFYDD) and Rhys (*see* RHYS AP GRUFFYDD), succeeded their half-brother Cadell as joint princes or lords of Deheubarth on his resignation in 1153.

Gruffydd ap Rhys II, Prince or Lord of Deheubarth (d.1201) The eldest son of RHYS AP GRUFFYDD ('The Lord Rhys'), Prince or Lord of DEHEUBARTH, and his wife Gwenllian, daughter of MADOG AP MAREDUDD, PRINCE OF POWYS, who succeeded his father in 1197 and was recognized by the English authorities. His short reign was occupied in his attempts to combat the growing ambitions of his brother Maelgwn, Lord of Ceredigion, and GWENWYNWYN, PRINCE OR LORD OF SOUTHERN POWYS. In 1189 he married Maud or Matilda, daughter of William de Braose and his wife Maud de S. Valerie. He died while still a young man on 25 July 1201, and was buried in Strata Florida Abbey, leaving two young sons, Rhys Ieuanc (who died in August 1222 and was buried at Strata Florida), and Owain (who died on 18 January 1236 and was buried at Strata Florida, leaving issue). His wife survived him, but the date of her death is unknown. She, too, was buried at Strata Florida. Gruffydd was the last semi-independent ruler of Deheubarth.

Gruffydd Maelor I, Prince or Lord of Northern Powys (d.1191) The second son of MADOG AP MAREDUDD, PRINCE OF POWYS and his wife Susanna, daughter of GRUFFYDD AP CYNAN, KING OF GWYNEDD, who received Maelor and Ial (Bromfield and Yale) on his father's death in February 1160 and later added Nanheudwy on the death of his (illegitimate) half-brother Owain Fychan in 1187 and other lands in a new subdivision with another half-brother, Owain Brogyntyn. He married his cousin Angharad, daughter of OWAIN GWYNEDD, KING OF GWYNEDD, and died in 1191, leaving two sons, Madog (*see* MADOG AP GRUFFYDD) and Owain.

Gruffydd Maelor II, Lord of Powys Fadog (d.1269) The eldest son of MADOG AP GRUFFYDD, LORD OF NORTHERN POWYS and his wife Gwladus or Isota, daughter of Ithel ap Rhys, King of Gwent, who succeeded his father as ruler of northern Powys in 1236. He married Emma, widow of Henry Touchet, and daughter of Henry Audley, and died in 1269, leaving four sons. The

Welsh hero OWAIN GLYN DŴR was his great-great-grandson.

Guinevere, Queen In Arthurian legend the queen of King ARTHUR. The name is an anglicization of the Welsh Gwenhwyfar. In the fullest development of the legend she has been expanded into three successive wives of Arthur bearing the same name. The first is said to have been the daughter of Corytus or Gwryd Gwent (or alternatively and somewhat unexpectedly of the King of Biscay) and to have been brought up by 'her near relative' Cador, Duke of Cornwall, King Arthur's half-brother, at Tintagel. She was, almost needless to say, a paragon of beauty and all the virtues. In the legend she accompanied her husband on an expedition to Scotland and was taken prisoner and confined in Dunbar Castle, where she died. She was buried in Meigle in Angus. The second Guinevere was the daughter of Uther ap Credawgal and married Arthur at Carlisle. She was as beautiful and good as her predecessor and shared King Arthur's tomb at Glastonbury. The third Guinevere was the daughter of a Pictish king. She, too, was beautiful, but far from good, being grossly unfaithful to her husband with his nephews among others. After Arthur's death she is said to have become a nun at Caerleon and to have died in 600, being buried at Amesbury, where her supposed tomb was excavated in the 16th century, according to the historian Rapin.

Gundred, Countess of Warren (d.1085) This lady, long supposed to have been a daughter of WILLIAM I THE CONQUEROR or of his wife MATILDA OF FLANDERS by a previous alliance, is now believed to have been neither. She was the sister of Gherbod the Fleming, Earl of Chester, and, according to some authorities, the daughter of Gherbod, Advocate of St Bertin. She was married before 1078 to William de Warrenne, first Earl of Warren and Surrey, and died at Castle Acre, Norfolk, on 27 May 1085, leaving two sons and two daughters. Her husband survived her until 24 June 1089. Both were buried in the monastery of St Pancras, which they had founded at Lewes in Sussex. Their lead coffins were found in October 1845 during the construction of a cutting for the Lewes to Brighton railway. They were deposited in Southover Church, where they may still be seen. Gundred is one of the most controversial figures in British history and a vast amount has been written on the vexed question of her parentage.

Gunpowder Plot Conspiracy to blow up the Houses of Parliament on 5 November 1605 when JAMES I was present to open Parliament in person. The conspirators were a number of Roman Catholic gentry, led by Robert Catesby, and the plan was to follow it up with a rising in the Midlands. The plot was discovered when one of the conspirators, Tresham, wrote to his friend Lord Monteagle to warn him to absent himself from Parliament on that day. A search of the vaults beneath Parliament was made, and Guy Fawkes, the conspirator who had been deputed to lay and light the trail, was discovered and arrested. The conspirators were rounded up and eventually tried, hanged, drawn and quartered. Ever since, a search has been carried out by the Yeomen of the Guard on the eve of opening Parliament and the fifth of November has become known as 'Guy Fawkes Night' or 'Bonfire Night' when throughout the country effigies of Guy Fawkes are burned on bonfires accompanied by firework displays. Children still delight in constructing 'Guys' and demanding 'A penny for the Guy' from passers-by when they display them in the streets. A form of thanksgiving for delivery from the 'Gunpowder Treason' was not omitted from English Prayer books until 1859.

Gwenwynwyn, Prince or Lord of Southern Powys (d.1216) The son of OWAIN CYFEILIOG, PRINCE OF SOUTHERN POWYS and his first wife Gwenllian, daughter of OWAIN GWYNEDD, KING OF GWYNEDD, who succeeded his father in 1195 and greatly extended his territory in 1197 by acquiring the lordship of Arwystli. The area he ruled became known as Powys Wenwynwyn after him, as northern Powys became known as Powys Fadog from MADOG AP GRUFFYDD. Gwenwynwyn made a great bid for independence, but was deprived of his lands by King JOHN in 1208. They were restored to him in 1210, and in 1215 he was obliged to swear an oath of allegiance to LLYWELYN THE GREAT. His failure to observe this oath led to his exile in the following year, and he died abroad in 1216. He married Margaret, daughter of Robert Corbet, of Caus, and left two young sons: Gruffydd, who was invested with most of his father's lands by HENRY III in 1241 and later transferred his allegiance to LLYWELYN III; and Madog.

Gwynne, Eleanor (1650–87) Famous mistress of CHARLES II, popularly known as 'Nell Gwynne' and 'Sweet Nell of Old Drury', who was born at Hereford on

2 February 1650, the daughter of Thomas Gwynne, said to have been a soldier, and Eleanor Smith. She first appeared on the stage in 1665 and gained great popularity as a comedienne. The story that she sold oranges in the pit at Drury Lane cannot be substantiated. She attracted the attention of the king and left the stage in 1682, after she had borne him two sons, Charles Beauclerk, later Duke of St Albans, and James Beauclerk, who died young.

Nell had a ready wit, which she put to good purpose. She said the king was her 'Charles the third' as she had already had two previous lovers named Charles. Her great rival was the king's French mistress, Louise de Kéroualle, and on one occasion the royal entourage was passing through London when the mob mistook Nell's coach for that of the Frenchwoman, whom they detested as a Catholic, and began to shout abuse. Nell put her head out of the coach window and called out: 'Good people, pray desist; I am the Protestant whore.' On another occasion when the king, accompanied by Louise who was wearing an enormous hat, was attending the theatre, Nell came on to the stage wearing a hat that completely swamped her and provoked enormous applause from the audience. Nell had no ambition to be ennobled herself but is said to have obtained a title for her elder son by threatening to throw the child from a window when the king was passing beneath and crying that she had no use for the 'little bastard'. The king rushed forward, calling out 'Save the Earl of Burford'. He did indeed receive that title in December 1676.

Nell's mother fell into a ditch near Westminster when in a drunken stupor and was drowned. Her daughter accorded her a magnificent funeral at St Martin-in-the-Fields on 30 July 1679. Towards the end of his life the king is said to have contemplated creating Nell Countess of Greenwich, and among his reported last words were 'Let not poor Nelly starve'. Nell suffered a stroke at the early age of 37 in March 1687 and died on 14 November 1687 at her house at 79 Pall Mall, which the king had given her. She was buried at St Martin-in-the-Fields. Nell Gwynne is said to have been instrumental in persuading Charles to found the Royal Hospital at Chelsea as a home for old soldiers.

H

Haemophilia Inherited disease associated with the British royal family in which the blood fails to clot and the sufferer is subject to prolonged bleeding from the slightest cut and severe and painful internal bleeding resulting from a minor knock or injury. The disease affects only men but is transmitted through females, although the daughter of a haemophiliac may transmit it to her male offspring. The defective gene that has been responsible for the occurrence of haemophilia in the descendants of Queen VICTORIA apparently originated with her. Her youngest son, Prince Leopold (*see* ALBANY, DUKE OF), was a sufferer, and at least three of her daughters were carriers. Today the disease can be treated by Factor VIII, a protein involved in the clotting of blood, which can be produced from donated blood.

Hammer of the Scots Nickname of EDWARD I, referring to the severity of his military campaigns in Scotland.

Hampton Court Palace Magnificent red-brick royal palace on the Middlesex side of the Thames above Kingston, about 15 miles south-west of London, which was built by HENRY VIII's Chancellor Cardinal Wolsey and was completed in 1517, when Wolsey entertained the king and CATHERINE OF ARAGON there. It was reputedly the largest house in England (said to have over 1000 rooms for guests alone) and its beauty soon aroused the king's envy. When Wolsey fell out of favour in 1529, he attempted to reinstate himself by giving the palace and its entire contents to the king, but it was to no avail and Wolsey died two years later at Leicester Abbey while journeying to London to face a charge of high treason. The palace became Henry's favourite residence and he spent much time there. The future EDWARD VI was born there, JANE SEYMOUR his mother dying there in childbirth soon afterwards, and Henry married his fifth and sixth queens there. For his recreation he added a tilt-yard and a royal tennis court to the palace complex. The ghost of CATHERINE HOWARD, screaming for mercy from her husband, is said to haunt the gallery leading to the Chapel Royal of the palace to this day.

The palace remained a favourite residence with the Stuart monarchs, and Cromwell, too, lived there as Lord Protector. WILLIAM III and Mary intended to make Hampton Court their principal residence and engaged Sir Christopher Wren to design and build a new suite of state apartments, which were completed under Queen ANNE. The palace continued to be a favourite summer residence until the reign of GEORGE II, the last sovereign to live there. GEORGE III and Queen CHARLOTTE preferred the simpler style of KEW.

Hampton Court has been open to the public since the reign of Queen VICTORIA. It contains a number of 'grace and favour' apartments occupied by pensioners of the crown. The Hampton Court Conference, held at the palace on 14 January 1604, was convened by JAMES I to consider the complaints of the Puritan clergy, who had presented him with the Millenary Petition, seeking radical changes in the Prayer Book that would not have been acceptable to most of the English clergy, the universities or a large number of the laity. The king himself was greatly opposed to the Puritans, whom he regarded in the same light as the Presbyterians in Scotland, and very few of the practices of which they had complained were disallowed. James's high-handed treatment of the Puritan leaders, Reynolds and Chaderton, led to an increase of the opposition of those members of Parliament who sought reforms in the Church of England.

Hanover, House of General designation of the dynasty that succeeded to the British throne in 1714 by virtue of the ACT OF SETTLEMENT of 1701. Also referred to as the House of Brunswick or the House of Guelph, it was, in fact, not of German but of Italian origin, sharing a male line of descent with the House of Este from Adalbert of Este, who lived early in the tenth century. In 1055 Azzo II, Marchese d'Este, married

Kunigunde (or Chuniza), daughter and heiress of Welf II, Count of Altdorf, and thus acquired the Welf (or Guelph) possessions in Germany. Later generations of the family acquired Bavaria, Saxony and Brunswick, and Heinrich the Lion, Duke of Saxony and Bavaria, married Matilda (*see* MATILDA, PRINCESS, DUCHESS OF SAXONY AND BAVARIA), eldest daughter of HENRY II in 1168. GEORGE I was their direct descendant in the male line, but his claim to the British throne was derived through his mother SOPHIA, ELECTRESS OF HANOVER, granddaughter of JAMES I. Like most German reigning families, the House of Brunswick divided and subdivided many times before the introduction of primogeniture. The branch that acquired the British throne was the ultimate junior line of Brunswick-Celle, which obtained the dignity of Elector of Hanover in 1692. It also held the title of Arch-Treasurer of the Holy Roman Empire, which, in the abbreviated form *S.R.I.A.Th.et El.*, appeared on the coins of the first three Hanoverian monarchs.

Hardicanute, King of England (*c*.1018–42) The son of King CANUTE and EMMA OF NORMANDY, who was born in England in about 1018 and was generally regarded as his father's heir, his half-brothers Sweyn and Harold (*see* HAROLD I HAREFOOT) being considered of dubious legitimacy. Hardicanute, or Harthacnut as the name is often rendered, is first mentioned in the ANGLO-SAXON CHRONICLE in 1023, when in June of that year he attended with his mother the translation of the relics of St Aelfheah, Archbishop of Canterbury, from London to Canterbury. In 1028 he accompanied his father to Denmark and was made titular king there, although he was only 10 years old. He appears to have remained in Denmark and was certainly there when his father died in November 1035. He was reluctant to return to England, and his half-brother Harold was elected by the council to reign jointly with him and was acknowledged as sole king in 1037.

In 1039 Hardicanute left Denmark and joined his mother in Bruges. On receiving the news of Harold's death the following year, he set out with a fleet of 60 ships to claim his inheritance and landed at Sandwich. He was crowned at Canterbury on 18 June 1040. The imposition of crippling taxes soon alienated the people who had solicited his return, and in the words of the Chronicle, 'he never did anything worthy of a king while he reigned'. He never married and died suddenly in 1042 at a wedding feast at Lambeth: 'as he stood at his drink and ... suddenly fell to the ground with a horrible convulsion; and those who were near thereto took hold of him, but he never spoke again, and passed away on 8 June'. He was buried with his father at Winchester and was succeeded by his much older half-brother EDWARD THE CONFESSOR, who had returned to England and been acknowledged as his heir the previous year.

Harold I Harefoot, King of England (*c*.1016–40) The second son of King CANUTE by his first wife or concubine Elfgifu of Northampton, whom he repudiated in order to marry EMMA OF NORMANDY, who was born in England in about 1016. He was nicknamed 'Harefoot' from his fleetness of foot. Harold's elder brother SWEYN was appointed to govern Norway with their mother's assistance, but Harold remained in England and on his father's death in 1035 was chosen by the Council to act as regent or co-ruler with his half-brother HARDICANUTE, the acknowledged heir, who was absent in Denmark. Two years later, Hardicanute being still abroad, Harold was recognized as sole king and crowned at Oxford. One of his first acts was to banish his stepmother Emma, who went into exile at Bruges. His reign was otherwise uneventful, and he died at Oxford on 17 March 1040, aged about 24. He was buried in London at St Clement Danes, but his half-brother and successor Hardicanute had his body disinterred, beheaded and flung into a marsh. Harold never married, but there is some evidence that he had a concubine, named Elfgifu like his mother. She is said to have borne him a son Aelfwine, who founded the monastery of Sainte-Foi at Conques in Aquitaine in about 1060.

Harold II, King of England (*c*.1022–66) The second son of GODWIN, EARL OF WESSEX and his wife Gytha, a kinswoman of King CANUTE, who was born about 1022. He rose to a position of prominence early in the reign of EDWARD THE CONFESSOR, who married his sister EDITH, and was associated with his father in many of his campaigns. In 1045 his father obtained the earldom of East Anglia for him and in the following year he was awarded half the lands forfeited by his rebellious elder brother Sweyn. He shared in his family's disgrace in 1051 and went into exile in Ireland, where he raised a fleet and sailed to join his father to ravage the Somerset coast and eventually sailed to London, where they were reconciled to the king and reinstated in favour.

On Godwin's death in April 1053 Harold succeeded to the earldom of Wessex and all his other possessions. In 1055 he was responsible for the undeserved banishment of Earl Aelfgar of East Anglia, who went to Ireland and raised a force with which he sailed to Wales and joined forces with GRUFFYDD AP LLYWELYN with the object of invading England. Harold arranged a peace and Aelfgar was restored to his earldom. Harold added the earldom of Hereford to his possessions in 1058 and it was probably in the same year that he made a pilgrimage to Rome. On his return he founded and endowed WALTHAM ABBEY in Essex, which was consecrated in 1060. He next turned his attention to the subjugation of Gruffydd ap Llywelyn and, with his brother Tostig, invaded Wales. They seized and sacked Rhuddlan, putting Gruffydd to flight and when the unfortunate Welsh king was killed by his own men in August 1063, his head was cut off and taken to Harold.

In sailing back from Wales, Harold was shipwrecked on the French coast and delivered up by Count Guy of Ponthieu to Duke William of Normandy (see WILLIAM I THE CONQUEROR), who extracted an oath from him, causing him to swear it unwittingly on concealed holy relics, that he would support William's claim to England on the death of Edward the Confessor. At the same time William betrothed Harold to one of his young daughters. Harold returned to England and, heedless of his betrothal to the Norman princess, married Ealdgyth, the widow of Gruffydd and daughter of Aelfgar in 1065. Prior to this he had lived in concubinage for many years with Eadgyth Swanneshals (Edith the Swan-necked), who had borne him a large family.

Harold's brother Tostig had become extremely unpopular through his oppressive rule in his earldom of Northumbria, and Harold secured his deposition and exile. He was replaced by Harold's brother-in-law Morcar, a brother of Ealdgyth, whom he hoped would support him in his bid for the Crown. King Edward died on 5 January 1066 and Harold was at once elected king by the nobles (though he had no valid hereditary claim) and crowned at WESTMINSTER ABBEY immediately after Edward's burial on 6 January. Soon after April his exiled brother Tostig crossed to the Isle of Wight and gathered men and provisions to set out on a raiding expedition eastwards along the south coast. On hearing this news, Harold

gathered a large army and set out for Sandwich. Tostig then sailed away northwards and eventually arrived in Scotland, where MALCOLM III received him in friendly fashion and allowed him to stay.

After mustering his troops at Sandwich, Harold went on to the Isle of Wight and stayed there the whole summer, anticipating an invasion from William of Normandy. By 8 September provisions ran out and Harold disbanded his army and returned to London. There he received news that Harald Hardrada, King of Norway, had landed in the north and been joined there by Tostig. He attempted to pacify Tostig by offering him a third of the kingdom, but to the Norwegian king he would offer only 'six feet of ground' and no deal could be struck. Harold hastily reassembled his army and, in the words of the ANGLO-SAXON CHRONICLE 'marched northward, day and night'. Meanwhile, his allies and brothers-in-law, Edwin and Morcar, gathered a large Mercian force and did battle with the invaders on 20 September. There were great losses on both sides, but eventually the Mercians were put to flight and Harald and Tostig entered York and took hostages before returning to their ships. Harold reached York a few days later and marched to Stamford Bridge, where he encountered the Norwegians and succeeded in inflicting a crushing defeat on them on 25 September, Harald Hardrada and Tostig both being killed. The remnants of the Norwegian army struggled back to their ships, and after Harald Hardrada's son Olaf had sworn an oath to maintain peace and friendship with Harold, they were allowed to sail away.

On 29 September William of Normandy landed at HASTINGS and Harold was obliged to muster the remains of his exhausted army and begin to march south, gathering reinforcements on the way. He reached Senlac, near Hastings, and was in the process of fortifying a position on a hill there when the Norman army set upon him on 14 October. The battle was fierce and 'there was great slaughter on both sides'. The Normans finally gained the victory by the stratagem of pretending flight. Harold and his brothers Gurth and Leofwine were killed. Traditionally Harold's eye was pierced by an arrow, but this seems to have arisen through a misinterpretation of the battle scene depicted in the BAYEUX TAPESTRY. A careful examination of this reveals Harold being felled by a sword blow and it is a nearby figure who has the arrow in his eye (though possibly it took both an arrow in the eye and sword blows to finish Harold off). William ordered Harold's body to be buried on the sea shore, but there is a strong tradition that his former concubine, Edith the Swan-necked, sought it out and was allowed to take it to his foundation of Waltham Abbey for burial. A noble who boasted of hacking off the dead Harold's leg was dismissed by William for this ignoble act.

Harold had one son, Harold, by his wife Ealdgyth. The boy is said to have been born posthumously at the end of 1066 and to have been living in 1098. Ealdgyth was deprived of all her property and entered a convent. The date of her death is unknown, but she is said to have been buried at Stortford in Hertfordshire, where she was regarded locally as a saint. Of Harold's children by Edith the Swan-necked, the sons, Godwin, Edmund, Magnus and Ulf, all survived the Conquest and probably went abroad, as did their sister, Gytha, who eventually married Vladimir Monomakh, Great Prince of Kiev. Another daughter, Gunhild, became a nun at Wilton. Nearly 300 years later Harold's blood returned to the throne of England in the persons of EDWARD III and Queen Philippa (*see* PHILIPPA OF HAINAULT, QUEEN OF ENGLAND), both of whom descended from Gytha (*see* Appendix XVI).

Hastings, Battle of The battle on 14 October 1066 in which WILLIAM I THE CONQUEROR defeated HAROLD II and thereby took possession of the English throne. Harold's army fought on foot, defending a strong position, but were ultimately overwhelmed by the attacks of the Norman cavalry and infantry. In the course of the battle Harold was killed.

Hatfield House Ancient royal manor in Hertfordshire, acquired by HENRY VIII, where ELIZABETH I was confined as a princess during the trial of her admirer Lord Seymour in 1548 and again during the latter part of the reign of MARY I. In 1558, she was allegedly sitting reading beneath an oak tree in the park at Hatfield House when messengers from London arrived to tell her that Mary was dead and she was now queen. JAMES I later exchanged Hatfield for THEOBALDS PALACE, and the new owners, the Cecil family, used bricks from the Old Palace, of which one wing containing the Great Hall still remains, to construct a magnificent new house there. Hatfield is open to the public and among the many treasures on display are Elizabeth I's garden hat, gloves and stockings.

Heir apparent The position of heir apparent to the throne can be held only by the male heir of the body of the reigning sovereign or by the daughter of a male heir apparent who has died in his regnant parent's lifetime leaving no male issue. The nearest instance of a female heir apparent would have been Princess Charlotte (*see* CHARLOTTE OF WALES, PRINCESS), the only daughter of George, Prince of Wales (later GEORGE IV), had he predeceased his father GEORGE III.

Heir presumptive The position of heir presumptive to the throne is held by an heir who is not the son of the reigning sovereign, since it is presumed that while the sovereign lives he or she may have male issue, regardless of age. Thus, WILLIAM IV was heir presumptive to his brother GEORGE IV, and his niece VICTORIA was his heir presumptive. The present queen was heir presumptive to her father GEORGE VI, the possibility of his having male issue never being ruled out.

Helena, Princess (1846–1923) The third daughter and fifth child of Queen VICTORIA and Prince ALBERT, who was born at BUCKINGHAM PALACE at five minutes to three in the afternoon of 25 May 1846 and was baptized Helena Augusta Victoria by the Archbishop of Canterbury in the chapel there on 25 July following. Her godparents were the Duchess of Orléans (represented by the Duchess of Kent), the Duchess of Cambridge and the Hereditary Grand Duke of Mecklenburg-Strelitz. She was almost three years old when her mother was shot at while driving down Constitution Hill. In writing to her uncle King Leopold of the Belgians, the queen said: 'Lenchen [the princess's nickname in the family] ... says, "Man shot, tried to shoot dear Mamma, must be punished".' The princess was educated under the care of the royal governesses, Lady Lyttelton (until 1851) and Lady Caroline Barrington.

On 20 June 1865 the 19-year-old princess deputized for her widowed mother in holding a 'drawing-room' at ST JAMES'S PALACE, the presentations at which, by the queen's command, were considered equivalent to presentations to the queen herself. In February of the following year the queen announced Princess Helena's engagement to Prince Christian of Schleswig-Holstein. Parliament voted her a dowry of £30,000 and £6000 per annum. The marriage took place in the private chapel at WINDSOR CASTLE on 5 July 1866. The bride, who was attended by eight unmarried daughters of dukes, marquesses and earls, wore 'a rich white satin dress and train with deep flounces of Honiton lace ... trimmed with knots of orange blossom and myrtle'. Prince Christian was the third son of Christian, Duke of Schleswig-Holstein-Sonderburg-Augustenburg, and his wife Countess Louise Sophie Danneskiold-Samsoe and was born at Augustenburg on 22 January 1831. As a great-grandson of CAROLINE MATILDA, QUEEN OF DENMARK he was his bride's third cousin. At Victoria's wish the couple made their home in England. Prince Christian was naturalized a British subject and nominated a Knight of the GARTER four days after his wedding.

Victoria's hopes that Princess Helena would become the ideal 'daughter at home' were to some measure disappointed. Prince and Princess Christian although dutifully accompanying the queen to Balmoral and Osborne when requested to do so, much preferred the privacy of their own home at Cumberland Lodge in Windsor Park, where the prince cultivated his roses, bred doves, smoked shag tobacco and went shooting. He was reported to be a dull man with no conversation and the tedious habit of counting to 30 before making a decision. He lost an eye in a shooting accident with his brother-in-law Prince Arthur (see CONNAUGHT, PRINCE ARTHUR, DUKE OF) and thereafter took pride in displaying his case of glass eyes to visitors. Victoria found fault with Lenchen's defections and expressed her displeasure in spiteful comments in letters to her eldest daughter the Crown Princess of Prussia: 'Helena is 26 today. She looks much older!'. It must have been a relief all round when Princess BEATRICE[2] took over the position of 'daughter at home'.

Princess Helena had six children: (1) Prince Christian Victor Albert Louis Ernest Anthony, who was born at Windsor Castle on 14 April 1867, made a career in the army and died of fever at Pretoria while serving in the South African War on 29 October 1900; (2) Prince Albert John Charles Frederick Alfred George, who was born at FROGMORE HOUSE on 26 February 1869, became head of the ducal house of Schleswig-Holstein in 1921 and died unmarried at Berlin on 27 April 1931; (3) Princess Victoria Louise Sophia Augusta Amelia Helena (later known as Princess Helena Victoria and in her family as Thora), who was born at Frogmore House on 3 May 1870 and died unmarried at 10 Fitzmaurice Place, Berkeley Square, London, on 13 March 1948; (4) Princess Franzisca Josepha Louise Augusta Marie Christina Helena (later

known as Princess Marie Louise and in her family as Louie), who was born at Cumberland Lodge on 12 August 1872, married at St George's Chapel, Windsor, on 6 July 1891, Prince Aribert Joseph Alexander of Anhalt, from whom she was divorced in 1900, and died at 10 Fitzmaurice Place, Berkeley Square, London, on 8 December 1956; (5) Prince (Frederick Christian Augustus Leopold Edward) Harold, who was born at Cumberland Lodge on 12 May and died there on 20 May 1876; and (6) a son, stillborn on 7 May 1877.

Princess Helena was President of the Royal British Nurses' Association and founded the Princess Christian Nursing Home for Officers at Windsor in 1894. She also founded the Royal School of Needlework at South Kensington in 1872 and became its first President.

Prince Christian died at Schomberg House, Pall Mall, London, on 28 October 1917 and Princess Helena died there also on 9 June 1923. Both were buried at Frogmore. Princess Helena's two daughters, known as 'the orphans', were inseparable and continued their mother's charitable work. Princess Marie Louise, who, in the words of her uncle EDWARD VII, returned to England after her divorce 'the same as she went', published an entertaining but unrevealing book of reminiscences entitled *My Memories of Six Reigns* in 1956.

Hengest, King of Kent (d.488) Founder of the Anglo-Saxon kingdom of Kent, who was, according to the pedigree recorded in the ANGLO-SAXON CHRONICLE, the son of Wihtgils, the son of Witta, the son of Wecta, the son of WODEN, a semi-mythical god-king. Hengest and his brother HORSA were invited to Britain from Jutland by the British King VORTIGERN, who required their assistance to protect his borders and repel the raids of the Picts and Scots, which had become more frequent after the withdrawal of the Romans from Britain early in the fifth century. The traditional date for the arrival of the brothers with their three longships is 449, but it is now believed to have been some years earlier and NENNIUS dates it in 428. They landed at Ebbsfleet in Kent and received a grant of land from Vortigern in return for their services. They turned against him, however, and fought a battle at Aylesford, Kent, in which Horsa was killed. The date assigned to this by the Chronicle is 455, and in 457 Hengest and his son Aesc or Oeric Oisc fought another battle with the Britons at Crayford, where they 'slew four thousand men; and the Britons then forsook Kent and fled to London in great terror'. In 465 Hengest and Aesc are recorded as fighting 'against the Welsh near Wippedesfleot [a place which has not been identified]'. In 473 they fought them again 'and captured innumerable spoils'. Hengest presumably died in 488, for in that year it is recorded that 'Aesc succeeded to the kingdom'. The romantic story of Hengest's daughter Rowena (Ronwen) and her marriage to Vortigern belongs to legend rather than to history.

Henrietta Anne, Duchess of Orléans

(1644–70) The fifth daughter and ninth and youngest child of CHARLES I and Queen HENRIETTA MARIA, who was born at Bedford House, Exeter, on 16 June and baptized in Exeter Cathedral on 21 July 1644, the city governor, Sir John Berkeley, standing as her godfather and two of her mother's ladies in waiting, Lady Dalkeith and Lady Poulett, as her godmothers. At the time of her birth the CIVIL WAR was at its height, her father was at Buckingham (he did not receive news of her birth until August) and Exeter was besieged by the Earl of Essex. Soon afterwards, the queen escaped to France, but she was obliged to leave the baby behind with Lady Dalkeith. Exeter was captured by Fairfax in April 1646 and the little princess and her governess were taken to London and lodged at ST JAMES'S PALACE, whence Lady Dalkeith eventually contrived to take the little princess in secrecy to rejoin her mother in Paris later in 1646.

Henrietta Maria brought up her daughter as a Roman Catholic in spite of her Anglican baptism, and at her confirmation the name Anne was added as a compliment to the princess's aunt, Anne of Austria, Queen Regent of France. She was always known in her family by the diminutive 'Minette'. After the Restoration in 1660 the princess, now 16, returned to England with her mother. Samuel Pepys escorted his wife to Whitehall on 22 November 1660 to see Henrietta Maria and her two daughters dining and commented: 'the Princess Henrietta is very pretty, but much below my expectation; and her dressing of herself with her hair frized short up to her ears, did make her seem so much the less to me'.

In January 1661 the princess and her mother set out to return to France, and on the 11 January Pepys recorded: 'This day comes news, by letters from Portsmouth, that the Princess Henrietta is fallen sick of the meazles on board the London, after the Queen and she was under sail. And so was forced to come back again into Portsmouth harbour; and in their way, by negligence of the pilot, ran upon the Horse sand.' Fortunately, the attack of measles was not a severe one and on the 15 January Pepys was able to report: 'This day I hear the Princess is recovered again.' The journey to France was resumed on the 27 January.

The princess had been betrothed to her first cousin, Philippe, Duke of Orléans, the only brother of Louis XIV of France, and they were married in the chapel of the Palais Royal in Paris by Daniel de Cosnac, Bishop of Valence, on 31 March 1661. The Duke, who was born at St Germain-en-Laye on 21 September 1640, was an effeminate homosexual and neglected his young wife for his male favourites. However, her charm and vivacity, combined with a wisdom beyond her years, made her a close friend and confidante of her brother-in-law Louis XIV, who often consulted her on affairs of state. The Duke and Duchess of Orléans had four children: (1) Marie Louise, who was born at the Palais Royal on 27 March 1662, was married in 1679 to Carlos II, King of Spain, and died without issue at Madrid on 12 February 1689; (2) Philippe Charles, Duke of Valois, who was born at Fontainebleau on 16 July 1664 and died at the Palais Royal on 8 December 1666; (3) a daughter, who was born and died at Versailles on 9 July 1665; (4) Anne Marie, who was born at St Cloud on 27 August 1669, was married in 1684 to Vittorio Amedeo II, King of Sardinia, and died at Turin on 26 August 1728, leaving issue.

Princess Henrietta was the patron of Molière, Corneille and Racine. In 1670 Louis XIV sent her on a mission to her brother CHARLES II to negotiate the Secret Treaty of Dover, whereby Charles pledged himself to support the French king in any claims he might pursue to the Spanish monarchy. Madame, as she was known in France, returned to Paris and on 27 June 1670 wrote to Sir Thomas Clifford (later 1st Lord Clifford of Chudleigh), one of the signatories of the Secret Treaty: 'This is the ferste letter I have ever write in inglis. You will eselay see it bi the stile and the ortografe.' Two days after writing this she fell ill and died in agony at St Cloud at about three o'clock in the morning on 30 June 1670. Poison was suspected, but it is more likely that the cause of her death was peritonitis resulting from a perforated duodenal ulcer. She was buried at St Denis on 21 August 1670. She died the most lamented person in both France and England, according to the Earl of Rochester.

The descendants of Princess Henrietta's daughter the Queen of Sardinia became the lineal representatives of the Royal House of Stuart in 1807, but being Roman Catholics were precluded from any right to the throne by the ACT OF SETTLEMENT.

Henrietta Maria of France, Queen of England (1609–69) The consort of CHARLES I, who was the third daughter and sixth and youngest child of Henri IV, King of France and Navarre, and his second wife Marie de'Medici, daughter of Francesco I, Grand Duke of Tuscany. She was born at the Hôtel du Louvre in Paris on 26 November 1609 and was not quite six months old when her father was assassinated in his carriage while driving through the streets of Paris on 14 May 1610.

Henrietta Maria was a little over 14 when negotiations for her marriage to Charles, Prince of Wales, were opened in 1624. By the time they were completed and the proxy marriage took place at Paris on 1 May 1625, Charles was king. The new queen landed at Dover and the marriage was completed at Canterbury on 13 June 1625. She did not attend her husband's coronation on 2 February 1626 and was never crowned herself because of the difference in religion.

The early years of the marriage were unhappy. Charles had undertaken to relieve the penal laws imposed on English Roman Catholics as part of the marriage treaty, but now found excuses not to do so. In response, Henrietta Maria sought to disrupt Anglican services at court by careering through the royal congregation with a pack of beagles. Her husband was almost as much under the influence of the Duke of Buckingham as his father had been, but the favourite's assassination at Portsmouth on 23 August 1628 removed a barrier, and the young couple soon developed a closer relationship, which was to ripen into a deep and abiding love for each other. In May 1629 the queen was frightened by a mastiff, which jumped at her while she was passing through a corridor of GREENWICH PALACE. She went into premature labour and her first child, Charles James, was born and died almost at once. Just over a year later the future CHARLES II was born and his birth was followed by those of seven more children, of whom two died young.

Henrietta Maria (as she is always referred to today, though to her contemporaries in England she was Queen Mary) delighted in the court amusements of the time and, like her mother-in-law before her, enjoyed taking part in masques and dramatic entertainments. She took little interest in politics or religion until 1637, when she appointed an agent to reside at the papal court and received a papal agent accredited to her. This man, a Scotsman named George Cann, began making conversions among the nobility and gentry, causing alarm in Protestant circles.

The queen gave the king her whole-hearted support in his struggles with the Commons and in his schemes to raise money. She was impeached by Parliament on 23 May 1643, but managed to join Charles at Edgehill and accompany him to Oxford. On 3 April 1644, when seven months pregnant, she was compelled to leave the king at Oxford and made her way to Exeter where she gave birth to her youngest child, HENRIETTA ANNE, on 16 June 1644. Soon afterwards she escaped to France, leaving her baby behind, and was well received by her sister-in-law Anne of Austria, the Queen Regent for her son Louis XIV. Her years in exile were passed in caring for her children. Rumours that she had contracted a private marriage with her secretary Lord Jermyn were probably unfounded, but her close relationship with him led to her partial estrangement from her children.

After the Restoration, Henrietta Maria returned to England and received a Parliamentary grant of £30,000 a year as compensation for the loss of her dower-lands and a matching sum as a pension from the king. Pepys saw her at court on 22 November 1660 and described her as a 'very little plain old woman, and nothing more in her presence in any respect nor garb than any ordinary woman'. She was only 50 at this time, but her troubles had aged her.

The Queen Mother returned to France in January 1661 to attend the marriage of her daughter Henrietta to the Duke of Orléans. She came back in the summer of 1662 and resumed her residence at Somerset House, but she found life in England uncongenial and the climate damaging to her health and so returned to France again in June 1665. She settled at Colombes, near Paris, and died there on 31 August 1669, probably from a massive overdose of opium taken to relieve the pain of the cancer from which she had suffered for four years. She was buried in the royal basilica of St Denis, where her tomb was despoiled in the French Revolution.

Henrietta of York, Princess (1669) The third daughter and seventh child of James, Duke of York (later JAMES II) and his first wife Anne HYDE, who was born at Whitehall 'at thirty-five minutes past seven at night' on 13 January 1669. She was named after her grandmother Queen HENRIETTA MARIA and her godparents were the Duke of Ormonde, the Marchioness of Dorchester and the Countess of Devonshire. The infant princess died at ST JAMES'S PALACE on 15 November and was buried in the royal vault in Henry VII's Chapel at WESTMINSTER ABBEY on 19 November 1669.

Henry, Duke of Gloucester see GLOU-CESTER, HENRY, DUKE OF.

Henry, Duke of Lancaster see LANCASTER, HENRY, DUKE OF.

Henry, Earl of Lancaster see LANCASTER, HENRY, EARL OF.

Henry, Prince[1] (c.1257) The sixth son and ninth and youngest child of HENRY III and ELEANOR OF PROVENCE, who died in his first year and was buried in WESTMINSTER ABBEY.

Henry, Prince[2] (1268–74) The second son of EDWARD I and his first wife ELEANOR OF CASTILE, who was born shortly before 6 May 1268, probably at Windsor. He died at Guildford, Surrey, on or about 16 October and was buried at WESTMINSTER ABBEY on 20 October 1274.

Henry I, King of England (1068–1135) The fourth and youngest son of WILLIAM I THE CONQUEROR and MATILDA OF FLANDERS, who was born at Selby in Yorkshire in about September or October 1068 (the only one of their children to be born in England), his mother having accompanied William on his expedition to subjugate the north. Like many youngest sons, he became his mother's favourite and on her death in 1083 she left him her English estates, which, however, he was not allowed to hold during his father's lifetime. Meanwhile he is reputed to have acquired a good education, learning to read and write Latin and also studying English and English law. It might be surmised that this was undertaken with a view to his entering the Church, often the destiny of youngest sons. His learning was to earn him the sobriquet of 'Beauclerc' (fine scholar), of which he became very proud, and in later life he was to declare that 'an unlettered King was but a crowned ass'. Another nickname, 'Lion of Justice', referred to his reform of administration.

Henry was knighted by his father at Westminster on Whitsunday (24 May) 1086 and after the king's death the following year he became one of those barons who suffered from the Conqueror's decision to leave Normandy to Robert (see ROBERT (III) CURT-HOSE, DUKE OF NORMANDY) and England to William. Until Robert resigned Normandy to William in 1096, Henry was constantly being forced to choose between his two overlords, and whichever side he came down on, he was likely to annoy the other. Once England and Normandy were re-united under WILLIAM II RUFUS, Henry was able to serve the king, and he was fortuitously present in the New Forest on the day his brother was killed on 2 August 1100. The following day, after William's burial at Winchester, such councillors as were at hand elected Henry king and, after securing the treasury, he immediately left for London, where on 6 August he was crowned in WESTMINSTER ABBEY by Maurice, Bishop of London.

Henry's first act as king was to issue a charter promising a return to his father's ways, and to restore Anselm to the Archbishopric of Canterbury (Anselm had gone into exile during William II's reign, following quarrels with the king over the rights of the Church). Henry's next act was to seek a wife and his choice very expediently fell upon Edith (renamed Matilda (see MATILDA OF SCOTLAND, QUEEN OF ENGLAND) in honour of his mother), the elder daughter of MALCOLM III CANMORE, KING OF SCOTS by St MARGARET, who was the granddaughter of EDMUND IRONSIDE. He thus reinforced the strain of Saxon blood in the royal family. The marriage and the coronation of the new queen took place at Westminster Abbey on 11 November 1100.

The vexed question of lay investiture of ecclesiastical estates threatened relations between Church and State for several years. Anselm refused to do homage to the king for the archiepiscopal estates, claiming he held them from the pope. The king would not give way and Anselm was deprived of his fiefs and again forced into exile. A compromise was reached in 1107 when the king's sister, ADELA, COUNTESS OF BLOIS, suggested that the bishops should pay homage for fiefs held of the king, who in his turn would allow clerical investiture. Another act that did much to mend relations between the king and his bishops was his apparently spontaneous decision, at Easter 1105, to have his beard shaved off after one of the French bishops criticized facial hair as a sign of sinfulness and begged his royal listeners to remove theirs. According to a contemporary account, 'when he had finished speaking the king consented in a mood of elation, as did all his magnates, and the bishop, ready for action, immediately drew scissors from his cloak-bag and proceeded to cut the hair, first of the king, and then of ... most of the magnates with his own hands.'

Henry was a wise ruler, a good judge of men and a skilled diplomat. It was his policy to choose his councillors and officials from the lower ranks of society and ennoble them to counteract the power of the great barons. The affairs of Normandy occupied the early years of his reign. Robert had returned from the Crusade but proved such an ineffective ruler that his barons revolted and invited Henry to come to their aid. Robert was taken prisoner at Tinchebrai and Normandy passed under Henry's rule. More troubles in Normandy and war with France continued to occupy the next few years. In 1109 Henry's foreign policy triumphed in the betrothal of his only legitimate daughter, Matilda (see MATILDA, 'LADY OF THE ENGLISH', EMPRESS), to the Emperor Henry V, the marriage taking place in 1114.

In 1120 Henry's only legitimate son, William (see WILLIAM 'THE ATHELING', DUKE OF NORMANDY), was tragically drowned with his entourage in the wreck of the *White Ship* when returning from Normandy. Henry, it is said, never smiled again. Queen Matilda had died in 1118, and in 1122 Henry took a second wife, ADELIZA OF LOUVAIN, daughter of Godfrey, Count of Louvain, but the marriage was to remain childless. At Christmas 1126 he designated his daughter, the widowed Empress Matilda, as his successor, and the following May he chose a second husband for her in the person of the young and handsome GEOFFREY PLANTAGENET, son of the Count of Anjou, who was 10 years or more her junior.

Henry was continually travelling from England to Normandy and back throughout his reign. He left England for the last time on 1 August 1135. An eclipse the next day was seen as an evil portent and, in the words of the ANGLO-SAXON CHRONICLE, 'men ... said that some important event should follow upon this; and so it did, for in that very year the King died in Normandy'. At the end of November Henry was at his royal hunting-box at St Denis-le-Fermont, near Gisors, where, says Henry of Huntingdon, 'he devoured lampreys which always disagreed with him, though he was excessively fond of them, and when his physicians forbade him to eat them the King did not heed their advice'. A severe case of ptomaine poisoning followed and Henry died on 1 December. He was 67, a good age for those days, though far short of the 80 years attained by his eldest brother Robert, who had ended his days in prison in Cardiff Castle a year earlier.

Henry's body was brought back to England and interred in Reading Abbey, which he had founded. No trace of his tomb remains today, the site being covered by a car park. 'He was,' says the Anglo-Saxon Chronicle, 'a good man, and was held in great awe. In his days no man dared to wrong another. He made peace for man and beast.' The last reference calls to mind the Woodstock menagerie, which Henry brought together, the first English zoo. This included lions, camels, leopards, lynxes and even a porcupine, many of the animals having been brought back to England by returning Crusaders. In his interest in natural history, as in many other things, he was a man far in advance of his time. William of Malmesbury remembered him as 'inferior in wisdom to no king in modern times; and, as I may almost say, he clearly surpassed all his predecessors in England'.

Henry's marriage to Matilda produced only two surviving children, that to Adeliza none, but a number of mistresses bore him a large illegitimate progeny of at least 21 children (more than any other English monarch), several of whom made a mark in the world, especially Robert, Earl of GLOUCESTER, who was to play an important part in the next reign. One of his daughters, Sibylla, married ALEXANDER I, KING OF SCOTS, and others made advantageous marriages among the Norman nobility.

The only contemporary depictions of Henry are coins and his great seal. Neither can be said to be a true likeness, but they, and a lively imagination, helped to inspire the portrait of Henry engraved by George Vertue in the 18th century.

Henry II, King of England (1133–89) The eldest son of GEOFFREY PLANTAGENET, COUNT OF ANJOU AND MAINE and his wife Matilda (see MATILDA, 'LADY OF THE ENGLISH', EMPRESS), widow of the Emperor Henry V and only legitimate daughter of HENRY I, who was born at Le Mans on 25 March 1133.

During the civil war in England waged between STEPHEN and Matilda, Geoffrey Plantagenet took the opportunity to acquire Normandy from the preoccupied Stephen and in 1150 invested his son Henry FitzEmpress, as he was often called, with the duchy. The following year, Geoffrey died and the young duke also succeeded to the counties of Anjou and Maine. In 1152 Henry was seduced by the newly divorced Queen of France, ELEANOR OF AQUITAINE, a woman 11 or so years his senior, and their subsequent marriage at Bordeaux on 18 May added further to his French dominions. Stephen's agreement to his claim to the English throne the next year and his accession on Stephen's death in October 1154 made him the ruler of a greater empire than any of his predecessors. He was crowned at WESTMINSTER ABBEY on 19 December 1154.

The early years of Henry's reign were spent in restoring law and order and recovering the Crown lands and prerogatives dissipated by Stephen. In this Henry was ably assisted by the Church, and a brilliant young cleric Thomas à Becket, a protégé of Archbishop Theobald of Canterbury, rose swiftly to power as the king's chief adviser. Plans to invade Ireland in 1155 fell through, but MALCOLM IV, KING OF SCOTS was forced to restore the northern counties of England that had been ceded to his grandfather DAVID I. An invasion of North Wales took place in 1157, followed in 1159 by a campaign in France to assert Queen Eleanor's claim to the county of Toulouse. This proved unsuccessful and an uneasy peace was concluded with Eleanor's former husband Louis VII, whose daughter Margaret (by his second wife) was betrothed to Henry and Eleanor's eldest surviving son.

Henry returned to England in 1163 and almost at once began a quarrel with the Church that was to occupy the next few years of his reign. Henry had raised his Chancellor Thomas à Becket to the Archbishopric of Canterbury in 1162, and in order to show that he was no mere cipher of the king, Becket set out to prove his independence. An argument developed between them over the issue of whether clergy who committed crimes ('criminous clerks') should be tried in ordinary courts of law or only in church courts. Attempts at negotiation failed, and in 1164 Becket was forced to leave the country, while Henry impounded the revenues of the archbishopric. Eventually, in spite of Henry's finesse, the threat of a papal interdict forced a reconciliation and Becket returned to England in 1170. The well-known story of Henry's exasperated utterance 'will no one rid me of this turbulent priest?' leading to Becket's murder in his own cathedral at the hands of four of Henry's knights on 29 December 1170, was disastrous to Henry's cause against the Church, but he cannot be considered altogether culpable. He was stricken with remorse and his public penance at Becket's tomb, while expediently obtaining papal absolution at the price of a complete surrender over the matters in dispute, exhibited a genuine sorrow at the loss of a once dear and trusted friend. According to his contemporary Arnulf, Bishop of Lisieux, he excited fears for his health by donning sackcloth and ashes in repentance and undergoing three days' starvation: 'At times he fell into a stupor, after which he would again utter groans and cries louder and more bitter than before. For three whole days he remained shut up in his chamber and would neither take food nor admit anyone to comfort him, until it seemed from the excess of his grief that he had determined to contrive his own death.' Subsequently he walked barefoot to the cathedral, supplicated himself in prayer and ordered his bishops to punish him with strokes of the lash. Legend has it that when the four knights guilty of the murder halted at the archbishop's home to partake of a meal, the table shook so violently that the saddle-packs they had laid on it were repeatedly thrown off in horror at their presence.

In 1170 Henry had his eldest surviving son, a boy of 15 also named Henry (see HENRY 'THE YOUNG KING'), crowned at Westminster Abbey, imitating a custom that had been adopted at the French court to ensure a peaceful succession. Louis VII took exception to the fact that his daughter Margaret, the 'Young King's' wife, had not also been crowned, and to satisfy him the ceremony was repeated at Winchester, with Margaret participating, in August 1172. At the banquet that followed the coronation Henry II served his son himself, remarking that 'No other King in Christendom has such a butler'. 'It is only fitting,' came the pert reply from his son, 'that the son of a Count should wait on the son of a King.' Unfortunately, young Henry did not live to become Henry III, dying long before his father in 1183. His only child died in infancy and Margaret remarried and ended her days as Queen of Hungary.

The latter part of Henry's reign was taken up by quarrels with and between his sons, stirred into rebellion by their mischief-making mother from whom he had separated. In 1189 Henry was at Tours when he received the news that his youngest and favourite son JOHN was in league with his enemies. It broke his heart and moved him to observe that his illegitimate son Geoffrey had proved more faithful than his real off-spring: 'Baseborn indeed have my other children shown themselves; this alone is my true son!' At 56 he was prematurely aged, worn out by the strenuous exertion of trying to hold together his unwieldy empire. On 30 June he was struck down by fever, yet never-theless on the 4 July set out to meet Philippe of France at Colombières. While the two kings spoke, still mounted, a sudden thunderclap caused Henry's horse to rear and throw him. He made his peace with Philippe and was carried in a litter to the cas-tle of Chinon. His last two days were embit-tered by wrangling with a deputation of monks from Canterbury come to demand further concessions for their order. Nearing his end, Henry asked to be carried before the altar of the castle church where, cursing the day he was born and calling down heaven's vengeance on his sons, he suffered a haem-orrhage and died almost immediately. He was buried in the Abbey of Fontevraud and succeeded by his third son RICHARD I.

Henry's effigy, though stylized, gives some impression of his appearance. Sturdily built with a large head, he was cleanshaven, had grey eyes and had inherited the red hair of his Norman ancestors, wearing it cut short. His nickname 'Curtmantle' was de-rived from the short continental cloak he wore, which appeared strange to English eyes. Essentially a man of action, athletic, energetic and self-disciplined, Henry stands out among his contemporaries. We are told he spoke not only Latin and French but also had a good knowledge of all languages 'from the French sea to the Jordan'. His mother, who retained a great influence on him until her death in 1167, had taken care with his education and he was well-grounded in law and history. It was said that he was never without a bow or a book in his hand. Although a man of strong passions, hasty, and often bad-tempered and not above man-handling his advisers physically, Henry's good qualities outweighed the lesser and he was undoubtedly a vigorous administrator and the dominant figure of his day in western European politics.

Apart from his large family by Queen Eleanor, Henry acknowledged two natural sons, William de Longespée, Earl of Salis-bury, who died on 7 March 1226, and Geoffrey, Bishop-elect of Lincoln from 1173 to 1182 and Archbishop of York from 1191 until his death on 18 December 1212.

Henry III, King of England (1207–72) The elder son of King JOHN and ISABELLA OF ANGOULÊME, who was born at Winchester Castle on 1 October 1207. On the death of his father in October 1216, the throne of England was occupied by a child for the first time since before the Conquest. Queen Isabella and her children were residing at Gloucester when John died and, since the greater part of eastern England was in the hands of Louis of France and the rebel barons, it was thought expedient to have the nine-year-old Henry crowned as soon as possible. Since the regalia were at West-minster and therefore not available, and John's personal state crown had been lost in the Wash, the young king was crowned in Gloucester Cathedral on 28 October by the Bishop of Winchester with a gold torque (or bracelet, according to some accounts) belonging to his mother. The regency was exercised by William Marshal, Earl of Pem-broke, until his death in 1219 and then by Hubert de Burgh. The loss of William Marshal was deeply felt by Henry, with whom he had been very close. He was inclined to see his friend's death as yet another punishment for the murder of Thomas à Becket many years before, remarking when he inspected William Marshal's dead body, 'Alas, woe is me, is the blood of blessed Thomas the martyr not even yet avenged?'

The king's person and education (his mother having retired to her native land at the first opportunity and remarried) were entrusted to Peter des Roches, Bishop of Winchester. Hubert and the bishop were soon to become deadly rivals. The French invaders were expelled and the rebel barons brought to heel by the end of 1217, and on Whitsunday (17 May) 1220 Henry was crowned for a second time in WESTMINSTER ABBEY with the full ceremonial. In order to secure the resumption of the royal castles and demesnes that had passed into private hands during the recent civil war, Henry was formally declared of age by Pope Honorius III in 1223, but his personal rule did not commence until 1227 when he was 20. Even then, Hubert de Burgh retained a great influence until July 1232, when he was dismissed as Justiciar, accused of filling his own pockets from the royal treasury and other malpractices, and imprisoned. Although he probably was guilty of some of these charges, the king was really using him as a scapegoat for the failure of his own ineffectual expedition to France to recover some of the continental possessions lost by

John. Peter des Roches, who had prudently left the kingdom on the declaration of Henry's majority, now returned to power and appointed his fellow Poitevins to high offices, initiating the long period of bad government for which the weak-willed Henry's reign is best known.

When the barons, headed by Edmund Rich, Archbishop of Canterbury, finally demanded the expulsion of the Poitevins in 1234, Henry assumed the administration himself, filling the high offices of state with his own men. His extortionate taxation (directed especially at the Jews), disastrous foreign policy and the favouritism shown to his wife ELEANOR OF PROVENCE's foreign relations and his own half-brothers, brought matters to a head and the lay barons of the kingdom found a leader in the person of Henry's brother-in-law, Simon de Montfort, Earl of Leicester. In the ensuing civil war Henry and his son Edward (see EDWARD I) were defeated and captured by de Montfort at Lewes in 1264 and the king was forced to summon a parliament and undertake to rule with the advice of a council of barons. The tide of battle at Lewes turned against Henry when he was duped into charging an empty litter that he assumed was carrying de Montfort himself, thus exposing his own flank to attack. While the king submitted, 'the Lord' Edward continued to lead the opposition and de Montfort was killed at the battle of Evesham in 1265. Thereafter Edward and Henry's brother, Richard of Cornwall (see CORNWALL, RICHARD, EARL OF), concluded a peace with the remaining rebels.

For the rest of his life Henry remained but a cipher and the forced inactivity eventually resulted in premature senility. The death of his beloved brother Richard in April 1272 was a mortal blow. While praying at St Edmund's shrine in Suffolk, Henry 'began to wax somewhat crasie', in the words of Holinshed. He recovered enough to call a council there, but suffered a relapse and was taken 'with all speed' to London, where he died at the Palace of Westminster on 16 November 1272. He was 65 years old and had reigned for 56 years. By his own directions he was interred in the original coffin of EDWARD THE CONFESSOR, who had been reburied in a more magnificent one, 'having with his usual simplicity', says Agnes Strickland, 'an idea that its previous occupation by the royal saint had made it a peculiarly desirable tenement'. His heart was sent to Fontevraud.

If Henry was a bad king, he was not a bad man, possessing none of his father's viciousness. The troubled realm he inherited would have needed a very strong ruler indeed to restore stability. Henry was not the man for the job and it remained for his far abler son and brother to accomplish it. What Henry lacked in statesmanship was largely compensated for by a cultivated mind and a patronage of literature and the arts, which had been neglected by his immediate predecessors. His rebuilding of Westminster Abbey, a tribute to his profound veneration for Edward the Confessor, whose relics he personally assisted in carrying to their new shrine on 13 October 1269, was his greatest achievement, and it stands today as his most eloquent memorial. His great piety, for which he was famous, was sometimes a hindrance, however – when visiting the French king he insisted upon hearing mass from every priest whom he met on the journey and was consequently very late in arriving (steps were taken when Henry was next due to visit to remove all priests from the vicinity of the royal route). Like Henry I he also showed an interest in natural history and his zoo at the TOWER OF LONDON included the first elephant ever seen in England, buffaloes, leopards, a camel, a bear and a lion.

Henry was the first sovereign to use a distinguishing numeral on some of his coins, the inscription on his silver pennies reading 'Henricus Tertius'. His appearance may be deduced from his magnificent tomb effigy, which, though stylized, probably represents a genuine likeness.

Henry IV, King of England (1366–1413)

The fourth son of John of Gaunt, Duke of LANCASTER (fourth son of EDWARD III) and his first wife Blanche, younger daughter and co-heiress of Henry, 4th Earl and 1st Duke of Lancaster, who was born at Bolingbroke Castle, Lincolnshire, on 4 April 1366. The deaths of his three elder brothers made Henry Bolingbroke his father's heir and as such he bore the courtesy title of Earl of Derby. He was created a Knight of the GARTER in 1377 and was married at Arundel Castle at the age of 14 between July 1380 and March 1381 to an 11-year-old heiress, Mary de Bohun, whose father Humphrey was 7th Earl of Hereford, 6th Earl of Essex and 2nd Earl of Northampton. She bore seven children in quick succession and died at the birth of the last at Peterborough Castle on 4 July 1394.

Mary's elder sister had married Henry's uncle, Thomas of Woodstock, Duke of

GLOUCESTER, and Henry supported his uncle and brother-in-law in his armed revolt against RICHARD II in 1387, but was later induced by his father to change sides. The spirit of adventure sent him to serve with the Teutonic Knights in Lithuania for a while and to visit Venice, Cyprus and Jerusalem. On his return to England he joined his father and the king against Gloucester and as a reward was created Duke of Hereford on 29 September 1397. Early in 1398, however, he quarrelled with the Duke of Norfolk, who accused him of treason, and challenged him to settle the matter by combat at Coventry. As the fight was about to start, the king intervened and banished both contestants from the kingdom. Henry went to Paris and bided his time. On his father's death in February 1399 he found the excuse to return secretly to recover his estates, which the Crown had confiscated in spite of promises to the contrary from Richard. While the king was in Ireland, Henry landed in Yorkshire and was joined by the Percys. Richard was abandoned by his followers, surrendered at Flint in August, and was forced to resign the crown to Henry by Parliament on 29 September 1399. Henry was crowned at WESTMINSTER ABBEY on 13 October. Superstitious commentators noted that following the coronation the new king was much troubled with head lice and that he could grow no hair on his head for some months afterwards – a portent of ills to come, it was claimed.

The crown gained by usurpation was indeed an uneasy one, as Shakespeare was to point out. The 13 years of Henry's reign were occupied by warfare of one sort or another. OWAIN GLYN DŴR's spirited bid for Welsh independence made in 1400 took 10 years to put down. The French plundered the south coast and the Scots made incursions in the north. The Percys and the Mortimers organized two rebellions, and Archbishop Scrope of York, who gave them support, was among those executed for treason, an act for which Henry was regarded as an impious monster. To add to Henry's troubles, his second wife, JOAN OF NAVARRE, was suspected of witchcraft and he himself was afflicted with a disfiguring skin disease, probably a form of eczema but called 'leprosy' by his contemporaries. Critics of the king claimed that he had been struck down with his leprosy as a form of divine retribution immediately after ordering the execution of the Archbishop of York.

It had been prophesied that Henry would die in Jerusalem and he comforted himself with the knowledge that his death would thus be deferred until he went on his long-projected crusade to the Holy Land. On 20 March 1413 he was praying at EDWARD THE CONFESSOR's shrine in Westminster Abbey when he had a seizure and was carried unconscious to the Jerusalem Chamber near the west door. Here he recovered consciousness and asked in what room he was. On being told its name, Holinshed tells us, he said: 'Lauds be given to the Father of Heaven, for now I know that I shall die here in this chamber; according to the prophecy of me declared, that I should depart this life in Jerusalem.' When it was thought that he was dead, his son (see HENRY V) was allowed to remove the crown lying on a chair close to where the king lay – only for the supposedly 'dead' king to rouse one last time and ask its whereabouts. When informed that the prince had taken it, Henry resigned himself to his fate and died shortly after.

Although Henry died in Westminster Abbey, where so many of his ancestors lay, his body was, at his own request, taken to Canterbury for burial near the tomb of the BLACK PRINCE and the last resting place of St Thomas à Becket. It was taken as far as Faversham by water, and Clement of Maidstone relates that a fierce storm sprang up during the journey and caused the superstitious crew to throw the king's body overboard and later substitute another. Henry's tomb was opened in 1832 and the account given in *Archaeologia* states that the outer coffin was of entirely different shape from that of the inner and that the space between them was filled with straw. No regalia was found with the body and on the inner coffin lay a cross fashioned from twigs bound together. Others, though, were satisfied that the body in Canterbury cathedral was indeed that of Henry, and marvelled at its excellent state of preservation, complete with a thick and matted beard 'of a deep russet colour' and an intact set of teeth, with just one fore-tooth missing, probably lost during the king's lifetime.

Henry's portraits are of one type only and probably based on a contemporary original. The effigy on his tomb at Canterbury accords well with the descriptions of him. He was as unprepossessing in person as his predecessor had been attractive. Short, stout, redhaired and bearded, he was lacking in kingly grace and dignity and regarded as uninspiring.

Henry V, King of England (1387–1422) The second, but first surviving, son of Henry,

Earl of Derby (later HENRY IV) and his first wife Mary de Bohun, who was born at Monmouth on 16 September 1387. Two days after his father's coronation he was created Prince of Wales, Duke of Cornwall and Earl of Chester on 15 October 1399, and on 10 November he was further created Duke of Aquitaine and Duke of Lancaster.

The story of Prince Hal's riotous youth is mostly an invention of Shakespeare and is not substantiated by any contemporary record, though there is equally no evidence that he was a pious, obedient son. Stories about how he boxed the ears of the Lord Chief Justice and about how he and other unruly friends liked to ambush and rob guests at the royal household – later to reimburse them generously for the losses and injuries sustained – seem to have been largely of Tudor, or later, origin. His profession of arms started early when he took part in the suppression of OWAIN GLYN DŴR's rebellion (at the age of 16, in 1403, he was wounded in the face by an arrow at the battle of Shrewsbury). His father's increasing ill-health obliged him to take a share in the government with his half-uncles Henry and Thomas Beaufort, but his policies differed from those of the king, who dismissed him from the Council in 1411. There was, however, no personal quarrel between father and son.

On his accession in March 1413 and following his coronation at WESTMINSTER ABBEY on 9 April, Henry – so legend has it – underwent something of a conversion and determinedly forsook his wild ways, pensioning off his former comrades (they were not allowed within 10 miles of him) and devoting himself to the serious and responsible business of kingship. He did not so much as touch the food laid out at his coronation banquet. Among those he is supposed to have cast off was the rascally Sir John Falstaff, though history insists that no such character actually existed (he may, however, just conceivably have had his origins in the real Sir John Oldcastle or in the old soldier Sir John Fastolf).

Henry set about restoring and maintaining order at home by cleverly diverting the interest of the great nobles to a renewal of the French war begun by EDWARD III. The story that he was provoked into taking up arms against the French after they jokingly sent him a set of tennis balls, suggesting that he stick to such 'childish' occupations until he was mature enough to contemplate such weighty matters, is probably apocryphal.

His expedition was crowned with success and the great victory of AGINCOURT on 25 October 1415 was followed by two years of careful preparation for further activity. Though later generations liked to depict him as a chivalrous and inspirational leader, the reality is less attractive, for he was quite ready to massacre French captives at Agincourt and laid waste captured towns and villages almost as a matter of course. He once remarked, indeed, that 'war without fire is like sausages without mustard'. In 1419, when he lay siege to Rouen he herded 12,000 old men, women and children who were hoping to leave the city into the moat round the city walls and left them there to die of hunger and exposure. To his critics he only replied, 'I am the scourge of God.' Normandy was conquered, its residents terrorized and treated with considerable barbarity, and by August 1419 the English forces had reached the walls of Paris. Negotiations for peace led to the Treaty of Troyes, whereby Henry was recognized as heir and regent of France, to the exclusion of the Dauphin, and received in marriage the mad King Charles VI's daughter CATHERINE OF FRANCE, the marriage taking place at Troyes on 2 June 1420.

Henry was now at the height of his power and a force to be reckoned with throughout western Europe (though his campaigns cost dear in terms of human lives and he was less popular at home than is usually assumed). He was much admired for his decisiveness, and it was said that he had only two answers to questions of military strategy: 'It shall be done' and 'It is impossible'. His influence, combined with that of the Emperor Sigismund, brought about the end of the Great Schism with the election of Pope Martin V, and Henry's next ambition was to launch a new Crusade to the Holy Land. Death overtook him before this could be accomplished. He had long been prone to attacks of dysentery, an almost unavoidable accompaniment to life on campaign in those insanitary days, and a particularly virulent attack struck him down at Bois de Vincennes near Paris on 31 August 1422. 'Death overcame the King when he was speaking to his nobles,' says the author of the *Memorials of Henry V*. His last words are said to have been to express the wish that he might live to rebuild the walls of Jerusalem. He was 35 years old.

Henry's body was dismembered, boiled in a cauldron and brought back to England for burial in Westminster Abbey. His chantry chapel lies immediately east of EDWARD THE CONFESSOR's shrine. The tomb was despoiled at the Reformation and at some stage the head of the effigy disappeared. It has recently been carefully restored.

Henry V was the last great warrior king of the Middle Ages. His personality is not attractive and he appears to have been stern and humourless. His portrait shows a lean, ascetic face with an over-large nose beneath a monkish haircut. There is an air of fanaticism about him well in keeping with the singleness of purpose with which he pursued the continuation of the French war. Probably his early death played a major role in the myth that has since accumulated around his name, as he died before the difficulties implicit in ruling both France and England did any serious damage to his reputation as a ruler.

Henry VI, King of England (1421–71) The
only child of HENRY V and CATHERINE OF FRANCE, who was born at WINDSOR CASTLE on 6 December 1421. He was Duke of Cornwall from his birth and was only eight months old when his father's death made him king in August 1422.

The baby king presided over Parliament seated in his mother's lap, but he was not always well behaved and threw a great tantrum in November 1423 when he was being brought from Windsor and lodged overnight at Staines. In the morning he was being carried to his mother's litter when 'he skreeked, he cried, he sprang, and would be carried no further; wherefore they again bore him to the inn, and there he abode ... all day'. The next day he was 'glad and merry of cheer' and the journey continued by extraordinarily slow stages with further overnight stops at Kingston and at Kennington. Some observers pointed out that the baby had protested loudly when the proposed journey was attempted on the Sabbath, but went meekly enough on the Monday, and claimed it as early evidence of the infant monarch's great piety.

Henry was crowned at WESTMINSTER ABBEY on 6 November 1429, exactly one month before his eighth birthday, and two years later was crowned King of France at Notre-Dame Cathedral in Paris, on 16 December 1431. He had the dubious distinction of being the only English claimant to the French throne to become *de facto* sovereign. Before Henry came of age on 12 November 1437, English rule in France had begun a steady decline with Joan

of Arc's campaign (he is said to have been present at her trial) and the death of the regent the Duke of Bedford. By 1453 only Calais remained of Henry V's conquests.

At home Henry concerned himself with his two great scholastic foundations, Eton College and King's College, Cambridge, laying the foundation stones of both buildings. This 'good and gentle creature' was better fitted for a life of piety and learning than that of a monarch. He never swore, eschewed all forms of fashionable dress, favouring instead the simple habit of a farmer or merchant, and showed reluctance to accept expensive gifts from flatterers. He had a particular horror of seeing naked bodies, and took steps to ensure the chastity of members of his household. He seemed devoid, however, of any administrative skills and was entirely open to the machinations of his advisers, quickly running the Crown into severe debt.

At the age of 23 he was married by proxy at Nancy in March and in person at Titchfield Abbey, Hampshire, on 22 April 1445 to MARGARET OF ANJOU, who was to prove as strong as he was weak, being cast in the mould of ELEANOR OF PROVENCE and ISABELLA OF FRANCE[1], though without their worse features. Henry engineered things so that he was first introduced to Margaret in the disguise of a squire, so that he might examine her without her suspecting who he really was. He seemed satisfied enough with her and the marriage went ahead. After eight years of marriage (during which Henry was entirely faithful) a son was born, the birth following almost immediately on Henry's first attack of insanity. This attack lasted for over a year, during which time he was unable even to recognize the people before him or to respond to the arrival of his son. During his incapacity Richard, 3rd Duke of YORK, the next in line after Henry's son, reigned as Protector and proved far more competent, leading to the conclusion that 'if Henry's insanity had been a tragedy, his recovery was a national disaster'.

On Henry's recovery in 1455, the Duke of York was dismissed and Queen Margaret and Edmund Beaufort, Duke of Somerset, became all-powerful. Things came to a head between the rival Lancastrians and Yorkists and open warfare broke out, Somerset being killed at the first battle of St Albans on 22 May 1455. A peace of sorts was patched up, but four years later hostilities recommenced and on 10 July 1460 Henry was captured at Northampton and forced to recognize the Duke of York as his heir to the exclusion of his own son. The queen rallied the Lancastrian forces and won a victory at Wakefield in which Richard of York was slain (29 December 1460). The second battle of St Albans (17 February 1461) secured Henry's freedom (he is alleged to have laughed and sung insanely while the battle raged), but the Lancastrian triumph was shortlived. On 29 March 1461 the new Duke of York, Edward, defeated the king's forces in a snowstorm at Towton and Henry fled to take refuge in Scotland. The Duke of York had already been proclaimed king as EDWARD IV on 4 March, when Henry was formally deposed.

Henry returned from Scotland to take part in an abortive rising in 1464. A year later he was captured and taken as a prisoner to the TOWER OF LONDON, where he lived until a brief restoration engineered by Richard Neville, Duke of Warwick 'the King-maker', and known as the 're-adeption', brought him back as puppet sovereign in October 1470. Edward, who had fled to Burgundy, returned early in 1471 and in two battles regained the throne. His final victory at Tewkesbury was followed by the murder of Henry's son, Edward, on 4 May 1471.

The hapless Henry was returned to the Tower from whence his own death – allegedly from 'pure displeasure and melancholy' – was announced on 21 May 1471. He was, it appears, stabbed to death and the perpetrator of the crime was popularly believed to have been Edward's brother, Richard, Duke of Gloucester (later RICHARD III). Henry was first buried at Chertsey Abbey, his corpse being conveyed up the Thames by night, but it was later removed to St George's Chapel, Windsor, where he lies near his rival Edward, his tomb consisting of a plain black marble tablet bearing his name and the date in brass lettering. Henry's reign was one long tragedy, and he himself was a pathetic figure, afflicted in the same way as his maternal grandfather Charles VI of France, though not perhaps to such a degree. It has been suggested that the 'royal malady' PORPHYRIA was responsible for his condition. He is one of the saddest figures in the history of English royalty. He was well-meaning, courteous and honest and could have made a good king in different times had he not been cursed with his recurring mental affliction. Over the years repeated efforts have been made to have him canonized, so far unsuccessfully.

Henry VII, King of England (1457–1509)
The only child of Edmund Tudor, Earl of Richmond (half-brother of HENRY VI) and his wife Lady Margaret Beaufort (see RICHMOND AND DERBY, MARGARET BEAUFORT, COUNTESS OF), who was born at Pembroke Castle on 28 January 1457, nearly three months after the death of his father, whom he succeeded as Earl of Richmond at birth. His mother was only 13 years old when he was born and she lived at Pembroke Castle under the protection of her brother-in-law Jasper Tudor, who held it as Constable for the Lancastrians.

The castle was captured for the Yorkists by Lord Herbert on 30 September 1461 and Henry's custody and marriage were sold to Herbert for £1000 early the following year. His life appears to have continued much as before and he resided either at Pembroke or at the Herberts' castle at Raglan for the next few years. His mother had left to remarry (first to Henry Stafford, who died in 1471, then to Thomas, Lord Stanley), and Lord and Lady Herbert proved kind foster parents, bringing Henry up in their household as the intended husband of their daughter Maud and providing him with a good education.

The 're-adeption' of Henry VI in October 1470 brought Jasper Tudor back to Pembroke to fetch his nephew to meet the king in London and there is a tradition that Henry pursued his studies at his royal half-uncle's foundation at Eton. If so, it must have been for a very short time, for early in 1471 he returned to Wales with Jasper, who had received a commission to array Welsh forces. The battles of Barnet (14 April) and Tewkesbury (4 May) proved fatal to the Lancastrian cause, and Jasper and Henry, who had been unable to join forces with Queen Margaret and her other supporters, headed back for Pembroke, where they were besieged in the castle. They were allowed to escape through the good offices of a friend and made their way to Tenby, where they took a ship with the intention of going to France. Stormy weather drove them to land in Brittany, where they were accorded the protection of Duke François II.

The next 13 years of Henry's life were passed in Brittany and little is known of this period, during which he grew to manhood. EDWARD IV made several attempts to extradite the exiles, being particularly anxious to secure 'the only imp now left of Henry's brood', but Jasper and Henry succeeded in evading all such efforts.

After the rising against RICHARD III, culminating in the battle of BOSWORTH FIELD in August 1485 and Henry's impromptu coronation by Lord Stanley with the fallen Richard III's crest crown, the new king lost no time in consolidating his position. No one questioned his claim to be considered the heir of the House of Lancaster, though his mother had a prior one. He at once ordered the arrest and imprisonment in the Tower of his chief rival, Edward, Earl of Warwick, the son of the ill-fated George, Duke of CLARENCE, and then made his way to London, where he was received by the Mayor and Aldermen and escorted by them to St Paul's Cathedral. There he deposited his standards on the high altar and a solemn *Te Deum* was sung. On 30 October Henry's coronation took place at WESTMINSTER ABBEY. He was crowned by the octogenarian Cardinal Bourchier, Archbishop of Canterbury, who had officiated at the coronations of both Edward IV and Richard III. The new king did not neglect to reward his supporters, among them his uncle Jasper, who became Duke of Bedford and was married to a sister of the Queen Dowager ELIZABETH WOODVILLE, and his stepfather Lord Stanley, who became Earl of Derby.

Henry's first Parliament had been called for November and one of its first acts was to pass a bill confirming Henry's right to the throne and settling it on 'the heirs of his body lawfully comen'. The session ended in December with a petition from the Lords and Commons begging the king to marry Elizabeth (*see* ELIZABETH OF YORK, QUEEN OF ENGLAND), the eldest daughter of Edward IV, to which he was graciously pleased to accede. Henry had, in fact, already pledged himself to this marriage at Rennes in 1483. Now it remained to remove the stigma of bastardy from the intended bride and to obtain a papal dispensation for the marriage of persons related 'in the fourth degree of kinship and perhaps in the fourth degree of affinity'. Both these formalities being complied with, the marriage took place at Westminster on 18 January 1486. The new queen became pregnant almost immediately and her coronation was accordingly deferred until 25 November 1487.

Henry, apart from seeing himself as the lawful heir of the House of Lancaster and the husband of the lawful heiress of the House of York, also laid claim to a much older tradition. Through his Welsh grandfather he traced descent from ancient British kings and saw himslf as the lawful successor of the semi-mythical ARTHUR. He adopted the red dragon of Wales as one of the supporters of the royal coat of arms and

named his eldest son and heir Arthur to boost the tradition. Although Henry was only one-quarter Welsh by blood, he had been born in the principality and had spent his earliest years in Wales and then in Brittany, where the same traditions prevailed and the same language was spoken. In many ways he was a typical Celt, both in appearance and temperament.

During his reign Henry had to deal with two pretenders to the throne. The first was Lambert SIMNEL, who personated Edward, Earl of Warwick, the son of Edward IV's brother George, Duke of Clarence. Simnel gained the support of his putative aunt MARGARET OF YORK, DUCHESS OF BURGUNDY and repairing to Ireland was actually crowned in Dublin as Edward VI in 1487. On invading England in the same year, however, he was defeated and captured by Henry at Stoke-on-Trent. Henry showed great magnanimity in pardoning him and putting him to work as a turnspit in the royal kitchens. He was still living in 1525. The second pretender was Perkin WARBECK, a native of Tournai, who pretended to be Richard Plantagenet, Duke of YORK, the younger son of Edward IV. He gained support in Europe, and Margaret of Burgundy, the Emperor Maximilian and JAMES IV, KING OF SCOTS all recognized him as Richard IV of England. At the Scottish court he received the hand of Lady Catherine Gordon in marriage. After rallying support in Ireland, he landed in Cornwall and advanced as far as Exeter before he was captured in September 1497. He confessed his imposture, was imprisoned in the TOWER OF LONDON, and was eventually hanged after an attempted escape in 1499. The real Earl of Warwick, who made a bid for freedom at the same time, perished with him, but on the block as befitted his royal birth.

Henry's health, never very robust, began to fail in 1507, when he became subject to recurrent attacks of gout and asthma. His condition worsened steadily and he died at his new palace at Richmond, a place not ideally situated for a sufferer from respiratory troubles, on 21 April 1509, aged 52. His mother survived him until the June following, when she died at the age of 66.

Although the Venetian Ambassador was to sum up Henry after his death as 'a very great miser but a man of vast ability', it was a facile judgment. Henry, although parsimonious by nature, maintained a splendid court and spent lavishly on the building of RICHMOND PALACE (the old palace of Sheen having been destroyed by fire in 1497), and the rebuilding of BAYNARD'S CASTLE and GREENWICH PALACE. He also founded several religious houses and actively supported his mother's religious and educational foundations; but his greatest achievement and everlasting memorial is the exquisite chapel known by his name which he added to Westminster Abbey, and in which he and his queen lie entombed beneath Torrigiano's magnificent bronze monument.

Henry VII is the first English monarch whose portrait reveals something of his character. From the surviving contemporary portrait by Michael Sittow in the National Portrait Gallery, painted in 1504 or 1505, his lean Welsh face peers out through shrewd blue-grey eyes, while his thin-lipped mouth speaks of his parsimony. An impression of majesty, not apparent in the painted portrait, is given by the magnificent polychrome bust by Pietro Torrigiano and the tomb effigy, wherein he is the personification of the Renaissance prince. Henry's death mask also survives at Westminster Abbey, but the nose has been restored, not very successfully, leaving the impression of a flawed likeness. Henry's coins were the first to carry a portrait of the monarch that is more than just a stylized representation of a king.

Henry VIII, King of England (1491–1547)
The second son and third child of HENRY VII and ELIZABETH OF YORK, who was born at GREENWICH PALACE on 28 June 1491. Before he was five years old he had a goodly string of honours conferred upon him: Constable of Dover Castle and Lord Warden of the Cinque Ports (5 April 1493), Lieutenant of Ireland (12 September 1494), Knight of the BATH (31 October 1494), Duke of York (1 November 1494), Knight of the GARTER (17 May 1495) and also Earl Marshal of England and Warden of the Scottish Marches. At the age of 10 he played a prominent part in the marriage ceremonies of his brother ARTHUR, PRINCE OF WALES to CATHERINE OF ARAGON. It is said to have been his father's intention that he should enter the Church and eventually become Archbishop of Canterbury, but the death of Arthur less than five months after his marriage changed all this. Henry became heir apparent and automatically Duke of Cornwall on 2 April 1502. On 18 February 1503 his patent as Duke of York was cancelled and he was created Prince of Wales and Earl of Chester.

Henry was well educated in the classics, his tutors being John Skelton, the Poet Laureate, and William Hone. He was also a good linguist and musician, playing several instruments and composing both religious music and secular songs. The well-known air 'Greensleeves' is attributed to him. When he succeeded his father in April 1509, Henry was regarded as the most accomplished prince of the age. Handsome and athletic, he bore a strong resemblance to his maternal grandfather EDWARD IV and there was none of his father's lean asceticism about him.

One of Henry's first acts was to marry his widowed sister-in-law, Catherine of Aragon, the necessary papal dispensation being first obtained on the grounds that the first marriage was unconsummated. The new king and queen then proceeded from Greenwich to the Tower and thence to Westminster for their crowning on 24 June with all the usual ceremonies. Days were passed in jousting and making royal progresses and the reign of 'Bluff King Hal', the first English king to be styled 'Majesty', had begun.

Three years after his accession Henry reopened the Hundred Years' War, invading France and winning the battle of the Spurs with the aid of Austrian mercenaries. At home, the Scots invaded England but were soundly beaten at FLODDEN Field, where Henry's brother-in-law JAMES IV (the husband of his sister, Margaret (see MARGARET TUDOR, QUEEN OF SCOTS)) and the 'flower of the Scots nobility' were slain on 9 September 1513. These years saw the rise of Thomas Wolsey, the son of an Ipswich butcher, who, through the patronage of Sir Richard Nanfan, Deputy of Calais, had been brought to the notice of Henry VII, who gave him several ecclesiastical preferments. He was appointed Almoner to Henry VIII in 1509 and Canon of Windsor and Registrar of the Order of the Garter and a Privy Councillor in 1511. Other appointments followed, and in 1513 he accompanied Henry to Calais and became his chief adviser. In 1514 he became Archbishop of York and in 1515 received the Cardinal's hat from Pope Leo X. He became all powerful and the king relied on him in all things.

Henry thought of himself as no mean theologian and in 1520 published a book *The Defence of the Seven Sacraments (Assertio Septem Sacramentorum)* to refute the heresies of Martin Luther, which were beginning to gain ground on the continent. The book was presented to Pope Leo X, who

rewarded its author with the new title of
DEFENDER OF THE FAITH (*Fidei Defensor*),
conferred by papal bull on 11 October 1521.
It has been proudly borne by all Henry's
successors to the present day, regardless of
all the religious changes that have taken
place. It was also in 1520 that Henry held his
famous meeting with François I of France at
the FIELD OF THE CLOTH OF GOLD at Ardres,
near Calais, where, in a stage-managed
setting of unparalleled magnificence, the
two sovereigns took part in a solemn act
of reconciliation and concluded an uneasy
and shortlived peace.

Henry's marriage to Catherine of Aragon
was initially a happy one, but out of six
children born to them only one sickly girl
survived (*see* MARY I). By the mid-1520s it
became obvious that Catherine, who was
five and a half years older than Henry, was
now unlikely at the age of 40 to bear any
more. Henry was desperate for a male heir.
He toyed with the idea of making his illegitimate son Henry FitzRoy, Duke of RICH-
MOND, his heir but then thought better of it
and decided that the only way was to divorce
the queen and marry again. Henry was soon
able to delude himself that his lack of a son
was a sign of divine retribution for marrying
his brother's widow, albeit that the necessary dispensation had been obtained, and
instructed Wolsey to open negotiations with
the Holy See to have the marriage annulled.
Catherine fought the petition tooth and nail
and was supported by her nephew the
Emperor Charles V. Wolsey's failure to procure the divorce from Rome after several
years of protracted negotiations earned him
the animosity of the king's paramour, ANNE
BOLEYN, who was eager to become queen,
and brought about his dismissal as Chancellor. A more far-reaching consequence of
the whole business was the exasperated
Henry's break with Rome, which was to lead
to the establishment of the Reformation in
England.

In 1533 Henry nominated Thomas Cranmer to the primatial see of Canterbury and
the appointment was confirmed by Rome.
Cranmer begged the king to be allowed to
decide Henry's 'great matter', as the divorce
suit was called, and in May he took it upon
himself to declare the marriage to Catherine
null and void. Henry had already jumped
the gun, for Anne had become pregnant by
him in December 1532, and on 25 January
1533 he had gone through a secret marriage
ceremony with her, which Cranmer's pro-
nouncement validated retrospectively. The
new queen's coronation was rushed through

on 1 June, and on 7 September she gave
birth to a daughter (*see* ELIZABETH I), much
to Henry's disappointment.

Henry's Reformation Parliament confirmed his title as 'of the Church of England
on Earth Supreme Head' and copies of the
new English translation of the Bible were
ordered to be placed in every church. In all
other respects, however, there was little
alteration in the old order of worship, the
Latin mass and all other ceremonies being
retained.

The year 1536 saw the death of Catherine
of Aragon, which her cruelly insensitive ex-
husband celebrated by dressing in bright
yellow and ordering a thanksgiving mass
followed by feasting, dancing and jousting.
It also saw the execution of Anne Boleyn,
who had been superseded in the king's affections by one of her own maids of honour, the
sly JANE SEYMOUR. The delivery of a mal-
formed stillborn son had sealed Anne's fate,
and she had been accused of adultery and
incest. The same year saw the commencement of the Dissolution of the Monasteries,
which had become immensely rich and
powerful. Henry desperately needed
money, as always, and aided by his new
Chancellor, Thomas Cromwell, saw the
spoliation of the monasteries as an easy
means of obtaining it. There was the added
factor, too, that the religious foundations
were likely to be hotbeds of pro-Roman
intrigue.

Henry married Jane Seymour as his third
wife and in due course she produced the
longed-for male heir (*see* EDWARD VI),
unfortunately dying 12 days later. Because
she was the mother of his son, Henry was to
regard her more highly than any of his other
wives, but he was not inconsolable and
ambassadors abroad were instructed to
make inquiries at the courts to which they
were accredited for a possible fourth bride.
Henry's choice at first alighted upon the 16-
year-old widowed Duchess of Milan,
Christina of Denmark, whose splendid portrait that Holbein was commissioned to
paint for the king now hangs in the National
Gallery. Christina was a great-niece of
Catherine of Aragon. She was a spirited girl
and is said to have refused Henry's suit by
remarking that if she had two heads the
King of England might be welcome to one of
them, but, alas, she had only one.

Henry was to remain a widower for over
two years and his fourth marriage was to
prove the shortest of the six. He married
ANNE OF CLEVES in January 1540, having
previously seen her only in Holbein's

flattering portrait. When he saw her in the flesh, Henry described her as a 'Flanders mare', but was obliged to marry her anyway – though he had the marriage annulled in July. The match led to the fall of Thomas Cromwell, who was arrested, charged with treason and heresy, and executed on 28 July. This was also the day on which Henry married his fifth wife, CATHERINE HOWARD, a first cousin of Anne Boleyn. Catherine was nearly 30 years Henry's junior and the once-handsome and much-admired king was now an obese monster, prematurely senile and stinking from an ulcerated left leg, the result of syphilis, which he had acquired early in life. Syphilis had first appeared in Europe in Spain in 1493, when Columbus returned from America with several members of his crew infected and it soon spread throughout Europe. The hypothesis has been put forward that Arthur, Prince of Wales, was infected and passed the disease on to Catherine of Aragon (in spite of the marriage never being properly consummated), who in turn infected Henry. Catherine's maternity record, and the fact that her only surviving child Mary was an obvious congenital syphilitic, tend to bear this out, while Henry's physical and moral degeneration throughout his reign leave little doubt as to the cause. As one writer has put it, he changed 'from a young man of great promise into a violent, brutal and ill-balanced tyrant'. Henry's fifth marriage was to founder in less than two years and Catherine, convicted of adultery, was sent to the block on Tower Green.

Henry now required a nurse rather than a wife and hearing good reports of the twice-widowed Catherine, Lady Latimer (see CATHERINE PARR), who had devotedly cared for her second husband and his family, made her his sixth and last wife in July 1543. It is an indication of the extent to which the blood of England's medieval kings had become diffused that all Henry's six wives descended (as did he, of course) from EDWARD I, and it is also, perhaps, noteworthy that his four English wives were all (with a varying number of 'greats') aunts of DIANA, PRINCESS OF WALES. Catherine Parr proved the good nurse Henry had hoped for and a kind stepmother to her three oddly assorted stepchildren. Nevertheless, her downfall was plotted and almost accomplished by opponents of her enthusiasm for the Protestant faith.

Henry's health was not helped by his excessive gluttony and in his 56th year he was to succumb at last to his many ailments.

In January 1547 he was dying and was able to ponder aloud on his misdoings. After some urging, he agreed that Cranmer should be sent for, but when the archbishop arrived at Whitehall he found the king beyond speech and able only to press his hand when asked to give a sign that he trusted in God. He died soon afterwards early in the morning of 28 January 1547. The news of his death was withheld for three days, while the Council debated the fate of the Duke of Norfolk, under sentence of death in the Tower, and finally decided to spare him. Henry's embalmed body in its massive coffin was conveyed to Windsor and buried beside that of Jane Seymour. He had made plans for a magnificent tomb to be erected for them both, but they were never carried out. There is an unsubstantiated story that Mary I had her father's body disinterred and burnt.

Henry was the founder of Trinity College, Cambridge, and endowed five regius professorships at the university, redistributing some of the monastic revenues gained through the Dissolution. He was also a builder and embellisher of palaces, Bridewell, Whitehall, St James's, Hampton Court (acquired from Cardinal Wolsey) and Nonsuch all being built or enlarged at his behest. Henry VIII is the one king whose likeness is instantly recognizable in his portraits, almost all of which evolve from the type made so familiar by the genius of Holbein. The large square face, the small eyes staring out morosely beneath the feathered hat, the red-gold beard, the slashed and bejewelled attire, the bulging codpiece, and the stance with hands on hips and legs well splayed are instantly familiar. The second Tudor monarch is undoubtedly the best known English king and the story of his six wives has fired the popular imagination for four centuries.

Henry IX The style assumed in 1788 by Prince Henry Benedict STUART, Cardinal Bishop of Frascati, following the death of his brother Prince Charles Edward STUART, who had been styled Charles III.

Henry Frederick, Prince of Wales (1594–1612) The eldest son and first child of James VI, King of Scots (later JAMES I, KING OF ENGLAND) and ANNE OF DENMARK, who was born at Stirling Castle on 19 February 1594 and received the names of his paternal and maternal grandfathers. He succeeded as Duke of Rothesay and Prince and Steward of Scotland at birth. In spite of objections from his mother, which the king overruled, he was placed under the guardianship of the Earl of Mar. On his father's accession to the English throne in March 1603, Henry became Duke of Cornwall and later in that year accompanied his mother to London. He matriculated at Magdalen College, Oxford, in 1605 and grew up exhibiting signs of great promise. Apart from an aptitude for learning, he excelled at all sports, particularly riding, swimming and tennis. He was inclined to be delicate, however, suffering from giddiness and nose bleeds, and it appears that he overtaxed his strength. It has also been suggested that he may have inherited the 'royal malady' of PORPHYRIA.

Henry was created Prince of Wales and Earl of Chester on 4 June 1610 and tentative negotiations were begun to find him a wife. A Spanish bride was the most considered, but princesses of Savoy and France were also in the running. In 1612 Henry took a lively part in the court festivities held in honour of the Elector Palatine, who had come to court his sister Elizabeth (see ELIZABETH, PRINCESS, QUEEN OF BOHEMIA), but he was failing visibly and his physical weaknesses were being noted by his attendants. His final illness began on 25 October, when he took to his bed. He was submitted to all the crude medical practices of the day, purges, emetics, cuppings and bleedings, and even had recourse to Sir Walter Ralegh's cordial, a nostrum which that gentleman concocted from many secret ingredients, some of which he had brought back from South America. All was to no avail, and the prince grew steadily weaker. His fever was probably typhoid and to avoid contagion the members of his family were forbidden to see him. His last words are said to have been, 'Where is my dear sister?'. He died at St JAMES'S PALACE on 6 November 1612 and was buried with great ceremony at WESTMINSTER ABBEY a month later.

Henry of Almayne (1235–71) The second but eldest surviving son of Richard of Cornwall (see CORNWALL, RICHARD, EARL OF), King of the Romans, and his first wife Isabella Marshal, who was born at Haughley Castle, Suffolk, on 2 November 1235 and baptized at his father's foundation, Hailes Abbey. He was styled Henry of Cornwall, but after his father's election as King of the Romans or German King, was more often known as Henry of Almayne, a corruption of Allemagne. He accompanied his father to France in 1247 and 1250 and was present at his coronation as King of the Romans at Aachen on 17 May 1257, when he

was knighted by him. Originally a supporter of Simon de Montfort, he later joined his cousin Prince Edward (see EDWARD I) and commanded the left wing of the royal army at the battle of Lewes on 14 May 1264, when he gave himself up as a hostage. The following year he was sent to France to treat with Louis IX and in 1266 he commanded an expedition against Earl Ferrers.

He married at Windsor on 15 May 1269, Constance, the childless widow of the Infante Alfonso of Aragon (son and heir of King Jaime I), and eldest daughter and co-heiress of Gaston VII de Monçada, Vicomte de Béarn, and his first wife Mathe, daughter of Boson de Mastas, Seigneur de Cognac. Henry had taken the cross before his marriage and shortly after it set out on a crusade with Prince Edward. On his return journey he was murdered while attending mass in the church of San Silvestro at Viterbo on 13 March 1271 by his cousins Simon and Guy de Montfort in vengeance for the death of their father at the battle of Evesham (although Henry had not been present). His body was brought back to England and was buried at Hailes Abbey on 21 May 1271, while his heart, encased in a gold cup, was buried near the shrine of EDWARD THE CONFESSOR in WESTMINSTER ABBEY. He died before his father and without issue. Henry's widow Constance died in about 1299.

Henry of Scotland, Earl of Huntingdon (c.1115–52) The second but only surviving son of DAVID I, KING OF SCOTS and Matilda (see MATILDA, QUEEN OF SCOTS), daughter and heiress of Waltheof, Earl of Northampton and Huntingdon, who was born about 1114 or 1115. He succeeded to the earldom of Huntingdon on his father's resignation of that honour in 1136. After fighting on the Scottish side at the battle of the Standard in 1138, he received the earldom of Northumberland (excluding the cities of Newcastle and Bambrugh) on the conclusion of peace in 1139. In the same year he married ADA, daughter of William de Warenne, 2nd Earl of Surrey and Warenne.

Henry spent several years in England, becoming a favourite with King STEPHEN, and founded the Abbey of Holmcultram in Cumberland in 1150. He died before his father on 11 June 1152 and was buried at Kelso Abbey. He had the reputation of being handsome, virtuous and devout. Of his three sons, two, MALCOLM IV and WILLIAM THE LION became Kings of Scots. His widow Ada died in 1178.

Henry 'the Young King' (1155–83) The second son of HENRY II and ELEANOR OF AQUITAINE, who was born at Bermondsey Palace, London, on 28 February 1155. He became his father's heir the following year on the death of his elder brother William. At the age of five, on 2 November 1160, he was married in Normandy to the two-year-old Margaret (Marguerite) of France, daughter of his mother's first husband Louis VII by his second wife Constance of Castile. Henry was educated under the guidance of his father's Chancellor Thomas à Becket and in 1170, when he was 15, his father decided to emulate the French practice for ensuring the succession by declaring him associate king and having him crowned at WESTMINSTER ABBEY by Roger of Pont l'Évêque, Archbishop of York, on 14 June 1170. Louis VII took exception to the fact that his daughter had not been crowned with her husband and to appease him the ceremony was repeated for both Henry and Margaret at Winchester Cathedral by Rotrou, Archbishop of Rouen, on 27 August 1172.

In spite of his titular rank, the young king's father refused to endow him with lands or allow him to participate in the government, so he went off to the French court and sided with his father's enemies. Father and son were reconciled in 1174. Henry's and Margaret's only child, John, was born at Paris on 19 June and died on 22 June 1177. In 1182 Henry made war on his brother Richard (later RICHARD I), who had been invested with the duchy of Aquitaine, and also took up arms against their father, but he was struck down by fever and died at Martel on 11 June 1183, expressing penitence on his deathbed. He was buried at Le Mans, but was later transferred to Rouen Cathedral. His widow married in 1185, as his second wife, Bela III, King of Hungary, and died at Acre in Palestine in 1197 or 1198.

Heptarchy The name given to the Anglo-Saxon kingdoms of England, literally meaning 'the rule of seven', although the number of kingdoms varied and there were sometimes more and sometimes fewer than that number. The kingdoms were quite independent of each other but formed a loosely knit confederation under the leadership of one king, usually the most powerful among them, who was acknowledged as a sort of 'head king' with the title of BRETWALDA.

Herleve The mother of WILLIAM I THE CONQUEROR. There are several variants of her name and she is usually stated to have been the daughter of Fulbert, a tanner or furrier of Falaise in Normandy, by his wife Doda. She became the mistress of Duke Robert of Normandy and bore William in about 1027 and possibly a daughter. She later married Herluin de Conteville, a Norman nobleman, and had further children, including ODO, BISHOP OF BAYEUX.

Hlothere, King of Kent (d.685) The son of King EORCENBERHT and Sexburg of EAST ANGLIA, he was named after his Merovingian great-grandfather Chlothacar (Clotaire) II, King of the Franks. He succeeded his brother EGBERT I in 673 and from c.676 ruled jointly with Suaebherd, son of SEBBI, King of Essex, with whom he probably formed an alliance to repel the Mercians, who 'ravaged Kent' in that year, according to the ANGLO-SAXON CHRONICLE. Early in 685 Hlothere's nephew EADRIC, the son of Egbert I, rebelled against him with South Saxon backing, and in the battle that ensued Hlothere was wounded, and, according to BEDE, 'died as his wounds were being dressed' on 6 February 685. Nothing is known of any wife or children, and Eadric succeeded to the throne.

Holyroodhouse Royal residence in eastern Edinburgh, which was originally a house of Augustinian canons, founded beneath Arthur's Seat by DAVID I in the twelfth century. David presented the community with a relic of the True Cross, in consequence of which the abbey was dedicated to the Holy Cross or Rood. The abbey was used as an occasional residence by medieval Scottish kings and was greatly altered and enlarged by JAMES IV, who established Edinburgh as the undisputed capital of Scotland and was determined to construct a palace of suitable magnificence. Further building work was carried out under JAMES V. The palace was the principal residence of MARY, QUEEN OF SCOTS and her son JAMES VI, and it was here in 1566 that the horrific murder of Mary's secretary David Riccio took place in the queen's presence (it is said that the bloodstains proved ineradicable and could be discerned centuries later).

After James IV's succession to the English throne in 1603 Holyrood ceased to have a regular occupant for nearly 200 years, although some rebuilding and remodelling was carried out between 1671 and 1680. Bonnie Prince Charlie (see Charles Edward STUART) stayed at the palace in 1745, and his pursuer William Augustus, Duke of CUMBERLAND did the same the next year. In 1822 the palace was the scene of many of the festivities connected with GEORGE IV's visit to

Scotland. Queen VICTORIA started the custom, maintained by her successors, of staying at Holyrood for a short period every year and holding a garden party and other events. She also had the royal apartments opened to the public from the 1850s. The Dukes of Hamilton are Hereditary Keepers of Holyroodhouse, and it is the duty of the incumbent duke to present the keys of the palace to the visiting sovereign. The Abbey Church, now a roofless ruin, was the venue of several coronations and the burial place of many kings and queens.

Honi Soi Qui Mal y Pense The medieval French motto of the Most Noble Order of the GARTER. It is usually translated as 'Evil be to him who evil thinks', but would be more accurately rendered as 'Evil to him who thinks ill of it'. According to the legend the words were uttered by EDWARD III when he retrieved the garter of the Countess of Salisbury, which had fallen from her leg at a court ball.

Honours of Scotland The name given to the Scottish regalia, now kept at Edinburgh Castle and consisting of the crown, sceptre, sword and other items.

Horsa (d.455) The brother of HENGEST, whom he accompanied from Jutland to England at the invitation of the British King VORTIGERN, traditionally in 449. He assisted his brother in founding the kingdom of Kent and was killed in battle at Aylesford in 455.

Howard, Catherine, Queen of England *see* CATHERINE HOWARD, QUEEN OF ENGAND.

Hyde, Anne, Duchess of York (1638–71) The first wife of James, Duke of York (later JAMES II) and the mother of MARY II and Queen ANNE, who was the eldest daughter of Edward Hyde, 1st Earl of Clarendon, Lord High Chancellor of England, and his second wife Frances Aylesbury, and was born at Cranborne Lodge, near Windsor, on 22 March 1638. In 1654 she was appointed a maid of honour to MARY, PRINCESS OF ORANGE, the eldest daughter of CHARLES I, and it was while serving at her court that she was seduced by the princess's brother James, Duke of York and became pregnant. It was later alleged that the duke had pledged himself to marry her at Breda on 24 November 1659.

After the Restoration and the return of the court to London, James and Anne were secretly married by his chaplain at Worcester House, London, on 3 September 1660. Their first child, Charles, Duke of CAMBRIDGE, was born there on 22 October following. The news of the marriage infuriated Anne's father and caused great consternation in the royal family, but CHARLES II refused to have the marriage annulled and, after the initial scandal had died down, the new Duchess of York played a leading role at court. She was no beauty and Pepys described her as 'a plain woman'. She was often referred to as 'ugly Anne Hyde', and her husband's penchant for ill-favoured women once caused his brother Charles II to remark that he thought the duke's mistresses were imposed upon him by his confessor as a penance.

Anne gave birth to four sons and four daughters, but only the first two daughters (both of whom were to become queen) survived infancy. In 1670 Anne was received secretly into the Roman Catholic Church and she was instrumental in influencing her husband, who had possessed strong leanings since his days in exile, to do the same a year or two later. James's many infidelities made his wife unhappy and she comforted herself in buying jewellery and over-eating. Her last child, CATHERINE, was born at Whitehall on 9 February 1671 and Anne died seven weeks later at ST JAMES'S PALACE on 31 March 1671, aged only 33. She was buried at WESTMINSTER ABBEY on 5 April 1671. Bishop Burnet in his *History of his Own Times* judged her as 'generous and friendly; but was too severe an enemy'. She was a patron of the artist Peter Lely, who painted many portraits of her.

Hywel Dda (the Good), King of All Wales (d.950) The elder son of Cadell ap Rhodri, King of Seisyllwg, whom he succeeded in 909. He had already succeeded as King of Dyfed some five years earlier in right of his wife Elen, daughter and heiress of Llywarch ap Hyfaidd, King of Dyfed. He did homage to EDWARD THE ELDER in 918 and to ATHELSTAN in 926 and in 928 went on a pilgrimage to Rome. In 942 he succeeded to the kingdom of Gwynedd following the death of his cousin IDWAL FOEL. Hywel is known as 'the law-giver of Wales', having compiled a code of laws that remained in force until the English conquest by EDWARD I. He was also the only Welsh ruler to mint his own coinage of silver pennies. Hywel died in 950 and was eulogized by the *Brut y Tywysogion* (Chronicle of the Princes) as 'the head and glory of all the Britons'. He was succeeded by his three sons, Rhodri, Edwin and Owain (*see* OWAIN AP HYWEL DDA), who reigned jointly.

I

Iago ab Idwal ap Meurig, King of Gwynedd (d.1039) The son of Idwal (d.996), son of Meurig (d.986), the youngest son of IDWAL FOEL, who was restored to the throne of Gwynedd in 1033 after a series of usurpations. After a reign of six years he was murdered in 1039 and the throne was usurped by GRUFFYDD AP LLYWELYN. Iago married Afandreg, daughter of Gwair ap Pill, a descendant of Llywarch Hen, and had, besides two daughters, a son Cynan, who sought refuge in Ireland, where he married Rhanullt of Dublin and became the father of GRUFFYDD AP CYNAN, who was destined to restore the glory of his house.

Iago ab Idwal Foel, King of Gwynedd (d. after 979) The eldest son of IDWAL FOEL, KING OF GWYNEDD and Mereddon, daughter of Cadwr ap Cadwr Wenwyn, who was driven out of Gwynedd with his brothers on their father's death in 942. He and his brother Ieuaf were restored as joint rulers on the death of HYWEL DDA in 950, but they soon began a struggle for supremacy and Ieuaf was defeated and driven out in 969. Iago was among the vassal kings who submitted to EDGAR at Chester in 973. He was deposed and imprisoned by his nephew, Hywel, the son of Ieuaf, in 979 and the date of his death is unknown. He had two sons, Cystennin Ddu and Owain, and probably a daughter, Angharad, who married Lluddica ap Tudur Trefor.

Iceni Celtic tribe that occupied Suffolk and Norfolk, their chief town being Venta Icenorum (Caistor), near Norwich. They were ruled by a dynasty of kings who struck a large and varied coinage. An early ruler, known only from his coins, was Anted. One of his successors, PRASUTAGUS, became a client-king under the Romans and it was his widow BOUDICCA or Boadicea who led the last great revolt against Roman rule.

Ich Dien Motto, meaning 'I serve' in German, which has been used by the Princes of Wales since the time of Edward the BLACK PRINCE, who is said to have adopted it and the crest of three ostrich feathers from the arms of the blind King John of Bohemia, who fell at the battle of Crécy in 1346. The story is unsubstantiated and other sources state that the emblem and motto were borne by the native princes of Wales before the Edwardian conquest. Modern heraldic opinion is that the three ostrich feathers, originally shown separately on a black flag, originated with the Black Prince's mother, PHILIPPA OF HAINAULT.

Ida, King of Bernicia (d.559) Founder of the kingdom of BERNICIA, who was the son of Eoppa, whose lineage is taken back to WODEN by the ANGLO-SAXON CHRONICLE, which records in 547 that 'Ida, from whom sprang the royal race of the Northumbrians, succeeded to the kingdom and reigned twelve years'. The circumstances by which he obtained or established the kingdom are nowhere recorded. NENNIUS implies that Ida had but one queen, named Bearnoch, and she was the mother of six sons, ADDA, Ethelric, Theodric, Ethric, Teuthere and Osmaer. He also had six sons by concubines, Ogg, Occa, Alric, Ecca, Osbald or Oswald, and Scor or Sogor. On his death in about 559 Ida was succeeded by the mysterious GLAPPA, perhaps also a son, who reigned for one year only and was followed by Adda.

Idwal Foel (the Bald), King of Gwynedd (d.942) The elder son of ANARAWD AP RHODRI, KING OF GWYNEDD, whom he succeeded in 916. He accepted English overlordship in 918. He died during an unsuccessful revolt against the English in 942. His sons were expelled and Gwynedd passed to his cousin HYWEL DDA, but two of his sons, IAGO and Ieuaf, were restored to the kingdom after Hywel's death in 950.

Indian Empire, Most Eminent Order of the Order of chivalry instituted by Queen VICTORIA on 31 December 1877 to commemorate her proclamation as Empress of

India. It was intended to be conferred for services rendered to the Indian Empire. The Order, which was enlarged in 1886, 1887, 1892, 1897, 1902, 1911, 1915, 1920, 1927 and 1939, consisted of the sovereign and three classes, Grand Commander (GCIE), Knight Commander (KCIE), and Companion (CIE). The insignia of a Knight Grand Commander consisted of: (1) a collar of gold, formed of elephants, lotus flowers, peacocks in their pride and Indian roses, with the Imperial Crown in the centre, the whole linked together by chains; (2) a star comprised of five rays of silver with a smaller ray of gold between each of them, the whole alternately plain and scaled, issuing from a gold centre, having thereon Queen Victoria's effigy within a purple circle inscribed *Imperatricis Auspiciis* in letters of gold, the circle ensigned by an Imperial Crown, also gold; (3) a badge, consisting of a rose enamelled gules, barbed vert and having in the centre Queen Victoria's effigy as in the star; (4) a mantle of purple satin, lined with and fastened by a cordon of white silk, with purple silk and gold tassels attached and having a representation of the Star of the order on the left side; (5) a ribbon of imperial purple, four inches in width. The insignia of a Knight Commander consisted of a badge of the same pattern but of smaller size, suspended around the neck from a purple ribbon two inches in width, and a breast star. The insignia of a Companion consisted of an even smaller badge suspended around the neck from a purple ribbon one and a half inches in width. The collar of a Knight Grand Commander was returnable at death to the Central Chancery of the Orders of Knighthood at ST JAMES'S PALACE. No appointments to the Order have been made since 14 August 1947.

Indulf, King of Scots (d.962) The son of CONSTANTINE II, who succeeded his cousin MALCOLM I as king on the latter's murder by the people of Moray in 954. He had previously reigned as sub-king of Strathclyde under Malcolm. He met his own death in battle with the Danes. His son CULEN succeeded to the throne in 966 but was himself murdered in 971, the fourth Scots king in succession to die violently.

Ine, King of Wessex (d. after 726) The son of Cenred, described as a sub-king (*subregulus*) by Florence of Worcester, a descendant of King CEAWLIN, who succeeded his kinsman CAEDWALLA on his abdication in 688. In 694 he received compensation from the Kentishmen for the burning to death of his

predecessor's brother Mul. Ine was notorious for his riotous, luxury-loving ways and nothing his wife Ethelburga could say would persuade him to adopt a more moral lifestyle. In the end, following a particularly wild visit to a country house, the queen had the place filled with cattle dung and farm animals and then contrived the return of her husband, who was astonished at the sudden transformation of the scene of his excesses. When he asked what the meaning of it all was, his wife calmly pointed out that there was no evidence now of the previous day's debauchery – and that all who lived in such a manner would themselves 'consume away' in similar fashion. Ine took the hint and determined to live more respectably from then on. Subsequently he built a new monastery at Glastonbury and became a great benefactor of the Church. He also issued a law code, detailing punishments for particular crimes.

The royal couple were childless, and in 726 Ine abdicated in favour of his wife's brother, ETHELHEARD, who was also of the royal lineage, and went on pilgrimage to Rome, where he died soon after. Ine's brother Ingild, whose death is recorded in 718, was an ancestor of King EGBERT. He also had two sisters, Cwenburga (Cwenburh) and Cuthburga (Cuthburh), who married ALDFRITH, KING OF NORTHUMBRIA, but parted from him and founded the nunnery at Wimborne in Dorset, becoming its first abbess.

Inverness, Cecilia Letitia Underwood, Duchess of (*c*.1788–1873) The eighth daughter of Arthur Saunders Gore, 2nd Earl of Arran, and the second by his third wife Elizabeth, only daughter of Richard Underwood, of Dublin, who was born probably in Ireland in about 1788. The exact date of her birth has not been discovered, but she is not listed in Lodge's *Peerage of Ireland* published in 1789, which records the birth of her brother John in February 1787, he then being the youngest of her father's children.

Lady Cecilia Gore was married at the Earl of Arran's house in Dover Street, London, on 14 May 1815, to Sir George Buggin, a city magnate and a widower aged 55, who had been knighted at ST JAMES'S PALACE on 31 May 1797. They lived together at his house in Great Cumberland Place, Marylebone, until his death on 12 April 1825 left her a childless widow. Within the next few years Lady Cecilia Buggin became a close friend of the eccentric Prince Augustus

Frederick, Duke of SUSSEX, the sixth son of GEORGE III, who had long been separated from his illegal wife Lady Augusta Murray, who died on 4 March 1830. On 2 May 1831 Lady Cecilia Buggin assumed her mother's maiden name of Underwood in lieu of that of Buggin by Royal Licence and it is believed that on that date she and the Duke of Sussex went through a form of marriage at her house in Great Cumberland Place. As the duke had not complied with the requirements of the ROYAL MARRIAGES ACT of 1772, the marriage remained null and void in law and there is no record of it having taken place. Many people, including the Duke of Wellington, did not believe there had been a marriage, but Lady Cecilia's conduct was impeccable and she was accepted by most members of the royal family as the duke's wife.

On 10 April 1840 Queen VICTORIA created her Duchess of Inverness, the title being taken from the duke's secondary title Earl of Inverness. The creation is said to have been made at the duke's earnest request and as a reward for agreeing to yield precedence to the queen's husband Prince ALBERT. The marriage appears to have been a very happy one and the duchess, known to her husband as 'Ciss', became 'quite a personage in London society. She was small of stature, old-fashioned in dress, and quaint, rather than distinguished, in appearance, but her kindness of heart and general *bonhomie* secured for her a large circle of friends'. The Duke of Sussex died at KENSINGTON PALACE on 21 April 1843 and at his own request was buried at Kensal Green Cemetery rather than at Windsor in order that his wife might eventually lie beside him. Queen ADELAIDE with characteristic kindness called on the widow and reported by letter to Queen Victoria: 'I have been with the poor Duchess of Inverness on my way to Town, and found her as composed as possible under the sad circumstances, and full of gratitude to you and all the family for all the kindness which she had received. I pity her very much. It must be her comfort to have made the last years of the Duke's life happy, and to have been his comfort to the last moment.'

The Duchess of Inverness lived on at Kensington Palace for many years, noted for her generosity and hospitality, included in family events and asked to stand godmother to royal children. She died at the Palace on 1 August 1873 and was buried with her husband at Kensal Green.

Iorwerth Drwyndwn, Prince of Gwynedd (d. *c*.1174) The eldest son of OWAIN GWYNEDD, KING OF GWYNEDD and his first wife Gwladus, daughter of Llywarch ap Trahaearn ap Caradog, who succeeded to the throne of Gwynedd on the death of his father in November 1170. His sobriquet *Drwyndwn* means 'Flatnose'. He had to contend for power with his half-brothers, and after the battle of Pentraeth in Anglesey a division of territory took place, in which Iorwerth received Arfon and probably Nanconwy. Soon afterwards he was driven out of Gwynedd and died in Powys. He is said to have been buried at Llandudclud (now known as Penmachno) in the Conwy Valley. Iorwerth married Marared, daughter of MADOG AP MAREDUDD, KING OF POWYS, and their only son was LLYWELYN THE GREAT, the last great independent Welsh ruler.

Isabella, Roman Empress and Queen of Sicily (1214–41) The second daughter and fourth child of King JOHN and ISABELLA OF ANGOULÊME, who was born in 1214. She was married at Worms on 20 July 1235 to Friedrich II, Roman Emperor and King of Sicily, becoming his third wife. He was her senior by about 20 years, having been born on 26 December 1194. Isabella had four children: Jordan, who was born at Ravenna in 1236 and died an infant; Agnes, who was born and died in 1237; Heinrich, who was born on 18 February 1238 and died unmarried in May 1254; and Margarethe, who was born at Foggia on 1 December 1241 and married in 1256 to Albert, Landgrave of Thuringia, by whom she had issue. The Empress Isabella died in childbirth at Foggia on 1 December 1241 and was buried at Andria in the kingdom of Naples. Matthew of Westminster, recording her death, refers to her as 'the hope and singular joy of the English'. The Emperor Friedrich in announcing her death to his brother-in-law HENRY III referred to Isabella's surviving son and daughter tempering his grief. He did not marry again and died at Firenzuola on 13 Decembeer 1250.

Isabella of Angoulême, Queen of England (*c*.1188–1246) The consort of King JOHN, who was the only daughter and heiress of Aymer Taillefer, Count of Angoulême, and his wife Alice, daughter of Pierre de Courtenay, the youngest son of Louis VI, King of France. She was born at Angoulême in about 1188 and at the age of 12 was betrothed to Hugues de Lusignan, son and heir of Hugues IX, Count of La Marche.

She was living at the Château de Lusignan as Lusignan's affianced bride when King John, who had recently obtained the annulment of his marriage to ISABELLA OF GLOUCESTER, saw her, became infatuated, and carried her off 'screaming with terror' to Bordeaux. This is the romantic version of events; the reality was a little different. Dazzled by the prospect of their daughter becoming a queen, Isabella's parents connived at breaking off her betrothal to Lusignan and the compliant clergy, headed by the Archbishop of Bordeaux, declared that there was no impediment to her union with John and solemnized the marriage forthwith on 24 August 1200. John returned to England with his new bride and she was crowned queen at WESTMINSTER ABBEY by Hubert Walter, Archbishop of Canterbury, on 8 October 1200.

The first few years of Isabella's marriage were passed in a round of pleasure, accompanying the king on his journeys about his dominions. Her first child, the future HENRY III, was not born until 1207, and the next two followed soon after. John was not a faithful husband and Isabella was, if not blatantly unfaithful herself, at least flirtatious when she fancied. John's jealousy was frequently aroused, and on one occasion he is said to have hanged one of his wife's supposed lovers over her bed. By 1212 John's suspicions of the queen had become so great that he had her placed in confinement at Gloucester, but the following year a reconciliation took place after Isabella had succeeded to her father's county of Angoulême. Two more daughters were born in 1214 and 1215 respectively.

Queen Isabella was residing at Gloucester with her children when John died in 1216, and on receiving the news she at once took steps to have her elder son proclaimed king and crowned, sending Richard, the younger boy, to Ireland for safety. In July 1217 Isabella returned to France to take up residence in her native city of Angoulême. Here she met her old fiancé Hugh de Lusignan, now Count of La Marche. He had never married, and a proposed betrothal between him and Isabella's 10-year-old daughter Joan was swiftly set aside 'because her age is so tender' and he was advised to 'take a wife from whom he might speedily hope for an heir'. Accordingly he married the mother, and Isabella became a bride again in 1220 when she was about 32. The marriage took place without Henry III's consent and, although he was only 13, he found it an excuse to deprive his mother of her dower. It

was a year before the breech was healed and the arrears of jointure paid.

Isabella bore a large family of five sons and at least three daughters to her second husband. Of the sons, Hugh XI succeeded his parents in La Marche and Angoulême, Guy fell at the battle of Lewes, William became Earl of Pembroke and loyally served his half-brother Henry III and nephew EDWARD I, and Aymer became Bishop of Winchester in 1250. In 1242 Isabella and her husband became implicated in a plot against the life of Louis IX of France and were arraigned to answer before him at a court of enquiry. Isabella remained seated on her horse at the door of the court and, when she heard that matters were likely to go against her, spurred homewards in a terrible rage. When she had calmed down, after attempting to stab herself and tearing her head-dress to shreds, she sought refuge in the Abbey of Fontevraud where she remained for the rest of her life. Her husband and son managed to patch up matters with Louis, while Matthew Paris relates that 'the Poitevins and French, considering her the origin of the disastrous war with France, called her by no other name than Jezebel, instead of ... Isabel'.

All things considered, Isabella was a fitting mate for John. She died at Fontevraud on 31 May 1246 and was buried in the common graveyard of the abbey. However, Henry III, visiting his mother's grave some years later, had her body moved into the choir of the abbey church and commissioned the fine effigy that is the only near contemporary likeness of her. Isabella's second husband survived until 1249, when he fell fighting in the Crusades.

Isabella of France, Queen of England[1]

(1295–1358) The consort of EDWARD II, who was the eldest daughter of Philippe IV, King of France, and his wife Jeanne I, Queen of Navarre, and was thus the daughter of two sovereigns. She was born, probably at Paris, in 1295 and was affianced to the future Edward II at the age of four. Papal dispensation for the marriage was obtained in 1303 and it was solemnized at Boulogne on 25 January 1308. The bride's portion from her father was £18,000 (a vast amount in those days), and she was to have the reversion of the dower settled on her aunt Queen Margaret (see MARGARET OF FRANCE, QUEEN OF ENGLAND) by EDWARD I. The bride's trousseau was magnificent and contained two gold crowns set with jewels, gold and silver cups, gold spoons, 50 silver porringers, and 12 large and 12 small silver dishes, as well as dozens of dresses of cloth of gold, cloth of silver, velvet, taffeta and other materials, furs, household linen and much more. The presents that her father bestowed on Edward were promptly passed to his favourite Gaveston, 'whose passion for finery was insatiable', and the king's marked partiality for him started the rift that was to exist throughout the marriage. At Isabella's coronation in WESTMINSTER ABBEY on 25 February 1308 it was noted that Gaveston 'was dressed more magnificently' than the king himself.

Isabella gave birth to her first child, the future EDWARD III, in 1312. Three more children followed at well-spaced intervals, a sign that relations between husband and wife were not all they should be, in an age when annual pregnancy was the norm.

The TOWER OF LONDON was a royal palace as well as a prison at this period and it was there that Isabella first saw and fell in love with a state prisoner, Roger Mortimer. He was under sentence of death but the queen used her influence to have this sentence commuted to life imprisonment, and in August 1323 she connived at his escape from the Tower and flight to France. The following year things came to a head between the queen and the king's favourites, the Despensers, and she left Edward, who nevertheless foolishly despatched her and their son Edward on a mission to France in September 1325. She at once joined her lover Mortimer in Paris and commenced the long and sordid process that was to end in Edward II's deposition and murder. Her duplicity and mendacity were such that when her brother the king of France finally had her conduct brought to his notice, he at once ordered her to quit the country and she was compelled to go to Hainault, where the count and countess gave her a good reception. When Isabella had gathered an army, she set sail for England, landing at Harwich on 25 September 1326. She was joined by Henry of Lancaster and many barons and knights and was, of course, accompanied by Mortimer, whom she placed in command of her forces. Events moved swiftly and the king's deposition was accomplished by January 1327.

Isabella shed hypocritical tears for her husband at the coronation of her son Edward III, but the murder of Edward II later in the year brought about a reaction of public feeling against her. She was by now living openly with Mortimer. Eventually Edward III was forced to take action and, in spite of his mother's cry, 'Fair son, have mercy on the gentle Mortimer!', as he was literally snatched from her arms at Nottingham Castle, Mortimer was taken and paid for his crimes at Tyburn, having the distinction of being the first person to be executed there. Edward spared his mother a public disgrace but she was obliged to take up residence at Castle Rising in Norfolk and live there quietly, occasionally visited by the king, until her death on 22 August 1358. Her body was taken to London and buried in Grey Friars Church, where Mortimer's body had been consigned many years previously. 'Carrying her characteristic hypocrisy even to the grave,' says Agnes Strickland, 'she was buried with the heart of her murdered husband on her breast'. Isabella's statuette forms one of the 'weepers' on the tomb of her son John of Eltham and her head also appears as a carving in Winchelsea Church, but the most spirited likeness of her is in a roof boss in Bristol Cathedral, which conveys much of the sensuality and ruthlessness that earned her the sobriquet of 'the she-wolf of France'.

Isabella of France, Queen of England[2] (1389–1409)

The second consort of RICHARD II, who was the second daughter and third child of Charles VI, King of France, and his wife Isabella (or Isabeau, as she is usually called) of Bavaria. She was born at the Hôtel du Louvre in Paris on 9 November 1389. She was almost seven years old when her marriage to the widowed Richard II, her senior by over 22 years, was arranged to cement the peace with France, and the marriage took place in the church of St Nicholas at Calais on All Saints' Day, 1 November 1396. They embarked for England a few days later and Isabella made her state entry into London on 13 November. The crowd that collected to see her was so great that nine people were crushed to death on London Bridge. It might have been supposed that Richard, mindful of the ordeal of his own coronation, would have spared his child-bride from undergoing the same, but strangely he did not and she was duly crowned at WESTMINSTER ABBEY on 8 January 1397, although no details of the ceremony have been preserved.

Isabella's chief residence in England was at WINDSOR CASTLE, where one of the king's de Coucy cousins was her chief companion and preceptress. Richard himself visited her frequently and a strong affection and companionship grew up between the disparate couple of this unconsummated marriage.

On Richard's deposition Isabella was confined at Sonning by HENRY IV and to her great distress kept in ignorance of her husband's fate. Henry seized her jewels and divided them among his own children and induced the Council to declare that she had no right to any dower as QUEEN DOWAGER. Her return to France was eventually arranged and she sailed from Dover on 1 July 1401. In the succeeding years Henry IV made several attempts to procure her in marriage for the future HENRY V, but the French royal family declined and eventually Isabella was betrothed to her cousin Charles of Angoulême, son of Louis, Duke of Orléans, amid 'banquets, dancing, jousts, and other jollities'. Their marriage took place at Compiègne on 29 June 1406. In November 1407 she became Duchess of Orléans when her father-in-law was murdered in the streets of Paris by the Duke of Burgundy.

Isabella enjoyed a short but happy married life with her second husband, dying at Blois on 14 September 1409 within a few hours of the birth of her first child, Jeanne, who later became Duchess of Alençon. She was buried in the Abbey of St Saumer at Blois, whence her body was transferred to the church of the Celestines in Paris in about 1624. Her husband survived her by many years, 23 of them spent as a prisoner in the TOWER OF LONDON following his capture after the battle of AGINCOURT. He was a poet of some merit and composed several verses in Isabella's memory. He remarried twice and died on 4 January 1465.

Isabella of Gloucester (d.1217) The first wife of King JOHN, who was the third and youngest daughter and co-heiress of William FitzRobert, Earl of Gloucester, and his wife Hawise, daughter of Robert de Beaumont, Earl of Leicester. She was married at Marlborough on 29 August 1189 to Prince (later King) John, the youngest son of HENRY II. Isabella and John were second cousins, both being great-grandchildren of HENRY I, and for that reason their marriage had been forbidden by Baldwin, Archbishop of Canterbury, but they appealed to Rome and the ruling was annulled in England. Henry II had taken the Honour of Gloucester and the earldom into his own hands on the death of Isabella's father in 1183, but after her marriage (and the death of Henry), it was granted to her as one of her father's co-heiresses.

Isabella and John were evidently ill-matched. They had no children and on his accession to the throne in 1199 he lost no time in seeking an annulment of their marriage on the grounds of consanguinity, which he obtained through the Archbishop of Bordeaux and the Bishops of Poitiers and Saintonge, in spite of the fact that the marriage had been authorized by Rome in the first place. Isabella was never acknowledged as queen and John kept her a state prisoner for several years. Eventually she was remarried under compulsion from the king between 16 and 26 January 1214 to Geoffrey de Mandeville, 5th Earl of Essex, from whom the king extracted 20,000 marks to buy her in marriage and thus obtain the earldom of Gloucester *jure uxoris*. He was one of the Magna Carta sureties in 1215 and died from the wounds he received in a tournament in London on 23 February 1216. Because he died in a state of rebellion against the king, the Honour of Gloucester was forfeited to the Crown, but on 17 September 1217 writs were issued for the return to Isabella of all the lands she had held before the war between the king and the barons, she having returned to her allegiance.

Isabella married thirdly in about October 1217, as his second wife, Hubert de Burgh, 1st Earl of Kent, and died a few days later on 14 October 1217. She was buried in Canterbury Cathedral. Hubert survived her for many years, dying at Banstead, Surrey, on 12 May 1243.

Isabella of York, Princess (1676–81) The sixth daughter of James, Duke of York (later JAMES II) and the second by his second wife MARY OF MODENA, who was born at ST JAMES'S PALACE at five minutes to eight in the morning on 18 August (28 August new style) 1676. She was named after her great-grandmother Isabella, Duchess of Modena, and her godparents were the Duchess of Monmouth, the Countess of Peterborough and the Earl of Danby, Lord High Treasurer (later Duke of Leeds). On 8 November 1677 the infant princess became a godmother herself, being represented by her governess Lady Frances Villiers at the baptism of her brother Charles, Duke of CAMBRIDGE. Princess Isabella was a delicate but beautiful child, and there is a charming portrait of her playing with a lamb by Sir Peter Lely, now in the Royal Collection at Hampton Court. She died at St James's Palace on 2 March 1681, when her parents were absent in Scotland and, in her father's own words, 'could not have the satisfaction of seeing and assisting her in her sickness'. Years later her mother told the nuns of Chaillot, 'If she had lived she might have run great dangers ... I console myself with the thought that I have more angels to pray for me'. The princess was buried in the vault of MARY, QUEEN OF SCOTS at WESTMINSTER ABBEY on 4 March 1681. James II named his royal yacht *Isabella* in memory of his daughter.

J

James I, King of England (1566–1625) The only son of MARY, QUEEN OF SCOTS and her second husband Henry, Lord DARNLEY, who was born at Edinburgh Castle on 19 June 1566. The story that the queen's child was stillborn, or died at birth, and that a child of her illegitimate half-brother the Earl of Moray was substituted may be safely discounted. At his baptism, the baby prince, who became Duke of Rothesay and Prince and Steward of Scotland at birth, received the names Charles James in honour of his godfather King Charles IX of France (Mary's erstwhile brother-in-law), and his maternal grandfather JAMES V. He was to be the first British sovereign to bear more than one Christian name.

James was only eight months old when his father was murdered at Kirk o' Field on 10 February 1567. Mary's suspected involvement and her marriage at Holyrood on 15 May to James Hepburn, Earl of Bothwell, led to her forced abdication on 24 July and James's proclamation as James VI of Scots. The one-year-old child was solemnly crowned at Stirling by Adam Bothwell, Bishop of Orkney, on 29 July. He was consigned to the care of the Earl of Mar and later to that of Sir Alexander Erskine and received a good education from the historian and poet George Buchanan. During his reign in Scotland James was controlled by powerful nobles and the extreme Protestant clergy of the Kirk, and was little more than a pawn in their political machinations.

In a series of ceremonies lasting from 20 August 1589 to 21 January 1590, James married Princess ANNE OF DENMARK, daughter of King Frederik II, and this rather plain, characterless and somewhat masculine lady made an ideal consort for him. He had grown up with practically no female society and his affections tended to centre on his own sex, though whether he ever practised homosexuality is debatable. His own appearance was unattractive, with a large head with rheumy eyes topping an ungainly and ill-proportioned body. He was bow-legged and suffered from the 'royal malady' PORPHYRIA, as had his mother. The disease takes its name from the dark purple hue that the urine of its sufferers acquires after standing a little while, and James was to describe his own urine as resembling rich Alicante wine.

James was generally accepted as the heir to the English throne and ELIZABETH I, when dying, signified her assent that he should succeed her. A messenger, Sir Robert Carey, set off for Scotland to inform James of his accession. The new king set out for London immediately, and he and his queen were crowned in WESTMINSTER ABBEY on St James's Day, 25 July 1603. As the first sovereign to reign over both England and Scotland, James often employed the title of King of Great Britain (in the preamble to the Authorized Version of the Bible, for example), but his official style by which he was proclaimed was 'King of England, Scotland, France and Ireland, Defender of the Faith', and another 100 years were to elapse before the words 'Great Britain' officially became part of the royal style and title.

Having escaped from the control of the Scottish lords and clergy, James was determined to exert his authority as ruler in his new kingdom. In order to do this he began to propound the theory of the 'divine right of kings', maintaining that the king was above the law and answerable only to God. He was enough of a statesman, however, not to press his claims too far. He did not confront Parliament head-on when it consistently refused to vote him extra funds, but turned instead to other ways of raising money. In 1616 he instituted the order of baronets, a new hereditary honour between knighthood and the peerage, and sold the dignity for £1,080. His feelings about Parliament were not, however, warm, and he once famously remarked of the House of Commons: 'I am surprised that my ancestors should ever have allowed such an institution to come into existence.'

In 1605 an attempt by Catholic sympathizers to blow up the king and Parliament at the state opening on 5 November was discovered, and the conspirators, including Guy (or Guido) Fawkes, who was to have fired the trail, were rounded up and executed (*see* GUNPOWDER PLOT). James was terrified by the conspiracy against him and for some days refused to leave his rooms, where he allowed only trusted fellow-Scots to attend him. The plot brought a new wave of anti-Catholic feeling, and for a while Parliament felt amicable towards their Protestant king and voted him an extra subsidy. The extreme Puritans, however, pushed for further religious reforms, including the abolition of bishops. James, who had suffered under the rule of the extreme Protestants in Scotland, was determined to oppose this, believing that his power would be reduced, and was wont to say, 'No Bishop, no King'.

James's eldest son, HENRY FREDERICK, PRINCE OF WALES, a young man of great promise, died of typhoid in November 1612, at the age of 18, and his second son Charles (*see* CHARLES I) became heir to the throne. The following year James's only surviving daughter Elizabeth (*see* ELIZABETH, PRINCESS, QUEEN OF BOHEMIA) was married to the Elector Palatine and left to live in Germany. Queen Anne died in 1619, but James was little moved by the event, his affections by then being entirely centred on George Villiers, whom he had first met in 1614 and advanced from honour to honour, culminating in the Dukedom of Buckingham in 1623. To James he was 'Steenie' from a fancied resemblance he saw to the figure in a painting of the martyrdom of St Stephen. Other courtiers with whom he had a, to some, suspiciously close attachment included Robert Carr, Earl of Somerset.

James had always been self-indulgent where food and drink were concerned – his fondness for fruit caused him to suffer badly from diarrhoea – and early in 1625 he was stricken with many distressing symptoms. There was the usual suspicion of poison, but kidney failure or dysentery combined with a stroke seems to have been the immediate cause of the king's death, which took place at Theobald's Park, Hertfordshire, on 27 March 1625. Having reigned in England for 22 years, he was buried in Westminster Abbey and his funeral is said to have cost the enormous sum of 'above £50,000' and to have been 'the greatest ... that was ever known in England'.

James was labelled 'the wisest fool in Christendom' by the Spanish ambassador, though other contemporaries admired the king as 'the English Solomon'. A naturally intelligent man, he had many abilities, though he was lazy and a slow beginner, not learning to talk until he was three and for the rest of his life retaining a stammer and a strong Scottish accent. This did not mean that he always appreciated intelligence in others, however: once, when a young girl skilled in several languages was introduced to him he remarked only, 'Can she spin?' As an adult he was a prolific author, penning, among other things, 'A Diatribe Against Tobacco', in which he attacked smoking as 'a custom loathsome to the eye, hateful to the nose, harmful to the brain, dangerous to the lungs, and in the black, stinking fume thereof, nearest resembling the horrible Stygian smoke of the pit that is bottomless'. Also celebrated was his *Basilikon Doron*, a treatise on the art of government addressed to his son Henry. Another work by his hand was a widely read treatise on demonology and witchcraft, a subject in which he was profoundly interested (as James VI of Scotland he had been deeply influenced by the discovery of an apparent witchcraft plot against his life and personally attended the interrogation of the suspects, who perhaps rather conveniently implicated his rival, the Earl of Bothwell). Even more influential was the 'King James Bible', which he commissioned from 54 scholars in 1604; the finished Bible became the most important book in the English language and maintained its high status as the standard version of the Bible for some four centuries.

James was, however, irresolute as monarch and was often prone to depression. Acquaintances found him ill-mannered and coarse as well as a physical and moral coward, weaknesses that probably had their roots in his unsettled childhood.

James I, King of Scots (1394–1437) The third and youngest but only surviving son of ROBERT III and ANNABELLA DRUMMOND, who was born at DUNFERMLINE in December 1394. He became heir apparent on the death of his brother David, Duke of ROTHESAY in March 1402, and by a charter dated at Perth on 10 December 1404 received from his father a grant for life of all the lands belonging to the office of Steward of Scotland, which included Rothesay and the whole of the isle of Bute, the earldom of Carrick, and the baronies of Renfrew and Kyle. He was known, however, only as Steward or Prince of Scotland.

On 4 April 1406 when he was on the way to France to complete his education, he was captured at sea by English sailors and taken as a prisoner to London. By chance his father had died on the same day and James was declared King of Scots by the Estates of the Kingdom at Perth in June 1406. His uncle Robert Stewart, Duke of ALBANY, acted as Governor of the Kingdom until his death in 1420, when he was succeeded in that office by his son Murdoch, 2nd Duke of Albany. James was kept prisoner in England until 1424. He occupied his time in writing poetry, the most famous of his poetical works being *The Kingis Quair*. He also fell in love with Lady JOAN BEAUFORT, elder daughter of John Beaufort, 1st Duke of Somerset, and they were married at St Mary Overy, Southwark, on 2 February 1424. Shortly thereafter James obtained his release, and he and his bride returned to Scotland, where they were crowned at Scone by the Bishop of St Andrews, on 21 May 1424.

James at once set out to crush the power of Albany, who was attainted and beheaded in May 1425. He also forced the submission of Alexander, Lord of the Isles, in 1429. His aim was to strengthen the power of the crown and effect internal peace, curbing the power of the lawless nobility. War with England broke out and an English army was defeated at Piperden, near Berwick, in 1436. The same year an English fleet was thwarted in its attempt to capture James's eldest daughter, the 12-year-old Princess Margaret, on her way to France to marry the dauphin. This was followed by an abortive attempt on James's part to capture Roxburgh. A conspiracy to murder the king was formed, its leaders being his half-uncle Walter, Earl of Atholl, and Sir Robert Graham, and on the night of 21 February 1437 they broke into James's apartment at Perth and murdered him in his bed. The bar to the door of the apartment had been removed and the heroic story of Catherine Douglas, one of the queen's ladies, vainly attempting to hold the door by thrusting her arm through the bolt holes is well known. Her arm was broken, but she was known ever after as 'Catherine bar-lass'.

James was buried in the Carthusian Church at Perth. He had been an enlightened ruler for his day, carrying out many social reforms and enforcing good laws. His widow married Sir James Stewart, known as 'The Black Knight of Lorne', as her second husband, and died at Dunbar Castle on 15 July 1445.

James II, King of England (1633–1701) The third, but second surviving, son and fourth child of CHARLES I and Queen HENRIETTA MARIA, who was born at ST JAMES'S PALACE on 14 October 1633. He was designated Duke of York from his birth, but not formally created so until 27 January 1643, having already been elected and invested a Knight of the Garter at York on 20 April 1642. With his brother Charles (later CHARLES II) he accompanied their father in the campaigns of the CIVIL WAR and was handed over to Parliament on the surrender of Oxford in 1646. He managed to escape to Holland in 1648 and, after Charles II's defeat at Worcester in 1651, volunteered for the French army and later for the Spanish. He was a brave soldier and a good commander and gave loyal service to those for whom he fought. When king, his brother Charles appointed him a Privy Councillor and Lord High Admiral of England in 1649 and Earl of Ulster on 10 May 1659.

James shared his brother's strong sexuality, but his penchant was for ugly women and Charles was wont to say jokingly of some of James's mistresses that his confessor must have given them to him as a penance. While still in exile, he fell in love with the very plain Anne HYDE, a maid of honour to his sister the Princess of Orange, and the daughter of Edward Hyde (later Earl of Clarendon and Lord Chancellor), one of Charles's most ardent supporters. The girl was far below James in situation but he pledged himself to her in secret at Breda in a ceremony later held to have been a marriage on 24 November 1659. Anne became pregnant in 1660 and when her father discovered this, the story of the 'secret marriage' at Breda came out. The king was consulted, and James and Anne were married publicly at Worcester House, London, on 3 September 1660, seven weeks before the birth of their first child, a boy who lived less than a year.

At the Restoration James was created Lord High Admiral of England, Ireland and Wales, and of the towns and marches of Calais, Normandy, Gascony and Aquitaine, and was also appointed Constable of Dover Castle and Lord Warden of the Cinque Ports, positions that he held until the passing of the Test Act in 1673 compelled him to relinquish them as a Roman Catholic. He was created Duke of Albany in Scotland on 31 December 1660. James had long had leanings towards the Roman Catholic Church and in 1670 both he and his wife were secretly received into it. Like many converts, he was to become an ardent fanatic in his zeal for his faith. James distinguished himself as a naval commander, winning victories over the Dutch in 1665 and 1672.

Anne died of complications following the birth of her eighth child CATHERINE OF YORK in 1671 and James found a second wife in the person of the Italian Princess MARY OF MODENA, whom he married in 1673. In the next few years James was gradually rehabilitated in the offices he had been forced to resign because of his Catholicism, and after serving as Lord High Commissioner to the Parliament of Scotland in 1681, was reappointed Lord High Admiral in 1684. Attempts to exclude him from the succession in favour of his daughter Mary (*see* MARY II), a staunch Protestant married to her cousin the Prince of Orange, were thwarted by Charles II, on whose death on 6 February 1685 James ascended the throne.

Although he openly acknowledged his Catholicism, James opened his reign well by summoning a Parliament, appointing his Protestant brother-in-law Laurence Hyde, Earl of Rochester, as Lord High Treasurer, and banishing Charles II's French mistress the Duchess of PORTSMOUTH, an agent of Louis XIV. James and Mary were crowned on St George's Day 23 April 1685 following the Anglican rite (but omitting the communion), having been privately crowned and anointed following the Catholic rite in their chapel at Whitehall the previous day.

On 11 June 1685, James, Duke of MONMOUTH, the eldest of Charles II's many illegitimate children, landed at Lyme Regis, claiming the throne as the Protestant champion, and was proclaimed king at Taunton on 20 June. James's forces were sent against him and Monmouth's army was defeated at Sedgemoor on 5 July. Monmouth was discovered cowering under a hedge and taken to London, where he threw himself on James's mercy, to no avail. On 17 July he was beheaded in the Tower, the executioner bungling the job and causing him undue suffering before his head was finally hacked from his shoulders. The other rebels were dealt with by the 'Bloody Assize' of Judge Jeffreys, 230 being executed and several hundred more transported for life, imprisoned, fined or flogged.

James was now determined on a course of bringing England back to Catholicism and as a first step issued a Declaration of Indulgence removing restrictions imposed on those who did not conform to the established Church of England. Seven bishops who protested against this were imprisoned in the Tower and tried for seditious libel but were acquitted on 30 June 1688. The country might have tolerated James, knowing that his heirs were his daughters the Protestant Mary and ANNE, but on Trinity Sunday 10 June 1688, the queen, who had no surviving children, gave birth to a son at St James's Palace. Rumours were at once circulated to the effect that the child was supposititious and had been smuggled into the queen's bed hidden in a warming-pan. These were completely false, but many people believed them. James's son-in-law (who was also his nephew) William, Prince of Orange (later WILLIAM III), landed at Brixham on 5 November 1688 with the vowed intent of safeguarding the Protestant interest and gathered many supporters on his march to London. Deserted on all sides, James panicked. He sent his wife and baby son to France and followed himself on 11 December, dropping the great seal of England into the Thames as he was ferried to the boat that was to take him to France. He was recognized at Sheerness and brought back to Faversham, but managed (or was allowed) to make good his escape a few days later, accompanied by his natural son, the Duke of Berwick. Parliament meeting on 28 January 1689 was to declare that James had abdicated the throne on 11 December, the day he first attempted to leave the country.

The exiled king, with his wife and baby son, settled down at the palace of St Germain-en-Laye near Paris, made over to their use by his cousin Louis XIV, and a court in exile was soon set up. James was determined to regain his throne and landed in Ireland with a French force in 1689. He held a Parliament in Dublin and remained *de facto* King of Ireland until defeated by William at the battle of the Boyne on 1 July 1690, when he was forced to withdraw again to France. An interesting reminder of these times is the 'gun money' that James struck from melted down brass cannon to pay his troops. The coins are dated by month as well as by year and are now much sought after collectors' items.

James spent the rest of his life in France, planning further invasions that never happened and devoting himself to religious observances. He found great consolation in the little daughter the queen bore him in 1692 and was also comforted by correspondence with his daughter Anne, who could never quite reconcile her conscience with the betrayal of her father. The exiled king died at St Germain from a cerebral haemorrhage on 6 September 1701, and was first buried in the church of the English Benedictines in Paris, but later removed to the parish church of St Germain, where his tomb was despoiled during the French Revolution.

James II possessed much less of the Stuart charm than his elder brother Charles and also lacked his sense of humour. He was good-looking but his looks were spoiled in later life by a cynical sneer, which is apparent in almost all his portraits.

James had a number of illegitimate children, including four by Arabella Churchill (1649–1730), sister of the 1st Duke of Marlborough, of whom James FitzJames, Duke of Berwick (1670–1734) became a celebrated military commander, fighting in his father's and later in the French service. He has many descendants. James II's daughter by another of his mistresses, Catherine Sedley (1657–1717), was Catherine Darnley (c.1682–1743), who married John Sheffield, Duke of Buckingham. She was so proud of being the daughter of a king that on her deathbed she extracted a promise from her attendants that, should she become unconscious, they would not presume to sit down in her presence until she was actually dead.

James II, King of Scots (1430–60) The younger twin son of JAMES I and JOAN BEAUFORT, who was born at Holyrood on 16 October 1430 and became Duke of Rothesay and Prince and Steward of Scotland on the death in infancy of his elder twin Alexander very soon thereafter. He was called 'James of the Fiery Face' on account of a birth mark. He became king in his seventh year on the assassination of his father and was crowned at Holyrood by Michael Ochiltree, Bishop of Dunblane, on 25 March 1437. His mother removed him to Stirling in 1439, but he was kidnapped and brought back to Edinburgh by Sir William Crichton, who contended for his custody with Sir Alexander Livingstone. Livingstone formed an alliance with William Douglas, 8th Earl of Douglas, and they secured the young king's liberty in 1443 and captured Edinburgh Castle from Crichton in 1445.

On 3 July 1449 James was married at Holyrood to MARY OF GUELDRES, the only daughter of Arnold, Duke of Gueldres. She bore him eight children. Crichton regained the king's favour, and after Livingstone and his family were tried and executed in 1450, James killed Douglas with his own hand on discovering his confederacy with Crawford

and Ross, stabbing him at Stirling in February 1452. The new Earl of Douglas, James, attempted to continue the struggle with his brothers, but they were defeated at Arkinholm in 1455 and attainted, their lands being annexed to the crown in the same year. James invaded Northumberland in 1456 but concluded a truce with HENRY VI in 1457.

In spite of the warlike nature of most of James's reign, he found time to establish the University of Glasgow in 1451 and to carry out important legal reforms by appointing supreme central courts to meet at Edinburgh, Perth and Aberdeen and establishing annual circuits of the justiciary court in his Parliament of 1458. In 1460 the king led a force to besiege Roxburgh Castle, but on 3 August he was accidentally killed by the bursting of a cannon. He was buried at Holyrood.

James III Style assumed by Prince James Francis Edward STUART on the death of his father JAMES II in 1701.

James III, King of Scots (1452–88) The eldest son of JAMES II and MARY OF GUELDRES, who was born at St Andrews Castle in May 1452 (not at Stirling on 10 July 1451 as formerly accepted). He became Duke of Rothesay and Prince and Steward of Scotland at birth and succeeded his father at the age of eight. He was crowned at Kelso Abbey by James Kennedy, Bishop of St Andrews, on 10 August 1460, one week after his father's death. The government was carried on by guardians, of whom Robert Boyd, 1st Lord Boyd, conspired with his brother Sir Alexander Boyd to obtain possession of the king's person and was made sole Governor of the Realm by Act of Parliament on 25 October 1466.

Boyd negotiated James's marriage to MARGARET OF DENMARK, daughter of Christian I of Denmark, and the secession of Orkney and Shetland to Scotland on 8 September 1468. While he was absent from Edinburgh for this purpose, James seized power and Boyd, his son the Earl of Arrran, husband of the king's sister Mary, and his brother Alexander were attainted for high treason for their abduction of the king and deprived of all their honours, being forced to flee the country. Nevertheless, James went ahead with the marriage to Margaret, which was solemnized at Holyrood on 13 July 1469, and they had three sons.

In 1479 the king's two brothers, Alexander Stewart, Duke of ALBANY, and John, Earl of MAR, gave trouble and both were imprisoned. Mar died in confinement, but Albany escaped to France, where he intrigued with Louis XI to provoke a new English invasion in 1480. Albany continually changed sides and eventually had to be exiled again. The death of EDWARD IV of England in 1483 ended the threat of further invasions and James was left in peace, but his extravagance and his partiality for unworthy favourites provoked a rising among the nobles, leading to his defeat at the battle of Sauchieburn in June 1488. After the battle the king sought refuge in a cottage at Milltown, near Bannockburn, but he was pursued and murdered there on 11 June 1488. He was buried at Cambuskenneth Abbey.

James was a great patron of the arts and literature, and the poet Robert Henryson flourished in his reign, being to Scotland what Chaucer was to England.

James IV, King of Scots (1473–1513) The eldest son of JAMES III and MARGARET OF DENMARK, who was born on 17 March 1473 and became Duke of Rothesay and Prince and Steward of Scotland at birth. He was only 15 years old when the insurgent lords placed him at their head and he was crowned at Scone by William Scheves, Archbishop of St Andrews, on 26 June 1488, just 15 days after his father's murder, for which he did penance wearing an iron belt, which led to his nickname 'James of the Iron Belt'. The rebels continued to conduct the government for a time, acting with energy and decision, but when James took over he placed much reliance on Sir Andrew Wood of Largo, who became overseer of public works and was instrumental in building up the navy.

In 1493 and 1494 James was occupied in the subjugation of John, Lord of the Isles, but after completing that enterprise successfully became involved in trouble with England through his support for the pretender Perkin WARBECK, on whose behalf he made several border raids in 1496. A seven-year truce was concluded on 30 September 1496, and on 8 August 1503 James was married at Holyrood to Margaret (see MARGARET TUDOR, QUEEN OF SCOTS), the eldest daughter of HENRY VII of England. The following year he instituted a daily council to hear civil cases at Edinburgh, confirmed the privileges of the burghs, secured fixity of tenure by the 'feu' statutes and revoked all acts prejudicial to the Crown and the Church. He gave assistance to Denmark against the Swedes and the Hanseatic League in 1507 and 1508 and

maintained the alliance with England, in spite of national opposition, as long as his father-in-law Henry VII lived.

In 1511, however, relations between James and his brother-in-law HENRY VIII became strained. James signed a treaty with Louis XII of France in 1512 and despatched a fleet to assist him against Henry. The capture of two Scottish ships by Sir Edward Howard exacerbated matters, and James invaded Northumberland with a large force when Henry was campaigning in France. He captured several castles but was finally defeated and slain at FLODDEN by Thomas Howard, Earl of Surrey, on 9 September 1513. His body was taken to London and buried at Sheen Abbey, Surrey.

James was an accomplished man with a keen interest in education and scientific experiment. In addition to his six children by Queen Margaret, he had several natural children, among them Alexander, who became Archbishop of St Andrews at the age of 12 and Chancellor of Scotland at 17 and who was killed at Flodden aged about 20, and James, Earl of Moray, who became Lieutenant General of the Realm in 1535.

James V, King of Scots (1512–42) The third, but eldest surviving, son of JAMES IV and MARGARET TUDOR, who was born at Linlithgow on 10 April 1512 and became Duke of Rothesay and Prince and Steward of Scotland at birth, his two elder brothers, James and Arthur, already having deceased. He was almost 18 months old when his father's death at FLODDEN made him king and he was crowned at Stirling on 21 September 1513. His father's first cousin, John Stewart, Duke of ALBANY, returned from France to take up the regency in 1515, and Queen Margaret was obliged to surrender it to him and allow her son to be taken from Stirling to Edinburgh, where he was educated by some of the leading scholars of the day, Gavin Dunbar, Dean of Moray (later Archbishop of Glasgow), John Bellenden, the poet, Sir David Lindsay, Lyon King of Arms, and James Inglis, Abbot of Culross. He thus became one of the most accomplished and cultivated rulers of his day.

In 1524 James's mother had him proclaimed competent to rule, but he remained under the control of his stepfather, Archibald Douglas, 6th Earl of Angus, until 1528, when James Beaton, Archbishop of St Andrews, aided his escape from Falkland and the influence of the Douglas family was ended. James spent some time in crushing the power of the nobles and liked to go about the country disguised as a farmer ('the Gudeman of Ballengeich') to meet his subjects and discuss their problems at first hand. He also founded the College of Justice in 1532. On 1 January 1537 James was married at Notre-Dame Cathedral in Paris to MADELEINE OF FRANCE, third daughter of François I, King of France, but his 16-year-old bride soon fell a victim to the Scottish climate and died at Holyrood on 7 July 1537.

James married again the following year. His bride was MARY OF GUISE, widow of Louis II, Duke of Longueville, and daughter of Claude I de Lorraine, Duke of Guise. The marriage was solemnized at St Andrews on 12 June 1538. Meanwhile, James was again beset by troubles. His relationship with his uncle HENRY VIII of England was never an easy one, and he also had to contend with the hostility of his nobles and those who wished him to support the Reformation, to which he was greatly opposed. When war broke out between England and France in 1542, the renewal of hostilities between England and Scotland became inevitable. The Scottish forces were routed at Solway Moss and 12,000 prisoners taken in November 1542. James fled back to Edinburgh and thence to Falkland Castle, where, overcome with grief and shame, he fell ill and took to his bed. There he received the news that the queen, who had already borne two sons who died in infancy, had been delivered of a daughter. 'It came with a lass [a reference to the 'Maid of Norway'] and it will go with a lass', was the king's comment as he turned his face to the wall and died on 14 December 1542. He was buried at Holyrood.

Besides his only surviving legitimate child, Mary (see MARY, QUEEN OF SCOTS), who succeeded him, James left a number of natural children, at least nine sons and two daughters. The most famous of the sons was James Stuart, 1st Earl of Moray, later Regent of Scotland, while others were Robert Stuart, 1st Earl of Orkney, and John Stuart, Lord Darnley.

James VI, King of Scots see JAMES I, KING OF ENGLAND.

James VII, King of Scots see JAMES II, KING OF ENGLAND.

James VIII Style assumed by Prince James Francis Edward STUART as King of Scots after the death of his father JAMES II and VII in 1701.

Jane, Queen of England (1537–54) Lady Jane Grey, the 'nine days queen', who was the second, but eldest surviving, daughter of Henry Grey, Duke of Suffolk and Marquess of Dorset, and his wife Lady Frances Brandon, eldest daughter and co-heiress of Charles Brandon, Duke of Suffolk, and his wife Mary (see MARY TUDOR, QUEEN OF FRANCE AND DUCHESS OF SUFFOLK), sometime Queen of France, third daughter of HENRY VII. She was born at Bradgate, Leicestershire, in October 1537 and was extremely well educated. By her early teens she had become something of a bluestocking, learned in Greek, Hebrew and Latin, and also a staunch adherent of the Protestant Reformation. Roger Ascham, the distinguished Cambridge scholar and one-time tutor to the future ELIZABETH I, visited Jane's parents' house at Bradgate and reported finding her reading Plato's *Phaedo* in Greek, while the rest of her family were disporting themselves in the park.

When EDWARD VI lay dying, the Protector Northumberland, well knowing and fearing the Catholic reaction that would come about under the Princess Mary, induced the king to nominate Lady Jane Grey as heiress presumptive on 21 June 1553. This nomination excluded not only the king's half-sisters Mary and Elizabeth and the descendants of his aunt MARGARET, QUEEN OF SCOTS, but also Lady Jane's own mother, Frances, Duchess of Suffolk. Just one month before the nomination, the wily Northumberland had arranged Lady Jane's marriage to his sixth son, Lord Guilford Dudley, a callow youth of 16 or 17, the ceremony having taken place at Durham House, London, on Whitsunday, 21 May 1553.

Jane was reluctant to accept the crown forced upon her by her ambitious father-in-law, but was publicly proclaimed queen with much pomp after Edward VI's death had been made public on 10 July 1553. At her state entry into the TOWER OF LONDON her train was carried by her mother and the diminutive Jane wore specially raised shoes to give her height. Jane showed some spirit in adamantly refusing the suggestion that her husband, for whom she apparently had little affection, should be proclaimed king with her. Whether or not she would have remained unyielding on this point is academic, for her reign lasted only nine days and she was deposed on 19 July 1553. The nobility were incensed by Northumberland's presumption and the people on the whole wanted Mary, not Jane, as their queen.

Northumberland's army was dispersed without bloodshed and he was attainted and beheaded on Tower Hill on 22 August 1553. Jane and Guilford were arraigned, convicted of high treason, and confined in the Tower. They were innocent victims of the overwhelming ambition of their parents and it was only with reluctance and after much heart-searching that MARY I agreed to their execution. The young couple had been drawn closer together in their adversity, and as Lord Guilford walked to his death on Tower Hill on the morning of 12 February 1554, Jane bade him farewell from her window. A little later she saw his headless body being returned to the Tower in a cart, his head in a cloth. She was accorded the privilege of a more private execution on Tower Green later the same day and met her end with calm fortitude, though when blindfolded she showed some signs of distress when she could not find the block with her groping hands. The luckless pair were buried in the Chapel of St Peter-ad-Vincula within the Tower.

Jane Seymour, Queen of England (*c.*1505–37) The third consort of HENRY VIII, who was the daughter of Sir John Seymour of Wolf Hall, Savernake, Wiltshire, and his wife Margery, daughter of Sir Henry Wentworth, of Nettlestead, Suffolk. She was born at Wolf Hall in about 1505. Although her parents did not belong to the higher ranks of the aristocracy, she could claim a line of royal descent through her mother and the famous Henry 'Hotspur', Lord Percy, and her maternal grandmother, Anne Saye, was a half-sister of Elizabeth Tilney, the maternal grandmother of ANNE BOLEYN, to whom she was thus half second cousin. With these court connections Jane served as a maid of honour to both CATHERINE OF ARAGON and Anne Boleyn. In her portraits she does not appear attractive, with a large nose and runaway chin, but she set out to ensnare Henry and seduce him from Anne Boleyn in a manner that does her no credit. She evidently knew how to appeal to the king in a way he found irresistible by striking a simple little-girl pose. She is said, however, to have resisted Henry's attempts to make her his mistress and made it clear that only on marriage would he enjoy her favours.

During Anne's trial and execution, Jane discreetly withdrew from court to her father's house, Wolf Hall. Henry set out for there the moment he heard the guns at the Tower announcing Anne's death, and they were formally betrothed on the following day. Ten days later, on 30 May 1536, the marriage took place quietly in the Queen's Closet at York Place. Henry's plans for the coronation of his new queen had to be postponed because of an outbreak of plague in London and were later deferred on account of her pregnancy, so in the event she was never crowned. Jane's one memorable act in the 17 months she was queen was to effect a reconciliation between Henry and his daughter Mary (*see* MARY I), whom she had known in her days as maid of honour to Catherine of Aragon.

Early in 1537 Jane became pregnant and on 12 October, to Henry's joy, she gave birth to a much longed-for son and heir (*see* EDWARD VI) at Hampton Court. Henry at once ordered celebrations on a massive scale and the infant prince's christening was attended by his half-sisters, Mary and Elizabeth (*see* ELIZABETH I), and by his mother, who was carried on a litter with her long train looped over the back. The excitement was too much for her: she became ill with puerperal fever and died 12 days after her son's birth on 24 October. Thomas Cromwell blamed the queen's death on eating 'things that her fancy called for'. She was buried in St George's Chapel, Windsor, on 12 November 1537. Henry's plans to erect a magnificent monument over her tomb never materialized and in less than 10 years and three wives later, he was laid at her side.

Joan, Princess[1] (1265) The third child of EDWARD I and his first wife ELEANOR OF CASTILE, who was born in January 1265 and died shortly before 7 September 1265, on which date her grandfather HENRY III ordered 'a good and fair cloth-of-gold' to be provided to cover her tomb in WESTMINSTER ABBEY.

Joan, Princess[2] (1335–48) The second daughter and third child of EDWARD III and PHILIPPA OF HAINAULT, who was born at Woodstock before 30 May 1335, on which date the sum of £66.13s.4d was paid to the messenger who brought the news of the birth to the king. While she was still very young, a marriage to Duke Friedrich of Austria was arranged, but the negotiations were broken off for political reasons, and Joan was affianced instead to the Infante Pedro of Castile, son and heir of Alfonso XI. She set out for Spain and the marriage was planned to take place at Bayonne on 1 November 1348. When the princess and her party reached Bordeaux, they discovered that the Black Death had broken out there. They hurried on to Loremo, but it was too late and Joan died there of the plague on

2 September 1348. She was buried in Bayonne Cathedral.

Joan, Princess of Gwynedd (d.1237) The natural daughter of King JOHN by an unknown mother, who was betrothed to LLYWELYN FAWR, PRINCE OF GWYNEDD in 1204 and married to him in the spring of the following year. She acted as an intermediary between her husband and the English Crown between 1211 and 1232. In 1229 she became involved in an amorous intrigue with her son's father-in-law, William de Braose (or Breos), who was hanged for his part in the affair on 3 May 1230. Joan was imprisoned for a short time, but later released by Llywelyn, who appears to have been genuinely fond of her. She died at Aber on 2 February 1237 and was buried at Llanfaes in Anglesey, where her husband founded a Franciscan friary in her memory. A stone coffin, reputedly hers, was taken from Llanfaes at the Dissolution and is now in St Mary's Church at Beaumaris. Joan is known to have had only one child, DAFYDD II, who succeeded his father as Prince of Gwynedd in 1240.

Joan, Princess of Wales (1328–85) The only daughter of Edmund of Woodstock, 1st Earl of KENT and his wife Margaret, Baroness Wake, who was born on 29 September 1328. In 1346, at the age of about 18, she was betrothed to Sir Thomas de Holand (or Holland), but the marriage was not proceeded with and by 15 October 1348 she had become the wife of William de Montacute, 2nd Earl of Salisbury. It was as Countess of Salisbury that Joan, who was known as 'The Fair Maid of Kent' from her beauty, became a prominent figure at the court of her cousin EDWARD III and the legendary loss of her garter at a court ball and its retrieval by the king is said to have inspired the foundation of the Order of the GARTER.

On 13 November 1349 Joan's marriage to the Earl of Salisbury was annulled by Papal Bull on the grounds of her pre-contract with Sir Thomas de Holand, to whom she was ordered to return. On the death of her brother John, 3rd Earl of Kent in December 1352, Joan succeeded him as Countess of Kent, Baroness Woodstock and Baroness Wake, and her husband was summoned to Parliament in right of his wife. The marriage produced three sons and two daughters before Thomas died in Normandy on 26 or 28 December 1360. Joan remained a widow for less than a year and was remarried at Windsor on 10 October 1361 to her first cousin once removed, EDWARD, PRINCE OF

WALES, known to posterity as 'The Black Prince', the eldest son and heir of Edward III. Joan accompanied her husband on his French campaigns and their two sons, EDWARD OF ANGOULÊME and the future RICHARD II, were both born in France. Edward died at Westminster in June 1376, and on the death of Edward III a year later, Joan's son became king. One of the last acts of Joan's life was to act as mediator between her son the king and John of Gaunt, Duke of LANCASTER in 1385. She died at Wallingford Castle, Berkshire, on 7 August 1385. Sandford's *Genealogical History of the Kings of England* relates that 'her corpse was embalmed and wrapped in lead, and ordered to be honourably entombed in the church of the Friars Minors at Stamford'. A roof boss in the Black Prince's Chantry in Canterbury Cathedral is said to be a representation of Joan.

Joan, Queen of Scots[1] (1210–38) The eldest daughter and third child of King JOHN and ISABELLA OF ANGOULÊME, who was born on 22 July 1210 and was married at York on 18 June 1221 to ALEXANDER II, KING OF SCOTS. She had no children and died in or near London while on a visit to her brother HENRY III on 4 March 1238. She was buried in the convent church at Tarrant Crawford, Dorset. On 7 December 1252 Henry III ordered 'an image of our sister' to be made and set up over her tomb, but no trace of it remains.

Joan, Queen of Scots[2] (1321–62) The younger daughter and fourth and youngest child of EDWARD II and ISABELLA OF FRANCE[1], who was born in the TOWER OF LONDON on 5 July 1321 and was consequently called 'Joan of the Tower'. Her marriage to David, the son and heir of ROBERT I, KING OF SCOTS, took place at Berwick-on-Tweed on 17 July 1328, she being only seven and her bridegroom only four years of age. Because the marriage concluded peace between England and Scotland, Joan became known as 'Joan Makepeace'. David succeeded his father as DAVID II on 7 June 1329, and the new king and queen were anointed and crowned at Scone on 24 November 1331, the right to receive anointing having been granted to the Scottish kings by Pope John XXII on 13 June 1329. Queen Joan had no children and died at Hertford when on a visit to her brother EDWARD III on 7 September 1362. She was buried in Grey Friars Church in London.

Joan, Queen of Sicily

Joan, Queen of Sicily (1165–99) The third and youngest daughter and seventh child of HENRY II and ELEANOR OF AQUITAINE, who was born at Angers in October 1165. On 13 February 1177, at the age of 11, she was married at Palermo to William II, King of Sicily, and crowned queen the same day. The only child of the marriage was Bohemond, Duke of Apulia, who died an infant in 1181. King William died at Palermo on 18 November 1189 and two years later Joan went to Messina to meet her mother, who was escorting BERENGARIA OF NAVARRE on her way to marry RICHARD I. The Queen of Sicily took over from her mother and accompanied her future sister-in-law to Cyprus, where the marriage took place at Limasol in May. Joan remained with her brother and his wife throughout the Crusade, and when they returned from the Holy Land she and Berengaria sailed on a different ship from the king. They landed at Naples and proceeded to Rome, where they stayed for a year until the Pope gave them a safe-conduct to travel to Marseilles. There Joan met and fell in love with Raymond VI, Count of Toulouse, already the widower of one wife and the divorced husband of two, and they married in Rouen in October 1196. Joan had two sons by her second marriage and died shortly after the birth of the younger on 4 September 1199, assuming the religious habit on her deathbed. She was buried at Fontevraud. Count Raymond married a fifth time and died in August 1222.

Joan Beaufort, Queen of Scots

Joan Beaufort, Queen of Scots (d.1445) The consort of JAMES I, KING OF SCOTS, who was the elder daughter of John Beaufort, 1st Duke of Somerset (the legitimated son of John of Gaunt, Duke of LANCASTER, and consequently a half-brother of HENRY IV), and his wife Margaret, third daughter of Thomas de Holand, 2nd Earl of Kent. The place and date of her birth appear to be unknown. James I met her and wooed her while he was held prisoner in London, and they were married at the church of St Mary Overy, Southwark, on 2 February 1424. James was released on 28 March and they set out for Scotland, where they were crowned at SCONE on 21 May 1424. Joan gave birth to two sons and six daughters. She was at Perth when her husband was murdered there on 21 February 1437 and was herself slightly wounded. In 1439 she made a second marriage to Sir James Stewart, known as 'The Black Knight of Lorne', and was obliged to give up the custody of her son JAMES II, her dowry and Stirling Castle by Sir Alexander Livingstone, the king's guardian. She had three sons by her second marriage and died at Dunbar Castle on 15 July 1445 being buried with her first husband in the Carthusian Church at Perth.

Joan of Acre, Princess, Countess of Gloucester and Hereford

Joan of Acre, Princess, Countess of Gloucester and Hereford (1272–1307) The 8th child of EDWARD I and his first wife ELEANOR OF CASTILE, who was born at Acre in Palestine in the spring of 1272 when her parents were taking part in the Crusades. She was married at WESTMINSTER ABBEY on 30 April 1290 to Gilbert de Clare, 3rd Earl of Gloucester and 7th Earl of Hereford, the divorced husband of Alice de Lusignan, a half-sister of HENRY III. Joan gave birth to a son and three daughters in quick succession before her husband died at Monmouth Castle on 7 December 1295 and was buried in Tewkesbury Abbey.

A little over a year later, in January 1297, Joan contracted a second marriage in secret to Ralph de Monthermer, who had been her first husband's esquire. When news of this marriage was made known to her father, he was so infuriated that he threw the crown or coronet he was wearing on the fire and ordered Ralph to be imprisoned at Bristol, at the same time confiscating all the lands and castles that Joan had inherited from her first husband. However, the Bishop of Durham acted as a mediator and the king accepted his new son-in-law by August 1297 when he was summoned to Parliament as Earl of Gloucester and Hereford in right of his wife. Joan had two sons and two daughters by her second marriage and died at Clare in Suffolk on 23 April 1307, being buried in the Augustinian priory there. The earldoms of Gloucester and Hereford passed to her son by her first husband, and Ralph de Monthermer was summoned to Parliament as Lord Monthermer. He married again and died on 5 April 1325, having had no issue by his second wife.

Joan of Navarre, Queen of England

Joan of Navarre, Queen of England (c.1370–1437) The second wife and consort of HENRY IV, who was the fourth and youngest daughter of Charles II (the Bad), King of Navarre, and his wife Jeanne, eldest daughter of Jean II, King of France, and was born at Pamplona in about 1370. She was named after her mother and her paternal grandmother Jeanne II, Queen of Navarre, and her name was anglicized as Joan or Joanna after she became Queen of England. Joan was only about three years old when she lost her mother on 3 November 1373 and no more than 16 when she was married to Jean V (the Valiant), Duke of Brittany at Saillé on 2 September 1386. Born in 1337, he was her senior by over 30 years and had already been married twice, first to Mary (*see* MARY, PRINCESS, DUCHESS OF BRITTANY), fourth daughter of EDWARD III, and secondly to Joan Holland, the half-sister of RICHARD II. Both marriages had been childless, but the last to Joan of Navarre produced nine children, four sons and five daughters.

On the death of the Duke of Brittany at Nantes on 1 November 1399, Joan became regent of the duchy for her eldest son Duke Jean VI until he came of age (at 12) and was invested at Rennes on 22 March 1401. Henry IV had visited the Breton court during his exile in 1399. He evidently made a great impression on the duchess, in spite of his rather unattractive appearance, and she determined to marry him should the opportunity ever arise. Now freed of her responsibilities, she applied to the Pope at Avignon for a dispensation to marry anyone she pleased within the fourth degree of consanguinity and this was granted on 20 March 1402. She then sent an emissary to England to conclude matters with Henry, who appears to have been quite compliant, and the proxy marriage (with her male emissary standing in for the bride) took place at Eltham Palace on 3 April.

Matters were now complicated by the fact that whereas Joan supported and had obtained her dispensation from Pope Benedict XIII at Avignon, Henry supported the rival Pope Boniface IX at Rome. Eventually things were settled to the satisfaction of all parties. Joan assumed the title of queen and set out for England, accompanied by her two youngest daughters, Marguerite and Blanche, and a large Breton and Navarrese suite. The crossing, in January 1403, was a rough one, taking five days, and the party was forced to land at Falmouth rather than at Southampton as had been intended. They then went on to Winchester where Henry met them and the marriage took place in the cathedral on 7 February. A feature of the elaborate wedding-breakfast was a pair of crowned panthers and a pair of crowned swans formed out of sweetmeats. Such things were known as 'subtleties' and were produced between courses in much the same way as a sorbet might be today. Joan's entry into London and her coronation at WESTMINSTER ABBEY on 26 February were celebrated with all the customary ceremonies.

Although Joan was no more than 35 at the time of her marriage and Henry about 37, she bore no more children and it has been suggested that some early form of birth control was used, since both had had large families by their previous partners. The seemingly unnatural lack of progeny may well have contributed to the suspicion of witchcraft that the people entertained against the queen. In this connection it must be remembered that Joan had been Duchess of Brittany, where many curious old superstitions and ceremonies are held and observed to this day.

Joan maintained an excellent relationship with her stepchildren and was frequently visited by her own offspring. She obviously held her first husband in high regard, as in 1408 an alabaster monument was made for him at her behest and shipped to Brittany to be erected over his tomb at Nantes. Agnes Strickland states that Joan's 'besetting sin' was avarice, and she certainly amassed a large fortune, being liberally dowered both in Brittany and in England.

The high esteem in which Joan was held by her stepson HENRY V is evidenced by the fact that he appointed her, whom he termed 'his dearest mother', to act as regent when he departed to continue the war in France in 1415. When the news of the victory of AGINCOURT was received in London, Joan, with the Mayor and Aldermen and a large retinue, walked in solemn procession from St Paul's to Westminster to make a thanksgiving offering at St Edward's shrine. Her feelings must have been very mixed, because one of her sons-in-law (the Duke of Alençon) fell fighting on the French side, while her son Arthur, later to succeed his brother as Duke of Brittany, had been taken prisoner and was to be brought back to England to languish for many years in the Tower and later at Fotheringay.

In 1417 Henry was still referring to Joan as 'that excellent and most dear lady, the Queen our mother', but in the following year, when Henry was again absent in France and his brother John, Duke of BEDFORD was acting as regent, she was suddenly arrested at Havering atte Bower in Essex and was taken to Pevensey Castle, 'being accused by certain persons of an act of witchcraft, which would have tended the King harm'. Joan's accuser was her own confessor, John Randolf, whose motivation is not clear. The queen was deprived of all her property and dower and was then kept in close confinement without trial until July

1422 when she was released and her dower was restored.

The rest of Joan's life was lived out quietly and she died at her favourite residence at Havering atte Bower on 9 July 1437, aged about 67. 'Also the same year', adds the Chronicle of London, 'died all the lions in the Tower, the which was nought seen in no man's time before out of mind'. The implication is that the witch-queen's familiars did not survive her. Joan was buried with Henry IV at Canterbury. Her alabaster effigy depicts a small, well-made woman with a trim figure and a long, slender neck.

John, King of England (1167–1216) The fifth son and eighth and youngest child of HENRY II and ELEANOR OF AQUITAINE, who was born at Beaumont Palace, Oxford, on 24 December 1167. He was born when his mother was well over 40 and was destined to become and to remain her favourite child. He inherited or acquired many of her characteristics. What he did not inherit or acquire was any patrimony, as did his elder brothers, and his nickname 'Lackland' is said to have been bestowed on him by his father. John grew up a dandy, a gourmet and a womanizer, dedicated to a sybaritic existence and entirely unprincipled. His parents looked on his youthful escapades with indulgence and doubtless extricated him from many scrapes. At the age of 18 John was sent to Ireland to complete the conquest there, but he was soon recalled when his ridiculing of the long beards and style of dress of the Irish princes and chieftains aggravated an already delicate situation.

RICHARD I seems to have had a soft spot for his young brother, and on his accession in 1189 conferred upon John the county of Mortain in Normandy. He also arranged his marriage on 29 August 1189 with an English heiress, Isabella (see ISABELLA OF GLOUCESTER), the granddaughter of Robert, Earl of GLOUCESTER (HENRY I's bastard son), who had been such a staunch supporter of the Empress MATILDA. The marriage at once encountered ecclesiastical difficulties because the couple were second cousins, and the Archbishop of Canterbury declared the marriage void and placed their lands under an interdict. John at once appealed to the pope and managed to get the decision reversed. However, there was little or no love between the pair and they soon ceased to live together.

Though fond of John, Richard was well aware of his weaknesses and at first excluded him from any part in the government when he left for the Crusade, appointing a Norman, William de Longchamp, as Chancellor and principal regent. John lost no time in identifying himself with the people, who resented the Chancellor's arrogant, French ways. With the assistance of his half-brother Geoffrey, Archbishop of York (one of Henry II's bastards), he led a force to seize London, where he promptly won over the citizens by granting them the right to elect a mayor. Longchamp fled, disguised as a woman, and was about to sail from Dover when the advances of an over-amorous sailor discovered him. John was so amused on hearing of this incident that he allowed him to go.

Despite John's scheming against him, Richard was ever forgiving and on his deathbed named John as heir. By the rules of primogeniture, ARTHUR, DUKE OF BRITANNY, the posthumous son of John's elder brother GEOFFREY should have succeeded, but he was only 11 years old and the succession of a child in those times was to be avoided if possible.

John was invested as Duke of Normandy at Rouen on 25 April 1199. In the course of the solemn ceremony, he dropped the spear, part of the ducal regalia, and this was afterwards taken as a portent of the loss of the duchy five years later. After this he set out for England and his coronation at Westminster on 27 May 1199, at which the archbishop, Hubert Walter, delivered an oration arguing that the election of a sovereign was more important than hereditary right. John's next step was to rid himself of his now unwanted wife, who had not been acknowledged as queen. An annulment was easily procured on the old grounds, and after a whirlwind courtship John married ISABELLA OF ANGOULÊME, a 12-year-old girl with whom he had become infatuated while campaigning in France. Neither was to be a model of fidelity (John himself fathered some seven or eight illegitimate children).

The murder of his nephew and rival, Arthur of Brittany, at Rouen in April 1203 was carried out at John's instigation (legend has it that he killed him with his own hands) and aroused the fury of Philippe II, King of France, who, as overlord of both Brittany and Normandy, declared John's duchy forfeit and began an invasion. Château-Gaillard, the key to Rouen, fell in March 1204 and in June the French king entered Rouen. The once mighty Angevin empire had shrunk to a fragment.

In 1205 John began a quarrel with the

Church when he refused to accept Pope Innocent III's nomination of Stephen Langton as Archbishop of Canterbury in preference to John, Bishop of Norwich, his own nominee and a personal friend. His intransigence in this matter led in 1208 to a papal interdict being laid over the whole country and his own excommunication. John was forced to submit at last and humiliatingly resign his kingdom to the pope and receive it back again as a fief of the papacy before the interdict and excommunication were ended in May 1213. In August that year John flung himself at the feet of Archbishop Langton and, after pleading forgiveness for his wrongs, was temporarily reconciled with his bishops.

In 1214 John conducted another campaign in France and suffered a catastrophic defeat at Bouvines. During his absence the barons banded together under the leadership of Stephen Langton to protest against the longstanding misgovernment of the realm. This culminated in the best known event of John's reign, his forced sealing of the Magna Carta at Runnymede, near Windsor, on 15 June 1215. The charter defined the rights of the Church, the barons and the people. In essence it declared that the Church was free to choose its own bishops; that no money over and above certain regular payments was to be exacted from the king's feudal tenants without their previous consent; and that no freeman was to be punished except in accordance with the laws of the land. John was infuriated by this forced agreement and claimed that he had acted under duress. He gained the backing of the pope who had once excommunicated him and received his blessing to gather an army and fight the barons, who for their part called in Louis of France, the heir to the French throne. Louis landed at Sandwich and proceeded at once to London where the barons made him their leader and promised him the throne. Once again civil war was rife in the land and a year of indecisive skirmishing ensued.

Journeying through East Anglia with his band, John attempted to cross the Wash from Norfolk to Lincolnshire but misjudged the tides so that the whole of his baggage train was lost, including his crown and many valuables. The story has inspired treasure hunters ever since, but nothing was ever recovered except a small crest crown from a helmet. It is possible, indeed, that the story is an invention and that the regalia were in fact stolen as the king lay on his deathbed (a contemporary recorded looting going on in his last hours). The loss of the crown jewels affected John so greatly that Matthew Paris says: 'He fell into such deep despondency ... that being seized with a sharp fever he became seriously ill. But he aggravated the discomfort of his illness by his disgusting gluttony, for that night by indulging too freely in peaches and copious draughts of new cider he greatly increased his feverishness.' Next day John was suffering from dysentery, but he managed to ride as far as Sleaford, where he took to a litter and was carried to Newark Castle. Here 'in a day or two' he died on the night of 18 October 1216, aged nearly 49. Another version of his death claims that he was poisoned by a monk at Swinstead Abbey, Lincolnshire, after he was heard vowing that within six months he would see to it that a loaf of bread that now cost a half penny would then cost 20 shillings.

John was buried in Worcester Cathedral, clad as a monk and, at his own request, as near the shrine of St Wulfstan as possible. Later his tomb was moved to the centre of the choir, where his effigy may be seen today. Though not contemporary, it conveys a strong impression of character. John's personality was a complex one and latterly he has found some apologists, not least for his achievements in reforming the administration of his realm. He was regarded as cruel and avaricious by many of his contemporaries but possessed a sense of humour and could occasionally show acts of mercy and generosity.

John, Prince[1] *see* JOHN, KING.

John, Prince[2] (*c*.1250–6) The fourth son and sixth child of HENRY III and ELEANOR OF PROVENCE, who was born in about 1250 and died in or before 1256. He was buried in WESTMINSTER ABBEY.

John, Prince[3] (1266–71) The eldest son and fourth child of EDWARD I and ELEANOR OF CASTILE, who was born at Windsor on the night of 13–14 July 1266. He died at Wallingford, Berkshire, on 3 August 1271, while in the care of his uncle, Richard, Earl of CORNWALL, to whom his father had entrusted his children when he left for the Crusade in 1270. He was buried in WESTMINSTER ABBEY on the north side of EDWARD THE CONFESSOR's shrine on 8 August 1271.

John, Prince[4] (1871) The third son and sixth and youngest child of Albert Edward, Prince of Wales (later EDWARD VII) and ALEXANDRA OF DENMARK, who was born prematurely at SANDRINGHAM HOUSE, Norfolk, on 6 April 1871. He was extremely frail and was baptized Alexander John Charles Albert. Had he lived he was to have been known by the second name. He survived for 24 hours only and died on 7 April 1871. His loss was a cause of great grief to both his parents. He was buried in Sandringham churchyard.

John, Prince[5] (1905–19) The fifth son and sixth and youngest child of GEORGE V and Queen MARY OF TECK, who was born at York Cottage, Sandringham, at five minutes past three in the morning on 12 July 1905. He received the names of John Charles Francis at his baptism. For the first four years of his life he appeared to be perfectly healthy, but unfortunately he began to have epileptic fits, which gradually worsened. Until 1917 he grew up with his brothers and sister, moving with them and their parents from one royal residence to another. In that year, however, his doctors advised that he should be segregated from them as his fits distressed his siblings. Accordingly, an establishment was set up at Wood Farm, Wolferton, near Sandringham, and Prince John lived there under the devoted care of his nurse 'Lalla' Bill. He also received much affection from his grandmother Queen ALEXANDRA. On the morning of 18 January 1919 he suffered a severe seizure and died peacefully in his sleep at 5.30 that afternoon. His parents received the news at nearby Sandringham, and Queen Mary recorded in her diary: 'The news gave me a great shock, tho' for the poor little boy's restless soul, death came as a great release.' Prince John was buried next to his uncle of the same name in Sandringham churchyard on 21 January. 'Now our two Johnnies rest side by side', his grandmother wrote to Queen Mary.

John Balliol, King of Scotland see BALLIOL, JOHN.

John of Eltham, Earl of Cornwall see CORNWALL, JOHN OF ELTHAM, EARL OF.

John of Gaunt, Duke of Lancaster see LANCASTER, JOHN OF GAUNT, DUKE OF.

Jordan, Dorothea (1761–1816) Stagename adopted by the actress Dora or Dorothy Bland, the third daughter of Francis Bland, an itinerant actor, and Grace, daughter of the Rev. Richard Phillips, incumbent of Trelethyn in the diocese of St David's, who became mistress of WILLIAM IV. Her father was the son of a distinguished Irish judge of the Prerogative Court in Dublin and the descendant of a Yorkshire family that had settled in Ireland. The judge strongly disapproved of his son's acting career and even more so of the marriage that he contracted when under age to Grace Phillips, who had travelled to Dublin with her sister, both intent on becoming actresses. He had the marriage declared void, but the young couple ignored this and continued to live together. They were in London when their daughter Dora was born on 22 November and baptized at St Martin-in-the-Fields on 5 December 1761.

Dora's parents separated in 1774 and she obtained employment in a Dublin milliner's shop to help maintain her mother and siblings. In 1777, however, she made her debut on the Dublin stage, using the stagename of Miss Francis. In the following year she appeared in Cork, where she was much admired for her comedy roles and her ability to play in male attire. She joined the company of Richard Daly and became pregnant by him in 1782, in which year she came to England and adopted the name 'Mrs Jordan', by which she is best known. She gave birth to a daughter, Fanny, in November 1782. She continued to play in the provinces until 1785, when she first appeared before a London audience as Peggy in *The Country Girl* at Drury Lane. Her success was immediate. About this time she met and fell in love with Richard Ford, the son of Dr James Ford, a part-proprietor of Drury Lane and obstetrician to Queen CHARLOTTE. The couple set up house together in Gower Street and Dora gave birth to three more children.

In 1790 Dora attracted the attention of the Duke of Clarence (later William IV). Her relationship with Ford was on the wane and she and the duke began a life of domestic bliss that was to endure until 1811 and produce 10 children (*see* FITZCLARENCE). It was alleged that state reasons were the underlying cause of the duke's demand for a separation and the shock was almost too great for Dora to bear. A yearly allowance of £4,400 was settled on her for the maintenance of herself and her daughters, with a provision that if she should resume her acting career the care of the duke's four daughters, together with £1,500 per annum allowed for them, should revert to their father. A few months later Mrs Jordan did resign the custody of the children and returned to the stage. The story was told that the duke demanded repayment of his money, but received in reply only a playbill, with the words, 'Positively no money refunded after the curtain has risen.' She made her last stage appearance at Margate in August 1815 and retired to France in great financial straits, having been ruined by settling the debts of her son-in-law Frederick Edward March, the husband of her elder daughter by Richard Ford. She took lodgings at Saint-Cloud and her health deteriorated rapidly. She died on 5 July 1816 and was buried in the public cemetery of Saint-Cloud.

The writer William Hazlitt, a fervent admirer, wrote: 'Her face, her tones, her manner were irresistible. Her smile had the effect of sunshine, and her laugh did one good to hear it. Her voice was eloquence itself; it seemed as if her heart was always at her mouth. She was all gaiety, openness and good-nature. She rioted in her fine animal spirits, and gave more pleasure than any other actress, because she had the greatest spirit of enjoyment in herself.'

Jubilees A 'Jubilee', a special time or season for celebration, was observed by the Jews once every 50 years and was a time during which slaves were liberated and alienated property was restored to its rightful owners. The word Jubilee (from which jubilation also stems) is derived ultimately from *yobhel*, the Hebrew word for the ram's horn that was blown to inaugurate the special year. The Jews probably borrowed the idea from the ancient Egyptians, whose Pharaohs celebrated similar anniversary festivals.

In Christian times a Jubilee was ordered to be observed every century by Pope Boniface VIII in 1300. Later popes decreed more frequent celebrations: Pope Clement VI every 50 years; Pope Urban VI every 33 years; and Pope Sixtus V every 25 years.

The first Jubilee to be so-called that was celebrated in the British Isles had no royal connotations. It was the Shakespeare Jubilee held at Stratford-on-Avon on three successive days in September 1769 and was the brain-child of David Garrick, who masterminded the proceedings. Forty years later a National Jubilee was held to mark the occasion of GEORGE III entering the 50th year of his reign on 25 October 1809. The manifestations of loyalty at that time and the series of events arranged on both national and local levels were somewhat subdued because of the king's failing eyesight and mental health throughout the year. However, commemorative medals were struck and souvenir pottery manufactured on a fairly extensive scale, and these now form collectors' items.

The death of the Prince Consort in December 1861 precluded the possibility of any celebration to mark the 25th anniversary of the accession of Queen VICTORIA, which might otherwise have taken place in the course of the following year, and it was not until the queen had completed the 50th year of her reign in 1887 that the first of the great modern royal Jubilees was celebrated. Queen Victoria's Golden Jubilee, which she herself was to refer to as 'this brilliant year', was an occasion of public rejoicing and magnificence such as had not been witnessed before in this country, enhanced as it was by the presence of many Indian princes and troops, as well as by the kings of Denmark, Belgium, Greece and Saxony, the crown princes of the German Empire, Austria, Portugal and Sweden, many other European princes and princesses, and, an exotic touch, the queen and crown princess of Hawaii, the latter of whom left in her delightful memoirs an engagingly naïve account of the great thanksgiving service in WESTMINSTER ABBEY and the other ceremonies that she attended. On 21 June, the actual Jubilee Day, London was illuminated at night and the country was crossed by beacon fires starting from the Malvern Hills. A laconic press report noted only 'two deaths recorded, and not many personal injuries'.

Ten years later Queen Victoria celebrated her DIAMOND JUBILEE, the 60th anniversary of her reign, in similar fashion. On this occasion the thanksgiving service was held at St Paul's Cathedral. The queen was now too infirm to negotiate the cathedral steps and it was therefore decided that her carriage should draw up before the steps, on which the robed Archbishop of Canterbury and cathedral clergy would be assembled to conduct the short service. This arrangement greatly outraged the queen's cousin, Grand Duchess Augusta of Mecklenburg-Strelitz (*see* AUGUSTA, PRINCESS, GRAND DUCHESS OF MECKLENBURG-STRELITZ), who in a letter to her niece May (the future Queen MARY OF TECK) made her own forthright comment: 'After 60 years Reign, to thank God in the Street!!! who *can* have started such an idea, and how could the Queen adopt it?'.

London was destined not to see another Jubilee for nearly 40 years, when it was decided to mark the 25th anniversary of the accession of GEORGE V in 1935 with a Silver Jubilee, the first of its kind. The arrangements for this occasion followed very closely those of Queen Victoria's two Jubilees. The king and Queen Mary drove in a carriage procession from BUCKINGHAM PALACE to a thanksgiving service in St Paul's Cathedral and the king, who was actually in failing health and was to die the following January, was greatly touched by the genuine signs of affection for him that appeared on all sides. 'I'd no idea they felt like that about me,' he wrote in his diary. 'I am beginning to think they must really like me for myself.'

The Silver Jubilee of ELIZABETH II was celebrated in 1977. If George V's had been a final manifestation of the old British Empire in all its glory and exuberance, that of his granddaughter was to set the pattern for the more restrained, though no less impressive, display of the new Commonwealth, with a mixture of both formal and more relaxed festivities, ranging from public services to countless street parties and a bonanza for souvenir manufacturers.

Julian (1271) The name given by the historian John Stow to the daughter of EDWARD I and ELEANOR OF CASTILE, who was born at Acre in Palestine in 1271 and died there in the autumn of the same year. There is no contemporary source for her name and she has also been identified with 'Katherine, daughter of King Edward', whose anniversary was kept at Canterbury on 5 September.

K

Katherine *see* CATHERINE.

Kendal, Charles (Stuart), Duke of (1666–7) The third son and fifth child of James, Duke of York (later JAMES II) and his first wife Anne HYDE, who was born at ST JAMES'S PALACE on 4 July 1666. His godparents were his three-year-old brother James, Duke of CAMBRIDGE, James, Duke of MONMOUTH, and Lady Ossory. He was designated Duke of Kendal and was to have been created Baron of Holdenby, Earl of Wigmore and Duke of Kendal, but no patent was ever enrolled. He died at St James's Palace at the age of 10 months on 22 May and was buried in the royal vault at WESTMINSTER ABBEY on 30 May 1667.

Kendal, Ehrengard Melusine von der Schulenburg, Duchess of (1667–1743) Mistress of GEORGE I, who was the daughter of Gustav Adolf von der Schulenburg, of an illustrious Altmark family, traceable to the 13th century, and his first wife, Petronella Ottilie von Schwencke. She was born at Emden on 25 December 1667 and became a maid of honour to SOPHIA, ELECTRESS OF HANOVER in 1690. By the following year she had become the mistress of Sophia's son George Louis. She was tall and thin and the Electress called her a *malkin* (a hop-pole or scarecrow). Later, in England, she was to acquire the nickname 'The Maypole'.

Melusine was a woman of some culture, interested in music and the theatre, and she made herself agreeable to her lover in contrast to the stormy relationship he enjoyed with his wife Sophia Dorothea (*see* SOPHIA DOROTHEA OF CELLE). She bore him three daughters, but they were never openly acknowledged as such, two of them, Anna Louise Sophie (1692–1773) and Petronella Melusine (1693–1778), being brought up as the children of Melusine's sister Margarethe Gertrud and her husband (and distant cousin) Friedrich Achaz von der Schulenburg, and the third, Margarethe Gertrud (1701–26), as the child of another

sister, Sophie Juliane, and her husband Rabe Christoph von Oeynhausen.

On George's accession to the British throne in 1714, Melusine accompanied him to England and was naturalized a British subject in 1716. On 18 July that year she was created Baroness of Dundalk, Countess and Marchioness of Dungannon, and Duchess of Munster for life in the peerage of Ireland, and on 19 March 1719 she was further created Baroness of Glastonbury, Somerset, Countess of Feversham, and Duchess of Kendal, also for life, in the peerage of Great Britain. Finally, on 1 January 1723 she was created Princess (Reichsfürstin) von Eberstein by the Emperor Karl VI at George's request. This lends some weight to the widespread belief that Melusine was secretly married to the king, and it was rumoured that the Archbishop of York had performed the ceremony. Sir Robert Walpole said of her that she 'was as much Queen of England as ever any was'.

Melusine was extremely useful to the king, acting as his hostess and cultivating the friendship of English ladies with political influence. When George I made his last journey to Hanover, the Duchess of Kendal and her second daughter the Countess of Walsingham were part of the entourage and they arrived in Osnabrück on the morning of the king's death, 22 June 1727. The grief-stricken duchess returned to England, where the king had seen to it that she was well provided for financially, and in 1728 she bought a house at Twickenham, Middlesex, which she named Kendal House. Here she lived out the rest of her life, comforted by the companionship of a large bird (a raven in some accounts) in which she believed George's spirit had been reincarnated. She died at Kendal House on 10 May 1743 and was buried in the Grosvenor Chapel in South Audley Street, London.

Her eldest daughter, Anna Louise Sophie, was married in 1707 to Ernst August Philipp von dem Bussche-Ippenburg, but the marriage was unhappy and ended in divorce before 1714. Louise, as she was known, was created Countess (Reichsgräfin) von Delitz by the Emperor at her father's request in 1722. The youngest daughter, Margarethe Gertrud, known as *die schöne Gertrud*, or Trudchen, was married in 1722 to Albrecht Wolfgang, Count of Schaumburg-Lippe, and died of tuberculosis in 1726, leaving two sons.

Kennedy, Buttercup The unlikely name of the professional co-respondent who was cited by Mrs Wallis Simpson (later Duchess of Windsor) in her divorce suit from Ernest Simpson in 1936 (*see* EDWARD VIII).

Kenneth I Mac Alpin, King of Scots (d.859) The son of ALPIN, KING OF KINTYRE, whom he succeeded on his death in battle with the Picts in Galloway in August 834. He succeeded to the throne of DALRIADA in 841 and in 843 became King of the Picts on the death of his distant kinsman BRUDE VII, thus uniting the two kingdoms and becoming the first King of Scots or King of Alba, although he had to contend with several opposition Pictish kings for several years. He moved his capital from Argyll to SCONE. The name of his wife is unknown, but he had at least three children, CONSTANTINE I and AEDH, successively Kings of Scots, and a daughter who married Run, King of Strathclyde. Kenneth died in 858 or 859 and was succeeded by his brother DONALD I.

Kenneth II, King of Scots (d.995) The younger son of MALCOLM I, KING OF SCOTS, who succeeded his kinsman CULEN in 971. He spent his reign in extending and consolidating his kingdom. He was treacherously murdered at Fetteresso in 995 and buried on Iona. He left two sons, Dungal, who was killed by his kinsman Gillacomgain Mac-Kenneth in 999, and MALCOLM II, later king.

Kenneth III, King of Scots (d.1005) The son of King DUBH, who obtained the throne after killing his predecessor CONSTANTINE III at Rathinveramon in 997. He was himself killed in battle by his *tanist* MALCOLM II at Monzievaird, near the banks of the Earn on or about 25 March 1005. He had three sons: (1) Giric, Mormaer or Regulus under his father, with whom he was killed; (2) Gillacomgain, who killed Dungal, the son of KENNETH II, in 999; and (3) Boite, who had a son, whose son was murdered by Malcolm II in 1033, and a daughter, Gruoch, the famous 'Lady Macbeth'.

Kensington Palace Royal residence west of Hyde Park, London. MARY II bought Kensington House from Heneage Finch, 1st Earl of Nottingham for £18,000 in 1689, hoping that the clearer air away from central London would be beneficial to her husband's asthma. Sir Christopher Wren enlarged the house into a palace and it became the favourite London residence of WILLIAM III and Mary, who both died there. Queen ANNE added the orangery, designed by Vanbrugh, and GEORGE I and GEORGE II both commissioned further enlargements. The palace was the birthplace of Queen VICTORIA and Queen MARY OF TECK. Since the reign of Queen Victoria it has been divided into a number of apartments assigned to various members of the royal family (currently including Princess MARGARET, COUNTESS OF SNOWDON). This usage led the Duke of Windsor (EDWARD VIII) to christen it 'the aunt heap'. The state apartments are open to the public.

Kent One of the kingdoms of the Saxon HEPTARCHY.

Kent, Earls and Dukes of The royal earls and dukes of Kent are here dealt with chronologically.

1. **Odo, Earl of Kent** *see* ODO, BISHOP OF BAYEUX.

2. **Edmund of Woodstock, Earl of Kent** (1301–30) The sixth and youngest son of EDWARD I and the younger son of his second wife MARGARET OF FRANCE, who was born at Woodstock on 5 August 1301. His half-brother EDWARD II granted him various castles, manors and lands, and on his 19th birthday, 5 August 1320, he was summoned to Parliament by writ, whereby he became Lord Woodstock. On 28 July 1321 he was created Earl of Kent. He served the king well in many capacities, accompanying him on his expedition to Scotland in 1322 and raising troops to fight in various campaigns. In 1325 he accompanied Queen ISABELLA OF FRANCE[1] and Edward, Prince of Wales (later EDWARD III) to France and went with them to Hainault to take part in the negotiations for the prince's marriage to PHILIPPA OF HAINAULT. He returned to England with the queen and prince in September 1326 and took part in the council held at Bristol on 26 October to appoint the Prince of Wales regent and 'custos' of the kingdom. The following day he acted as an assessor at the trial of the Despensers. He was present at the coronation of EDWARD III in February 1327 and received several grants of land including some of the forfeited property of the Despensers.

While on the continent Edmund had married, in December 1325, Margaret, widow of John Comyn, Lord of Badenoch (who was killed at Bannockburn on 24 June 1314), and only daughter of John Wake, 1st Baron Wake, and his wife Joan, daughter of William de Fiennes, Lord of Wendover, and they had two sons and one daughter. In 1329 Edmund, according to his own confession, was persuaded by an unnamed friar to believe that his half-brother Edward II was still alive and set about collecting forces to effect a restoration. He was apparently 'set up', to use a modern phrase, by Queen Isabella and her lover Mortimer, who feared his power and influence might turn against them and managed to arrange for letters of a treasonable nature written by Edmund to come into the king's hands. The earl was arrested at the Parliament of Winchester on 13 March 1330 and confessed to the conspiracy. He was condemned to death as a traitor on 19 March and executed outside the gates of Winchester Castle in the evening of the same day. He was buried in the church of the Friars Minor at Winchester but later removed to WESTMINSTER ABBEY.

His widow, after petitioning Parliament, was allowed to receive her dower. On 31 May 1349 she succeeded her brother Thomas as Baroness Wake but died of plague on 29 September the same year.

3. **Edmund, 2nd Earl of Kent** (*c*.1326–31) The elder son of Edmund of Woodstock (*see above*), who was born about 1326 and was sent with his mother, sister and new-born brother to Salisbury Castle after the execution of his father and detained there in the custody of the sheriff of Wiltshire until further orders. On 7 December 1330 a petition on his behalf was presented to Parliament and the king restored all his father's lands and decreed that he should not lose the title of earl, since his father had 'been at all times good and loyal although deceived by wicked men'. The young earl did not enjoy his restored honours for long, dying before 5 October 1331.

4. **John, 3rd Earl of Kent** (1330–52) The younger son of Edmund of Woodstock (*see above*), who was born at Arundel Castle on 7 April 1330, almost three weeks after his father's execution. He succeeded his brother as 3rd Earl of Kent in 1331 and was only 16 when EDWARD III, who was then besieging Calais, sent a message to John's mother requesting her to send him to his assistance with as many men as he could muster. On 23 June 1349 John paid homage

to the king and received livery of his father's lands. In September of the same year he succeeded his mother as 4th Baron Wake and on 10 April 1351, having come of age, he paid homage again and received livery of all the lands that his father and mother had held in chief. He had already been summoned to a Council and to Parliament while still under age.

He married by papal dispensation, granted on 3 April 1348, Elizabeth, daughter of Wilhelm V, Margrave (later Duke) of Jülich, by his wife Jehanne of Hainault, a sister of Queen PHILIPPA OF HAINAULT. There were no children of the marriage and John died on 26 or 27 December 1352. He was buried in the church of the Grey Friars at Winchester.

His widow married on 29 September 1360, Sir Eustace d'Aubrécicourt (or Dabridgecourt), and had two sons by him. Sir Eustace died soon after 1 December 1372. Elizabeth lived on one of the Earl of Kent's manors at Bedhampton, near Portsmouth, and it was probably there that she died on 6 June 1411. At her own request she was buried with her first husband at Winchester.

5. **Joan, Countess of Kent** *see* JOAN, PRINCESS OF WALES.

6. **Edward, Duke of Kent** (1767–1820) The father of Queen VICTORIA, who was the fourth son and fifth child of GEORGE III and Queen CHARLOTTE. He was born at Buckingham House, St James's Park, London, on 2 November 1767 and baptized at ST JAMES'S PALACE on 30 November, his godparents being the Hereditary Prince of Brunswick, his maternal uncle Prince Carl of Mecklenburg-Strelitz, his aunt the Hereditary Princess of Brunswick, and his great-aunt the Landgravine of Hesse-Cassel, all represented by proxies. Prince Edward was educated under the Rev. John Fisher (later Bishop of Exeter and of Salisbury) and was then sent to the continent to study under Baron von Wangenheim at Lüneburg and Hanover. His father provided an allowance of £5,000 a year, but the baron allowed him only a pittance for pocket money and intercepted his letters home, causing the prince to borrow and run into debt, a state in which he was to remain all his life.

Prince Edward entered the Hanoverian Guards as a Cadet in February 1785 and trained at the College at Geneva, where he became an enthusiastic admirer of military discipline. He was appointed a Colonel in the army on 30 May 1786, aged 18. He returned home without his tutor's permission in January 1790, thereby incurring his father's displeasure, and he was granted an interview of only a few minutes before departing to serve at Gibraltar, where he joined the 7th Foot under Major-General Charles O'Hara, the Lieutenant-Governor. His service there rendered him unpopular because of his strictness, and his regiment repeatedly mutinied. In 1791 the prince was sent to Canada with his regiment, and while there he distinguished himself under General Sir Charles (later Earl) Grey during the expedition in the French West Indies, showing conspicuous bravery commanding the flank division during the storming of Martinique. He was promoted to Major-General in 1793 and Lieutenant-General in 1796. In 1798 he had a severe fall from his horse and was allowed to return to England on sick leave.

On 24 April 1799 he was created Duke of Kent and Strathearn and Earl of Dublin. He was promoted to General on 10 May 1799 and in July returned to Canada as Commander-in-Chief of the Forces in North America, which appointment he held until 1800, when he was thrown from his curricle when it overturned on hitting a tree stump and he was again obliged to return to England on sick leave.

He was appointed Governor-General of Gibraltar on 24 March 1802, but his desire to repress irregularities and enforce subordination, particularly his suppression of the drink shops, while pleasing to the civil population, led to serious consequences. Having refused a request from the soldiers of the garrison to celebrate Christmas Eve as a holiday, and having put the deputation that brought it under arrest, the men became mutinous. Christmas Day passed in confusion and on the following night the duke headed his regiment against the rebels. Blood was shed before peace was restored and the ringleaders rounded up. The duke was recalled to England in May 1803, although he retained the governorship for the rest of his life.

The duke, who was promoted to Field Marshal in 1805, took up residence at Castle Hill Lodge, Ealing, where he maintained an establishment greatly beyond his means. While in Canada he had met a French Canadian lady, Julie de St Laurent, a girl of respectable family, and she became his mistress and wife in all but name, presiding over his household for 27 years. She was referred to by the duke's sisters as 'Edward's French lady'. Contrary to stories that are still widely believed, the union produced no issue, although the duke had fathered a child, Adélaïde Victoire Auguste, born at Geneva on 15 December 1789 to one Adélaïde Dubus (who died in childbirth). The girl died between Marseille and Gibraltar in June or July of the following year. When the death of Princess CHARLOTTE OF WALES necessitated the marriages of the hitherto unmarried sons of George III to provide an heir to the throne, is said to have read the news of the duke's engagement to the Dowager Princess of Leiningen in the newspaper while seated at the breakfast table and to have been seized with violent hysterics. The duke was genuinely attached to her and felt the forced separation keenly. He saw that she was provided with an income of £500 a year, and she retired to live in Paris, where she was known as the Comtesse de Montgenet.

The Duke of Kent married at Coburg, on 29 May 1818, Marie Louise Victoire, widow of Emich Carl, 2nd Prince of Leiningen, and fourth daughter of Franz Friedrich Anton, Duke of Saxe-Coburg-Saalfeld. On their return to England they went through a second ceremony at KEW PALACE before the ailing Queen CHARLOTTE on 13 July 1818. In September the duke and duchess set out for Amorbach, where she was regent of the principality of Leiningen for her young son, but on discovering that she was pregnant they determined on returning to England, which they did in April 1819. They took up residence in an apartment at KENSINGTON PALACE and it was there that Victoria was born on 24 May 1819.

Towards the end of the year the need to economize, coupled with the idea that sea air would benefit the duchess's health, caused the duke to lease Woolbrook Cottage, Sidmouth, and the family moved there in December 1819. Early in January the duke caught a cold, but insisted in going out for a walk, during which he got thoroughly wet and chilled. He became feverish and delirious and his condition was aggravated by the bleeding and cupping advocated by Dr William Maton, the physician who was sent from London to treat him. The duke became increasingly exhausted and died at ten o'clock in the morning on 23 January 1820. He was buried in St George's Chapel, Windsor, on 12 February 1820. He left only debts.

7. **George, Duke of Kent** (1902–42) The fourth son and fifth child of GEORGE V and

Queen MARY OF TECK, who was born at York Cottage, Sandringham, Norfolk, on 20 December 1902 and baptized George Edward Alexander Edmund by the Rt Rev. Francis Paget, Bishop of Oxford, his god-parents being his grandfather EDWARD VII, his great-uncle Prince Waldemar of Denmark, Prince Louis of Battenberg (later 1st Marquess of Milford Haven), his grand-mother Queen ALEXANDRA, his great-aunt the Dowager Empress of Russia, and his great-aunt Princess HELENA. With his elder brothers and sister he attended the corona-tion of their parents on 22 June 1911 and in a squabble with his brothers on the return journey to BUCKINGHAM PALACE was forced to sit on the floor of the coach that conveyed them. He received his early education from private tutors and in 1918 entered the Royal Naval College at Dartmouth.

Prince George's service career was with the Royal Navy. He was promoted to Lieutenant in 1926, Commander in 1934, Captain in 1937 and Rear Admiral in 1939. He was also a Major-General in the Army and a Personal ADC to his brother GEORGE VI from 1937 until his death. He was created a Knight of the GARTER in 1923 and later received many more honours. His marriage was a love match. He married at WEST-MINSTER ABBEY, on 29 November 1934, Princess Marina of Greece and Denmark, third and youngest daughter of Prince Nicholas of Greece and Denmark, and his wife Grand Duchess Helen Vladimirovna of Russia. The Anglican service in the Abbey was followed by a Greek Orthodox cere-mony in the private chapel of Buckingham Palace. Preceding his marriage, Prince George was created, on 12 October 1934, Duke of Kent, Earl of St Andrews and Baron Downpatrick.

In the year following his marriage Prince George served as Lord High Commissioner to the General Assembly of the Church of Scotland and in 1938 he was nominated Governor-General and Commander-in-Chief of the Commonwealth of Australia, but did not proceed because of the threaten-ing war. During the Second World War the duke served in the Intelligence Division of the Admiralty from 1939 to 1940 and with Training Command RAF from 1940 to 1942. On 25 August 1942 he set out by air to inspect RAF establishments in Iceland, but in adverse weather conditions the aeroplane crashed into a hillside at Morven in north-west Scotland and the duke was killed instantaneously. His funeral took place at St George's Chapel, Windsor, on 29 August and his coffin was deposited in the Royal Tomb House until it was removed to the royal burial ground at Frogmore on the eve of his widow's funeral in 1968. He left three children: Prince Edward, who succeeded him as Duke of Kent (see below); Princess ALEXANDRA OF KENT; and Prince MICHAEL OF KENT. His widow, Princess Marina, who was born at Athens on 30 November 1906, died from an inoperable brain tumour at Kensington Palace on 27 August 1968.

8. **Prince Edward, 2nd Duke of Kent** (1935–) The elder son of Prince George of Kent (see above) and Princess Marina of Greece and Denmark, who was born at 3 Belgrave Square, London, on 9 October 1935 and baptized Edward George Nicholas Paul Patrick at the private chapel in Buckingham Palace on 20 November 1935. He was only six when he succeeded his father as second Duke of Kent in August 1942. He was educated at Eton, Le Rosey in Switzerland and at the Royal Mili-tary Academy, Sandhurst, where he was awarded the Sir James Moncrieff Grierson foreign language prize and also passed the French interpretership examination. Whereas his father chose to make his service career with the Royal Navy, the second duke did so with the Army, being commissioned a Lieutenant in the Royal Scots Dragoon Guards (Carabiniers and Greys) in 1955 and retiring as a Lieutenant-Colonel in 1976. He was promoted to Major-General in 1983 and to Field Marshal in 1993 and has been a personal ADC to his cousin ELIZABETH II since 1966.

The duke took his seat in the House of Lords on 9 December 1959 and became a Knight of the GARTER on his 50th birthday in 1985. He has acted as COUNSELLOR OF STATE on several occasions and has repre-sented the Queen at the independence cele-brations of Sierra Leone in 1961, Uganda in 1962, The Gambia in 1965, and Guyana and Barbados in 1966, and at the coronation of the King of Tonga in 1967. He is Grand Master of the United Grand Lodge of Freemasons of England and patron or presi-dent of many charitable and other organiza-tions as well as being Chancellor of the University of Surrey since 1977.

The duke married at York Minster on 8 June 1961, Katharine Lucy Mary, only daughter of Sir William Arthington Wors-ley, 4th Baronet, and his wife Joyce Morgan, daughter of Sir John Fowler Brunner, 2nd Baronet. The Duchess of Kent, who was born at Hovingham Hall, Yorkshire, on

22 February 1933, is Chancellor of Leeds University, Controller Commandant of the WRAC (with the rank of Major-General), Colonel-in-Chief of several regiments, patron of Kent County Playing Fields Association, of the Spastics Society (now SCOPE), and of the Samaritans among other charities. She has been Royal Patron of Age Concern England since 1993. On 14 January 1994 she became the first member of the royal family to be received into the Roman Catholic Church for over 300 years. By a stroke of irony the duchess is also a direct descendant of the Lord Protector Oliver Cromwell through his fourth daughter Frances.

The Duke and Duchess of Kent have three children: George Philip Nicholas, Earl of St Andrews, who was born on 26 June 1962 and was married on 9 January 1988 to Sylvana Palma, daughter of Maximilian Karl Tomaselli and formerly wife of John Paul Jones, having a son and two daughters; Lady Helen Marina Lucy Windsor, who was born on 28 April 1964 and was married on 18 July 1992 to Timothy Verner Taylor, having one son; and Lord Nicholas Charles Edward Jonathan Windsor, who was born on 25 July 1970.

Keppel, Alice Frederica (1869–1947) Mistress of EDWARD VII, who was the ninth and youngest daughter of Sir William Edmonstone, 4th Baronet, and his wife Mary Elizabeth Parsons. On 1 June 1891 she married Lieutenant-Colonel the Hon. George Keppel, third son of the 7th Earl of Albemarle. Their daughter Violet was born on 6 June 1894 and it was probably soon after that event that Alice first attracted the attention of Albert Edward, Prince of Wales, and became his mistress. Their relationship was widely known in court circles but was conducted with discretion and both the Princess of Wales and Colonel Keppel chose to turn a blind eye. 'Mrs G.K.', as she was referred to by certain members of the royal household, was both beautiful and witty. 'A royal mistress should curtsey first – and then jump into bed', is one of the remarks attributed to her. What could have been an embarrassing situation arose on one occasion at Biarritz in the course of a large luncheon party attended by King Edward. A Portuguese duchess idly picked up the place-card of the man seated next to her and said, 'Kep-pel ... Kep-pel ... How very odd of you to have the same name as the King's mistress'. It was, of course, Alice's husband.

On 24 May 1900 Alice gave birth to her second daughter, Sonia Rosemary, widely believed to be the Prince of Wales's child, although never acknowledged as such. She grew up to become the grandmother of Camilla Parker Bowles, whose name was frequently linked in the press with that of CHARLES, PRINCE OF WALES during the break-up of his marriage.

When Edward VII lay dying at BUCKINGHAM PALACE in May 1910 Queen ALEXANDRA in a typically gracious gesture sent for Mrs Keppel and led her by the hand to the king's bedside to make her farewells. Mrs Keppel survived the Edwardian age and two world wars. Commenting on the events leading up to the abdication of EDWARD VIII she observed, 'We did it better in *my* day.' She died on 11 September 1947 and her husband survived her a little over two months, dying on 22 November following.

Kew Palace Royal residence in Kew Gardens, London, which was originally known as the Dutch House before being first leased by Queen Caroline (*see* CAROLINE OF ANSBACH) in 1728. The neighbouring White House was acquired by FREDERICK LOUIS, PRINCE OF WALES in 1731. The two houses were used as one by George III and Queen CHARLOTTE, until the White House was demolished in 1802 and a new, much grander palace was built, designed by James Wyatt in the Gothic style. This was never finished and was knocked down in 1827–8. The Dutch House still survives and is now open to the public. The garden surrounding Kew Palace is now the Royal Botanic Garden and has long been open to the public.

King's Champion The lords of the manor of Scrivelsby in Lincolnshire held that manor by the service of exercising the office of King's Champion at coronations. The service consisted of riding fully armed into WESTMINSTER HALL during the coronation banquet and issuing a challenge to anyone who might dispute the sovereign's title to the throne. The office belonged originally to the Marmion family and passed by marriage to the Dymokes in the reign of EDWARD III. Sir John Dymoke successfully claimed the right to act as Champion at the coronation of RICHARD II in 1377, and his descendants continued to do so until the coronation of GEORGE IV, the last occasion on which the banquet was held. No claim was made at the coronations of WILLIAM IV and Queen VICTORIA, but Frank Scaman Dymoke claimed to exercise the office at the coronation of

EDWARD VII. Since the banquet was not revived, he served instead as Standard Bearer of England and acted in the same capacity at the coronations of GEORGE V (1911) and GEORGE VI (1937). He died in August 1946. The present holder of the office is his grandson, Lieutenant-Colonel John Lindley Marmion Dymoke, the Honourable the Queen's Champion and Standard Bearer of England, who served at the coronation of ELIZABETH II in 1953.

King's Evil Popular name for tuberculosis of the lymphatic glands of the neck, formerly known as scrofula. It was believed that the condition could be cured by the sovereign's touch in the exercise of a mystic healing power derived from EDWARD THE CONFESSOR. The custom was also observed in France. An elaborate religious ceremony evolved in which the sovereign stroked the necks of the afflicted persons and hung a specially minted coin known as a 'touch piece' around their necks. The last sovereign to perform the ceremony in England was Queen ANNE, and Dr Samuel Johnson was among those 'touched' by her in 1712, when he was a child. The Stuart pretenders continued the practice in exile and Prince Charles Edward STUART held a healing ceremony in Edinburgh in 1745.

Knighthood Admission to one of various orders, which can be granted only by the specific command of the sovereign. Unlike other honours, knighthoods cannot be won through reason of birth alone but are usually conferred for military or other services rendered. In medieval times it was customary for a knight to progress to the rank by serving under a lord as a page and esquire before finally winning the right to bear arms. Prior to the reign of HENRY III, knights were obliged to perform military service in return for the honour, which could also be bestowed by barons and princes of the Church as well as the reigning king or queen.

The oldest of the various orders of knighthood is the Order of the GARTER, though the Order of the Hospital of St John of Jerusalem also has ancient origins. Another order is the Sovereign Military Order of Malta, a Roman Catholic religious order (though this has no official standing). Better known are the Order of the THISTLE, the Order of the BATH, the Order of the BRITISH EMPIRE, the ROYAL VICTORIAN ORDER, the Order of the STAR OF INDIA and the Order of ST MICHAEL AND ST GEORGE, No new admissions have been made to the two Indian orders and the Irish order of ST PATRICK since the two countries achieved independence. Knights who are not attached to a specific order are known as knights bachelor. *See also* ACCOLADE.

L

Lady in waiting General term applied to those ladies who are appointed by the queen, the queen mother and other female members of the royal family to act as personal attendants and companions when undertaking official duties. In the case of queens, the ladies are divided into Ladies of the Bedchamber and Women of the Bedchamber, the former being peeresses and the latter ladies of lesser rank. *See also* BEDCHAMBER CRISIS.

Lancaster, Earls and Dukes of The royal earls and dukes of Lancaster are here dealt with chronologically.

1. **Edmund 'Crouchback', Earl of Lancaster** (1245–96) The second son and fourth child of HENRY III and ELEANOR OF PROVENCE, who was born in London on 16 January 1245 and who, as his nickname implies, was afflicted with a spinal deformity from birth. He was only nine years old when the Papal Legate, Albert, offered him the kingdom of Sicily on 7 March 1254, the offer being confirmed by Pope Innocent IV on 14 May 1254. The boy's father was overwhelmed by this honour and at once ordered a great seal to be engraved for Edmund as King of Sicily. At the end of May, Edmund and his mother proceeded to Bordeaux and on 18 October 1255, according to Matthew Paris, Edmund was invested with the kingdom of Sicily and Apulia by the bishop of Bologna. He never obtained possession of the kingdom, however, for the pope concluded a peace with Manfred, the rival claimant for the kingdom, and allowed him to retain possession. Although Henry renounced Sicily on Edmund's behalf in June 1257, the claim lingered on for several years, and it was not until the summer of 1264 that Edmund and his father were absolved by the pope of all their obligations in respect of Sicily.

Edmund spent his early years in travelling to and from France with his mother, gathering mercenaries and money to fight in his father's struggle with the barons. After Simon de Montfort had been killed at Evesham, Edmund had a charter, dated 26 October 1265, granting him and the heirs of his body the honour of Leicester and all the lands that had been held by de Montfort. He did not, however, assume the title of Earl of Leicester. Further grants of castles and lands followed, including the honour, county, castle and town of Lancaster on 30 June 1267.

In 1268 Edmund took the cross with his elder brother Edward (*see* EDWARD I, KING OF ENGLAND) but did not proceed immediately to the Holy Land. On 8 or 9 April 1269 he was married at WESTMINSTER ABBEY to Aveline, only surviving daughter and heiress of William de Forz, Count of Aumale, by his wife Isabel, elder daughter of Baldwin de Reviers, Earl of Devon. He finally reached Jerusalem in 1271, but returned by the end of the following year. His wife died childless at Stockwell on 10 November 1274 and was buried in Westminster Abbey, where her tomb may still be seen on the north side of the sanctuary. Edmund married secondly, at Paris between 27 July and 29 October 1276, Blanche, widow of Henri I, King of Navarre, and only daughter of Robert I, Count of Artois (third son of Louis VIII, King of France), by his wife Mahaut, daughter of Henri II, Duke of Brabant. She bore him three sons, THOMAS and HENRY, both successively Earls of Lancaster (*see below*), and John, Lord of Beaufort, and Nogent Lartauld, who was born before May 1286 and died unmarried in France before 1327, and a daughter, Mary, who died young.

Edmund was a faithful supporter of his brother Edward I and was appointed commander in Wales in August 1277. He captured and executed LLYWELYN III in 1282. The rest of his life was spent busily in England and in France, where at the time of his death he was Lieutenant of Aquitaine. He died at Bayonne, while besieging Bordeaux, on 5 June 1296. His body was returned to England and buried in

Westminster Abbey near that of his first wife. His widow, who was probably born between 1245 and 1250, died in Paris on 2 May 1302. Her body was probably brought to England and interred in the convent of sisters of St Clare, which she had founded in Aldgate.

2. **Thomas, 2nd Earl of Lancaster** (*c*.1279–1322) The eldest son and successor of Edmund, Earl of Lancaster (*see above*), and his second wife Blanche, who was born in about 1279 or 1280 and was still a minor when he succeeded his father in 1296. He was considered of full age on 8 September 1298, when he rendered homage to his uncle the king and had seisin of his father's lands, being appointed Sheriff of Lancashire in the same year. Thomas served in a variety of minor capacities throughout the remainder of EDWARD I's reign and at the coronation of his cousin EDWARD II on 25 February 1308 carried Curtana, the Sword of Mercy. The following year he was appointed Steward of England.

In 1310 he joined the confederation of nobles in opposition to Piers Gaveston, the king's favourite, and was present when Gaveston was beheaded on 19 June 1312. He was ordered to appear before the king at Westminster, but refused and joined forces with the Earls of Hereford and Warwick to march on London. They were stopped at Ware, however, and in December the papal legates intervened to effect a peace between them and the king. On 16 October 1313 Thomas was pardoned for his part in Gaveston's execution. He was appointed the King's Lieutenant and Chief Captain of all the forces against the Scots in the Marches on 8 August 1315. At the Parliament held at Lincoln in February 1316, Thomas was appointed chief counsellor to the king, but he neglected public business to attend to his private affairs.

On or before 28 October 1294 he had married a 13-year-old heiress, Alice, daughter of Henry de Lacy, 3rd Earl of Lincoln, and his first wife Margaret, daughter and heiress of Sir William Longespée, a claimant to the earldom of Salisbury. There were no children and in 1317 Alice was abducted, apparently not unwillingly, by Sir Richard de St Martin, a knight of the Earl of Surrey, who connived at the abduction. It was claimed that Alice had been pre-contracted to Richard before her marriage to Thomas and she agreed that this was so. Thomas engaged in a private war to regain his wife, but did not succeed in so doing and according to some

accounts their marriage was annulled in 1318. Thomas was in violent opposition to the Despensers, the king's favourites, and took up residence in his castle at Pontefract, where he marshalled his forces and was soon in a state of open rebellion against the king. His men laid siege to the king's castle of Tickhill and captured it in February 1322. They then marched to Burton-on-Trent where they were defeated by the royal forces on 10 March. Thomas and the remainder of his army made their way to Boroughbridge, where they were completely defeated by Sir Andrew de Harcla and Thomas himself was taken prisoner on 16 March. He was taken back to Pontefract and there beheaded in the presence of the king on 22 March 1322. He was buried in the Priory of St John at Pontefract.

In a short while thereafter Thomas began to be regarded as a martyr. On 3 February 1327 he was rehabilitated and the sentence against him annulled. EDWARD III built a chapel on the site of his execution and on three occasions requested the pope to canonize Thomas, but his request was never complied with – perhaps not unjustly, since although Thomas had become a popular hero through his opposition to Edward II's misgovernment, his motives were by no means altruistic.

Thomas's widow (or former wife) Alice, who was born probably at Denbigh on 25 December 1281, married secondly, in about 1331, Eubule l'Estrange, Lord Strange, who died on 8 September 1335. She married thirdly, before 23 March 1336, Hugh de Fresnes, Lord Fresnes, who died in the following December or January. Alice died on 2 October 1348 and was buried with her second husband at Barlings Abbey.

3. **Henry, 3rd Earl of Lancaster** (*c*.1281–1345) The second son of Edmund 'Crouchback', 1st Earl of Lancaster (*see above*), who was born at Grosmont Castle, Monmouth, in about 1281. He married before 2 March 1297, Maud, daughter and heiress of Sir Patrick de Chaworth, of Kidwelly, and his wife Isabella, daughter of William Beauchamp, 1st Earl of Warwick. Shortly after his marriage Henry had livery of Monmouth and his father's lands beyond the Severn and in the next few years served with the king in Flanders and in Scotland. He carried the Rod with the Dove at the coronation of Queen Isabel on 25 February 1308. Henry took no part in the rebellion of his brother Thomas and after the latter's execution petitioned the king for the earl-

doms of Lancaster and Leicester. The earldom and honour of Leicester (with the exception of Kenilworth Castle) were allowed to him by a writ of livery on 29 March 1324.

In September 1326 Henry joined the queen and Mortimer against EDWARD II and at the council held at Bristol on 26 October to elect Prince Edward as Keeper of the Realm, he was acknowledged as Earl of Lancaster and Leicester. He was sent in pursuit of Edward II, who had fled to Wales, and captured him at Neath, being then made responsible for his custody at Kenilworth, where he was present when the king was forced to abdicate. He was present at the coronation of EDWARD III, whom he knighted and of whom he was appointed guardian and chief counsellor. The queen and Mortimer usurped his authority and after attempting to form a confederacy against them, Henry was obliged to submit to their superior numbers. From 1329 to 1330 he was sent on an embassy to France, and it was probably while there that he became blind. On the downfall of Mortimer in October 1330 he was received back into the king's favour and on 27 March 1332 he was granted the sum of 500 marks yearly for the better maintenance of his estate. Thereafter he remained in favour for the rest of his life, fulfilling such offices as his blindness permitted.

His wife Maud had died between 19 February 1317 and 3 December 1322, and was buried at Mottisfont Priory. She had borne him one son and six daughters. Henry remarried, on an unknown date, Alix, widow of Jean, Sieur d'Arcies sur Aube et de Chacenay, and daughter of Jean de Joinville, Seneschal of Champagne (the chronicler of St Louis) and his second wife Alix de Risnel. There were no children of this marriage. Earl Henry died at Leicester on 22 September 1345 and was buried 'with great state' on the south side of the high altar of Newark Abbey, Leicester.

4. Henry 'Wryneck', 4th Earl and 1st Duke of Lancaster (c.1314–61)

The only son of Henry, 3rd Earl of Lancaster (see above), and his first wife Maud de Chaworth, who was born at Grosmont Castle, Monmouthshire, in about 1314. Some authorities date his birth much earlier, to 1299 or 1302, but the later date seems preferable since he did not begin to take any part in public affairs until his father went blind in 1330. In September 1333 his father granted him Kidwelly, Grosmont and other lordships

west of the Severn. He was summoned to a council at Nottingham in 1335 and on 16 March 1337 he was created Earl of Derby. He accompanied EDWARD III on many of his campaigns in Scotland and on the continent. He succeeded his father as Earl of Lancaster, Earl of Leicester and Steward of England in 1345 and was a Founder Knight of the Order of the GARTER in 1348. On 20 August 1349 he was created Earl of Lincoln and on 6 March 1351 he was created Duke of Lancaster, this being the second dukedom created in England (the first being that of Cornwall). The duchy carried palatine jurisdiction.

Henry went on many diplomatic missions, to the pope, the King of Castile, Prussia, Poland and the King of Navarre. On 5 April 1359 he was created Earl of Moray by DAVID II, KING OF SCOTS. In the course of a lifetime of faithful service to his king and country, 'the good duke', as he became known, found time to be the benefactor of many religious foundations, among them adding to his father's foundation of the Collegiate Church of St Mary the Greater at Leicester. He is also regarded as the founder of Corpus Christi College, Cambridge.

Henry married in about 1334, Isabel, daughter of Henry, 1st Lord Beaumont, and his wife Alice, daughter of Sir Alexander Comyn. She possibly bore him one son, who died in infancy, and also two daughters, Maud and Blanche, who became their father's co-heiresses.

The duke died of the plague at Leicester on 24 March 1361 and was buried on the south side of the high altar of Newark Abbey, Leicester. His widow survived him and was buried with him, but the date of her death is unknown. Their elder daughter, Maud, who was born on 4 April 1339, married first, on 1 November 1344, Ralph, son and heir of Ralph, Lord Stafford, and became a widow at the age of eight in 1348. She married secondly, in the King's Chapel at Westminster in 1352, Wilhelm I, Duke of Bavaria, Count of Zeeland, Holland and Hainault, a nephew of Queen PHILIPPA, and died without issue on 10 April 1362, of plague, but reputedly from poison administered at the instigation of her sister's husband John of Gaunt (see below). Duke Henry's younger daughter, Blanche, who was born on 25 March 1345, married John of Gaunt as his first wife.

5. John of Gaunt, Duke of Lancaster (1340–99)

The fourth son of EDWARD III and PHILIPPA OF HAINAULT, who was born at the

Abbey of St Bavon in Ghent probably in March 1340. On 20 September 1342 he was created Earl of Richmond and at the age of 10 he was on board his brother the Prince of Wales's ship during a sea battle off Winchelsea. He married, in the Queen's Chapel at Reading on 19 May 1359, Blanche, younger daughter of Henry 'Wryneck', Duke of Lancaster (*see above*). In the same year he took part in his father's French campaign. He was summoned to Parliament as Earl of Richmond in November 1360 and was nominated a Knight of the GARTER in 1361. On the death of his father-in-law he came into possession of one half of the duke's estates, including the castle and honour of Lancaster, and he was summoned to Parliament as Earl of Lancaster and Richmond on 14 August 1361. In the following year, the death of his sister-in-law without issue brought him the other half of the estates, including the honour and earldom of Leicester, and on 13 November 1362 John was created Duke of Lancaster.

John accompanied his brother, Edward, Prince of Wales, on his Spanish expedition and in June 1369 was appointed the King's Lieutenant in the north of France. His wife Blanche died at Bolingbroke Castle on 12 September 1369 and was buried in St Paul's Cathedral, London. In September 1371, John married secondly, at Roquefort in Guienne, Constance, the elder surviving daughter and co-heiress of Pedro I, King of Castile and Leon, and his mistress (whom he claimed to have married secretly) Maria de Padilla. In right of his new wife, John assumed the style of King of Castile and Leon, but he was never able to obtain possession of the kingdom and in May 1388 resigned his claim in favour of the *de facto* king Enrique III, who later became his son-in-law.

In August 1373 John invaded France and marched unopposed from Calais to Bordeaux. He negotiated a truce with France, concluded at Bruges on 27 June 1375. At the coronation of his nephew RICHARD II in July 1377, the duke acted as High Steward and presided over the Court of Claims. As Earl of Leicester he carried the Sword of Mercy (Curtana) and as Earl of Lincoln carved at the king's table at the coronation banquet. In the following years he led expeditions against French marauders on the south coast and into Scotland. It was while he was absent in Scotland that his palace in London was attacked and burned by Wat Tyler and his insurgents.

On 2 March 1390 John was created Duke

of Aquitaine in Parliament with palatinate rights. His wife Constance, who was born at Castro Kerez in 1354, died at Leicester Castle on 24 March 1394 and was buried in St Mary's Church (the Newark) there. John spent from September 1394 to December 1395 looking after his interests in Guienne. Following his return, he contracted a third marriage, at Lincoln on or soon after 13 January 1396, to his long-time mistress, Catherine Swynford, who had been governess to his daughters. The four children she had already borne him were declared legitimate by the pope and legitimated by Act of Parliament on 9 February 1397. They bore the surname of Beaufort, from the castle in Champagne where they were born.

The duke's busy life of service continued until his death at Leicester Castle on 3 or 4 February 1399. He was buried with his first wife Blanche in St Paul's Cathedral, where their tomb with its alabaster effigies was destroyed in the Great Fire of London.

John of Gaunt was a man of culture and refinement, an amateur poet and a friend of Chaucer, who was married to a sister of the duke's last wife. He was also a patron of Wycliffe, approving and encouraging his translation of the Bible into English. The duke had four sons and three daughters by his first wife, one son and one daughter by his second, and three sons and one daughter by his third. He also had an illegitimate daughter by Marie de St Hilaire, Blanche, who married Sir Thomas Morieux.

6. **Henry of Bolingbroke, 2nd Duke of Lancaster** *see* HENRY IV.

7. **Henry of Monmouth, Duke of Lancaster** *see* HENRY V.

8. Since the dukedom of Lancaster merged in the Crown on the accession of HENRY V in 1413 it has never again been conferred. In Lancashire the loyal toast takes the form of 'The Queen, Duke of Lancaster'. Queen VICTORIA used the title 'Countess of Lancaster' as an incognito when travelling abroad.

Lancaster, House of The general designation of the branch of the PLANTAGENETS that reigned from 1399 to 1461 in the persons of HENRY IV, HENRY V and HENRY VI.

Leopold, Prince, Duke of Albany *see* ALBANY, PRINCE LEOPOLD, DUKE OF.

Leopold of Saxe-Coburg, Prince (1790–1865) The third son of Franz Friedrich Anton, Duke of Saxe-Saalfeld-Coburg, and his second wife, Auguste Caroline Sophie, daughter of Heinrich XXIV, Count Reuss-Ebersdorf, who was born at Coburg on 16 December 1790 and received the names of Leopold Georg Friedrich. As a young man he entered the Russian service and served with distinction throughout the Napoleonic wars. In 1814 he accompanied the allied sovereigns to London and there met Princess CHARLOTTE OF WALES, the only daughter of the Prince Regent (later GEORGE IV). After serving in the army of the Rhine in 1815, Leopold returned to London to become Charlotte's accepted suitor. He was naturalized a British subject and appointed a Knight of the GARTER and a General in the Army, although a proposal to created him Duke of Kendal came to naught. The couple were married at CARLTON HOUSE on 2 May 1816 and thereafter took up residence at Claremont House, near Esher in Surrey, where they led a blissfully happy and care-free existence until the princess died on 6 November 1817 after being delivered of a stillborn son.

Leopold, who was devastated by his wife's death, stayed on in England and was destined to become the mainstay of his widowed sister VICTORIA, DUCHESS OF KENT and a father figure to her daughter, the future Queen VICTORIA, who was to consult her 'Uncle Leopold' on all matters both public and private for the remainder of his life. In 1830 Leopold declined the crown of Greece, but later agreed to accept that of the newly formed Kingdom of Belgium in June 1831, entering Brussels and taking the oath on 21 July. He married secondly, at Compiègne on 9 August 1832, Louise Marie Thérèse Charlotte Isabelle, eldest daughter of Louis Philippe I, King of the French, and they had three sons and one daughter.

Leopold proved a wise and efficient ruler and was widely respected throughout Europe. He died at the palace of Laeken, outside Brussels, on 10 December 1865, and was buried beside Queen Louise Marie, who had died at Ostende on 11 October 1850, in the Royal Tomb House at Laeken on 16 December. He had never converted from the Lutheran faith and consequently the portion of the tomb allotted to him remained unconsecrated by the Roman Catholic Church.

Linlithgow Palace Royal residence, now ruined, at Linlithgow in Lothian region, south-east Scotland. The first timber palace or manor house at Linlithgow ('the loch of the wet valley') was built on a promontory

into the loch by DAVID I (1124–53). The rents of the lordship of Linlithgow were from his time onwards settled on the Scottish queens as a jointure or dowry. EDWARD I occupied Linlithgow during his Scottish campaign and replaced the wooden building with a stronger one, which was recaptured by the Scots in 1313 and later destroyed by ROBERT BRUCE. DAVID II again rebuilt it and most of the town, but his work was destroyed by fire in 1424. JAMES I, on his return from England in that year, commenced the rebuilding, which was to continue intermittently for the next century. From 1461 to 1462 the palace was the residence of the English king HENRY VI and Queen MARGARET OF ANJOU, who fled to Scotland after their defeat at Towton.

JAMES IV gave the palace to his wife MARGARET TUDOR and their son, the future JAMES V, was born there in 1512. A legend has it that Queen Margaret arranged for a man purporting to be St John to appear before the king in Linlithgow chapel to warn him not to go to war with England. If so, it was to no avail. When James V brought his second wife MARY OF GUISE to Linlithgow following their marriage, she was to declare that she had never seen so princely a place. MARY, QUEEN OF SCOTS was born at Linlithgow and it became a favourite residence of JAMES VI, who continued its building. After his accession to the English throne, however, the palace fell into a state of disrepair and partially fell into ruin. Some repairs were effected and the palace was still habitable in 1746, when William Augustus, Duke of CUMBERLAND's army bivouacked there after the battle of Falkirk. Unfortunately, the soldiers omitted to smother the fires and after they left the palace was gutted by fire on 31 January 1746. It remains a roofless and picturesque ruin.

On 11 June 1914 GEORGE V and Queen MARY OF TECK held a court in the Lyon Hall, and in 1954 ELIZABETH II held a reception in the ruins. The palace ruins and grounds are open to the public.

Lisle, Arthur Plantagenet, Viscount (c.1462–1542) The illegitimate son of EDWARD IV by the widowed Elizabeth, Lady Lucy, daughter of Thomas Wayte, a Hampshire landowner, who was probably born in about 1462. He appears to have lived with his mother at court until the age of 10 and then with one of her family in Hampshire. In 1501 he joined the household of his half-sister ELIZABETH OF YORK and on her death in 1503 he joined that of HENRY VII.

He became a favourite and close companion of his half-nephew HENRY VIII and on 12 November 1511 married Elizabeth, widow of Edmund Dudley (who was beheaded on 18 August 1510), and daughter of Edward Grey, Viscount Lisle, by his first wife Elizabeth Talbot, Baroness Lisle in her own right. Arthur was knighted on 14 October 1513 and acted as Sheriff of Hampshire from 1513 to 1514. In 1519 his wife succeeded her niece Elizabeth as Baroness Lisle and on 25 April 1523 Arthur was created Viscount Lisle. He was nominated a Knight of the GARTER in 1524 and appointed Vice-Admiral of England in 1525. He continued in high favour, accompanying Henry VIII to Calais and serving as governor thereof from 1533 to 1540. He acted as pantler at the coronation of ANNE BOLEYN, was Lord Warden of the Cinque Ports from 1536 until his death and was appointed a Privy Councillor in 1540. His wife died in about 1525 and he married secondly, in 1529, Honor, widow of Sir John Basset (who died 31 January 1528), and daughter of Sir Thomas Grenville, by his first wife Isabel, daughter of Otes Gilbert.

In 1540 Lisle became the victim of a conspiracy to discredit him. He was ordered to surrender the keys of Calais and return to England, where he was imprisoned in the Tower on suspicion of treason in May 1540. His innocence of the charge being finally established, he was pardoned at the end of February 1542 and his release ordered, but the joy and excitement this occasioned proved too much for a man in his 80th year and Lisle died in the Tower on 3 March 1542. He was buried in the Chapel of St Peter ad Vincula. His widow died at Tehidy, Cornwall, in 1566.

Lord Lisle left three daughters by his first wife: Frances, who married first, her step-brother John Basset, and secondly, Thomas Monk, of Potheridge, Devon, by whom she was the great-grandmother of General Monk, who played a leading role in the restoration of CHARLES II; Elizabeth, who married Sir Francis Jobson; and Bridget, who married William Carden, of Kent. The letters written to and by Lord Lisle during his service as Lord Deputy of Calais have been published and provide a fascinating insight into the lives and manners of Tudor times.

Little gentleman in black velvet Jacobite toast referring to the mole whose hill caused WILLIAM III's horse to stumble and throw him, thus precipitating his illness and death.

Llywelyn (I) ap Seisyll, King of Deheubarth and Gwynedd (d.1023) The son of an otherwise completely unrecorded Seisyll and Prawst, daughter of Elisse, a younger son of ANARAWD AP RHODRI, KING OF GWYNEDD, who married ANGHARAD FERCH MAREDUDD, daughter and heiress of MARE-DUDD AB OWAIN AP HYWEL DDA, King of Deheubarth and Gwynedd and succeeded his father-in-law in 999. He made himself ruler or overlord of all Wales, defeating Aeddan ap Blegywryd and his four sons in 1018 and an Irish pretender Rhain, who claimed he was a son of King Maredudd, in 1022. He died in the following year, leaving a son Gruffydd (*see* GRUFFYDD AP LLYWE-LYN), who later obtained the throne. The *Brut y Tywysogion* calls Llywelyn 'the supreme and most praiseworthy king of all Britain. And in his time, as the old men were wont to say, the whole land from the one sea to the other was fruitful in men and in every kind of wealth, so that there was no one in want nor anyone in need within his territory; and there was not one township empty or desolate.'

Llywelyn (II) Fawr ('the Great') ap Iorwerth, Prince of Gwynedd (1173–1240) The son of IORWERTH DRWYNDWN, PRINCE OF GWYNEDD and his wife Marared (or Margaret), daughter of MADOG AP MARE-DUDD, KING OF POWYS, who was probably born at Dolwyddelan, the royal manor of Nantconwy. He was only about a year old when his father died and the throne of Gwynedd was usurped by Iorwerth's half-brother DAFYDD I in 1174. Llywelyn was probably taken to Powys and brought up under the protection of his maternal relatives there. In 1194 he gathered a force and defeated Dafydd, gaining a share in the government of Perfeddwlad and sole rule there in 1197. He captured Mold in 1199 and by 1203 had regained the whole of Gwynedd, being finally acknowledged as overlord by all the other Welsh princes.

In 1205 he married Joan (*see* JOAN, PRINCESS OF GWYNEDD), the natural daughter of JOHN, KING OF ENGLAND, but in spite of this, hostilities with England broke out in 1210. Wales was invaded and some territory lost temporarily. However, these areas were regained in 1212 and over the next six years Llywelyn captured Carmarthen, Cardigan and Montgomery, the great strongholds of the Marches, although they were lost again in 1223. Llywelyn acquired Builth from William de Breos in 1229 and recaptured Cardigan in 1231. In 1230 he assumed the style of 'Prince of Aberffraw and Lord of Snowdon' and in 1234 a successful treaty with England, the 'Pact of Middle', brought lasting peace.

Llywelyn had an only son by Joan, Dafydd (see DAFYDD II), and in 1229 he got the boy's half-uncle HENRY III to acknowledge him as his sole heir and successor, to the detriment of an elder son, Gruffydd, born to him by Tangwystl, daughter of Llywarch Goch of Rhos. Dafydd was apparently Llywelyn's only child by Joan, who died in 1237, but he also had five daughters for whom he arranged advantageous marriages. They were: Gwenllian, married to William de Lacy; Helen, married first, to John le Scot, Earl of Chester, and secondly, to Robert de Quincy; Gwladus *Ddu* ('the Black'), married first, to Reginald de Breos, and secondly, to Roger Mortimer, of Wigmore; Margaret, married first, to John de Breos, and secondly, to Walter Clifford; and Angharad, married to Maelgwn Fychan, son of Maelgwn ap Rhys, Lord of Ceredigion. It is interesting to note that the present CHARLES, PRINCE OF WALES descends from the last four of these ladies, whose blood united in the issue of HENRY VII and ELIZABETH OF YORK. Francis Jones, the late Wales Herald Extraordinary, referred to this fact as 'The Genealogical Triumph of Llywelyn the Great' (see Appendix XXX).

Llywelyn died at Aberconwy on 11 April 1240 and was buried in the abbey there, of which he had been a great benefactor.

Llywelyn (III) ap Gruffydd, Prince of Wales (d.1282) The second son of GRUFFYDD AP LLYWELYN (elder son of LLYWELYN THE GREAT) and his wife Senena, who is first heard of in the entourage of his half-uncle Prince DAFYDD II in 1245 and appears to have been his designated heir. Following Dafydd's death in February 1246, Llywelyn succeeded and concluded the peace of Woodstock with HENRY III of England in 1247. For the first eight years of his reign he had to share power with his elder brother Owain, but he defeated him and their younger brother DAFYDD at Bryn Derwin in 1255 and set about reuniting his realm. He received the homage of all the other Welsh princes (with the exception of GRUFFYDD AP GWENWYNWYN, who submitted later in 1263) in 1258 and assumed the style of Prince of Wales, being officially recognized as such by Henry III, by the peace of Montgomery in 1267.

Llywelyn was married at Worcester on 13 October 1278 to Eleanor, daughter of Simon de Montfort, Earl of Leicester, and his wife Eleanor (see ELEANOR, PRINCESS, COUNTESS OF PEMBROKE AND LEICESTER), youngest daughter of King JOHN. The match had been contracted as far back as 1265, when Llywelyn had joined de Montfort in his rebellion, and had then been postponed because of the bride's forcible detention at Windsor by her cousin EDWARD I. However, the king was present at the wedding. Eleanor, who was born at Kenilworth about the end of September 1252, gave birth to a daughter Gwenllian on 19 June 1282 and died in childbirth then or shortly after. She was buried at Llanfaes.

The uneasy peace with England was ended when Llywelyn's brother Dafydd attacked Hawarden on Palm Sunday (22 March) 1282. Llywelyn was campaigning near Builth when he was killed on the banks of the Irfon by a man who was unaware of his identity. His head was hacked from his body and sent to London for public display. The rest of his body was buried in the Cistercian Abbey of Cwm Hir. Llywelyn's death marked the end of Welsh independence and he is remembered as 'Llywelyn the Last'. His only child Gwenllian became a nun at Sempringham and died there on 7 June 1337.

Looty Queen VICTORIA's pet pekingese dog, so called because it had been looted from the imperial palace in Peking in the course of one of the Chinese wars.

Lord-in-waiting A political appointment in the royal household.

Lord Protector Title generally used until Tudor times for persons appointed to act as regents for sovereigns during their minorities. Under the COMMONWEALTH it became the title of head of state assumed by Oliver Cromwell and his son, Richard Cromwell.

Louis, Louisa (1771–1838) The devoted dresser of Princess CHARLOTTE OF WALES and later equally devoted to Queen VICTORIA, who was born at Erbach in 1771. Queen Victoria in reminiscences that she wrote in 1872 says that 'Louie', as she was known, was 'beloved and respected by all who knew her' and that she was 'the only really devoted Attendant of the poor Princess, whose governesses paid little real attention to her – and who never left her, and was with her when she died'. Mrs Louis died in London on 15 April 1838 and Queen Victoria, writing to her uncle King LEOPOLD of the Belgians two days later, said: 'I don't think I have *ever* been so much overcome or distressed by anything, almost, as by the death of this my earliest friend; it is the first link that has been broken of my first and infantine affections.' The queen erected a tablet to her memory in St Martin-in-the-Fields.

Louisa, Princess, Queen of Denmark (1724–51) The fifth daughter and ninth and youngest child of GEORGE II and CAROLINE OF ANSBACH, who was born at Leicester House, London, between four and five o'clock in the evening of 7 December (18 December new style) 1724. When she was 18 a marriage was arranged for her with Crown Prince Frederik of Denmark. She left ST JAMES'S PALACE on 19 October and arrived in Hanover on 27 October 1743. Her proxy marriage was solemnized there three days later, her brother William Augustus, Duke of CUMBERLAND standing in for the bridegroom. Princess Louisa then proceeded to Denmark and was married in person at Christiansborg on 30 November/ 11 December 1743. Just under three years later the death of her father-in-law Christian VI and her husband's succession as Frederik V made her Queen of Denmark in August 1746.

Louisa had two sons (of whom the elder died young) and three daughters. Although court life in Denmark blossomed under Frederik's reign, his queen was not happy. She missed her English family and, although generally acknowledged to be the best looking of her parents' daughters, was neglected by her husband. She died at Christiansborg Castle on 8 December 1751 after undergoing a painful operation for a rupture, similar to that which had killed her mother. She was buried in Roskilde Cathedral. Her widower remarried and died at Copenhagen on 14 January 1766.

Louisa Anne, Princess (1749–68) The third daughter and seventh child of FREDERICK LOUIS, PRINCE OF WALES and Augusta of Saxe-Gotha (*see* AUGUSTA, PRINCESS OF WALES) who was born at Leicester House, London, at quarter to nine in the morning of 8 March (19 March new style) 1749 and baptized there on 1 April (11 April new style), her godparents being her uncle by marriage the Hereditary Prince of Hesse and her aunts the Princess of Orange and the Queen of Denmark, all represented by proxies. She grew up to be delicate and consumptive and Horace Walpole said that she 'never appeared more than an unhealthy child of thirteen or fourteen'. When she was 15 a marriage was projected between her and Duke Adolf Friedrich IV of Mecklenburg-

Strelitz, the brother of her sister-in-law Queen CHARLOTTE, but the princess's health did not allow matters to proceed. Another suitor was her cousin the Prince of Orange, but that match also had to be abandoned. The princess's malady grew worse and she died at her mother's residence CARLTON HOUSE, London, on 13 May 1768. She was buried in the royal vault in Henry VII's Chapel at WESTMINSTER ABBEY on 21 May.

Louisa Maria Theresa Stuart, Princess (1692–1712) The eighth and youngest daughter of JAMES II and fourth by his second wife MARY OF MODENA, who was born in exile at St Germain-en-Laye, near Paris, on 28 June 1692. She was baptized in the Chapel Royal of St Louis there, receiving the names of Louise Marie, that of Theresa probably being added later at her confirmation. Her godparents were Louis XIV, King of France, and Elisabeth Charlotte, Duchess of Orléans. The ladies of the French court were astounded to see such a young baby unswaddled and clad in shoes and stockings for the ceremony. James II regarded his youngest child as a consolation sent to him in his exile and took a tender farewell of her on his deathbed in September 1701, bidding the nine-year-old girl: 'Consider virtue as the greatest ornament of your sex. Follow close the great pattern of it, your mother, who has been, no less than myself, overclouded with calumny; but Time, the Mother of truth, will, I hope, at last make her virtues shine as bright as the sun.'

'La Consolatrice', as the princess became known, grew up to be a high-spirited and engaging child under the guidance of her governess Lady Middleton and her mother, who also gave her lessons. She was a complete contrast to her less attractive brother, Prince James, who was admonished by the Earl of Perth: 'Why do you have to learn by study the affability which your sister has by nature?' Louisa's godmother, the Duchess of Orléans, described her as resembling her mother, 'but her eyes are more beautiful than the Queen's. She is as sweet and gentle as a lamb'. She was also said to bear a resemblance to her aunt HENRIETTA ANNE, DUCHESS OF ORLÉANS. She was popular at the French court, where she enjoyed dancing and attending the opera. At one time a match was proposed between her and Louis XIV's grandson, the Duke of Berry, but it came to naught and Louisa said, 'While the queen lives, I am too happy to be near her. I cannot support the thought of our separation.'

In April 1712 Prince James and Princess Louisa both fell ill with smallpox and although he recovered, she grew steadily worse and died at St Germain at nine o'clock in the morning of 18 April. She was buried with her father in the church of the English Benedictines in the Rue Faubourg St Jacques in Paris. They were both reburied at St Germain after the French Revolution. There is a charming portrait by Largillière of Louisa with her brother in the National Portrait Gallery in London. There are also portraits of her by an unknown artist in the National Galleries of Scotland and by Hyacinthe Rigaud at Sizergh Castle.

Louise, Princess, Duchess of Argyll (1848–1939) The fourth daughter and sixth child of Queen VICTORIA and Prince ALBERT, who was born at BUCKINGHAM PALACE at eight o'clock in the morning of 18 March 1848. She was baptized by the Archbishop of Canterbury (Dr Sumner) in the private chapel of the palace on 13 May, receiving the names Louisa Caroline Alberta, but in later years the first name by which she was known took the form of Louise. Her godparents were the Duchess of Saxe-Meiningen (for whom Queen ADELAIDE stood proxy), the Hereditary Grand Duchess of Mecklenburg-Strelitz (*see* AUGUSTA, PRINCESS, GRAND DUCHESS OF MECKLENBURG-STRE-LITZ, for whom the Duchess of Cambridge stood proxy) and Duke Gustav of Mecklenburg-Schwerin (for whom Prince Albert stood proxy). Princess Louise grew up to be the most gifted of Queen Victoria's children. She early displayed an artistic bent and was instructed in sculpture by Mary Thornycroft. Among the princess's works is the life-sized seated figure of her mother that stands outside KENSINGTON PALACE.

After she came of age, Louise represented her widowed and reclusive mother on several important occasions, notably at the opening of the Thames Embankment with her brother the Prince of Wales on 13 July 1870. On 9 February 1871, Queen Victoria opened Parliament in person and was accompanied by Princess Louise, whose engagement she announced. The princess had broken with precedent in her choice of a husband. He was John George Edward Henry Douglas Sutherland Campbell, Marquess of Lorne, eldest son of the 8th Duke of Argyll, and had been born at Stafford House, London, on 6 August 1845. The court of Berlin disapproved of the match, considering it one of unequal birth, but when Lord Lorne was told of this by the queen his haughty reply was: 'Ma'am, my ancestors were kings when the Hohenzollerns were parvenus.' The marriage took place at St George's Chapel, Windsor, on 21 March 1871, the bride, arrayed in white satin and Honiton lace, being given away by her mother, her brother, the Prince of Wales, and her uncle, the Duke of Saxe-Coburg and Gotha.

Parliament voted Louise the same dowry of £30,000 and £6,000 per annum as her elder sisters. Lord Lorne was appointed Governor-General of Canada in 1878 and his wife accompanied him there. While in Canada she had a serious tobogganing accident in which one of her ears was ripped off and thereafter her hair was always carefully arranged to cover the disfigurement. The couple returned to England in 1883 and took up residence at Kensington Palace. There were no children of the marriage, which, in spite of its romantic start, did not turn out particularly happily. The marquess apparently had other proclivities and rumour has it that Princess Louise had some of the ground floor windows of Kensington Palace blocked up, either to prevent him from an easy escape at night or to put a stop to him wistfully gazing on the forbidden fruit strolling in Kensington Gardens.

The princess continued to occupy herself with her artistic interests. She modelled the monument to her brother-in-law Prince Henry of Battenberg at Whippingham Church, Isle of Wight, was an Honorary Fellow of the Royal Society of Painters in Water Colour, and contributed to artistic journals under the name of 'Myra Fontenoy'. She also studied under the sculptor Sir Joseph Boehm, who died suddenly when she was visiting him in his studio in 1890, giving rise to some scandalous speculation.

Lord Lorne succeeded his father as 9th Duke of Argyll on 24 April 1900. He died at Kent House, Cowes, Isle of Wight, on 2 May 1914. Princess Louise occupied herself with many charitable works and made her apartments at Kensington Palace a centre for artists. She lived on into the reign of her grand-nephew GEORGE VI and died at Kensington Palace on 3 December 1939. She was cremated at Golders Green Crematorium and her ashes were buried (in a full-sized coffin) in the Royal Burial Ground at Frogmore.

Louise, Princess Royal, Duchess of Fife (1867–1931) The eldest daughter and third child of Albert Edward, Prince of Wales (later EDWARD VII) and ALEXANDRA of Denmark, who was born at Marlborough House, London, at half past six in the morning of 20 February 1867 and was baptized there by the Archbishop of Canterbury on 10 May. Of her impressive array of godparents, her grandmother the Queen of Denmark and the Grand Duchess of Mecklenburg-Strelitz (see AUGUSTA, PRINCESS, GRAND DUCHESS OF MECKLENBURG-STRELITZ) were both present, the others, all represented by proxies, were her aunts, the princesses ALICE, HELENA and LOUISE, the King of the Hellenes, the Crown Prince of Prussia, the Duke of Schleswig-Holstein-Sonderburg-Glücksburg, Landgrave Friedrich of Hesse-Cassel, and Prince Edward of Saxe-Weimar.

Princess Louise and her two younger sisters, VICTORIA and MAUD, grew up under the wing of their extremely possessive mother. They were all intensely shy and were referred to by other members of the royal family as 'the whispering Waleses'. Princess Louise followed the example of her aunt and namesake by choosing a husband from the ranks of the nobility. In June 1889 she became engaged to Alexander William George Duff, 6th Earl of Fife, only son of James Duff, 5th Earl of Fife, and his wife Lady Agnes Georgiana Elizabeth Hay, second daughter of the 18th Earl of Errol and his wife Elizabeth FITZCLARENCE, third natural daughter of WILLIAM IV and Mrs JORDAN. The marriage took place in the private chapel at BUCKINGHAM PALACE on 27 July 1889, and on the same day the bridegroom was created Duke of Fife and Marquess of Macduff. Most of their early married life was spent at East Sheen Lodge, described as the duke's 'suburban seat'. It was there on 16 June 1890 that Louise was delivered of her first child, a stillborn boy. The following year, on 17 May, she gave birth there to a daughter named Alexandra Victoria Alberta Edwina Louise; and on 3 April 1893, also at East Sheen Lodge, to her third and last child Maud Alexandra Victoria Georgina Bertha.

Although the Duke of Fife, born at Edinburgh on 10 November 1849, was 17 years older than his wife, they were a well-matched pair, both enjoying a quiet life of country pursuits and salmon fishing at their Scottish residences, Mar Lodge and Duff House. On 9 November 1905 Princess Louise was declared Princess Royal, the fifth to bear that title, and on the same day her daughters, who had hitherto been styled Lady Alexandra and Lady Maud Duff, were granted the title of Princess with the style of 'Highness' and precedence immediately after all members of the royal family bearing the style of 'Royal Highness'. This was unprecedented and it is said that when Garter King of Arms told King Edward that such a thing could not be done, he received the laconic command, 'Do it!'.

In December 1911 the Princess Royal with her husband and daughters set out to spend the winter in Egypt and the Sudan as they had done for several years, considering the climate beneficial to Louise's always delicate health. Their ship, the P&O liner *Delhi*, went aground in heavy seas off the coast of Morocco. The Fife family were rescued by a boat sent out by HMS *Edinburgh*, but it became swamped by the huge waves and sank beneath them. The family were only saved by their lifebelts and managed with help to reach the shore. The whole incident was described by Louise in a dramatic letter to her brother GEORGE V. The family went on to Khartoum and Cairo, where a few weeks later the Duke of Fife caught a chill, which developed into pneumonia, and he died on 29 January 1912. His body was returned to England and buried first at St George's Chapel, Windsor, but later transferred to Mar Lodge.

When it had become apparent that he and his wife were unlikely to have any further issue, he had had a further creation as Duke of Fife and Earl (not Marquess, this time) of Macduff with special remainder to his daughters and the heirs male of their bodies in 1900. Consequently, on his death Princess Alexandra succeeded as Duchess of Fife in her own right. She later married Prince ARTHUR OF CONNAUGHT. Princess Maud, known as 'little Maudie' in the family, later married Charles Alexander Carnegie, 11th Earl of Southesk, and their son James succeeded his aunt as 3rd Duke of Fife on her death in 1959. Louise, Princess Royal, died at her London residence, 15 Portman Square, on 4 January 1931. She, like her husband, was buried first at St George's Chapel, Windsor, and later transferred to Mar Lodge.

Louise of Stolberg *see* ALBANY, LOUISE, COUNTESS OF.

Lucius, King of Britain (d.AD156) Legendary king who, according to BEDE, wrote to Pope Eleutherius (c.174–80) 'asking to be made a Christian by his direction'. This story is based on a confusion with that of Agbar IX, *alias* Lucius, King of Edessa, who probably sent emissaries to the pope and was later converted. GEOFFREY OF MON-MOUTH has elaborated the story, making Lucius the only son and successor of King Coilus, and naming the priests sent by Eleutherius as Faganus and Duvianus. He further states that Lucius died at Gloucester in 156, which is about 18 years before Eleutherius became pope. He says he left no heirs.

Lulach, King of Scots (c.1032–58) The son of Gillacomgain, Mormaer of Moray, and his wife Gruoch, daughter of Boite (or Bodhe), the youngest son of KENNETH III, who was born in about 1032. He was still an infant when his father was burned alive in his hall and his mother married his successor MACBETH, later King of Scots. After Macbeth's defeat and death at the hands of MALCOLM III in August 1057, his followers took Lulach to SCONE and set him on the royal seat as king. The struggle against Malcolm was hopeless, however, and Lulach was killed at Essie in Strathbogie on 17 March 1058. He was buried on Iona.

Lulach was called 'the Simple', perhaps because of his naïvety in believing he could overcome the superior forces of his enemies. By an unknown wife he left a son, Maelsnectai, who succeeded him as Mormaer of Moray but who was expelled by Malcolm III in 1078 and died a monk in 1085. Lulach also had a daughter (name unknown), who married Aedh (or Heth), set up as Mormaer of Moray in 1078, and who had two sons and a daughter, from whom several lines can be traced.

M

Macbeth, King of Scots (*c*.1005–57) The son of Findleach, Mormaer of Moray, who seized the Scottish throne in 1040. It used to be asserted that his mother was a daughter of MALCOLM II, but this is no longer accepted by historians. He succeeded his cousin Gillacomgain as Mormaer of Moray in 1032 and about the same time married his widow Gruoch, the daughter of Boite (or Bodhe), a son of KENNETH III. It was in her right that he claimed the throne. Macbeth was commander of the forces of DUNCAN I and, encouraged by his wife if we are to believe Shakespeare, murdered him at Bothnagowan (now Pitgaveny), near Elgin, on 14 August 1040 and seized the throne. Duncan's two young sons went into exile and Macbeth's position was secure enough to enable him to make a pilgrimage to Rome in 1050. He was, in fact, a good ruler and popular with his subjects. In 1054 Siward, Earl of Northumberland, invaded Scotland and defeated Macbeth in battle, establishing Duncan's son Malcolm (*see* MALCOLM III) as king of Cumbria. Three years later Malcolm's forces made a further inroad and Macbeth was killed at Lumphanan, Aberdeenshire, on 15 August 1057. He was buried on Iona but his ghost, lamenting the murder of Duncan, is said to haunt Glamis Castle. Macbeth had no children of his own, but his stepson LULACH rallied his supporters and reigned in opposition to Malcolm for seven months.

The somewhat hostile approach taken by Shakespeare to the historical Macbeth may have been influenced by the fact that tradition suggested that JAMES I could claim descent from Banquo, one of Macbeth's victims. The story of Birnam Wood moving to Dunsinane and thus heralding Macbeth's death, meanwhile, may have been borrowed from the legend of the evil Lord Soulis of Hermitage Castle, Roxburghshire, who was warned by a spirit called Redcap Sly to 'beware the coming tree': subsequently his enemies concealed their numbers by carrying branches and defeated him, after which he was wrapped in lead and boiled to death.

Madeleine of France, Queen of Scots (1520–37) The first consort of JAMES V, who was the third daughter of François I, King of France, and his first wife Claude, eldest daughter of Louis XII, King of France, and was born at St Germain-en-Laye on 10 August 1520. She was married to James V at Notre-Dame Cathedral in Paris on 1 January 1537 and returned with him to Scotland, where she soon fell victim to the harsh Scottish climate and died at Holyrood of a galloping consumption on 7 July 1537. She was buried at Holyrood.

Madog ap Gruffydd, Lord of Northern Powys (d.1236) The elder son of GRUFFYDD MAELOR I and his wife Angharad, daughter of OWAIN GWYNEDD, KING OF GWYNEDD, who succeeded his father in 1191 and reigned jointly with his younger brother Owain until the latter's death in 1197. His realm became known as Powys Fadog after him. He vacillated as a supporter of his cousin LLYWELYN THE GREAT for many years, finally adhering to his cause in 1215. Madog married Gwladus, or Isota, daughter of Ithel ap Rhys, King of Gwent, and died in 1236, being buried in the Cistercian Abbey of Valle Crucis, which he had founded near Llangollen. After his death his realm became fragmented by partition among his five sons, GRUFFYDD MAELOR II, Gruffydd Iâl (d.1238), Maredudd (d.1256), Hywel (d.1268?) and Madog Fychan (d.1269). Madog also left a daughter Angharad.

Madog ap Maredudd, Prince (or King) of Powys (d.1160) The eldest son of MAREDUDD AP BLEDDYN, PRINCE OF POWYS and his first wife Hunydd, daughter of Eunydd (or Efnydd) ap Gwernwy, who succeeded his father in 1132 and formed an alliance with the English to protect his realm from the advancing ambitions of OWAIN GWYNEDD, his brother-in-law. This proved unsuccessful and he lost control of many of his lands, but in 1157 he supported HENRY II in his assertion of authority in North Wales and regained much that he had lost. He died at Winchester on or about 9 February 1160 and was buried at Tysilio Church at Meifod. By his wife Susanna, fourth daughter of GRUFFYDD AP CYNAN, KING OF GWYNEDD he had two sons, Llywelyn, who died in 1160, and GRUFFYDD MAELOR I, and two daughters, Marared, who married IORWERTH DRWYNDWN, PRINCE OF GWYNEDD and became the mother of LLYWELYN THE GREAT, and Gwenllian, who married RHYS AP GRUFFYDD, PRINCE OF DEHEUBARTH. Madog also had three natural sons, of whom Owain Brogyntyn was the ancestor of several prominent North Welsh families.

Maelgwn Gwynedd, King of Gwynedd (d.c.547) The son of Cadwallon *Lawhir* (the Long-handed) and great-grandson of CUNEDDA WLEDIG, who, as 'Maglocunus, the island dragon', is one of the five British kings harangued by St GILDAS. GEOFFREY OF MONMOUTH calls him 'Malgo' and says he was the fourth king to reign after ARTHUR, accounting him a brave warrior and a generous man but 'hateful to God, for he was given to the vice of sodom'. He was nicknamed *Hir* (the Tall). As a young man Maelgwn evidently travelled to the north, where he formed an alliance with a Pictish princess, conjecturally a younger sister of DRUST III, GARTNAIT III and CALTRAM, sucessive Kings of the Picts, and became the father of BRUDE I, KING OF THE PICTS and a daughter Domelch, who married Aed, son of GABRAN, KING OF DALRIADA.

Maelgwn returned to North Wales and obtained the kingdom by the overthrow of a maternal uncle, who has not been identified. He further incurred the wrath of the Church by murdering his wife and carrying off a nun, who had previously been married to his nephew. Soon after this he is said to have repented of his evil ways and for a short period entered a monastery. After his return to power, the country was beset by the 'yellow plague'. In an endeavour to escape it, Maelgwn took refuge in a church at Rhos, where, according to legend, he 'beheld the Yellow Plague through the keyhole in the church door and forthwith died'. Maelgwn's wife, according to the genealogies was Sanan, daughter of Cyngen Glodrydd ap Cadell Ddyrnllug, King of Powys. Presumably she is the wife he murdered. His son and successor, RHUN AP MAELGWN, was illegitimate, the son of Gwallwen ferch Afallach, perhaps the abducted nun.

Maelgwn also had other children, including a daughter St Eurgain, whose mother was a daughter of Sawyl Benisel, a great-grandson of Coel Hen.

Magna Carta *see* JOHN, KING OF ENGLAND.

Maid of Honour A junior LADY IN WAITING, chosen from among the unmarried daughters of the nobility and gentry to attend on queens. If untitled, maids of honour were granted the courtesy prefix of 'Honourable', which was retained for life. The last queen to appoint maids of honour was Queen MARY OF TECK.

Maid of Norway Popular name for MARGARET, QUEEN OF SCOTS.

Maiden all for Lorne Romantic reference to Princess Louise (*see* LOUISE, PRINCESS, DUCHESS OF ARGYLL) when she became engaged to the Marquess of Lorne.

Malcolm I, King of Scots (d.954) The son of DONALD II, who succeeded his kinsman CONSTANTINE II on his abdication in 942 and concluded a treaty with EDMUND I, KING OF ENGLAND. He was killed by the men of Moray in 954 and was buried on Iona. His sons, DUBH and KENNETH II, both became king.

Malcolm II, King of Scots (c.954–1034) The younger son of KENNETH II, who was born in about 954 and named after his grandfather MALCOLM I. He reigned as King of Strathclyde from 990 to 995 and again from 997 to 1005, when he succeeded KENNETH III, whom he had defeated and killed at Monzievaird on or about 25 March 1005. He annexed Lothian after the battle of Carham in 1018 and obtained the kingdom of Strathclyde for his grandson DUNCAN I. Malcolm died at Glamis on 25 November 1034 and was buried on Iona. He had no male issue and was succeeded by the son of his elder daughter Bethoc. His younger daughter, Donada, married as his second wife, Sigurd II Digri, Jarl of Orkney and Caithness. Older historians credited him with another daughter, the mother of MACBETH, but this is no longer accepted.

Malcolm III Canmore (Great Head or Chief), King of Scots (c.1031–93) The eldest son of DUNCAN I and Sibylla of Northumbria, who was born about 1031. On his father's accession to the Scottish throne in 1034 he was made King of Strathclyde, although no more than three years old. He was forced into exile in England after his father's murder by

MACBETH in 1040, but after he grew up raised an army and, with the help of Siward, Earl of Northumberland, conquered Lothian in 1054. He defeated and killed Macbeth at Lumphanan in August 1057 and LULACH at Essie in March 1058, thereby becoming the unrivalled King of Scots. He was crowned at SCONE on 25 April 1058. It was probably in the following year that he married Ingibiorg, widow of Thorfinn II, Earl of Caithness and Jarl of Orkney, and daughter of Finn Arnesson of Vrjar, Jarl of Halland, and his wife Bergljot, daughter of Halfdan Sigurdsson, half-brother of Olav II 'the Saint', King of Norway. She bore him three sons, DUNCAN II, Malcolm and Donald, and died before 1069, when Malcolm was married at DUNFERMLINE to his second wife, St MARGARET, by whom he had six other sons and two daughters.

Malcolm did homage to WILLIAM I THE CONQUEROR of England in 1072 and to WILLIAM II in 1091. In 1093 he invaded Northumberland and was treacherously killed at Alnwick on 13 November 1093. He was buried first at Tynemouth, but his body was later removed to Dunfermline by his son ALEXANDER I.

Malcolm IV the Maiden, King of Scots (1142–65) The eldest son of HENRY OF SCOTLAND, EARL OF HUNTINGDON and his wife Ada de Warenne (*see* ADA, COUNTESS OF HUNTINGDON), who was born on 20 March 1142. His father died when he was only 10 years old in June 1152, and in May of the following year Malcolm succeeded his grandfather DAVID I as King of Scots. He was crowned or enthroned at SCONE 'according to the custom of the nation'. Malcolm was nicknamed 'the Maiden' from his youth and girlish complexion. He was compelled to surrender Northumberland and Cumberland to HENRY II of England in 1157 and, as an English baron, served in the expedition against Toulouse in 1159. From 1160 to 1164 he was engaged in suppressing rebellions at home. He never married and died at Jedburgh on 9 December 1165. He was buried at DUNFERMLINE and was succeeded by his brother WILLIAM THE LION.

Mar, John Stewart, Earl of (1457–79) The fourth and youngest son of JAMES II, KING OF SCOTS and MARY OF GUELDRES, who was born probably in about July 1457 and was created Earl of Mar and Garioch between 21 June 1458 and 25 June 1459. He attended the Parliament that met in the Canongate, Edinburgh, in March 1479 and died unmar-

ried soon afterwards. A legend has it that he was murdered by being bled to death on the order of his brother JAMES III, but it is probable that he died of natural causes.

Maredudd The Welsh rulers of this name are here dealt with chronologically.

1. **Maredudd ab Owain ap Hywel Dda, King of Deheubarth and Gwynedd** (d.999) The son of OWAIN AP HYWEL DDA, whom he succeeded as sole ruler of DEHEUBARTH in 986, three elder brothers having already predeceased their father. In the same year he reunited Gwynedd to Deheubarth. He exercised strong leadership against the Saxons and the Danes. His only son Cadwallon, died in 992 and Maredudd was succeeded on his death in 999 by LLYWELYN AP SEISYLL, the husband of his daughter ANGHARAD FERCH MARE-DUDD.

2. **Maredudd ab Owain ab Edwin, King of Deheubarth** (d.1072) The son of Owain ab Edwin ab Einon ab Owain ap Hywel Dda, who gained the throne of DEHEUBARTH following the death of GRUFFYDD AP LLYWE-LYN in August 1063. He spent his whole reign in opposing the Norman invasion but finally allowed the occupation of Gwent and was rewarded by grants of land in England in 1070. He was killed on the banks of the Rhymney in battle with a fellow prince in 1072. His only son, Gruffydd, lived in exile on his father's English estates and was killed while attempting to regain his patrimony from RHYS AP TEWDWR in 1091.

3. **Maredudd ap Bleddyn, Prince of Powys** (d.1132) The son of BLEDDYN AP CYNFYN, KING OF GWYNEDD AND POWYS and Haer, daughter of Cillin ap y Blaidd Rhudd, of Gest, who succeeded to Powys and reigned jointly with his brothers, surviving them all and finally uniting all Powys under his sole rule. He married first, Hunydd, daughter of Eunydd (or Efnydd) ap Gwernwy, and had three sons, MADOG AP MAREDUDD, Gruffydd and Hywel. Maredudd's second wife was Efa, daughter of Bletrws ab Ednowain Bendew, by whom he had another son, Iorwerth Goch (the Red), who submitted to HENRY II and received manors in Shropshire. Maredudd died in 1132 and was succeeded by his eldest son Madog.

4. **Maredudd ap Gruffydd ap Rhys, Prince of Deheubarth** (1130/1–55) The son of GRUFFYDD AP RHYS, PRINCE OF DEHEU-BARTH and his wife Gwenllian, daughter of GRUFFYDD AP CYNAN, KING OF GWYNEDD,

who was born in Ireland in 1130 or 1131, when his parents were living there in exile. He was only six years old when his father died in 1137 and at the age of 16 assisted his half-brother Cadell to expel the Normans from southern Ceredigion. When Cadell was severely wounded by a band of marauders in 1151 he resigned DEHEUBARTH to Maredudd and his younger brother RHYS AP GRUFFYDD jointly. Maredudd gained a reputation as a capable leader but died prematurely in 1155, leaving Rhys as sole ruler.

Margaret, Princess[1] *see* MARGARET, QUEEN OF SCOTS.

Margaret, Princess[2] (1472) The fourth daughter and fifth child of EDWARD IV and ELIZABETH WOODVILLE, who was born on 10 April 1472 and died at the age of 8 months on 11 December 1472. She was buried in Edward the Confessor's Chapel (the Capella Regnum) in WESTMINSTER ABBEY.

Margaret, Princess[3] (1598–1600) The second daughter and third child of James VI, King of Scots (later JAMES I of England) and ANNE OF DENMARK, who was born at Dalkeith Palace on 24 December 1598 and baptized at Holyrood on 15 April 1599. She died at Linlithgow in March 1600, and was buried at Holyrood.

Margaret, Princess, Countess of Pembroke (1346–61) The fifth and youngest daughter and tenth child of EDWARD III and PHILIPPA OF HAINAULT, who was born at WINDSOR CASTLE on St Margaret's Day, 20 July 1346. Froissart asserted that she was born at Calais, but an entry in the Issue Roll of 1350 refers to one Agnes Pore as nurse to 'Margaret of Windsor', the king's daughter. She was married at the Queen's Chapel, Reading, on 19 May 1359 to John Hastings, 2nd Earl of Pembroke, and died soon after 1 October 1361. She was buried at Abingdon, Berkshire. The Earl of Pembroke married secondly, before 26 March 1371, Anne, daughter of Walter, 1st Lord Manny, and MARGARET, DUCHESS OF NORFOLK.

Margaret, Princess, Countess of Snowdon (1930–) The younger daughter of GEORGE VI and Queen Elizabeth (*see* ELIZABETH THE QUEEN MOTHER), who was born at Glamis Castle, Angus, the seat of her maternal grandfather the Earl of Strathmore on 21 August 1930. She was baptized in the private chapel at Buckingham Palace in October and named Margaret Rose, the second name being that of her mother's sister Countess Granville, who was one of her godmothers. The princess was educated privately with her elder sister Princess Elizabeth (*see* ELIZABETH II) and was six years old when the abdication of her uncle EDWARD VIII (*see* ABDICATION CRISIS) brought her father to the throne. In May 1937 she attended the coronation of her parents wearing the dress, small robe and coronet that had been specially designed for the king's daughters for the occasion. The two princesses were appointed ladies of the Order of the CROWN OF INDIA (CI) in 1947, these being the last two appointments made to that order before the dissolution of the Indian Empire.

Princess Margaret was the chief bridesmaid at the wedding of her sister in 1947. She was appointed GCVO in the coronation honours of 1953. Soon afterwards it emerged in public that the princess had formed an attachment for Group Captain Peter Townsend, who served as an equerry to both her father and her sister. He had been divorced, however, and after much soul-searching the princess issued a statement to the effect that 'mindful of the teachings of the church' she had decided not to marry him. The announcement was received with a great deal of sympathy. A few years later Princess Margaret married at WESTMINSTER ABBEY, on 6 May 1960, Antony Charles Robert Armstrong-Jones, son of Ronald Owen Lloyd Armstrong-Jones, sometime High Sheriff of Caernarvonshire, by his first wife Anne (who married secondly the 6th Earl of Rosse), only daughter of Lieutenant-Colonel Leonard Charles Rudolph Messel, of Nymans, Handcross, Sussex. He was created Viscount Linley and Earl of Snowdon on 6 October 1961, and appointed GCVO in 1969 for the part he played in organizing the investiture of the Prince of Wales at Caernarvon in that year.

Princess Margaret and Lord Snowdon had two children, David Albert Charles, who bears the courtesy title of Viscount Linley, born at Clarence House on 3 November 1961, and Lady Sarah Frances Elizabeth Armstrong-Jones (now Lady Sarah Chatto), born at Kensington Palace on 1 May 1964. After several years, however, the press began to focus on evident problems in the marriage, with much speculation about the princess's unhappiness and her alleged weakness for alcohol as a result. Much was also made of her friendships with many leading figures in London's 'fast' set of the 1960s. The princess refused to satisfy the curiosity of the media, once commenting, 'I've been misreported and misrepresented since the age of seventeen and I gave up long ago reading about myself', but the couple finally announced their decision to separate in 1976 and the marriage was dissolved by divorce in 1978.

Princess Margaret has been the recipient of several foreign orders, has represented the queen on many occasions overseas, is Colonel-in-Chief of several regiments and is president or patron of many charitable organizations. She received the Royal Victorian Chain in 1990. She lives in an apartment at KENSINGTON PALACE, London, and also spends some time each year in the Caribbean island of Mustique.

Margaret, Princess, Duchess of Brabant (1275–1333) Probably the seventh daughter and tenth child of EDWARD I and his first wife ELEANOR OF CASTILE, who was born at WINDSOR CASTLE on 15 March 1275. At the age of 15, on 9 July 1290, she was married at WESTMINSTER ABBEY to Jean, the son and heir of Jean I, Duke of Brabant, who succeeded his father as Duke Jean II in May 1294. She had a dower of £3,000 per annum. Duke Jean was born on 27 September 1275 and died at Tervueren on 27 October 1312, being buried in the Collegiate Church of Sainte-Gudule at Brussels. He was succeeded as duke by his and Margaret's only child, Jean III (1300–55). Margaret survived her husband many years and was still living on 11 March 1333, but probably died soon thereafter. She was buried with her husband at Brussels.

Margaret, Princess, Duchess of Norfolk (*c*.1320–99) The elder daughter and co-heiress of Thomas of Brotherton, Earl of Norfolk (son of EDWARD I) and his first wife Alice Hayles, who was born in about 1320. Royal assent for her marriage to John de Segrave, 4th Baron Segrave, was given on 3 March 1327. In 1338 Margaret succeeded her father as Countess of Norfolk, and her marriage was consummated at about the same time. She had two daughters, Elizabeth, later Lady Mowbray, and Anne, later abbess of Barking.

Lord Segrave died on 20 March 1353 and was buried at Chacombe Priory, Northamptonshire. His widow married secondly, shortly before 30 May 1354, Walter Manny, 1st Baron Manny, who died at Great Chesterford, Essex, between the 8 and 15 January 1372 and was buried in Grey Friars' Church, London, of which he and his wife were great benefactors. The issue of this marriage was a son Thomas, who died

before his father, and a daughter Anne, who married John Hastings, 2nd Earl of Pembroke, the widower of EDWARD III's daughter MARGARET, COUNTESS OF PEMBROKE. On the death of her niece Joan, Countess of Suffolk, without surviving issue in 1375, Margaret became the sole heir of her late father. As such she claimed to execute the office of Marshal of England by deputy at the coronation of RICHARD II but the claim was disallowed. However, the office of Earl Marshal was eventually granted to her grandson Thomas de Mowbray by charter in January 1386 and on 29 September 1397 he was created Duke of Norfolk in Parliament. The same day his grandmother was created Duchess of Norfolk for life.

She survived her new honour less than two years, dying on 24 March 1399. She was buried with her second husband in the choir of the Grey Friars' Church in London.

Margaret, Queen of Scots (1283–90) The only daughter of Eric II (Magnusson), King of Norway, by his first wife Margaret, only daughter of ALEXANDER III, KING OF SCOTS, who was born in Norway shortly before 9 April 1283, the date on which her mother died from complications following her birth. On 28 January 1284 the death of her uncle ALEXANDER, PRINCE OF SCOTLAND, left her as the only legitimate heir of her grandfather Alexander III and she was acknowledged by the nobles as heir to the kingdom. She succeeded her grandfather on 19 March 1286, but did not set out for Scotland until 1290. She was taken ill on the voyage and put ashore in Orkney, where she died on or about 26 September 1290. Her body was returned to Bergen for burial. Margaret, who was known as 'The Maid of Norway', had been betrothed since 1287 to Prince Edward (later EDWARD II), son of EDWARD I of England. Her death left the Scottish throne vacant with no clear heir among 13 competitors (*see* SCOTTISH SUCCESSION). A pretender, claiming to be Margaret, appeared in Bergen in 1301 and was burnt at the stake.

Margaret, St, Queen of Scots (1046–93) The second consort of MALCOLM III CANMORE, KING OF SCOTS, who was the eldest child of Edward 'the Exile' (the son of EDMUND II IRONSIDE, KING OF ENGLAND) and his wife AGATHA[1], daughter of Liudolf, Margrave of Westfriesland. Through her mother, Margaret had widespread connections with many of the reigning families of Europe. Her parents were probably married in Kiev in 1043 or 1044 and a year or so later accompanied another exiled prince, Andrew, in his successful attempt to gain the throne of Hungary, which had been held by usurpers since the death of St Stephen in 1038. It was at Andrew's court that Margaret was born in 1046 and her birth was followed by that of her sister Christina in 1052 and her brother EDGAR 'THE ATHELING' in 1055 or early in 1056.

In 1054 the childless EDWARD THE CONFESSOR sent a messenger to Hungary to recall his half-nephew and potential heir Edward and his family to England. The journey was delayed because of Agatha's pregnancy, and the family did not arrive in England until 1056. The ship for their journey was provided by Agatha's half-uncle, the Emperor Heinrich III. Very soon after their return Edward 'the Exile' died, leaving his widow and three young children under the protection of Edward the Confessor. When the king died in January 1066, Margaret's brother Edgar was only 10 years old and, although the person with most right to the throne, was passed over, the powerful HAROLD II becoming king in his place. After the Norman Conquest in October 1066, there was an attempt to set Edgar on the throne, but his followers submitted to WILLIAM I at Berkhamsted. Agatha's advisors thought it expedient for her and her children to seek refuge in Scotland, which was offered to them by King Malcolm and they set sail from Monkwearmouth in Northumberland in the summer of 1067, landing safely on the north shore of the Firth of Forth at a point subsequently known as St Margaret's Hope. The party set out on foot for the royal residence at DUNFERMLINE, four and a half miles away. After they had journeyed for two miles, Margaret sat down to rest on a stone later known as St Margaret's stone. In Dunfermline they were well received by the king and occupied an honoured place at his court.

Malcolm's wife Ingibiorg died (or in some accounts was repudiated) in 1069 and he asked Edgar for the hand of his elder sister. Margaret's thoughts were concentrated on becoming a nun and it took a little time to overcome her scruples, but Malcolm was persistent and she finally agreed to the marriage, which took place at Dunfermline in 1069 or 1070. Margaret and Malcolm were both persons of great piety and their marriage was evidently a happy one, producing six sons and two daughters, all of whom were carefully educated by their mother. Margaret was residing at Edinburgh Castle

when she received the news of the death in battle at Alnwick of her husband and the mortal wounding of her eldest son Edward. The shock was too great and she died on 16 November 1093. She was buried in the Abbey Church of the Holy Trinity, which she had founded, at Dunfermline. St Margaret was canonized by Pope Innocent IV in 1250.

Margaret Beaufort *see* RICHMOND AND DERBY, COUNTESS OF.

Margaret of Anjou, Queen of England (1429–82) The consort of HENRY VI, who was the second daughter and fifth child of 'Le bon roi René', Count of Anjou and titular King of Naples and Sicily, by his first wife Isabelle, in her own right Duchess of Lorraine, and was born at Pont-à-Mousson in Lorraine on 23 March 1429. Her childhood must have been unsettled, as her parents went through many vicissitudes as sovereigns without a throne. Her education was partly entrusted to her paternal grandmother, Yolande of Aragon. Her marriage to Henry VI was negotiated by Beaufort and after the proxy marriage at Nancy in March 1445 the 16-year-old bride set out for England. The channel crossing was a rough one and Margaret was violently sea-sick, being carried ashore at Porchester in the middle of a thunderstorm on 8 April 1445. She rested for a few days at Portsmouth and then went to Southampton where she fell ill with what appears to have been chickenpox. Recovered from this, she joined Henry and the marriage was solemnized at Titchfield Abbey on 22 April 1445. Her coronation at WESTMINSTER ABBEY took place on 30 May following.

Margaret was generally acknowledged to be a beauty, but Henry does not appear to have been a very demanding husband. Probably he was not highly sexed and it was eight years before the first and only child of the marriage appeared. As an intelligent and energetic woman, Margaret soon realized that she would have to take on most of the sovereign's duties, and she allied herself to the Beaufort–Suffolk faction. She also shared Henry's scholastic interests to some extent, and in 1448 she founded Queen's College (now Queens' College), Cambridge.

The birth of Margaret's son Edward in October 1453 followed closely on Henry's mental aberration. Richard, 3rd Duke of YORK, superseded in the succession by the queen's child, lost no time in spreading rumours to the effect that the boy was either the result of an intrigue between Margaret and Somerset, or an entirely supposititious child of low birth. These rumours she angrily refuted. The king's condition appeared so hopeless that Richard of York was constituted Protector by Parliament on 27 March 1454. By November Henry's condition began to improve and by Christmas he was almost entirely recovered and it was with joy that he saw his infant son for the first time. The queen now took over the management of affairs, caused the king to dissolve Parliament and mustered an army to attempt to crush the Yorkists. Her efforts on behalf of her husband and son were indefatigable but doomed to failure. She must often have felt exasperated and frustrated by her husband's inertia.

The defeat at Towton in 1461 sent Margaret into exile in Scotland with Henry and the young Edward, but her restless spirit soon sent her to France to appeal for aid from Louis XI, who was her first cousin as well as being first cousin to Henry VI. She returned after five months with Pierre Brezé, the seneschal of Normandy, and a company of French, and attempted to invade Northumberland but was beaten at Hexham. After being befriended and protected by a robber, she made good her escape to France, accompanied by her son. They possessed only the clothes they stood up in and were practically destitute. The exiled queen did not give up hope. After living for nearly seven years in reduced circumstances near Verdun, her father and other members of her family finally arranged a meeting with Louis XI at Tours. On his persuasion she was reconciled with the Earl of Warwick, and their alliance was cemented by the marriage of the Prince of Wales to Warwick's daughter Anne. Warwick and his force landed at Dartmouth. EDWARD IV, unable to oppose them, fled to Holland, and Henry VI's brief restoration ensued.

The final defeat of the Lancastrians at Tewkesbury, followed by the murder of the Prince of Wales, ended all Margaret's hopes. She was brought before Edward IV at Coventry and despatched to London forthwith. Henry VI's murder took place on the very night his wife entered the Tower as a prisoner, and she is said to have seen his body carried past her window. Margaret was removed from the Tower to Windsor and thence to Wallingford Castle, where the sum of five marks weekly was allotted for her maintenance. Her father King René worked tirelessly to procure her release and finally, by surrendering some of his Provençal pos-

sessions to Louis XI, was able to raise the ransom of 50,000 crowns demanded by Edward IV. The tragic queen was released in November 1475 and escorted by slow stages to Sandwich, where she embarked for France and landed at Dieppe early in January 1476. She went to Rouen and there signed a renunciation of her dower. Only then was she allowed to join her devoted father at his country retreat, La Maison de Reculée, near Angers. Her tribulations had left their mark and the queen's once lovely face was disfigured by a scaly eczema.

In 1480 Margaret's father died and she went to live with an old family retainer, François de la Vignolles, at his Château de Dampiere, near Saumur, and there, after a residence of less than two years, she died on 25 August 1482. She was only 53 but had the appearance of a worn-out old woman. The saddest of England's queens was buried with her parents in Angers Cathedral. She has no memorial.

Margaret of Connaught, Princess, Crown Princess of Sweden (1882–1920) The elder daughter and eldest child of Prince Arthur, Duke of CONNAUGHT (third son of Queen VICTORIA), and Louise Margaret of Prussia, who was born at Bagshot Park, Surrey, at ten past three in the afternoon on 15 January 1882. She was baptized by the Archbishop of Canterbury in the private chapel at WINDSOR CASTLE on 11 March following and received the names Margaret Victoria Augusta Charlotte Norah. She had the usual impressive array of godparents, her grandmother the queen, the German Empress, the German Crown Princess, and her grandmother Princess Friedrich Karl of Prussia (the last three all represented by proxies), the German Emperor, the Prince of Wales (later EDWARD VII), her great-grandfather Prince Karl of Prussia and her grandfather Prince Friedrich Karl of Prussia (the first and the last two being represented by proxies).

The princess was always known to her family as 'Daisy'. She was particularly charming and attractive, and when her father was serving in Cairo she met Prince Gustaf Adolf of Sweden, Duke of Skåne, eldest son of the Crown Prince, and they became engaged. The royal consent for the marriage was given on 20 March 1905 and the marriage took place at St George's Chapel, Windsor, on 15 June 1905. The honeymoon was spent at Saighton in Cheshire and in Ireland. In December 1907 the death of his grandfather, Oscar II, made

Daisy's husband Crown Prince of Sweden. Although she did not find life in Sweden always easy, she had a happy marriage and gave birth to four sons and one daughter. She was pregnant with her sixth child when a sudden ear infection, spreading to the throat, put an end to her life at Stockholm on 1 May 1920. Her death was so sudden and unexpected that a rumour that she had committed suicide in a fit of depression began to circulate and still finds some credence.

The Crown Prince married secondly, on 3 November 1923, Lady Louise MOUNT-BATTEN (formerly Princess Louise of Battenberg). He succeeded his father as Gustaf VI Adolf in October 1950 and died on 15 September 1973.

Margaret of Denmark, Queen of Scots (1456–86) The consort of JAMES III, KING OF SCOTS, who was the only daughter of Christian I, King of Denmark, and his wife Dorothea, daughter of Johann III, Elector of Brandenburg, and was born on 23 June 1456. Her marriage to the 17-year-old James III took place at Holyrood on 10 July 1469 and she brought the Orkney and Shetland Isles as part of her dowry. Margaret gave birth to three sons: the future JAMES IV, KING OF SCOTS; James, Duke of Ross (1476–1504); and John, Earl of Mar (1479–1503). She died at Stirling on 14 July 1486, and was buried at Cambuskenneth Abbey.

Margaret of England, Queen of Scots (1240–75) The first consort of ALEXANDER III, KING OF SCOTS, who was the eldest daughter and second child of HENRY III, KING OF ENGLAND and ELEANOR OF PROVENCE and was born at WINDSOR CASTLE on 29 September 1240. She was only 11 years of age when she was married at York on 26 December 1251 to Alexander III, who was 11 months her junior and was knighted by his father-in-law on the occasion. Margaret's first child, a daughter also named Margaret, was born while she was on a visit to her parents at Windsor in February 1261. Her birth was followed by those of two sons, Alexander at Jedburgh in January 1264, and David in March 1273. Neither was destined to live to succeed to the throne. Queen Margaret died 'of decline' at Cupar Castle, Fife, on 17 February 1275. She was buried at DUNFERMLINE.

Margaret of France, Queen of England (1279–1318) The second consort of EDWARD I, who was the younger daughter of Philippe III, King of France, and his second wife Marie, daughter of Henri III, Duke of Brabant, and was born probably at Paris in 1279. After the death of ELEANOR OF CASTILE in 1290, Edward I appeared to be an inconsolable widower for several years. His second marriage, at the age of 60 to a girl 40 years his junior, seems to have been at the instance of Philippe IV of France, the bride's half-brother. Margaret's elder sister Blanche was originally intended for Edward, but Margaret was substituted for reasons that are not clear. When all was agreed she sailed for England, landing at Dover on 8 September 1299. The couple were married at Canterbury two days later. In October she made her state entry into London and progressed from the Tower to Westminster accompanied by the Mayor and Aldermen and 300 burgesses. As was customary, the conduits in Cheapside flowed with wine and rich cloths were hung from all the windows on the route. However, Edward never got around to arranging for Margaret's coronation and she was the first queen since the Conquest not to be consecrated and crowned.

Edward was still a handsome and vigorous man and Margaret appears to have been quite content with her elderly bridegroom. She bore him two sons, Thomas (see NOR-FOLK, THOMAS OF BROTHERTON, EARL OF) and Edmund (see KENT, EDMUND OF WOOD-STOCK, EARL OF), who were both to play a part in history, and a daughter (named after the lamented Eleanor), who died young. Margaret accompanied Edward on his campaigns, as Eleanor had done, and was probably with him when he died at Burgh-on-Sands in July 1307. She was on excellent terms with her stepson EDWARD II, and travelled to Boulogne to attend his wedding to her niece in January 1308. Returning to England, she took up residence at Marlborough Castle and devoted herself to charitable works. She died there on 14 February 1318, still under 40, and was buried in the church of the Grey Friars in Newgate Street, London, of which she was a co-founder.

Her monument, together with those of nine other members of the royal family interred there, was sold for £50 by an avaricious Lord Mayor in the reign of ELIZABETH I and consequently lost. Likenesses of Queen Margaret are preserved in stone carvings at Lincoln Cathedral and in Winchelsea Church and by a statuette on the tomb of John of Eltham in WESTMINSTER ABBEY.

Margaret of Scotland, Princess, Dauphine of France (1424–45) The eldest daughter and eldest child of JAMES I, KING OF SCOTS and JOAN BEAUFORT, who was born in December 1424. At the age of four she was contracted at Perth on 19 July 1428 to marry Louis, Dauphin of France, the son and heir of Charles VII. The contract was ratified by treaty at Chinon on 30 October 1428. In 1436 Margaret travelled to France and the marriage was solemnized in the cathedral at Tours on 24 June 1436. Margaret found no happiness in her marriage to the parsimonious and cold-natured Louis and her sole consolation was in writing poetry. She had no children and died at Châlons-sur-Marne on 16 August 1445. She was buried first in Châlons Cathedral but later transferred to the chapel of the Holy Sepulchre in the Abbey Church of St Laon. Her widower succeeded his father as Louis XI in 1461 and died in 1483, having married Charlotte of Savoy as his second wife.

Margaret of York, Duchess of Burgundy (1446–1503) The third daughter and sixth child of Richard Plantagenet, 3rd Duke of YORK, and his wife Cicely Nevill, who was born at Fotheringay on 3 May 1446. After her brother had ascended the throne as EDWARD IV her hand was sought in marriage by Charles 'the Bold', Duke of Burgundy, and she became his third wife at Damme, near Bruges, on 3 July 1468, the ceremony being conducted by the Bishop of Salisbury. Margaret's magnificent marriage crown, enamelled with white roses and adorned with many pearls, is preserved in Aachen Cathedral, to which she later presented it. The total cost of the items of her trousseau and the trappings of her entourage amounted to £2,450.6s.8d., a vast sum in those days.

Margaret presided over her husband's court at Bruges for the next nine years, gaining a reputation as a patroness of the arts and a great bibliophile, employing William Caxton as a translator. She had no children of her own, but was a kind stepmother to her husband's only child Marie, who was destined to succeed her father as sovereign Duchess of Burgundy and to die prematurely in 1482 as the result of a fall from her horse. Duke Charles was killed in combat before Nancy on 5 January 1477 and was buried in the church of Notre-Dame at Bruges. After his death, Margaret resided at Malines, where five years later she took over the care of her step-grandchildren, Philip

and Margaret of Austria, after the death of their mother.

For many years she intrigued against the new Tudor dynasty in England, supporting in turn the pretenders Lambert SIMNEL and Perkin WARBECK, but eventually she agreed to accept the inevitable and undertook to abstain from any action to help those who might rebel against HENRY VII. One of the last acts of Margaret's life was to stand as godmother to her step-great-grandson the future Emperor Charles V, who was named after her late husband. She died at Malines on 23 November 1503 and was buried in the church of the Cordeliers there.

Margaret Plantagenet, Countess of Salisbury (1473–1541) The younger daughter and second child of George, Duke of CLARENCE and his wife Isabel Nevill, who was born at Farley Castle, Somerset, on 14 August 1473. She was married before 22 September 1494 to Sir Richard Pole, son of Sir Geoffrey Pole, and his wife Edith, the daughter of Sir Oliver St John and half-sister of Margaret, Countess of RICHMOND, the mother of HENRY VII. There were four sons and one daughter of the marriage. Following the execution of her brother Edward, Earl of Salisbury and Warwick on 24 November 1499, Margaret became the sole heir of her father.

After the accession of HENRY VIII in 1509 she enjoyed high favour for a time. The king declared her Countess of Salisbury on 14 October 1513 and later appointed her godmother and governess to his daughter Mary (later MARY I). Margaret was a strong character and her sturdy spirit of independence eventually angered the king. She was accused of conducting a treasonable correspondence with her son Cardinal Pole, arrested on a charge of high treason and attainted and imprisoned in the TOWER OF LONDON in June 1539. Two years later she was beheaded without trial on Tower Hill, on 27 May 1541. She refused to place her head on the block, saying, 'So should traitors do, and I am none', and the executioner, a young boy, was obliged to 'hack her head and shoulders to pieces'. She was buried in the Chapel of St Peter ad Vincula in the Tower.

Margaret was regarded by many, including her son Cardinal Pole, who was destined to become Archbishop of Canterbury in the reign of Queen Mary I, as a martyr to the true faith.

Margaret Tudor, Queen of Scots (1489–1541) The consort of JAMES IV, KING OF

SCOTS, who was the eldest daughter and second child of HENRY VII, KING OF ENGLAND and ELIZABETH OF YORK and was born at the Palace of Westminster on 29 November 1489. She was baptized in St Margaret's Church, Westminster, on the day after her birth, her godparents being her paternal grandmother the Countess of Richmond (after whom she was named), the Duchess of Norfolk and John Morton, Archbishop of Canterbury. She was almost 14 when she was married and crowned at Holyrood on 8 August 1503 to the 30-year-old James IV. Her first child, James, was born in February 1507 and died a year later. A daughter, born in July 1508, died shortly after birth without being named, and a second son, Arthur, followed in October 1509, only to die in July 1510. Margaret's fourth child, born in April 1512, survived to become the future JAMES V, and a second unnamed daughter was born prematurely and died immediately in 1513. The queen was again pregnant when King James was killed at the battle of FLODDEN, and she gave birth to her fourth son and sixth child, Alexander, Duke of Ross on 30 April 1514. Alexander died at the age of 18 months.

On the death of James IV, Margaret became regent and guardian of her young son James V. She had to contend with great opposition but managed to conclude peace with England in 1514. On 6 August 1514 Margaret married at Kinnoul, as his second wife, Archibald Douglas, 6th Earl of Angus, and the following year she was besieged at Stirling and compelled to give up the regency and the person of the young king to John Stewart, Duke of ALBANY. She managed to escape to England and at Harbottle Castle, Northumberland, gave birth to a daughter, Margaret (later Countess of Lennox) on 18 October 1515. In 1517 Margaret returned to Edinburgh, hoping to regain her dower and access to her son, but in this she was unsuccessful. For the next few years she was constantly changing sides, and in a series of manoeuvres she regained the regency and took the king to Edinburgh. Angus, from whom she had been estranged, was again admitted to the Council of Regency in 1523 and continued to exercise supreme power after his stepson had gained his legal majority at the age of 14 in 1526, being made High Chancellor of Scotland in August 1527.

Meanwhile, Margaret had transferred her affections to Henry Stewart, 1st Lord Methven and married him immediately after obtaining a divorce from Angus on 11 March 1527. She and her new husband contrived to bring about Angus's forfeiture for high treason in 1528, and he went into exile in England, where he was befriended by his brother-in-law HENRY VIII, who had little love for his sister. Margaret and Methven then became James V's chief advisers and were influential in concluding peace with England in 1534. Shortly after this James accused his mother of taking bribes from England. Her last years were spent in an unsuccessful attempt to obtain a divorce from Methven, complaining to her brother Henry that he had squandered her lands and profits on his own family. In 1537 she attempted to escape to England, but was overtaken and brought back to Methven Castle, where she remained until her death from 'palsy' on 18 October 1541. She was buried in the Carthusian monastery of St John at Perth. Her only issue by Lord Methven was a daughter who died in infancy.

Agnes Strickland in her *Lives of the Queens of Scotland* says of Margaret that she had 'no education, scarcely any religion, and was guided entirely by her instincts, which were not of an elevated character'. Her portrait was painted by Holbein.

Mary, Princess[1] (1279–1332) The youngest but one of the daughters of EDWARD I and his first wife ELEANOR OF CASTILE and probably their 13th child, who was born at Woodstock on 11 or 12 March 1279. She entered the Benedictine convent at Amesbury, Wiltshire, where her grandmother ELEANOR OF PROVENCE had taken the veil, and was dedicated there on 15 August 1285, being professed a nun at the end of 1291, perhaps on 8 December (the feast of the Conception of the Virgin). She died at Amesbury on 29 May 1332 and was buried there.

Mary, Princess[2] (1466–82) The second daughter and second child of EDWARD IV and ELIZABETH WOODVILLE, who was born at WINDSOR CASTLE in August 1466. She was affianced to Frederik (later King Frederik I of Denmark), son of Christian I, King of Denmark, but died before the marriage could take place. She died at Greenwich on 23 May 1482 and was buried in St George's Chapel, Windsor.

Mary, Princess[3] *see* MARY I, QUEEN OF ENGLAND.

Mary, Princess[4] *see* MARY, QUEEN OF SCOTS.

Mary, Princess[5] (1605–7) The third daughter and seventh child of JAMES I and ANNE OF DENMARK, who was born at GREENWICH PALACE at about four o'clock in the morning on 6 April 1605 and baptized there by the Archbishop of Canterbury on 5 May, her godparents being her father's cousin Lady Arabella Stuart, the Countess of Northumberland, her maternal uncle Ulrik, Duke of Holstein, and her cousin the 2nd Duke of Lennox. Princess Mary died at Stanwell Park, Middlesex, the seat of Lord Knyvet, whose wife Elizabeth was her governess, on 16 September 1607, and was buried on 23 September in Henry VII's Chapel, WESTMINSTER ABBEY. Her monument bears her effigy clad in a dress with ruff and farthingale reclining on one elbow and gazing into the cradle of her baby sister SOPHIA[1], which lies alongside. The month of her death is wrongly given as December in her monumental inscription.

Mary, Princess[6] *see* MARY II, QUEEN OF ENGLAND.

Mary, Princess, Countess of Boulogne (*c*.1136–82) The second daughter and fifth and youngest child of King STEPHEN and MATILDA OF BOULOGNE, who was born in about 1136. She entered the religious life and became a nun and eventually abbess of Romsey in Hampshire, where she remained until 1159, when the death of her brother William left her the sole surviving child of her parents and Countess of Boulogne in her own right. It was probably in the following year that Mathieu of Alsace, son of Thierry, Count of Flanders, carried her off from the convent and married her, becoming Count of Boulogne in her right. It seems highly probable that she was dispensed from her vow of chastity to do so, since her two daughters were regarded as legitimate and the elder, Ida, succeeded to the county of Boulogne, her right thereto being undisputed. After nine years of marriage, however, Mary began to have scruples about her married state and obtained an annulment to enable her to return to the religious life, which she did at St Austrebert, near Montreuil. Mathieu married again two years later and died from a wound received at the siege of Driencourt on 24 July 1173. He was buried at St Judoc in Ponthieu. Mary died at St Austrebert in 1182 and was buried there.

Mary, Princess, Duchess of Brittany (1344–61) The fourth daughter and ninth child of EDWARD III and PHILIPPA OF HAINAULT, who was born at Waltham, near Winchester, on 10 October 1344. She was married at Woodstock in the summer of 1361 to Jean V 'the Valiant', Duke of Brittany. Her wedding dress, according to the Wardrobe Account of Edward III, was made of 'four cloths of gold of Lucca and three baldekyn furred of miniver [part of which was a gift from the King of France], and ermine'. The princess did not survive her marriage very long, dying in the autumn of the same year, shortly after Garter robes had been provided for her on 1 October. She was buried at Abingdon Abbey, Berkshire. Duke Jean remarried twice, his third and last wife being Jeanne, or JOAN OF NAVARRE, who later married HENRY IV. He died at Nantes on 1 November 1399.

Mary, Princess, Duchess of Gloucester (1776–1857) The fourth daughter and eleventh child of GEORGE III and Queen CHARLOTTE, who was born at the Queen's House, St James's Park, at seven o'clock in the morning on 25 April 1776. She was baptized by the Archbishop of Canterbury on her mother's birthday, 19 May, in the Great Council Chamber of ST JAMES'S PALACE, her godparents being the Duchess of Saxe-Gotha, Princess Friederike of Mecklenburg-Strelitz and Prince Friedrich of Hesse-Cassel, all represented by proxies. Mrs Delany described her at the Queen's Lodge, Windsor, in her fourth year as 'a most sweet child ... in cherry-coloured tabby, with silver leading strings ... She could not remember my name, but making me a very low curtsey said, "How do you do, Duchess of Portland's friend? And how does your little niece do? I wish you had brought her."'

Princess Mary made her debut at court on the occasion of her father's birthday ball on 4 June 1791. Fanny Burney, who saw her, said: 'She looked most interesting and unaffectedly lovely; she is a sweet creature, and perhaps, in point of beauty, the first of this truly beautiful race.' Her portrait by Gainsborough does much to confirm this opinion. The princess and her other unmarried sisters spent most of their time as satellites to their mother, who was loath to lose any of them in marriage. The first Earl of Malmesbury, writing of Princess Mary in November 1801, described her as 'all goodhumour and pleasantness. Her manners are perfect, and I never saw or conversed with any Princess so exactly what she ought to be'.

Princess Mary had passed her 40th birthday when she married at the Queen's House,

St James's, on 22 July 1816, her first cousin, William Frederick, 2nd Duke of GLOU-CESTER, who was three months her senior. The marriage, although remaining child-less, proved an extremely happy one. It ended with the duke's death at Bagshot Park, Surrey, on 30 November 1834.

Princess Mary, Duchess of Gloucester, was a great favourite with all the members of the royal family and particularly with her niece Queen VICTORIA. She was noted for her charm and kindness throughout her long life and took great pleasure in society. In the last 10 years of her life she exhibited signs of senility from time to time. Queen Victoria writing to King LEOPOLD (*see* LEOPOLD OF SAXE-COBURG) of the Belgians on 16 May 1848, reported: 'The poor Duchess of Gloster [*sic*] is again in one of her nervous states, and gave us a dreadful fright at the Christening [of Princess Louise] by quite forgetting where she was, and coming and kneeling at my feet in the midst of the service. Imagine our horror!'

Princess Mary died, the last survivor of her parents' 15 children, at Gloucester House, Piccadilly, at a quarter past five in the morning on 30 April 1857, five days after her 81st birthday. She was buried in the Gloucester vault in St George's Chapel, Windsor, on 8 May 1857.

Mary, Princess, Landgravine of Hesse-Cassel (1723–72)

The fourth daugher and eighth child of GEORGE II and Queen CARO-LINE, who was born at Leicester House, London, between eight and nine o'clock in the evening on 22 February (5 March new style) 1723. She was carefully brought up by her mother and, after her death, by her elder sister Princess CAROLINE. According to a contemporary she was 'a lover of reading, and far more solicitous to improve the mind than to adorn the body'.

A marriage was arranged for her with Friedrich, Hereditary Prince of Hesse-Cassel, the only surviving son and heir of Wilhelm VIII, Landgrave of Hesse-Cassel. The princess was voted a marriage portion of £40,000 by Parliament, and the proxy marriage took place at the Chapel Royal, St James's, in the evening of 8 May (19 May new style) 1740, the bride's brother William Augustus, Duke of CUMBERLAND standing proxy for the bridegroom. Princess Mary sailed from Greenwich on 6 June and trav-elled via Holland to Cassel, where she was married in person on 28 June. Her husband, although tall and handsome, was profligate and brutal, and the princess's married life

was a most unhappy one. She gave birth to four sons, the youngest being born in September 1747. The couple separated in February 1755 following his conversion to Roman Catholicism. In 1760 he succeeded his father as reigning Landgrave Friedrich II of Hesse-Cassel and Mary's second, but eldest surviving, son Wilhelm became reigning Count of Hanau with his mother as regent until 13 October 1764. As such, she struck silver coins bearing her name, includ-ing a very handsome thaler and half-thaler with her portrait bust on the obverse and the arms of Hesse-Cassel and Great Britain on the reverse. She died there on 14 January 1772 at seven o'clock in the morning and was buried in the Reformed Church there.

The Landgrave Friedrich was married secondly, on 10 January 1773, to Philippine, daughter of Friedrich Wilhelm, Margrave of Brandenburg-Schwedt, but had no fur-ther issue. He died at Schloss Weissenstein on 31 October 1785.

Mary, Princess, Queen of France and Duchess of Suffolk (1496–1533)

The third daughter and fifth child of HENRY VII and ELIZABETH OF YORK, who was born at RICH-MOND PALACE on 18 March 1496. As a child she was affianced to the Archduke Charles of Austria (later the Emperor Charles V), but it came to nothing, and in 1514 her brother HENRY VIII, in order to cement a newly concluded treaty of peace with France, arranged her marriage to Louis XII. The French king, although only 52, was already decrepit and considered an old man. His second wife, Anne of Brittany, had died in January 1514, and as Louis gazed upon her lying in her coffin he cried out: 'Go make the vault big enough for us two. Before the year is out I shall be with her, to keep her company.' His words came true, but before they did so he had acquired a third wife in the person of Mary Tudor. The marriage took place at Abbeville on 9 October 1514, the ceremony being performed by Cardinal de Brie, Bishop of Limoges, who also crowned the new queen at St Denis on 5 November 1514. Louis had entered into the marriage reluctantly, but when he discov-ered that his 18-year-old bride was charm-ing, beautiful and vivacious, his enthusiasm for the match knew no bounds. According to a contemporary, Louis 'reported that he had performed marvels' on his wedding night. 'At least, that is what he said for he was not very virile,' is the wry comment.

After her coronation Mary made her state entry into Paris, where feasting and dancing continued for several weeks until the king, having exhausted himself in his efforts to be a good husband, fell ill and died rather suddenly at the Palais du Tournelles on 1 January 1515. Witty Parisians said that the King of England had 'sent a mare [Mary] to the King of France to take him quickly and gently to heaven or hell'. Louis lay beside Anne as he had predicted.

Mary was able to assure Louis's son-in-law and successor François I that she was not with child and found consolation without delay in the arms of one of her English gentlemen, Charles Brandon, Duke of Suffolk, whom she married secretly at the Hôtel Cluny in Paris on 3 March 1515. He was a favourite of her brother Henry VIII and had already had two, if not three, matrimonial entanglements. The couple returned to England to face the wrath of Henry VIII, but Wolsey managed to calm the king down and Mary and Suffolk were publicly married at the Grey Friars' Church, Greenwich, on 13 May 1515. They had three children: Henry, Earl of Lincoln, who was born on 11 March 1516 and died in March 1534; Lady Frances Brandon, who was born at Hatfield, Hertfordshire, on 16 July 1517, married Henry Grey, Duke of Suffolk, and became the mother, among others, of Lady Jane Grey, the 'nine days queen' (*see* JANE, QUEEN OF ENGLAND); and Lady Eleanor Brandon, who was born in about 1520 and married Henry Clifford, 2nd Earl of Cumberland.

Mary died at Westhorpe Hall, Suffolk, on 25 June 1533, 'between the hours of seven and eight in the morning'. She was buried 'with great state' in the Abbey Church of Bury St Edmunds. After the Dissolution of the Monasteries she was reburied in St Mary's Church, Bury St Edmunds, where Queen VICTORIA placed a window in her memory in 1881. The Duke of Suffolk married a fourth (or fifth) wife and died at Guildford Palace, Surrey, on 22 August 1545. He was buried at St George's Chapel, Windsor, 'at the King's own Charge'.

Mary, Princess Royal, Countess of Harewood (1897–1965)

Mary, Princess Royal, Countess of Harewood (1897–1965) The only daughter and third child of GEORGE V and Queen MARY OF TECK, who was born at York Cottage, Sandringham, at half past three in the afternoon of 25 April 1897. She was baptized by the Archbishop of York in the parish church of St Mary Magdalene, Sandringham, on 7 June and received the names Victoria Alexandra Alice Mary, although she was always known by the last name. Her god-parents were her great-grandmother Queen VICTORIA; her grandmothers the Princess of Wales (later Queen ALEXANDRA) and the Duchess of Teck; her great-aunt the Dowager Empress Maria Feodorovna of Russia; her aunt Princess VICTORIA; her great-uncle the King of the Hellenes; her grandfather the Prince of Wales (later EDWARD VII); and her uncle Prince Francis of Teck.

Princess Mary was educated privately. The First World War effectively put an end to the era when princesses married princes from foreign (usually German) royal families, and on 28 February 1922 Princess Mary was married at WESTMINSTER ABBEY to Henry George Charles Lascelles, Viscount Lascelles, who succeeded his father as 6th Earl of Harewood in October 1929. They had two sons, George Henry Hubert, later 7th Earl of Harewood, and the Hon. Gerald David Lascelles. Princess Mary's early married life was spent at Chesterfield House in London and at Goldsborough Hall, near Knaresborough, until her husband's succession to the earldom, when they moved to Harewood House, near Leeds. Lord Harewood was 15 years older than his wife, having been born on 6 September 1882, but widespread rumours that their marriage was not a happy one are refuted by their elder son in his memoirs *The Tongs and the Bones*. He says that they 'got on well together and had a lot of friends and interests in common'. Both were devoted to country pursuits.

Princess Mary was declared Princess Royal on 1 January 1932, following the death of her aunt Princess Louise (*see* LOUISE, PRINCESS ROYAL, DUCHESS OF FIFE), the previous holder of that title, the year before. As she grew older she became more and more like her mother Queen Mary in character and temperament, coupled with an acute shyness. Lord Harewood died at Harewood House on 23 May 1947. The Princess Royal acted as a COUNSELLOR OF STATE on many occasions and represented her niece ELIZABETH II at independence celebrations in Trinidad (1962) and Zambia (1964).

On 28 March 1965 Princess Mary, who for some time had suffered from heart murmurings, went for a walk in the grounds of Harewood House, accompanied by her son Lord Harewood and two of her grandsons. She stumbled and fell and her son supported her to a seat while his sons ran back to the house to get a car to take her back. Before it arrived she died peacefully in his arms. She was buried with her husband in the family vault at Harewood parish church.

Mary, Princess Royal, Princess of Orange

(1631–60) The eldest daughter and third child of CHARLES I and HENRIETTA MARIA, who was born at ST JAMES'S PALACE on 4 November 1631 and – as she seemed unlikely to live – was baptized immediately by Dr Laud, Bishop of London (later Archbishop of Canterbury), her godparents being the Bishop of Lincoln and the Countesses of Carlisle and Denbigh. She was the first princess to bear the title of princess royal.

Princess Mary was in only her 10th year when she was married at the Chapel Royal, Whitehall, on 2 May (12 May new style) 1641 to Willem, Hereditary Prince of Orange, who was just approaching his 15th birthday. The following February the princess, accompanied by her mother, sailed from Dover to Holland, where she received a warm welcome not only from her parents-in-law, but also from her aunt ELIZABETH, QUEEN OF BOHEMIA and such of her children as were then residing at The Hague. The marriage ceremony was repeated at The Hague on 4 November 1643. In March 1647 Mary's father-in-law died and her husband succeeded him as Willem II, Prince of Orange and Stadhouder of the United Provinces of the Netherlands. The following year they welcomed Mary's two exiled brothers Charles and James at their court.

In 1650 Mary was expecting her first child when Willem fell ill with smallpox. He died on 27 October 1650 and was buried at Delft. Mary's son was born on her 19th birthday, 4 November (14 November new style) 1650, and named William Henry (see WILLIAM III). Mary was appointed her son's guardian, but she was unpopular with the Dutch, who tended to side with Cromwell and resented the unfailing help she gave to her brothers and their followers. On the outbreak of war between Holland and England in 1652, Mary was forbidden by the States General to receive them altogether. However, she visited CHARLES II at Cologne and Paris in 1656.

In 1658 she became sole regent of the principality of Orange, but was opposed by Dona, the town governor. Her cousin Louis XIV came to her aid and captured Orange in 1660. In May 1660, amid great rejoicing, the princess saw her brothers depart at Scheveningen on the Restoration of Charles II. She travelled to England herself in September and landed at Margate. The court was in mourning for her brother Henry, Duke of GLOUCESTER, but her surviving brothers, Charles II and the Duke of York (later JAMES II), travelled down the Thames in barges to meet her.

She did not live to enjoy the pleasures of the Restoration court. On 20 December Pepys recorded in his diary that she had fallen ill with smallpox. The following day he noted that she was 'dangerously ill' and reported a rumour (false as it happened) that she had secretly married Henry Jermyn (later Earl of Dover), the Duke of York's Master of the Horse. The Princess Royal died at WHITEHALL PALACE at four o'clock in the afternoon on 24 December 1660. Two days later Pepys dined with Lady Sandwich, 'who at table did tell me how much fault was laid upon Dr Frazer [Alexander Fraizer, physician in ordinary to Charles II] and the rest of the Doctors, for the death of the Princess'. The princess was buried in Henry VII's Chapel at WESTMINSTER ABBEY on 29 December 1660.

Mary, Queen of Scots

(1542–87) Mary Stuart, the only daughter and third and youngest child of JAMES V, KING OF SCOTS and his second wife MARY OF GUISE, who was born at LINLITHGOW PALACE on 8 December 1542. The death of her father one week later made her Queen of Scots with the Earl of Arran as Lord Governor or regent. On 1 July 1543 an agreement was reached with HENRY VIII of England that in due course Mary should marry his son, the future EDWARD VI. Fearing the possibility of an abduction to England, Mary and her mother were taken to Stirling Castle on 27 July and on 9 September 1543, although only nine months old, Mary was crowned in the Chapel Royal there, the crown being held over her head. Mary was placed under the guardianship of Lord Erskine.

With the English invasion in September 1547, Mary and her mother were again moved for safety to Inchmahome Priory, where they stayed for three weeks until the danger had abated and they returned to Stirling, where they remained until February 1548, when they moved to Dumbarton Castle on the Clyde. The hostilities initiated by Henry VIII forced the Scots to abandon the English marriage project, and in July 1548 the Scots Parliament gave approval for Mary's marriage to the four-year-old Dauphin François, son and heir of Henri II, King of France. The French king sent a ship to convey his prospective daughter-in-law to France, and she set sail on 7 August, without her mother, but with a suite that included Lord Erskine, her governess Lady Fleming and the famous 'Four Maries', her maids-of-honour, Mary Beaton, Mary Fleming, Mary Livingston and Mary Seton. The party landed at Roscoff on the French coast on 13 August and joined the French court, where Mary's education was completed. She learned French, Latin, Greek, Italian and Spanish, as well as music, dancing, singing, drawing and needlework, and became an accomplished young woman.

Her maternal grandmother, Antoinette, Duchess of Guise and her Guise uncles took a lively interest in her welfare and upbringing and she became greatly attached to them. Her mother visited her in 1550 and stayed for a year. Mary's wedding to François took place in the open air before Notre-Dame Cathedral in Paris on 24 April 1558 and was a magnificent ceremony, attended by the French court and witnessed by many onlookers. A year later Mary's father-in-law was injured by a splintered lance at the tournament held to celebrate the marriage of his daughter Elisabeth to PHILIP II, KING OF SPAIN, and he died 10 days later on 10 July 1559. Mary's husband succeeded him as François II and Mary found herself Queen of France as well as of Scotland. As she was already a crowned and anointed queen, she did not participate in her husband's coronation at Rheims on 8 September 1559, but watched the ceremony from a tribune in the cathedral. François reigned for less than 18 months. He had always been delicate and his attachment to Mary, a healthy, sensuous girl of great charm, sapped his feeble strength still further. In November 1560 he became seriously ill with headaches and fainting fits, and from the description of his symptoms it is clear that he was suffering from meningitis. His surgeons carried out an horrific operation of trepanning but could do nothing to save him and he continued screaming unceasingly until he died at Orléans on 5 December 1560, just over one month short of completing his 17th year.

Mary was a childless widow at the age of 18. She had also lost her mother, who had taken over the regency of Scotland in 1554 and died in June 1560. Mary determined on returning to Scotland the following year and landed at Leith in August 1561. On 19 August she took up residence in the Palace of HOLYROODHOUSE at Edinburgh. During her absence in France the Protestant Reformation had been preached in Scotland by John Knox and proclaimed by the Parliament in August 1560, so Mary returned to a Scotland very different from the one she had left as a child. Although she continued to have mass celebrated in her private chapel, Mary did not make any attempt to interfere with the new reformed religion that Parliament had established and for four years she pursued a wise and successful policy, negotiating with ELIZABETH I of England and making progresses throughout the country, in the course of which her good looks and charm gained her much support from the people. She was a keen huntswoman and also played the then new game of golf.

The question of a second marriage became imperative and after considering Don Carlos of Spain (a match strongly disapproved by John Knox, who harangued Mary in no uncertain terms) and Robert Dudley, Earl of Leicester, Mary became infatuated with her cousin Henry Stuart, Lord DARNLEY, and married him at Holyrood on 29 July 1565. Mary very soon became disillusioned with the uncouth Darnley, who was created Duke of Albany, Earl of Ross and Lord Ardmannoch and entitled 'king', although excluded from all share in the government. Mary became pregnant towards the end of the year and found solace in the company of David Riccio, an Italian musician whom she appointed her secretary. Darnley and several of the principal nobles suspected that Riccio was the queen's lover, which he may have been, and formed a conspiracy to do away with him. On 9 March 1566 Riccio was at supper with the queen and her ladies at Holyrood, when the conspirators, headed by Darnley, burst into the room, dragged him from her side and despatched him in the ante-chamber. Mary herself was roughly handled, but did not miscarry as the conspirators may have hoped she would. All the conspirators except Darnley were banished, although he was ostensibly forgiven.

On 19 June 1566 Mary gave birth to a son (see JAMES I, KING OF ENGLAND) at Edinburgh and he was baptized with Catholic rites in December, receiving the names of Charles James, the first after his godfather Charles IX of France, Mary's erstwhile brother-in-law. In the same month, December, the exiled conspirators were allowed to return. They had now conceived a hatred of Darnley, by whom they felt they had been betrayed, and his days, too, were numbered. Mary, meanwhile, was beginning to be drawn to James Hepburn, 4th

Earl of Bothwell, an attractive rogue and a married man, as well as one of the most powerful noblemen in Scotland. Bothwell entered into a bond with the Earls of Argyll and Huntly to rid Mary of her husband. The result was Darnley's murder at Kirk o' Field beside the city walls of Edinburgh, when the house in which he was staying was blown up in the early hours of the morning of 10 February 1567. It was generally believed that Mary had prior knowledge of the deed, but she was probably innocent.

In April 1567 she went to visit her baby son at Stirling and on her way back to Edinburgh was abducted by Bothwell, probably not unwillingly, and carried off to Dunbar Castle. Events moved swiftly. Bothwell divorced his wife on 3 May and on 15 May he and Mary were married at Holyroodhouse. Three days before the marriage Bothwell was created Duke of Orkney, but he was never associated with Mary as titular King of Scots as both François and Darnley had been. The marriage aroused great anger among the Scottish nobles opposed to Bothwell and brought Scotland to the verge of civil war. The queen and Bothwell left Edinburgh to gather an army in his territory and on their return met with the Scottish lords and their followers at Carberry, east of Edinburgh, on 15 June 1567. After a day of discussion Mary surrendered herself to the lords and Bothwell went back to Dunbar. Mary was taken to Lochleven Castle, where she remained a prisoner for nearly a year. While there, she miscarried twins. Bothwell moved northwards, attempting to rally support, but eventually was forced to flee the country. He sought refuge in Denmark, but was imprisoned by the Danish King Frederik and held in solitary confinement at Dragsholm Castle, where 11 years later, on 14 April 1578, he died insane. He was buried in Faarevejle Church, near Dragsholm, where his remains were later exhumed and placed on public display. In 1976 there was an abortive move to return his body to Scotland.

Mary was forced to abdicate in favour of her son on 24 July 1567. She occupied her time at Lochleven in needlework and was allowed to exercise in the castle grounds. On 2 May 1568 her supporters engineered her escape and she was rowed across the loch to meet them. She managed to raise an army but on 13 May was defeated at Langside by the forces of her half-brother the regent Moray. She fled southwards and on 16 May sailed across the Solway Firth to Workington, determined to seek the aid of Elizabeth. She was taken to Carlisle Castle, where she remained for two months before moving to Bolton Castle and thence from castle to castle, being kept as a state prisoner. She was unable to refrain from plotting and eventually it became her undoing through her involvement in the Babington Plot in 1586. She was tried for conspiring to bring about the assassination of Elizabeth and condemned to death.

It was only with great reluctance that Elizabeth signed the death warrant of the cousin she had never met, and Mary was beheaded on 8 February 1587 in the great hall of FOTHERINGAY CASTLE, where she had last been confined. When the executioner lifted her head, her red wig fell off and it was seen that her hair had become quite white, although she was only in her early forties. Her body remained at Fotheringay for six months until at Elizabeth's order it received a state funeral 'with all the trophies of a Sovereign Queen' and was buried in Peterborough Cathedral on 1 August 1587. Queen Elizabeth expressed sorrow for the 'miserable accident' that had taken place. After Mary's son had succeeded Elizabeth on the English throne he had his mother's body disinterred and brought to WESTMINSTER ABBEY, where, in 1612, it was reburied in a vault on the south side of King Henry VII's Chapel, parallel with the tomb of Elizabeth on the north side. Mary's tomb bears her full-length effigy. James also ordered the demolition of Fotheringay Castle, the scene of his mother's execution.

Mary I, Queen of England (1516–58) The second daughter and fifth child of HENRY VIII and his first wife CATHERINE OF ARAGON, who was born at GREENWICH PALACE on 18 February 1516. She was the only child of her parents to survive infancy, her birth having been preceded by those of a stillborn daughter, two short lived sons and a stillborn son. It was followed by that of another stillborn daughter in 1518. Her father's initial disappointment at her being a girl was tempered by his hope of further issue to come, but it was not to be. Mary was given her own court at Ludlow Castle with many of the prerogatives usually given to a Prince of Wales. She was placed in the charge of the Countess of Salisbury, a Plantagenet cousin and the mother of Cardinal Pole, who was to play such a leading part in Mary's later life. She studied Greek, Latin, French, Italian, science and music. There were some tentative marriage plans to

François I of France and to her cousin the Emperor Charles V (whose son she was eventually to marry), but they came to naught.

Mary was a sickly child and suffered from severe headaches and defective eyesight, being almost certainly a congenital syphilitic. All her portraits confirm this and Dr Maclaurin wrote in his book *Mere Mortals*: 'Any doctor looking at the portrait of her wizened, lined, and prematurely aged face would probably say "That woman must have been a hereditary syphilitic".' Mary's childhood and young womanhood were made wretched not only by her ill-health but by the protracted divorce proceedings of her parents and the subsequent humiliations to which she and her mother were subjected. She was devoted to her mother but was not allowed to be with her at her death.

In 1533 Mary was declared illegitimate and sent to Hatfield to live with her baby half-sister Elizabeth (the future ELIZABETH I) under the care of ANNE BOLEYN's aunt Lady Shelton. She seems to have borne no grudge against the baby and even to have had some genuine sisterly feeling for her, which speaks well for her character. After the execution of Anne Boleyn, Mary was reconciled to her father and induced to acknowledge that her mother's marriage to him had been unlawful and she herself, therefore, was illegitimate. She also outwardly acknowledged the king as head of the Church and on these terms was received back at court. In 1537 she stood as godmother to her half-brother the future EDWARD VI, and acted as chief mourner at the funeral of her stepmother, Queen JANE SEYMOUR.

CATHERINE PARR's influence drew the royal family closer together in 1544 and Mary was reinstated in the line of succession to the throne. It was with Catherine's encouragement, too, that she translated Erasmus's Latin paraphrase of St John at this time. After Henry VIII's death his three children remained on friendly terms with each other in spite of their great differences in age and religious belief. When the Act of Uniformity in 1549 made use of the new Prayer Book compulsory, Mary refused to comply and continued to have the Latin mass celebrated in her household. The attempt to divert the succession to Lady Jane Grey (*see* JANE, QUEEN OF ENGLAND) on Edward VI's death was a direct result of this intransigence.

When Edward VI died in June 1553,

Mary was at Framlingham Castle, Suffolk, and on hearing that the country was in her favour, set out for London, where she made a triumphant entry accompanied by her half-sister Elizabeth. All support for Jane melted away and Mary's succession was unchallenged. She at once ordered the release of the Duke of Norfolk and Stephen Gardiner from the Tower, restoring the latter to the see of Winchester and making him Chancellor. It was Gardiner, too, who officiated at her coronation at WESTMINSTER ABBEY on 1 October.

Throughout her reign Mary devoted herself singlemindedly to the restoration of the old order, the Latin mass and papal supremacy. Her first Parliament abolished Edward VI's religious laws and firmly reasserted her own legitimacy. It was essential that the new queen, already 37, should marry as soon as possible to provide an heir to the throne other than her half-sister Elizabeth, whose religious leanings were doubtful. The Earl of Devon was suggested as a possible bridegroom, but Mary had set her heart on marrying the heir to the Spanish throne, PHILIP II, son of her one-time suitor Charles V, who was a widower, 11 years her junior. The Commons, backed by Gardiner, begged her to reconsider, fearing the threat to English independence that might be posed by such a match. Mary was adamant and her persistence led to a rebellion headed by Sir Thomas Wyatt, who marched on London, but was promptly defeated and executed. The marriage plans went through and Mary and Philip were married in Winchester Cathedral on 25 July 1554. At Mary's instance Philip received the title of king and all official documents and Acts of Parliament were to be dated in their joint names. His head also appeared on the coinage, face to face with hers. Jointly the king and queen had the longest style of any British sovereign:

> Philip and Mary, by the Grace of God, King and Queen of England and France, Naples, Jerusalem and Ireland, Defenders of the Faith, Princes of Spain and Sicily, Archdukes of Austria, Dukes of Milan, Burgundy and Brabant, Count and Countess of Flanders, Habsburg and Tyrol.

The marriage was not a success, for although Mary fell deeply in love with Philip, he found her repellent and complained of the disgusting odour emanating from her nose. This was another indication of possible congenital syphilis resulting from syphilitic rhinitis attended by bone ulceration and the formation of malodorous crusts. After 14 months Philip returned to Spain in August 1555 leaving a disconsolate Mary deluding herself with a false pregnancy.

Mary's rigorous attempts to eradicate Protestantism resulted in the so-called 'Marian Persecutions', in the course of which some 300 Protestants including Cranmer, Ridley, Latimer and Hooper suffered death for their faith. Bishop Bonner of London was particularly active in the persecutions. He was later to be deprived of his bishopric under Elizabeth and to die in prison. It must be stated, however, that the number of Protestants who suffered death or persecution under Mary was more than balanced by the number of Catholics who were to suffer under Elizabeth.

In 1557 Philip returned to England and was joyfully received by Mary at Greenwich. She at once agreed to join with Spain in war against France and as a result lost Calais, England's last remaining Continental possession. Philip left again in July 1557 and was never to return.

Mary had come to rely heavily on her kinsman Cardinal Pole, who became Archbishop of Canterbury in 1556 in succession to Cranmer and had acted as the pope's legate in reconciling the Church of England to Rome. In November 1558 both queen and cardinal fell ill with influenza. In the queen's case her condition was aggravated by her grief over Philip's absence and the loss of Calais. 'When I am dead,' she said, 'you will find the words "Philip" and "Calais" engraved upon my heart.' She died, very peacefully and heartened by visions of children 'like angels', at ST JAMES'S PALACE on 17 November 1558, and Cardinal Pole died at Lambeth the following day. She was buried in Westminster Abbey.

Mary's character has been so obscured by the reports of her ferocious persecutions in pursuit of her fanatical mission to restore Catholicism, that the pathetic, frustrated, chronically sick, unloved woman has been overlooked. She had some of her father's fire and greatness and, blessed with health, might have achieved her design. Instead her whole life was an unmitigated tragedy and she has gone down in history as 'Bloody Mary', an unjust epithet, for she was not by nature a cruel or vindictive woman, albeit a bigoted one, determined to bring England back to papal obedience. The Venetian ambassador, describing her a year before her death, found her a 'seemly' woman and 'never to be loathed for ugliness, even at her

present age', but detected that she had a tendency to 'a very deep melancholy, much greater than that to which she is constitutionally liable'.

Mary II, Queen of England (1662–94) The eldest daughter and second child of James, Duke of York (later JAMES II) and his first wife Anne HYDE, who was born at ST JAMES'S PALACE at 'past one of the clock in the morning' on 30 April 1662 and baptized in the Chapel Royal, St James's, on 9 May following, her godparents being the Duchess of Buckingham, the Duchess of Ormonde and her father's cousin Prince RUPERT, Duke of Cumberland. She grew up with her younger sister Anne (later Queen ANNE) and because their other siblings were all short lived, they were destined to be virtually the only two occupants of their nursery. Their education was very rudimentary.

The Lady Mary of York, as she was then known, was only 15 years old when she was married in a strictly private ceremony, which took place at nine o'clock at night in her bedchamber at St James's Palace on 4 November 1677, to her first cousin, William Henry, Prince of Orange (see WILLIAM III). The marriage, which was conducted by Dr Compton, Bishop of London, took place in the presence of the king and queen and the bride's father and stepmother. Mary was an unhappy bride, for apart from the fact that she towered over her short, asthmatic bridegroom, the idea of leaving home appalled her. Her aunt Queen Catherine (see CATHERINE OF BRAGANZA) sought to comfort her by saying, 'Child, when I came to England I had not even seen the King', to which Mary replied, 'Madam, you came into England, but I am going out of England'.

In spite of this inauspicious beginning, the marriage turned out well and the couple soon became devotedly attached to each other. Mary adapted well to life in Holland, taking an interest in planning gardens and assiduously collecting blue and white china. Sadly, there were to be no children (possibly because Mary's father had had syphilis as duke of York) although Mary miscarried on at least two occasions. The marriage was, however, briefly endangered in 1685, when news of William's relationship with his mistress Betty Villiers, publicized by the agents of James II, became widely known. In response, William assured his wife that the rumours were without foundation and Mary, apparently 'completely disarmed' by his denials, burst into tears and allowed herself to be reconciled.

The death of CHARLES II and the accession to the throne of Mary's father in 1685 made Mary heiress presumptive and as long as she retained this position her father's Catholicism was tolerated, since it was known that Mary was a staunch Protestant. Matters changed in 1688, though, when James's queen, MARY OF MODENA, gave birth to a son who seemed likely to live and who displaced Mary in the succession. William set out to safeguard the Protestant succession and, after landing at Brixham on 5 November 1688, marched on London. James panicked and fled the country in December, having sent his wife and baby son on ahead. After an interregnum of two months the throne was offered to William and Mary jointly, and they were proclaimed king and queen on 13 February 1689. The throne was initially offered to Mary alone, with William to become her prince consort, but neither Mary nor William was willing to agree to such an arrangement. Their coronation, on 11 April 1689, was unique as a duplicate coronation chair and duplicate items of regalia had to be provided for the ceremony, at which the Bishop of London, who had married them, officiated, since Archbishop Sancroft, who had crowned James II, had scruples about crowning another sovereign in James's lifetime. Mary had behaved very badly on her arrival in England, running through WHITEHALL PALACE recently vacated by her father and stepmother, 'laughing and jolly as to a wedding', as Evelyn recorded, and bouncing on the beds in triumph. Her sister Anne adopted a very different attitude.

Mary played no part in public affairs except during William's absences abroad when she was left in charge. She was not particularly intelligent and leaned towards Puritanism in religion, doubtless influenced by her encounter with Calvinism during her early married life in Holland. To this end, she abolished the sung services in the Chapel Royal at Whitehall. Her preferred residences were HAMPTON COURT and KENSINGTON PALACE, and she was largely responsible for the construction of the ornamental water known as the Serpentine in Kensington Gardens.

In December 1694 Mary fell ill with smallpox. She was dosed with 'Venice treacle', a celebrated panacea of the day containing no fewer than 64 ingredients, but grew progressively worse and died at Kensington Palace on 28 December 1694.

Her funeral took place at WESTMINSTER ABBEY on 5 March 1695 and was attended by members of both Houses of Parliament, another unique occurrence, because up till that time Parliament had always been dissolved on the death of a sovereign. 'Never was so universal a mourning,' Evelyn recorded, 'all the Parliament men had cloaks given them, and 400 poore women; all the streetes hung, and the middle of the streete boarded and cover'd with black cloth. There were all the nobility, Mayor, Aldermen, Judges, etc.' Purcell composed the music for Queen Mary's funeral and the total cost of the whole ceremony was a staggering £50,000. Evelyn had revised his opinion of Mary since her accession, remarking that her debts were very small and that she was 'an admirable woman'.

Mary Adelaide of Cambridge, Princess, Duchess of Teck (1833–97) The younger daughter and third and youngest child of Prince Adolphus, Duke of CAMBRIDGE (seventh son of GEORGE III) and Augusta of Hesse-Cassel, who was born at Hanover on 22 November 1833 and named Mary Adelaide Wilhelmina Elizabeth. Her first two names were those of her aunts and godmothers, Princess MARY, DUCHESS OF GLOUCESTER and Queen ADELAIDE. At the time of her birth, the princess's father was Viceroy of Hanover, but he relinquished that post in 1837 when the death of WILLIAM IV brought about the separation of the kingdom of Hanover from the British crown, and the family returned to England. Following the death of her father in 1850, Princess Mary Adelaide and her mother the Duchess of Cambridge went to live at Cambridge Cottage, Kew, a house facing Kew Green.

From her early youth the princess was excessively stout and she was known to her cousin Queen VICTORIA as 'Fat Mary', often being the butt of disparaging remarks in the queen's family correspondence. However, her joviality and general air of gruff benevolence were to render her extremely popular with the ordinary people.

At the age of 17 Princess Mary Adelaide made her first appearance in society at the official opening of the Great Exhibition in 1851 and for the next 15 years she and her mother led a very full social life. The princess's large size led many of her family to consider her unmarriageable. She was described as 'that mountain of a girl' and the US Minister estimated that she must weigh at least 250 pounds. Carriage springs were said to 'groan' under her, and on one occasion when dancing at Orleans House, Twickenham, with the Comte de Paris she careered into another girl and knocked her flat on her back.

After tentative marriage projects with Prince Oscar of Sweden, the King of Sardinia, and others, a serious suitor for Princess Mary Adelaide's hand appeared when she was 32 in the person of Prince Franz of Teck, the only son of Duke Alexander of Württemberg, who had contracted a morganatic marriage with a Hungarian, Countess Claudine Susanne Rhèdey. Claudine, who had been created Countess of Hohenstein and had given birth to three children, had been killed at a military review when her horse threw her and she was trampled to death by a squadron of galloping cavalry. In 1863 her son Franz, who had been born at Esseg (now Osijek in the former Yugoslavia), and not at Vienna as often stated, on 27 August 1837, was created Prince of Teck and granted the qualification of 'Serene Highness' (HSH). He had found favour with the Emperor and Empress of Austria and served as an officer in the Imperial Gendarmerie Guard. It was at Vienna that he met Albert Edward, Prince of Wales (later EDWARD VII), who took a liking to him and invited him to visit England, which he did in March 1866 at a time when Princess Mary Adelaide was in Germany visiting her sister the Grand Duchess of Mecklenburg-Strelitz. The Cambridge family, seeing an opportunity to marry her at last, sent her back post-haste to London, where, after a very short acquaintance, she accepted the tall, dark, good-looking young man's proposal in the Rhododendron Walk in Kew Gardens and they became engaged on 10 April.

Queen Victoria approved of the prospective bridegroom as 'very gentlemanlike and certainly very good looking' and the marriage took place at Kew Church on 12 June 1866. The couple were to enjoy a very happy marriage although they remained chronically hard up, chiefly through Princess Mary Adelaide's extravagances and impetuous generosity. They were allotted an apartment in KENSINGTON PALACE and it was there that their four children were born: Victoria Mary (later Queen MARY OF TECK) on 26 May 1867; Adolphus (later 2nd Duke and Prince of Teck and 1st Marquess of Cambridge) on 13 August 1868; Francis (Frank) on 9 January 1870 (died 22 October 1910); and Alexander (Alge) (later Earl of Athlone) on 14 April 1874. The family

moved to White Lodge in Richmond Park by 1870.

In September 1871 the King of Württemberg raised Teck to a dukedom and from thenceforth the couple became duke and duchess of Teck. Princess Mary Adelaide became popular in the area of her new residence, encouraging her children to play in the park with the children of the gamekeepers and lodgekeepers. She would also frequently call on the wife of one of the lodgekeepers and invite her to accompany her in her carriage for an afternoon drive. It was not for nothing that she became known as 'The People's Princess'.

For many years Princess Mary Adelaide was occupied in caring for her mother, who became a chronic and very querulous invalid yet managed to live to the age of 92. From September 1883 until May 1885 the Tecks were obliged to live in Florence in an attempt to economize and retrench. They took their daughter with them and the stay undoubtedly gave her that lifelong love of art that was to be one of her main interests.

In 1884 the Duke of Teck suffered some kind of seizure brought on partly by money worries and partly by his constant fretting over his morganatic status and his obsessional idea that but for that he would have been heir presumptive to the crown of Württemberg. Fortunately, he recovered quite rapidly. On 1 July 1887 he was granted the style of 'Highness' (HH) by Royal Warrant. The culminating triumph of Princess Mary Adelaide's life was the marriage in 1893 of her daughter May to the Duke of York (later GEORGE V) (after first being engaged to his elder brother the Duke of Clarence (see CLARENCE, ALBERT VICTOR, DUKE OF), who died before their marriage could take place), and the knowledge that she would one day be queen and the mother of future sovereigns.

Princess Mary Adelaide's health began to fail in the summer of 1896. In April 1897 she underwent a serious emergency operation at White Lodge. She made a speedy recovery and was able to appear in Queen Victoria's DIAMOND JUBILEE procession on 22 June 1897. On 25 October her daughter noted in her diary, 'Mama was not feeling quite well'. The next day she was very much worse and her medical advisers decided that another emergency operation was called for. Mr Allingham, the surgeon, operated at half past midnight and at 3 am on 27 October 1897 Princess Mary Adelaide died of heart failure. The operations had been to relieve an intestinal obstruction, which does not appear to have been of a cancerous nature. She was buried in the Royal Tomb House at St George's Chapel, Windsor, on 4 November. The Duke of Teck became more and more unbalanced after his wife's death, and, died at White Lodge on 20 January 1900.

Mary of Gueldres, Queen of Scots

(1433–63) The consort of JAMES II, KING OF SCOTS, who was the second of the three daughters of Arnold, Duke of Gueldres, and his wife Catherine, daughter of Adolf I, Duke of Cleves. She was educated at the court of Philippe the Good, Duke of Burgundy, and was married to James II at HOLYROODHOUSE on 3 July 1449, being crowned queen the same day. There were four sons and two daughters of the marriage. After James II had been killed by the bursting of a cannon at the siege of Roxburgh in August 1460, Queen Mary became regent for her eight-year-old son JAMES III. She at once took him with her to Roxburgh and successfully captured the castle. In the following year she gave hospitality to HENRY VI of England and MARGARET OF ANJOU when they sought refuge after their defeat at Towton.

Queen Mary died on 1 December 1463 and was buried in the Collegiate Church of the Holy Trinity (which she had founded) in Edinburgh. The church was demolished in 1848 and a female skeleton, thought to be the queen's, was reinterred at Holyroodhouse and placed in the royal vault there in 1898.

Mary of Guise, Queen of Scots (1515–60)

The second consort of JAMES V, who was the eldest daughter and first child of Claude I de Lorraine, Duke of Guise, and his wife Antoinette, eldest daughter of François de Bourbon, Duke of Vendôme, and was born at Bar-le-Duc on 20 November 1515. She was brought up at the Château de Joinville and enjoyed a happy childhood as the eldest of a large family of brothers and sisters. To complete her education she was sent to the Poor Clares' Convent at Pont-au-Mousson, where her paternal grandmother, Philippa of Gueldres, Duchess of Lorraine, had become a nun.

Mary grew up to be a tall, handsome, red-haired woman and when she left the convent she joined the ducal court of her uncle the Duke of Lorraine at Nancy. In March 1531 she accompanied other members of her family to St Denis to attend the coronation of Queen Eléonore, the second wife of François I and made her début at the French

court, riding in the new queen's train when she made her state entry into Paris. Mary enjoyed life at the French court for the next two and a half years until she married, at the Louvre on 4 August 1534, Louis II, Duke of Longueville, Grand Chamberlain of France, a young man of considerable wealth and property. The marriage proved to be a happy one and Mary's first child, François, was born at Amiens on 30 October 1535.

The following year the Duke and Duchess of Longueville went to Paris to attend the wedding of Princess Madeleine (see MADELEINE OF FRANCE, QUEEN OF SCOTS), the king's eldest daughter, to James V, King of Scots, and Mary thus met for the first time the man who was to become her second husband. Mary's happiness came to an end on 9 June 1537, when her husband died at Rouen of a virulent fever, leaving her a widow at 21. Her second son was born posthumously on 4 August 1537 and named Louis. He survived only four months. It was François I of France who proposed that Mary should marry his widowed son-in-law James V. She had another suitor in the person of HENRY VIII of England, then the widower of JANE SEYMOUR (he had heard that Mary was 'lusty and fair' with a dowry of 30,000 francs a year). When the French ambassador to England asked him why he was eager to marry her, Henry said that it was because she was big and he had need of a big wife. When this was reported to Mary, she commented, 'I may be big in person, but my neck is small!' The negotiations for Mary's marriage to James were speeded up, the dowry was fixed at 150,000 livres, and James applied to the Pope for a dispensation since he and Mary were third cousins, both being great-great-grandchildren of Arnold, Duke of Gueldres. The proxy marriage took place at Châteaudun on 9 May 1538, Robert, Lord Maxwell acting for the King of Scots.

Mary sailed from Le Havre on 10 June and reached Scotland on Trinity Sunday, 16 June. She landed at Balcomie in Fife and lodged overnight in the castle there. The next morning James and a large retinue rode out from St Andrews, 10 miles north, to meet her and escort her back. The marriage took place in St Andrews Cathedral on 18 June 1538. Mary's coronation at Holyrood took place on 22 February 1540 when she was six months pregnant. It was a magnificent occasion, with Cardinal Beaton officiating, and the queen's crown and sceptre were made to order at a cost of £45. Soon after the coronation the court moved to Stirling and thence to St Andrews, where

Mary's child, James, Duke of Rothesay, was born on 22 May 1540. On 24 April 1541 Mary gave birth to another son, Robert, Duke of Albany, at Falkland Castle. A week after his birth news arrived from St Andrews that Prince James was mortally ill. His father set out to see him at once, but when he arrived the child was already dead. To add to the tragedy, the new baby also died, leaving the parents desolate.

In November 1542 Mary was at Linlithgow awaiting the birth of her fifth child, when James's army was defeated by the English at Solway Moss. The king, who had not been present at the battle himself, left Lochmaben where he had been encamped and rode northwards. He stopped at Linlithgow, where Mary was unable to comfort him, 'his mind near gone through dolour and care' as it was reported, and he soon left her and rode on to Falkland Castle, where he became feverish and delirious and took to his bed. On 8 December the queen gave birth to a daughter. A week later James died and the baby had become MARY, QUEEN OF SCOTS.

A struggle for the regency between the Earl of Arran and Cardinal Beaton, who had the queen's support, ended with Arran being proclaimed Lord Governor of Scotland on 3 January 1543 and Beaton being appointed Chancellor a week later. The widowed queen and her daughter remained at Linlithgow until July 1543, when they moved to Stirling, where the baby queen's coronation took place in September. In the same month Mary of Guise was appointed as the principal member of the Council of Regency to assist and advise Arran, whose power was greatly reduced. She kept a brilliant court with 'dancing, singing, playing and much merriness'. Her acceptance of French offers of help led to war with England again breaking out and after the murder of Cardinal Beaton in 1546, Mary, with the support of the Douglases, became the most powerful figure in Scotland.

The Scottish defeat at the battle of Pinkie in September 1547 left the country in a parlous state. Arran, as regent, was completely useless and Mary again sought French aid. The outcome was the betrothal of the little queen to the French Dauphin and once Parliament had agreed to this, the younger Mary was sent to France. The war with England was pursued until peace was finally concluded in April 1550. Mary's father the Duke of Guise died in the same month and in September she set out on a visit to France,

where she spent a year, happily reunited with her children, her mother and her other relations. Sadly, however, the visit was marred by the death of Mary's son, François, Duke of Longueville, who died in her arms from a virulent fever.

Mary returned via England, where she was received with great honour and entertained at Hampton Court and at Westminster by EDWARD VI. The Queen Dowager returned to Edinburgh by land and spent the next two years in a bid to become the sole regent of Scotland. In this she was successful. Arran, who had been created Duke of Châtelherault by the king of France, came to an agreement with Mary, and on 12 April 1554 he resigned his office and she was solemnly invested as Queen Regent at the Tolbooth in Edinburgh.

Mary, an extremely capable woman, had achieved her life's ambition and set out to bring justice, peace and prosperity to her adopted country – though she had to contend with the unrest occasioned by the Protestant Reformation, which had taken root in Scotland. In 1559 John Knox commenced his fiery sermons, stirring his congregations to break up images and desecrate churches, much to Mary's distress. By the end of the year the whole country was on the verge of civil war with the former regent Châtelherault siding with the Protestants and gaining aid from England, where ELIZABETH I had now become queen. Mary obtained French aid to fortify Leith, which was threatened with siege by the English, and early in November she returned to Edinburgh, where soon after she fell seriously ill, apparently with a valvular heart disease.

The English army invaded Scotland in March 1560, and on 1 April Mary and her entourage deemed it prudent to remove from HOLYROODHOUSE into Edinburgh Castle. There she received various emissaries treating for peace and continued to conduct the business of the kingdom, although she was daily growing weaker. She summoned her last council on 7 June and died about half an hour after midnight on 11 June 1560. She was only 44 years old and was survived by her mother. After she had been embalmed and placed in a lead coffin, she lay in St Margaret's Chapel within the castle until March 1561, when she was taken to Leith and placed on board a ship bound for France. Her final resting place was to be the convent of St Pierre at Rheims, where her sister Renée was abbess. The monument erected over her tomb was destroyed in the French Revolution.

Queen Mary was undoubtedly a good and well-intentioned woman and a capable ruler, but the times were against her as well as the virulence of Knox, who said that the sight of a crown on her head was as unseemly 'as to put a saddle upon the back of an unruly cow'.

Mary of Modena, Queen of England

(1658–1718) The second wife and queen consort of JAMES II, who was the only daughter of Alfonso IV, Duke of Modena, of the great House of Este, and his wife Laura Martinozzi, a niece of the famous Cardinal Mazarin, and was born at Modena on 25 September 1658. There is a discrepancy over her names, which are usually given as Mary Beatrice Eleonora, but Agnes Strickland says she was baptized Mary Beatrice Anne Margaret Isabella. Perhaps the name Eleonora was added at her confirmation, as was often the case.

As a girl Mary had the intention of becoming a nun, having had a strict religious upbringing, but largely through the influence of Louis XIV she was proposed as a possible second wife for James, Duke of York. The negotiations being successfully completed, she set out for England after a proxy marriage at Modena on 30 September 1673. She visited the French court *en route*, where her charm, beauty and air of distinction gained much approval, and was married to James on arrival at Dover on 21 November 1673. 'I have brought you a new playmate,' said James to his daughters Mary and Anne on presenting their stepmother to them. There was less than four years between the two Marys, and the three teen-age girls got on well together and formed a warm friendship. In the first nine years of her marriage the Duchess of York gave birth to four children, of whom only one, the Princess Isabella (*see* ISABELLA OF YORK, PRINCESS) survived more than a few months, and she died in her fifth year. Mary also suffered four miscarriages.

On the death of CHARLES II Mary became Queen Consort, and she was crowned with James at WESTMINSTER ABBEY on 23 April 1685. It was noted that she joined in the responses in the Anglican service, whereas James remained tight-lipped. As a 'cradle Catholic', the queen did not share his bigotry. Her diadem, two crowns, sceptre and ivory rod were all made for her coronation, replacing items that had been broken up under the Commonwealth.

In 1687 Mary announced that she was again pregnant after a gap of five years, and the outcome was the birth of her son James Francis Edward on 10 June 1688 (enemies claimed the baby was an imposter introduced to the royal bed by means of a warming pan). Later in the year she was obliged to flee with the baby (*see* STUART, PRINCE JAMES FRANCIS EDWARD) to France as James was ousted in what became known as the 'GLORIOUS REVOLUTION'. The exiled Queen of England was greatly admired at the French court and when she gave birth to a daughter, Princess Louisa Maria (*see* LOUISA MARIA THERESA STUART, PRINCESS), on 28 June 1692, the French ladies were astonished to see the tiny baby dressed in little shoes and stockings for her baptism. Doubtless there was a rush to emulate this example of English chic.

After James II's death in September 1701, his widow, who received an annual pension of 100,000 francs from Louis XIV, was regarded as Queen Regent until the coming of age of her son 'James III'. She frequently retreated to the convent of Chaillot where the nuns became the recipients of her confidences and recorded many of her reminiscences.

In 1712 Queen Mary had the great sorrow of losing her only surviving daughter, an attractive girl of 20, who succumbed to smallpox. She lived on another six years and died of cancer at St Germain-en-Laye on 7 May 1718, aged 59. She was buried in the convent of Chaillot among her beloved nuns.

Mary of Scotland, Princess, Countess of Boulogne

(d.1116) The younger daughter of MALCOLM III, KING OF SCOTS and St MARGARET, who was married in 1102 to Eustace III, Count of Boulogne. She had one son, who died young, and one daughter, MATILDA OF BOULOGNE, who married King STEPHEN. She died on 31 May 1116 and was buried at BERMONDSEY ABBEY. Count Eustace died after 1125.

Mary of Teck, Queen of Great Britain

(1867–1953) The consort of GEORGE V, who was the only daughter and eldest child of Francis, Prince and Duke of Teck, and his wife Princess MARY ADELAIDE OF CAMBRIDGE, and was born at KENSINGTON PALACE, London, at midnight on 26 May 1867. She was baptized by the Archbishop of Canterbury in the palace chapel on 27 July and received the names Victoria Mary Augusta Louisa Olga Pauline Claudine Agnes. To her family she was always to be known as 'May'. Her godparents were her mother's cousin, Queen VICTORIA (for whom Princess Mary Adelaide stood proxy), her maternal grandmother the Duchess of Cambridge, and Albert Edward, Prince of Wales (later EDWARD VII and her father-in-law).

May's father was a morganatic scion of the royal house of Württemberg, his father Duke Alexander having married a Hungarian Countess Claudine Rhèdey, who was not considered his equal in birth, so that their children were not regarded as being fully of royal birth and were ineligible to succeed to the kingdom of Württemberg. This fact so played on May's father's mind that he eventually lost his reason, and it was to colour her whole life also, for although she attained the highest possible rank as Queen of Great Britain and Empress of India, she was forever conscious of her inferior birth, which would have rendered her virtually unmarriageable in the ranks of continental royalty. It was probably for this reason that she over-compensated by becoming the stiff, unbending regal figure, overawing all with whom she came in contact.

Few who saw the stately figure of Queen Mary in later life could have imagined that in her childhood she had been something of a tomboy. As the only sister of three lively brothers, she climbed trees and played cricket with them and the children of the gamekeepers and lodgekeepers of Richmond Park, where her parents resided at White Lodge. May's mother, the Duchess of Teck, known behind her back to the queen and other members of the royal family as 'Fat Mary', was a large, jolly, generous lady, who often found herself in pecuniary difficulties. At one time, in order to economize, she moved to Florence with her family, and it was there that Mary acquired the interest in art that was to remain with her all her life, although it must be admitted that her taste was far from impeccable. In later life she was to acquire 'art treasures' in magpie fashion, and many stories are told of the unscrupulous way in which she would cajole friends and even casual acquaintances into donating to her collection objects to which she had taken a fancy. After her death the Victoria and Albert Museum arranged an exhibition of some of her possessions, and precious jewelled objets and bibelots by Fabergé and others were displayed cheek-by-jowl with sentimental watercolours of rustic cottages with hollyhocks clustering round the door.

Princess May became the unprotesting fiancée of the rather unsavoury Prince Eddy (see CLARENCE), and on his death was passed on, as it were, to his younger brother George, a much more suitable match. They were married at the Chapel Royal, ST JAMES'S PALACE, on 6 July 1893. She was a young woman of great tact and well able to handle the rather difficult mother-in-law she acquired in 'motherdear'. As Queen Mary, which she became on her husband's accession to the throne in 1910, May, who was never a beauty (she herself was to say that she was far too like her great-grandmother Queen CHARLOTTE ever to be considered good-looking), acquired a regal bearing and dignity of carriage surpassing that of any other queen. She could wear jewels superbly and in profusion, and on her they never looked vulgar as they would on other women. Following her death at Marlborough House at 10.15 in the evening on 24 March 1953 Sir Winston Churchill, paying tribute in the House of Commons, was to say, 'She looked like a Queen and she acted like a Queen'.

As Queen Mother, Queen Mary spent the years of the Second World War in the safety of Badminton House, the Gloucestershire seat of the Duke of Beaufort, who had married her niece Lady Mary Cambridge. Years later the Duchess was to be asked which part of the house Queen Mary had occupied. 'All of it,' was the laconic reply. At Badminton the old queen was photographed in her inevitable toque and caped coat 'helping' the woodmen to cut down trees in a series of artlessly posed photographs. She found the drawing-room rather too distant from the 'usual offices' for her comfort and had a commode installed behind a screen at one end of the room. She would retire behind this whenever she felt the need, regardless of the assembled company who had to continue making embarrassed and loud conversation until she reappeared.

Queen Mary loved the theatre and the cinema, and both before and after the Second World War her distinctive Daimler motor car was to be seen parked outside various suburban cinemas, where she had ventured to see a particular film that had been recommended to her, thus avoiding the fuss that would have surrounded her attendance at a West End performance.

One of Queen Mary's failings was her inability to express her feelings for her children in any outward form. She did care for them deeply and had the great sorrow of seeing three of her five sons die before her. Prince JOHN[5], the youngest, was an epileptic and his mother was able to regard his death as a 'happy release', but the deaths of the Duke of Kent (see KENT, GEORGE, DUKE OF) on active service and of GEORGE VI were an added burden in her old age. The defection, as she saw it, of her eldest son David (see EDWARD VIII) also grieved her deeply, although she never ceased to love him as much as ever.

Queen Mary was buried in St George's Chapel, Windsor, beside George V in a tomb in the nave surmounted by their recumbent effigies clad in the robes of the Order of the GARTER.

Matilda, 'Lady of the English', Empress
(c.1103–67) The only legitimate daughter of HENRY I and his first wife MATILDA OF SCOTLAND, who was born at Winchester in about 1103 and may have been a twin with her brother WILLIAM 'THE ATHELING', DUKE OF NORMANDY. The late Gerald Paget, in his book *The Lineage and Ancestry of HRH Prince Charles, Prince of Wales*, states that she was born on 7 February 1102 and William on 5 August 1103 without citing any authority. The first date is impossible as Queen Matilda is known to have given birth to a premature infant in July 1101.

Matilda was originally named Alice or Aethelic, but her name was later changed to that of her mother. She was still a child when her father arranged a very grand marriage for her to the Emperor Heinrich V. The ceremony took place at Mainz on 7 January 1114 and Matilda was crowned Empress the same day by the Archbishop of Cologne. Her husband, who was her senior by more than 20 years, died at Utrecht on 23 May 1125, leaving her a childless widow, and she returned to England where the death of her brother William in the wreck of the *White Ship* (or *Blanche Nef*) had left her as her father's sole legitimate offspring. Henry obliged the English barons to take an oath of fealty to his daughter as heiress presumptive to the crown at Christmas 1126, her cousin STEPHEN being one of those to do so (though many agreed privately that they found Matilda haughty and superior and resented her assumption of influence). The following year Henry arranged a second marriage for his daughter to Geoffrey V, Count of Anjou and Maine (see GEOFFREY PLANTAGENET), the ceremony taking place at Le Mans on 22 May 1127. Matilda was a somewhat reluctant bride, and, although she retained the style of empress for the rest of her life, she evidently felt that marriage to a brash young count, who was more than 10 years

her junior, was somewhat beneath her. However, the required object of the marriage was attained by the birth of three sons.

On the death of Henry I in December 1135 and Stephen's usurpation of the throne, Matilda at once protested. She gathered forces and landed in England in the autumn of 1139, being ably supported by her half-brother, Robert, Earl of GLOUCESTER, and several powerful barons. In the course of the civil wars that ensued, Stephen was captured at Lincoln in February 1141 and imprisoned at Bristol. His brother Henry, Bishop of Winchester, turned against him and a legatine council of the English church held at Winchester declared Stephen deposed and proclaimed Matilda 'Lady of the English' on 7 April 1141. Although she had possession of the royal regalia, she was never crowned as queen. The struggle continued, and Stephen's supporters, who had managed to capture Robert of Gloucester, exchanged him for Stephen. First one side and then the other gained the upper hand for several years to come. At times, the person of the empress herself was in some danger: in 1141, for instance, she escaped from Devizes only by having herself disguised as a corpse, while in 1142 she made a 'miraculous' escape from Oxford Castle by means of a rope and wearing a white cloak to blend in with the winter landscape. Matilda's husband conquered Normandy in 1144 and Matilda withdrew there some years later.

In 1153 her eldest son Henry (see HENRY II), now grown to manhood, took her place and was joined by all her old supporters. This time the matter was settled without further bloodshed and by the Treaty of Westminster it was agreed that Stephen should retain the crown for life and that Henry should succeed him, which he did on Stephen's death in October the following year. A rumour recounted by Matthew Paris has it that Stephen, not Geoffrey, was the real father of Henry, having conducted an amorous intrigue with Matilda, but the relevant dates render it unlikely.

Matilda, whose name is often rendered as Maud, lived to see her son firmly established on the English throne. She died at Rouen on 10 September 1167. She was buried first in the convent of Bonnes Nouvelles and thence transferred to the Abbey of Bec, where her body was reinterred before the high altar in 1282. Her remains were discovered and again reburied in 1847.

Matilda, Princess[1] see MATILDA OF SCOT-
LAND, QUEEN OF ENGLAND.

Matilda, Princess[2] (d. before 1112) One of
the daughters of WILLIAM I THE CON-
QUEROR and MATILDA OF FLANDERS. She is
mentioned in Domesday Book, which
records that her chamberlain Geoffrey held
lands of the king in Hampshire. A circular
letter issued by the nuns of the Holy Trinity
at Caen in June 1112 announcing the death
of their abbess refers to Matilda and her sisters Adelais and Constance as being dead.
She was almost certainly unmarried.

Matilda, Princess[3] see MATILDA, 'LADY OF
THE ENGLISH', EMPRESS.

Matilda, Princess[4] (c.1133–c.1135) The
elder daughter of King STEPHEN and
MATILDA OF BOULOGNE, who was born in
about 1133. While still an infant she was
contracted in marriage to Waleran, Count of
Mellent, said to have been 30 years her
senior. She died in about 1135 and if before
her great-uncle HENRY I cannot be considered a princess of England. She was buried
in the Priory Church of the Holy Trinity
within Aldgate, London, and her mother
later founded and endowed the hospital and
church of St Katherine by the Tower for the
repose of her soul and that of her brother
Baldwin.

**Matilda, Princess, Duchess of Saxony and
Bavaria** (1156–89) The eldest daughter and
third child of HENRY II and ELEANOR OF
AQUITAINE, who was born in London in
June 1156 and baptized in the Priory
Church of the Holy Trinity within Aldgate
by Theobald, Archbishop of Canterbury.
She was married at St Peter's Cathedral,
Minden, on 1 February 1168 to Heinrich V
'the Lion', Duke of Saxony and Bavaria, her
senior by some 27 years, whose first marriage to Klementia of Zähringen had been
annulled in 1162. Matilda became the
mother of four sons and two daughters.
Through her youngest son, Wilhelm, who
was born at Winchester during a visit to
England in 1184, she became the ancestress
in direct male line of the House of HANOVER,
which was to ascend the British throne in
1714. Matilda died at Brunswick on 28 June
1189 and was buried in the Cathedral of St
Blasius there. Her husband survived until 6
August 1195 and was buried with her.

Matilda, Queen of Scots (c.1071–c.1130)
The consort of DAVID I, KING OF SCOTS, who
was the eldest daughter and heiress of
Waltheof, Earl of Northampton and
Huntingdon, and his wife Judith, daughter
of Lambert, Count of Lens, and his wife
Adelaide or Adeliz, sister or half-sister of
WILLIAM I THE CONQUEROR, and was born
in about 1071 or 1072. She married first, in
about 1090, Simon de St Liz, who became
Earl of Huntingdon and Northampton in
her right and died at the Cluniac Priory of
La Charité-sur-Loire in about 1111 when
on the way to Jerusalem. They had two
sons, Simon, later Earl of Huntingdon and
Northampton, and Waltheof, Abbot of
Melrose, and a daughter Matilda or Maud,
who married Robert fitzRichard. Matilda
married secondly, in 1113 or 1114, David of
Scotland, who held the earldoms of Huntingdon and Northampton in her right. In
April 1124 he succeeded his brother
ALEXANDER I on the Scottish throne.
Although over 40 at the time of her second
marriage, Matilda had four more children,
Malcolm, who died young, HENRY, EARL OF
HUNTINGDON, and Claricia and Hodierna,
who both died unmarried. Queen Matilda
died between 23 April 1130 and 22 April
1131 and was buried at Scone Abbey.

Matilda of Boulogne, Queen of England
(c.1105–52) The consort of King STEPHEN,
who was the only daughter and heiress of
Eustace III, Count of Boulogne, and his
wife MARY, the younger sister of MATILDA
OF SCOTLAND, the first queen of HENRY I.
She was born probably at Boulogne between
1103 and 1105. On her father's death
Matilda succeeded to the county of Boulogne and Henry I arranged her marriage to
his nephew Stephen of Blois. The wedding
probably took place at Westminster in 1125,
and in the course of the next 10 years
Matilda gave birth to three sons and two
daughters. When Stephen usurped the
English throne in December 1135, his wife
was to prove one of his most active and
staunch supporters throughout his long
struggle with the Empress Matilda (see
MATILDA, 'LADY OF THE ENGLISH', EM-
PRESS), who was first cousin to both of them.
Matilda followed Stephen to England, her
journey perhaps delayed by the birth of her
youngest child Mary, and was crowned
at WESTMINSTER ABBEY on Easter Day,
22 March 1136. She was as strong and
resourceful as Stephen was weak and indecisive. It was she who recaptured London
for him from the Empress Matilda's forces
and later forced the empress's withdrawal
from the siege of Winchester, leading to
Stephen's release in 1141 in exchange for
Robert of Gloucester. Had she not died at

Hedingham Castle, Essex, on 3 May 1152 the dispute over the crown might well have continued and there would have been no Treaty of Westminster. Stephen was even more of a broken reed without her and survived her by a little over two years. Matilda was buried at Faversham Abbey in Kent, which Stephen had founded and where he and their son EUSTACE were also laid to rest.

Matilda of Flanders, Queen of England

(c.1031–83) The consort of WILLIAM I THE CONQUEROR, who was the daughter of Baldwin V, Count of Flanders, and his wife Adèle, daughter of Robert II, King of France, and was born in Flanders in about 1031. She was a direct descendant of ALFRED THE GREAT, whose daughter Elfthryth had married Count Baldwin II of Flanders, and this fact doubtless added to her desirability as a bride for William. Matilda was a lady of diminutive stature whose early life is surrounded by mystery. When William first sought her hand, she is said to have rejected him with the crushing retort that she would not have a bastard for her husband. In retaliation William burst into her apartment in her father's castle at Lille and, dragging her across the room by her hair, gave her a sound beating. His daring on this occasion, we are told, so impressed her that she at once changed her mind and accepted his hand.

There were strong papal objections to the marriage, the reasons for which have never been clear. There are some indications that Matilda was not free to marry because she had already been betrothed to Brihtric Meaw, a young Saxon nobleman who visited her father's court as an emissary of EDWARD THE CONFESSOR. There is also the possibility that she had compromised herself with a Flemish commoner named Gherbod and given birth to two children – Gherbod, who later received the Earldom of Chester, and Gundred, who married William de Warenne, Earl of Surrey. This has been the subject of controversy over several centuries and still continues to exercise the minds of historians and genealogists. Married to William at last at Eu in 1053, and with dispensation finally granted by Pope Nicholas II in 1059, Matilda became an exemplary wife and mother.

She was a woman of great capability, and William had no hesitation in leaving her in charge as regent of Normandy during his absences in England. William first returned to Normandy after the conquest in March 1067 and remained until early December. It was during the last days of his stay that the future HENRY I must have been conceived. Matilda, although pregnant, left Normandy to join William in England in the spring of 1068 and was crowned at Winchester on Whitsunday (11 May). Her coronation banquet is said to have been the first at which the KING'S CHAMPION made his appearance to challenge any who might dispute the king's right to the throne.

Matilda accompanied William to the north of England and gave birth to the future Henry I at Selby, probably in September 1068. He was almost certainly her last child. She remained in England until the following year, when she returned to Normandy for good and busied herself with the affairs of the duchy and her religious foundations at Caen and Rouen. In 1083, Matilda aged about 52, fell ill, and William hastened from England to be at her side. She died at Caen on 2 November 1083 and was buried there in her foundation of the Holy Trinity. Her magnificent tomb was desecrated by the Calvinists in 1562 and later restored in simpler fashion only to be destroyed again during the French Revolution.

Matilda of Scotland, Queen of England

(1079/80–1118) The first consort of HENRY I, who was the elder daughter of MALCOLM III, KING OF SCOTS and his second wife St MARGARET and was born at DUNFERMLINE in 1079 or 1080. As a child she was sent to be educated under the care of her mother's sister, Christina, abbess of Romsey, in Hampshire and expected to take the veil there when her hand in marriage was suddenly demanded by the recently acceded Henry I. His choice was motivated by Matilda's descent from the Saxon kings rather than for any other consideration, and the marriage and the new queen's coronation were solemnized at WESTMINSTER ABBEY by Archbishop Anselm on 11 November 1100. Matilda had originally borne the Saxon name Edith, but before her marriage she adopted the name Matilda, a compliment to Henry's deceased mother. In the July following her marriage, Matilda gave birth prematurely to an infant, which did not survive, and in the succeeding years her children William (see WILLIAM 'THE ATHELING', DUKE OF NORMANDY) and Matilda (see MATILDA, 'LADY OF THE ENGLISH', EMPRESS) were born at Winchester, possibly (though not certainly) twins. Matilda, true to her convent upbringing and following the footsteps of her mother, St

Margaret, was given to good works. She built a leper hospital at St Giles-in-the-Fields, London, and founded the Augustinian priory at Aldgate. On 1 May 1118 she died at Westminster and was buried in the abbey. All trace of her tomb has disappeared.

Maud, Princess, Queen of Norway (1869–1938) The third and youngest daughter and fifth child of Albert Edward, Prince of Wales (later EDWARD VII) and ALEXANDRA OF DENMARK, who was born at Marlborough House, London, at 12.20 am on 26 November 1869. She was baptized there by the Bishop of London on Christmas Eve and received the names Maud Charlotte Mary Victoria. Her godparents were her aunts the Grand Duchess (later Empress) Maria Feodorovna of Russia and the Crown Princess (later Queen) of Denmark, the Duchess of Nassau, the Princess of Leiningen, the Duchess of INVERNESS, King Carl XV of Sweden and Norway, her uncle Prince Leopold (later Duke of ALBANY), the Prince (later Duke) of Teck, and Count Gleichen (Prince Victor of Hohenlohe-Langenburg), most of whom were represented by proxies.

Princess Maud was more lively and high-spirited than either of her elder sisters and was known in her family as 'Harry'. As a young girl she fell in love with Prince Francis of Teck, the brother of her future sister-in-law Queen MARY OF TECK, but although charming, he was an entirely unsuitable match for her, being noted for his gambling debts, general fecklessnes and his flagrant liaison with the Countess of Kilmorey, a much older woman, on whom he was later to bestow his mother's emeralds, to the horror of his family. To get him out of Maud's way, he was despatched to India and Queen VICTORIA took a hand in selecting a suitable husband for her grand-daughter. The successful candidate was Maud's first cousin, Prince (Christian Frederik) Carl Georg Waldemar Axel of Denmark, the second son of the Crown Prince (later King Frederik VIII) of Denmark. Born at Charlottenlund on 3 August 1872, he was almost three years younger than his bride. The engagement was announced on 29 October 1895 and the wedding took place in the private chapel of BUCKINGHAM PALACE on 22 July 1896. Maud wore a dress and train of white satin with a belt of silver embroidery and a wedding veil of old lace, a present from her grandmother the queen. She was attended by eight bridesmaids, all drawn from her close family. The honeymoon was spent at Appleton Hall, Norfolk, not far from Sandringham, and Maud was so reluctant to leave her parents and England that they were still there five months later. However, Prince Carl had to resume his duties with the Danish navy and they left for Denmark in December 1896.

They took up residence in the Bernstorff Palace, which Maud attempted to make as like Sandringham as possible. She had a delicate constitution and found the Danish winters extremely trying, so that she endeavoured to visit England as often as possible. Her only child was born at APPLETON HOUSE on 2 July 1903 and named Alexander Edward Christian Frederick, but his name was changed to Olav after his parents became King and Queen of Norway. In 1905 Norway declared its independence from Sweden in a bloodless revolution, and on 16 November 1905 the Norwegian government offered the throne to Prince Carl, which he accepted with the backing of Sweden, Denmark and Great Britain and a referendum by the Norwegian people, the result of which was overwhelming. He assumed the name King Haakon VII and with Queen Maud and their son entered the capital Christiania (which reverted to its old name of Oslo) on 25 November. Two days later he took the oath to the constitution and the king and queen were crowned in Trondheim Cathedral on 22 June 1906. The coronation was attended by Maud's brother and sister-in-law (later GEORGE V and Queen Mary). Maud's weakness in her legs prevented her from walking in the solemn procession to the cathedral, but she managed the rest of the ceremony well and her sister-in-law reported in a letter to her aunt AUGUSTA, Grand Duchess of Mecklenburg-Strelitz: 'The Coronation ceremony was fine and impressive – Very well done and both Charles and Maud did it all in a dignified manner and both looked very well with the Crowns on their heads.'

Maud did not take easily to being a queen, disliking all royal ceremonial, and this often made her appear stiff and cold on state occasions. At home, however, she was more relaxed and indulged in the passion for practical jokes common to many of her family. She interested herself in women's rights and the welfare of unmarried mothers. Every winter she returned to Appleton House to escape from the Norwegian climate.

Queen Maud attended the coronation of her nephew GEORGE VI at WESTMINSTER

ABBEY in May 1937, driving there and back in the glass coach with her sister-in-law Queen Mary. Her legs had evidently strengthened since the day of her own coronation as Queen Mary reported: 'Maud and I proceeded up the Abbey to the Royal Box.'

On 20 November 1938 Queen Maud died suddenly and unexpectedly of heart failure following an operation in a London nursing home three days earlier. Her body was taken to the chapel at Marlborough House, where she had been christened, and thence was conveyed by gun-carriage to Victoria Station to travel by rail to Portsmouth and then by sea to Oslo for burial. King Haakon, who was destined to spend the years of Norway's occupation by the Germans heading a government in exile in London from 1940 to 1945, died at Oslo on 21 September 1957.

Maundy Money The bestowing of commemorative coins to invited members of the public by the reigning monarch on the Thursday before Easter, a custom said to date from the reign of EDWARD II. The word Maundy is derived from the first word of the church office for that day, *Mandatum*, which commemorates Christ washing his disciples' feet and giving them the commandment to love one another. The ceremony originally consisted of washing the feet of 12 beggars and distributing alms and clothing to as many old men and old women as the years of the sovereign's age. JAMES II was the last monarch to observe the ceremony of foot washing, but the giving of alms has continued to the present day.

For many years the sovereign's role in the ceremony was delegated to the Lord High Almoner and the service took place in the Chapel Royal, Whitehall, and later at WEST-MINSTER ABBEY. From the reign of CHARLES II the alms have taken the form of silver pennies and four, three, two and one pence pieces are specially struck for this purpose. In 1909 EDWARD VII ordered the numbers struck of these coins to be strictly limited to those required for the ceremony with a few extra sets for members of the royal family and all those taking part in the ceremony, so that they have become comparatively rare collectors' items. The distribution by the sovereign in person was revived by GEORGE V in 1932 and has been continued ever since. ELIZABETH II initiated the custom of making the distribution in a different cathedral each year to enable people in different areas to participate in the ceremony. The Lord High Almoner and the other clergy who take part are girt with towels over their vestments in allusion to the long discontinued foot-washing aspect of the rite.

Mercia Anglo-Saxon kingdom situated in the central part of England, between NORTH-UMBRIA to the north and WESSEX to the south, with EAST ANGLIA on its eastern border and Wales on its western side. It was founded in about 585 by Creoda and rose to prominence under PENDA, a great pagan warrior king. His sons embraced Christianity and enlarged their realm. The greatest king of Mercia was OFFA, but after his death in 796, the kingdom declined and was eventually absorbed into the kingdom of Wessex.

Merit, Order of An order instituted by letters patent of EDWARD VII on 23 June 1902, limited to 24 members. The order carries no special title or personal precedence and can be conferred on both men and women. The badge consists of a cross of red and blue enamel of eight points, having the words 'For Merit' in gold letters within a laurel wreath on a blue enamel centre. The reverse of the badge has the royal cipher in gold also within a laurel wreath on a blue enamel centre and the whole is surmounted by an imperial crown enamelled in colour. If the order is conferred on members chosen for naval or military distinction two silver swords with gold hilts are placed saltirewise between the angles of the cross. Men wear the badge round the neck suspended from a parti-coloured ribbon of Garter blue and crimson, two inches broad. Ladies wear the badge on a bow of the same ribbon on the left shoulder except when in uniform, when it is worn in the same manner as by gentlemen. Holders of the order are entitled to the post-nominal letters of OM and to attach a facsimile of the badge and ribbon to their arms.

Merry Monarch Epithet popularly applied to CHARLES II, evoking the relaxation in public morality that followed the Restoration and reflecting the monarch's own pleasure-loving tastes.

Mey, Castle of Property in the Highland Region bought by Queen ELIZABETH THE QUEEN MOTHER as a private residence in the early days of her widowhood and restored by her over a period of three years. It was formerly called Barrogill and was built for the Bishops of Caithness, passing to the Earls of Caithness after the Reformation.

Michael of Kent, Prince (1942–) The younger son and third and youngest child of Prince George, Duke of KENT (fourth son of

GEORGE V) and of Princess Marina of Greece and Denmark, who was born at Coppins, Iver, Buckinghamshire, on 4 July 1942. As he was born on American Independence Day his parents invited Franklin Delano Roosevelt, 31st President of the United States, to become one of his godfathers and he was christened Michael George Charles Franklin. He never knew his father, who was killed on 25 August 1942.

Prince Michael was educated at Eton and the Royal Military Academy at Sandhurst. He was commissioned into the 11th Hussars (now the Royal Hussars) in 1963 and served as foreign attaché in the liaison section of the Ministry of Defence from 1968 to 1970, with the United Nations Force in Cyprus in 1971, with the Defence Intelligence Service from 1974 to 1976, with the Army Recruiting Directorate from 1976 to 1978, and as GSO Defence Intelligence Staff from 1978 to 1981, when he retired with the rank of Major.

Prince Michael is president of the British Bobsleigh Association, the Society of Genealogists, the Royal Patriotic Fund Corporation, the Soldiers', Sailors' and Airmen's Families Association and other bodies. He married at Vienna City Hall on 30 June 1978, Baroness Marie Christine Agnes Hedwig Ida von Reibnitz, only daughter of Baron Günther Hubertus von Reibnitz and Countess Maria Anna (Marianne) Szapáry de Muraszombath, Széchysziget et Szápar. She was born at Karlsbad (Karlovy Vary) on 15 January 1945 and was formerly married to Thomas Troubridge, which marriage was annulled. Prince and Princess Michael's marriage was blessed at Lambeth Palace Chapel by the Archbishop of Canterbury on 30 October 1978 and validated by the Roman Catholic Church at Westminster Cathedral on 30 July 1983. Since Princess Michael is a Roman Catholic, Prince Michael has lost his rights of succession to the throne, but they pass to the two children of the marriage, Lord Frederick Michael George David Louis Windsor, who was born at St Mary's Hospital, Paddington, on 6 April 1979, and Lady Gabriella (Ella) Marina Alexandra Ophelia Windsor, who was also born at St Mary's Hospital on 23 April 1981. Prince Michael was appointed a Knight Commander of the ROYAL VICTORIAN ORDER (KCVO) on his 50th birthday in 1992.

Mistress of the Robes Title borne by the female head of the household of a queen, queen mother or QUEEN DOWAGER. The appointment is almost invariably held by a duchess, who acts as chief lady-in-waiting at the state opening of Parliament and is in attendance on great state occasions. A Mistress of the Robes is alone among all other peeresses in being permitted to have the train of her peeress's coronation robe decorated with embroidery, usually of heraldic significance.

Monmouth, James Scott, Duke of (1649–85) The eldest of the many natural children of CHARLES II, who was born at Rotterdam on 9 April 1649. His mother, Lucy Walter, who was born at Roch Castle, Pembrokeshire, between 1628 and 1631 and died at Paris in September or October 1658, was the daughter of William Walter and his wife Elizabeth Prothero, both descended from respectable Welsh families with aristocratic connections. Although Charles II acknowledged the paternity of her son James, there was some reason to believe that the real father may have been Robert Sydney. Lucy did not enjoy a good reputation, and the king did not acknowledge her daughter Mary, born at The Hague on 6 May 1651, as his child, although Lucy claimed she was. Charles got possession of James, however, and handed him over to the care of his mother Queen HENRIETTA MARIA. In about 1657 the boy was placed in charge of William Crofts, Baron Crofts of Saxham, and thereafter he bore the surname of Crofts. He was educated at Port Royal in Paris and was brought to England in 1662.

James's charm and good looks made him a favourite with all at court and a grand marriage with an heiress was arranged for him, in anticipation of which he assumed the name of Scott and was knighted. He was provided with an annual income of £8,000 by being granted the monopoly of the export of all new drapery for 31 years, and on 14 February 1663 he was created Baron Scott of Tindale, Earl of Doncaster and Duke of Monmouth. On 28 March 1663 he was nominated a Knight of the GARTER (installed 22 April).

He married at the London house of her stepfather the Earl of Wemyss on 20 April 1663, Anne Scott, in her own right Countess of Buccleuch, daughter of Francis Scott, 2nd Earl of Buccleuch, and his wife Lady Margaret Leslie, daughter of John Leslie, 6th Earl of Rothes. On the day of the marriage Monmouth was created Duke of Buccleuch, Earl of Dalkeith and Lord Scott of Whitchester and Eskdale.

Monmouth served in the fleet under his uncle the Duke of York at Solebay on 3 June 1665 and as Captain of a troop of horse and of the 1st Life Guards. He became a Privy Councillor in 1670 and a Scottish Privy Councillor in 1674. His father sent him on an embassy to Paris and Utrecht in 1672 and in the same year he commanded the British auxiliaries sent to help Louis XIV in his campaign against the Dutch. Various appointments followed over the next few years, including those of Lord High Chamberlain of Scotland, Master of the Horse, Chancellor of Cambridge University and Captain-General of all land forces in England, Wales and Scotland.

In 1678 the bogus claims that a 'Popish Plot' existed, whereby Catholics would massacre Protestants and overthrow the Protestant monarchy, caused a popular outcry for a Protestant succession to the throne and the recognition of Monmouth as legitimate. Charles II's response was to issue a proclamation to the effect that the only wife he had ever married was Queen Catherine (see CATHERINE OF BRAGANZA). Monmouth was then sent to Scotland to repress the rising of the Covenanters, in which he succeeded. This only added to his popularity and his father, displeased by his claims to legitimacy, recalled him from his Scottish command and ordered him to go into exile in Holland. He returned without permission in November 1679 and was received by the populace 'with bonfires and the ringing of bells', although the king refused to see him and deprived him of most of his positions. Monmouth defied his father's commands to go abroad again and between June and October made a tour of the West Country to gauge likely support there.

In the course of the next two years several attempts to effect a reconciliation between father and son failed. In 1682 Monmouth toured the Midlands and was arrested at Stafford on the king's orders and brought to London. He was released on bail and became a tool of Shaftesbury, who implicated him in the Rye House Plot to assassinate the king and the Duke of York. When it was discovered in June 1683 Monmouth went into hiding. In his absence he was found guilty of high treason, but he managed to negotiate a pardon by offering to inform against his confederates. He was forbidden to come to court, however, and after spending a few weeks living quietly in the country went to Holland, where he was when Charles II died in February 1685. He at once asserted his right to the throne and

planned a simultaneous invasion of England and Scotland.

On 11 June 1685 he landed at Lyme Regis and was proclaimed king at Taunton on 20 June. His army was totally defeated at Sedgemoor on 5 July. Monmouth fled from the battlefield, leaving his followers to their fate, and, disguised as a labourer, was found cowering in a ditch three days later. He was taken to London, having been attainted of treason on 16 June, and after grovelling at JAMES II's feet and unsuccessfully pleading for his life was confined in the TOWER OF LONDON and beheaded on Tower Hill on 15 July 1685. He was buried in the Chapel of St Peter ad Vincula in the Tower. His English peerages were forfeited by the act of attainder, but the Scottish ones were not affected and continued to be held by his widow and to pass to their descendants.

The duchess, who was born at Dundee on 11 February 1651, married secondly, on 6 May 1688, Charles Cornwallis, 3rd Baron Cornwallis, who died on 29 April 1698. She died at Dalkeith on 6 February 1732, and was succeeded in the Scottish peerages by her grandson, Francis Scott, who was restored to the English peerages (with the exception of the dukedom of Monmouth) by Act of Parliament on 21 March 1743. It is interesting to note that Monmouth's blood has returned to the royal family in the persons of Princess Alice, Duchess of Gloucester, the Princess of Wales and the Duchess of York, who all descend from him.

Monmouth, although possessed of great personal charm, lacked intelligence and was in many ways a weak and despicable character, easily led. He was a notoriously bad husband and lived openly with Henrietta, Baroness Wentworth, whom he described as his 'wife before God'. He also had four illegitimate children, who bore the surname of Crofts, by Eleanor, daughter of Sir Robert Needham. The youngest of these children, Henrietta, married Charles Powlett, 2nd Duke of Bolton.

Mother of the Maids Title given in the time of ELIZABETH I to Blanche Parry, who was appointed to act as chaperon to and to look after the general well-being of the queen's maids of honour. It was later borne by other ladies who held the position.

Mountbatten The anglicized version of the German BATTENBERG, which was adopted by the English members of that family in 1917 when they were required to relinquish all German names and titles at the behest of GEORGE V. The family sprang from the morganatic union of Prince Alexander of Hesse (1823–88) and the Polish Countess Julie von Hauke (1825–95), who was created Princess of Battenberg with the qualification of Serene Highness. Their eldest son, Prince Louis Alexander of Battenberg (1854–1921), was born in Graz, Austria, but was naturalized in Great Britain and joined the British navy in 1868, serving as a commodore with the Mediterranean Fleet and as director of naval intelligence before rising to the post of First Sea Lord at the outbreak of the First World War. Anti-German prejudice obliged him to reliquish his naval post during the war, but he was promoted to admiral in 1919. He married his first cousin once removed, Princess Victoria of Hesse (1863–1950), whose mother was Princess Alice (*see* ALICE MAUD MARY, PRINCESS, GRAND DUCHESS OF HESSE), the second daughter of Queen VICTORIA. On relinquishing his German titles he was created Marquess of Milford Haven, Earl of Medina and Viscount Alderney. His younger son, Louis Mountbatten, 1st Earl MOUNTBATTEN OF BURMA, recalled that his father was staying at his elder son's house when he learned that the change of name and title had been approved by the king. He wrote in the visitors' book, 'June 9th arrived Prince Hyde, June 19th departed Lord Jekyll'.

The present (4th) Marquess of Milford Haven is the great-grandson of the 1st Marquess and Countess Mountbatten of Burma (the second holder of the title) is his grand-daughter. The name Mountbatten was also assumed by his grandson Prince Philip of Greece and Denmark (*see* EDINBURGH, DUKE OF) (son of his elder daughter Alice) prior to his marriage to Princess Elizabeth (now ELIZABETH II).

Another line of Mountbattens stems from the third son of Prince Alexander of Hesse and the Princess of Battenberg, Prince Henry (1858–96), who married Queen Victoria's youngest daughter Princess BEATRICE[2]. Their sons assumed the Mountbatten name in 1917, the eldest, Alexander, being created Marquess of Carisbrooke, Earl of Berkhamsted and Viscount Launceston. These titles became extinct on his death without male issue in 1960.

Mountbatten of Burma, Louis, 1st Earl (1900–79) The younger son of Prince Louis of Battenberg (*see* MOUNTBATTEN) and Princess Victoria of Hesse (grand-daughter of Queen VICTORIA), who was born at WINDSOR CASTLE on 25 June 1900 and was named

Louis Francis Albert Victor Nicholas. At his christening he knocked the spectacles off the nose of his great-grandmother Queen Victoria when she was holding him. 'Dickie', as he came to be known within the family circle, trained at Dartmouth Naval College and joined the Royal Navy in 1916. On 18 July he was married at St Margaret's Church, Westminster to the Hon Edwina Cynthia Annette Ashley, elder daughter of the 1st Baron Mount Temple, who had been born at Broadlands, Romsey, Hampshire, on 28 November 1901, and who later served with distinction with the Red Cross during the Second World War and became superintendent-in-chief of the St John Ambulance Brigade in 1942.

'Dickie', who bore the title of Lord Louis Mountbatten from 1917, enjoyed a hugely successful naval career (though he did acquire something of a reputation for causing accidents of one kind or another) and during the Second World War was appointed chief of Combined Operations Command (1942). In 1943 he was made supreme commander for the Allies in SE Asia, masterminding the defence of India (1944) and the reconquest of Burma (1945). He also played a crucial role in the preparations for D-Day in 1944. When the Japanese finally sued for peace, it was Mountbatten who accepted the surrender at Singapore.

With peacetime, Mountbatten was entrusted with another sensitive task – presiding over the transition to independence of India in the capacity of last Viceroy (1947), supported by his wife – who formed invaluable friendships with both Nehru and Gandhi – as his Vicereine. His success in this role was acknowledged that same year with his creation as Earl Mountbatten of Burma and Baron Romsey (he had been created Viscount Mountbatten of Burma the previous year). Subsequently, Mountbatten returned to the Admiralty and, like his father before him, rose to the post of First Sea Lord (1954). In 1959 he was appointed chief of the defence staff.

Mountbatten's debonair charm and skills as a statesman made him a great favourite with both GEORGE VI and his successor ELIZABETH II, who much valued his advice. Long after his official retirement in 1965, he was also credited with bestowing the benefit of his extensive experience upon the young CHARLES, PRINCE OF WALES as he was prepared for his future role of king. With years of training behind him, he was rarely caught out by the media – when, for instance, in the 1960s US chat show host Johnny Carson asked him on television (despite agreeing beforehand not to do so) what he thought the US President should do about Vietnam, Mountbatten delivered the riposte: 'I'd tell the British to keep their noses out of it.'

On 21 February 1960 Lady Mountbatten died unexpectedly at Jesselton, British North Borneo, while on an official tour on behalf of the St John Ambulance Brigade. At her own request, she was buried at sea. The royal family and the nation as a whole were deeply shocked when Lord Mountbatten himself, together with other members of his party, were murdered by an IRA bomb placed on his small boat while fishing off Mullaghmore, a favourite retreat near his summer home, Classiebawn Castle in County Sligo, Ireland, on 28 August 1979. He was buried in Romsey Abbey. His elder daughter Patricia succeeded him, assuming the title of Countess Mountbatten of Burma.

Mylius, Edward Publisher of a libel alleging that GEORGE V while serving in the navy as a young man had contracted a secret marriage at Malta in 1890 with the daughter of Admiral Culme-Seymour. The story had first appeared in the *Star* newspaper in 1893 and was then treated as a joke, the Duke of York (as George V then was) saying to his fiancée Princess May of Teck, 'I say, May, we can't get married after all! I hear I have got a wife and three children!' The journalist Edward Mylius dug the story up again in 1910 and published it in a scurrilous French paper. He was prosecuted for criminal libel, found guilty and sentenced to 12 months' imprisonment.

Nechtan I Morbet, King of the Picts
(d.*c*.481) One of the shadowy early Pictish kings whose name cannot be disentagled from legend. He was apparently a Christian as he is said to have dedicated Abernethy to St Bridget in the presence of her pupil Darlugdach, abbess of Kildare.

Nechtan II Neithon, King of the Picts
(d.621) A son of Gwyddno Garanhir, a descendant of Coroticus, King of Strathclyde, who held land in Cardigan and Irb, sister of DRUST IV, he succeeded his kinsman GARTNAIT IV in about 594 and died in 621. He had three brothers, Rhvawn Befr (killed at Catraeth *c*.596), St Elfin (a probable patron of the bard Taliesin) and Isaac (also killed at Catraeth), and two sisters through whom the Pictish succession was passed on.

Nechtan III, King of the Picts (d.732) The son of Derile by a sister of BRUDE III, he succeeded his brother BRUDE IV in 706. About four years later he accepted the Roman date of Easter under the guidance of Abbot Ceolfrid of Monkwearmouth and Jarrow. In 724 Nechtan abdicated and became a monk, but in 728 he emerged from his monastery, deposed ALPIN I and resumed the throne for a year until he was deposed in his turn by his nephew OENGUS I. He returned to the monastic life and died in 732.

Nennius (*fl.c.*800) Early British historian, who is traditionally identified as the author of the Latin work known as the *Historia Brittonum*. He is believed to have lived on the Welsh/Mercian border and to have been a pupil of Elfodd (d.809), 'chief bishop in the land of Gwynedd', who introduced the observance of Roman Easter into the Welsh church. The work attributed to Nennius is a very valuable source of information on the history and genealogies of ancient Britain and early Anglo-Saxon England.

Nest, Princess (*fl.*1120) The 'Helen of Wales', as she has been called, who was the daughter of RHYS AP TEWDWR, KING OF DEHEUBARTH and his wife Gwladus, daughter of Rhiwallon ap Cynfyn. In about 1100 she married Gerald of Windsor. They had three sons, William, Maurice and David, and a daughter, Angharad, who became the mother of Giraldus Cambrensis, the author of *Itinerarium Kambriae*. In 1109 Nest was abducted and carried off from her husband's house by her kinsman Owain ap Cadwgan, which event earned her her nickname. Gerald avenged himself by leading the party that slew Owain in 1116. Nest also had a liaison with Stephen, Constable of Cardigan Castle, by whom she had a son Robert FitzStephen, one of the conquerors of Ireland. She was also at one time the mistress of HENRY I, to whom she bore a son Henry FitzRoy, claimed as an ancestor by the Irish family of FitzHenry. Nest's date of death is unknown, but she was still living in 1136 and probably for several years afterwards.

Nevill, Anne, Queen of England *see* ANNE NEVILL, QUEEN OF ENGLAND.

New Zealand, Order of An Order instituted by ELIZABETH II in 1987 with membership limited to 20 persons living at any one time. Members may use the letters ONZ after their names. Appointments are made for outstanding services to the Crown and people of New Zealand in a civil or military capacity.

Niall of the Nine Hostages, High-King of Ireland (*fl.*AD400) The son of Eochaid Mugmedon, King of Tara (*fl.*AD360), and his concubine Cairenn (Carina), a girl of Romano-British origin who had been carried off in a slave raid, who was, according to legend, born beside a well, where his mother left him for fear of Queen Mongfind, Eochaid's wife and the mother of his elder sons, Brion, Fiachra and Ailill. Niall was rescued and fostered by a poet named Torna, who eventually took him to his father's court, where he was recognized and was able to better his mother's lot. Eochaid organized a contest to decide which of his sons was most worthy to succeed him by sending them into a burning smithy and telling each one to bring out whatever he considered to be of greatest value. Niall won by rescuing the anvil, tongs, bellows and other tools of the smith's trade.

There are other confusing and conflicting legends. One tells that after the death of Eochaid, Mongfind, who had the reputation of being a witch, contrived to get her brother, Crimthann mac Fidaig, King of Munster, elected high-king in preference to Niall, whose election to that office had been agreed. When Crimthann went on a royal progress, Mongfind divided the land among her sons and planned to poison her brother at the feast held to celebrate his return. Her evil back-fired, however, for Crimthann became suspicious and she was compelled to drink the poisoned draught herself.

Emerging from this myth and legend it can be said that Niall gained at least a nominal suzerainty over the whole of Ireland and he was possibly the Irish king who campaigned against the Roman general Stilicho in 399. His sobriquet of Noígiallach ('of the nine hostages') is said to have been given after he had obtained nine hostages, one each from the five Irish provinces and four from Britain, where he is said to have made seven raids, being killed on the last by a king of Leinster. His body was taken back to Ireland and buried at Ochan, that is Faughan Hill between Kells and Navan in County Meath. He was succeeded as high-king by Nath I, the son of his half-brother Fiachra, who was followed in turn by Niall's son Lóeguire (who died around 463). The high-kingship was held by Niall's descendants for many years, alternating between the Northern Uí Néill and the Southern Uí Néill branches. St Columba, the apostle of Scotland, belonged to the former and the hereditary lay abbots of Dunkeld were of the same lineage (*see* CRINAN).

Nine Days' Queen Nickname applied to Lady Jane Grey, queen of England for just nine days (*see* JANE, QUEEN OF ENGLAND).

Nonsuch Palace Former royal palace in Surrey built at vast expense by HENRY VIII from April 1538 and still uncompleted at his death in 1547. Constructed on the site of the village of Cuddington (which was cleared for the new building), it was intended to rival the Château de Chambord in France and consisted of three courts set within 2000 acres of land about six miles south-east of HAMPTON COURT. The name 'Nonsuch' (or 'Nonesuch') was intended to indicate that there was no other place like it anywhere in the civilized world. ELIZABETH I stayed at the palace on many occasions, though her predecessor MARY I had already exchanged it with Henry Fitzalan, 12th Earl of Arundel, for land in Suffolk. Having passed back into royal ownership in 1603, it was given by JAMES I to his wife ANNE OF DENMARK and was used as a hunting lodge by both James and CHARLES I. CHARLES II installed his mistress Barbara Villiers at the palace, but in 1682 she sold it to Lord Berkeley, who demolished it. The site is now occupied by Nonsuch Park.

Normandy, House of The dynasty that ruled England from 1066 until 1154, although STEPHEN, the last Norman king, really belonged to the house of Blois and was Norman only through his mother. The ducal house of Normandy was founded by Rolf or Rollo the Ganger, a Norse sea-rover who carried out a number of raids on the northern coast of France. He was finally granted the duchy of Normandy as a fief of the crown by Charles III the Simple, King of France, in 911, accepting Christian baptism and taking the name Robert in the following year. His ancestors can be traced with near certainty to the early Yngling kings of Sweden. Rollo is credited with having contemptuously tipped the French monarch backwards off his throne when he came to do homage for his fief, and he and his successors were well-nigh independent sovereigns, paying lip-service to the French crown. WILLIAM I THE CONQUEROR was Rollo's great-great-great-grandson.

Northumbria The northernmost kingdom of the Saxon HEPTARCHY, which was formed by the union of the kingdoms of DEIRA and BERNICIA. It was at its zenith during the reigns of EDWIN (616–33), OSWALD (634–41) and OSWY (641–70), respectively the fifth, sixth and seventh BRETWALDAS. The kingdom began to decline soon after Oswy's death, and the last recorded king was EGBERT II, who died in about 878. The country was then absorbed into the Scandinavian kingdom of York.

O

Oak-Apple Day Designation given to 29 May, CHARLES II's birthday and the day of his Restoration in 1660. It was observed as a public holiday until the middle of the 19th century. It refers to the king's hiding in an oak tree at BOSCOBEL HOUSE during his escape after the battle of Worcester. Charles contemplated founding a new order of Knights of the Royal Oak, but the plans did not materialize.

Octavius, Prince (1779–83) The eighth son and thirteenth child of GEORGE III and Queen CHARLOTTE, who was born at the Queen's House, St James's Park (later BUCKINGHAM PALACE), on 23 February 1779 and baptized in the Great Council Chamber of ST JAMES'S PALACE on 23 March, his godparents being the Duke of Brunswick, the Duke of Mecklenburg-Schwerin and Louise, Duchess of Saxe-Weimar, all of whom were represented by proxies. He grew into a beautiful child and was a great favourite with his father. However, the prince became consumptive and died of complications following his inoculation for smallpox at KEW PALACE on 3 May 1783. He was buried in the royal vault in Henry VII's Chapel at WESTMINSTER ABBEY on 10 May, but removed thence to the new Royal Tomb House at St George's Chapel, Windsor, on 20 February 1820. 'There will be no Heaven for me if Octavius is not there', said his father as reported by Mrs Delany. Prince Octavius's portrait by Gainsborough is at WINDSOR CASTLE.

Odo, Bishop of Bayeux (*c*.1030–97) The half-brother of WILLIAM I THE CONQUEROR, being the elder son of his mother HERLEVE by Herluin de Conteville (whom she married after her liaison with Duke Robert II of Normandy had ended), who was born in Normandy in about 1030. He had become Bishop of Bayeux by 23 April 1050, although not more than 20 years old. Odo played an active role in the preparations for his half-brother's invasion of England in 1066 and was present at the battle of

HASTINGS. He was rewarded by a grant of over 500 manors, the earldom of Kent and the wardenship of Dover Castle.

Odo acted as regent during William's absences in Normandy and was the builder of many castles throughout the land. His severe oppresion of the poor led to a revolt in Kent, which was quelled only when William returned. Odo's cupidity and greed led him to misappropriate many manors and other property, some of which he was compelled to surrender. Although warlike, he found time to interest himself in ecclesiastical affairs both in England and in Normandy, but he seems to have been at his happiest when called upon to undertake military expeditions such as the suppression of the rebellion led by the Earls of Norfolk and Hereford in 1075 or avenging the murder of Bishop Walcher in Northumberland in 1080, on which occasion he harried the countryside over a large area and raided the treasury of Durham Cathedral.

Power went to Odo's head and it was his ambition to become pope, to which end he sent bribes to influential men in Rome and attempted to raise a band of Normans in England to accompany him to Italy. When William heard of this he had him arrested and sent over to Normandy, where he was imprisoned at Rouen until 1087 when William on his deathbed ordered his release. Odo was present at the Conqueror's funeral and then accompanied his nephew WILLIAM II back to England, where the earldom of Kent was restored to him. He soon began to intrigue to depose William and place ROBERT III, DUKE OF NORMANDY on the throne in his place. After plundering the king's lands in Kent, Odo was forced to flee from Tonbridge Castle and seek refuge with his brother Robert, Count of Mortain, at Pevensey, where they were besieged for six weeks until forced to surrender. Odo was sent under guard to Rochester with the intention of surrendering it to the king, but the garrison seized him and his escort and put them in chains. The king besieged the castle and when it finally surrendered Odo was banished from England for good. He went to Normandy and became the principal adviser of his nephew Duke Robert.

In November 1095 Odo attended the Council of Clermont, at which Pope Urban II proclaimed the First Crusade, and the following February was present at the Council of Rouen, where the decrees of the Council of Clermont were promulgated. In September 1096, although about 66 years old, he set out on the Crusade with Duke Robert. He was taken ill on the way and died at Palermo in February 1097, being buried in Palermo Cathedral. He left an illegitimate son, John, who, according to Orderic Vitalis, occupied a position of great esteem at the court of HENRY I on account of his eloquence and probity.

It was Bishop Odo who is now believed to have been responsible for commissioning the BAYEUX TAPESTRY, depicting the events leading up to and including the Norman Conquest.

Oengus I, King of the Picts (d.761) The son of one Urguist, or Fergus, by a sister of BRUDE IV and NECHTAN III, he was *regulus* (sub-king) of Fortrinn when he deposed his uncle Nechtan and seized the throne in 729, in the same year defeating and killing DRUST VI, who attempted to regain the kingdom. In 734 he deposed Dungal, King of Lorn and in 741 defeated and killed Indrechtach, King of Kintyre. In 750, however, Oengus was himself defeated and deposed at Mugdock, near Glasgow, by TEUDUR, King of Strathclyde. In 752 he defeated and killed his successor BRUDE V, regaining the throne, which he retained until his death in 761. Oengus married his second cousin, a sister of ALPIN I, and had two sons, Brude, who died in 736 and TALORCAN III.

Oengus II, King of the Picts (*fl*.789–834) A son of FERGUS, King of DALRIADA, by a sister of CINIATH II and ALPIN II, he succeeded his brother CONSTANTINE I as *regulus* of Fortrinn in 789 and as King of the Picts in 820 and reigned until 834. His wife may have been a Pictish princess because his elder son Eoganan reigned from 836 to 839, when he, together with his younger brother Branm, was killed at Fortrinn, by Danish invaders.

Offa, King of Essex (d. after 709) The son of King SIGHERE and the legendary St OSYTH, who succeeded his father's cousins SIGE-HEARD and Swaefred on an unknown date after 694. In 709 he abdicated in favour of his kinsman SAELRED and went to Rome with his kinsman COENRED, King of MER-CIA. BEDE says he was 'a very handsome and lovable young man who the entire nation greatly hoped would inherit and uphold the sceptre of the kingdom. But, fired by an equal ardour, he left his wife, lands, family and country for the sake of Christ and his Gospel'. At Rome the two former kings 'entered upon the monastic life, and at last attained the long-desired vision of the blessed Apostles in heaven'.

Offa, King of Mercia (d.796) The son of Thingfrith (sometimes given as Wingferd), a scion of the Mercian royal house descended from a brother of PENDA, KING OF MERCIA and his wife Marcellina, who was named after his remote ancestor, Offa, King of Angel, and has sometimes been referred to by historians as Offa II. According to the ANGLO-SAXON CHRONICLE and Henry of Huntingdon, he could claim ultimate descent from WODEN himself. He obtained the throne of Mercia in 757 after defeating and putting to flight BEONRED, who had succeeded King ETHELBALD earlier that year.

Offa was one of the greatest of the Saxon kings. He brought practically the whole of England under his sway in the course of a long reign of 39 years, adopted the style of *rex totius Anglorum patriae* and was addressed as 'King of the English' by Pope Adrian I. Among Offa's achievements were the construction of Offa's Dyke, an earthwork stretching from the Wye to the Dee to withhold the incursions of Welsh marauders, and the compilation of a code of laws which was later adapted by ALFRED THE GREAT. A more ominous development was the first arrival on British shores of Danish pirates.

Offa struck a handsome coinage and the head of his Queen CYNETHRYTH also appears on some of his coins. This is unique in England and doubtless emphasizes Offa's imperial aspirations, as the Roman emperors had been in the habit of depicting their wives and other members of their families on the coinage. Offa also took the unprecedented step (for England) of having his only son EGFRITH anointed king in his father's lifetime, in 787.

Offa died on 29 July 796 and was succeeded by Egfrith, whose reign lasted only 141 days.

Oiscings Designation of the dynasty that ruled the Saxon kingdom of KENT. It is derived from the name of the second king of the line, Oeric Oisc, the son and successor of HENGEST.

Old King Cole *see* COEL, KING.

Old Pretender The name by which the Hanoverians usually referred to Prince James Francis Edward STUART, the Jacobite claimant to the British throne.

Orb An item of regalia consisting of a globe of gold, often jewelled, and surmounted by a cross. The present royal orb was part of the regalia re-made for the coronation of CHARLES II. A second orb was made for the coronation of MARY II as joint sovereign in 1689. Both orbs were displayed on Queen VICTORIA's coffin, the second one being said to symbolize the Empire of India. A QUEEN CONSORT does not receive an orb.

Osbald, King of Northumbria (d.799) Of unknown lineage, Osbald gained the throne in 796 but was expelled after a reign of 27 days. According to Symeon of Durham he died in 799.

Osbert, King of Northumbria (d.867) Of unknown lineage, he ascended the throne *c*.848. He was expelled in 862–3 in favour of Ælla, 'a king not of royal birth', according to the ANGLO-SAXON CHRONICLE, though Symeon of Durham says he was Osbert's brother. He was apparently restored in 866 or 867 and seems to have shared the power with Ælla. Both the kings were killed when they attempted to retake York from the Norse invaders on 21 March 867.

Osborne House The favourite home, on the Isle of Wight, of Queen VICTORIA. Victoria first visited the Isle of Wight with her mother in 1831, when they stayed at Norris Castle, a mock medieval residence in Cowes. They stayed there again in 1833 and obviously gained a favourable impression of the island. Years later, when the queen and Prince ALBERT were seeking a seaside residence other than Brighton, which they both disliked, they consulted the Prime Minister, Sir Robert Peel, on the matter and he discovered that the Osborne estate (the name a corruption of Austerbourne), near East Cowes, was for sale at £30,000. In the course of a cruise the royal family had made in the summer of 1843, Albert had been charmed by the Isle of Wight and consequently negotiations were opened with Osborne's owner, Lady Isabella Blachford, for its purchase (agreed at just under £28,000).

Matters were delayed for various reasons and it was not until October that the royal family took up residence. They were delighted with the place and additional land was later acquired from Winchester College in order to make the estate commercially viable. Prince Albert eschewed the employment of architects and drew up his own plans for the building of a new house with the assistance of the master-builder Thomas Cubitt, a Norfolk man. The final result was an elegant Italianate palace, where the queen and her family could lead the simple life they enjoyed amid pleasant surroundings. The new building was ready for occupation in September 1846 and the queen wrote in her diary: 'All is so convenient, spacious and well carried out. Mr Cubitt has done it admirably ... It seems to be like a dream to be here now in our house, of which we laid the first stone only 15 months ago.'

In 1890 a new wing was added to the house and its principal drawing-room became known as the Durbar Room, since it was designed in Indian-Saracenic style and was later used to house the vast variety of artefacts the queen received as presents from the Indian princes on the occasion of her DIAMOND JUBILEE.

Queen Victoria died at Osborne in January 1901. Her son and successor EDWARD VII gave part of the house to be used as a convalescent home for serving and retired officers, but the private apartments remained closed until 1954, when ELIZABETH II had them opened to the public.

Osburga (Osburh) (d.*c*.855) The daughter of Oslac, Ealdorman of Hampshire, the royal cup-bearer (*pincerna*) and a descendant of the Jutish brothers Stuf and Wihtgar (to whom their uncle CERDIC, KING OF WESSEX had given the Isle of Wight). She became the first wife of King ETHELWULF and presumably the mother of all his children, certainly of ALFRED THE GREAT, according to whose biographer Asser she was 'a most religious woman, noble in character and noble by birth'. She was also a woman of some learning and able to read. Asser relates that she showed her children a book of English poetry and promised to give it to the first one who could learn to read it. Alfred won the prize. Unless she was divorced, as some authorities claim, Osburh must have died in about 855, since Ethelwulf married again in 856.

Osred I, King of Northumbria (*c*.696–716) The son of King ALDFRITH and his wife Cuthburh, sister of INE, KING OF WESSEX, who was born in about 696 and ascended the throne on his father's death in December 704, when he was about eight years old according to BEDE. He reigned 11 years and was killed 'to the south of the border' of NORTHUMBRIA and MERCIA in 716 and was succeeded by COENRED.

Osred II, King of Northumbria (d.794) The son of King Alchred and his wife Osgearn or Osgifu, a sister of King Elfwald I, whom he succeeded in 788. He was deposed and imprisoned by his uncle's predecessor King ETHELRED I, who thus regained the throne in 790. Osred escaped and sought refuge in the Isle of Man, but returned in an attempt to regain the throne and was 'seized and slain' on 14 September 794. He was buried at Tynemouth.

Osric, King of Northumberland (d.729) The son of ALCHFRITH, sub-king in DEIRA, and Cyneburg of MERCIA, although some accounts make him the son of King ALD-FRITH and brother of King OSRED I. He succeeded his kinsman King COENRED in 718 and reigned for 11 years. He was killed on 9 May 729 and succeeded by CEOLWULF, the brother of Coenred.

Oswald, St, King of Northumbria (604–41) The son of Ethelfrith, King of Northumbria, and his second wife Acha, daughter of AELLA, KING OF DEIRA, who was born about 604. In 617 his father was killed by RED-WALD, KING OF EAST ANGLIA, and Edwin of Deira was established as King of Northumbria (*see* EDWIN, KING OF NORTHUMBRIA). Oswald and his brothers were driven into exile. Oswald spent the remainder of his youth in the Hebrides and was converted to Christianity at Iona. After Edwin had been killed by PENDA, KING OF MERCIA in October 632, Oswald returned to England and in 633 succeeded his half-brother Eanfrith on the throne of BERNICIA, to which he had been restored after Edwin's death. Oswald also annexed DEIRA on the death of King OSRIC the same summer. He 'mustered an army small in numbers but strong in the faith of Christ' and defeated CADWALLON, KING OF GWYNEDD in a battle fought near Hexham in 634, inspiring his small force by placing a cross on the battlefield before the fight was joined.

Peace being restored, Oswald sent to Scotland asking to be sent a bishop to preach the gospel in his kingdom. He was sent St Aidan, whom he established as Bishop of Lindisfarne. Aidan was not fluent in English and Oswald himself acted as an interpreter of his sermons, having 'obtained perfect command of the Scottish tongue during his long exile'. He married Cyne-burg, daughter of CYNEGILS, the first Christian King of WESSEX, and they had one son, Ethelwald, later King of Deira.

Oswald is reckoned as the sixth BRET-WALDA, or overlord, of the HEPTARCHY. His reign was all too short. Penda of Mercia again invaded and Oswald was killed in battle at Maserfeld (Oswestry) on 5 August 641. He was buried at Bardney. 'His holiness and miracles,' says the ANGLO-SAXON CHRONICLE, 'were afterwards abundantly made manifest throughout this island, and his hands are at Bamburgh uncorrupted.' BEDE elaborates this by relating a story to the effect that Oswald and Aidan were dining together one Easter when a servant brought news of a crowd of poor and needy clamouring for alms in the street outside. The king 'at once ordered his own food to be taken out to the poor, and the silver dish to be broken up and distributed among them'. Aidan was so moved by this act of generosity that he seized Oswald's right hand and exclaimed, 'May this hand never wither with age'. Bede says that the hand and arm remained uncorrupted and were preserved in a silver casket and venerated as relics in St Peter's Church, Bamburgh. Oswald was succeeded by his half-brother OSWY.

Oswin, King of Deira (d.651) The son of King OSRIC, who was associated in the royal dignity by OSWY, KING OF NORTHUMBRIA and given DEIRA to rule in 644. BEDE says he was 'a man of great holiness and piety' and 'of handsome appearance and lofty stature, pleasant in speech and courteous in manner ... generous to high and low alike'. In spite of this, he fell out with Oswy and the two kings raised armies and prepared to fight each other. On seeing that Oswy's forces were superior to his, Oswin disbanded his army near Catterick and sent his men home. Accompanied by one faithful soldier named Tondhere, he sought asylum in the house of a noble named Hunwald, whom he believed to be his friend. Hunwald betrayed him to Oswy, however, and Oswin and Tondhere were put to death by Oswy's commander Ethelwin at Gilling in Yorkshire on 20 August 651. A monastery was later built on the spot in atonement and 'prayers were ... offered ... daily for the souls of the two kings, both slayer and slain alike'. Oswin was succeeded as King of Deira by ETHELWALD, the son of King OSWALD.

Oswini, King of Kent (*fl*.688/90) Known only from charters, he is one of the obscure kings of unknown lineage who reigned jointly after the death of HLOTHERE.

Oswulf, King of Northumbria (d.758/9) The son of King EADBERHT, on whose abdication he succeeded to the throne in 757 or 758. He reigned for less than a year and was killed by his own bodyguard on 24 or 25 July 758 or 759. His wife was named Richthryth and he had a son Elfwald, who was later king, and a daughter Osgyfu, who married King Alchred and was the mother of King OSRED II.

Oswy, King of Northumbria (c.612–70) The son of King Ethelfrith by an unknown third wife or concubine, although some authorities state that his mother was Acha of DEIRA. He succeeded his brother or half-brother OSWALD as King of BERNICIA only in 641, but succeeded in annexing Deira in 654 and becoming king of a united Northumbria. He was acknowledged as seventh BRETWALDA or overlord of the HEPTARCHY and between 654 and 657 also annexed MERCIA after defeating and killing PENDA. He made incursions into the north and brought the British kingdom of Strathclyde and the Scottish kingdom of DALRIADA into subjugation as well as annexing much of the Pictish kingdom.

In spite of being such a warlike king, Oswy was assiduous in his attention to religious affairs and presided over the Synod of Whitby, which adopted the observance of Roman Easter. Oswy's first wife was Riemmelth, daughter of Royth, son of Rum. She was the mother of ALCHFRITH, who reigned as sub-king in Deira from 654 to 664 and died before his father, leaving a son OSRIC, later king. Riemmelth was probably also the mother of Alchfled, who married PEADA, KING OF MERCIA. Oswy's second wife was EANFLED, the daughter of King EDWIN. She was the mother of his successor EGFRITH, Elfwine, sub-king in Deira c.664–79, Osthryth, who married ETHELRED, KING OF MERCIA, and Elfleda, abbess of Whitby, who died in 713 or 714. By a concubine named Fina, Oswy was also the father of ALDFRITH, who succeeded Egfrith as king. Oswy died on 15 February 670.

Osyth, St, Queen of Essex (fl.c.680) The daughter of Frithwold, a sub-king in Surrey, and his wife Wilburga, daughter of PENDA, KING OF MERCIA, who married SIGHERE, KING OF ESSEX and was the mother of OFFA, KING OF ESSEX. After her husband's death in about 683 she founded a nunnery at Chich (now called St Osyth), where she died, murdered according to later legend, by Danish pirates. Her feast day is 7 October.

Owain I, King of Strathclyde (fl.641) The son of Beli I, King of Strathclyde, by an unknown first wife, who succeeded his father in 641. In 643 he defeated and killed Domnall Brecc, the Scottish King of DALRIADA. The date of Owain's death is unknown. He left three sons, Gwriad and DYFNWAL I, successively kings of Strathclyde, and Elfin, all of whom became the ancestors of later kings.

Owain II, King of Strathclyde (fl.760) The son and successor of King DYFNWAL II in 760. The length of his reign is unknown. He was succeeded by his son Riderch II.

Owain III, King of Strathclyde (fl.926) The son of King DYFNWAL V (formerly Donald), of the House of Alpin, who succeeded his father in about 926. The following year he acted as host at the conference of British kings held at Dacre. In 937 he allied himself with his uncle CONSTANTINE III, KING OF SCOTS and Olaf Guthfrithsson, King of Dublin, against ATHELSTAN, King of WESSEX, who, however, won a complete victory over them at the battle of Brunanburh. The date of Owain's death is unknown. He was succeeded by his son DYFNWAL VI.

Owain IV the Bald, King of Strathclyde (d.1018) The youngest son of King DYFNAL VI, who obtained the kingdom of Strathclyde by cession from MALCOLM II, KING OF SCOTS in 1005. He remained Malcolm's ally but was killed at Carham on the Tweed in the course of their successful campaign against Uhtred of Northumberland. He apparently had no children and Strathclyde became an apanage for Malcolm's grandson Duncan (DUNCAN I, KING OF SCOTS).

Owain ap Gruffydd, Prince or Lord of Deheubarth (d.1236) The younger son of GRUFFYDD AP RHYS, PRINCE OF DEHEUBARTH and his wife Matilda, daughter of William de Breos, who succeeded his father in July 1201, while still a child, and reigned jointly with his elder brother Rhys Ieuanc until the latter's death in August 1222. Their uncles, Rhys Gryg and Maelgwn Fychan, had designs on their territory, but they were protected by the Prince of Gwynedd and received additional lands when a new division of DEHEUBARTH was effected in 1216. Owain married a daughter of Gwion Sais, and had a son Maredudd. He died at Strata Florida on 18 January 1236 and was buried in the abbey there with his parents and brother.

Owain ap Hywel Dda, King of Deheubarth
(d.988) The third and youngest son of
HYWEL DDA and his wife Elen, daughter and
heiress of Llywarch ap Hyfaidd, King of
Dyfed, who succeeded his father and
reigned jointly with his elder brothers,
Rhodri (d.953) and Edwin (d.954), until
their deaths left him as sole ruler. He married Angharad, daughter of Llywelyn ap
Merfyn ap Rhodri Mawr, and had five sons:
Cadwallon (d.966), Einion (d.984), Llywarch, Iestyn and MAREDUDD AB OWAIN.
Owain died in 988 and was succeeded by his
youngest son.

**Owain Cyfeiliog, Prince of Southern
Powys** (c.1125–97) The son of Gruffydd ap
Maredudd, Lord of Mawddy, and his wife
Gwerfyl, daughter and heiress of Gwrgeno
ap Hywel, Lord of Caer or Clydewen, who
was born about 1125 and was only about
three years old when his father died in 1128.
His uncle, MADOG AP MAREDUDD, PRINCE
OF POWYS gave Cyfeiliog to Owain and his
younger brother Meurig in 1149, and on
Madog's death in February 1160, Owain
succeeded him in southern Powys. He
joined with the other Welsh princes in
opposing HENRY II, but made peace with
England in 1167. He was excommunicated
for refusing to support the Crusade in 1188.

He married first, Gwenllian, daughter
of OWAIN GWYNEDD, KING OF GWYNEDD,
and had two sons, GWENWYNWYN and
Caswallon. Owain's second wife was a
daughter of RHYS AP GRUFFYDD. He abdicated in 1195 in favour of his son
Gwenwynwyn and retired to the Cistercian
monastery of Strata Marcella, which he had
founded in 1170. He died and was buried
there in 1197.

**Owain Glyn Dŵr (Glendower), Prince of
Wales** (c.1354–1416) The last champion of
Welsh independence, who was the son of
Gruffydd Fychan II, Lord of Glyndyfrdwy
and Cynllaith Owain in northern Powys,
and his wife Elen, daughter and co-heiress
of Thomas ap Llywelyn, of the royal line of
DEHEUBARTH (and thus the representative
of several of the old royal lines). He was born
in about 1354 and in about 1383 married
Margaret, daughter of David Hanmer, of
Maelor, who bore him a large family. Some
of Owain's early years were spent in London
studying law and later serving as a soldier.
In 1386, he appeared as a witness in the
famous Scrope versus Grosvenor dispute
regarding armorial bearings.

In 1400 Owain gathered together a group
of kinsmen with the intent to liberate Wales
from the English yoke and was proclaimed
Prince of Wales on 16 September. By 1404
he had achieved a considerable measure of
success, having burned Cardiff, captured
Harlech and Aberystwyth and held a
Parliament at Machynlleth. He concluded a
treaty with France and his army was reinforced by 2500 French troops, who marched
with him as far east as Worcester. Other
supporters attracted to him included his
captives Lord Grey of Ruthin and Lord
Edmund Mortimer as well as the Earl of
Northumberland and his son Harry
'Hotspur'. In the following year, however,
following the return of the French (with
their booty), the tide began to turn and
Owain eventually became a fugitive, occasionally carrying out border raids. He disappeared from history in 1412. Legend has it
that he died somewhere in the mountain
fastnesses of central Wales, never captured
by the English, but others believe he spent
his last years in the house of his daughter
Alice Scudamore at Monnington in
Herefordshire and that it was there that he
died in 1416.

Owain Gwynedd, King of Gwynedd
(c.1100–70) The second son of GRUFFYDD
AP CYNAN, KING OF GWYNEDD and
Angharad, daughter of Owain ab Edwin,
who was born in about 1100. As a young
man he and his elder brother Cadwallon
(d.1132) fought to restore the prosperity of
their father's realm and added the cantrefs
of Meirionydd, Rhos, Rhufoniog and
Dyffryn Clwyd to his dominions. Owain
succeeded his father in 1137 and over the
next 12 years continued to annexe territory.
In 1157, however, he suffered a defeat
by HENRY II's invading army and shortly
thereafter did homage to the English king,
changing his own style from king to prince.
In the general uprising of 1165 he destroyed
the royal strongholds in Tegeingl and
re-established his power along the Dee
estuary, but did not attempt to reassert his
independence.

Owain married first, Gwladus, daughter
of Llywarch ap Trahaearn ap Caradog, and
had two sons, IORWERTH DRWYNDWN and
Maelgwn. He incurred the displeasure of
the Church by his second marriage to his
first cousin Christina, daughter of Gronw
ab Owain ab Edwin. She also bore him two
sons, DAFYDD I and Rhodri. By other
women Owain had at least six other sons and
two daughters. He died on 28 November
1170 and was buried in Bangor Cathedral.

P

Page A male servant in a royal household, whose duties consist in acting as an usher and in conveying messages. Pages are quite distinct from Pages of Honour, young boys of good family who are appointed to act as train bearers to the sovereign on such occasions as the State Opening of Parliament, the Garter Ceremony and so on and wear an 18th-century style costume in the royal livery colours of red and gold.

Paris, Matthew (c.1200–59) Benedictine monk of St Albans who compiled a chronicle of the events of his day that is a valuable and often vivid source of information on HENRY III's reign.

Parisii The earliest Celtic tribe known to have invaded Britain. They came from a region of Gaul around Paris and settled in Yorkshire in about the second century BC, establishing a kingdom that was still flourishing at the time of the Roman conquest of Britain.

Parliament The supreme legislature, which consists of the sovereign and the three estates of the realm, the Lords Spiritual, the Lords Temporal and the Commons. It evolved from the councils called together by early kings (see WITENAGEMOT) and the first Parliament of England was summoned to meet at Westminster on 28 January 1265 after Simon de Montfort, Earl of Leicester, had defeated HENRY III at the battle of Lewes. The two-chamber system of House of Lords and House of Commons developed throughout the Middle Ages and has continued through many modifications to the present day. The British Parliament is popularly known as 'The Mother of Parliaments' as it provided a model that was adopted and adapted by many other nations throughout the world.

Parr, Catherine see CATHERINE PARR.

Peada, King of Mercia (d.656) The eldest son of PENDA, KING OF MERCIA and his wife Cynewise, who was made ruler (princeps) of the Middle Angles by his father and according to BEDE was a 'noble young man, well deserving the title and dignity of a king'. He wished to marry Alchfled, the daughter of OSWY, KING OF NORTHUMBRIA, but her father would not agree to her marriage with a pagan. Peada, whose sister Cyneburg was already married to Oswy's son ALCHFRITH, undertook instruction in the Christian faith under their influence and became an enthusiastic convert. He was baptized in 653 by Finan, Bishop of Lindisfarne, at a place that Bede calls 'At-Wall', which was probably Walton or Walbottle, near Newcastle. He returned home with four priests, 'chosen for their learning and holy life, to instruct and baptize his people'. After Penda had been killed in battle with Oswy in November 654, Oswy took over the kingdom of Mercia but granted Peada his son-in-law the kingdom of South Mercia, south of the river Trent. Peada was not destined to enjoy a long rule, for at Eastertide in April 656 he 'was foully assassinated through the treachery, it is said, of his own wife'. He left no issue.

Penda, King of Mercia (c.575–654) The son of PYBBA and grandson of Creoda (founder of the Mercian kingdom, according to Henry of Huntingdon), who succeeded his kinsman Ceorl on the Mercian throne in about 626, according to the ANGLO-SAXON CHRONICLE, or about 632 as implied by BEDE. As he was said to have been 50 years old at his accession, the year of his birth can be assigned to between 575 and 582.

Penda was a great pagan warrior king, who made his realm the most powerful state of the Saxon HEPTARCHY. He defeated and killed EDWIN, KING OF NORTHUMBRIA in 633, subjugated the East Saxons and defeated and killed OSWALD, KING OF NORTHUMBRIA in 642, but was himself overcome and slain by Oswald's brother and successor OSWY at Winwidfeld on 15 November 654. After his death his sons accepted Christianity.

Penda's wife was named Cynewise and they had at least three sons, PEADA, WULFHERE and ETHELRED, all successively kings, and three daughters, Cyneburga, who married ALCHFRITH, son of Oswy, King of Northumbria, Cyneswith, who became a nun, and Wilburga, who married Frithwold, a sub-king in Surrey and became the mother of St OSYTH.

Philip, Prince, Duke of Edinburgh *see* EDINBURGH, PRINCE PHILIP, DUKE OF.

Philip II, King of Spain (1527–98) The husband of MARY I, who has the unique distinction of being the only king consort in English history. The first-born child of the Holy Roman Emperor Karl (Charles) V, who was also King Carlos I of Spain, and of his wife Isabel, daughter of King Manuel I of Portugal, he was born at Valladolid on 21 May 1527. He married first, at the age of 16, on 13 November 1543, his first cousin Maria, daughter of João (John) III, King of Portugal. She died on 12 July 1545, four days after the birth of her only child Don Carlos.

Mary I, Philip's first cousin once removed and his senior by 11 years, chose him to be her husband against the wishes of Parliament and the country in general, and the marriage took place at Winchester Cathedral on 25 July 1554. Mary chose to follow the Spanish custom by which the husbands of titled ladies took on their spouse's rank (a custom that still obtains in Spain) and in her eyes at least he was co-regent with her. Philip's name and effigy appeared with Mary's on the coinage and all acts of Parliament and legal documents were dated in their joint names.

Philip's portraits do not show him as very prepossessing, and contemporary accounts of his character serve only to confirm this – yet he captivated Mary, who after many years of frustration fell in love with all the ardour of a young girl. His callous and cruel treatment of her was to break her heart (excusable though his aloofness might have been to some extent on account of Mary's congenital syphilis). Not least of his misdemeanours was his outrageous flirting with her half-sister Elizabeth (later ELIZABETH I). Once having got a foothold in England, Philip was determined to keep it and thought it expedient to pave the way for a possible future matrimonial alliance with his sickly wife's designated successor. Philip was an even more bigoted Catholic than Mary and the persecutions and burnings of 'heretics' in Spain throughout his reign far exceeded anything seen in England.

After Mary's death in November 1558 – at which her widower professed to feel 'a reasonable regret' – Philip felt he had a claim on the English throne and in the 1580s began immense preparations for an invasion of England. The fleet that he prepared for this purpose, and arrogantly named the 'Invincible Armada', was thrown into disorder by a storm and completely destroyed by the English fire ships under the command of Howard of Effingham.

Philip married again twice. His third marriage on 22 June 1559 was to Elisabeth, daughter of King Henri II of France. She bore him two daughters and died on 3 October 1568. Philip married fourthly, on 12 November 1570, his own niece, Anna Maria, daughter of Maximilian II, Holy Roman Emperor, and his wife, who was Philip's sister Maria. She bore him three sons (who died young), followed by his eventual successor Philip III and a daughter (who also died young), and died on 26 October 1580.

Philip moved the Spanish capital from Toledo to Madrid and died aged 71 on 13 September 1598 after a long and painful illness, covered in boils and in a verminous condition, in the great monastery palace of El Escorial, which he had built. He was buried in the monastery, which was to become the last resting-place of all future kings and queens of Spain.

Philippa, Princess, Queen of Denmark (1394–1430) The second daughter and seventh and youngest child of HENRY IV and his first wife Mary de Bohun, who was born at Peterborough Castle on 4 July 1394. She was five years old when her father became king and her position was greatly enhanced thereby. An offer for her hand was forthcoming from Erik XIII of Pomerania, King of Denmark, Sweden and Norway. Philippa proceeded to Lund with a large train and was married there on 26 October 1406, her coronation taking place there on 1 November. In 1429, 23 years after her marriage, Queen Philippa was delivered of a stillborn child. She never fully recovered her health and retired to the convent of Vadstena, where she died on 6 January 1430. She was buried in the convent church. King Erik, who was born in 1381 or 1382, died at Rügenwalde Castle in Pomerania on 3 May 1459.

Philippa of Clarence, Princess, Countess of March (1355–78) The only child of Lionel of Antwerp, Duke of CLARENCE (third son of EDWARD III) and his first wife Elizabeth, daughter of William de Burgh, 3rd Earl of Ulster, who was born at Eltham

Palace, Kent, on 16 August 1355 and named after her grandmother Queen PHILIPPA OF HAINAULT, who was one of her godparents. She was in only her fourth year when she was married at the Queen's Chapel, Reading, shortly after 15 February 1359 to Edmund Mortimer, 3rd Earl of March, Marshal of England and Lieutenant of Ireland. The bridegroom, who was only seven, having been born on 1 February 1352, succeeded his father in the year following the marriage. Child marriages such as this were, of course, not consummated until the parties reached years of maturity.

Philippa's first child, Elizabeth, was born at Usk on 12 February 1371. She was followed by Roger, born at Usk on 1 September 1373, Philippa, born at Ludlow on 21 November 1375, and Edmund, born at Ludlow on 9 November 1377. Philippa died, probably as a result of complications following the last birth, on or shortly before 7 January 1378. She was buried at Wigmore, Herefordshire, the burial place of the Mortimers. Her husband, who was appointed Lieutenant of Ireland by RICHARD II on 22 October 1380, died at Cork on 26 or 27 December 1381, and his body was brought back to Wigmore for burial.

From the death of her grandfather Edward III on 21 June 1377 until her own death six months later, Philippa occupied the position of heiress presumptive to the throne, and her elder son was declared heir to the throne by Richard II in 1387. It was through descent from him that the Yorkist claim to the throne derived.

Philippa of Gloucester, Princess (c.1389–c.1399) The fourth and youngest daughter of Thomas of Woodstock, Duke of GLOUCESTER (seventh and youngest son of EDWARD III) and his wife Eleanor de Bohun, who was born about 1389 and died before 3 October 1399, not being mentioned in the Inquisition post-mortem of her mother, who died on that day.

Philippa of Hainault, Queen of England (1311–69) The consort (and second cousin) of EDWARD III, who was the third daughter of William III, Count of Holland and Hainault, and his wife Jeanne, daughter of Charles, Count of Valois, a son of Philippe III, King of France. Philippa was born, probably at Valenciennes, on 24 June 1311. She was first considered as a possible bride for the future Edward III when she was only eight. Bishop Stapeldon of Exeter was sent to inspect her on behalf of Edward's parents and reported back in minute detail:

The lady ... has not uncomely hair, betwixt blue-black and brown. Her head is clean-shaped; her forehead high and broad, and standing somewhat forward. Her face narrows between the eyes, and the lower part of her face is still more narrow and slender than the forehead. Her eyes are blackish-brown and deep. Her nose is fairly smooth and even, save that it is somewhat broad at the tip and flattened, yet it is no snub-nose. Her nostrils are also broad, her mouth fairly wide. Her lips somewhat full, and especially the lower lip. Her teeth which have fallen and grown again are white enough, but the rest are not so white. The lower teeth project a little beyond the upper; yet this is but little seen. Her ears and chin are comely enough. Her neck, shoulders and all her body and lower limbs are reasonably well shapen; all her limbs are well set and unmaimed; and nought is amiss so far as a man may see. Moreover, she is of brown skin all over, and much like her father; and in all things she is pleasant enough, as it seems to us.

The bishop goes on to add that she was 'neither too tall nor too short' for her age, and that she was 'of fair carriage and well taught in all that becometh her rank'. Edward was able to check the truth of this report for himself when he and his mother were guests at the court of Hainault in 1326. Philippa was then 15 and Edward 14. Evidently he liked what he found and after a papal dispensation for the marriage had been sought and obtained from Avignon in September 1327, Philippa set out for England, arriving in London two days before Christmas. Edward was in the north with his army, and Philippa, with a large suite in attendance, rode to meet him. The marriage took place in York Minster on 24 January 1328, and the queen's coronation at WESTMINSTER ABBEY took place on 20 February 1328.

The royal manor of Woodstock was to become Philippa's favourite residence and the birthplace of four of her 12 children. Her eldest child, Edward, was born there on 15 June 1330 and Philippa chose to feed the baby herself, going against the current fashion for employing wet-nurses. Like other medieval queens, Philippa accompanied her husband on his campaigns and the birthplaces of some of her children testify that she was not to be deterred in so doing by pregnancy. She had a kindly nature and was able to restrain her husband and eldest son on many occasions when their tempers got the better of them. She interceded for the lives of the carpenters whose stand collapsed at the great tournament in Cheapside held to celebrate the birth of the BLACK PRINCE and later, in an episode celebrated as a subject for pictures and statues, pleaded successfully for the lives of the six burghers of Calais who came to surrender the town to Edward III.

The queen's great amiability gained her a popularity not enjoyed by any of her predecessors. Her homely features and comfortable, motherly figure are well apparent in Master Hennequin of Liège's fine alabaster effigy on her tomb in Westminster Abbey. A lively carving of the younger Philippa, wearing an elaborate crown, is to be seen on one of the misericordes in the Chapel of the Royal Foundation of St Katherine in east London.

Philippa died in her late fifties of a 'dropsical malady' that had afflicted her for about two years. Froissart describes her deathbed, with her hand in that of the king, and her youngest son Thomas, a boy of 14, standing by her bed.

The Queen's College, Oxford, was founded in Philippa's honour by her chaplain Robert d'Eglesfield and established by Royal Charter in 1341. Agnes Strickland ends her life of Philippa thus:

> The close observer of history will not fail to notice that with the life of Queen Philippa the happiness, the good fortune, and even the respectability of Edward III and his family departed; and scenes of strife, sorrow and folly distracted the court where she had once promoted virtue, and presided with well-regulated magnificence.

Philippa of Lancaster, Queen of Portugal

(1360–1415) The eldest daughter of John of Gaunt, Duke of LANCASTER (fourth son of EDWARD III) and his first wife BLANCHE OF LANCASTER, who was born at Leicester on 31 March 1360. She was married at Oporto on 2 February 1387 to João (John) I, King of Portugal, the marriage being arranged by her father to gain an ally in his campaign to conquer Castile and Leon, which he claimed through his second wife Constance. A beautifully illuminated manuscript in the British Museum depicts the marriage. Philippa wears the tall pointed head-dress of the day and has three maids of honour, while her father and stepmother, both regally clad, look on. 'Dona Filipa', as Philippa was to become known in Portugal, became one of that country's best loved queens. Austere and pious by nature, she brought about a much needed reform in court life, and she and the king brought up their large family with care. João had had two natural children born before his marriage, but after it had taken place appears to have remained faithful to Philippa, although on one occasion court gossip informed the queen that he had strayed. He was able to convince her that

this was not so and wryly commemorated the event by having one of the royal apartments decorated with a design of chattering magpies, which may be seen to this day in the palace of Sintra.

Philippa had six sons and two daughters, the best known of her children being her fourth son, Prince Henrique (Henry) 'the Navigator', who financed and fitted out expeditions and voyages of discovery (although never himself setting out to sea). In 1415 Philippa's three eldest surviving sons, anxious to prove their mettle in battle and scorning their father's offer to hold a tourney for them, eventually persuaded him to launch an attack on the port of Ceuta in north Africa. They were about to sail when Philippa was struck down by the plague. She died at Odivelas, near Lisbon, on 19 July 1415, arming and exhorting her sons from her deathbed. They set out five days after her death and Ceuta fell after only one day, becoming the first Portuguese possession in Africa. Queen Philippa was buried at Batalha Abbey, where her husband was laid beside her after his death at Lisbon on 14 August 1433.

Placentia *see* GREENWICH PALACE.

Plantagenet, House of General name given to the dynasty that ruled England from 1154 until 1485. The male line of the counts of Anjou can be traced from Geoffrey I of Château-Landon, Count of Gâtinais, who married Beatrice de Macon. Their son Geoffrey II married Ermengarde, the heiress of Anjou, about the first quarter of the 11th century. Her family had reigned as counts of Anjou for about 200 years. Geoffrey and Ermengarde's grandson, Count Fulk or Foulques V, resigned Anjou and Maine (the latter county acquired by his first marriage) to his eldest son Geoffrey and went off to the Crusades, where he married his second wife, Melisande, Queen of Jerusalem, becoming king in her right and dying at Acre in 1144. Geoffrey, who remained to rule Anjou and Maine, acquired the nickname Plantagenet from the sprig of broom (*planta genista*) that he habitually wore in his cap. It was he who married HENRY I's daughter Matilda (*see* MATILDA, 'LADY OF THE ENGLISH', EMPRESS) and became the ancestor of the Plantagenet kings.

Characteristics common to nearly all of the Plantagenet monarchs included a hot-tempered disposition. This was credited by some to the legend that they were descended from the fairy Melusine, daughter of Satan, who had married an early ancestor of the counts of Anjou. St Bernard of Clairvaux was moved by this legend to observe, 'From the Devil they came and to the Devil they will return'.

Porphyria Hereditary metabolic disorder that was for many years associated with the British royal family. The disorder is characterized by the dark purple colour acquired by the urine of sufferers, caused by the pigment porphyrin, the name of which is derived from the Greek word for purple, *porphyra*. Attacks of the disease are accompanied by severe abdominal pain and mental confusion. It is now believed that GEORGE III's madness was caused by acute intermittent porphyria, a condition unknown to 18th-century doctors. The hereditary character of the disease has led to it being described as 'the royal malady' and it can be shown to have afflicted several of King George's forebears and descendants. MARY, QUEEN OF SCOTS and her son JAMES I were sufferers, and the disease probably accounted for the madness of Charles VI of France, from whom they were descended through his daughter CATHERINE OF FRANCE. Further back, it has been suggested that porphyria may have been the mysterious disease from which ALFRED THE GREAT suffered intermittently.

Portsmouth, Louise Renée de Penancoët de Kéroualle, Duchess of (1649–1734) French mistress of CHARLES II, who was the elder daughter of Guillaume de Penancoët, Comte de Kéroualle, and his wife Marie-Anne, daughter of Sebastien de Ploeuc, Marquis de Timeur et de Kergolay, and was born at Kéroualle in September 1649. Both parents belonged to distinguished Breton families with widespread connections with French and Breton nobility. Louise was appointed a MAID OF HONOUR to HENRIETTA ANNE, DUCHESS OF ORLÉANS in 1668 and accompanied her on her visit to England in 1670, where she first attracted the notice of Charles II. After Henrietta's death later that year, Louise was sent back to England by Louis XIV virtually as a spy, with instructions to captivate the king. She played the part admirably, resisting Charles's advances at first and finally becoming his mistress at Euston, Suffolk, where she was staying as a guest of Lady Arlington while the king was at the races at Newmarket in October 1671.

On 29 July 1672 she gave birth to a son, Charles Lennox, later Duke of Richmond. The following year, on 19 August 1673,

having been naturalized by act of Parliament, Louise was created Baroness Petersfield, Countess of Fareham and Duchess of Portsmouth for life, and in December Louis XIV gave her the fief of Aubigny in Berry.

Louise remained Charles II's mistress for the rest of his life, all the time acting as Louis XIV's agent. Her only great rival for the king's affections was Nell GWYNNE, who lost no opportunity to ridicule her and make fun of the preposterous fashions she adopted. She wore such large hats, for instance, that the cockney wits made play on her name, calling her 'Madame Cartwheel'. The diarist John Evelyn referred to Louise as 'that famous beauty, but in my opinion of a childish, simple and baby face'.

Louise paid several visits to France to report to Louis XIV and he rewarded her services in January 1684 by raising her fief of Aubigny to a Duché-Pairie of France and creating her Duchess of Aubigny with remainder to her natural son the Duke of Richmond. After Charles II's death in 1685, Louise remained in England until July 1688, when she retired to Aubigny. She sought permission to visit London in 1697, but WILLIAM III intimated that she would not be allowed to land.

Louise's extravagance and love of gambling led to chronic financial difficulties in spite of a substantial pension paid by Louis XIV, and she was forced to sell her estates in Brittany. She made her last visit to England in 1716 to claim her arrears of pension. A story is told of her meeting at the court of GEORGE I with the Countess of Orkney, a former mistress of William III, and the Countess of Dorchester, a former mistress of JAMES II and a noted wit, who exclaimed 'Who would have thought that we three whores should have met *here!*' At this time Louise was apparently still as enchanting and lively as ever.

She returned to France and died in Paris on 14 November 1734, being buried there in the Rieux family chapel in the church of the Discalced Carmelites. Her French dukedom of Aubigny passed to her grandson, the 2nd Duke of Richmond, her son having predeceased her.

Prasutagus, King of the Iceni (d.AD60) Ruler of the Iceni, the powerful Celtic tribe that inhabited Norfolk and Suffolk. He was possibly the successor of a ruler named Anted (known only from coins) and became an ally and client king of the Romans following the conquest of AD43. On his death in 59 or 60 he left his dominions jointly to Rome and his two daughters, but the Roman authorities usurped full power, the daughters were raped by Roman officers, and their mother BOUDICCA (or Boadicea) was flogged. This succession of events led to Boudicca's revolt, a serious uprising against Roman rule.

Princes in the Tower Popular designation given to the youthful EDWARD V and his brother Richard Plantagenet, Duke of YORK, who are believed to have met their deaths by foul play while held prisoner in the TOWER OF LONDON in 1483.

Princess Royal Title that is bestowed only upon the first-born daughter of a sovereign, and borne uniquely during the lifetime of the holder. Thus, the eldest daughter of a reigning sovereign may not bear the title during the lifetime of the eldest daughter of a preceding sovereign who may hold it. ELIZABETH II, for example, although the first born daughter of GEORGE VI, could have been declared Princess Royal only in the event of her aunt Princess MARY, COUNTESS OF HAREWOOD dying before the king, and Princess ANNE was similarly ineligible until the death of Princess Mary.

The title of Princess Royal is not created by Letters Patent under the Great Seal but is granted by Royal Warrant entered at the COLLEGE OF ARMS. It seems likely, though by no means certain, that an eldest daughter born to a reigning sovereign would bear the style from birth provided there was no existing holder. The seven princesses who have borne the title of Princess Royal are:

1. Princess MARY, PRINCESS OF ORANGE, eldest daughter of CHARLES I, who was born on 4 November 1631 and died on 24 December 1660, having been married to Willem II, Prince of Orange, who died in 1650. When she was first styled Princess Royal is uncertain, but it was probably at the instigation of her mother Queen HENRIETTA MARIA in imitation of the usage of the French court, where the eldest daughter of the king was styled 'Madame Royale'. She died at Whitehall and the burial register of WESTMINSTER ABBEY gives her the style of Princess Royal.

2. Princess ANNE, eldest daughter of GEORGE II, who was born on 2 November 1709 and who died on 12 January 1759, having been married to William IV, Prince of Orange, since 1734. She appears to have been styled Princess Royal from the date of her father's accession in June 1727, armorial bearings being conferred on her in that style by Royal Warrant dated 30 August 1727.

3. Princess CHARLOTTE, eldest daughter of GEORGE III, who was born on 29 September 1766 and died on 6 October 1828, having been married to Friedrich I, King of Württemberg since 1797. She appears to have been styled Princess Royal from her birth, armorial bearings being conferred in that style.

4. Princess VICTORIA, eldest daughter of Queen VICTORIA, who was born on 21 November 1840 and died on 5 August 1901, having been married to Friedrich III, German Emperor and King of Prussia since 1858. She was styled Princess Royal from her birth, armorial bearings being granted 19 January 1841, when she was two months old. She was also heiress presumptive to the throne until the birth of her brother Albert Edward (later EDWARD VII) in 1841.

5. Princess LOUISE, DUCHESS OF FIFE, eldest daughter of EDWARD VII, who was born on 20 February 1867 and died on 4 January 1931, having been married to the 1st Duke of Fife since 1889. She was declared Princess Royal by Royal Warrant dated 9 November 1905. The Warrant also provided that her two daughters, Lady Alexandra and Lady Maud Duff, 'shall at all times hold and enjoy the style title and attribute of Highness prefixed to such respective styles or titles of Honour as may belong to them ... and ... shall bear the style of Princess prefixed to their respective Christian names and shall take hold and enjoy during the term of their natural lives ... the Precedence and Rank following, that is to say, immediately after all Members of Our Royal Family enjoying the style of Royal Highness.' This additional mark of honour is said to have been granted at the earnest request of their mother and did not meet with the universal approval of the royal family or the College of Arms. Princess Alexandra, Duchess of Fife (who succeeded her father in the dukedom under special remainder) was to attain even higher rank by her marriage to Prince ARTHUR OF CONNAUGHT; but Princess Maud of Fife (as she was styled) was to marry Lord Carnegie (later 14th Earl of Southesk) and when enquiries were made of her uncle GEORGE V as to how she was to be styled after her marriage, he replied tartly that she was 'only a Duff'. She consequently reverted to the style she had held from birth, being known as Lady Maud Carnegie until her husband's accession to the Earldom of Southesk and as Countess of Southesk thereafter until her death in 1945.

6. Princess MARY, COUNTESS OF HAREWOOD, only daughter of GEORGE V, who was born on 25 April 1897 and died on 28 March 1965, having been married to the 6th Earl of Harewood since 1922. She was declared Princess Royal by Royal Warrant dated 15 December 1931 (made public 1 January 1932), almost a year after the death of her aunt the previous Princess Royal. The Warrant carried no instructions regarding the style of the princess's two sons.

7. Princess ANNE, only daughter of ELIZABETH II, who was born on 15 August 1950 and declared Princess Royal by Royal Warrant dated 13 June 1987.

The last three Princesses Royal were declared by Royal Warrant as each had been born during the lifetime of the previous holder of the title. The daughters of George III and Queen Victoria were quite rightly styled Princess Royal from the moment of their births when they were the only persons eligible to hold the title. The case of George II's daughter Anne is curious, however, as her aunt Queen SOPHIA DOROTHEA of Prussia, the only daughter of George I, was alive when she was first styled Princess Royal and indeed, for many years after, dying only 18 months before her niece. Had George I seen fit to declare his daughter Princess Royal, Anne would have had to wait until 1757 before she became eligible to receive the honour. Doubtless George I felt that since his daughter was already a queen the title of Princess Royal could add nothing to her dignity. The only other person entitled to the style but who did not receive it was the eldest daughter of JAMES II, Princess Mary, later MARY II. As she was already married to the Prince of Orange and living in Holland at the time of her father's accession to the throne in 1685, the question was probably never considered.

Privy Council A body of advisers to the sovereign on affairs of state. Its members are entitled to the style of 'Right Honourable' and the post-nominal letters PC. The Lord President of the Council is the fourth great officer of state and is always a prominent member of the cabinet.

Proclamations Public announcements issued by the sovereign in council to declare war, dissolve or prorogue Parliament, etc. On the death of a sovereign the succeeding sovereign is proclaimed at several points in London, where the proclamation is read by a member of the COLLEGE OF ARMS, and in the chief cities of the country, where it is read by the Lord Mayor, Mayor or other civic authority.

Pybba, King of Mercia (d.*c*.606) The second king of MERCIA, according to most authorities, succeeding his father Creoda *c*.593. His wife is not named in any of the pedigrees, but he had three sons, PENDA, Eowa and Coenwalh (the two latter both being ancestors of later Mercian kings), and two daughters, who married CENWALH, King of Wessex and CADWALLON AP CADFAN, King of Gwynedd respectively. Pybba, who was a pagan, died *c*.606 and was succeeded by 'a kinsman' named Ceorl, about whom there is very little information.

Q

Queen Anne's Bounty Government charity that was first set up under Queen ANNE in 1703 to administer funds set aside to augment the stipends of the poorer clergy, build parsonage houses, deal with the dilapidations thereof and so on.

Queen Anne's Children The number of Queen ANNE's children has become one of the enduring myths of history. The number usually stated is 18 and this figure can be arrived at by carefully noting all her recorded pregnancies, whatever their outcome, as follows:

1. A daughter, stillborn on 12 May 1684.
2. Mary, who was born at Whitehall on 2 June 1685, died at WINDSOR CASTLE on 8 February 1687 and was buried in Henry VII's Chapel, WESTMINSTER ABBEY.
3. Anne Sophia, who was born at WINDSOR CASTLE on 12 May 1686, died there on 2 February 1687 and was buried in Henry VII's Chapel, Westminster Abbey.
4. A miscarriage between 20 January and 4 February 1687.
5. A son, miscarried on 22 October 1687 and buried in Westminster Abbey the same day.
6. A miscarriage on 16 April 1688.
7. William, Duke of GLOUCESTER, who was born at HAMPTON COURT PALACE on 24 July 1689 and died at Windsor Castle on 30 July 1700.
8. Mary, who was born at ST JAMES'S PALACE on 14 October 1690, lived only two hours and was buried in Westminster Abbey.
9. George, who was born and died at Syon House, Brentford, Middlesex on 17 April 1692.
10. A daughter, miscarried at Berkeley House, St James's Street, London on 23 March 1693 and buried in Westminster Abbey.
11. A miscarriage on 21 January 1694.
12. A daughter (called 'Anne' in a foreign source), miscarried on 18 February 1696.
13, 14. A double miscarriage of a son 'of seven months grown' on 20 September 1696 (buried at St George's Chapel, Windsor) and on the following day of a foetus 'of two or three months'.
15. A daughter, miscarried on 25 March 1697.
16. A miscarriage early in December 1697.
17. A son (called 'Charles' in a foreign source), miscarried on 15 September 1698 at 'about six months'.
18. A son or daughter, miscarried on 25 January 1700, recorded as a daughter buried at Westminster Abbey on 27 January 1700.

Queen Consort The wife of a male sovereign.

Queen Dowager The widow of a male sovereign who is not the mother of his successor. The most notable Queen Dowagers have been CATHERINE OF BRAGANZA and ADELAIDE OF SAXE-MEININGEN.

Queen Mother The widow of a male sovereign who is the mother of his successor. The last three to bear the title have been Queen ALEXANDRA, Queen MARY OF TECK and Queen ELIZABETH THE QUEEN MOTHER. It should perhaps be noted that Queen Mary ceased to be Queen Mother on the death of her son GEORGE VI and the succession of her granddaughter ELIZABETH II. Strictly speaking, she then became QUEEN DOWAGER, although she was sometimes referred to as Queen Grandmother. In the Prayer Book liturgy she was simply referred to as Queen Mary.

Queen Regnant A female sovereign in her own right.

Queen's Service Order of New Zealand Order instituted by ELIZABETH II in 1975 to reward community service and public services in the Dominion of New Zealand. There are two classes or divisions: Companions of the Queen's Service Order (QSO), limited to 30 appointments a year, with precedence after the OBE; and the Queen's Service Medal (QSM), with precedence after the Queen's Gallantry Medal and before the BEM.

R

Redwald, King of East Anglia (d.c.617) The son of TYTILA, KING OF EAST ANGLIA, whom he succeeded in about 593. He is counted as the fourth BRETWALDA or overlord of Saxon England. He gave refuge to EDWIN, King of Deira, and assisted him to gain the throne of NORTHUMBRIA in 616. According to BEDE, Redwald was baptized in Kent as a young man, 'but to no good purpose; for on his return home his wife and certain perverse advisers persuaded him to apostatize from the true Faith. So his last state was worse than his first: for ... he tried to serve both Christ and the ancient gods, and he had in the same temple an altar for the holy sacrifice of Christ side by side with an altar on which victims were offered to devils'. The name of Redwald's wife is unrecorded, but she had a son SIGEBERHT (who succeeded his half-brother) by a previous alliance and two sons by Redwald: Raegenhere, who was killed in the battle with Ethelfrith of BERNICIA in 616, and EARP-WALD, who succeeded his father. Redwald died in or soon after 617 and is believed to be the king commemorated by the pagan ship burial at Sutton Hoo, near Ipswich.

Redwulf, King of Northumbria (fl.844) Of unknown lineage, he expelled ETHELRED II in 844 and reigned for only a short time until Ethelred was restored in the same year. Coins of Redwulf are known.

Rhodri Mawr (the Great), King of all Wales (d.877) The son of Merfyn Frych and his wife Nest, daughter of Cadell ap Brochwel, King of Powys, who succeeded his father as King of Gwynedd in 844 and his maternal uncle Cyngen as King of Powys in 855. He married Angharad, daughter of Meurig ap Dyfnwallon, King of Seisyllwg, and after the death of her brother Gwgon in 872 added that realm to his kingdom as well. Rhodri was killed fighting the Saxons in 877. He left a number of sons, of whom the eldest ANARAWD AP RHODRI continued the line of Gwynedd, and the second, Cadell, became King of Seisyllwg, which later

united with Dyfed to become the kingdom of DEHEUBARTH.

Rhodri Molwynog, King of Gwynedd (d.754) The son of Idwal Iwrch, whom he apparently succeeded on an unknown date. He died in 754, leaving two sons, Hywel and Cynan, who reigned jointly after him.

Rhun ap Maelgwn Gwynedd, King of Gwynedd (fl.550) The natural son of MAEL-GWN GWYNEDD by Gwallwen, daughter of Afallech, who succeeded his father as King of Gwynedd in about 550. He is often called Rhun Hir ('the Tall'). He is said to have led an army as far north as the river Forth in retaliation for raids made on Arfon. The pedigrees name his wife as Perwyr, daughter of Rhun Ryfeddfawr, a descendant of Coel Hen. He is said to have been succeeded by his son Beli, but GEOFFREY OF MONMOUTH makes Beli his brother, which would seem more likely chronologically since Sir J.E. Lloyd pointed out that the number of generations between Maelgwn and CADWALADR is rather too great for the period covered. Geoffrey of Monmouth also credits Rhun with a daughter who married Hoel II, King of Brittany, and had issue.

Rhydderch ab Iestyn, King of South Wales (d.1033) Usurper of the thrones of both North and South Wales after the death of LLYWELYN AP SEISYLL in 1023, who reigned until he was killed by the Irish in 1033, when the legitimate lines were restored.

Rhydderch Hael (The Generous), King of Strathclyde (d.603 or 612?) The son of King Tudwal Tudclyd ap Clynnog ap Dyfnwal Hen and Nefydd, daughter of Brychan, Prince of Manau Guotodin, who is said to have been baptized in Ireland and to have been a friend of St Columba. After succeeding his father in Strathclyde, Rhydderch allied himself with his cousin URIEN RHEGED and others in a campaign against Hussa, King of BERNICIA, besieging him in Lindisfarne in about 585. Rhydderch figures in many traditional stories and legends. He married Langueth, heiress of

Cadzow, and had one son, Constantine, who succeeded him. Rhydderch is said to have died at Partick very shortly after St Kentigern, whose death took place on 13 January 603 according to one source, or in about 612 in another. A late tradition says he was buried at Aber-erch.

Rhys ab Owain ab Edwin, King of Deheubarth (d.1078) The son of Owain ab Edwin ab Einion, who succeeded his brother MAREDUDD AB OWAIN in 1072 and in 1075 was implicated in the death of BLEDDYN AP CYNFYN, KING OF GWYNEDD AND POWYS. He was defeated at Goodwick by the usurper TRAHAEARN AP CARADOG in 1078 and later in the same year was killed by Caradog ap Gruffydd. He was succeeded by his second cousin, RHYS AP TEWDWR.

Rhys ap Gruffydd, Prince or **Lord of Deheubarth** (1132–97) The younger son of GRUFFYDD AP RHYS, PRINCE OF DEHEUBARTH and his wife Gwenllian, daughter of GRUFFYDD AP CYNAN, KING OF GWYNEDD, who was born in Ireland in 1132. He was only four years old when his father died in 1137 and had also lost his mother the previous year, when she was killed leading her men in an attack on the Norman castle of Kidwelly. Until 1153 DEHEUBARTH was ruled by his much older half-brothers, ANARAWD AP GRUFFYDD until 1143 and then Cadell, under whom Rhys and his brother MAREDUDD AP GRUFFYDD fought as teenagers. Cadell abdicated and went to Rome in 1153, leaving Maredudd and Rhys as joint rulers of Deheubarth, and Maredudd's death in 1155 made Rhys the sole ruler.

In a rule lasting long over 40 years, Rhys strengthened and consolidated his position, which, in spite of his submission to HENRY II in 1158, became one of pre-eminence in South Wales. He gained much territory and was created Justice of South Wales. As a vassal of England he discontinued the titles of king and prince and was known simply as 'The Lord Rhys' (*Yr Arglwydd Rhys*). He adopted Norman dress and manners at his court and gave his patronage to the newly emerging religious orders. He built castles, founded abbeys and presided at the eisteddfod held at Cardigan in 1176.

He married Gwenllian, daughter of MADOG AP MAREDUDD, PRINCE OF POWYS, and had eight sons: GRUFFYDD AP RHYS (his successor), Maredudd Ddall (who died in 1239), Cynwrig (who died in 1237), Rhys Gryg (who died in 1234), Maredudd, Lord of Cantref Bychan (who died in 1201), Maelgwn, Lord of Ceredigion (who died in

1230), Hywel Sais (who died in 1204) and Maredudd, Archdeacon of Cardigan (who died in 1227). He also had one daughter, Gwenllian, who married Ednyfed Fychan ap Cynwrig, Seneschal of Gwynedd (who died in 1246), and was ancestor of the House of TUDOR. Rhys died on 28 April 1197 and was buried in St David's Cathedral.

Rhys ap Tewdwr, King of Deheubarth (d.1093) The son of Tewdwr ap Cadell ab Einion, a descendant of HYWEL DDA, who succeeded his second cousin RHYS AB OWAIN in 1078. In 1081 he was expelled by Caradog ap Gruffydd, but managed to regain the throne later the same year with the aid of GRUFFYDD AP CYNAN, KING OF GWYNEDD. A few years later Rhys became a vassal of WILLIAM I THE CONQUEROR, to whom he paid a tribute of £40 a year for DEHEUBARTH. In 1088 he was forced to take refuge in Ireland after his realm was invaded by Powys, but he gathered Danish aid there and was able to return and defeat his rivals. Rhys spent the rest of his reign contending with various rebels and was killed while resisting a Norman advance at Aberhonddu, Brecon, in April 1093. He married Gwladus, daughter of Rhiwallon ap Cynfyn, and had two sons, GRUFFYDD, his successor, and Hywel, and a daughter NEST.

Richard, Duke of Gloucester *see* GLOUCESTER, RICHARD, DUKE OF.

Richard, 3rd Duke of York *see* YORK, RICHARD, 3RD DUKE OF.

Richard, Earl of Cambridge *see* CAMBRIDGE, RICHARD, EARL OF.

Richard, Earl of Cornwall *see* CORNWALL, RICHARD, EARL OF.

Richard, Prince (*c*.1247–before 1256) The third son of HENRY III and ELEANOR OF PROVENCE, who was born in about 1247 and was dead by 1256. He was buried in WESTMINSTER ABBEY on the south side of the choir, where several of his siblings also lie.

Richard I 'Coeur de Lion', King of England (1157–99) The third son and fourth child of HENRY II and ELEANOR OF AQUITAINE, who was born at Beaumont Palace, Oxford, on 8 September 1157. As the second surviving son of his father, he grew up with little prospect of succeeding to the throne until the death of his elder brother HENRY 'THE YOUNG KING' in June 1183. Meanwhile, he had been invested as Duke of Aquitaine (his mother's inheritance) in 1172 before reaching the age of 15 and shown his military prowess by besieging and taking the seemingly impregnable fortress of Taillebourg in 1179. In the autumn of 1187 news reached Europe of Saladin's crushing defeat of the Christian forces at Hattin in July and, fired with enthusiasm, Richard took the Cross, vowing to devote the rest of his life to the reconquest of the Holy Land. Before leaving Europe, however, Richard had a stormy meeting with his father and King Philippe II of France, to whom he did homage for his French possessions, much to his father's annoyance.

On Henry II's death Richard set out for England, pausing at Rouen to be invested with the Duchy of Normandy and receive the fealty of his Norman barons in July. Arriving in England, he proclaimed a general amnesty and was crowned at WESTMINSTER ABBEY on 3 September 1189. A unique feature of the ceremonial, recorded by Roger of Hoveden, was that Richard himself took the crown from the altar and handed it to Archbishop Baldwin before the act of crowning. The coronation celebrations were marred, however, by a violent persecution of the London Jews, who had been forbidden to attend the coronation, and this massacre was followed by similar outbreaks in Lincoln, Norwich and York. Concerned with little but raising money to pursue the Crusade, Richard paid scant heed and returned to Normandy before Christmas. Before he left he responded to criticisms of the amount of money he had taken from the people of London with the lighthearted remark, 'If I could have found a buyer I would have sold London itself'.

At last, in July 1190, the Crusade headed by Richard and Philippe of France set out and made its way across Europe. By October they had reached Messina, where further delays took place and Richard did penance for vice. With regard to this penance, Richard was once warned by a priest to rid himself as soon as possible of his three daughters – when Richard protested that he did not have any daughters, the cleric told him his daughters were 'ambition, avarice and luxury'. Richard retorted, somewhat tartly, that in that case he would give his ambition to the templars, his avarice to the monks and his luxury to the prelates.

Although it has been denied by a recent biographer, it seems likely that Richard was homosexual. His marriage was probably never consummated and throughout his life preachers were to thunder at him to beware the fate of Sodom. His friendship with Philippe of France was intense and seems to

have caused some concern to his father, who expressed alarm at the fact that the pair were reported to eat at the same table, share the same dish and sleep in the same bed. However, he did have one well-attested illegitimate son, Philip, so there must have been at least one heterosexual episode in his life. Richard's mother Eleanor was probably aware of her son's tendencies and hastened to provide him with a young bride. Her choice fell on BERENGARIA OF NAVARRE, whose own brother had probably been one of Richard's early lovers. The marriage took place at Limasol in Cyprus on 12 May 1191 and was followed immediately by Berengaria's coronation as Queen of England.

The Crusade proceeded but failed to recapture Jerusalem, and the only significant achievement of the campaign was the capture of Acre in 1191 (itself marred by arguments among the Crusaders and by a massacre of the defeated foe). After his supporters (very much against his wishes) concluded a truce with Saladin, the Saracen leader, Richard sailed for home in October 1192, having enjoyed no more than a brief glimpse of his goal, Jerusalem (legend insists he covered his eyes with his shield so that he would not have to look further upon the distant city he had failed to recover for Christianity). Wrecked in the Adriatic, he set out incognito to cross Europe by land, but was detected in Austria when one of his servant boys was tortured into revealing the identity of his disguised master. Another story claims that when first arrested, the unrecognized Richard opted to work as a kitchen hand, roasting meat on a spit, in the hope that he would be thought a person of no consequence – but was betrayed by the rings he wore on his fingers. Whatever the case, Richard was found out and flung into prison at the castle of Dürnstein for 15 months by Duke Leopold of Austria, whom he had rashly insulted in the Holy Land.

The romantic story has often been told of how the minstrel Blondel sought out Richard's place of imprisonment by travelling throughout Austria singing one of Richard's own songs until he heard the refrain taken up from a barred window. He is then said to have got employment at the castle in order to communicate with his royal master and negotiate a ransom for him. This may be true, though there is no reliable source to corroborate the story. At any rate, the huge ransom demand was finally met and Richard returned to London in March 1194 to find that his brother JOHN (forewarned of Richard's arrival by a message from Philippe of France, that read, 'Look to yourself; the devil is loose') had been depleting the treasury and planning to supplant him. John was both charming and good looking, and Richard readily forgave him, exclaiming, 'You are a child!'

During Richard's absence, his continental possessions had been threatened by his enemies, including the King of France, who had returned from the Crusade earlier than Richard. The years after his return from imprisonment were spent in regaining lost territory and strengthening his hold over his continental possessions. During this period he constructed the great fortress of Château-Gaillard in Normandy and is said to have been his own architect. Its purpose was to guard the border between Normandy and France.

In March 1199 Richard was laying siege to the town of Châlus in Limousin, where he claimed possession as the ultimate suzerain, but the local landlord had refused to give it up. One morning while riding before the town walls Richard was struck on the right shoulder by an arrow loosed from the battlements by a crossbowman. He made light of the wound and continued the siege, successfully taking the town several days later and ordering that all the defenders, with the exception of the man who had wounded him (one Bertrand de Gurdun), be put to death. His physician Marchadeus had made a bungling job of removing the arrow, however, and the wound turned gangrenous. The king died on 6 April, nursed at the last by his mother Queen Eleanor. Before he died he forgave Bertrand de Gurdun for his death and promised him he should go free, with compensation of one hundred shillings – only for Bertrand, so legend claims, to be flayed alive and then hanged on the orders of Marchadeus once the king was dead. Marchadeus paid for his mishandling of the case with his life a few days later. Richard was buried at Fontevraud near his father. His heart, as was then frequently the custom, was buried separately at Rouen.

It is curious that Richard 'Lionheart' should be regarded as a national hero and have been chosen to typify English monarchy in the fine statue erected outside the Houses of Parliament, since he spent less time in and took less interest in his country than any other king before or since.

Richard II, King of England (1367–1400)

The younger son of EDWARD OF WOOD-STOCK, PRINCE OF WALES ('The Black Prince') and his wife Joan, Countess of Kent ('The Fair Maid of Kent') (see JOAN, PRINCESS OF WALES), who was born at Bordeaux on 6 January 1367, and was consequently known in his youth as 'Richard of Bordeaux'. It was rumoured that he was born without a skin and spent his early weeks being nourished in a goat's skin. As he grew up he developed a stammer, which he never overcame. The death of his elder brother Edward in 1372 left him the only surviving child of his parents. He could have had no memories of his grandmother Queen Philippa (see PHILIPPA OF HAINAULT), who died when he was only two years old, and whatever impressions he had of his family would have been derived from memories of his stern father, who died when he was nine, his lecherous old grandfather EDWARD III, his flighty but loving mother and his assortment of uncles and half-siblings. His father entrusted his education to an old soldier, Sir Simon Burley, who instilled in him a love of literature and music, as well as a sense of the importance of his royal office.

After his father's death Richard was created Prince of Wales, Duke of Cornwall and Earl of Chester on 20 November 1376 and invested at Westminster on Christmas Day. He was nominated a Knight of the GARTER on 23 April 1377 and two months later succeeded his grandfather as king. The dignitaries of the day saw nothing incongruous in submitting a boy of 10 to the long ceremonial of anointing and coronation preceded by fasting, and the little king was so exhausted after the ceremony on 16 July 1377 that he had to be carried from the Abbey to WESTMINSTER HALL on the shoulders of his attendants. Superstitious spectators at the coronation remarked upon the loss of one of his shoes as he walked or was carried in procession, and prophesied from this unlucky occurence that he would incur the wrath of the Commons during his reign. When he also lost one of his golden spurs, the same spectators foretold that his armies would rebel against him, and when a gust of wind blew the crown from his head they were agreed that in due course he would be forced from the throne before his reign was over. During his minority the government was carried on by a council of regency.

In 1381 the Peasants' Revolt led by Wat Tyler against the imposition of a tax of a shilling a head on all persons over 15 was the occasion of a remarkable act of bravery from Richard, who at the age of just 14 rode out to meet them at Smithfield and was personally able to pacify them. The minority ended in 1382 and the king was married at St

Stephen's Chapel in the Palace of Westminster on 20 January to ANNE OF BOHEMIA, with whom he fell deeply and passionately in love – and for whom he agreed to pay a colossal loan to her brother Wenceslas. Unfortunately the marriage was to remain childless and the queen's death, probably from plague, in 1394 drove Richard so wild with grief that he had SHEEN PALACE, where she died, razed to the ground. When the Earl of Arundel turned up late for the queen's funeral and then asked to be excused before the end, the outraged Richard struck him down with a baton and had him thrown into the TOWER OF LONDON. This was not the only instance in which Richard's naturally hot temper showed itself: in 1385, for instance, it was only with difficulty that others present prevented the king, in a fit of anger, running the Archbishop of Canterbury through with a sword after the latter had voiced complaints about the king's favourites.

Richard's reign was a troubled one throughout, his uncles of Lancaster, York and Gloucester continually vying for power with an eye on the eventual succession. While Richard remained childless, the heir to the throne was Roger Mortimer, Earl of March, the grandson of his uncle Lionel, Duke of CLARENCE, but his claim, although officially recognized by Richard in 1387, was hardly likely to remain uncontested. On 1 November 1396 Richard married again, to ISABELLA OF FRANCE[2], but his bride was a child and not likely to produce an heir for several years. Richard became fond of her, but she filled the position of a sister more than a wife. Undoubtedly what Richard needed emotionally was a father-figure, and this was supplied, after Sir Simon Burley had been impeached and beheaded by the king's opponents in 1388, by Robert de Vere, 9th Earl of Oxford, successively created Marquess of Dublin (the first English marquessate) and Duke of Ireland. The king worshipped Robert, a dashing aristocrat who was only five years older than himself. Their association was probably quite innocent, but it aroused intense jealousy and hostility from the royal uncles and others, who had Robert charged with treason. He managed to escape to the continent where he was killed in a boar hunt in 1392. The sorrowing Richard had his body brought back to England and buried with great solemnity (he even had the coffin opened so that he could gaze one last time upon the face of his dead friend and clasp his fingers). Another favourite, who was similarly resented for his

closeness to the king, was Michael de la Pole, who was also driven abroad.

In 1396 Richard concluded peace with France, but his attempt to do away with parliamentary government and establish a royal autocracy proved his final undoing and he was deposed in favour of his cousin Henry Bolingbroke (later HENRY IV) on 29 September 1399 and imprisoned, first, at Leeds Castle and then in Pontefract Castle. Here he completely lost the will to live and, refusing to eat, starved himself to death, dying on or about 14 February 1400. A final rebuff was delivered to the doomed king when his faithful greyhound deserted him and subsequently found its way to Henry's chambers, where it was allowed to sleep on the royal bed. Inevitably false rumours that he had been murdered were circulated and to refute them his body was brought to London and paraded through the streets on an open bier. He was buried beside his beloved Queen Anne in the tomb he had carefully ordered for them both in WESTMINSTER ABBEY. Shakespeare's Richard is murdered, but examination of the king's supposed skeleton in 1871 did not appear to support this version of events. Another theory (hotly contested by Henry IV's supporters) claimed that the king evaded death at Pontefract and instead escaped to Scotland, where he finally died in Stirling Castle.

Richard is perhaps the most tragic of all English kings. His reign began with great promise but after he attained his majority it proceeded from failure to failure, not always of his making. His portrait in Westminster Abbey and tomb effigy both have an air of melancholy. He was only 33 when he died. Lasting legacies of his reign include the rebuilding of Westminster Hall and improvements at York Minster and Canterbury Cathedral.

Richard III, King of England (1452–85) The eighth and youngest son and 11th child of Richard Plantagenet, 3rd Duke of YORK, and his wife the redoubtable Lady Cicely Nevill, who was born at FOTHERINGAY CASTLE on 2 October 1452 (after a pregnancy of two years, according to his later critics). All that remains of Fotheringay today is a single lump of masonry on top of a grassy knoll. Attached to it are plaques commemorating the two most notable events to take place within its walls, the birth of Richard and the beheading of MARY, QUEEN OF SCOTS. Richard was only eight years old when his brother EDWARD IV was proclaimed king in March 1461, and he was created Duke of Gloucester on the eve of Edward's coronation. He proved himself a loyal and loving brother and fought bravely in the later stages of the civil war, culminating in the battle of Tewkesbury.

On 12 July 1472 Richard was married at Westminster to the widow of Edward, Prince of Wales, ANNE NEVILL, the younger daughter of Warwick 'the King-maker'. Her elder sister, Isabel, had married Richard's brother George, Duke of CLARENCE, three years earlier. These marriages caused a rift between the brothers because George was desirous of retaining all the Warwick estates for himself. Richard was suspected of being implicated in Clarence's death in the Tower in 1478, but the charge remains unproven.

Edward IV's death made Richard Lord High Protector of the Realm for his nephew EDWARD V and he set out from York to meet Edward, who was coming from Ludlow, and proceeded to London. Edward was conducted by his maternal uncle Earl Rivers and his half-brother Sir Richard Grey. When the parties met up at Stony Stratford, these two were seized by Richard, who had long chafed under the ascendancy of the Woodville faction, and he took charge of the young king. On entering London, Richard presented Edward to the Lord Mayor and citizens as their king, himself evincing complete loyalty. The Woodville party was completely overthrown and Lord Hastings, who had previously supported Richard, grew apprehensive as he gained power and sought, with some members of the Council, to wrest Edward from Richard's control. The result was dramatic. Apprised of their intentions, Richard had Hastings and his fellow plotters arrested at a sitting of the Council and summarily beheaded on 13 June 1483. Their executions were followed 12 days later by those of Rivers and Grey, also without trial.

On 22 June 1483 Dr Shaw preached a sermon at St Paul's Cross, London, declaring Edward IV's marriage invalid and his children bastards, based on the information revealed by Bishop Stillington of Bath and Wells. As a result, Richard was offered the Crown by Parliament and proclaimed king on 26 June. Ten days later Richard and Anne were crowned in WESTMINSTER ABBEY by Cardinal Bourchier. The presumed deaths of Edward V and his young brother (the PRINCES IN THE TOWER) while held captive in the TOWER OF LONDON, probably some time in 1483 or 1484, have long been laid at Richard's door (as has that of HENRY

VI), but the evidence is circumstantial and like everything else to Richard's discredit was highly coloured by the Tudor propagandists, Polydore Vergil and Sir Thomas More.

Richard's hour of victory was soon overshadowed by sorrow occasioned by the death of his only legitimate son, another Edward, Prince of Wales, whose shadowy, sickly life of 10 years ended at Middleham Castle in Yorkshire on 9 April 1484, and was followed a year later by that of Queen Anne (poisoned by her husband, according to Richard's enemies). Richard then designated his nephew, John de la Pole, Earl of Lincoln, as heir presumptive. He was the eldest son of Richard's second sister, Elizabeth, Duchess of Suffolk (the possibility of a female succeeding to the throne in her own right was then still considered unfeasible).

Meanwhile, the Lancastrians were being rallied under the leadership of Henry Tudor, who landed at Milford Haven on 7 August 1485 and travelled through Wales gathering support. Richard was in the north and proceeded to Leicester with his army. On 21 August he rode out to meet Henry, who was encamped near Market Bosworth (*see* BOSWORTH FIELD). The night before the conflict, it was reported, Richard was tormented with terrible nightmares, in which he believed himself surrounded by demons. Battle was joined on the morning of 22 August. The king's army was twice the size of Henry's, but the turning point of the battle came when Lord Stanley and his 7000 men deserted Richard and went over to Henry. Richard fought bravely to the last, even after his horse was killed under him. He could have escaped, but proudly declared: 'I will not budge a foot; I will die King of England'. And so he did, attempting to fight his way through the press to reach Henry Tudor himself. The crest crown from his helmet fell or was hacked off and rolled away under a hawthorn bush, where Stanley picked it up and placed it on the head of the victorious Henry. The battle had lasted only two hours.

Richard's body, stripped of its armour, was laid across the back of a pack-horse and was taken in procession back to Leicester, arriving at nightfall. He was buried in Grey Friars Abbey in Leicester, but it proved a temporary resting place for at the Dissolution Richard's bones were dug up and thrown into the River Soar. His coffin was used as a horse-trough until this, too, was broken up and used to make steps down to the cellar of the White Horse Inn. In recent years the Richard III Society, dedicated to a wholesale reappraisal of the king's reign in the wake of Shakespeare's allegedly biased version of events, has placed a memorial to the king in Leicester Cathedral and there is also an inscription adjacent to the bridge over the River Soar.

Richard was a small, slightly built man, a complete contrast to his brother Edward. He had one shoulder slightly higher than the other, a malformation that has been magnified into the hump and crooked back so maliciously described by his detractors. His portraits reveal a not unpleasant face with a rather worried expression. He was only 32 when he died. That Richard III has gone down in history as the archetype 'wicked uncle' and an evil monster is due almost entirely to the effective hatchet job carried out by Tudor propagandists in the reigns of HENRY VII and HENRY VIII and perfected by Shakespeare in the reign of ELIZABETH I. In fact, he showed signs of being a very competent ruler, though he had little opportunity to confirm this, reigning for just 26 months. He had to wait nearly 300 years for his first apologist and found a doughty champion in the person of Horace Walpole, who in 1768 published his *Historic Doubts on Richard III*, in which he questioned Richard's guilt. Thereafter the move towards his rehabilitation has grown steadily and in the present century Josephine Tey's ingenious novel *The Daughter of Time*, in which a detective whiles away a forced sojourn in hospital by studying Richard's story and finding him innocent of all charges brought against him, has done more than anything else to win over people to Richard's cause. The flourishing Richard III Society, appropriately under the patronage of another Richard, Duke of Gloucester, holds regular meetings and lectures to promote the cause and enthusiastically visits Ricardian sites.

Richard of Normandy (*c*.1054–*c*.1081) The second son of WILLIAM I THE CONQUEROR and MATILDA OF FLANDERS, who was born in Normandy in about 1054. He was killed accidentally while hunting in the New Forest in about 1081 and was buried in Winchester Cathedral. He was unmarried.

Richmond, Henry FitzRoy, Duke of (1519–36) The natural son of HENRY VIII and Elizabeth, daughter of Sir John Blount, of Kinlet, Shropshire, who was probably born at Jericho, the manor house of Blackmore, Essex, in June 1519. Cardinal Wolsey acted as his godfather. On 7 June

1525 the boy was nominated a Knight of the GARTER and on 18 June he was created Earl of Nottingham and Duke of Richmond and Somerset with precedence over all other dukes except the king's lawful issue. His father had high hopes for him and very likely intended to legitimate him and make him heir to the throne if he had no legitimate son.

Richmond was appointed Lord High Admiral, Warden General of the Marches of Scotland, Lord Lieutenant of Ireland, Lieutenant of the Order of the Garter, Chamberlain of Chester and North Wales and Lord Warden of the Cinque Ports. He took his seat in the House of Lords at the age of 15 and accompanied his father to Calais on his meeting with King François I of France. He was married by dispensation dated 28 November 1533 to Mary, daughter of Thomas Howard, Duke of Norfolk, and his second wife Elizabeth, daughter of Edward Stafford, Duke of Buckingham, but the marriage was never consummated, probably because of the bridegroom's youth and ill-health.

The duke was present at the execution of ANNE BOLEYN in May 1536 and died of consumption on 22 July 1536. He was buried at Thetford, Norfolk. His widow had some trouble in establishing her right to dower, but eventually did so and served as a lady-in-waiting to ANNE OF CLEVES. She did not remarry and died on 9 December 1557.

Richmond and Derby, Margaret Beaufort, Countess of (1443–1509) The mother of HENRY VII, who was the only child of John Beaufort, Duke of Somerset (grandson of John of Gaunt, Duke of LANCASTER), and his wife Margaret, only daughter of John Beauchamp, 4th Baron Beauchamp of Bletsoe, and was born at Bletsoe, Bedfordshire, on 31 May 1443. She was just under a year old when her father died suddenly, by suicide as rumour had it, at Wimborne, Dorset, on 27 May 1444. Her wardship and marriage were granted by HENRY VI to William de la Pole, Earl of Suffolk, and in late January or early February 1450 he married her to his seven-year-old son John, a papal dispensation being granted on 18 August that year. A reclamation or dissolution of this marriage took place three years later, in 1453, and the king re-granted Margaret's wardship and marriage to his half-brothers Jasper and Edmund Tudor.

On an unknown date in 1455 Margaret married the 25-year-old Edmund, who had been created Earl of Richmond on 23 November 1452. By the convention of the day the marriage should not have been consummated until Margaret reached the age of 14, but Edmund was eager to secure a life-tenancy of his wife's inheritance, which would be his legally on the birth of a living child and would not wait. Margaret became pregnant and accompanied her husband to Wales, where he died at Carmarthen Castle on 3 November 1456. He was buried in the Greyfriars' Church in Carmarthen, but after the Dissolution of the Monasteries his body was removed to St David's Cathedral in 1536. His 13-year-old widow sought the protection of her brother-in-law Jasper Tudor, Earl of Pembroke, and it was at Pembroke Castle on 28 January 1457 that she gave birth to her only child, the future Henry VII. The birth was a protracted and difficult one and effectively incapacitated her as far as any future prospects of maternity were concerned.

On 3 January 1458 Margaret contracted a third marriage with her second cousin Lord Henry Stafford, second son of Humphrey Stafford, 1st Duke of Buckingham. He died on 4 October 1471 and in June 1472 Margaret married her fourth and last husband, Thomas, Lord Stanley, who was to be created Earl of Derby by his stepson Henry VII on 27 October 1485. He played a prominent role in Henry's path to the throne and it was he who picked up RICHARD III's crest crown from under a thorn bush on BOSWORTH FIELD and placed it on Henry's head. With the accession of her son Margaret came to occupy a position of great importance at court. She was the second lady in the land and was to all intents and purposes the queen mother. She became a great patron of learning, founding Christ's and St John's Colleges at Cambridge, and was truly a woman of the Renaissance.

The Earl of Derby died on 29 July 1504. Margaret survived her son Henry VII and headed the list of those appointed to make his funeral arrangements. On 23 June 1509 she witnessed the coronation procession of her grandson HENRY VIII from the latticed window of a rented house in Cheapside. After the coronation festivities she moved to Cheyneygates, part of the great palace complex at Westminster, and soon after fell ill, the result it was said of eating a cygnet, but more probably from exhaustion following the unaccustomed round of celebrations and feasting. Various remedies were administered but she died on 29 June 1509. She was buried in Henry VII's Chapel in WESTMINSTER ABBEY, where her tomb with her full-length effigy lying upon it was constructed

to the design of the Florentine sculptor Pietro Torrigiano and her epitaph, extolling her virtues and scholastic foundations, was composed by Erasmus.

Richmond Palace Royal palace rebuilt from the ruins of the burned-out SHEEN PALACE in Surrey by HENRY VII between 1499 and 1510. Renamed Richmond Palace after the king's earldom of Richmond in Yorkshire, the palace witnessed the death of Henry VII in 1509 and subsequently served as home to CATHERINE OF ARAGON and ANNE OF CLEVES. Other visitors included ELIZABETH I, EDWARD VI and MARY I, who spent her honeymoon with PHILIP OF SPAIN here. Elizabeth I died at Richmond Palace in 1603 and some years later CHARLES I gave it as a wedding present to HENRIETTA MARIA. Most of the palace was destroyed after the execution of Charles I in 1649. JAMES II had plans to renovate the palace, but these never materialized and all that now remains is the gateway on the Green and the restored buildings of the Wardrobe.

Ricsige, King of Northumbria (d.876) Of unknown origin, Ricsige succeeded EGBERT I in 873 and reigned for three years, dying in 876. His rule was probably confined to the area north of the Tyne. He may have been the father of Edred *filius Rixinci*, who according to Simeon of Durham killed a certain *princeps Eardulfus*, perhaps identifiable with Eadwulf, who seems to have ruled after EGBERT II.

Robert, Duke of Albany *see* ALBANY, ROBERT STEWART, DUKE OF.

Robert I (Bruce), King of Scots (1274–1329) The eldest son of Robert Bruce, Lord of Annandale and *jure uxoris* Earl of Carrick, and his wife Margaret, or Marjorie, daughter and heiress of Neil, 2nd Earl of Carrick, who was born at Writtle, near Chelmsford, Essex, on 11 July 1274. His paternal grandfather Robert de Brus (or Bruce), Lord of Annandale (*c*.1210–94) was one of the competitors for the crown of Scotland in 1291 (*see* SCOTTISH SUCCESSION). On 27 October 1292 Robert's father resigned the earldom of Carrick to him and he swore fealty to EDWARD I on 24 August 1296. In 1297 he fought with the English against William Wallace, but after changing sides more than once he joined the fighters for Scottish freedom and was chosen one of the guardians of the kingdom at Peebles on 19 August 1299.

Bruce succeeded his father as Lord Annandale in the spring of 1304, and for a time he resumed fealty to Edward I until learning that the king was planning his execution on information received from John Comyn, one of the rival competitors for the crown. He fled to Scotland and stabbed Comyn to death at Dumfries. He then assembled his followers at Lochmaben and proceeded to SCONE, where he was proclaimed king and the crown was placed on his head by Isabella, Countess of Buchan, 'in the presence, and with the consent of four bishops, five earls, and the people of the land' on 27 March 1306.

For a time things did not run smoothly for Robert. He was defeated at Methven in June and forced to become a wanderer in the Highlands and western isles, finally finding shelter on Rathlin Island off the north coast of Antrim. To this period belongs the well-known story of his finding inspiration to continue the struggle through watching the perseverance of a spider in constructing its web at the mouth of a cave in which he was hiding. (However, this story is almost certainly apocryphal since it was 'lifted' from a story originally attributed to the 'Black Douglas'.) In May 1307 he landed on the Carrick coast and defeated the Earl of Pembroke at Loudon Hill. In the course of the next two years he won back most of the country. The Scottish clergy recognized him as king in 1310, and in 1312 the king of Norway ceded the Hebrides to him. Raids into the north of England took place in 1312 and 1313, and on 24 June 1314 the decisive battle of Bannockburn, near Stirling, totally defeated the forces of EDWARD II and established Scottish independence. According to legend, the Monymusk Reliquary, containing the relics of St Columba, was carried into the battle.

Bruce's younger brother Edward, whom he had created Earl of Carrick in 1313, was invited to Ireland by some of the Ulster chieftains and crowned king of Ireland on 2 May 1316. He met with much opposition and Robert went to his aid in 1317 and helped him gain Limerick, but after he left the following year Edward was pushed back to Carrickfergus and was finally killed in battle at Dundalk on 14 October 1318. The English had conducted several border raids during Robert's absence and in retaliation he took Berwick and harried the north of England as far as Yorkshire. English aggression continued for several years and a gathering of Scottish nobles at Arbroath Abbey drew up a petition to Pope John XXII seeking his recognition of Scotland as an independent sovereign state. This petition, known as the Declaration of Arbroath, was allowed in 1323, but it was not until April 1328 that the Treaty of Northampton finally secured peace with England and acknowledged Scotland's independence.

Robert survived a little over a year after this, dying, of leprosy it is said, at Cardross Castle, Dumbartonshire, on 7 June 1329. His body was buried at DUNFERMLINE Abbey and his heart at Melrose.

Robert married first, in about 1295, Isabella, daughter of Donald, 6th Earl of Mar. Her mother, Helen, was the widow of Malcolm, 7th Earl of Fife, and is said to have been a daughter of LLYWELYN THE GREAT, Prince of Aberffraw and Lord of Snowdon, but she is not recorded in any of the Welsh genealogies. Robert and Isabella had one daughter, Marjorie, who in 1315 married Walter, 6th High Steward of Scotland, and became the mother of the future ROBERT II. Robert I married secondly, in 1302, Elizabeth, daughter of Richard de Burgh, 2nd Earl of Ulster, and his wife Margaret, daughter of Sir John de Burgh. She died at Cullen on 26 October 1327 and was buried at Dunfermline Abbey. By her, Robert had two sons, DAVID II, his successor, and John, who died young and was buried at Restennet Priory, Forfarshire, and two daughters, Matilda, who married Thomas Isaac and died at Aberdeen on 20 July 1353, leaving issue, and Margaret, who married William Sutherland, 5th Earl of Sutherland, and died in about 1346, leaving issue.

Robert II, King of Scots (1316–90) The first of the Stewart (or STUART) kings, who was the only child of Walter, 6th High Steward of Scotland, and his wife Marjorie, eldest daughter of ROBERT I and was born at Paisley on 2 March 1316, his mother dying at his birth. He was declared heir to the crown in default of male issue of his maternal grandfather by Parliament at SCONE on 3 December 1318. On 9 April 1326 he succeeded his father as 7th High Steward of Scotland. He acted as Guardian of the Kingdom (or regent) during DAVID II's absence in France in the years 1334–41 and his imprisonment in England in 1346–57.

On 22 February 1371 he succeeded his half-uncle David II (who was actually his junior by eight years) as king and was crowned at Scone by William de Landallis, Bishop of St Andrews, on 26 March 1371. Robert, who was nicknamed 'Auld Blearie' because of his bloodshot eyes, was a weak and feeble king, content to delegate power to his eldest son, John, Earl of Carrick (later ROBERT III). Hostilities with England were renewed in 1378 and carried on intermittently for the rest of Robert's reign. He died at Dundonald Castle, Ayrshire, on 19 April 1390 and was buried at Scone Abbey.

Robert married first, by dispensation dated at Avignon on 22 November 1347, Elizabeth, daughter of Sir Adam Mure of Rowallan and his wife Janet Mure of Fokeltie. She had already borne him nine children, who were legitimated *per subsequens matrimonium*. She died before 1355 and Robert married secondly, by dispensation dated 2 May 1355, EUPHEMIA, widow of John Randolph, 3rd Earl of Moray, and daughter of Hugh, 4th Earl of Ross, and his wife Margaret, daughter of Sir David Graham of Montrose. Euphemia was crowned at Scone by Alexander de Kyninmund II, Bishop of Aberdeen, in 1372 and died in 1387, having had two sons and two daughters by Robert. Robert's youngest daughter by his first wife was Jean, who married first Sir John Keith and secondly, in 1376, Sir John Lyon, Chamberlain of Scotland, by whom she became an ancestor of Queen ELIZABETH THE QUEEN MOTHER. Sir John Lyon was killed on 4 November 1382, and Jean married thirdly, in 1384, Sir James Sandilands of Calder, by whom she also had issue.

Robert III, King of Scots (*c*.1337–1406)

The eldest son of ROBERT II and Elizabeth Mure (who subsequently became his wife thereby legitimizing their offspring), who was born in about 1337 and named John. He was created Earl of Carrick by DAVID II on 22 June 1368 and after his father's accession was declared heir to the crown by decree of Parliament at SCONE on 27 March 1371, the day after his father's coronation. He exercised power throughout most of his father's reign. Towards the end of it he met with a serious accident, being kicked by a horse, which left him crippled and also mentally impaired.

He succeeded his father in April 1390 and assumed the style of Robert III, the name of John being considered an unlucky one for kings. His coronation took place at Scone Abbey on 14 August 1390. Because of his infirmities Robert delegated all his powers to his brother Robert Stewart, Duke of ALBANY. In 1398 a faction wished to replace Albany by the king's son and heir, David, Duke of ROTHESAY, who was appointed Lieutenant of the Kingdom in 1399, but he was seized by Albany in 1402 and imprisoned in Falkland Castle, where he soon after died mysteriously. Fearing for the safety of his surviving son James, the king sent him to France, but the ship that carried him was captured by the English and James was imprisoned in London. The news broke the old king's heart and he died at Rothesay on 4 April 1406. He was buried in Paisley Abbey.

Robert III married in 1366 or 1367, ANNABELLA DRUMMOND, daughter of Sir John Drummond of Stobhall. She died at Scone Palace in about October 1401 and was buried at DUNFERMLINE Abbey. She bore three sons, David, Robert (who died in infancy) and James (*see* JAMES I), and four daughters, Margaret, Mary and Elizabeth, who all married, and Egidia, who died unmarried.

Robert (III) Curthose, Duke of Normandy

(*c*.1051–1134) The eldest son and probably the first child of WILLIAM I THE CONQUEROR and MATILDA OF FLANDERS, who was born in Normandy in about 1051. He was invested with the county of Maine in 1069, but his father refused to give him actual possession of the county. This led him into a state of rebellion for several years, but he finally submitted to his father and was recognized as heir to Normandy, succeeding as Duke Robert III on William's death in September 1087. In 1096 he joined the First Crusade, pledging his duchy to his brother WILLIAM II for five years for the sum of 10,000 marks. He distinguished himself in the Holy Land and returned home in 1100, reaching Normandy in September.

In the course of the journey home he was married at Apulia to Sibylla, daughter of Geoffrey, Count of Conversano, a scion of the Norman house of Hauteville. The death of William Rufus had freed Robert from the necessity of redeeming his pledge. He concluded a treaty with his brother HENRY I and ceded the county of Evreux to him in 1104. His mismanagement of Normandy led to an invasion by Henry in 1105 and Robert was defeated and taken prisoner at the battle of Tinchebrai on 28 September 1106. The rest of his life was spent in captivity in England. The story that he was blinded is almost certainly untrue and his existence was probably an agreeable one, since he lived to be well over 80, a very great age for those days.

He died at Cardiff Castle on 10 February 1134 and was buried in Gloucester Cathedral, where he is commemorated by a monument of much later date. His wife Sibylla had died at Rouen in February or March 1103 and was buried at Caen. They had two sons, WILLIAM 'CLITO', COUNT OF FLANDERS and Henry, who was killed while hunting in the New Forest. Robert also had two natural sons, Richard and William, and a natural daughter who married Élie de St Saen.

Roehenstart Surname assumed by the three natural and legitimated children of Charlotte Stuart, Duchess of ALBANY (herself the natural daughter of Prince Charles Edward STUART) and Ferdinand Maximilien Mériadec de Rohan, Archbishop of Cambrai (1738–1813). The name is presumed to be contrived from a combination of the names of Rohan and Stuart. The three children were:

1. Charlotte Maximilienne Amélie Roehenstart, who was born about 1781 and married at Paris on 9 August 1804, Jean Louis Lugle Luglien Cousin de La Morlière (born at Montdidier, Somme, on 13 September 1763; died at Paris on 20 December 1846), son of Jacques Luglien Cousin de Beaunesnil and Marie Jeanne Renée de La Morlière. Her only son was born and died on 26 November 1806.
2. Victoire Adélaïde Roehenstart, who was born in about 1782.
3. Charles Edward Auguste Maximilien Roehenstart, called Count (de) Roehenstart, who was born probably on 4 May 1784 and married first, in 1818, Marie Antoinette Barbuoni (who was born in about 1790 and buried at St Marylebone, Middlesex, on 20 July 1821). Count Roehenstart married secondly, at St Pancras, Middlesex, on 13 December 1826, Louisa Constance, daughter of Bourchier Smith. He had no issue by either marriage and was killed in a carriage accident at Dunkeld, Scotland, on 28 October 1854. He was buried at Dunkeld Cathedral, where his grave is marked by a granite slab.

Roses, Wars of the Name given to the dynastic struggle between the Lancastrian and Yorkist branches of the PLANTAGENET dynasty, which occupied most of the 15th century. The name is taken from the badges worn by the two factions, the red rose for Lancaster and the white rose for York. The wars were finally brought to an end at BOSWORTH FIELD in 1485 when the Yorkist King RICHARD III was defeated and killed by his Lancastrian rival, who became HENRY VII. After the latter had married ELIZABETH OF YORK the two symbols were combined to form the so-called Tudor Rose.

Rothesay, David Stewart, Duke of (1378–1402) The eldest son of ROBERT III, KING OF SCOTS and ANNABELLA DRUMMOND, who was born on 24 October 1378. Soon after his father's accession to the throne in 1390 he was recognized as Earl of Carrick and on 28 April 1398 he was created Duke of Rothesay, his uncle Robert being created Duke of Albany at the same time and these being the first dukedoms to be made in Scotland. On 6 September 1398 David was also created Earl of Atholl. He married at Bothwell Church in February 1400, Marjorie, eldest daughter of Archibald Douglas, 3rd Earl of Douglas, and his wife Jean, daughter of Thomas Moray of Bothwell. His uncle the Duke of Albany grew jealous of his growing power and had him arrested on the pretext of some misdemeanor and imprisoned in Falkland Castle, where he died on 26 March 1402. His death was probably caused by dysentery but there were the inevitable rumours that his uncle had had him poisoned. He was buried in Lindores Abbey.

The duke had no children, and his widow married in 1403 Sir Walter Haliburton, Younger of Dirletoun. She died before 11 May 1421, leaving issue by him.

Rothesay, Duke of Traditional title for the HEIR APPARENT to the Scots throne, which since its first inception in 1398 has descended in similar fashion to the dukedom of Cornwall in England and since the union of the Crowns in 1603 has been held by the same individuals.

Royal Marriages Act Act of Parliament passed in 1772 at the behest of GEORGE III after two of his brothers had contracted, without his consent, what he considered entirely unsuitable marriages. It attempts to regulate the marriages of all the descendants of GEORGE II, except the issue of princesses who have married into foreign families, by requiring them to obtain the consent of the sovereign in council. If consent is refused, the person in question, being aged 25 or over, may give notice to the PRIVY COUNCIL and may marry after a lapse of 12 months unless both houses of Parliament signify their disapproval. Marriages contracted in infringement of this are void. The act was so hastily drawn up and loosely worded that modern legal opinion tends to consider it inoperative since the exempting clause now covers all those who might otherwise come within its scope.

Royal Victorian Order Order instituted by Queen VICTORIA on 21 April 1896. It consists of the Sovereign, a Grand Master, Ordinary Members and such Honorary Members as the Sovereign shall from time to time appoint, the members being divided into five classes and designated respectively: Knights and Dames Grand Cross (GCVO),

Knights and Dames Commanders (KCVO or DCVO), Commanders (CVO), Members of the Fourth Class (now styled Lieutenants; LVO) and Members of the Fifth Class (MVO). Under date of 29 May 1936, a Warrant was issued consolidating the Statutes of the Order so as to permit bestowal upon women:

The persons to be admitted as Ordinary Members of this Order shall be such persons, being male or female subjects of the British Crown, who, having rendered extraordinary, or important, or personal service to the sovereign, merit royal favour; and the Honorary members of the several classes consist of those foreign princes and persons upon whom the sovereign may think fit to confer the honour of being received into the Order.

The number of the members is unlimited, and the anniversary of the order is the 20th day of June every year, being the day of Queen Victoria's accession to the throne.

The Queen's Chapel of the Savoy has been the Chapel of the order since 1938, but because of its small size services of the order, which are held at irregular intervals, usually take place at St George's Chapel, Windsor.

Rupert of the Rhine, Prince, Duke of Cumberland (1619–82) The third son and fourth child of Friedrich V, Elector Palatine of the Rhine and King of Bohemia, by his wife ELIZABETH, QUEEN OF BOHEMIA, daughter of JAMES I, who was born at Prague during his parents' brief tenure of the kingdom of Bohemia on 27 December 1619. He was educated at Leyden University and served as a volunteer under the Prince of Orange in the invasion of Brabant in 1635. The following year he visited England and received an honorary MA from Oxford University. Returned to the Netherlands, he was present at the siege of Breda in 1637, but during the invasion of Westphalia was taken prisoner by the imperial forces near Wesel and detained for three years at Linz. Following his release, he came to England and was naturalized on 19 January 1642. His uncle, CHARLES I, appointed him General of the Horse in 1642 and he was also nominated a Knight of the GARTER in that year.

Prince Rupert served as a dashing royalist commander throughout the CIVIL WAR, commanding the right wing of the king's horse at the battle of Edgehill and taking Cirencester. He made an unsuccessful attempt to take Bristol in March 1643, but took Birmingham the following month and won a great victory at Chalgrove in June, followed by the capitulation of Bristol in

July and Newbury in September. On 24 January 1644 he was created Earl of Holderness and Duke of Cumberland. He relieved Newark in March 1644, defeated the Parliamentarians at Stockport in May and took Liverpool in June. In the same month, however, he failed to relieve York and suffered a defeat at the battle of Marston Moor. Though a feared cavalry commander on the field, complete with pet dog (a poodle) slung across his saddle, he failed repeatedly to curb his victorious troops from cutting through the enemy lines and then throwing themselves upon the Parliamentarian baggage trains, an easy target, thus effectively removing themselves from the field of battle. His dog, called Boy, was killed during the defeat at Marston Moor.

Appointed President of the Council in Wales, Master of the Horse and Commander-in-Chief of the Royal Army in 1644, he suppressed a rising in Wales in February 1645 and relieved Chester, taking Leicester in May 1645. He distinguished himself at the Royalist defeat at Naseby in June 1645 and thereafter occupied Bristol and urged the king to make peace in July. On 11 September 1645 he surrendered Bristol to Fairfax and, losing royal favour thereby, was deprived of his commission in October. On the capitulation of Oxford in January 1646, Prince Rupert was ordered to leave England and went to France.

After a period commanding the English troops in the French service, he accompanied his cousin Charles, Prince of Wales (the future CHARLES II) to Holland in 1648. He commanded the fleet sent to assist Ormonde in Ireland in 1649 and relieved the Scilly Isles, but was blockaded by Blake at the mouth of the Tagus in 1650. He managed to escape into the Mediterranean and for the next two years occupied himself in making a piratical cruise to Barbados. Returned to Europe, he served as Master of the Horse to the exiled Charles II from 1653 to 1655 and was sent by him as an envoy to Vienna in June 1654.

Rupert returned to England at the Restoration in 1660 and was appointed a Privy Councillor and commissioner for the government of Tangier in 1662. He was a patentee of the Royal African Company in 1663 and as Admiral of the White served under his cousin the Duke of York (later JAMES II) at Solebay on 3 June 1665. The prince was appointed Constable of WINDSOR CASTLE in 1668, Lord Lieutenant of Berkshire in 1670 and of Surrey in 1675, holding those appointments until his death. At the outbreak of the second Dutch war in 1672 he was Vice-Admiral of England, being promoted Admiral of the Fleet in 1673. He served as First Lord of the Admiralty from 1673 to 1679.

Rupert was described by Gramont in the following terms: 'brave and courageous even to rashness; but cross-grained and incorrigibly obstinate; his genius was fertile in mathematical experiments, and he possessed some knowledge of chemistry; he was polite even to excess unseasonably, but haughty and even brutal when he ought to have been gentle and courteous; he was tall, and his manners were ungracious; he had a dry, hard-favoured visage, and a stern look even when he wished to please.' The invention of mezzotint engraving is attributed to Prince Rupert, and John Evelyn recorded in his Diary on 13 March 1661: 'Prince Rupert shew'd me with his owne hands the new way of graving called *Mezzo Tinto*, which afterwards by his permission I publish'd in my

History of Chalcography; this set so many artistes on worke, that they soone ariv'd to that perfection it is since come, emulating the tenderest miniatures.' Pepys had a poor opinion of Prince Rupert's abilities as Commissioner for Tangier, however, saying that he 'do nothing but swear and laugh a little, with an oathe or two, and that's all he do'.

Prince Rupert, whose portrait was painted by Van Dyke and Lely, died at his house in Spring Gardens, Westminster, on 29 November 1682, and was buried in WESTMINSTER ABBEY on 6 December following. He never married but left a natural son, Dudley Bard, by Frances Bard, daughter of Viscount Bellomont. Dudley was killed at the siege of Buda on 13 July 1686, aged about 20. Prince Rupert also had a daughter, Ruperta, by the actress Peg Hughes. She was born in 1671 and was left most of her father's property. She married General Emanuel Scrope Howe, brother of the 1st Viscount Howe, and left issue.

S

Saebert, King of Essex (d.616/7) The son of SLEDDA, KING OF ESSEX and his wife Ricula, sister of ETHELBERT I, KING OF KENT, who succeeded his father sometime before 604 and was converted to Christianity through the influence of his maternal uncle Ethelbert. He founded the episcopal see of London, the first bishop Mellitus being consecrated by St Augustine, and in conjunction with his uncle built the first St Paul's Cathedral. Saebert died in 616 or 617 and was buried in St Paul's. He was succeeded by his three sons, SEXRED, SAEWARD and another unnamed, who reigned jointly and rejected Christianity.

Saelred, King of Essex (d.746) According to the genealogies, a son of SIGEBERHT II, though this seems chronologically impossible and he was more likely a grandson or great-grandson. He succeeded OFFA, KING OF ESSEX on his abdication in about 709 and reigned until 746, when he was 'slain' in unknown circumstances. His son SIGERIC reigned later.

Saethryd, Abbess of Brie (*fl.c.*650) The step-daughter of ANNA, KING OF EAST ANGLIA, being the daughter of his wife Saewara by an unknown first husband, who was sent to France to be educated and entered the convent of Brie, eventually becoming its abbess. She was succeeded in that office by her half-sister Ethelburga.

Saeward, King of Essex (d.*c.*617) The second son of King SAEBERT, who succeeded his father and reigned jointly with his elder brother SEXRED and his unnamed younger brother. The three brothers had not been converted to Christianity like their father, but demanded that Bishop Mellitus should give them communion. He refused to do so unless they agreed to be baptized. According to BEDE they retorted: 'We refuse to enter that font and see no need for it; but we want to be strengthened with this bread.' Mellitus was adamant and the brothers expelled him from their kingdom. Shortly afterwards they were defeated and killed in battle with the West Saxons. Saeward was succeeded by his son SIGEBERHT I.

St Edward's Crown The crown of England, originally the crown of EDWARD THE CONFESSOR, which was used as the coronation crown of subsequent sovereigns until CHARLES I. It was broken up with the rest of the regalia under the COMMONWEALTH. A new St Edward's crown was made for the coronation of CHARLES II and possibly incorporated some fragments from the old crown. It has been used as the coronation crown of most subsequent sovereigns, with one or two notable exceptions (including Queen VICTORIA and EDWARD VII) and is publicly displayed with the other items of regalia in the TOWER OF LONDON.

St Edward's Staff An item of regalia. The original is said to have been EDWARD THE CONFESSOR's walking staff and was probably taken from his tomb in WESTMINSTER ABBEY. In an inventory of 1606 it is described as 'a long Scepter with a Pike of Steele in the bottome' and this description served as a model when the new set of regalia was made for CHARLES II's coronation. However, its exact function had been forgotten and it was merely carried before the sovereign with the other regalia and then placed on the altar. From sundry references it would appear that the staff was handed to the later medieval kings by the Abbot of Westminster when they visited the abbey in state, much in the same way as the Lord Mayor of London surrenders the city sword when the monarch pays official visits to the city.

St George's Chapel *see* WINDSOR CASTLE.

St James's Palace The principal London residence of English and British sovereigns for over two centuries, which was built by HENRY VIII, who bought the land in 1532 from the Hospital of St James, a foundation for the care of 'leprous maidens'. Henry enclosed St James's Park and built the red-brick palace of which the presence chamber, the chapel royal, the guard room and the great gatehouse still remain. The palace was enlarged by Sir Christopher Wren, who added the great staircase.

St James's Palace has been the birthplace of five sovereigns, CHARLES II, JAMES II, MARY II, ANNE and GEORGE IV. Charles II made it his principal residence after the Restoration and laid out St James's Park. Birdcage Walk, which skirts one side of the park, was so named because the pelicans presented to Charles by the Russian ambassador were housed there. George IV had the lake remodelled by John Nash and also The Mall leading up to BUCKINGHAM PALACE, which he intended to make his principal residence. After the palace ceased to be a royal residence, Queen VICTORIA continued to hold drawing-rooms there until 1865 and it was also the scene for royal levées until the outbreak of the Second World War. Foreign ambassadors are still accredited to 'The Court of St James's'. The palace is now occupied by the Lord Chamberlain's Department but also has apartments occupied by CHARLES, PRINCE OF WALES and the Duke and Duchess of KENT.

St Michael and St George, The Most Distinguished Order of Order of chivalry instituted by the Prince Regent on behalf of GEORGE III in 1818. It has been enlarged and extended 17 times, the last time being in 1974. It is conferred on British subjects and British protected persons, 'who may hold, or have held high and confidential offices, or may render or have rendered extraordinary and important services (other than military) within or in relation to any part of the British Dominions or Territories under British Protection or Administration, and in reward for important and loyal services in relation to foreign affairs'. The order is limited to 120 Knights or Dames Grand Cross (GCMG), 390 Knights or Dames Commanders (KCMG or DCMG), and 1775 Companions (CMG), exclusive of any honorary or additional members who may be appointed.

The insignia of a GCMG consists of a star of seven rays of silver with a small ray of gold between each of them and over all the cross of St George with a representation of the Archangel St Michael trampling upon Satan in the centre, within a blue circle inscribed with the motto *Auspicium melioris aevi* in gold letters, a collar of gold formed alternately of lions of England royally crowned, of Maltese crosses of white enamel, and of the ciphers SM and SG (also alternately), having in the centre the imper-

ial crown over two winged lions, each holding in his forepaw a book and seven arrows, the whole linked together by small gold chains; the badge consisting of a cross of fourteen points enamelled silver and edged with gold, having in the centre a representation of St Michael on one side and of St George on the other. The badge is either attached to the collar or to a four-inch-wide Saxon blue ribbon with a scarlet central stripe worn across the right shoulder to the left side. The mantle is of Saxon blue satin, lined with scarlet silk and tied with a cordon of blue and scarlet silk and gold with two tassels and with an embroidered representation of the star of the order on the left side. The star and badge of a KCMG or DCMG are similar in design but smaller, the badge being suspended round the neck by men or from a bow on the left shoulder by women. The insignia for a CMG is a smaller badge worn in the same manner. The chapel of the order is in St Paul's Cathedral, London.

St Patrick, Most Illustrious Order of Order of chivalry instituted by GEORGE III on 5 February 1783 for the kingdom of Ireland and revised in 1905. It has not been conferred since the partition of Ireland.

Sandringham House A private residence, in Norfolk, of the royal family, which was bought by Albert Edward, Prince of Wales (later EDWARD VII) in 1862 and rebuilt by him in 1870 with subsequent enlargements. It is a large, sprawling red-brick building of completely undistinguished appearance and has been described as reminiscent of a convalescent home for railway workers. Nevertheless, it has remained a favourite country retreat for four generations of the royal family (especially at Christmas) and GEORGE V and GEORGE VI both died there. The grounds extend to some 20,000 acres.

Sceptre An item of regalia of very ancient origin. Two sceptres are presented to the sovereign in the coronation ceremony: the Sceptre with the Cross, made for the coronation of CHARLES II and embellished by the addition of the largest diamond in the world, which was set in its head in 1907; and the Sceptre with the Dove (also known as the Rod of Equity and Mercy), a much plainer artefact, which is placed in the sovereign's left hand and later exchanged for the ORB. QUEEN CONSORTS also receive two sceptres: the Queen's Sceptre with the Cross, made for the coronation of MARY OF MODENA; and the Queen's Ivory Rod, made at the same time. Both sceptres are retained in the procession from the abbey as a queen consort is not invested with an orb in the English coronation rite.

Scone, Stone of Large block of sandstone, also known as the 'stone of destiny' and the 'fatal stone', upon which Scottish kings were formerly enthroned. The stone was said to be that on which the Patriarch Jacob slept at Bethel when he had his vision of angels ascending and descending. In the course of its history the stone is supposed to have travelled to Egypt, Spain and thence to Ireland, where it was set up on the Hill of TARA and became the centre of the inauguration ceremonies of the high-kings of Ireland, being said to utter a groaning noise when the rightful monarch sat on it and to have remained silent under a usurper. Such a stone still stands at Tara, so it must have been a duplicate that, in the continuation of the legend, was taken to Scotland, built into the walls of Dunstaffnage Castle, and finally deposited at Scone (a village near Perth and once the capital of the Picts) by KENNETH MAC ALPIN in 850.

In 1296 the English king, EDWARD I, removed the stone in the course of his Scottish campaigns and brought it back to London. He dedicated the stone to EDWARD THE CONFESSOR, his patron saint, and commissioned Master Walter of Durham to construct a wooden chair – the coronation chair – to contain it for a fee of 100 shillings. Since then every English sovereign has been crowned seated in the coronation chair, with the exceptions of MARY I, who was crowned in a chair sent to her by the pope, and MARY II, for whom, as joint sovereign, a duplicate chair without the stone was constructed. Both chairs are exhibited in WESTMINSTER ABBEY near the Confessor's shrine and have been much defaced and vandalized by Westminster schoolboys and others who have carved their initials on them over the centuries. The original coronation chair was taken to Westminster Hall for the inauguration of Oliver Cromwell as Lord Protector. It was also used by Queen VICTORIA at the abbey service of thanksgiving on the occasion of her Golden Jubilee in 1887.

In 1950 the Stone of Scone made the headlines when it was stolen by Scottish nationalists in protest at English domination. The stone was taken north of the border but was later recovered by the authorities and returned to Westminster in February 1952. In 1996 it was announced that the stone was to be returned to Scotland, but would be brought back to London for subsequent coronations. The announcement has met with a certain amount of opposition from the abbey authorities, backed by historians and members of the public.

Scottish Succession On the death of MARGARET, QUEEN OF SCOTS, 'the Maid of Norway', in September 1290 there was no clear heir to the Scottish throne, which was disputed by 13 competitors, who agreed to submit their claims to the arbitration of EDWARD I, King of England. The 13 competitors, in the order in which their names were recorded in the Great Roll of Scotland on 3 August 1291, were:

1. Floris V, Count of Holland (d.27 June 1296), who claimed as son of Willem II, Count of Holland, son of Floris IV, Count of Holland, son of Willem I, Count of Holland, son of Floris III, Count of Holland, by his wife Ada, daughter of Henry, Earl of Huntingdon.
2. Patrick de Dunbar, 7th Earl of Dunbar (d.10 October 1308), who claimed as son of Patrick, 6th Earl, son of Patrick, 5th Earl, son of Patrick, 4th Earl, by his wife Ada, natural daughter of King WILLIAM THE LION. The 4th Earl of Dunbar was son of Waltheof, 3rd Earl, son of Gospatrick, 2nd Earl, son of Gospatrick, 1st Earl of Dunbar.
3. William de Vesci, Baron de Vesci, who claimed as son of William de Vesci, son of Eustace de Vesci, by his wife, Margaret, natural daughter of King WILLIAM THE LION.
4. William de Ros, 2nd Baron de Ros (d.15 August 1316), who claimed as son of Robert de Ros, 1st Baron de Ros, son of William de Ros, of Hamlake, son of Robert de Ros, by his wife Isabella, natural daughter of King WILLIAM THE LION.
5. Robert de Pinkeney, who claimed as son of Henry de Pinkeney, son of Henry de Pinkeny, by his wife Alicia, daughter of John Lindesay, by his wife Marjorie, an alleged natural daughter of Henry, Earl of Huntingdon.
6. Nicholas de Soules, who claimed as son of Ermengarde, daughter of Alan Durward, by his wife Marjorie, natural daughter of ALEXANDER II.
7. Patrick Galithly, who claimed as son of Henry Galithly, a natural son of King WILLIAM THE LION.
8. Roger de Mandeville, who claimed as son of Agatha, daughter of Robert Wardone, by his wife Aufrica, daughter of William de Say, by his wife Aufrica, natural daughter of King WILLIAM THE LION.
9. John Comyn, Lord of Badenoch, who claimed as son of John Comyn, son of Richard Comyn, son of William Comyn, son of Richard Comyn, by his wife Hextilda, daughter of Uhtred of Tyndale, by his wife Bethoc, daughter of King

Donalbane (*see* DONALD III, KING OF SCOTS).

10. John de Hastings, 2nd Baron Hastings (d.1313), who claimed as son of Henry de Hastings, 1st Baron Hastings, son of Henry de Hastings by his wife Ada, fourth daughter of DAVID, EARL OF HUNTINGDON.
11. John BALLIOL.
12. Robert de Brus, whose grandson eventually succeeded as ROBERT I (BRUCE).
13. Eric II, King of Norway, who claimed as father and heir of the deceased Queen Margaret.

The interregnum was ended on 17 November 1292 when Edward I pronounced at Berwick in favour of John Balliol.

Sebbi, King of Essex (d.*c*.695) The younger son of King SAEWARD, who reigned jointly with his nephew SIGHERE in succession to their kinsman SWITHELM from about 683. When the kingdom was ravaged by plague, Sighere reverted to paganism, but Sebbi 'remained faithful [to Christianity] and ended his days happily'. After reigning for 30 years Sebbi was afflicted with a mortal disease and decided to abdicate and become a monk, his wife becoming a nun at the same time. He received the monastic habit from Waldhere, Bishop of London, and died soon afterwards, in about 695. BEDE relates a story of the stone sarcophagus that had been prepared for his burial but was found to be too short, miraculously enlarging to fit his body. He was buried in St Paul's Cathedral.

Sexburga (Seaxburh), Queen of Wessex (*fl.*672–4) The second wife of King CENWALH, whom she succeeded on the throne of Wessex in about 672, this being the only known instance of a QUEEN REGNANT in Saxon times. Nothing further is known of her beyond the fact that she reigned for about one year and either died or was deposed in 674, when she was succeeded by her husband's kinsman CENFUS.

Sexred, King of Essex (*fl.*616–17) The eldest son of King SAEBERT, whom he succeeded jointly with his two younger brothers in about 616. He remained a pagan and was killed in battle with the West Saxons in about 617, apparently childless.

Seymour, Jane *see* JANE SEYMOUR, QUEEN OF ENGLAND.

She-wolf of France, The Popular nickname of ISABELLA OF FRANCE[1].

Sheen Palace Royal residence at Sheen, Surrey, which was associated with royalty as far back as the 12th century. A favourite residence of EDWARD III, who died there in 1377, the manor house at Sheen became Sheen Palace in the 14th century. It was at Sheen that RICHARD II and ANNE OF BOHEMIA were reputed to play host daily to some 10,000 guests at their court. When Anne died of plague in 1394 the grief-stricken Richard had most of the palace pulled down. It was rebuilt, however, by HENRY V and subsequently HENRY VI and EDWARD IV often held court there. The palace was destroyed by fire in 1499, after which it was rebuilt by HENRY VII and renamed RICHMOND PALACE.

Sigeberht, King of East Anglia (d.*c*.634) The stepson of King REDWALD, who was exiled in Gaul during the reign of his half-brother EARPWALD and while there was converted to Christianity. After Earpwald's murder by one Ricbert in 627 or 628, the realm 'relapsed into heathendom' for three years until Sigeberht, 'a devout Christian and a man of learning', returned from Gaul and gained possession of the throne. He brought about the re-conversion of EAST ANGLIA and established the episcopal see of Dunwich with Felix as Bishop. Sigeberht abdicated in about 634 and became a monk at Bury St Edmunds. When PENDA, KING OF MERCIA invaded East Anglia soon after, Sigeberht was forced by his former subjects to leave the monastery and lead them into battle, in which he 'refused to carry anything more than a stick'. He and his kinsman and successor Ecgric were both killed and their army dispersed.

Sigeberht, King of Wessex (d.*c*.757) The son of a sub-king named Sigeric and a kinsman of King CUTHRED, whom he succeeded in about 756. The following year he was deposed by CYNEWULF and the councillors of Wessex 'for unlawful actions', the nature of which is unspecified. He retained Hampshire, but after killing the ealdorman there was driven into the weald, where he was stabbed by a herdsman 'at the stream at Privett'. His death was later avenged by his brother Cyneheard who slew Cynewulf.

Sigeberht I the Little, King of Essex (d. before 653) The elder son of King SAEWARD, whom he succeeded in about 617, probably while still very young, hence his epithet of Parvus or 'the Little'. Nothing is known of his deeds. He was dead by 653, when he was succeeded by his kinsman Sigeberht II. He had a son, SIGHERE, who was later king.

Sigeberht II the Good, King of Essex (d.*c*.660) The son of Sexbald, a younger son of King SLEDDA, he succeeded his kinsman

SIGEBERHT I c.653 and restored Christianity to Essex before his death c.660.

Sigeheard, King of Essex (d. before 709) The son of King SEBBI, whom he succeeded in 694 or 695, reigning jointly with his brother Swaefred. He was dead by 709. He had a son Sigemund, whose son Swithred later became king.

Sigered, King of Essex (d. after 825) The son of King SIGERIC, whom he succeeded in 798 or 799. Like his father he ruled as an underking of Mercia until 825, when he sought the protection of EGBERT, KING OF WESSEX, who absorbed Essex into his realm.

Sigeric, King of Essex (d. after 798) The son of King SAELRED, who succeeded his kinsman King Swithred on an unknown date after 758. In 797 or 798 he abdicated in favour of his son SIGERED and went to Rome, where he died.

Sighere, King of Essex (d.683) The son of King SIGEBERHT I, who reigned jointly with his uncle SEBBI from about 665. His wife was St OSYTH, daughter of Frithwold, sub-king in Surrey, and Wilburga, a daughter of PENDA, KING OF MERCIA, and their son OFFA was later king of Essex for a short period.

Simnel, Lambert (c.1475–1525) The son of a baker in Oxford, where he was born in 1474 or 1475, who claimed the throne in the guise of Edward, Earl of Warwick, the son and heir of George, Duke of CLARENCE. As a boy he was trained in the imposture by Richard Simon, a priest. He was taken to Ireland by Simon in 1486 and after gathering support in opposition to the rule of HENRY VII was proclaimed king as Edward VI and crowned in Dublin in 1487. He received the support of his alleged aunt MARGARET OF YORK, DUCHESS OF BURGUNDY, who furnished him with troops, and they landed in Lancashire early in June 1487, but met a crushing defeat a few days later at Stoke-on-Trent. Lambert was captured and imprisoned but because of his youth was later pardoned by Henry VII, who gave him a place in his household, first as a scullion in the royal kitchens and later as a falconer. He died in 1525.

Simpson, Mrs see ABDICATION CRISIS; EDWARD VIII.

Sledda, King of Essex (d. before 604) The son of King AESCWINE, whom he succeeded before 587. He married Ricula, sister of ETHELBERT I, KING OF KENT, and was the father of King SAEBERT and of Sexbald,

several of whose descendants later reigned in Essex.

Snowdon, Antony Armstrong-Jones, Earl of see MARGARET, PRINCESS, COUNTESS OF SNOWDON.

Sobieska, Maria Casimire Clementina (1702–35) The consort of the titular King James III and VIII (see STUART, Prince James Francis Edward), who was the fifth daughter of Prince Jakob Ludwik Sobieski (son of the heroic warrior King Jan III of Poland, who saved Europe from the Turks) and his wife Hedwig Elisabeth, seventh daughter of Philip Wilhelm, Elector Palatine of the Rhine, and was born on 18 July 1702. Her contract of marriage to Prince James was dated at Ohlau in Silesia on 22 and 23 July 1718, but the princess was detained at Innsbruck on her way to Italy and escaped and managed to continue the journey only with great difficulty. The proxy marriage took place at Bologna on 9 May 1719 and the couple were married in person by the pope at Montefiascone on 1 September 1719. After the births of their two sons in 1720 and 1725, Clementina was completely neglected by her husband, who incurred much criticism thereby. She found solace in religious observances, driving in her coach from one church to another to attend as many masses and benedictions as she could in the course of one day. She died at Rome on 18 January 1735 and was buried in St Peter's.

Sobieski-Stuart Surname assumed by two brothers, John Hay Allen (1797–1872) and Charles Stuart Hay Allen (1799–1880), who claimed that their father, Captain Thomas Allen, RN (1773–1852), was the legitimate son of Prince Charles Edward STUART and his wife Louise of Stolberg-Gedern (see ALBANY, LOUISE, COUNTESS OF), who had been adopted and brought up as the son of Admiral John Carter Allen (d.1800). The claim has been exhaustively studied and completely refuted. The brothers were wildly eccentric, wore Highland dress and amassed a large and varied collection of Stuart relics. They became well-known figures in London Society and both used the title 'Count d'Albanie'. Their claims were never taken seriously by anybody except themselves. Both married, but only the younger had issue and descendants in the female line are still extant.

Sophia, Electress of Hanover (1630–1714) The fifth and youngest daughter and twelfth child of Friedrich V, Elector Palatine and

'Winter' King of Bohemia, and his wife Elizabeth, the eldest daughter of JAMES I, who was born at The Hague when her parents were living in exile in Holland on 14 October 1630. She was baptized there on 30 January 1631, the States of Friesland acting as her godfather. In her own lively memoirs Sophia says that various names were written on slips of paper and one drawn to decide the one she should have, so that she got her name by chance. She is said to have become 'one of the most Accomplished Ladies in Europe'.

After an early engagement to a brother of the king of Sweden, which was broken off through the machinations of Cromwell, Sophia was married at Heidelberg on 30 September 1658 to Ernst August, Hereditary Prince of Brunswick-Lüneburg, later Prince Bishop of Osnabrück and Duke and Elector of Hanover, and they had seven sons and one daughter. Ernst August died at Herrenhausen on 23 January 1698.

On 12 June 1701 the ACT OF SETTLEMENT settled the Crown of England after Queen ANNE and the heirs of her body on the Electress Sophia and the heirs of her body, being Protestants, and on the death of WILLIAM III in 1702 she accordingly became heiress presumptive, a position that she occupied until her death. Sophia died quite suddenly while walking in the gardens at Herrenhausen on 8 June 1714 and was buried in the Leineschloss Church at Hanover on the following day. Her sarcophagus was removed to the mausoleum in the grounds of Herrenhausen in 1957 as the Leineschloss Church had been severely damaged during the Second World War. Two months after her death her eldest son succeeded to the throne as GEORGE I.

Sophia, Princess[1] (1606) The fourth daughter and eighth and youngest child of JAMES I and ANNE OF DENMARK, who was born at GREENWICH PALACE at three o'clock in the morning on 22 June 1606. She was hastily baptized the following day, receiving the name of her maternal grandmother Queen Sophia of Denmark, and died soon afterwards. She was buried in Henry VII's Chapel at WESTMINSTER ABBEY on 26 June 1606, and her tomb is marked by a monument representing a baby lying in a cradle.

Sophia, Princess[2] (1777–1848) The fifth daughter and twelfth child of GEORGE III and Queen CHARLOTTE, who was born at Buckingham House (now BUCKINGHAM PALACE) on 3 November 1777 and baptized at ST JAMES'S PALACE on 1 December,

her godparents being the Duchess of Brunswick, the Duchess of Meckenburg-Schwerin and Prince August of Saxe-Gotha, all of whom were represented by proxies. Princess Sophia and her brother Prince OCTAVIUS were both inoculated for smallpox in the spring of 1783 and sent to Kew to be under the observation of the surgeon, Pennel Hawkins. The princess suffered no ill effects but Prince Octavius 'caught cold just when the eruption should have come out, and died'.

As a child Princess Sophia was moved enough on being told about prisons and the hard lot of prisoners to offer to give her allowance 'to buy bread for the poor prisoners'. Her parents were so struck by her generous thought that they augmented the amount given. The princess grew up under the shadow of her father's recurring attacks of PORPHYRIA. Princess Sophia never married but did have a natural son, Captain Thomas Garth, born at Weymouth, Dorset in the summer of 1800, whose probable father General Thomas Garth (d.1829), one of George III's equerries, adopted and brought up. Scurrilous rumours were later circulated that the child's father was Sophia's own brother Ernest, Duke of CUMBERLAND. It is said that when she was pregnant at Weymouth her father, noticing her increasing girth, enquired as to the cause and was told that it came from eating roast beef and was later cured by sea-bathing.

Princess Sophia lived quietly with her mother Queen Charlotte and on the queen's death in 1818 was left Lower Lodge at New Windsor, but did not take it up. She enjoyed an allowance of £13,000 per annum allotted to her by Parliament, but her finances came under the control of Sir John Conroy, who fleeced her of so much money to buy property for himself that at her death she only left £1,607.19s.7d., apart from her furniture and a few worthless shares. Sir John Conroy's frauds did not come to light until after his death in 1854.

The princess's eyesight failed towards the end of her life and she took up crochet work as an occupation. She was described by Baroness Bunsen, who visited her, as 'never complaining, always cheerful, talking of the many blessings she had to be thankful for'. She spent much time in the companionship of her sister Princess MARY, DUCHESS OF GLOUCESTER, and her brother the Duke of SUSSEX and his wife the Duchess of INVERNESS. Princess Sophia died at her house in Vicarage Place, Kensington, at 6.30 in the evening of 27 May 1848. At her own request she was buried at Kensal Green Cemetery opposite her brother the Duke of Sussex. Her tomb is marked by a fine monument surmounted by a sarcophagus bearing a representation of her coronet.

Sophia Dorothea, Princess, Queen of Prussia (1687–1757) The only daughter of GEORGE I and SOPHIA DOROTHEA OF CELLE, who was born at Hanover on 16 March (new style 26 March) 1687. She was only eight when her mother was disgraced and divorced and thereafter was brought up by her paternal grandmother the Electress SOPHIA OF HANOVER at Herrenhausen. She was married by proxy at Hanover on 14 November and in person at Berlin on 28 November 1706 to her first cousin, Friedrich Wilhelm, Crown Prince of Prussia, the only surviving son and heir of Friedrich I, King of Prussia, and his second wife, Sophie Charlotte, only daughter of Ernst August, Elector of Hanover.

Sophia Dorothea became Queen of Prussia on 25 February 1713, when her father-in-law died and her husband succeeded him as Friedrich Wilhelm I. They had a large family of seven sons and seven daughters. Sophia Dorothea, however, was the least maternal of women and her eldest daughter, Wilhelmine, Margravine of Bayreuth, says of her in her *Memoirs*: 'My mother never loved any of her children. She cared for them only as they served her ambitious purposes.' She was probably bereft of all feeling as the wife of a brutal and insensitive husband, who bullied her and their children unmercifully. In his own strange way, he was devoted to her, and his daughter writes that when he was dying 'he had himself rolled in his chair to the queen's room. Not having thought the danger imminent, she was still asleep. "Get up," the king said to her, "I have only a few hours to live and I wish to have the happiness of dying in your arms." He died at Berlin on 31 May 1740 and was buried at Potsdam 'with all possible pomp and splendour' on the order of his son and successor Friedrich II (Frederick the Great), who desired 'that none might say that his father's memory had been rendered less dear to him by that which had formerly taken place between them'.

Sophia Dorothea survived her husband for 17 years and died at the palace of Monbijou, near Berlin, on 28 June 1757. She was buried at Potsdam.

Sophia Dorothea of Celle (1666–1726) The wife of GEORGE I, who is often referred to as 'the uncrowned queen', though whether or not she can be considered a queen of Great Britain is debatable. Her divorce from George at Hanover in 1694 is generally thought to have been ineffective as far as British law was concerned, and had she survived George it is very likely that she would have been recognized as Queen Mother and brought to England by her son GEORGE II, who believed in her innocence.

Sophia Dorothea was born at Celle on 10 September 1666 and entered life with a distinct disadvantage, for although her father Duke Georg Wilhelm of Brunswick-Lüneburg-Celle was of royal birth, her mother Éléonore Desmiers d'Olbreuse was but a French Huguenot lady of a noble but untitled family. She was of such inferior rank to her husband that she had originally been known as Frau von Harburg when the duke entered into a 'marriage of conscience' with her in 1665 and it was not until 1674 that she was raised to the rank of a Countess of the Empire, finally becoming Duchess of Celle in 1675 on the legalization of her marriage. All this meant that Sophia Dorothea was regarded as unmarriageable by most of the ruling houses of Germany. In spite of being the only child of loving parents and having an upbringing surrounded with every comfort and luxury, she must continually have been aware of a terrible sense of inferiority. Her marriage to her cousin George Louis was arranged by their respective fathers and received some opposition from George's mother SOPHIA, ELECTRESS OF HANOVER, on account of the bride's maternal ancestry. However, it was solemnized at Celle on 22 November 1682, when Sophia Dorothea was 16 years old and George Louis was 22.

Having got over her initial objections, Sophia proved a kind mother-in-law and Sophia Dorothea, attractive and high-spirited, fitted well into her new family. In December 1683 she gave birth to her first child, the future GEORGE II, and in 1687 a daughter, named after her mother, completed the family.

One day in 1689, Sophia Dorothea's brother-in-law Carl Philipp brought a friend to meet her, a Count Philipp Christoph von Königsmarck. One year older than Sophia Dorothea, he was an officer in the Hanoverian service, handsome, dashing and debonair, a complete contrast to George Louis. By now the marriage that had started so well was beginning to come apart. George Louis had come under the spell of his Melusine (see KENDAL, DUCHESS OF) and was frequently away on campaigns, and it did not take long for Sophia Dorothea to become infatuated with Königsmarck. Opinions are still divided as to whether they actually became lovers in the physical sense and Sophia Dorothea was to maintain to the end of her life that they were not, though the letters they exchanged tend to suggest that they were.

The affair became an open scandal and the couple ignored the warnings of their friends and relations to bring it to an end. Matters came to a head in 1694 when rumours that the lovers planned to elope became rife. On the night of 11 July, while George Louis was away visiting his sister in Berlin, Königsmarck was seen to enter the palace in Hanover and head for the princess's apartments. He was never seen again and the generally accepted story is that he was intercepted and murdered by a group of zealous young officers, anxious to safeguard the reputation of the Electoral House. His body, weighted with stones, was apparently sunk in the Leine. The following day Sophia Dorothea was ordered to be confined to her apartments, where incriminating letters from Königsmarck were found hidden in curtain linings. The Elector Ernst August and his brother Duke Georg Wilhelm of Celle agreed, when confronted with the evidence, that a divorce must be arranged on the safe grounds of Sophia Dorothea's refusal to continue to cohabit with George Louis. A specially convened tribunal of jurists and Lutheran Church officials obligingly declared the marriage dissolved on 28 December 1694.

Meanwhile, Sophia Dorothea had been removed to Ahlden, a castle in her father's territory of Celle, where she lived in hope of being allowed to rejoin Königsmarck, of whose fate she was kept ignorant, after the divorce was completed. She was soon to be disillusioned. The terms of the divorce provided that she, as the guilty party, was not to be allowed to remarry and furthermore was to be denied access to her children. Her father refused to see her and she was destined to remain a virtual prisoner at Ahlden for the rest of her life.

Sophia Dorothea's long captivity of over 30 years, arduous though it must have been, was never an excessively harsh one and many of the conditions were relaxed as time passed. She enjoyed an adequate income, enabling her to live in a style befitting her rank, and was even allowed to drive out in her coach for short distances under escort. She could receive visitors, including her mother, who constantly sought to procure her release, even asking Queen ANNE to intercede on the grounds that her daughter's situation was unfitting for the mother of a future king of Great Britain. It was all to no avail. George I himself is said to have offered her the chance of rehabilitation, but legend has it that she refused this offer with the words, 'If what I am accused of is true, I am unworthy of his bed; and if it is false, he is unworthy of mine.'

Her days of boredom and loneliness were ended only when she died at the age of 60 on 2 November (13 November new style) 1726. She was buried with her parents at Celle.

Sophia Matilda of Gloucester, Princess (1773–1844) The elder daughter and first child of William Henry, Duke of GLOUCESTER (brother of GEORGE III) and his wife Maria Walpole, who was born at Gloucester House, London at eight o'clock in the evening on 29 May 1773. She was baptized on 27 June, her godparents being her uncle and aunt the Duke and Duchess of Cumberland (see CUMBERLAND, PRINCE HENRY FREDERICK, DUKE OF) and her aunt CAROLINE MATILDA, QUEEN OF DENMARK (represented by proxy). Her uncle the king had been asked to be a godfather, but he was still incensed by her parents' marriage and refused. However, the princess grew up to be on friendly terms with her cousins, the children of George III, and Fanny Burney, who met her when she was visiting the royal family after her retirement from Queen CHARLOTTE's service, describes her as 'very fat, with very fine eyes, a bright, even dazzling bloom, fine teeth, a beautiful skin, and a look of extreme modesty and sweetness. Her dress was perfectly simple, though remarkably elegant.'

Princess Sophia Matilda remained unmarried, her mother's humble origin making it virtually impossible for her to find a husband among the ranks of most German reigning families. As the great-grandchild of a sovereign, the princess was styled 'Highness', but after her brother the 2nd Duke of Gloucester had married their cousin Princess Mary (see MARY, PRINCESS, DUCHESS OF GLOUCESTER), the fourth daughter of George III, she received a Royal Warrant dated 23 July 1816 to the effect that she 'shall henceforward upon all occasions whatsoever be styled and called "Her Royal Highness" before such other styles and titles as do or hereafter may belong to her'. For many years she held the office of Ranger of Greenwich Park and resided at the Ranger's House, Blackheath. She was a godmother to Queen VICTORIA's second daughter, Princess Alice (*see* ALICE MAUD MARY, PRINCESS, GRAND DUCHESS OF HESSE), in June 1843.

The princess died peacefully after a short illness at the Ranger's House on 29 November 1844. She was buried in the Gloucester Vault in St George's Chapel, Windsor, on 10 December 1844.

Star of India, Most Exalted Order of the Order of chivalry instituted by Queen VICTORIA in 1861 and enlarged nine times thereafter. The dignity of Knight Grand Commander (GCSI) was conferred on princes or chiefs of India, or on British subjects for important and loyal service rendered to the Indian Empire. The second class of Knight Commander (KCSI) and the third class of Companion (CSI) were conferred for services in the Indian Empire of not less than 30 years in the department of the Secretary of State for India. No appointments to the order have been made since 14 August 1947.

Stephen, King of England (*c*.1096–1154) The third son of Stephen (Etienne), Count of Blois and Chartres, and his wife ADELA, one of the daughters of WILLIAM I THE CONQUEROR, who was born at Blois in about 1096. From the fact that the arms attributed to him by later heralds are blazoned as gules, a sagittarius or (or, in some versions, gules, three sagittarii or) it has been conjectured that he may have been born under that sign of the zodiac, but it may equally refer to the fact that he ascended the throne under that sign.

Stephen was still a child when his father was killed at Ramleh on 19 May 1102 while participating in the First Crusade. He was brought up by his energetic and capable mother, who acted as regent of the counties of Blois and Chartres during the minority of Stephen's elder brother Count Thibaut IV. He also became a favourite of his uncle HENRY I, who endowed him with lands in England and with the counties of Mortain and Alençon. In 1125 a brilliant marriage was arranged for him with the niece of Henry's first queen, Matilda (*see* MATILDA OF SCOTLAND, QUEEN OF ENGLAND), the only daughter and heiress of Eustace III, Count of Boulogne, the marriage probably taking place at Westminster.

In 1126 Stephen was the first of the lay barons to swear to acknowledge his cousin, the Empress Matilda (*see* MATILDA, 'LADY OF THE ENGLISH', EMPRESS), heiress to England and Normandy. He again swore fealty on the birth of her son Henry (later HENRY II) in 1133. In spite of these solemn oaths, on the death of his uncle, at the beginning of December 1135 Stephen left his county of Boulogne (but a day's journey from south-east England) and went straight to London, where he secured the support of the citizens, claiming that his royal uncle had changed his mind about the succession on his deathbed and given the crown to him. He was crowned on St Stephen's Day, 26 December 1135, by William de Corbeil, Archbishop of Canterbury.

Matilda protested against Stephen's succession but he was recognized by Pope Innocent II. Stephen secured the royal treasury with the aid of his brother Henry of Blois, Bishop of Winchester, and set about bribing many of his opponents, including his wife's uncle, DAVID I, KING OF SCOTS. At the same time he gained popular support by promising to restore the laws of EDWARD THE CONFESSOR, a promise never to be fulfilled. Baronial insurrections and wars with the Scots (terminating in Stephen's victory at the battle of the Standard in 1138) occupied the early years of the reign.

Matilda landed in England in the autumn of 1139, where she was ably supported by her half-brother Robert, Earl of GLOUCESTER (who had earlier attended Stephen's court but later defected), and was joined by several powerful barons. In the course of the civil wars that ensued, Stephen was captured at Lincoln in February 1141 and imprisoned at Bristol. The defeat at Lincoln (in the course of which the king fought with prodigious courage) was predicted by superstitious followers before battle was even joined when a wax taper offered by Stephen to his bishop during mass broke and the vessel containing the Host fell from the altar. His brother, Bishop Henry, turned against him and a legatine council of the English Church held at Winchester declared Stephen deposed and proclaimed Matilda 'Lady of the English' on 7 April 1141.

Stephen's supporters continued the struggle and having managed to capture Robert of Gloucester, exchanged him for Stephen, who had himself re-crowned on the anniversary of his first coronation. This was still not an end to the strife that ravaged the country, Stephen and Matilda alternately gaining the upper hand. In 1144 Stephen lost Normandy to Geoffrey of Anjou, Matilda's husband. A feud with the papacy led to an interdict in 1148, not raised until 1151. In 1152 Stephen sought to secure the succession in his own family by crowning his son EUSTACE, following a practice in use in France, but the pope refused to sanction this coronation.

Matilda had retired to Normandy, but her son Henry, now grown to manhood, took her place in 1153 and was joined by all her old supporters. This time the matter was settled without further bloodshed and by the Treaty of Westminster it was agreed that Stephen should retain the crown for life and that Henry should succeed him.

The following year Stephen, now 57 or 58, was at Dover when he was seized with what appears to have been an acute attack of appendicitis, aggravated by bleeding piles, and he died in great agony at Dover Castle on 25 October 1154. He was buried with his wife and son Eustace, who had both predeceased him, in Faversham Abbey, his own foundation.

Stephen was a sad figure, but most of his troubles were of his own making or the result of his weakness of character. Although brave in battle, he was politically inept, completely lacking the deviousness of his uncle Henry I, an essential for survival in those days. According to the ANGLO-SAXON CHRONICLE the years of warfare that characterized Stephen's reign were a cause of much grief and 'Men said openly that Christ and His saints slept'. Stephen was generally more popular than Matilda, however, and it was proudly claimed that he was the handsomest man in England, chivalrous and generous and not, apparently, above sitting down to eat with his humblest subjects.

Stephen's coinage is of inferior quality to that of his predecessors; on his coins he is depicted in profile facing right and George Vertue based his famous engraving of Stephen on this likeness. Stephen was survived by his two youngest children, WILLIAM OF BLOIS and MARY, COUNTESS OF BOULOGNE, who successively held their mother's county of Boulogne.

Stuart, House of The family that ruled Scotland from 1371 and England from 1603 to 1714. The Stuarts were of Breton origin, the family tracing its descent from Flaald, Seneschal of Dol in Brittany, who was living in 1080. His son, Alan FitzFlaald settled in England, where he married and had three sons, the second of whom, William FitzAlan, became ancestor of the earls of Arundel. Alan's eldest son, Walter, settled in Scotland where he became High Steward and died in 1177. The high stewardship of Scotland became hereditary and Walter's grandson, Walter, 3rd High Steward,

became known by the surname of Stewart. The sixth High Steward, also named Walter, married Marjorie Bruce, the eldest daughter of ROBERT I (BRUCE), KING OF SCOTS and their son Robert succeeded his maternal half-uncle DAVID II as ROBERT II in 1371. The spelling Stuart, which has become more familiar in England, was a corruption of the French version of the name, Steuart, and was widely adopted in the 17th century, doubtless being considered more fashionable.

Stuart, Prince Charles Edward (1720–88) 'Bonnie Prince Charlie', the 'Young Pretender' or 'Young Chevalier', who was the elder son of Prince James Francis Edward STUART (*see below*) and his wife Princess Clementina SOBIESKA and was born at the Palazzo Muti-Papazurri, Rome, on 31 December 1720, being baptized the same day by the names Charles Edward Louis John Casimir Silvester Maria. As the firstborn son of the titular King James III and VIII, he was styled Prince of Wales and Duke of Cornwall, etc. from birth. On Christmas Day 1723 his father invested him with the Order of the THISTLE, he being already considered a knight of the Order of the GARTER by virtue of being Prince of Wales.

Prince Charles Edward was brought up at his father's court in exile in Rome with every thought directed towards the recovery of the British throne. To this end he landed at Eriskay in Scotland on 25 July 1745, launching the so-called FORTY-FIVE rebellion, initially with just seven friends though he was quickly joined by many supporters from the Highlands. He was proclaimed Prince Regent on 12 August 1745 and, cheered by 700 Cameron clansmen, raised his father's banner at Glenfinnan on 19 August. He entered Edinburgh amid scenes of great rejoicing on 17 September. While holding court at HOLYROODHOUSE he received the news that Lieutenant-General Sir John Cope was marching from Stirling against him. The Highlanders surprised the Hanoverians at Prestonpans and forced them into flight after a battle lasting only 10 minutes. Instead of following this victory up, however, Charles returned to Edinburgh to resume the interrupted round of court life, which he apparently enjoyed greatly.

He was subsequently joined by Lords Kilmarnock, Cromarty, Balmerino and others and began the march south. He reached Derby on 4 December 1745 and took the town without a shot being fired. When the news reached London there was considerable panic, and GEORGE II himself had the royal yacht discreetly prepared to take the royal family to France. No more than 300 English supporters had joined the Young Pretender's force, however, and without the anticipated support of more English Jacobites it became dangerous to proceed any further away from the Scottish border. At Derby, the prince was lodged in a house in Full Street and it was there, after much argument, that he gave in to his generals and after two days began the retreat to Scotland with William Augustus, Duke of CUMBERLAND's army in hot pursuit. The Jacobites took Stirling and obtained a last victory at Falkirk Muir in January 1746, when they routed the army of Lieutenant-General Henry Havling. The Duke of Cumberland arrived in Edinburgh on 30 January and proceeded thence to Aberdeen and to Inverness, which he made his headquarters. The Jacobite army marched to Nairn in a snowstorm, but by this time had become a sorry, ill-fed band, largely owing to Prince Charles's indecisive leadership and his failure to delegate authority to the more competent Lord George Murray, his second-in-command.

The two armies met at Culloden Moor at dawn on 16 April 1746. The Highlanders (5000 strong) were outnumbered by almost two to one and after a long, hard-fought battle (the last on British soil) were completely defeated, putting an end to the Jacobite cause for good. Prince Charles Edward, whose main asset was his youthful good looks, made good his escape from the battlefield and went into hiding in the Hebrides, constantly on the move for some five months with a price of £30,000 on his head. Among his most loyal attendants during this time was Flora MacDonald, who disguised the prince as 'Betty Bourke', an Irish spinning-maid, in order to conceal his identity from his enemies (though he nearly betrayed himself when without thinking he hoisted up his skirts in order to cross a river, thus revealing his masculine legs). In the end it became clear that he had no future in Scotland and on 19 September he boarded a ship to take him back to France. His supporters, deserted by their leader, were harried mercilessly by Cumberland's men and the rebel clans were devastated. Flora MacDonald was imprisoned in the TOWER OF LONDON for her part in the prince's escape, but was eventually released under

the Act of Indemnity of 1747 (she died in 1790).

The rest of the prince's life was a sad story of decline, degradation and drunkenness (a favourite tipple was Drambuie, which to this day is known as 'Prince Charles Edward's liqueur'). For several years he was accompanied by his mistress Clementina WALKINSHAW, who bore him a daughter in 1753 (see ALBANY, CHARLOTTE, DUCHESS OF), but they later separated. Other mistresses included his cousin the Duchess of Montbazon and the Princess of Talmont. On 1 January 1766 his father died and Charles Edward assumed the style of 'King Charles III'. He was still unmarried and as his only brother was a Cardinal, he now gave his mind to securing a bride and continuing the Stuart line. His choice fell on Princess Louise Maximilienne of Stolberg-Gedern (see ALBANY, LOUISE, COUNTESS OF) and they were married by proxy in Paris on 28 March and in person at the Palazzo Compagnani, Marefoschi, Macerata, on 17 April 1772. Not yet 20, she was over 30 years his junior, and although the marriage appeared to start well, it soon foundered. The desired children never came, and after a sordid wife-beating episode the couple separated for good. Swinburne, in his *Courts of Europe*, describes the prince and his wife thus: 'He goes regularly to the theatre, and always falls asleep at the end of the first act, being generally intoxicated. His face is red and his eyes fiery, otherwise he is not an ill-looking man. The Countess is not handsome, being black and sallow, with a pug nose.'

Charles Edward's last years were solaced by the presence of his legitimated daughter Charlotte, who joined him in Rome, where he died in the Palazzo of his birth, a victim of his debaucheries, on 31 January 1788. To the end he expressed his regrets at having been defeated in 1746, commenting sadly, 'I should have died with my men at Culloden'. He was buried with his father in the crypt of St Peter's, Rome.

Stuart, Prince Henry Benedict, 'Cardinal of York' (1725–1807) The younger son of Prince James Francis Edward STUART and Princess Clementina SOBIESKA and brother of Charles Edward STUART, the 'Young Pretender', who was born at the Palazzo Muti-Papazurri in Rome on 6 March 1725 and was baptized by Pope Benedict XIII by the names Henry Benedict Thomas Edward Maria Clement Francis Xavier. He was styled Duke of York from birth.

On 25 October 1745 he was appointed 'Generalissimo of the King's forces in Great Britain and Ireland' and from December 1745 until April 1746 was stationed at Dunkirk in nominal command of the French expeditionary force that was poised to sail to the support of his brother Prince Charles Edward, but never actually did so. He later saw service under the Comte de Clermont at the siege of Antwerp.

Much to his father's displeasure, Henry was bent on a religious life. He received the tonsure from Pope Benedict XIV on 30 June 1747 and on 3 July was created Cardinal Deacon with the title of Santa Maria in Campitelli. He was ordained deacon and sub-deacon in August and priest on 1 September 1748. The Cardinal held various appointments at the papal court and on 19 November 1758 was consecrated Archbishop of Corinth *in partibus infidelium*. He was named Bishop of Frascati on 7 July and enthroned on 13 July 1761.

Henry took the side of his sister-in-law Louise on her separation from Prince Charles Edward, but withdrew his support of her on hearing of her intrigue with the Italian poet Alfieri and was again on good terms with his brother and with his legitimated niece Charlotte, Duchess of ALBANY. On the death of Prince Charles Edward in January 1788, Henry assumed the style of 'King Henry IX' and struck a medal bearing the legend: *Non Desideriis Hominum sed Voluntate Dei* (Not by the Desire of Men but by the Will of God).

When the French entered Rome in February 1798, the Cardinal fled first to Naples and then to Venice, where he lived on restricted means until January 1800, when GEORGE III, hearing of his plight, granted him a pension of £4,000 a year, which was continued until his death. The Cardinal was able to return to Frascati in July 1801 and in September 1803 was made Dean of the Sacred College and Bishop of Ostia and Velletri.

Henry died in his episcopal palace at Frascati on 13 July 1807 and was buried in the crypt of St Peter's, Rome, with his father and brother. Out of gratitude for the pension he had received he left the Stuart sapphire and other jewels to the British crown. He was the last legitimate male descendant of ROBERT II, KING OF SCOTS.

Stuart, Prince James Francis Edward (1688–1766) The sixth and youngest son of JAMES II and the second by his second wife MARY OF MODENA, who was born at ST JAMES'S PALACE on 10 June 1688, becoming Duke of Cornwall and Duke of Rothesay, etc. at birth. He was baptized by Catholic rites in the Chapel Royal, St James's, on 15 October, his godparents being the Queen Dowager CATHERINE OF BRAGANZA and Pope Innocent XI (represented by the papal nuncio). He was styled Prince of Wales, but never formally so created. His birth led to the GLORIOUS REVOLUTION, which ensured the Protestant succession by forcing King James and his wife and son into exile in France and setting the baby prince's Protestant half-sister MARY II and her husband WILLIAM III on the throne as joint-sovereigns. Such was the unwillingness of the Protestant faithful to accept that Mary of Modena now had a male heir, rumours abounded to the effect that the child was an imposter, smuggled into the queen's bed in a warming-pan.

Prince James, popularly known as the 'Old Pretender', grew up at Saint Germain, the residence allotted to the exiles by Louis XIV, and on his father's death in September 1701 he was proclaimed there as King James III and VIII. His mother was designated queen regent until he came of age. James was a serious and rather humourless young man, though not lacking some of the Stuart charm, which always assured his unfortunate family many adherents. He served with the French army, distinguishing himself at the battles of Oudenarde and Malplaquet, during the War of the Spanish Succession. His half-sister Queen ANNE would have preferred him as her successor rather than the Hanoverian George and was working to that end when death overtook her in August 1714.

In the following year James made an attempt to gain the throne in a campaign that became known to history as the FIFTEEN. He sailed from Dunkirk and landed in disguise at Peterhead. He was joined by the Earl of Mar with his army and proceeded to SCONE, where he was actually crowned in September 1715, although no details of the ceremony have been preserved. He intended to winter in Perth, but the advance of the Duke of Argyll obliged him to abandon the cause and to sail from Montrose to Gravelines. He arrived back at St Germain on 22 February 1716, accompanied by Mar, whom he appointed as his chief minister. His supporters back in Scotland were ruthlessly hounded by the armies of GEORGE I and many of the leaders, including Lord Derwentwater and Lord Kenmuir, were executed.

After his mother's death in 1718, Prince James settled in Rome. Negotiations were begun to find him a bride and the choice fell on Maria Casimire Clementina, the fifth daughter of Prince Jakob Ludwik Sobieski (the eldest son of the great warrior Jan III, King of Poland). They were married by proxy at Bologna on 9 May 1719 and in person by Pope Clement XI at Montefiascone, near Viterbo, on 1 September 1719. The couple had two sons, Charles Edward and Henry, but the marriage was a fairly loveless one and Clementina died in January 1735. James again had hopes of regaining his father's throne in 1745, when Charles Edward launched the abortive FORTY-FIVE rebellion, but again they were dashed.

Prince James died at Rome on 1 January 1766 and was accorded a funeral with full royal honours in St Peter's, where he was buried in the crypt. GEORGE III commissioned the sculptor Canova to design a monument to mark the tomb of his Stuart cousins and this was completed in 1819. It is interesting to note that had James succeeded his father in the normal way and continued to reign until his death, he would have been the longest reigning British monarch.

Sussex, Augustus Frederick, Duke of

(1773–1843) The sixth son and ninth child of GEORGE III and Queen CHARLOTTE, who was born at Buckingham House (now BUCKINGHAM PALACE) on 27 January 1773 and baptized at ST JAMES'S PALACE on 25 February, his godparents being Ernst II, Duke of Saxe-Gotha, Prince Georg of Mecklenburg-Strelitz and Princess Louise of Hesse, all of whom were represented by proxies. Prince Augustus was educated by tutors in England and then at the University of Göttingen. He was nominated a Knight of the GARTER on 2 June 1786.

After Göttingen the prince went on to study in Italy and at Rome met and became enamoured of Lady Augusta Murray, second daughter of John Murray, 4th Earl of Dunmore, and his wife Lady Charlotte Stewart, daughter of Alexander Stewart, 6th Earl of Galloway. Without seeking his father's consent, Prince Augustus married her, in contravention of the ROYAL MARRIAGES ACT, on 4 April 1793, repeating the ceremony on their return to London at St George's, Hanover Square, on 5 December 1793. Lady Augusta, who was born in London on 27 January 1768, was exactly five years older than her husband. The king was greatly incensed by the marriage, and it was declared null and void by the Court of

Arches on 3 August 1794. Nevertheless, the couple continued to live together. A son, Augustus Frederick d'Este was born in Essex on 13 January 1794 and a daughter, Augusta Emma d'Este, at Lower Grosvenor Street, London, on 11 August 1801. The marriage, combined with the prince's connection with the Whig party, completely alienated him from his father and from the court, and it was not until 27 November 1801 that he was created Duke of Sussex, Earl of Inverness and Baron Arklow and granted an income of £12,000 a year, which was later increased to £18,000.

On 13 October 1806 Lady Augusta assumed the surname de Ameland by Royal Licence and subsequently was usually styled Countess de Ameland. She and the duke later became estranged and she died at Ramsgate, Kent, on 5 March 1830 and was buried there. On or about 2 May 1831 the duke contracted a second irregular marriage with Lady Cecilia Letitia Underwood (see INVERNESS, DUCHESS OF).

The duke became Grand Master of Freemasons in 1811 and President of the Society of Arts in 1816 and was President of the Royal Society from 1830 to 1839. He was a steady friend and benefactor to art, science and literature, and his presence as chairman at dinners or meetings for the benefit of public charities might always be reckoned on. Though not very learned himself, he valued learning and his library was very extensive, containing probably the richest private collection in England of Bibles in different languages and editions. The duke was regarded with great affection by his niece Queen VICTORIA, and he was delighted when she created his wife Duchess of Inverness in April 1840 as a mark of her appreciation of the duke agreeing to yield precedence to Prince ALBERT. That same year he gave Victoria away at her wedding (inspiring wits to remark, 'The Duke of Sussex is always ready to give away what does not belong to him').

The Duke of Sussex died of erysipelas at KENSINGTON PALACE on 21 April 1843 and at his own request was buried at Kensal Green Cemetery in order that his wife might eventually rest beside him, which he feared might not have been permitted at Windsor. His son by his first marriage became a colonel in the army and unsuccessfully claimed the dukedom in 1843. He died unmarried at Kensington Gore, London, on 28 December 1848. The duke's daughter, Augusta Emma, married on 13 August 1845, as his second wife, Thomas Wilde, 1st

Baron Truro, who was Lord High Chancellor from 1850 to 1852. She died in London without issue on 21 May 1866.

Sweyn Forkbeard, King of England (*c*.970–1014) The son of Harald Bluetooth, King of Denmark, probably by his second wife Tove, daughter of Mistivoj, Prince of the Wends, who was born in Denmark in about 970. He succeeded his father as king of Denmark in about 986. In 994 he joined Olaf Trygvesson, King of Norway, in a raid on England, sailing up the Thames and besieging London until ETHELRED II and his council bought them off for £16,000. In 1002 Sweyn attacked his former ally and added Norway to his dominions. On St Brice's Day, 13 November 1002 Ethelred ordered the massacre of all the Danes in England, fearing that they were about to seize the kingdom. Among those killed at Oxford was Sweyn's sister Gunhild, the wife of Ealdorman Pallig, who was also slain. Sweyn renewed his attack on England in 1004, sacking and burning Norwich. After a temporary withdrawal occasioned by a famine the following year, he returned and in the course of the next few years brought the whole of England under his rule, being acknowledged as king after Ethelred's flight in the autumn of 1013.

Sweyn's first wife, Gunhild, was the daughter of Mieszko I, Duke of Poland, and his first wife Dubravka, daughter of Boleslav I, Duke of Bohemia. Dubravka's brother Duke Boleslav II was a son-in-law of EDWARD THE ELDER if the identification of his wife based on numismatic evidence is a correct one. Gunhild was the mother of Harald, who reigned as King of Denmark from 1014 to 1019, and CANUTE, who accompanied his father to England and eventually came to rule a large Scandinavian empire.

Sweyn's second wife was Sigrid the Haughty, daughter of Skogul Toste. She had been divorced from King Eric the Victorious of Sweden and had also been courted by Sweyn's companion-in-arms Olaf Tryvgesson, who had attempted to woo her with the present of a brass bracelet plated with gold. The wily queen detected the shoddiness of this at once and flung it back at him, whereupon he slapped her face and called her a 'heathen bitch'. He was a brave man, for only a little while before she had made some other prospective suitors drunk and then burned them alive in their lodging. This great lady bore Sweyn a daughter Estrith, or Astrid (later baptized as Margaret), who was to become the ancestor of the later sovereigns of Denmark.

Sweyn died at Gainsborough, following a fall from his horse, less than six months after gaining the kingdom on 3 February 1014. His body was taken back to Denmark and buried in Roskilde Cathedral.

Swithelm, King of Essex (d.*c*.665) The son of Sexbald or Sigebald, a brother of King SAEBERT, who succeeded his brother King SIGEBERHT II in about 660. He had been baptized by St Cedd at Rendlesham, King Ethelwald of EAST ANGLIA standing as his godfather. Swithelm died in about 665 and was succeeded by his kinsmen SIGHERE and SEBBI, who reigned jointly.

T

Talorc, King of the Picts (*fl*.641–53) The son of Wid Foith (son of BRUDE I) and a sister of King NECHTAN II, who succeeded his brother BRUDE II in about 641 and reigned until about 653.

Talorcan I, King of the Picts (d.656/7) The son of Eanfrith, King of BERNICIA, and a Pictish princess, apparently the elder sister of Kings GARTNAIT V, BRUDE II and TALORC, who succeeded the last in 653 and died in 656 or 657, being succeeded by his nephew BRUDE III.

Talorcan II, King of the Picts (d. after 782) The son of Drostan by a sister of ALPIN II, he reigned as an opposition king from 780 to 782, when he was killed or driven out by TALORCAN III.

Talorcan III, King of the Picts (d. after 784) The younger son of OENGUS II by a sister of ALPIN I, he was *regulus* of Atholl probably from 752 until 782, when he killed or drove out his rival TALORCAN II and set himself up as king of the Picts in opposition to DRUST VII. He was deposed or killed in 784.

Talorcan IV, King of the Picts (*fl*.693–9) The son of Fethal or Wtheil and a daughter of Conall MacAidan, King of Argyll, by a sister of CANAUL COEM, he reigned in opposition to his kinsman DRUST VIII from 834 to 836.

Tara The site, in County Meath, of the ancient seat of the High Kings of Ireland until the 6th century AD.

Tarrain, King of the Picts (*fl*.693–9) The son of Ainfrech and a sister of BRUDE III, whom he succeeded in 693. He was deposed by his cousin BRUDE IV in 697 and went to Ireland in 699.

Tasciovanus, King of the Catuvellauni (d. *c*.AD10) Probably a younger son of CASSIVELLAUNUS and the brother and successor of Androco. He enjoyed a long and peaceful reign and died in about AD10, when he was succeeded by his son CUNOBELINUS.

Teck, Duchess of *see* MARY ADELAIDE OF CAMBRIDGE, PRINCESS, DUCHESS OF TECK.

Theobalds Palace Mansion near Cheshunt in Hertfordshire, which belonged to Robert Cecil, 1st Earl of Salisbury, before being acquired as a royal residence. JAMES I took a fancy to the building and in 1607 exchanged the Old Palace at HATFIELD for it. It became his favourite residence and he died there in March 1625. The building fell into decay during the CIVIL WAR and was sold by CHARLES II. Nothing remains of the house, but the park is open to the public and contains old Temple Bar, which was removed there from the City in 1760.

Thistle, Most Ancient and Most Noble Order of the The principal order of chivalry for Scotland, which, according to legend, was founded by King Achaius, himself a legendary figure. JAMES II, KING OF SCOTS is said to have 'revived' an Order of St Andrew in 1452, but his son and successor JAMES III was probably the true founder. The Order subsequently lapsed and was refounded as the Order of the Thistle by JAMES II, KING OF ENGLAND in 1687 and again by Queen ANNE in 1703. It consists of the sovereign and 16 knights, plus such royal knights and extra knights who may be admitted from time to time by special statutes.

The insignia of the Order are: (1) the star, consisting of a St Andrew's cross of silver with rays emanating between the points of the cross and in the centre upon a field of gold, a thistle of green heightened with gold and surrounded by a circle of green bearing the motto *Nemo me impune lacessit* in gold letters; (2) the collar of gold, consisting of thistles intermingled with sprigs of rue and pendant from the centre the figure of St Andrew in gold with green gown and purple surcoat bearing before him his cross enamelled white and having round the images rays of gold going out from it in the form of a glory; (3) the mantle of dark green velvet lined with white taffeta and tied with cords and tassels of green and gold, with a representation of the star of the order on the left shoulder; (4) the badge of gold enamelled, having on one side the image of St Andrew as described above and on the other a thistle, enamelled gold and green with the flower reddish, worn attached to a dark green ribbon passing over the left shoulder and resting on the right hip; (5) the hat of black velvet, ornamented with white osprey plumes.

The chapel of the Order is in St Giles's Cathedral, Edinburgh, and the Chancery at the Court of the Lord Lyon, HM New Register House, Edinburgh.

Thomas of Woodstock, Duke of Gloucester see GLOUCESTER, THOMAS OF WOODSTOCK, DUKE OF.

Tincommius, King of the Atrebates (*fl.*15BC) One of the three sons of COMMIUS, who received Sussex as his share of his father's realm and was recognized by the Emperor Augustus in about 15BC. His coins bear the title of *Rex* (King).

Togodumnus, King of the Catuvellauni (*fl.*AD50) The son of CUNOBELINUS, whom he succeeded in about AD40. He resisted the Roman invasion in 43 and was probably killed at the battle of the Medway. The struggle was carried on by his brother CARATACUS.

Touch Pieces see KING'S EVIL.

Tower of London The great fortress overlooking the Thames in London, which was begun by WILLIAM I THE CONQUEROR, who commenced the construction of its principal building, the White Tower, in 1078 (an old tradition tells that the mortar used was mixed with blood). This initial building was completed by his son WILLIAM II and the keep, the biggest in the country after Colchester, is 90 feet high with walls 15 feet thick. It is in pure Norman style and contains the Chapel of St John the Evangelist, an exceptionally beautiful part of the structure. The Tower complex of buildings was added to by RICHARD I, HENRY III, EDWARD I, RICHARD II and HENRY VIII.

The Tower served not only as a royal palace until the reign of CHARLES I, but also as a place of confinement for state prisoners, many of whom were beheaded on Tower Green (including Lady JANE Grey, ANNE BOLEYN and CATHERINE HOWARD). The Tower's first prisoner, Ralf Flambard, Bishop of Durham, who was incarcerated in 1101, was one of the few to make good his escape, leaving by means of a rope lowered from one of the windows after he had got the guards drunk. First to be beheaded on nearby Tower Hill was Sir Simon Burley, tutor to Richard II, in 1386.

Notable buildings of the Tower include: Traitors' Gate, the original access from the Thames, through which Sir Thomas More, Anne Boleyn, Catherine Howard, the Duke of MONMOUTH and many others passed to meet their doom (ELIZABETH I as princess also passed that way, but lived to tell the tale); the Bloody Tower, said to have been the scene of the murder of the 'Princes in the Tower' (*see* EDWARD V), and also the place of confinement of Sir Walter Raleigh for nearly 20 years; the Wakefield Tower, in which HENRY VI died in mysterious circumstances; the Chapel Royal of St Peter ad Vincula, rebuilt after a fire in 1512 and the burial place of many of those executed on Tower Green or Tower Hill; the Beauchamp Tower, which contains mural inscriptions carved by prisoners; and the Waterloo Block, formerly the Waterloo Barracks, built in 1845 and now housing, among other artefacts, the crown jewels. Until the reign of CHARLES II, new sovereigns set out from the Tower to proceed in great state to Westminster on the eve of their coronations.

As one might expect, stories of ghostly apparitions, including that of Anne Boleyn, abound. The Tower of London is open to the public and is one of the city's greatest tourist attractions. Among the sights enjoyed by visitors are the Tower's ravens (the last representatives of the royal menagerie once sited at the Tower), which are maintained by the Yeoman Warders. Legend has it that if the ravens ever leave, the British monarchy will come to an end.

Trahaearn ap Caradog, King of Gwynedd (d.1081) The son of Caradog ap Gwyn ap Collwyn, his mother apparently being a sister of Cynfyn ap Gwerstan (thus making him a first cousin of BLEDDYN AP CYNFYN), who was ruler of Arwystli by inheritance and on the death of Bleddyn in 1075 boldly seized the throne of Gwynedd. His authority was at once challenged by GRUFFYDD AP CYNAN, who, after initially defeating him at Dyffryn Glyngin in Meirionydd, was in turn defeated at Bron yr Erw and driven into exile in Ireland. Trahaearn followed this victory by invading South Wales in 1078 and killing King RHYS AB OWAIN at Goodwick. RHYS AP TEWDWR then formed an alliance with Gruffydd ap Cynan, returned from exile, and eventually defeated and killed Trahaearn at the battle of Mynydd Carn, an unidentified site possibly in Montgomeryshire, in 1081.

Trahaearn's wife was Nest, daughter of GRUFFYDD AP LLYWELYN according to the pedigrees, and they had five sons, Llywarch, Meurig, Griffri, Owain and Leuan. Llywarch's daughter Gwladus became the wife of OWAIN GWYNEDD and the grandmother of LLYWELYN THE GREAT. Trahaearn's descendants reigned in Arwystli until it was absorbed into Powys by GWENWYNWYN.

Trinovantes Celtic tribe that occupied the area around Colchester. They were conquered by CASSIVELLAUNUS, KING OF THE CATUVELLANNI shortly before Caesar's first visit to Britain (c.56BC). Caesar restored the son of the defeated king and exacted an undertaking from Cassivellaunus not to molest him. The tribe remained tributary to the Catuvellauni and joined with other tribes in the resistance to the Roman conquest in the first century AD.

Trooping the Colour Popular name for the sovereign's Birthday Parade, which is held every year on the monarch's official birthday, now always a Saturday in June. It takes place on Horse Guards Parade and culminates in the colour of one of the five regiments of foot guards being paraded through the ranks in the presence of the sovereign. It first took place to mark the sovereign's birthday in the reign of GEORGE III in 1805. The ceremony has become a great tourist attraction, with ELIZABETH II for many years attending the event riding her horse Burmese side-saddle (though in recent years she has opted to drive in a barouche, partly for security reasons). The parade is usually followed by the appearance of the royal family on the balcony at BUCKINGHAM PALACE and a fly-past by the RAF.

Tudor, House of The dynasty that ruled England from 1485 to 1603 and can be traced back in the male line, fairly reliably, through many generations to the Romano-British chief COEL Hen Godebog or Caelius Votepacus, 'Old King Cole' of the nursery rhyme, who held sway in the 4th century AD. HENRY VII's great-grandfather Maredudd ap Tudor was a first cousin of the great Welsh hero OWAIN GLYN DŴR, who made the last bid for Welsh independence in 1400, and Henry was the representative of several lines of Welsh kings and princes (as can be seen from the genealogical table in Appendix XXXI). Henry VII's grandfather Owen Tudor either married, or at any rate became the lover of, CATHERINE OF FRANCE, widow of HENRY V, and their eldest son Edmund was therefore a half-brother of HENRY VI. Edmund Tudor, Earl of Richmond, married Margaret Beaufort (*see* RICHMOND AND DERBY, MARGARET BEAUFORT, COUNTESS OF), the only child of John Beaufort, Duke of Somerset, and Henry was their only son. Henry's slender claim to the English throne was through his mother, the genealogical representative of John of Gaunt, Duke of LANCASTER (the fourth son of EDWARD III) and his third wife Katherine Swynford. The children had all been born before their marriage but were legitimated by RICHARD II, and this was confirmed by HENRY IV, but with the addition of a new clause *excepta dignitate regale*, which excluded them from any right of succession to the throne.

Tytila, King of East Anglia (d.c.593) The son and successor WUFFA, KING OF EAST ANGLIA, who is regarded as the first king of EAST ANGLIA by Florence of Worcester, Simeon of Durham and William of Malmesbury. Roger of Wendover, on the other hand, reckons Wuffa as the first king and assigns the date of Tytila's accession to 578 and of his death to 593. He was succeeded by his son REDWALD.

U

Underwood, Cecilia Letitia *see* INVERNESS, CECILIA LETITIA UNDERWOOD, DUCHESS OF.

Urien Rheged, King of Rheged (d.c.585) Semi-legendary British king who reigned in the area around the Solway Firth. According to the traditional pedigrees, he was the son of Cynvarch, King of Rheged, and Nyfain or Nevyn, daughter of Brychan, Prince of Manau Guotodin, a nephew of CUNEDDA WLEDIG. His male line ancestry is carried back to Coel Hen, who is said to have made himself the first king of Rheged. Urien fought the Bernicians, probably in alliance with Strathclyde. He was murdered at Aberleu, by Llovan Llawddivo at the instigation of Morcant, King of Aeron, in about 585. He left two sons, Owain, who succeeded him as king of Rheged and reigned until about 596, and Elfin.

Uther Pendragon, King of Britain The legendary father of King ARTHUR. According to GEOFFREY OF MONMOUTH he was the youngest of the three sons of Constantine II and his wife 'born of a noble family.' He and his brothers were educated by 'Guithelinus, Archbishop of London', and the eldest son, Constans, became a monk at Winchester. King Constantine was stabbed to death by a Pict and argument ensued as to which of his younger sons, Aurelius Ambrosianus or Uther, should succeed him. While this was going on, VORTIGERN, 'leader of the Gewissei', brought Constans out of his monastery and had him crowned king in London, later causing the assassination of Constans and usurping the throne himself. Aurelius Ambrosianus and Uther took refuge in Brittany, whence they returned a few years later and overthrew Vortigern, burning him to death in his tower.

Having established his rule, Aurelius Ambrosianus sent his brother with the wizard Merlin to bring back the 'Giants' Ring', which they did, and this became Stonehenge. Aurelius died at Winchester from the effect of poison and Uther succeeded him as king. Some years later he seduced Ygerna, the wife of Gorlois, Duke of Cornwall, by impersonating her husband with the aid of Merlin's magic. Gorlois was conveniently killed in a siege and Uther was thus enabled to marry Ygerna, who became the mother of Arthur and a daughter Anna. Eventually Uther became old and ill, but he had himself carried on a litter to St Albans, where his army defeated and killed Octa, King of Kent. However, the Saxons managed to poison the spring from which Uther drank and he died with about 100 of his men after imbibing the water. His body was taken to Stonehenge for burial inside the 'Giants' Ring'.

Almost all the details of Uther's life are a complete fabrication, but it does involve several historical figures, in particular his alleged brother and predecessor Aurelius Ambrosianus.

V

Verica, King of the Atrebates (*fl*.1st century BC) The youngest son of COMMIUS, who received the main tribal lands of the Atrebates in Hampshire in the division made after his father's death. He struck coins bearing his name based on Greek and Roman types. A later Verica, reigning in Surrey and Sussex, was deposed in the time of CLAUDIUS and went to Rome to beg the emperor to restore him to his kingdom. He may have been a descendant of the elder Verica.

Victoria, Duchess of Kent (1786–1861) The mother of Queen VICTORIA, who was the fourth daughter and seventh child of Franz Friedrich Anton, Duke of Saxe-Saalfeld-Coburg, and his second wife Auguste Caroline Sophie, daughter of Heinrich XXIV, Count Reuss-Ebersdorf, and was born at Coburg on 17 August 1786. She was named Marie Louise Victoire, but was always known by the last name, which became Victoria in England, where her names were usually given as Victoria Mary Louisa.

The princess was married at Coburg at the age of 17 on 21 December 1803 to Emich Carl, Hereditary Prince of Leiningen, the 40-year-old widower of her mother's sister Henriette. She bore him a son, Carl Friedrich Wilhelm Emich, later 3rd Prince of Leiningen, on 12 September 1804, and a daughter, Feodora, later Princess of Hohenlohe-Langenburg, on 7 December 1807. Victoria's husband succeeded his father as 2nd Prince of Leiningen in January 1807 and died at Amorbach on 4 July 1814, leaving her as the guardian of their two children and regent of the principality, most of which had been taken by Napoleon.

In 1816 Victoria's brother Leopold (*see* LEOPOLD OF SAXE-COBURG) married Princess CHARLOTTE OF WALES and the sisters-in-law began a friendly correspondence. Charlotte's uncle Edward, Duke of KENT made a trip to Germany in 1816 and armed with a letter 'not of introduction but of recommendation' from his niece, visited Amorbach, where he was so taken with Princess Victoria that he proposed marriage after a few days' acquaintance. Victoria's first marriage with an older husband had not been particularly happy and her first response was to reject the duke's offer, although he had made a good impression on her. The death of Princess Charlotte in November 1817 made the Duke of Kent's marriage a matter of paramount importance; he renewed his suit and Victoria wrote to accept his proposal on 25 January 1818. They were married by Lutheran rites in the Hall of the Giants at Schloss Ehrenburg, Coburg, on 29 May 1818. The couple set out for England four days later and were married in a second ceremony at KEW PALACE in the presence of the duke's mother Queen CHARLOTTE on 13 July 1818, the Duke and Duchess of Clarence being married at the same time. Victoria again wore her wedding dress of 'blonde silk lace', trimmed with orange blossom and white roses, which had cost £97.6s.0d.

After a few days spent with Prince Leopold at Claremont, the Duke and Duchess of Kent returned to his apartment in KENSINGTON PALACE, but in September economic reasons compelled them to return to Amorbach. By this time the duchess was already pregnant and her husband, convinced that 'the crown will come to me and my children', decided that the child must be born in England. After much negotiation and borrowing of money they set out at the end of March, arrived at Calais on 18 April and after waiting six days for a favourable wind embarked on the royal yacht on 24 April, making the crossing in less than three hours and arriving safely at Dover. They proceeded to Kensington Palace, where the future queen Victoria was born on 24 May 1819.

Eight months later the Duke of Kent died at Sidmouth in January 1820. He left nothing but debts and the duchess was penniless. Fortunately, her brother Prince Leopold came to the rescue and after her return to

Kensington Palace she was greatly cheered by the daily visits of her sister-in-law the Duchess of Clarence (later Queen ADELAIDE). GEORGE IV, who had detested his brother the Duke of Kent, refused to be of any assistance to his widow, in spite of pleas from his sister Princess MARY, DUCHESS OF GLOUCESTER. Apart from £6,000 a year voted by Parliament, Victoria and her infant daughter also received an allowance of £3,000 a year from Prince Leopold, who received £50,000 annually (settled on him when he married Princess Charlotte). The duchess's affairs were managed by Sir John Conroy, who had been an equerry to the duke. He gained a great ascendancy over her, and it was widely believed that he became her lover, though this was probably untrue. He was far from scrupulous in his management of financial affairs and misappropriated large sums entrusted to him by Princess SOPHIA, an inveterate mischiefmaker who reported to him on private matters within the royal family.

Princess Victoria conceived a strong dislike of Conroy, which affected her relations with her mother and after her accession to the throne she and the duchess became estranged for several years. The duchess's financial affairs were in a mess and the queen had to help her settle her debts, which amounted to some £55,000, with a payment of £30,000 from her Privy Purse. Sir John Conroy resigned from the duchess's household in 1839 and thereafter relations between mother and daughter began to improve slightly, although the duchess remained grumbling and demanding. She wished to live with the queen and Prince ALBERT at BUCKINGHAM PALACE after their marriage, but the queen refused to consider this and took a lease of Ingestre House, Belgrave Square, for her mother in April 1840. The duchess complained it was too small and five months later on the death of Princess AUGUSTA SOPHIA, the queen gave her CLARENCE HOUSE, St James's, and FROGMORE HOUSE at Windsor as residences.

In the same year the duchess acquired a new secretary and comptroller in the person of Colonel Sir George Couper, who managed to put her affairs in order and was greatly esteemed by her as well as by her daughter and son-in-law. He remained in charge of her affairs until his sudden death in February 1861, only two weeks before that of the duchess.

Since 1859 the Duchess of Kent had suffered recurring attacks of erysipelas and early in March 1861 her right arm was so swollen and painful that an operation was performed to afford her some relief, but a similar gathering on her left arm and side was observed. On the 15 March 1861 she lay on a sofa in her bedroom at Frogmore and was visited by the Prince Consort and then by the queen, who remained nearly all night and held her mother's hand as she died peacefully at 9.30 in the morning on 16 March 1861. The Duchess of Kent had desired to be buried in a mausoleum in the grounds of Frogmore House and had asked the Prince Consort to arrange for its design and erection. He commissioned Professor Ludwig Gruner, of Dresden, to make the design and the architect A. J. Humbert to carry it out. It was almost completed when the duchess died. It is a very pleasing circular, domed building standing on a grassy knoll, which covers the vault containing the sarcophagus. The upper part contains a full-length statue of the duchess standing and plaques on either side of the plinth bear the heads of her two husbands in low relief. Queen Victoria in characteristic fashion indulged in wild paroxysms of grief over her mother's death, which she expressed in epistolary outpourings to her uncle King Leopold. She was greatly moved to discover evidence of her parents' attachment to each other and of her mother's love for her in the contents of 'a little writing desk' which had belonged to her father.

Victoria, Princess (1868–1935) The second daughter and fourth child of Albert Edward, Prince of Wales (later EDWARD VII) and ALEXANDRA OF DENMARK, who was born at Marlborough House, London, at 4.25 in the morning on 6 July 1868. She was baptized there on 6 August by the Bishop of London, receiving the names Victoria Alexandra Olga Mary. Her godparents were her grandmother Queen VICTORIA (for whom the Duchess of Cambridge stood proxy), the Queen of the Hellenes (for whom Princess AUGUSTA, Grand Duchess of Mecklenburg-Strelitz stood proxy), the Queen Dowager of Denmark (widow of Christian VIII), the Grand Duchess Dowager of Mecklenburg-Strèlitz, Princess MARY ADELAIDE, Duchess of Teck, Princess Friedrich of Anhalt, Emperor Alexander II of Russia (for whom the Russian ambassador stood proxy), Grand Duke Alexander of Russia (later Emperor Alexander III), Prince Arthur (later Duke of CONNAUGHT), Prince Ludwig (later Grand Duke Ludwig IV) of Hesse and Prince Georg of Hesse-Cassel – a large and impressive array.

Princess Victoria was brought up with her elder sister Louise (see LOUISE, PRINCESS ROYAL, DUCHESS OF FIFE) and her younger sister Maud (see MAUD, PRINCESS, QUEEN OF NORWAY) to act as satellites to their beautiful mother, whose looks none of them was lucky enough to inherit. As a result they became excessively shy. First Louise and then Maud escaped into marriage, leaving Victoria at home as her mother's companion. She did have several suitors, including Prince Adolphus of Teck (brother of her future sister-in-law), Sir Arthur Davidson, one of her father's equerries, and Lord Roseberry, but for one reason or another all were considered 'unsuitable' by her parents, and the princess was destined to spend the greater part of her life in attendance on her mother, who would ring a bell to summon her to her side at all times of day and night. Victoria's cousin, Grand Duchess Olga of Russia, described her as little more than 'a glorified maid'.

Known in her family as 'Toria', the princess, probably as a result of her subservience, developed a sharp and often spiteful tongue. A particular butt for her remarks was her sister-in-law Mary (see MARY OF TECK), whom she would ridicule, poking fun at her artistic interests. Victoria was very close to her brother GEORGE V and like him was a complete Philistine, so that between them they could on occasion render Mary's life a misery.

The death of Queen Alexandra in 1925 enabled Victoria to order her own life at last at the age of 57. She bought a sprawling, undistinguished house called Coppins at Iver, Buckinghamshire, and lived there for the rest of her life. Her last years were occupied with health concerns, and she became something of a hypochondriac, indulging herself with neuralgia, migraines, indigestion, depression and a succession of colds and attacks of influenza. She died at Coppins on 3 December 1935 and was buried at Frogmore. King George mourned her sincerely and recorded in his diary: 'No one ever had a sister like her.' He survived her for only two months. Princess Victoria left Coppins to her favourite nephew, Prince George, Duke of KENT, and it was sold by his son in 1972.

Victoria, Princess Royal and German Empress (1840–1901) The eldest daughter and first child of Queen VICTORIA and Prince ALBERT, who was born at BUCKINGHAM PALACE shortly before two o'clock in the afternoon on 21 November 1840. She was baptized by the Archbishop of Canterbury in the throne room of the palace on 10 February 1841, receiving the names Victoria Adelaide Mary Louisa. Her godparents were Queen ADELAIDE, Princess MARY, DUCHESS OF GLOUCESTER, the Duchess of Kent, the King of the Belgians, the Duke of Sussex and her paternal grandfather, the Duke of Saxe-Coburg and Gotha (for whom the Duke of Wellington stood proxy). Princess Victoria was granted the style of PRINCESS ROYAL on 19 January 1841.

As a baby and small child she was known in her family as 'Pussy'. She was an engaging child, bright and quick to learn and soon became her father's favourite. In August 1855 she and her brother the Prince of Wales (later EDWARD VII) accompanied their parents to Paris on a state visit to the Emperor and Empress of the French. In the same year Vicky, as she had come to be called, although only 15, fell in love with Prince Friedrich Wilhelm of Prussia, whose father was heir to the Prussian throne. Her parents approved her engagement, which took place on 29 September 1855, but with some misgivings 'on account of her extreme youth'. The queen sent a message to the House of Commons on 18 May 1857 intimating her consent to the marriage and Parliament voted her the sum of £40,000 with an annuity of £8,000. The marriage took place in the Chapel Royal, St James's, on 25 January 1858 (Prussian suggestions that the wedding should take place in Berlin were greeted with outrage by Victoria). It was a real love match and the young couple were both fired with liberal ideals and a desire to bring constitutional monarchy to Prussia. Four sons and four daughters were born to them between 1859 and 1872.

In January 1861 the death of Friedrich Wilhelm IV brought Vicky's father-in-law to the throne of Prussia as Wilhelm I and she became Crown Princess. Her mother, who conducted a voluminous correspondence with her, always addressed her as 'Princess Royal and Crown Princess' rather than the other way about, thereby causing some annoyance in Prussian court circles. On 18 January 1871 Wilhelm I was proclaimed German Emperor (*Deutscher Kaiser*) at Versailles and Vicky became Crown Princess of the German Empire with the style of 'Imperial and Royal Highness'.

She was a woman of very strong opinions and not afraid to speak her mind, eschewing all tact and thereby incurring the inveterate enmity of Bismarck, the German

Chancellor. Her brother the Prince of Wales was to say that she was at her most British in Berlin and at her most Prussian in London. Her outspokenness and unshakeable belief that her opinions on every subject were the right ones brought her many enemies in addition to Bismarck. She could be violently partisan, as she demonstrated in the Franco-Prussian War, but it did not bring her popularity and it was generally believed that she exercised an undue influence on her husband.

In March 1888 the Emperor Wilhelm I died in Berlin at the age of 90 and Vicky's husband succeeded him, becoming Friedrich III, German Emperor and King of Prussia. He was already a dying man, having been stricken with cancer of the throat, which made him unable to speak in more than a whisper. His reign lasted only three months and he died at Potsdam on 15 June 1888 after undergoing much suffering, occasioned not least by the various treatments he received. Vicky's eldest son now became Emperor Wilhelm II.

Although devoted to his grandmother Queen Victoria, Wilhelm disliked his mother and subjected her to many slights and humiliations. In widowhood she assumed the rather curious style of the Empress Friedrich rather than that of Dowager Empress or Empress Victoria.

In 1900 the empress fell ill with cancer of the spine. She was not well enough to journey to England to visit her dying mother in January 1901, and she died at her residence Friedrichshof at 6.15 in the evening on 5 August 1901. Victoria was buried beside her husband in the Friedenskirche at Potsdam.

Victoria, Queen of Great Britain (1819–1901) The only child of Edward, Duke of KENT (fourth son of GEORGE III) and his wife Maria Louisa Victoria of Saxe-Coburg-Saalfeld, who was born at KENSINGTON PALACE, London, at a quarter past four in the morning on 24 May 1819 and was baptized by the Archbishop of Canterbury in the cupola room of the palace on 24 June, receiving the names Alexandrina Victoria. Her godparents were her uncle the Prince Regent (later GEORGE IV), Emperor Alexander I of Russia (in whose honour she received her first name and for whom the Duke of YORK stood proxy), her aunt CHARLOTTE, PRINCESS ROYAL AND QUEEN OF WÜRTTEMBERG (for whom Princess AUGUSTA SOPHIA stood proxy) and her maternal grandmother the Dowager

Duchess of Saxe-Coburg-Saalfeld (for whom Princess MARY, DUCHESS OF GLOUCESTER stood proxy).

Victoria was only eight months old when her father died at Sidmouth in January 1820, and she was brought back to Kensington Palace by her mother and her uncle Prince LEOPOLD (later King Leopold I of the Belgians), arriving there on the day of the death of her grandfather George III at Windsor. Very many years later one of her granddaughters was to ask her, rather thoughtlessly, if she had ever been shown to George III. 'What? Show a baby to a madman!' was the outraged response. Victoria was brought up very simply under her mother's guidance. Uncle Leopold was very much a father-figure and a great influence and she also had the companionship of her much older half-brother and half-sister, Prince Charles and Princess Feodora of Leiningen. Her governess from babyhood onwards was the Hanoverian Louise Lehzen, later created a Hanoverian baroness, who was to remain with her until after the queen's marriage, when her jealousy and penchant for mischief-making made her fall foul of Prince Albert and brought about her dismissal and her return to Germany with a pension of £800 a year.

Lehzen gave Victoria a very thorough grounding in most subjects but found her a somewhat slow learner at first. At the age of eight the princess was given a tutor, the Rev. George Davys (later Bishop of Peterborough), with whom she had daily lessons. She also had French and German tutors, a writing and mathematics master and a drawing master (Richard Westall, RA, who found she had a great talent), and she also had dancing lessons, which she loved, and lessons in music and singing. On the accession of Victoria's uncle WILLIAM IV in June 1830, she became heiress presumptive to the Crown. Only a few months before this she had discovered how near to the throne she was when Lehzen inserted a genealogical table in her history book. The princess perused this carefully and then said: 'I see I am nearer to the throne that I thought.' She then burst into tears, but composed herself and uttered her famous remark, 'I will be good.'

The Duchess of Kent took her daughter on a series of 'royal progresses' throughout the country, but incurred the king's displeasure by not allowing the princess to appear at court as often as he wished. Victoria came of age on reaching her 18th birthday in May 1837, much to the relief of William IV, who had dreaded the prospect of the Duchess of Kent becoming regent, as she would have done had he died while his niece was still a minor. A month later the king did die, and Victoria received the news of her accession to the throne at Kensington Palace, early in the morning while still in her night attire. She was crowned at WESTMINSTER ABBEY on 28 June 1838 and recorded her own impression of the ceremony in her diary. On the day that she became queen she demonstrated her determination to free herself from her mother's influence by ordering that her bed be removed from her mother's room, which they had hitherto always shared.

Prince Leopold had long since departed to become king of the Belgians, but Victoria was fortunate in finding another father-figure in her first prime minister, Lord Melbourne, upon whom she came to rely almost as much as she had on 'Uncle Leopold'. However, the greatest influence in her life was to be that of her cousin and husband, Prince ALBERT of Saxe-Coburg, to whom she was married at the Chapel Royal, St James's, on 10 February 1840. The prince was a man of culture and taste, a true polymath, and he moulded and shaped the character of his young wife completely. Victoria had inherited much of the temperament of her father and mother, including a strong sexuality, which Albert was to satisfy. He, strangely enough, has always been considered something of a prude, but his high moral standards precluded any extramarital activity of the kind heavily indulged in by his father and brother, both notorious womanizers. In any case, marriage to Victoria was a full-time occupation, exacting both physically and mentally. When the Prince Consort (as he had been created by Patent on 25 June 1857 – though Victoria wanted him to be called king consort) died at the age of 42 he had the appearance of a much older man. The cause of his death was attributed by his doctors to typhoid, but in recent years there has been some medical speculation as to whether he suffered from cancer or some other wasting disease.

The effect of the prince's death on the queen and her almost complete withdrawal from public life for the remaining 40 years of her reign are well documented and she was often referred to, at home and abroad, as 'The Widow of Windsor'. She found some comfort in her large and ever-growing family of children, grandchildren and great-grandchildren, and later in travel to the south of France, where she enjoyed the Mediterranean sunshine.

Victoria always preferred the company of men to that of women and her partiality for her Highland servant John BROWN was a matter of concern to her family and household. He treated the queen in a rough and familiar yet kindly manner, which she greatly relished, and in return he was allowed many privileges that infuriated the other members of the household. After Brown's death the queen was dissuaded from writing and publishing a personal memoir of him only with the greatest difficulty.

Almost as great an influence on the queen in her later years, and even more resented, was her Indian secretary, Abdul Karim, known as 'the Munshi', who claimed to be the son of a Surgeon-General in the Indian army. Victoria's favourite son, Prince Arthur, Duke of CONNAUGHT, made some investigations into the Munshi's origins when he was in India and discovered that he was in reality the son of a very lowly apothecary. The queen was so affronted when given this information that she would not speak to her son for several days. The Munshi was appointed a Companion of the Indian Empire (CIE) and a Companion of the ROYAL VICTORIAN ORDER (CVO) and was given a house near Windsor, which he soon filled with a number of Indian ladies, euphemistically described as his 'sisters, aunts and cousins' and a succession of pretty young 'nephews' with whom he was often photographed. Some of the photographs still hang in the corridors of OSBORNE HOUSE, the elegant Italianate palace on the Isle of Wight created by the Prince Consort and now (apart from being the repository of the many elaborate presents received by the queen from the Indian princes on the occasion of her Golden Jubilee) a convalescent home for naval officers.

Victoria's reign, a time when Britain reached a height of prestige around the world, probably saw more social changes than any other. The queen's proclamation as Empress of India at Delhi on 1 January 1877 marked the apogee of the British Empire and was a source of great pride and satisfaction to Victoria herself, as she could now feel herself on a par with the Emperors of Russia and Austria and the recently proclaimed German Emperor, to all of whom she considered herself vastly superior.

Victoria's relationship with her prime ministers was not always a smooth one (*see* BEDCHAMBER CRISIS). She especially disliked and distrusted the Liberals, and Gladstone, whom she termed a 'half-mad firebrand', was particularly scorned by her both in public and in private. At a royal wedding he once inadvertently entered the marquee where the queen was sitting and she was heard to ask in a loud voice, 'Does Mr Gladstone think this is a public tent?' On the other hand, the wily Conservative flatterer Disraeli could do no wrong in the queen's eyes. She offered to visit him on his deathbed but he declined this singular honour, remarking to his attendants with a last summoning-up of his ready wit that she would only want to give him a message for Albert and he would find the visit too tiring.

After 50 years on the throne the queen had become the most politically astute person in the kingdom and was able to advise and influence her ministers to a considerable extent. On one occasion the Secretary of State for War, Campbell-Bannerman (later prime minister under EDWARD VII) brought what he claimed to be some entirely new army schemes for the queen's approval. 'No, Mr Bannerman,' she said, 'Lord Palmerston proposed exactly the same thing to me in '52, and Lord Palmerston was wrong.' Lord Palmerston was another prime minister with whom Victoria did not get along.

At Victoria's accession the throne was far from secure. There was a strong republican movement and the queen was hissed at Ascot races on one occasion. By the end of the reign she had acquired a popularity greater than that enjoyed by any of her predecessors, and she was greatly moved on the occasion of her DIAMOND JUBILEE in 1897 to hear a man in the crowd shout out, 'Well done, old girl!'

Victoria enjoyed robust health throughout her life and had a hearty appetite, but in the last year of her life her health began to fail and she suffered from dyspepsia, insomnia, slight aphasia and weight loss. She journeyed to Osborne for the last time on 18 December 1900 and was exhausted by the journey, although she recovered somewhat a few days later. The final phase began on 16 January 1901 and the queen continued sinking and rallying until she died very peacefully, surrounded by her family, at 6.30 in the evening on 22 January 1901.

The queen had been greatly impressed, when visiting Germany in the early days of her marriage, by the mausoleum that was used as the burial place of the ducal family at Coburg, and determined that she herself would not be buried in the Royal Tomb House at Windsor constructed by George III. Accordingly, on the Prince Consort's death, the construction of an impressive mausoleum at FROGMORE was begun and there the queen and her husband rest side by side in a great sarcophagus surmounted by their recumbent effigies. A smaller mausoleum nearby houses the remains of Victoria's mother, the Duchess of Kent, while the grounds surrounding the Royal Mausoleum have been laid out as a burial ground for many of Victoria's descendants.

Victoria's death was an occasion of real and heartfelt grief for the majority of her subjects, most of whom had grown up in her reign and could remember no other. The 63-year span linked the age of the stagecoach, highwaymen and public executions (abolished in 1868) to the age of the motor car and the eve of the conquest of the air.

The saying 'We are not amused', which is frequently attributed to Queen Victoria, is apocryphal. She very often was amused, and the reminiscences of two of her granddaughters leave no doubt about this. One of them, Princess ALICE, COUNTESS OF ATHLONE, when interviewed on television in her old age, said that she once asked her grandmother if she had ever really said it and received a categorical denial. 'Wasn't it a pity?' was the princess's chuckling comment. On another occasion the queen was reportedly reduced to tears of laughter when she questioned Admiral Foley about the salvage of HMS *Eurydice*, which had gone down off Portsmouth – having satisfied her curiosity on the subject she then asked the admiral how her friend his sister was, only for the slightly deaf admiral to respond, 'Well, Ma'am, I am going to have her turned over, take a good look at her bottom and have it well scraped.'

The queen did, however, employ the royal 'we' on frequent occasions and this usage has been explained by her constant wish to associate her beloved husband Albert in every statement of opinion which she uttered, this being one way in which she felt she was keeping his memory alive after his death.

Victoria and Albert, Royal Order of Order for ladies instituted by Queen VICTORIA on 10 February 1862 and enlarged on 10 October 1864, 15 November 1865 and 15 March 1880. The Order consisted of four classes, and was not conferred after the death of Queen Victoria in 1901.

Vortigern British king or chief who, according to tradition, invited the Jutes HENGEST and HORSA to Britain to help him repel the incursion of the Picts from the north. His name is really a title signifying 'overlord'. In the Welsh pedigrees he is named Gwrtheyrn Gwrtheneu, son of Gwidol, son of Gwidolin, son of Gloyw Wallt Hir and is given a wife Severa, daughter of Macsen Wledig (otherwise the Roman Emperor Magnus Maximus who died in 388). They had four sons, Cateyrn, Gwerthefyr Fendigaid (or Vortimer), Pasgen (or Pascent) and Brydw, and an unnamed daughter who, from an incestuous union with her father, bore a son Faustus. According to GEOFFREY OF MONMOUTH, who followed NENNIUS, Vortigern fell in love with Hengest's daughter Renwein (or Rowena) and obtained her in marriage in exchange for the kingdom of KENT. This angered his people and he was deposed in favour of his son Vortimer. Renwein contrived to have Vortimer poisoned and Vortigern was restored to the throne, eventually being burned alive in his tower by Aurelius Ambrosius. Vortigern's third son Pascent later attempted to regain his father's kingdom but was defeated and killed at the battle of Menevia by UTHER PENDRAGON. Vortigern's story contains some elements of historicity.

Vortiporius (Voteporix), King of Dyfed
One of the kings of Britain who was castigated by GILDAS. In the Welsh pedigrees he is the son of Aircol Lawhir (Agricola the Longhanded). GEOFFREY OF MONMOUTH lists him as the third king to reign after ARTHUR and says that he beat the Saxons in battle and thereafter 'governed the people frugally and peacefully'. In 1895 a tombstone was discovered in the heart of Dyfed bearing an inscription in Latin capitals headed by a wheel cross (an indication that the person commemorated was a Christian) and reading: *Memoria Voteporigis protictoris*. The other side of the stone bears the name in Goidelic form 'Votecorigas'.

W

Wales, Prince of Title traditionally bestowed upon the HEIR APPARENT to the English throne. The title was instituted by EDWARD I for his son Edward (later EDWARD II), who was born at Caernarfon. According to legend the king promised to give the conquered Welsh people a prince who could not speak a word of English and accordingly presented to the populace his new-born infant son cradled in his shield. The English Princes of Wales have been as follows:

1. 1301–7 EDWARD OF CAERNARFON, fourth son of Edward I, who was granted the Principality of Wales and Earldom of Chester by charter on 7 February 1301 and succeeded his father as Edward II on 8 July 1307.
2. 1343–6 EDWARD OF WOODSTOCK ('The Black Prince'), eldest son of EDWARD III, who was created Prince of Wales and invested at Westminster on 12 May 1343 but died before his father on 8 June 1376.
3. 1376–77 Richard of Bordeaux, only surviving son of the preceding, who was created Prince of Wales, Duke of Cornwall and Earl of Chester on 20 November 1376 and succeeded his grandfather as RICHARD II on 21 June 1377.
4. 1399–1413 Henry of Monmouth, eldest surviving son of HENRY IV, who was created Prince of Wales, Duke of Cornwall and Earl of Chester on 15 October 1399 and succeeded his father as HENRY V on 20 March 1413.
5. 1454–71 Edward of Westminster, only son of HENRY VI, who was created Prince of Wales and Earl of Chester on 15 March 1454 and was killed after the battle of Tewkesbury on 4 May 1471.
6. 1471–83 Edward of Westminster, eldest son of EDWARD IV, who was created Prince of Wales and Earl of Chester on 26 June 1471 and succeeded his father as EDWARD V on 9 April 1483.
7. 1483–4 Edward of Middleham, only son of RICHARD III, who was created Prince of Wales and Earl of Chester on 24 August 1483 and died before his father on 9 April 1484.
8. 1489–1502 Arthur Tudor, eldest son of HENRY VII, who was created Prince of Wales and Earl of Chester and invested at Westminster on 29 November 1489 but died before his father on 2 April 1502.
9. 1504–9 Henry Tudor, second son of Henry VII, who was created Prince of Wales and Earl of Chester and invested at Westminster on 18 February 1504 and succeeded his father as HENRY VIII on 21 April 1509. Edward Tudor, only surviving son and heir of Henry VIII, was styled Prince of Wales and was about to be formally created Prince of Wales and Earl of Chester when he succeeded his father as EDWARD VI on 28 January 1547.
10. 1610–12 Henry Frederick Stuart, eldest son of JAMES I, who was created Prince of Wales and Earl of Chester and invested at Westminster on 4 June 1610 but died before his father on 6 November 1612.
11. 1616–25 Charles Stuart, second son of JAMES I, who was created Prince of Wales and invested at Whitehall on 4 November 1616 and succeeded his father as CHARLES I on 27 March 1625. (Charles James Stuart, eldest son of CHARLES I, born and died on 13 May 1629, was buried as 'Charles, Prince of Wales'.)
12. 1638–49 Charles Stuart, second son of CHARLES I, who was declared Prince of Wales and Earl of Chester around 1638 (though never formally so created) and succeeded his father as *de jure* King CHARLES II on 30 January 1649.
13. 1688 James Francis Edward Stuart, sixth and youngest but only surviving son of JAMES II, who was styled Prince of Wales from 4 July 1688, but was never formally so created, and went into exile with his parents in December 1688, succeeding his father as *de jure* King James III and VIII on 6 September 1701. Charles Edward (Louis John Casimir Silvester Maria) Stuart, elder son of the preceding, was styled Prince of Wales, etc., from his birth on 31 December 1720, succeeding his father as *de jure* King Charles III on 1 January 1766.
14. 1714–27 George Augustus, only son of GEORGE I, who was created Prince of Wales and Earl of Chester and invested at Westminster on 27 September 1714, succeeding his father as GEORGE II on 11 June 1727.
15. 1729–51 Frederick Louis, eldest son of GEORGE II, who was created Prince of Wales and Earl of Chester on 8 January 1729 and died in his father's lifetime on 20 March 1751.
16. 1751–60 George William Frederick, eldest son of the preceding, who was created Prince of Wales and Earl of Chester on 20

April 1751, succeeding his grandfather as GEORGE III on 25 October 1760.

17. 1762–1820 George Augustus Frederick, eldest son of George III, who was created Prince of Wales and Earl of Chester on 19 August 1762, succeeding his father as GEORGE IV on 29 January 1820.

18. 1841–1901 Albert Edward, eldest son of Queen VICTORIA, who was created Prince of Wales and Earl of Chester on 8 December 1841, succeeding his mother as EDWARD VII on 22 January 1901.

19. 1901–10 George Frederick Ernest Albert, second but only surviving son of Edward VII, who was created Prince of Wales and Earl of Chester on 9 November 1901, succeeding his father as GEORGE V on 6 May 1910.

20. 1910–36 Edward Albert Christian George Andrew Patrick David, eldest son of GEORGE V, who was created Prince of Wales and Earl of Chester on 23 June 1910 and invested at Caernarfon Castle on 13 July 1911, succeeding his father as EDWARD VIII on 20 January 1936.

21. 1958– CHARLES Philip Arthur George, eldest son of ELIZABETH II, who was created Prince of Wales and Earl of Chester on 26 July 1958 and invested at Caernarfon Castle on 1 July 1969.

Walkinshaw, Clementina (c.1720–1802) Mistress of Prince Charles Edward STUART ('Bonnie Prince Charlie'), who was the daughter of John Walkinshaw and Katherine Paterson and was born about 1720. Her father, a staunch Jacobite, named her after the bride of 'The Old Pretender'. Clementina was brought up in Rome and met Prince Charles Edward in Scotland in 1746, becoming his mistress soon thereafter. She joined him in Paris in 1752 and travelled about the continent with him under various aliases and generally passing as his wife. She gave birth to a daughter Charlotte (*see* ALBANY, CHARLOTTE, DUCHESS OF) at Liège in October 1753, and possibly also bore a son who died in infancy. She separated from the prince in 1760 because of his ill-treatment of her and received a pension from his father and later from his brother Prince Henry Benedict STUART, 'Cardinal of York'. When her daughter Charlotte joined her father in 1787 she acted as guardian to Charlotte's three illegitimate children by Ferdinand de Rohan. She used the title Countess d'Albestroff, but whether this was a legitimate title or not has never been established. In 1792 she settled in Switzerland and died at Freiburg on 27 November 1802, having survived her daughter by 13 years.

Waltham Abbey Abbey founded by Earl Harold Godwinsson in the reign of EDWARD THE CONFESSOR and consecrated in 1060. Harold, later King HAROLD II, was a generous benefactor of his foundation and according to tradition his body was taken there for burial after his death at the battle of HASTINGS in 1066. The abbey was partially destroyed in 1536.

Wantage The royal manor of the kings of WESSEX in Berkshire (now relocated in Oxfordshire), which is noted as the birthplace of ALFRED THE GREAT.

Warbeck, Perkin (1474–99) Pretender, of Flemish origin, who claimed to be Richard Duke of York, the son of EDWARD IV. He gained much support on the continent and was recognized as her nephew by MARGARET OF YORK, DUCHESS OF BURGUNDY. He was welcomed at Stirling by JAMES IV, KING OF SCOTS in November 1495 and received the hand of Lady Catherine Gordon in marriage. He proclaimed himself King Richard IV and after making several incursions into England, landed in Cornwall and advanced as far as Exeter, where he was captured in September 1497. He confessed his imposture at Taunton the following month and was conveyed to London where he was imprisoned in the Tower for two years. After an attempted escape he was hanged, drawn and quartered in November 1499.

Wessex A kingdom of the Saxon HEPTARCHY, which was founded by CERDIC, who became the first King of the West Saxons, or Wessex. It gradually expanded throughout the 6th and 7th centuries, until it covered most of southern England and in the reign of EGBERT (802–39) gained supremacy over NORTHUMBRIA and MERCIA. It reached its apogee under EDGAR, but after his death in 975 had to contend with a new wave of Danish invaders, who eventually usurped the throne.

Westminster Abbey The collegiate church of St Peter in Westminster, scene of all the coronations of English monarchs (with the exception of EDWARD V, JANE and EDWARD VIII) since 1066. According to tradition the first abbey church at Westminster was founded by Sebert, King of Essex, in 616 and miraculously consecrated overnight by St Peter himself. EDWARD THE CONFESSOR decided to refound the monastery in 1052 in redemption of his unfulfilled vow to make a pilgrimage to the Holy Land. The building was completed in 1065 and consecrated on Holy Innocents' Day, 28 December. By then Edward had fallen mortally ill and was probably unable to attend the ceremony, although some accounts say that he was carried to it on a litter. He died in January and was buried in his new foundation, his brother-in-law and successor HAROLD II being crowned there the same day, thus establishing the abbey as the coronation church of English kings. Edward was formally canonized in 1161.

In 1245 HENRY III, who had a great devotion to his predecessor, determined to rebuild the abbey on a much grander scale in early English Gothic style. The Confessor's body was translated to a new shrine behind the high altar, and when Henry died in 1272 he was buried nearby in what became known as the *Capella Regnum* (Chapel of the Kings) from the number of kings and queens buried there. Henry's rebuilding had come to a halt in 1265 when only the chancel, transepts and four bays of the nave had been completed, but work was renewed in the 14th century and the architect Henry Yevele completed it in the same style. HENRY VII rebuilt the Lady Chapel, which became better known as Henry VII's Chapel. He and his wife ELIZABETH OF YORK were both buried there in a magnificent Renaissance tomb designed by Pietro Torrigiano and the vaults beneath the chapel became the burial place for many of his successors and other members of the royal family until the death of GEORGE II in 1760, when it was superseded by St George's Chapel at WINDSOR CASTLE. During the English CIVIL WAR Cromwell showed his distaste for the monarchy and disrespect for the Church of England when he billeted his troops in the abbey.

The abbey was a Benedictine house, but the monks were expelled at the Dissolution of the Monasteries and after a short spell as the cathedral church of a bishopric, the abbey became the Collegiate Church of St Peter and a royal peculiar, which it has remained. The building was completed by the addition of two western towers designed by Nicholas Hawksmoor in 1745.

Besides members of the royal family, the abbey is also the resting place of many other notable people, including many of the most celebrated of the country's writers, who lie buried in Poets' Corner, and the 'Unknown Soldier', an unidentified body brought back from the battlefield of Flanders in the First World War. Items of interest kept within the abbey include the Coronation Chair, which incorporates the Stone of SCONE.

Westminster Hall Surviving remnant of the Palace of Westminster, which was begun by

CANUTE and much extended between 1095 and 1097 by WILLIAM RUFUS, who added the hall on a site adjacent to WESTMINSTER ABBEY. The hall was constructed on a scale hitherto unseen in England, though William boasted that it was 'but a bedchamber' to the palace he intended to build. The Palace of Westminster was a favourite residence of medieval kings, many of whom added to or embellished it. It became the meeting-place for PARLIAMENT and also the scene of state trials, including that of CHARLES I. Coronation processions were marshalled in the hall to proceed on foot on a raised walkway to the abbey and return after the crowning for the coronation banquet, which was last held at the coronation of GEORGE IV in 1821.

The hall, which survived the fire that destroyed most of Westminster Palace in 1834, was also used for the lying-in-state of GEORGE V, GEORGE VI, Queen MARY OF TECK and Sir Winston Churchill.

Wettin, House of The family to which Queen VICTORIA's consort Prince ALBERT belonged. The Wettins descended from one Burkhard, Count in the Grabfeld, who died in 908. His descendant Count Dedi I received grants of land from the Holy Roman Emperor Otto III in 997 and further territories were acquired by purchase, cession or marriage through the succeeding centuries. The family divided into two main branches, the Ernestine and the Albertine. The senior line obtained the dignity of Elector of Saxony but was forced to transfer it to the junior line after siding with the Protestant reformers at the Reformation, although the title of Duke of Saxony and many territories were retained. The duchy went into several divisions and its branches have provided Britain with a Princess of Wales (*see* AUGUSTA, PRINCESS OF WALES), a queen (ADELAIDE), a Duchess of Kent (VICTORIA) and a Prince Consort (ALBERT). The son of the last ascended the throne as EDWARD VII in 1901 and the House of Wettin or House of Saxony reigned in Great Britain until an outbreak of anti-German feeling engendered by the First World War induced GEORGE V to change the name of his 'House and Family' from Wettin to WINDSOR in 1917. Branches of the family have also provided rulers for Belgium, Bulgaria and Portugal.

Whitehall Palace The London residence of the archbishops of York on the north bank of the Thames just below Westminster, which was taken over by HENRY VIII after Cardinal

Wolsey's downfall. He changed its name from York Place to Whitehall and made it his principal London residence, employing Holbein to decorate his presence chamber with a mural depicting the triumph of the house of TUDOR and stocking his large wine cellar, which still remains beneath the Ministry of Defence. JAMES I employed Inigo Jones to build the Banqueting House between 1619 and 1622 and this building is now the only part of the palace still standing. CHARLES I was beheaded on a scaffold erected outside the Banqueting House, stepping directly onto it from a window. The palace continued as a royal residence under CHARLES II, JAMES II and WILLIAM III and MARY II, but two accidental fires in 1691 and 1698 (the second started by a careless Dutch laundry woman) destroyed the greater part of it and it was not rebuilt, KENSINGTON PALACE and HAMPTON COURT superseding it as favourite royal residences.

Wiglaf, King of Mercia (d.840) Of unknown origin, Wiglaf commenced his reign in 827, was driven out by EGBERT, KING OF WESSEX in 829, but recovered the kingdom in 830. He died in 840, leaving a son Wigmund, who married Elfleda, daughter of King CEOLWULF, and was the father of St Wistan and possibly of Eadburga, the mother-in-law of ALFRED THE GREAT. He was buried at Repton.

Wihtred, King of Kent (d.725) The son of King EGBERT I, he became king of Kent in the autumn of 690 according to BEDE, at first reigning jointly with Suaebhard until about 692. His reign followed a troubled period during which 'various alien kings and usurpers plundered the kingdom for a while'. Wihtred 'freed the nation from foreign invasion by his devotion and diligence'. He married three times, first to Cynegyth (mother of ETHELBERT II and EADBERT), secondly to Ethelburga, and thirdly to Werburga (mother of ALRIC), and died on 23 April 725, when he was succeeded by his three sons reigning jointly.

William, Prince[1] (1152–6) The eldest son of HENRY II and ELEANOR OF AQUITAINE, who was born in Normandy on 17 August 1152, just three months after his parents' marriage. He died at Wallingford Castle in Berkshire in about April 1156 and was buried at Reading Abbey.

William, Prince[2] (1256) The fifth son and eighth child of HENRY III and ELEANOR OF PROVENCE, who was born and died in about 1256. He was buried in the New Temple Church, London.

William I the Conqueror, King of England (1027/8–87) The first Norman king of England, who was the illegitimate son of Duke Robert the Devil or the Magnificent and was born at Falaise in 1027 or 1028. His father is said, in a romantically unlikely story, to have fallen in love with a young girl he saw washing clothes in a stream as he looked out from his castle at Falaise. He wooed her, installed her as his official mistress, and in due course she bore William and also probably a daughter. William's mother's name was HERLEVE, and her father, Fulbert, a citizen of Falaise, is usually described as a tanner, although opinions differ as to the exact rendering of his occupation, ranging from what we would now call an undertaker to furrier. Unions such as that between Duke Robert and Herleve had been by no means uncommon in the ducal House of Normandy. Its founder, Rollo the Ganger (reckoned as Duke Robert I from the name he received in Christian baptism) was succeeded by the son of one Popa, or Papie, the pagan wife or concubine he repudiated in order to marry the daughter of King Charles the Simple of France. When she died childless, Rollo resumed his relationship with Papie. Their son, Duke William Longsword, was also succeeded by the son of a concubine, Duke Richard the Fearless, who married his mistress Gunnor, the mother of all his children, after the death of his first wife. One of Gunnor's daughters was EMMA OF NORMANDY, who was twice queen of England. Gunnor's eldest son, Duke Richard the Good, was the first Duke of Normandy to be succeeded by undisputedly legitimate sons, first Duke Richard III, who reigned for just under a year, then Duke Robert II, William the Conqueror's father. The taint of bastardy, therefore, mattered very little where the ducal succession was concerned and it can hardly have had any psychological effect on William, as some have claimed.

William was only seven or eight years old when he succeeded to the duchy on the death of his father in 1035. His mother married Herluin de Conteville, a Norman noble, after her separation from Duke Robert and bore him two sons, who later, as Robert, Count of Mortain, and ODO, BISHOP OF BAYEUX and Earl of Kent, were to be among the staunchest supporters of their elder half-brother. William grew up under the protection of Alan, Count of Brittany,

Gilbert, Count of Brionne, and Osborn the Seneschal. All three fell victim to assassins. When William was still under 20 he defeated an attempt to wrest the duchy from his control by his cousin, Count Guy of Burgundy, and a faction of dissatisfied nobles.

In 1053 William made an advantageous marriage with MATILDA OF FLANDERS, the daughter of his neighbour, Count Baldwin of Flanders. There was some ecclesiastical objection to the marriage, which has never been satisfactorily unravelled, and it was not until 1059 that the Pope gave his approval. The couple expiated their 'sin' by founding two abbeys – the Abbaye-aux-Hommes (St Stephen's) and the Abbaye-aux-Dames (Holy Trinity) – at Caen. William and Matilda became devoted to each other and, in an age when marital infidelity was the norm, we hear of no mistresses, and the two bastards attributed to William can both be proved spurious.

William's marriage may well have been partly motivated by his growing ambition to gain the throne of England, for Matilda was a direct descendant of ALFRED THE GREAT. William had visited his first cousin once removed, EDWARD THE CONFESSOR, in 1051, when he had been well received and designated as Edward's successor. In 1064 fortune played into his hands when Harold, Earl of Wessex, was driven ashore on the coast of Ponthieu. He was received with great honour, but before sending him home William extracted an oath from him to uphold his claim to the English throne on the death of Edward.

Edward died and Harold was crowned king as HAROLD II in January 1066. William at once began careful preparations for an invasion. He was not hurried and, when he was ready to set sail in the late summer, was delayed further by an adverse wind. Harold, meanwhile, was forced to march north to deal with the Norwegian invasion and while he was away the wind changed and William landed with his troops at Pevensey on 28 September. He stumbled on leaping ashore, but allayed the fears of those of his supporters who saw this as an ill omen by holding aloft a handful of sand and shouting that he had already taken possession of his kingdom. William bided his time at HASTINGS and began constructing a castle there while waiting for Harold to arrive from the north. He may have thought that Harold would surrender easily, exhausted by his action against the Norwegians and his march south, but the battle, when it took place on 14 October, was hard fought, and after a full day's fighting ended only with Harold's death.

William marched to London with his victorious army, laying waste the land around the city until local resistance collapsed and the English nobles led by EDGAR ATHELING submitted to the Conqueror. On Christmas Day 1066 William was crowned at WESTMINSTER ABBEY by Aldred, Archbishop of York. The shouts of acclamation – in English as well as French – from the congregation inside the abbey alarmed the Norman guards stationed outside. Mistaking the noise for signs of an insurrection, they began a massacre of the Saxons living nearby, burning and pillaging their houses until the king himself appeared at the doorway of the abbey to quell the tumult.

Although the south and east of England quickly submitted to William's rule, over the next five years there were risings in various parts of the country. The south-west submitted in 1068, and the rebellion in the north of the Earls Edwin and Morcar was put down in person by William in 1069 and was followed by the 'harrowing of the north', a laying waste from York to Durham. A rising in the Isle of Ely led by Hereward the Wake was put down in 1071. During this period the Normans had to live like an army of occupation, building castles from which a few men could dominate the subject population.

Gradually during William's reign English lords were superseded by Norman and other French barons, and the continental system of feudal land tenure was introduced. In the Church, too, English bishops were replaced by continental prelates, and Lanfranc of Pavia, who was appointed Archbishop of Canterbury, reorganized the English Church on European lines. The Domesday Book, compiled by royal command in 1086, gave the king, as chief lord of this feudal system, an exact account of his power and resources for administrative purposes.

After 1071 William felt secure enough in England to turn again to his continental possessions, which were more vulnerable to attack than his island kingdom. His borders were continually threatened by his neighbours, the King of France and the Count of Anjou, who enlisted the support of William's disaffected eldest son ROBERT (III) CURTHOSE. The rest of William's reign was taken up with a series of intrigues by these enemies.

The French king's facetious remarks about William's excessive corpulence, enquiring when he expected to lie in, prompted him to threaten to 'set all France ablaze'. In 1087 the French garrison at Mantes made a raid into Normandy and William retaliated by sacking the town. As he was urging on his men, his horse stumbled on a hot cinder and he was flung violently against the high pommel of his saddle. He sustained grave internal injuries, probably a ruptured bladder, from which peritonitis ensued, and he died after much suffering at the Priory of St Gervais, near Rouen, on 8 September. He was succeeded by his son WILLIAM II.

William's burial in his foundation of St Stephen at Caen was fraught with incident. As the cortège neared the church, a citizen barred the way, claiming that it had been built on land illegally seized from his family and was appeased only by an on-the-spot payment of cash. On reaching the grave it was found that it had been made too small and the bearers, in attempting to force into it the already fast decomposing corpse burst it open so that a vile stench filled the church, causing all but the hardiest to flee, and the burial was completed by a handful of faithful retainers. The coffin was reburied in 1522 but was vandalized by Calvinists in 1562, leaving only William's thigh bone intact. This was thought to have been destroyed during the French Revolution, but it later was found in the old tomb and was reburied under a new tombstone in 1987.

The writer of the ANGLO-SAXON CHRONICLE, who knew William and at one time lived in his court, summed him up as 'a man of great wisdom and power, and surpassed in honour and in strength all those who had gone before him. Though stern beyond measure to those who opposed his will, he was kind to those good men who loved God ... He wore his royal crown three times a year as often as he was in England: at Easter at Winchester, at Whitsuntide at Westminster, at Christmas at Gloucester. On these occasions all the great men of England were assembled about him.' He was grasping and mendacious but a great ruler and far in advance of his times as a legislator.

William, who was about 60 at the time of his death, was a tall man of ruddy complexion, always inclined to corpulence and for most of his life probably clean-shaven. The only contemporary likenesses of him are in the BAYEUX TAPESTRY. Long popularly supposed to have been the work of Queen Matilda and her ladies, this is now believed to have been commissioned by William's half-brother, Odo, Bishop of Bayeux. The figures depicted in it are hardly portraits but do convey some idea of personality and appearance and, above all, costume.

William II Rufus, King of England (1056/60–1100) The third son of WILLIAM I and MATILDA OF FLANDERS, who was born in Normandy between 1056 and 1060. The death of his elder brother Richard, killed by a stag while hunting in the New Forest in about 1081, made him the Conqueror's second surviving son and his accession to the throne of England on his father's death in September 1087 shows that the principle of primogeniture had not yet been established. His eldest brother ROBERT (III) CURTHOSE, despite his rebellion against his father, inherited the Norman lands that his father had himself inherited, but William felt free to leave the land he had acquired by conquest to his favourite younger son, and Rufus was duly crowned at WESTMINSTER ABBEY on 26 September 1087.

Of the two, Rufus was probably the better choice for, despite his bad reputation, he did have some kingly qualities lacking in his brother. He was a good leader of men and a successful soldier. He resembled his father physically, his ruddy complexion and red hair earning him the sobriquet of 'Rufus', by which he is always known. However, whereas the Conqueror was always above reproach in his dealings, William Rufus exploited his position for his own benefit, and the extravagance of his court was in marked contrast to that of his father.

William's reputation has suffered because the Church – which kept most of the records of the time – disapproved of his lifestyle and the way in which he delayed the appointment of bishops and abbots in order to help himself to church revenues (the fact that he blasphemed with almost every sentence was also unlikely to impress the pious). Chroniclers write of William's debaucheries as being 'hateful to God and man', without being too specific. The implication is that he was a homosexual, and William of Malmesbury states that it was the fashion in William's court for young men to 'rival women in delicacy of person, to mince their gait, to walk with loose gestures and half naked'. William never married and there is no indication that he was ever interested in women.

For several years after his accession William campaigned in Normandy, alternately supporting his brother against the king of France and opposing him for the control of Normandy. This was one of William's primary concerns, for while England and Normandy were under separate rule, the barons who held land in both places found it well-nigh impossible to serve two lords. If they supported William, then his brother might deprive them of their Norman lands; if they supported Robert, then they were in danger of losing their English estates. The problem was temporarily solved when Robert decided to join the First Crusade and, in order to finance the expedition, pledged Normandy to William for 10,000 marks.

There is no doubt that William was unpopular, especially because of his treatment of the saintly Anselm, whom he had appointed Archbishop of Canterbury in a moment of panic in 1093 when he thought he was dying. William's opposition to the archbishop's attempts to reform the Church forced Anselm to leave the country, whereupon the king took over the revenues of the archbishopric. 'He was very harsh and fierce in his rule over his realm,' records the ANGLO-SAXON CHRONICLE, '... everything that was hateful to God and to righteous man was the daily practice in this land during his reign. Therefore he was hated by almost all his people and abhorrent to God.'

William's death in the New Forest has become the subject of much speculation, and there were certainly many mysterious and inexplicable circumstances surrounding it. On 2 August 1100 he rode out from Winchester on a hunting expedition accompanied by his younger brother Henry and several nobles and knights. According to most accounts, the king went in pursuit of a stag followed by Walter Tirel, a knight. The king shot an arrow at the stag but missed and called out to Walter to shoot, which he did, accidentally killing the king. This was the widely accepted version and, if true, could have been told only by Tirel, who later denied that he was present. Nobody was ever held to blame, so unloved was Rufus.

William's body was left in charge of a handful of peasants. They loaded it on to a farm cart and the next morning it arrived at Winchester Cathedral 'with blood dripping from it the whole way', according to William of Malmesbury. There it was interred with little ceremony (the clergy denying it religious rites) in the crossing under the tower, the collapse of which in the following year caused many heads to nod sagely, though the matter-of-fact William of Malmesbury adds 'it would have collapsed in any case ...

because it was badly built'. The spot where the fatal arrow struck the king is now marked by a memorial stone.

On a more positive note, William had started to rebuild the Palace of Westminster, and WESTMINSTER HALL was completed in his lifetime. When visitors exclaimed on its size he was wont to boast that it was 'but a bedchamber' to the palace he intended to build.

William III, King of England (1650–1702) The only child of William II, Prince of Orange, Stadhouder of the United Provinces of the Netherlands, and his wife MARY, PRINCESS ROYAL, the eldest daughter of CHARLES I, who was born at the Old Palace of the Counts of Holland at The Hague on 4 November 1650, eight days after the death of his father, and was named William Henry. He was educated at Leyden and at the age of 17 was admitted to the Council of State of the Dutch Provinces. He paid his first visit to England in 1670, meeting the eight-year-old cousin who was later to become his wife. Returning to the Netherlands he was appointed Captain General of the Dutch Forces and a little later Stadhouder of the United Provinces of the Netherlands, an office that had practically become hereditary in his family.

William returned to England and was married to Mary at ST JAMES'S PALACE on 4 November 1677. He was a most unprepossessing individual, undersized, asthmatic, hook-nosed and with a penchant for the society of young men, similar to that of his great grandfather JAMES I. The statuesque Mary towered above him. She was a handsome, though not pretty, woman inclined to plumpness, although never reaching the proportions of her sister ANNE. If the couple were ill matched physically, they were ideally suited in other ways, and William adored his rather formidable wife. There were no children, although Mary appears to have miscarried at least twice during her residence in Holland.

In 1688, following the birth of a son to JAMES II, William was invited by seven Whig peers to deliver England from the threat of 'Popery', and he landed at Brixham on 5 November 1688 and commenced to march on London, gathering many supporters on the way. James panicked and attempted to flee the country on 11 December, but although he was apprehended and brought back as far as Faversham, he was allowed to make his way to the continent a few days later. Parliament met on

28 January 1689 and declared that James had abdicated the throne on the day of his flight. William refused to accept the crown by right of conquest, yet was unwilling to play second fiddle to his wife, fond of her though he was. The solution was to offer the throne to William and Mary jointly. They were proclaimed king and queen on 13 February and crowned at WESTMINSTER ABBEY on 11 April 1689. A duplicate coronation chair and a duplicate set of regalia for Mary had to be hastily provided for the ceremony. To his everlasting credit, Archbishop Sancroft, who had crowned James II, declined to officiate in spite of having been one of the 'Seven Bishops' tried for seditious libel the year before, and the ceremony was performed by Henry Compton, Bishop of London.

The Bill of Rights was passed by Parliament to define the rights of the new king and queen and the Mutiny Act made Parliament supreme. James II landed in Ireland with a French force in an attempt to regain his throne, but was defeated by William at the battle of the Boyne on 1 July 1690, which was followed by the treaty of Limerick in 1691. William became a hero to the Irish Protestants, who referred to him affectionately as 'King Billy'. The Stuart cause in Scotland was effectively ruined after the death of Dundee, who had won the battle of Killiecrankie for James in 1689, but William's success there was marred by the terrible massacre of Glencoe in 1692. The English naval victory of La Hogue on 19 May 1692 put paid to all chance of direct aid to James from France. On the continent, however, the French armies were successful, and in August 1692 William was defeated at Steinkirk and later at Landen. He managed to retake Namur in 1695, but was unable to win a decisive victory over the French, and in 1697 England, France, Holland and Spain agreed the peace of Ryswick.

Mary died of smallpox on 28 December 1694 and William had a succession of fainting fits on receiving the news of her death. He continued to reign alone for the remainder of his life and from 1697 to 1700 was occupied with the question of the Spanish Succession, although war did not break out until after his death. Another great blow to him was the death of the little Duke of Gloucester (*see* GLOUCESTER, WILLIAM HENRY, DUKE OF[1]), the only surviving child of his sister-in-law Princess Anne in July 1700.

William was never popular with his English subjects, who found him too cold and serious. He was opposed by Parliament during his later years and was obliged to cancel his grants of land in Ireland to his Dutch favourites, Keppel and Bentinck. The ACT OF SETTLEMENT, passed in 1701, secured the Protestant succession to the throne after Mary's sister, Anne, and further curtailed royal power. William's reign marked the transition from personal government, as exercised by the Stuarts, to parliamentary government, which was to come into full flower under the Hanoverians.

In February 1702 William was riding at Hampton Court when his horse Sorrel stumbled on a mole hill and threw him, breaking his collar bone. After it had been set, he insisted on returning to KENSINGTON PALACE by coach, which aggravated his condition. He became feverish some days later and was put to bed but died of pleuro-pneumonia a few days later on 8 March 1702. He was buried in Westminster Abbey. The Jacobites toasted the 'little gentleman in black velvet' (the mole) who had brought about the death of their enemy.

William IV, King of Great Britain
(1765–1837) The third son of GEORGE III and Queen CHARLOTTE, who was born at Buckingham House, St James's Park, on 21 August 1765 and baptized William Henry in the Great Council Chamber at ST JAMES'S PALACE on 18 September, his godparents being his uncles William Henry, Duke of GLOUCESTER and Prince Henry Frederick (later Duke of CUMBERLAND) and his aunt AUGUSTA, DUCHESS OF BRUNSWICK. As the third son of George III and Queen Charlotte, there seemed little likelihood that Prince William Henry would ever be more than a royal duke. The fast-filling royal nursery was a lively place and the three noisy little boys must have been very trying; a nursemaid had to be dismissed for losing her temper with Prince William and banging his head against the wall.

As his immediate elder brother Prince Frederick was destined for an army career, so William's future was to be a naval one. He went to sea at the age of 14, serving under Captain (later Admiral) Robert Digby on board the *Prince George*, a 98–gun ship, as an ordinary able seaman at the relief of Gibraltar in 1779. In the following year he became a midshipman but, on his father's orders, received no privileges and was treated in every respect the same as his fellows. He was present with Admiral

Rodney at Cape St Vincent and was stationed in the West Indies and off Nova Scotia. He later transferred to HMS *Warwick* under the command of Captain Elphinstone (later Admiral Viscount Keith) with whom he saw action off the Delaware in 1782. He next joined Lord Hood in quest of the French fleet and became friendly with Nelson. Lord Hood's squadron returned to England in June 1783, and in the summer of 1785 the prince was appointed third lieutenant of the frigate *Hebe*. In 1786, as Captain of the *Pegasus* (28 guns), he sailed for Nova Scotia and thence to the Leeward Islands station, where he remained for several months under Nelson's command. The friendship between the two deepened, and on 22 March 1787 Prince William undertook the pleasant duty of giving away the bride when Nelson married Mrs Frances Nisbet, a doctor's widow.

The following December the prince returned to England and was appointed to command the frigate *Andromeda*, in which he returned for a short time to the West Indies. Fanny Burney gives a delightful account of him at this time, describing a visit he made to his sisters when he got rather drunk on champagne and told Queen Charlotte's formidable waiting woman, Mrs Schwellenberg, 'hold your potato jaw, my dear', when she remonstrated with him about his louche conduct.

Prince William had received the Order of the GARTER in 1782. On 20 May 1789 he was created Duke of Clarence and St Andrews and Earl of Munster by his father and subsequently took his seat in the House of Lords. The following year he was appointed Rear Admiral of the Blue and commanded HMS *Valiant* in home waters. He was to see no more active service afloat.

It was about this time that William formed a deep attachment for the actress Dorothea Bland, known professionally as 'Mrs Jordan' (*see* JORDAN, DOROTHEA). Over the next 20 years she had 10 children by him, whom he acknowledged and ennobled after his accession to the throne. They bore the surname FITZCLARENCE and the eldest boy was eventually created Earl of Munster.

In 1811 William, who had been promoted to Vice-Admiral in 1799, became Admiral of the Fleet in succession to Sir Peter Parker, and in that capacity hoisted his flag for the last time to escort Louis XVIII back to France and to receive the Emperor Alexander I of Russia and King Friedrich Wilhelm III of Prussia on board HMS *Impregnable*.

His happy life with Mrs Jordan ended abruptly in 1811 for reasons that have never been clear. Dorothea certainly had what would today be described as a 'drink problem', and this may well have been a contributory factor. She received an annual allowance of £4,000 for the maintenance of herself and her daughters, with the proviso that, should she resume her stage career, the cost of the care of the four youngest daughters and £15,000 allowed for them should revert to the duke. The shock of the separation was a great blow to Dorothea and, after an unsuccessful attempt to make a comeback on the stage, she went to France, where she suffered a complete physical and mental breakdown and died in a state of abject misery at St Cloud in July 1816. William's behaviour in this matter seems little in keeping with his kindly and generous nature, although it was the sort of conduct that might have been expected from almost any of his brothers.

In November 1817 the untimely death of Princess Charlotte plunged the nation into mourning and prompted the ageing progeny of George III into a frantic scramble to find brides and beget heirs to the throne. The Prince Regent was still married to his unloved and now childless Caroline and the Duke of York to his unloved and childless Frederica, so William at 52 and the unmarried father of 10 children, suddenly became one of the most eligible bachelors in Europe. For a time he assiduously courted an English heiress, Miss Sophia Elizabeth Wykeham, of Thame Park, Oxfordshire, but the regent would not give his consent to the marriage. His eventual choice of bride was a happy one for both himself and the nation and, although the object – to provide an heir – was sadly unfulfilled, Britain gained one of the most sympathetic queens ever to wear the crown (*see* ADELAIDE, QUEEN). William fell touchingly in love with his young wife, who was less than three years older than his eldest daughter, and she became devoted to him and, strangely, to her illegitimate stepchildren.

The death of George III made William second in line to the throne, and on the death of the Duke of York in 1827 he became heir presumptive and received a parliamentary grant raising his income to £40,000 a year. He was also appointed Lord High Admiral of England, a post specially revived for him, but resigned the office after the Duke of

Wellington raised objections to the expenses of William's progresses.

On 26 June 1830 GEORGE IV died and William became king. He wished at first to reign as Henry IX, but after it was pointed out to him that this style had been adopted by the Jacobite Cardinal Duke of York, who had died as recently as 1807, he agreed to become William IV. The coronation was subjected to so many government economies that it soon became lampooned and caricatured as the 'half-crownation'. The traditional processions on the raised footway from WESTMINSTER HALL to the Abbey and back again were abolished, as also was the coronation banquet with the challenge by the KING'S CHAMPION, never to be revived again. Queen Adelaide was obliged to provide the jewels for her own crown and other jewels had to be hired. Nevertheless, the coronation took place on 8 September 1831, almost exactly 70 years after that of the king's parents, the last king and queen to be crowned together.

William had become a garrulous old man, given to impetuous outbursts, yet he possessed some shrewd, statesmanlike instincts. The political position was fraught with difficulties. Wellington's administration was followed by that of Earl Grey, who brought in the Reform Bill. After its first rejection by the House of Lords, the king resolutely refused to create new peers to form a Whig majority but sent round a circular letter to the Tory peers, as a result of which 100 of them abstained from voting so that the Bill became law.

The king's personal tastes were simple and he retained many of the ways and habits of an old serving officer. He could not have been a more complete contrast to his brother and predecessor, and it was said of him that 'he would not know a picture from a window-shutter'. However, he did found the Royal Library at Windsor, not because he was a bibliophile, but because he felt the castle should have one, most of George III's books having gone to form the nucleus of what is now the National Library. From time to time the newspapers published rumours that the queen was pregnant, dismissed by the king, perhaps a little regretfully, as 'stuff and nonsense'. His heiress presumptive was his niece VICTORIA, the only child of the Duke of KENT (see KENT, EDWARD, DUKE OF). The king was fond of her but loathed her mother, the Duchess of Kent, whom he publicly insulted in a speech he made in August 1836 at a dinner to celebrate his 71st birthday. He replied after his health had been drunk by saying:

> I trust in God that my life may be spared for nine months longer, after which period, in the event of my death, no regency would take place. I should then have the satisfaction of leaving the royal authority to the personal exercise of that young lady [pointing to the Princess Victoria], the Heiress Presumptive of the Crown, and not in the hands of a person now near me, who is surrounded by evil advisers and who is herself incompetent to act with propriety in the station in which she would be placed. I have no hesitation in saying that I have been insulted – grossly and continually insulted – by that person, but I am now determined to endure no longer a course of behaviour so disrespectful to me. Among many other things I have particularly to complain of the manner in which that young lady has been kept away from my court: she has been repeatedly kept from my drawing rooms at which she ought always to have been present, but I am fully resolved that this shall not happen again. I would have her know that I am king, and that I am determined to make my authority respected, and for the future I shall insist and command that the Princess do upon all occasions appear at my court, as is her duty to do.

Consternation followed this outburst and it was only with the greatest difficulty that the Duchess of Kent was dissuaded from immediately ordering her carriage. The king's wish that his life might be spared for another nine months was granted.

In May 1837 William was reported to be suffering from asthma or hay fever. In a day or two pneumonia ensued and he died peacefully at 2.15 in the morning of 20 June 1837. A detailed description of the postmortem findings was published in *The Lancet* and revealed cirrhosis of the liver and heart disease as contributory causes of death. He was buried in the Royal Tomb House at Windsor.

Lord Grey gave an eloquent summing-up of William's character:

> A man more sincerely devoted to the interests of his country, and better understanding what was necessary for the attainment of that object, there never did exist; and if ever there was a sovereign entitled to the character, His Majesty may truly be styled a Patriot King.

William Augustus, Duke of Cumberland
see CUMBERLAND, PRINCE WILLIAM AUGUSTUS, DUKE OF.

William 'Clito', Count of Flanders
(1101–28) The elder son of ROBERT (III) CURTHOSE, DUKE OF NORMANDY (the eldest son of WILLIAM I THE CONQUEROR) and Sybilla of Conversano, who was born probably at Rouen in Normandy in 1101. In 1123 he married, or perhaps was only affianced

to, Sybilla, younger daughter of Fulk (Foulques) V, Count of Anjou and Maine (later King of Jerusalem) and his first wife Heremburge, daughter and heiress of Hélie I, Count of Maine. The marriage or betrothal was set aside the following year on the grounds of consanguinity. Sybilla, who was born in 1112, married in 1134, Thierry of Alsace, Count of Flanders, and died a nun in the Abbey of St Lazarus at Bethlehem in 1165. In the spring of 1127 William received the county of Flanders from Louis VI, King of France, and in January 1128 he married Joan (Giovanna), the half-sister of Queen Adelaide of France, who negotiated the match, being the daughter of Ranieri, Marquis of Montferrat, and his wife Gisla (Gisèle), widow of Umberto II, Count of Savoy and Maurienne, and daughter of Guillaume I, Count of Burgundy. In July 1128 William was wounded in a sortie at Alost and died five days later at the Abbey of St Bertin in St Omer on 27 July 1128. He was buried there. He left no children and the subsequent history of his widow is unknown.

William Frederick, Duke of Gloucester *see* GLOUCESTER, WILLIAM FREDERICK, DUKE OF.

William Henry, Duke of Gloucester *see* GLOUCESTER, WILLIAM HENRY, DUKE OF.

William of Blois, Count of Boulogne (c.1134–59) The third and youngest son and fourth child of King STEPHEN and MATILDA OF BOULOGNE, who was born about 1134. In about 1149 he married the 12-year-old Isabel, daughter and heiress of William de Warrenne, 3rd Earl of Warrenne and Surrey, and his wife Ela de Belesme. On the death of his elder brother EUSTACE IV in August 1153, William succeeded him in their mother's county of Boulogne. On the death of Stephen in the following October, he made no attempt to oppose the accession of HENRY II and accepted a knighthood from him. He is said by some authorities to have been killed at the siege of Toulouse on 11 October 1159, although others date his death as occurring in August 1160. He had no issue, and his widow married Hameline Plantagenet, natural son of Geoffrey, Count of Anjou, and consequently half-brother of Henry II. She had one son and three daughters by him and died on 13 July 1199, being buried in the chapter house of Lewes Priory, Sussex.

William of Hatfield, Prince (1337) The second son and fourth child of EDWARD III and PHILIPPA OF HAINAULT, who was born at Hatfield, Hertfordshire, before 16 February 1337 (the date of his mother's 'uprising'). He died on 3 July 1337 and was buried in York Minster.

William of Wales, Prince (1982–) The elder son of CHARLES, PRINCE OF WALES and DIANA, PRINCESS OF WALES, who was born at St Mary's Hospital, Paddington, on 21 June 1982 and baptized at Buckingham Palace on 4 August 1982 (the 82nd birthday of his great-grandmother Queen ELIZABETH THE QUEEN MOTHER) by the names William Arthur Philip Louis. Prince William, who is second in line to the throne, is being educated at Eton.

William of Windsor, Prince (1348) The sixth son and eleventh child of EDWARD III and PHILIPPA OF HAINAULT, who was born at WINDSOR CASTLE before 24 June 1348 (the date of his mother's 'uprising'). He was buried in St Edmund's Chapel, WESTMINSTER ABBEY, on 5 September 1348.

William 'the Atheling', Duke of Normandy (1102–20) The only son of HENRY I and his first wife MATILDA OF SCOTLAND, who was born at Winchester almost certainly in 1102 and was possibly a twin with his sister Matilda (*see* MATILDA, 'LADY OF THE ENGLISH', EMPRESS). He was acknowledged as his father's successor and was apparently completely indulged by him, growing up a wayward and strong-willed youth. In June 1119 he was married at Lisieux to Matilda (formerly called Alice, according to some), the elder daughter of Fulk (Foulques) V, Count of Anjou and Maine, and having had the duchy of Normandy bestowed on him by his father went there to be invested by Louis VI of France and to receive the homage of the Norman barons. He was accompanied by his father, his wife, and a large company, including several of his half-siblings, Henry I's natural offspring. At the Norman port of Barfleur, the custom of the party was solicited by the owner of a newly built ship, the *Blanche Nef* (the *White Ship*), who guaranteed a swift and safe passage. King Henry declined the offer, preferring to travel in his own ship, which he boarded with his daughter-in-law, but the impetuous William, probably already half-inebriated, chose to board the *Blanche Nef*, doubtless hoping to race his father across the Channel. He was accompanied by his half-brother Richard and many companions of both sexes. They had barely set sail on 25 November 1120 when the ship (allegedly steered by a drunken helmsman) struck a rock and was completely wrecked. The only survivor was a butcher of Rouen named Berold. King Henry was said to have been so affected by the loss of his son and heir that he never smiled again. William's widow, who was only about 13, never married again. She became a nun at Fontevraud and died as its abbess in 1154.

William 'the Lion', King of Scots (1143–1214) The second son of HENRY OF SCOTLAND, EARL OF HUNTINGDON and his wife ADA, COUNTESS OF HUNTINGDON, who was born in 1143, and following his father's death in 1152, was assigned the earldom of Northumberland by his grandfather DAVID I. On David's death in May of the following year, William became HEIR PRESUMPTIVE to his brother MALCOLM IV and succeeded him on his death on 9 December 1165. He was consecrated king at SCONE by Richard, Bishop of St Andrews, on 24 December 1165.

Malcolm IV had been compelled to surrender Northumberland, Cumberland and Westmorland to HENRY II of England and to acknowledge him as overlord. In 1173 William was won over to espouse the cause of the rebellious English barons by the offer of the return of Northumberland. He invaded England but was taken prisoner at Alnwick by the sheriff of York on 13 July 1174. By the Treaty of Falaise on 8 December 1174 he was obliged to acknowledge Henry II as his overlord and to surrender the castles of Edinburgh, Stirling, Roxburgh, Jedburgh and Berwick as security. He was released on 2 February 1175 and allowed to return to Scotland. In 1178 he founded Arbroath Abbey in memory of Thomas à Becket. Henry II restored the earldom of Huntingdon to William in 1185 and he resigned it to his younger brother David.

On 5 September 1186 at Woodstock, Oxfordshire, William married ERMENGARDE DE BEAUMONT, daughter of Richard, Viscount de Beaumont (son of Roscelin, Viscount de Beaumont, by his wife Constance, a natural daughter of HENRY I, KING OF ENGLAND), and she bore him one son and three daughters. William also had a number of illegitimate children, at least two sons and four daughters, from whom five of the competitors for the crown of Scotland in 1291 were descended (*see* SCOTTISH SUCCESSION). Scotland's independence was restored on payment of 10,000 marks by quit claim of RICHARD I at Canterbury

on 5 December 1189, and the castles of Roxburgh and Berwick were restored at the same time.

William lived to what was, for those days, the remarkable age of 70 or 71 and died at Stirling on 4 December 1214. He was buried in his foundation of Arbroath Abbey. Queen Ermengarde, who was considerably his junior, survived until 11 February 1234 and was buried at Balmerino Abbey in Fife.

Windsor, Duke and Duchess of *see* EDWARD VIII.

Windsor, House of The designation of the royal family since 17 July 1917, when it was adopted by GEORGE V for himself and his descendants by an Order in Council. The change was occasioned by the anti-German fever, almost amounting to hysteria, that swept the country in the middle of the First World War. The king's cousin and enemy, the German Emperor Wilhelm II, received the news of the change with amusement and sarcastically promised that he would arrange for a performance of 'The Merry Wives of Saxe-Coburg' to be staged at his court theatre. ELIZABETH II, at the beginning of her reign, confirmed that the dynasty would continue to be known as the House and Family of Windsor, but this was slightly modified on 8 February 1960 by the announcement that the third generation of her male line descendants should bear the surname MOUNTBATTEN-Windsor.

Windsor Castle The home of the royal family at Windsor, Berkshire. The first castle at Windsor was built by WILLIAM I THE CONQUEROR as one of a chain of castles to control the Thames Valley and the outskirts of London. It was an earth and timber construction on a hill above the site of an old Saxon palace. HENRY II replaced the wooden structure with the Round Tower and began work on a ring of stone buildings. The walls were completed under HENRY III, who also added the D-shaped towers that remain to this day. EDWARD III embarked on an extensive building programme with the help of William of Wykeham and made St George's Chapel in the castle the chapel of his new Order of the GARTER. The chapel was completely rebuilt by EDWARD IV in the perpendicular style made popular by his predecessor HENRY VI and was added to by HENRY VII and HENRY VIII. It has been the burial place of many kings and queens and also the scene of several royal weddings. The ALBERT MEMORIAL CHAPEL at the east end of St George's was originally built by

Henry VII, who intended that Henry VI should be buried there, but this plan never materialized, and it was restored by Queen VICTORIA in memory of Prince ALBERT, although he was not buried there. The latest addition to St George's has been the small memorial chapel containing the tomb of GEORGE VI.

The castle has been in continual use as a residence of English sovereigns. GEORGE IV employed James Wyatt and his nephew Jeffry Wyatville to make embellishments in the Gothic style. When the latter begged leave of the king to assume the name of Wyatville in lieu of Wyatt to distinguish him from the other architects in his family, George is said to have replied: 'Veal or mutton, call yourself what you like.' It was from Windsor that EDWARD VIII broadcast his famous abdication speech in 1936 (see ABDICATION CRISIS).

In 1993 the state apartments of the castle were seriously damaged by fire, but extensive restoration work has since been carried out. The state apartments, St George's Chapel and the home park are open to the public. The park, once a popular hunting ground for English monarchs, is said to be haunted by Herne the Hunter, a spectral rider with a pack of ghostly hounds who is traditionally supposed to be the reincarnation of the one-time keeper of the park, who was either hanged from 'Herne's Oak' on charges of sorcery by order of Henry VIII or who saved the life of RICHARD II when he was attacked by a wounded stag, was rewarded with the post of head keeper, but later hanged himself when his knowledge of hunting deserted him due to the malicious magic of rival keepers (sightings of Herne have been reported as recently as 1964).

Windsor Uniform A form of evening dress for men originally introduced by GEORGE III in 1777and worn by members of the royal family. The king chose its colours of dark blue with red collars and cuffs and gilt buttons bearing the royal cipher, which, with a few modifications, has continued to the present day.

Witenagemot The great council of the Anglo-Saxons, consisting of bishops, ealdormen of the shires, and others who were called together to advise the king and give approval to grants of land, the imposition of taxes and other matters. It also exercised judicial powers, although it was of little effect if the king chose not to accept its advice. It is generally regarded as the forerunner of PARLIAMENT.

Woden Mythical god-king who was claimed as a common ancestor by all the Anglo-Saxon dynasties. His name is derived from a Sanskrit root meaning 'to blow' and he was originally a supreme spirit or wind-god circulating everywhere. He was attended by two ravens who perched on his shoulder nightly and told him the news they had gathered during their daily flights. The maintenance of ravens in the TOWER OF LONDON may be a cult memory of this. His wife was Frigg, or Freya, and the ANGLO-SAXON CHRONICLE names seven sons as ancestors of the various dynasties. In Scandinavian myth his name became Odin.

Woman of the Bedchamber see LADY IN WAITING.

Woodville, Elizabeth see ELIZABETH WOODVILLE, QUEEN OF ENGLAND.

Wuffa, King of East Anglia (d.578) The first king of EAST ANGLIA, according to Florence of Worcester and Roger of Wendover, who dates his accession to 571. He was eighth in descent from WODEN according to the genealogies, and the East Anglian dynasty became known as the Wuffingas after him. According to Roger he died in about 578 and was succeeded by his son TYTILA.

Wulfhere, King of Mercia (d.674) The second son of PENDA, KING OF MERCIA, who restored Mercian independence in 657 after the kingdom had been ruled for three years by OSWY, KING OF NORTHUMBRIA. Wulfhere became a Christian and married Eormengild, a daughter of EARCONBERT, King of Kent, and his wife SEXBURGA, daughter of ANNA, KING OF EAST ANGLIA. Their children were COENRED, who became king of Mercia in 704, Behrtwald, and St Werburg, abbess of Ely, who died in about 700. Wulfhere died in 674 and was succeeded by his brother ETHELRED.

X,Y,Z

Xit The court dwarf of EDWARD VI, to whom he was in constant attendance. He figures largely as a character in Harrison Ainsworth's novel *The Tower of London*.

Yarmouth, Amalie Sophie Marianne von Wallmoden, Countess of (1704–65) Mistress of GEORGE II, who was the daughter of Johann Franz Dietrich von Wendt, a General in the Hanoverian service, and his wife Friederike Charlotte von dem Bussche and was born in Hanover on 1 April 1704. After the death of Queen CAROLINE in 1737, George brought her to England and installed her in ST JAMES'S PALACE, probably mindful of his promise to the queen that he would never remarry but only take mistresses. Madame de Wallmoden was granted an annuity of £3,000 for 31 years on the Irish List on 24 June 1738. At this time she was described as having 'fine black eyes, and brown hair, and very well shap'd; not tall, nor low, has no fine features, but very agreeable in the main'. Her husband, who had accompanied her to England, divorced her in 1739, and after being naturalized by Act of Parliament in February, she was created Baroness Yarmouth and Countess of Yarmouth for life on 24 March 1740. Horace Walpole said that she was 'inoffensive, and attentive only to pleasing [the king], and to selling peerages whenever she had an opportunity'. In spite of this somewhat dubious procedure, she appears to have been generally popular and made no enemies.

She returned to Hanover after the king's death in 1760 and died there on 19 October 1765. Her youngest child, Count Johann Ludwig von Wallmoden-Gimborn, born in Hanover on 22 April 1736, was almost certainly the king's, although he was never acknowledged as such either publicly or privately. He had a fairly distinguished career in the Hanoverian service and died on 10 October 1811. He has many descendants.

Yolande of Dreux, Queen of Scots (d.1322) The second consort of ALEXANDER III, KING OF SCOTS, who was the daughter of Robert IV, Count of Dreux, and his wife Beatrix de Montfort. She was married to Alexander at Jedburgh on 14 October 1285. He was accidentally killed five months later in March 1286, and in May 1292 Yolande (or Joleta, as her name is sometimes rendered) became the second wife of Arthur II, Duke of Brittany, to whom she bore one son and five daughters. She became a widow again on 27 August 1312 and died in 1322.

York, Cardinal *see* STUART, PRINCE HENRY BENEDICT, 'CARDINAL OF YORK'.

York, Dukes of The dukes of this name are here dealt with chronologically.

1. **Edmund of Langley, Duke of York** (1341–1402) The fifth son and seventh child of EDWARD III and PHILIPPA OF HAINAULT, who was born at King's Langley, Hertfordshire, on 5 June 1341 and baptized there by Michael, Abbot of St Albans, who was also his godfather with the Earls of Surrey and Arundel. He remained in his mother's guardianship until September 1354. In 1359–60 he participated in his father's French campaign and was a witness to the Treaty of Bretigny on 24 October 1360. He was nominated a Knight of the GARTER in 1361 and created Earl of Cambridge on 13 November 1362.

In the course of the next 10 years he took part with his brothers in various campaigns in France. He returned to England in 1371, and on or about 1 March 1372 he was married, probably at Hertford, to Isabel, younger surviving daughter and co-heiress of Pedro, King of Castile and Leon, by his mistress (or as he claimed, wife) Maria de Padilla. Edmund took part in further campaigns in France and served as Constable of Dover Castle and Warden of the Cinque Ports from June 1376 to February 1381. On 25 May 1377 he and his wife were granted FOTHERINGAY CASTLE in Northamptonshire and Anstey Castle in Hertfordshire. He was appointed chief commissioner for the defence of the Kentish coast on 30 June

1377, and at the coronation of his nephew RICHARD II on 16 July that year, he bore the sceptre with the dove. He was a chief commissioner to treat with the Bohemian envoys concerning the king's marriage in 1381 and commanded the English troops sent to Portugal against the Spaniards later in the same year, but met with little success. In 1385 he accompanied the king to Scotland and on 6 August was created Duke of York, being invested in Parliament at Westminster on 20 October. He received a grant of £1,000 a year for the support of the dukedom.

The Duchess of York, who was born at Morales or Tordesillas in about 1355, died on 23 December 1392 and was buried in the church of the Mendicant Friars (Dominicans) at King's Langley. She had borne him two sons and one daughter. Edmund married secondly, before 4 November 1393, Joan, daughter of Thomas de Holand, 2nd Earl of Kent (half-brother of Richard II), and his wife Alice, daughter of Richard FitzAlan, Earl of Arundel. There were no children of this marriage.

In 1399 Edmund acted as regent while the king was in Ireland and was prepared to oppose the landing of his nephew Henry of Bolingbroke (later HENRY IV), but he made peace with the usurper on 27 July and the new king appointed him a Privy Councillor and made him master of the royal mews and falcons with a grant of the lordship of the Isle of Axholme, Lincolnshire, on 10 October 1399.

Edmund died at his birthplace, King's Langley, on 1 August 1402, and was buried with his first wife. Their splendid armorial tomb, topped with black marble, was moved to the parish church in about 1575 and again re-sited in 1877. The duke's widow, who was born about 1380, remarried three times (to the 5th Baron Willoughby de Eresby, the 3rd Baron Scrope of Masham, and the 1st Baron Vesey) and died without issue on 12 April 1434.

2. **Edward of York, 2nd Duke of York** (1373–1415) The elder son of Edmund of Langley, Duke of York (*see above*), and his first wife Isabel of Castile, who was born in 1373 (on 25 March according to one authority). He was knighted at the age of four on the occasion of the coronation of his cousin RICHARD II in July 1377, was nominated a Knight of the GARTER in 1387 and was created Earl of Rutland on 25 February 1390. He served as Admiral of the North and West from 1391 to 1398, as Constable of the

TOWER OF LONDON in 1392, 1397–9 and 1406, as joint ambassador to France in 1395, as Constable of Dover Castle and Lord Warden of the Cinque Ports in 1396–8, as Governor of the Channel Islands in 1396, as Lord of the Isle of Wight and Governor of Carisbrooke Castle in 1397, as Constable of England 1398–9 and as joint ambassador to Scotland in 1399.

On 29 September 1397 he was created Duke of Albemarle, but he was deprived of the dukedom on 6 October 1399. He was Lieutenant of the Duchy of Aquitaine from 1400 to 1413 and Warden and Governor of North Wales in 1401. He succeeded his father as Duke of York in 1402, and in 1411 was joint founder of the Collegiate Church at Fotheringay. He was appointed Warden and Commissary-General of the East Marches towards Scotland and Captain of the Castle and Town of Berwick in 1414 and Constable and Marshal of the King's Army in France in September.

Edward's busy, over-crowded life was brought to an end on the field of AGINCOURT on 25 October 1415, when he was among the relatively few English casualties. He was buried at Fotheringay. The duke had married in about 1398, Philippa, second daughter and co-heiress of John de Mohun, 2nd Baron Mohun of Dunster, and his wife Joan, daughter of Bartholomew de Burghersh, 1st Baron Burghersh. She had already been married and widowed twice, first to Walter FitzWalter, 4th Baron FitzWalter (d.1386), and secondly to Sir John Golafré (d.1396). After Edward's death she was granted the Lordship of the Isle of Wight for life and is reputed to have married for a fourth time to one John Vesey. She died without issue on 17 July 1431 and was buried in the chapel of St Nicholas in WESTMINSTER ABBEY, where her monument may still be seen.

3. **Richard Plantagenet, 3rd Duke of York** (1411–60) The only son of Richard, Earl of CAMBRIDGE, and his wife Anne, daughter of Roger Mortimer, 4th Earl of March, who was born on 21 September 1411 and succeeded his uncle Edward as 3rd Duke of York in October 1415. In 1425 he succeeded his maternal uncle as Earl of March and Earl of Ulster, also inheriting the Lordship of Clare and lands in Ireland. He was knighted by HENRY VI at Leicester on 19 May 1426 and accompanied the king to France in 1430, being present at his French coronation in December 1431. He was nominated a Knight of the GARTER in 1433 and served as Lieutenant and Governor-General of

France and Normandy from 1436 to 1437 and from 1440 to 1447.

Richard assumed the surname PLANTA-GENET in 1448 and in 1450 assumed leadership of the Yorkist party, marking the beginning of the long dynastic struggle known as the Wars of the ROSES. At the first battle of St Albans on 22 May 1455, Richard's rival the Duke of Somerset was killed and the king taken prisoner. Richard was made Protector of the Realm from 19 November 1455 until 25 February 1456. Peace between York and Lancaster was temporarily effected in March 1458, when Richard walked with Queen Margaret (see MARGARET OF ANJOU) in the 'love-day' procession to St Paul's, but fighting broke out again in 1459 and Richard was attainted in November. Subsequently, his son the Earl of March, with the Earls of Salisbury and Warwick, seized London in July 1460 and the duke returned to claim the crown as the heir general of EDWARD III. A compromise was reached whereby his attainder was reversed and he was declared heir to the crown on 31 October 1460. Queen Margaret would have none of this, however, and assembled her army at Wakefield. Richard marched against it and the Yorkist army was defeated and he himself was killed on 30 December 1460.

Richard was buried first at Pontefract and his severed head, mockingly adorned with a crown of paper and straw, was set up on Micklegate Bar in York. It was later taken down and restored to the trunk. His son, EDWARD IV, had the body exhumed and reburied at Fotheringay on 30 July 1476.

Richard had married, in about 1437, Cicely, twelfth and youngest daughter of Ralph Nevill, 1st Earl of Westmorland, being his fifth daughter by his second wife JOAN BEAUFORT, half-sister of Henry IV. Born at Raby Castle on 3 May 1415, she was known as 'Proud Cis' and 'The Rose of Raby'. She lived to see two of her sons become king (Edward IV and RICHARD III) and her granddaughter become queen consort (ELIZABETH OF YORK) and died at Berkhamsted Castle on 31 May 1495. She was buried with her husband at Fotheringay.

4. **Edward Plantagenet, 4th Duke of York** see EDWARD IV.

5. **Richard Plantagenet, Duke of York** (1473–83?) The second son of EDWARD IV and ELIZABETH WOODVILLE, who was born at Shrewsbury on 17 August 1473 and created Duke of York on 28 May 1474. He was

nominated a Knight of the GARTER in May 1475 and further created Earl of Nottingham on 12 June 1476 and Earl of Warenne and Duke of Norfolk on 7 February 1478. At the age of five, on 15 January 1478, he was married at St Stephen's Chapel, Westminster, to Anne, only daughter and heiress of John Mowbray, 4th Duke of Norfolk and 9th Baron Mowbray, Earl Marshal of England, and his wife Elizabeth, daughter of John Talbot, 1st Earl of Shrewsbury. She was born at Framlingham, Suffolk, on 17 December 1472 and died at Greenwich on 19 November 1481, being buried in the Chapel of St Erasmus in WESTMINSTER ABBEY and thence transferred to the convent of the Minoresses in Stepney (where her body was discovered in the course of some building work in 1965 and reinterred in Westminster Abbey near the supposed bones of her boy husband).

After his father's death in 1483, Richard's mother took the Duke of York and his sisters into sanctuary at Westminster, but later gave him up at the demand of the PRIVY COUNCIL and he was taken to join his brother EDWARD V in the TOWER OF LONDON. The children of Edward IV and Elizabeth Woodville were declared illegitimate by Parliament on 25 June 1483 on the ground of the supposed invalidity of their parents' marriage and Edward was accordingly deposed in favour of his uncle, Richard, Duke of Gloucester, who ascended the throne as RICHARD III. The PRINCES IN THE TOWER were generally presumed to have been murdered in the Tower on Richard's instigation in or after July 1483. The bones of two children, corresponding in age to those of the princes, were discovered beneath a staircase in the Tower in the reign of CHARLES II and deposited in an urn in Westminster Abbey.

6. **Henry Tudor, Duke of York** see HENRY VIII.

7. **Charles Stuart, Duke of York** see CHARLES I.

8. **James Stuart, Duke of York** see JAMES II.

9. **Ernest Augustus, Duke of York** (1674–1728) The seventh son and eighth and youngest child of Ernest Augustus (Ernst August), Elector and Duke of Hanover and Duke of Brunswick-Lüneburg, and his wife Sophia, fifth and youngest daughter of Friedrich V, Elector Palatine and sometime King of Bohemia, and his wife Elizabeth, eldest daughter of JAMES I, who was born at

Osnabrück on 18 September 1674. He was president of the council of Hanover from 1714 to 1728 and was elected Prince-Bishop of Osnabrück in 1715. Since the Reformation the see and principality of Osnabrück had been ruled by Catholic and Protestant Bishops alternately. As the only surviving brother of GEORGE I he was nominated a Knight of the GARTER on 3 July 1716 and two days later was created Earl of Ulster and Duke of York and Albany. Dr John Mitchell, a visitor to Osnabrück in November 1717, wrote that the duke 'very much resembles his brother King George, but is fatter'. The duke died unmarried at Osnabrück on 14 August 1728.

10. **Prince Edward Augustus, Duke of York and Albany** (1739–67) The second son and third child of FREDERICK LOUIS, PRINCE OF WALES and Augusta of Saxe-Gotha (*see* AUGUSTA, PRINCESS OF WALES), who was born at Norfolk House, St James's Square, London, on 14 March (25 March new style) 1739 and baptized there by the Bishop of Oxford on 11 April, his godparents being the King of Prussia, the Duke of Brunswick-Wolfenbüttel and Friederike, Duchess of Saxe-Weissenfels, all represented by proxies. He was nominated a Knight of the GARTER in 1752 and entered the Royal Navy as a Midshipman in 1758. He served under Admiral Howe in the expedition to Cherbourg in August 1758 and in the Channel in 1759 and was promoted Captain in HMS *Phoenix* on 14 June 1759.

On 1 April 1760 he was created Earl of Ulster and Duke of York and Albany by his grandfather GEORGE II. Two days after his elder brother's accession to the throne as GEORGE III, he was appointed a Privy Councillor on 27 October 1760. He was promoted Rear Admiral of the Blue on 8 April 1761 and served off the Spanish and Portugese coasts and in the Channel in 1762 before being promoted Vice-Admiral of the Blue in 1766. In the same year he was appointed Keeper and Lieutenant of Windsor Forest.

In the summer of 1767 the duke was serving in the Mediterranean and caught cold after a dance given in his honour by Honoré III, Prince of Monaco. It turned to a 'malignant fever' and he died in the Palais Princier at Monaco on 17 September 1767. The room in which he died is still known as the York Chamber. His body was returned to England and buried in WESTMINSTER ABBEY on 3 November 1767. He was unmarried.

11. **Prince Frederick, Duke of York** (1763–1827) The second son of GEORGE III and Queen CHARLOTTE, who was born at St James's Palace on 16 August 1763 and baptized there on 14 September, his godparents being his uncle the Duke of York (*see above*), his grand-uncle the Duke of Saxe-Gotha, both represented by proxies, and his grand-aunt Princess AMELIA, who stood in person. He was only six months old when he was elected Prince Bishop of Osnabrück on 27 February 1764. He was nominated a Knight of the GARTER in 1771. On 1 November 1780 he was appointed a Brevet Colonel in the Army and was sent to Berlin to study military tactics in the school established there by Friedrich II (Frederick the Great), King of Prussia. He held various army appointments and was promoted Major-General in November 1782 and Lieutenant-General in October 1784.

On 27 November 1784 he was created Earl of Ulster and Duke of York and Albany. He returned to England in 1787, took his seat in the House of Lords and was appointed a Privy Councillor. On 26 May 1789 he fought a duel on Wimbledon Common with Lieutenant-Colonel Charles Lennox (later 4th Duke of Richmond), by whom he had been challenged. Lennox's shot 'grazed his royal highness's curl', but the duke discharged his pistol into the air. On 29 September 1791, Frederick was married at Berlin (the ceremony being repeated at the Queen's House in London on 23 November) to Frederica Charlotte Ulrica Catherine, the eldest daughter of Friedrich Wilhelm II, King of Prussia, and only daughter by his first wife, Elisabeth Christina Ulrica of Brunswick. The marriage was to remain childless.

In 1793 the duke was placed at the head of the British forces in Flanders and took part in the siege of Valenciennes, which was captured on 28 July. After a few more successes and several defeats by the French he was recalled to England in November 1794. He was made Field Marshal in February 1795 and Commander-in-Chief of the Forces in Great Britain and Ireland on 9 June 1801, a position which he held until March 1809, when a series of charges were preferred against him in the House of Commons by Colonel Wardle for having allowed his mistress Mary Anne Clarke to influence him in the disposal of army commissions. The duke was acquitted of any implication in corrupt transactions but was nevertheless compelled to resign as Commander-in-Chief. He was reinstated by his brother the Prince

Regent on 25 May 1811 and from then onwards exercised a rigid impartiality in the distribution of promotions. He attended to the rights and comforts of the private soldier, though enforcing strict discipline.

The care of the king's person was entrusted to the duke in 1819, and on his demise in 1820 Frederick became HEIR PRESUMPTIVE to the throne. He and his duchess lived apart in an amicable separation for many years. She was born at Potsdam on 7 May 1767 and died at her residence, Oatlands Park, Weybridge, Surrey, where she had lived surrounded by pet dogs, on 6 August 1820. She chose to be buried in a vault in Weybridge churchyard.

In his latter years the duke became a bitter opponent of Catholic emancipation, the subject of his last speech in the House of Lords. The duke died 'of dropsy' at Rutland House, Arlington Street, London, on 5 January 1827 (he had been staying with his friend the Duke of Rutland while his own house was being redecorated). The room in which he died now forms part of the cocktail bar of the Royal Over-Seas League. He was buried at St George's Chapel, Windsor, on 20 January 1827.

Frederick is the Duke of York remembered in the famous nursery rhyme:

> The Grand Old Duke of York,
> He had ten thousand men.
> He marched them up to the top of the hill;
> Then he marched them down again.

12. **George, Duke of York** *see* GEORGE V.

13. **Albert, Duke of York** *see* GEORGE VI.

14. **Prince Andrew, Duke of York** (1960–)
The second son and third child of ELIZABETH II and Prince Philip, Duke of EDINBURGH, who was born at BUCKINGHAM PALACE on 19 February 1960 and received the names Andrew Albert Christian Edward at his baptism at Buckingham Palace on 8 April 1960. He was educated at Gordonstoun, Lakefield College, Ontario, Canada, and at the Royal Naval College, Dartmouth. He subsequently attained the rank of Lieutenant Commander RN and served in the South Atlantic Campaign in 1982 as a helicopter pilot with HMS *Invincible*. He was appointed a Companion of the ROYAL VICTORIAN ORDER in 1979 and became a personal ADC to the queen in 1984. He is Colonel-in-Chief of several regiments and Admiral of the Sea Cadet Corps.

Prince Andrew was created Baron Killyleagh, Earl of Inverness and Duke of York on 23 July 1986, the day of his marriage at Westminster Abbey to Sarah Margaret FERGUSON, second daughter of Major Ronald Ivor Ferguson, of Dummer Down House, Dummer, Basingstoke, Hampshire, and his first wife Susan Mary, daughter of FitzHerbert Wright. The duke and duchess have two daughters: Princess BEATRICE OF YORK, born at the Portland Hospital, London, on 8 August 1988, and Princess EUGÉNIE OF YORK, born at the Portland Hospital on 23 March 1990.

The marriage of the Duke and Duchess of York attracted much critical attention in the late 1980s when a rift between the royal couple became increasingly evident and tales of difficulties between the outgoing duchess and the rest of the royal family were widely reported. In the face of intense media speculation, reinforced by rumours of extra-marital friendships, the Yorks announced an amicable separation in March 1992 and preparations were made for a divorce. A decree nisi was granted on 17 April 1996, followed by a decree absolute on 30 May 1996.

In 1993 the Duke of York assumed command of HMS *Cottesmore*, in February 1995 he was posted to HMS *Osprey*, and in July 1996 he was promoted to be second-in-command of HMS *Cumberland*.

York, House of The designation given to the branch of the House of PLANTAGENET that occupied the throne from 1461 to 1485. The Yorkist claim to the throne was not through direct descent from EDWARD III's son, Edmund of Langley, Duke of YORK, for he was born after John of Gaunt, from whom the House of LANCASTER derived its claim. In order to assert precedence over the Lancastrians, the claim was derived from John of Gaunt's elder brother, Lionel of Antwerp, Duke of CLARENCE, whose only child Philippa married Edmund Mortimer, Earl of March, and was the grandmother of Anne Mortimer, who married Richard of Conisburgh, Earl of CAMBRIDGE, son of Edmund of Langley. EDWARD IV, the first Yorkist king, was their grandson.

York, Viking Kingdom of The Viking or Scandinavian kingdom of York was founded in 875 or 876 by Halfdan, son of Ragnar Lodbrok. He was driven out a year or two later and is said to have been killed in Ireland. His successor, Guthfrith, is reputed to have reigned 14 years and died on 24 August 896. The next king, Siefred, struck coins at York in the late ninth and early tenth centuries, as also did one Canute (Cnut). Ethelwald, son of ETHELRED I, King of Wessex, took refuge in York after he was driven out of Wessex by his cousin EDWARD THE ELDER in 899 and was recognized as king there. He was killed at the battle of the Holme in 902 and power in York passed to Halfdan II and his brother's Eowils and Ivar, who reigned jointly until all three were killed at Tettenhall in 910. Between 912 and 915 Northumbria was invaded by Ragnald, whose mother was a daughter of Ivar the Boneless, eldest son of Ragnar Lodbrok. He captured York in 919 and acknowedged Edward the Elder as overlord in the same year. On his death in 921 he was succeeded by his presumed brother Sihtric Caoch, who married a sister of ATHELSTAN of Wessex in 926 and died the following year, when he was succeeded by his brother Guthfrith II. He was expelled by Athelstan, who maintained direct rule over York until his death in 939, when Guthfrith's son Anlaf (Olaf) became king. He married a daughter of CONSTANTINE III, King of Scots and died in 941, being succeeded by his cousin Anlaf Sihtricsson or Anlaf Cuaran, a son of Sihtric Caoch by an earlier wife than Athelstan's sister. Anlaf acknowledged EDMUND I of Wessex as overlord and was driven out of York in the summer of 943 by Ragnald,

brother of Anlaf Guthfrithsson, with whom he carried on a long struggle until both were expelled by Edmund. York then remained under the direct rule of Edmund and his brother and successor EDRED until 948, when Eric Bloodaxe of Norway seized power. He was driven out again soon after by Anlaf Sihtricsson, who returned from Ireland and remained in power until 952, when Eric again expelled him. He, in turn, was driven out by Edred and killed at Stainmore in 954, and thereafter Northumbria remained under the direct rule of Wessex after 80 turbulent years.

Zadok the Priest Coronation anthem sung immediately prior to the anointing at the coronation of every English and British sovereign since that of EDGAR in 973. The words are taken from verses 39 and 40 of the first chapter of the First Book of Kings: 'Zadok the priest and Nathan the prophet anointed Solomon King; and all the people rejoiced and said: God Save the King, Long live the King, May the King live for ever. Amen. Hallelujah.' Since the coronation of GEORGE II in 1727 the anthem has been sung to the exhilarating setting by George Frideric Handel (1685–1759).

APPENDIX I

Geoffrey of Monmouth's Kings of Britain

Brutus	Reigned 23 years
Locrinus	Son of Brutus; reigned 10 years
Gwendolen	Widow of Locrinus; reigned 15 years
Maddan	Son of Locrinus and Gwendolen; reigned 40 years
Mempricius	Son of Maddan; reigned 20 years
Ebraucus	Son of Mempricius; reigned 39 years; had 20 wives, 20 sons and 30 daughters
Brutus Greenshield	Son of Ebraucus; reigned 12 years; contemporary of Solomon
Leil	Son of Brutus Greenshield; reigned 25 years; founded Carlisle
Rud Hud Hudibras	Son of Leil; reigned 39 years; founded Canterbury, Winchester and Shaftesbury
Bladud	Son of Rud Hud Hudibras; reigned 20 years; founded Bath and tried to fly
Leir	Son of Bladud; reigned 60 years; founded Leicester; Shakespeare's King Lear
Cordelia	Daughter of Leir; reigned 5 years
Marganus I and **Cunedagius**	Sons respectively of Goneril and Regan, Leir's elder daughters; rebelled against their aunt and reigned together, dividing the kingdom, for two years. Cunedagius drove Marganus out and reigned alone for 33 years. Rome was founded during his reign
Rivallo	Son of Cunedagius
Gurgustius	Son of Rivallo
Sisillius I	Relationship to predecessor not stated
Jago	Nephew of Gurgustius
Kimarcus	Son of Sisillius I
Gorboduc	Relationship to predecessor not stated. His sons Ferrex and Porrex quarrelled as to which should succeed and the former was killed by the latter, who in his turn was killed by their mother Judon
Five unnamed kings	A period of civil war
Dunvallo Molmutius	Son of Cloten, King of Cornwall; reigned 40 years; established the Molmutine laws
Belinus	Son of Dunvallo Molmutius; fought with his brother Brennius
Gurguit Barbtruc	Son of Belinus
Guithelin	Relationship to predecessor not stated
Marcia	Widow of Guithelin; author of the *Lex Martiana*
Sisillius II	Son of Guithelin and Marcia
Kinarius	Son of Sisillius II
Danius	Brother of Kinarius
Morvidus	Illegitimate son of Danius
Gorbonianus	Eldest son of Morvidus
Archgallo	Brother of Gorbonianus; deposed
Elidurus	Brother of Archgallo; reigned 5 years and then restored the crown to
Archgallo	Reigned 10 years; died and was again succeeded by
Elidurus	Deposed by his two youngest brothers
Ingenius and **Peredurus**	Reigned together 7 years until Ingenius died; Peredurus then reigned alone until his death when
Elidurus	Reigned a third time until his death
An unnamed king	Son of Gorbonianus
Marganus II	Son of Archgallo
Enniaunus	Brother of Marganus II; deposed in the sixth year of his reign
Idvallo	Son of Ingenius
Runo	Son of Peredurus
Gerennus	Son of Elidurus
Catellus	Son of Gerennus
Millus	Relationship to predecessor not stated
Porrex	Relationship to predecessor not stated
Cherin	Relationship to predecessor not stated
Fulgenius	Son of Cherin
Edadus	Brother of Fulgenius
Andragius	Brother of Edadus
Urianus	Son of Andragius
Eliud **Cledaucus** **Clotenus** **Gurgintius** **Merianus** **Bledudo** **Cap** **Oenus** **Sisillius III** **Beldgabred**	Nothing recorded of these ten kings

355

Archmail	Brother of Beldgabred
Eldol	
Redon	
Redechius	Nothing recorded of these seven kings
Samuil	
Penessil	
Pir	
Capoir	
Digueillis	Son of Capoir
Heli	Son of Digueillis; reigned 40 years
Lud	Son of Heli; founded London
Cassivelaunu	Brother of Lud; the historical Cassivelaunus (Caswallon), who fought with Caesar in 55 and 54BC
Tenvantius	Son of Lud; can be equated with the historical Tasciovanus
Cymbeline	Son of Tenvantius; reigned over 10 years; can be equated with the historical Cunobelinus
Guiderius	Son of Cymbeline
Arvirargus	Brother of Guiderius
Marius	Son of Arvirargus
Coilus	Son of Marius
Lucius	Son of Coilus; converted to Christianity and d.AD156

Interregnum of about 150 years

Asclepiodotus	Duke of Cornwall; elected king by the people
Coel	Duke of Kaecolim (Colchester); killed Asclepiodotus and usurped the throne; the 'Old King Cole' of the nursery rhyme; can be equated with the historical Coel Hen Godhebog
Constantius	Married Coel's daughter Helen; equated with the Roman Emperor Constantius I
Constantine I	Son of Constantius; the Roman Emperor Constantine the Great
Octavius	Duke of the Gewissei; seized power while Constantine was in Rome; driven out by
Trahern	Brother of Coel; later killed by
Octavius	who regained the throne
Maximianus	Son of Ioelinus, brother of Coel; married the daughter of Octavius
Gracianus	A freedman; seized power on the death of Maximianus
Constantine II	Brother of Aldroenus, King of Brittany; invited to Britain and chosen king
Constans	Son of Constantine II
Vortigern	Usurped the throne; an historical figure
Vortimer	Son of Vortigern, whom he deposed; poisoned by his stepmother
Vortigern	Restored
Aurelius Ambrosius	Son of Constantine II; deposed Vortigern
Uther Pendragon	Brother of Aurelius Ambrosius
Arthur	Son of Uther Pendragon; the mighty King Arthur of legend; d. 542
Constantine III	Son of Cador, Duke of Cornwall and cousin of Arthur
Aurelius Conanus	Nephew of Constantine III; died in the third year of his reign
Vortiporius	Nothing recorded
Malgo	The historical Maelgwn Gwynedd, King of Gwynedd, who died about 550
Keredic	Nothing recorded
Three unnamed kings	Nothing recorded
Cadvan	The historical King of Gwynedd, Cadfan ab Iago, who reigned 616–c.625
Cadwallo	The historical Cadwallon, son of Cadfan; reigned c.625–633, although Geoffrey makes him reign 48 years
Cadwallader	The historical Cadwaladr Fendigaid, son of Cadwallon; reigned 654–664. Geoffrey makes him die at Rome in 689, confusing him with Caedwalla, King of Wessex

HERE GEOFFREY ENDS HIS HISTORY

Kings of the Catuvellauni and their Tentative Descendants

This pedigree is based on a hitherto unpublished study by the late Patrick Montague-Smith. If it is correct an unbroken line from Cassivelaunus to Elizabeth II can be shown.

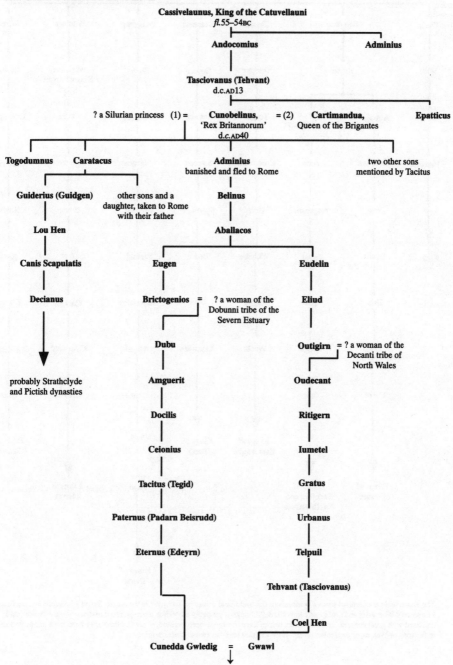

Cassivelaunus, King of the Catuvellauni
*fl.*55–54BC

Andocomius — **Adminius**

Tasciovanus (Tehvant)
d.c.AD13

? a Silurian princess (1) = **Cunobelinus,** = (2) **Cartimandua,** — **Epatticus**
'Rex Britannorum' Queen of the Brigantes
d.c.AD40

Togodumnus **Caratacus** **Adminius** two other sons
banished and fled to Rome mentioned by Tacitus

Guiderius (Guidgen) other sons and a **Belinus**
daughter, taken to Rome
with their father

Lou Hen **Aballacos**

Canis Scapulatis **Eugen** **Eudelin**

Decianus **Brictogenios** = ? a woman of the **Eliud**
Dobunni tribe of the
Severn Estuary

probably Strathclyde **Dubu** **Outigirn** = ? a woman of the
and Pictish dynasties Decanti tribe of
North Wales

Amguerit **Oudecant**

Docilis **Ritigern**

Ceionius **Iumetel**

Tacitus (Tegid) **Gratus**

Paternus (Padarn Beisrudd) **Urbanus**

Eternus (Edeyrn) **Telpuil**

Tehvant (Tasciovanus)

Coel Hen

Cunedda Gwledig = **Gwawl**

APPENDIX III

The Descendants of Woden

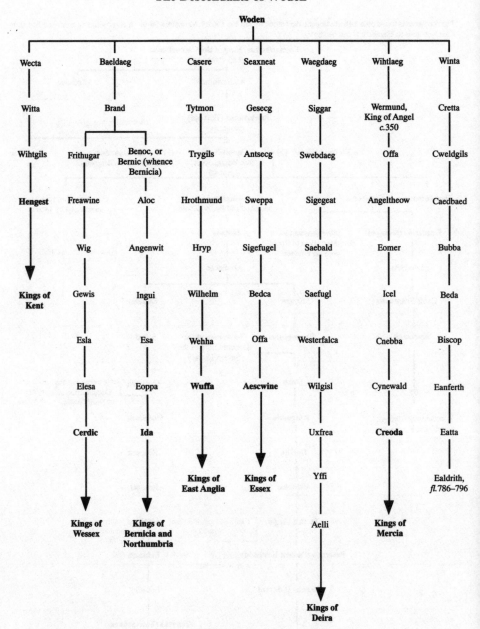

The above table is compiled from a synthesis of the traditional pedigrees recorded in the *Anglo-Saxon Chronicle*, and by Bede, Florence of Worcester and other early historians. Although it probably embodies much genuine material it must be accepted and used with great caution. In some cases names have obviously been omitted, while in others they have been duplicated and, in the case of Wessex in particular, interpolated to bring together two distinct traditions.

Kings of Kent

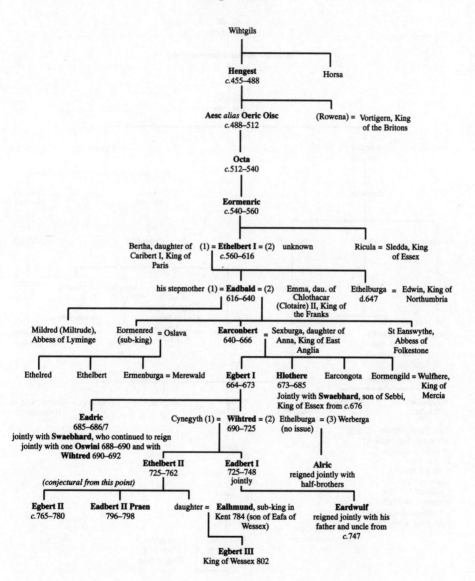

Several other kings of unknown, or different lineage reigned until 825, when the last of them, **Baldred**, was driven out by Egbert of Wessex.

Kings of Wessex from Cerdic to Egbert

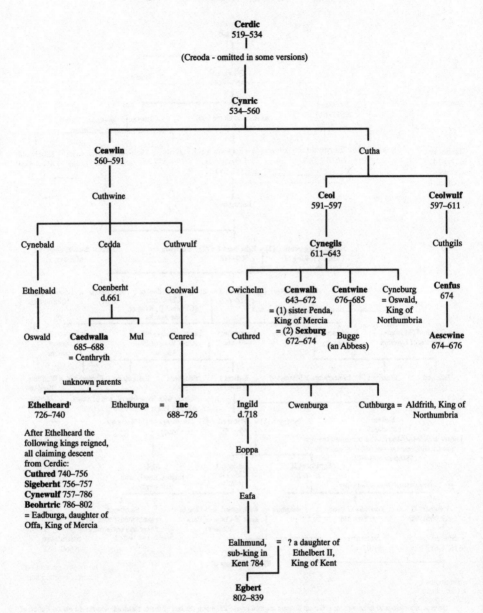

Cerdic
519–534

(Creoda - omitted in some versions)

Cynric
534–560

Ceawlin 560–591 | Cutha

Cuthwine | Ceol 591–597 | **Ceolwulf** 597–611

Cynebald | Cedda | Cuthwulf | **Cynegils** 611–643 | Cuthgils

Ethelbald | Coenberht d.661 | Ceolwald | Cwichelm | **Cenwalh** 643–672 = (1) sister Penda, King of Mercia = (2) **Sexburg** 672–674 | **Centwine** 676–685 | Cyneburg = Oswald, King of Northumbria | **Cenfus** 674

Oswald | **Caedwalla** 685–688 = Centhryth | Mul | Cenred | Cuthred | Bugge (an Abbess) | **Aescwine** 674–676

unknown parents

Ethelheard[1] 726–740 | Ethelburga = **Ine** 688–726 | Ingild d.718 | Cwenburga | Cuthburga = Aldfrith, King of Northumbria

After Ethelheard the following kings reigned, all claiming descent from Cerdic:
Cuthred 740–756
Sigeberht 756–757
Cynewulf 757–786
Beohrtric 786–802
= Eadburga, daughter of Offa, King of Mercia

Eoppa

Eafa

Ealhmund, sub-king in Kent 784 | = | ? a daughter of Ethelbert II, King of Kent

Egbert
802–839

[1]A.M.H.J. Stokvis, in *Manuel d'Histoire, de Généalogie et de Chronologie de Tous les États du Globe* (1889–93), without citing an authority, makes Ethelheard and Cuthred to be sons of Aescwine, Cynewulf to be a son of Ethelheard, and Beohrtric to be a son of Cynewulf.

Kings of East Anglia

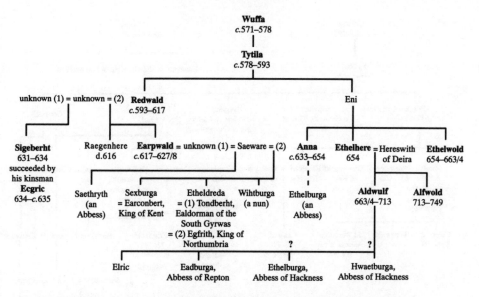

The names of several other kings are recorded, the last being **St Edmund**, who was murdered by the Danes in 870.

Kings of Essex

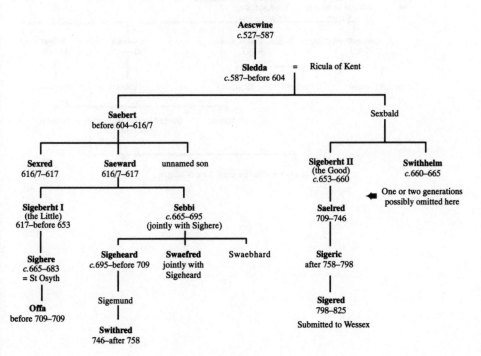

Kings of Mercia

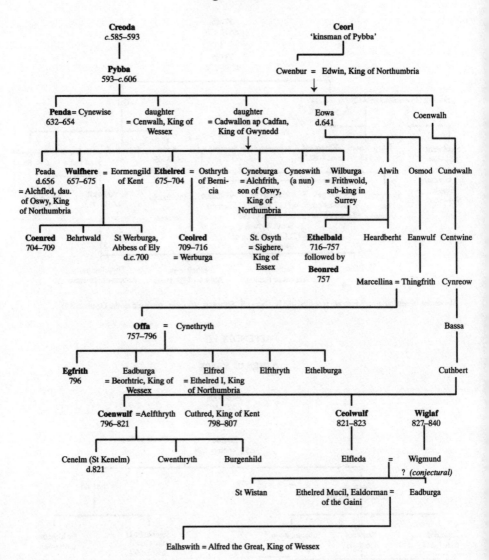

Kings of Deira

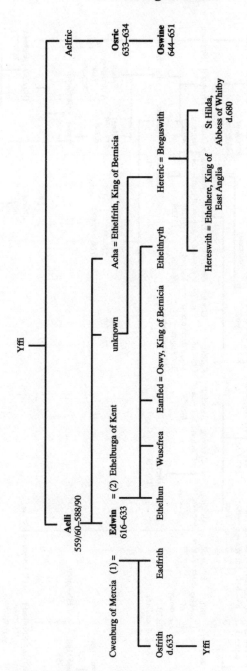

King Oswine was succeeded by Ethelwald of Bernicia who reigned until 654 when Deira was finally annexed to Bernicia.

Kings of Bernicia and Northumbria

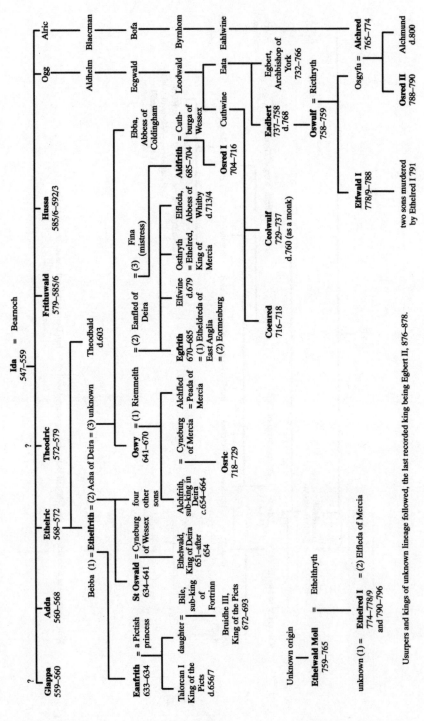

Kings of Wessex and All England

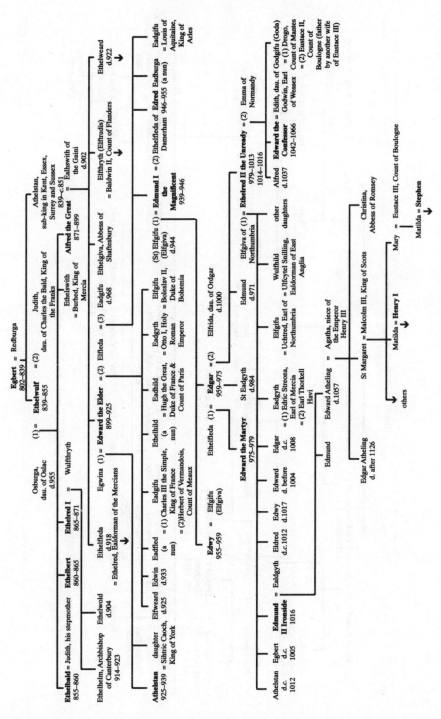

Anglo-Danish Kings

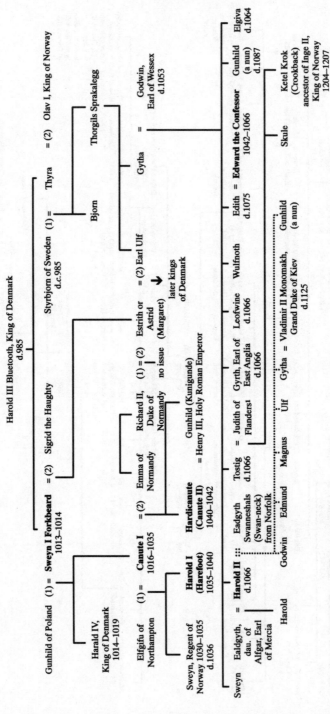

1 Judith's 2nd marriage was to Welf, Duke of Bavaria, and so she became an ancestor of the House of Hanover.

The Saxon/Norman Succession

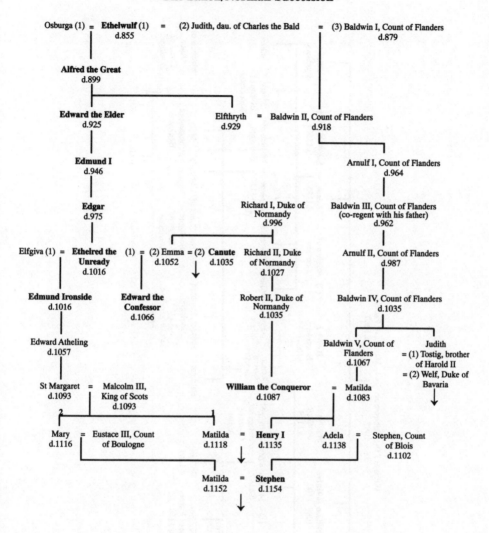

The Houses of Normandy and Blois

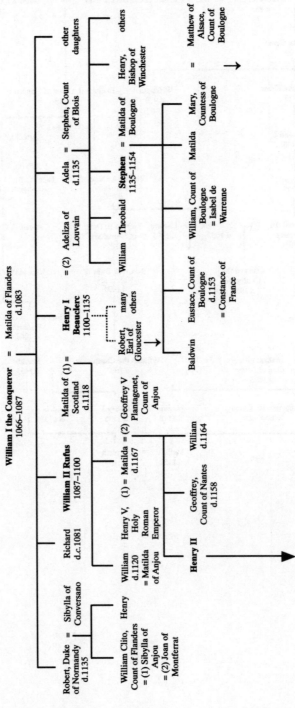

The House of Anjou (Plantagenet)

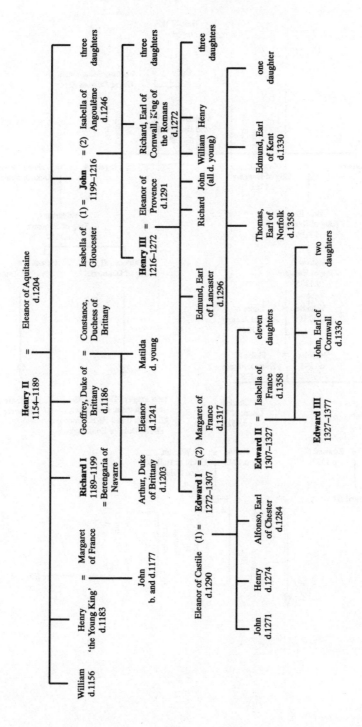

The Blood of Harold II Returns to England

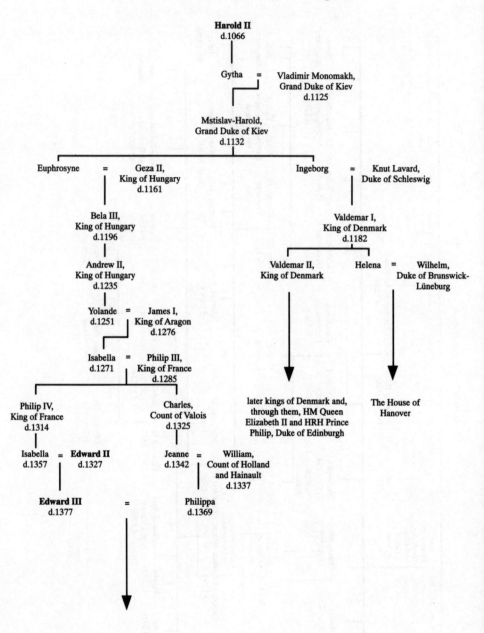

Harold II
d.1066

Gytha = Vladimir Monomakh,
Grand Duke of Kiev
d.1125

Mstislav-Harold,
Grand Duke of Kiev
d.1132

Euphrosyne = Geza II,
King of Hungary
d.1161

Ingeborg = Knut Lavard,
Duke of Schleswig

Bela III,
King of Hungary
d.1196

Valdemar I,
King of Denmark
d.1182

Andrew II,
King of Hungary
d.1235

Valdemar II,
King of Denmark

Helena = Wilhelm,
Duke of Brunswick-
Lüneburg

Yolande = James I,
d.1251   King of Aragon
d.1276

Isabella = Philip III,
d.1271   King of France
d.1285

Philip IV,
King of France
d.1314

Charles,
Count of Valois
d.1325

later kings of Denmark and,
through them, HM Queen
Elizabeth II and HRH Prince
Philip, Duke of Edinburgh

The House of
Hanover

Isabella = **Edward II**
d.1357   d.1327

Jeanne = William,
d.1342   Count of Holland
and Hainault
d.1337

Edward III =
d.1377

Philippa
d.1369

The Later Plantagenets

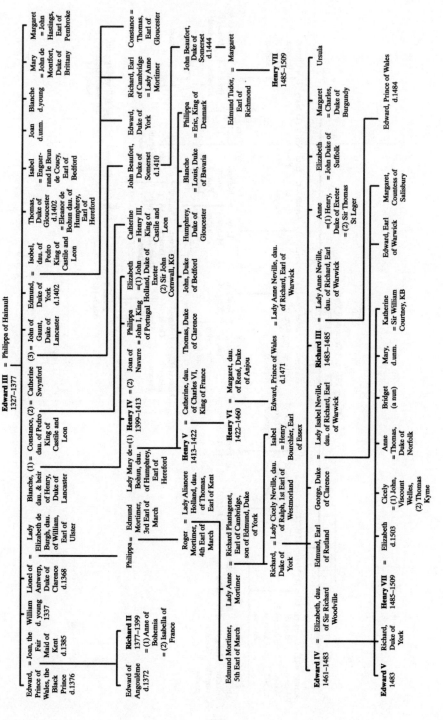

371

The House of Tudor

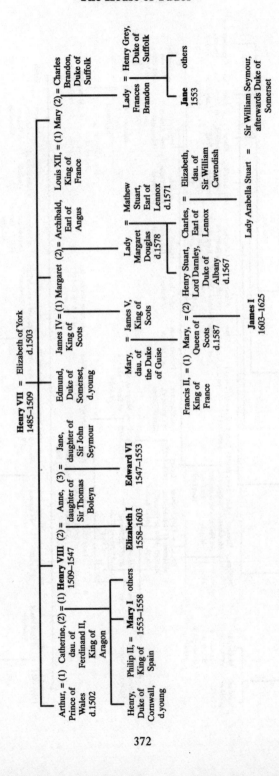

The House of Stuart

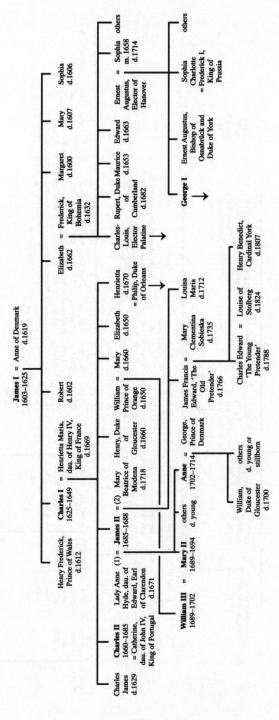

The House of Hanover

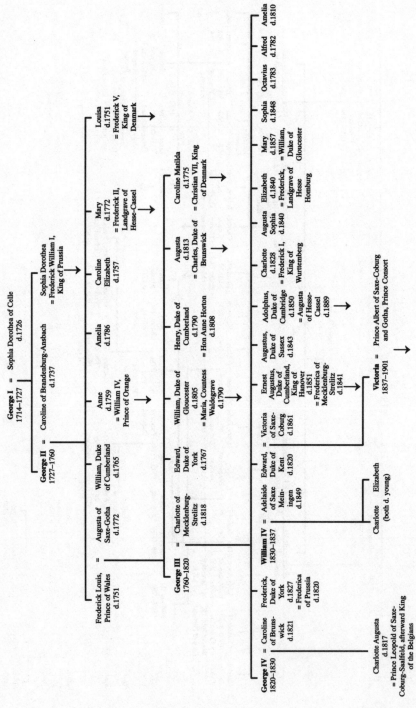

APPENDIX XXI

From Victoria to Elizabeth II

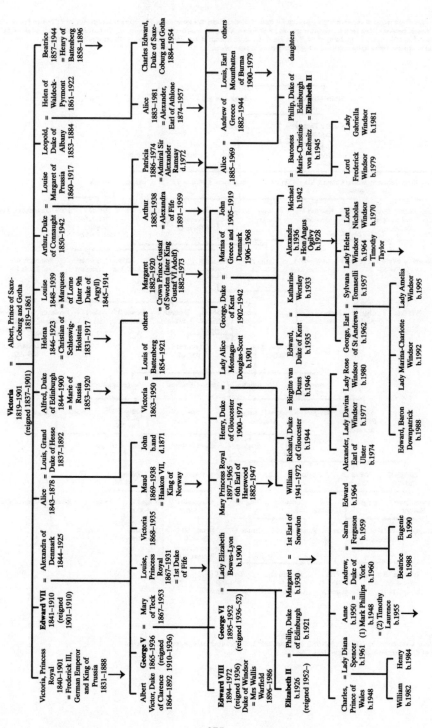

APPENDIX XXII

Kings of the Picts

The Picts were a people of unknown origin who occupied most of Scotland from time immemorial. They received the name of *Picti* ('Painted People') from the Romans because of their habit of painting or tattooing their bodies. A long list of mythical kings starting with Cruithne becomes historical about the middle of the fifth century. A peculiarity of the Pictish kingdom was the practice of matrilineal succession, the throne passing from brother to brother or to a maternal nephew. The pedigree here given is highly conjectural in many places.

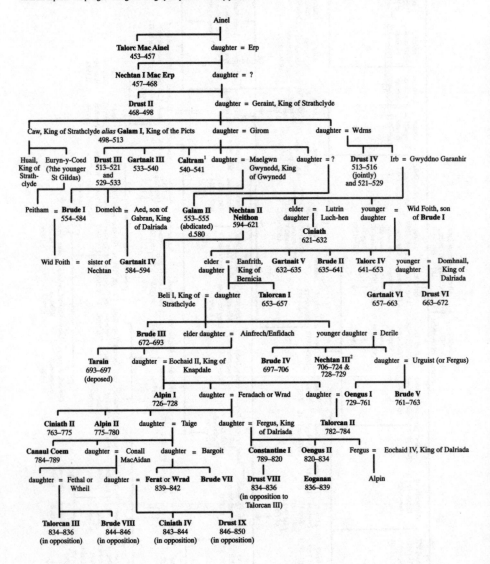

Notes:

1 Caltram was followed by **Talorc II** (541–552) and **Drust V** (552–553) who cannot be placed in the pedigree.
2 **Drust VII**, of unknown origin, reigned from 724–726.

Scottish Kings of Dalriada

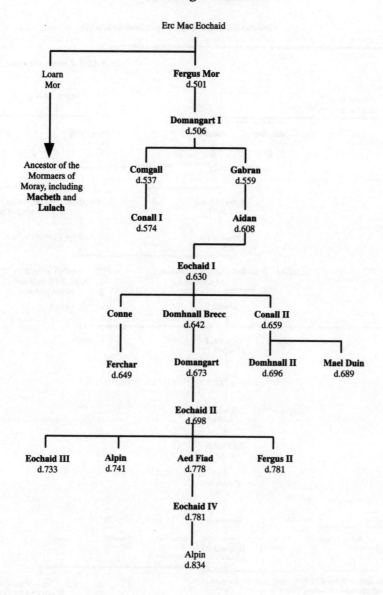

Erc Mac Eochaid

Loarn
Mor

Ancestor of the
Mormaers of
Moray, including
Macbeth and
Lulach

Fergus Mor
d.501

Domangart I
d.506

Comgall
d.537

Gabran
d.559

Conall I
d.574

Aidan
d.608

Eochaid I
d.630

Conne

Domhnall Brecc
d.642

Conall II
d.659

Ferchar
d.649

Domangart
d.673

Domhnall II
d.696

Mael Duin
d.689

Eochaid II
d.698

Eochaid III
d.733

Alpin
d.741

Aed Fiad
d.778

Fergus II
d.781

Eochaid IV
d.781

Alpin
d.834

Kings of Strathclyde

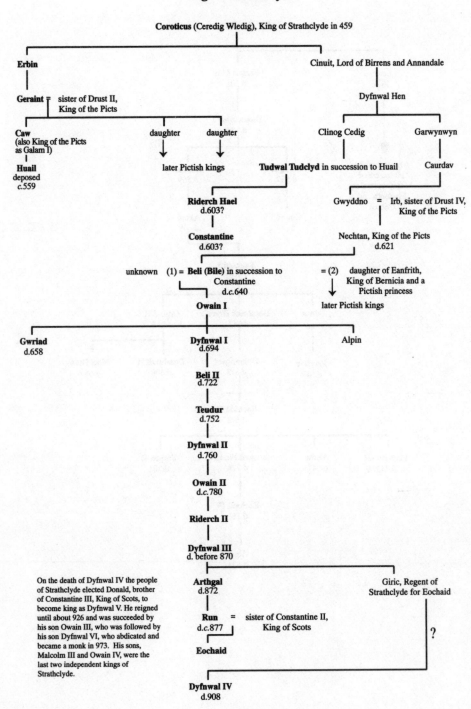

Coroticus (Ceredig Wledig), King of Strathclyde in 459

Erbin

Cinuit, Lord of Birrens and Annandale

Geraint = sister of Drust II, King of the Picts

Dyfnwal Hen

Caw (also King of the Picts as Galam I)

daughter

daughter

Clinog Cedig

Garwynwyn

Huail deposed *c.*559

later Pictish kings

Tudwal Tudclyd in succession to Huail

Caurdav

Riderch Hael d.603?

Gwyddno = Irb, sister of Drust IV, King of the Picts

Constantine d.603?

Nechtan, King of the Picts d.621

unknown (1) = **Beli (Bile)** in succession to Constantine d.*c.*640

= (2) daughter of Eanfrith, King of Bernicia and a Pictish princess

Owain I

later Pictish kings

Gwriad d.658

Dyfnwal I d.694

Alpin

Beli II d.722

Teudur d.752

Dyfnwal II d.760

Owain II d.*c.*780

Riderch II

Dyfnwal III d. before 870

On the death of Dyfnwal IV the people of Strathclyde elected Donald, brother of Constantine III, King of Scots, to become king as Dyfnwal V. He reigned until about 926 and was succeeded by his son Owain III, who was followed by his son Dyfnwal VI, who abdicated and became a monk in 973. His sons, Malcolm III and Owain IV, were the last two independent kings of Strathclyde.

Arthgal d.872

Giric, Regent of Strathclyde for Eochaid

Run = sister of Constantine II, d.*c.*877 King of Scots

?

Eochaid

Dyfnwal IV d.908

The House of Alpin

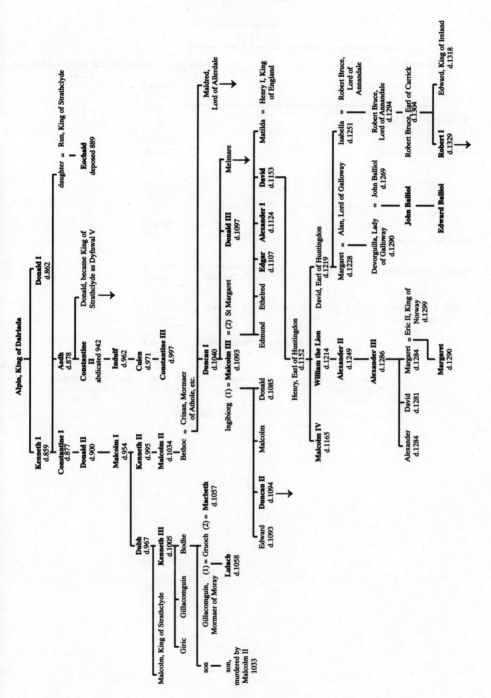

The Houses of Bruce and Stewart (Stuart)

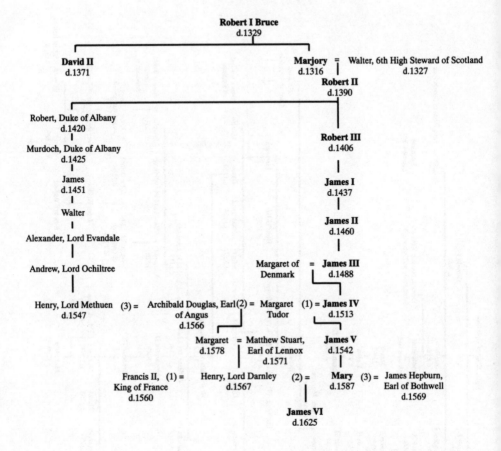

The Dynasty of Gwynedd

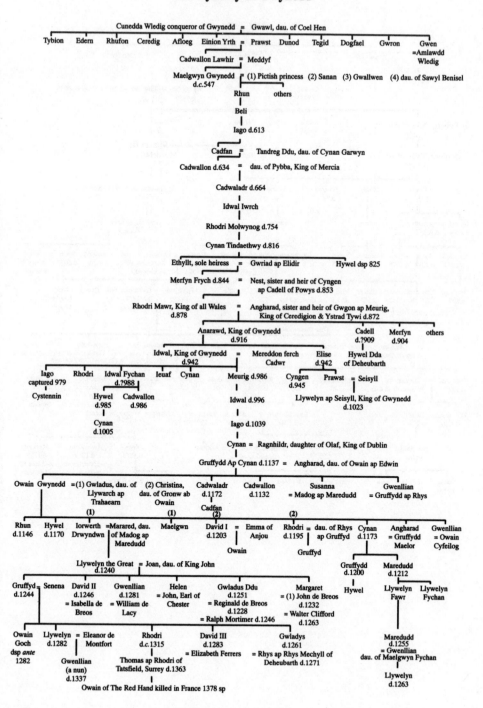

The Royal Line of Deheubarth

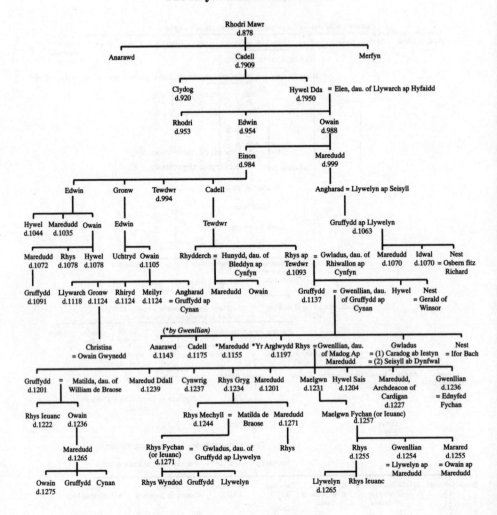

The Royal Line of Powys

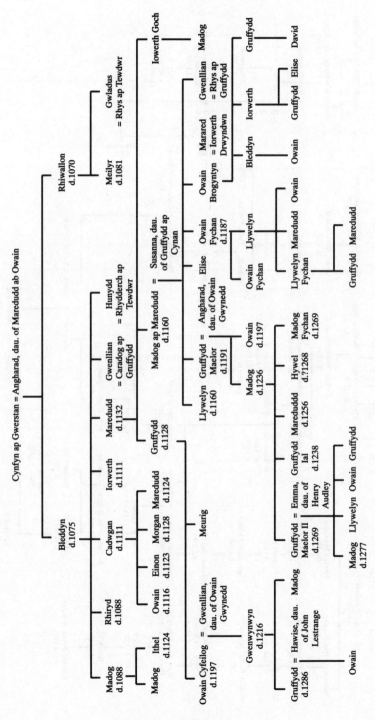

The Genealogical Triumph of Llywelyn the Great

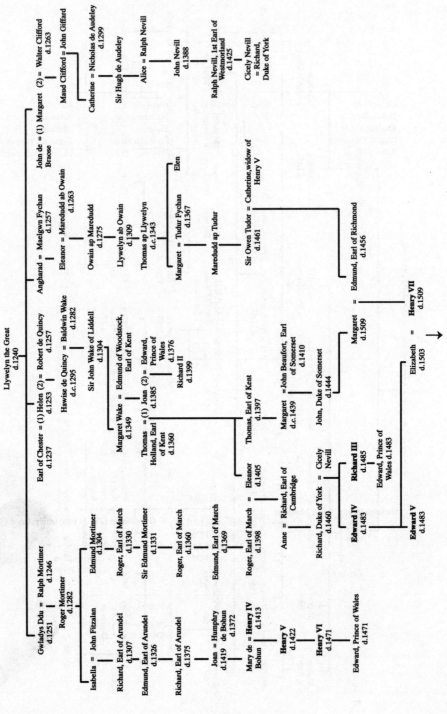

The Welsh Ancestry of Henry VII

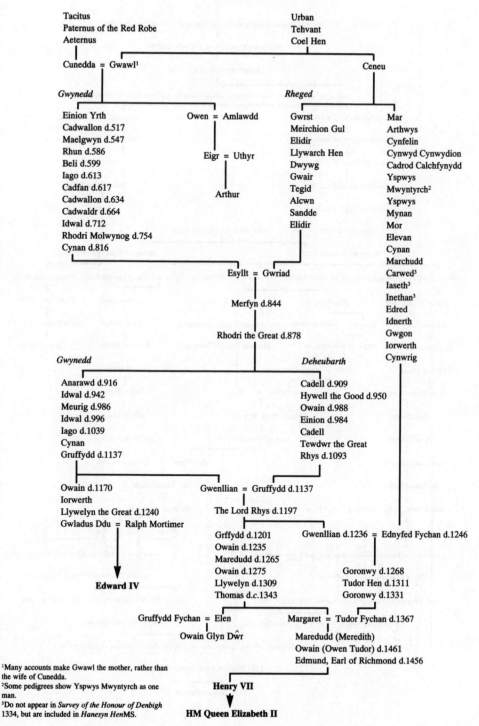

Tacitus
Paternus of the Red Robe
Aeternus

Urban
Tehvant
Coel Hen

Cunedda = Gwawl[1]

Ceneu

Gwynedd

Rheged

Einion Yrth
Cadwallon d.517
Maelgwyn d.547
Rhun d.586
Beli d.599
Iago d.613
Cadfan d.617
Cadwallon d.634
Cadwaldr d.664
Idwal d.712
Rhodri Molwynog d.754
Cynan d.816

Owen = Amlawdd

Eigr = Uthyr

Arthur

Gwrst
Meirchion Gul
Elidir
Llywarch Hen
Dwywg
Gwair
Tegid
Alcwn
Sandde
Elidir

Mar
Arthwys
Cynfelin
Cynwyd Cynwydion
Cadrod Calchfynydd
Yspwys
Mwyntyrch[2]
Yspwys
Mynan
Mor
Elevan
Cynan
Marchudd
Carwed[3]
Iaseth[3]
Inethan[3]
Edred
Idnerth
Gwgon
Iorwerth
Cynwrig

Esyllt = Gwriad

Merfyn d.844

Rhodri the Great d.878

Gwynedd

Deheubarth

Anarawd d.916
Idwal d.942
Meurig d.986
Idwal d.996
Iago d.1039
Cynan
Gruffydd d.1137

Cadell d.909
Hywell the Good d.950
Owain d.988
Einion d.984
Cadell
Tewdwr the Great
Rhys d.1093

Owain d.1170
Iorwerth
Llywelyn the Great d.1240
Gwladus Ddu = Ralph Mortimer

Gwenllian = Gruffydd d.1137

The Lord Rhys d.1197

Edward IV

Grffydd d.1201
Owain d.1235
Maredudd d.1265
Owain d.1275
Llywelyn d.1309
Thomas d.*c.*1343

Gwenllian d.1236 = Ednyfed Fychan d.1246

Goronwy d.1268
Tudor Hen d.1311
Goronwy d.1331

Gruffydd Fychan = Elen

Owain Glyn Dŵr

Margaret = Tudor Fychan d.1367

Maredudd (Meredith)
Owain (Owen Tudor) d.1461
Edmund, Earl of Richmond d.1456

[1]Many accounts make Gwawl the mother, rather than
the wife of Cunedda.
[2]Some pedigrees show Yspwys Mwyntyrch as one
man.
[3]Do not appear in *Survey of the Honour of Denbigh*
1334, but are included in *Hanesyn Hen*MS.

Henry VII

HM Queen Elizabeth II

Elizabeth II's Descent from the Dynasty of Powys and Owain Glyn Dŵr

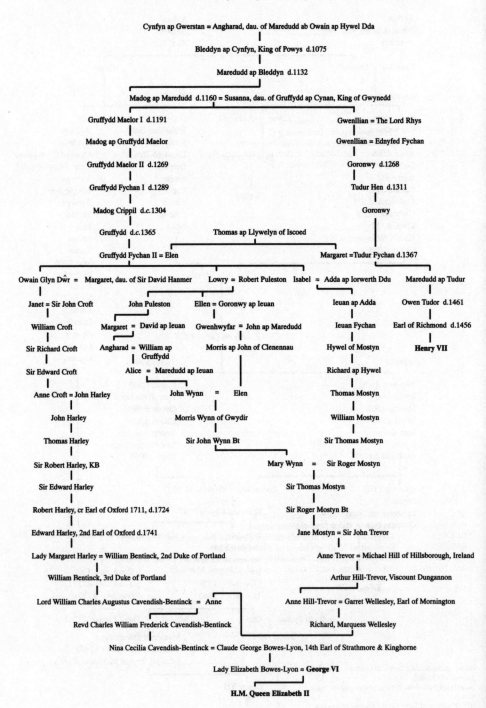

The High Kings of Ireland

The early dates and order of succession have been disputed

c.370–405	Niall of the Nine Hostages (King of Tara; traditional ancestor of claimants to the high kingship)
c.405–452	Nath Í mac Fiachrach (nephew of Niall)
452–463	Lóeguire (son of Niall)
463–482	Ailill Molt (son of Nath Í mac Fiachrach)
482–507	Lugaid (son of Lóeguire)
507–534	Muirchertaig I (great-grandson of Niall)
534–544	Tuathal Maelgarb (great-grandson of Niall)
544–565	Diarmait I (great-grandson of Niall)
565–566	Forggus (son of Muirchertaig I)
565–566	Domnall Ilchelgach (brother; co-regent)
566–569	Ainmire mac Sátnei (fourth in descent from Niall)
569–572	Báetán I (son of Muirchertaig I)
569–572	Eochaid (son of Domnall Ilchelgach; co-regent)
572–586	Báetán II mac Ninnedo (fourth in descent from Niall)
586–598	Áed (son of Ainmire)
598–604	Áed Sláine (son of Diarmait I)
598–604	Colmán Rímid (son of Báetán I; co-regent)
604–612	Áed Allán alias Áed Uaridnach (son of Domnall Ilchelgach)
612–615	Máel Cobo (son of Áed)
615–628	Suibne Menn mac Fiachnai (grandnephew of Muirchertaig I)
628–642	Domnall (son of Áed)
642–658	Cellach (son of Máel Cobo)
642–654	Conall Cáel (brother; co-regent)
658–665	Diarmait II (son of Áed Sláine)
658–665	Blathmac (brother; co-regent)
665–671	Sechnussach (son)
671–675	Cenn Fáelad (brother)
675–695	Fínsnechta Fledach mac Dúnchado (grandson of Áed Sláine)
695–704	Loingsech mac Óengusso (grandson of Domnall)
704–710	Congal Cennmagair (grandson of Domnall)
710–722	Fergal mac Máele Dúin (great-grandson of Áed Uaridnach)
722–724	Fogartach mac Néill (great-grandson of Diarmait II)
724–728	Cináed mac Írgalaig (fonrth in descent from Áed Sláine)
728–734	Flaithbertach (son of Loingsech; deposed, d.765)
734–743	Áed Allán (son of Fergal)
743–763	Domnall Midi mac Murchado (seventh in descent from Diarmait I)
763–770	Niall Frossach (son of Fergal; abdicated, d.778)
770–797	Donnchad Midi (son of Domnall Midi)
797–819	Áed Oirdnide (son of Niall Frossach)
819–833	Conchobar (son of Donnchad Midi)
833–846	Niall Caille (son of Áed Oirdnide)
846–862	Máelsechnaill I mac Máele Ruanaid (nephew of Conchobar)
862–879	Áed Findliath (son of Niall Caille)
879–916	Fiann Sinna (son of Máelsechnaill I)
916–919	Niall Glúndub (son of Áed Finliath)
919–944	Donnchad Donn (son of Fiann Sinna)
944–956	Congalach Cnogba mac Máelmithig (tenth in descent from Áed Sláine)
956–980	Domnall ua Néill (grandson of Niall Glúndub)
980–1002	Máelsechnaill II mac Domnaill (grandson of Donnchad Donn; deposed)
1002–1014	Brian Bóruma mac Cennétig (Dál Cais; King of Munster)
1014–1022	Máelsechnaill II mac Domnaill (restored; interregnum 1022–1072)
1072–1086	Tairrdelbach I (grandson of Brian Bóruma; King of Munster)
1086–1119	Muirchertach II (son)
1119–1121	Domnall ua Lochlainn (fourth in descent from Domnall ua Néill?; King of Ailech)
1121–1156	Tairrdelbach II (Ua Conchobair; King of Connact)
1156–1166	Muirchertaig III mac Lochlainn (grandson of Domnall ua Lochlainn)
1166–1186	Ruaidrí (son of Tairrdelbach II; deposed, d.1198)

After the deposition of the last High King the provincial and lesser regional kingships came under English domination.

Elizabeth II's Descent from Irish Kings

Ireland was divided into five main kingdoms, Ulster, Munster, Leinster, Connaught and Meath, each of which was again sub-divided into many petty kingdoms. A High King, or Supreme Monarch of Ireland, was elected from among the main kingdoms and inaugurated in an ancient ceremony on the hill of Tara. Brian Boru, King of Munster, became one of Ireland's greatest High Kings and was killed after the battle of Clontarf, in which he won a great victory over the Danes, in 1014. His descendants continued to reign as Kings of Munster until 1120 and thereafter as Kings of Thomond (North Munster) until they submitted to Henry VIII and were created Earls of Thomond, Barons of Inchiquin. King Henry II invaded Ireland in 1172 and was acknowledged as liege lord by the last native High King, Rory O'Connor, in 1175. The Kings of England then assumed the title of Lord of Ireland, which they bore until 1542, when Henry VIII changed the style to King by Act of Parliament.

Brian Boru, High King of Ireland 1002–1014

Tiege (Terence) d.1023 — Donnchad, King of Munster 1023–1064

Turlough, King of Munster 1064–1086 and High King of Ireland 1072–1086

Dearbforgail d.1080 = Dermot MacMailnamo, King of Leinster and High King of Ireland d.1072

Dermot, King of Munster 1116–1120 — Murchad, King of Leinster d.1090

Turlough, King of Thomond 1142–1167 — Donchad, King of Leinster d.1115

Enna, King of Leinster d.1126

Dermot MacMurrough, King of Leinster d.1171

Donnell More, King of Thomond d.1194 — Aoife (Eva) = Richard (Strongbow), Earl of Pembroke

Donough Cairbreach, King of Thomond 1239–1242 — Isabel = William Marshal, Earl of Pembroke

Conor Na Suidane, King of Thomond 1242–1258 — Eva = William de Braose

Tiege Caeluisce, King of Thomond — Maud = Roger Mortimer

Turlough, King of Thomond d.1306 — Edmund Mortimer, 1st Lord Mortimer

Mortogh, King of Thomond 1307–1343 — Roger Mortimer, 1st Earl of March

Mahon Moinmoy, King of Thomond 1343–1369 — Sir Edmund Mortimer

Brian Catha An Eanaigh, King of Thomond 1370–1399 — Roger Mortimer, 2nd Earl of March

Turlough Bog (the Soft), King of Thomond 1446–1459 — Edmund Mortimer, 3rd Earl of March d.1382

Teige An Chomard, King of Thomond 1461–1466 — Roger Mortimer, 4th Earl of March d.1398

Turlough Don, King of Thomond 1499–1528 — Lady Anne Mortimer = Richard, Earl of Cambridge

Murrough, last King of Thomond 1540–1543, 1st Earl of Thomond and Lord Inchiquin d.1551 — Richard, Duke of York

Dermod O'Brien, 2nd Lord Inchiquin d.1557 — **Edward IV**

Murrough O'Brien, 3rd Lord Inchiquin d.1573 — Elizabeth of York = **Henry VII**

Murrough O'Brien, 4th Lord Inchiquin d.1597 — Margaret = **James IV**, King of Scots

Dermot O'Brien, 5th Lord Inchiquin d.1624 — **James V**, King of Scots

Mary O'Brien = Dr. Michael Boyle, Archbishop of Armagh — **Mary**, Queen of Scots = Henry Lord Darnley

Eleanor Boyle = William Hill — **James VI of Scotland & I of England**

Michael Hill of Hillsborough, Ireland — Elizabeth = Frederick, King of Bohemia

Arthur Hill-Trevor, Viscount Dungannon — Sophia = Ernest Augustus, Elector of Hanover

Anne Hill-Trevor = Garret Wellesley, Earl of Mornington — **George I**

Richard, Marquess Wellesley — **George II**

Anne = Lord William Charles Augustus Cavendish-Bentinck d.1826 — Frederick, Prince of Wales

Revd Charles William Frederick Cavendish-Bentinck — **George III**

Nina Cecilia Cavendish-Bentinck = Claude George Bowes-Lyon, 14th Earl of Strathmore & Kinghorne — Edward, Duke of Kent

Victoria = Albert of Saxe-Coburg & Gotha (Prince Consort)

Edward VII

George V

Lady Elizabeth Bowes-Lyon = **George VI**

H.M. Queen Elizabeth II

APPENDIX XXXV

Coronations before the Norman Conquest

There are few specific references to coronations or inauguration rites of the early Anglo-Saxon kings, but the kings of Wessex were installed on the ancient Kings' Stone, which still stands near the parish church at Kingston-upon-Thames, Surrey.

Date of coronation	Person crowned	Place of coronation	Prelate or other officiant
?871	Alfred the Great	Kingston or Winchester	?Ethelred, Archbishop of Canterbury
8 June 900	Edward the Elder	Kingston	Plegmund, Archbishop of Canterbury
5 Sept. 925	Athelstan	Kingston	?Wulfhelm, Archbishop of Canterbury
16 Nov. 940	Edmund I	Kingston	Oda, Archbishop of Canterbury
? Jan. 956	Edwy	Kingston	Oda, Archbishop of Canterbury
11 May 973	Edgar and Elfrida	Bath Abbey	Dunstan, Archbishop of Canterbury, and Oswald, Archbishop of York
? July 975	Edward the Martyr	Kingston	Dunstan, Archbishop of Canterbury
14 April 979	Ethelred II	Kingston	Dunstan, Archbishop of Canterbury
?April 1016	Edmund II Ironside	St Paul's Cathedral	Lyfing, Archbishop of Canterbury
6 Jan. 1017	Canute	St Paul's Cathedral	?
? 1037	Harold I Harefoot	Oxford	?
18 June 1040	Hardicanute	Canterbury	Eadsige, Archbishop of Canterbury
3 April 1043	Edward the Confessor	Winchester Cathedral	Eadsige, Archbishop of Canterbury, and Ethelric, Archbishop of York
? Jan. 1045	Edith (wife of Edward) the Confessor	Winchester Cathedral	Eadsige, Archbishop of Canterbury
6 Jan. 1066	Harold II	Westminster Abbey	Stigand, Archbishop of Canterbury

Coronations since the Norman Conquest

Date of coronation	Person crowned	Place of coronation	Prelate or other officiant
25 Dec. 1066	William I the Conqueror	Westminster Abbey	Ealdred, Archbishop of York
11 May 1068	Matilda of Flanders (wife of William I)	Winchester Cathedral	Ealdred, Archbishop of York
26 Sept. 1087	William II Rufus	Westminster Abbey	Lanfranc, Archbishop of Canterbury
5 Aug. 1100	Henry I	Westminster Abbey	Maurice, Bishop of London
11 Nov. 1100	Matilda of Scotland (1st wife of Henry I)	Westminster Abbey	Anselm, Archbishop of Canterbury
3 Feb. 1122	Adeliza of Louvain (2nd wife of Henry I)	Westminster Abbey	Ralph d'Escures, Archbishop of Canterbury
26 Dec. 1135	Stephen	Westminster Abbey	William de Corbeil, Archbishop of Canterbury
22 March 1136	Matilda of Boulogne (wife of Stephen)	Westminster Abbey	William de Corbeil, Archbishop of Canterbury
25 Dec. 1141	Stephen said to have been recrowned		
19 Dec. 1154	Henry II	Westminster Abbey	Theobald, Archbishop of Canterbury
25 Dec. 1158	Eleanor of Aquitaine (wife of Henry II)	Worcester Cathedral	Theobald, Archbishop of Canterbury
14 June 1170	Henry 'the Young King' (son and heir of Henry II)	Westminster Abbey	Roger of Pont l'Eveque, Archbishop of Canterbury
27 Aug. 1172	Henry 'the Young King' recrowned with his wife Margaret of France	Winchester Cathedral	Rotrou, Archbishop of Rouen
3 Sept. 1189	Richard I	Westminster Abbey	Baldwin, Archbishop of Canterbury
12 May 1191	Berengaria of Navarre (wife of Richard I)	Chapel of St George, Limasol, Cyprus	John FitzLuke, Bishop of Evreux
27 May 1199	John	Westminster Abbey	Hubert Walter, Archbishop of Canterbury
8 Oct. 1200	Isabella of Angoulême (wife of John)	Westminster Abbey	Hubert Walter, Archbishop of Canterbury
28 Oct. 1216	Henry III	Gloucester Cathedral	Peter des Roches, Bishop of Winchester
17 May 1220	Henry III (recrowned)	Westminster Abbey	Stephen Langton, Archbishop of Canterbury
20 Jan. 1236	Eleanor of Provence (wife of Henry III)	Westminster Abbey	Edmund Rich, Archbishop of Canterbury
19 Aug. 1274	Edward I and Eleanor of Castile	Westminster Abbey	Edward Kilwardby, Archbishop of Canterbury
25 Feb. 1308	Edward II and Isabella of France	Westminster Abbey	Henry Merewell (alias Woodlock), Bishop of Winchester
1/2 Feb. 1327	Edward III	Westminster Abbey	Walter Reynolds, Archbishop of Canterbury
20 Feb. 1328	Philippa of Hainault (wife of Edward III)	Westminster Abbey	Simon Meopham, Archbishop of Canterbury
16 July 1377	Richard II	Westminster Abbey	Simon Sudbury, Archbishop of Canterbury
22 Jan. 1382	Anne of Bohemia (1st wife of Richard II)	Westminster Abbey	William Courtenay, Archbishop of Canterbury
8 Jan. 1397	Isabella of France (2nd wife of Richard II)	Westminster Abbey	Thomas Arundel, Archbishop of Canterbury
13 Oct. 1399	Henry IV	Westminster Abbey	Thomas Arundel, Archbishop of Canterbury
26 Feb. 1403	Joan of Navarre (2nd wife of Henry IV)	Westminster Abbey	Thomas Arundel, Archbishop of Canterbury

9 April 1413	Henry V	Westminster Abbey	Thomas Arundel, Archbishop of Canterbury
24 Feb. 1421	Catherine of France (wife of Henry V)	Westminster Abbey	Henry Chichele, Archbishop of Canterbury
6 Nov. 1429	Henry VI	Westminster Abbey	Henry Chichele, Archbishop of Canterbury
30 May 1445	Margaret of Anjou (wife of Henry VI)	Westminster Abbey	John Stafford, Archbishop of Canterbury
29 June 1461	Edward IV	Westminster Abbey	Cardinal Bourchier, Archbishop of Canterbury
26 May 1465	Elizabeth Woodville (wife of Edward IV)	Westminster Abbey	Cardinal Bourchier, Archbishop of Canterbury
6 July 1483	Richard III and Anne Neville	Westminster Abbey	Cardinal Bourchier, Archbishop of Canterbury
30 Oct. 1485	Henry VII	Westminster Abbey	Cardinal Bourchier, Archbishop of Canterbury
24 Nov. 1487	Elizabeth of York (wife of Henry VII)	Westminster Abbey	John Morton, Archbishop of Canterbury
24 June 1509	Henry VIII and Catherine of Aragon	Westminster Abbey	William Warham, Archbishop of Canterbury
1 June 1533	Anne Boleyn (2nd wife of Henry VIII)	Westminster Abbey	Thomas Cranmer, Archbishop of Canterbury
20 Feb. 1547	Edward VI	Westminster Abbey	Thomas Cranmer, Archbishop of Canterbury
1 Oct. 1553	Mary I	Westminster Abbey	Stephen Gardiner, Bishop of Winchester
15 Jan. 1559	Elizabeth I	Westminster Abbey	Owen Oglethorpe, Bishop of Carlisle
25 July 1603	James I and Anne of Denmark	Westminster Abbey	John Whitgift, Archbishop of Canterbury
2 Feb. 1626	Charles I	Westminster Abbey	George Abbot, Archbishop of Canterbury
23 April 1661	Charles II	Westminster Abbey	William Juxon, Archbishop of Canterbury
23 April 1685	James II and Mary of Modena	Westminster Abbey	William Sancroft, Archbishop of Canterbury
11 April 1689	William III and Mary II (joint sovereigns)	Westminster Abbey	Henry Compton, Bishop of London
23 April 1702	Anne	Westminster Abbey	Thomas Tenison, Archbishop of Canterbury
20 Oct. 1714	George I	Westminster Abbey	Thomas Tenison, Archbishop of Canterbury
11 Oct. 1727	George II and Caroline of Brandenburg-Ansbach	Westminster Abbey	William Wake, Archbishop of Canterbury
22 Sept. 1761	George III and Charlotte of Mecklenburg-Strelitz	Westminster Abbey	Thomas Secker, Archbishop of Canterbury
19 July 1821	George IV	Westminster Abbey	Charles Manners Sutton, Archbishop of Canterbury
8 Sept. 1831	William IV and Adelaide of Saxe-Meiningen	Westminster Abbey	William Howley, Archbishop of Canterbury
28 June 1838	Victoria	Westminster Abbey	William Howley, Archbishop of Canterbury
9 Aug. 1902	Edward VII and Alexandra of Denmark	Westminster Abbey	Frederick Temple, Archbishop of Canterbury, and William Dalrymple Maclagan, Archbishop of York
22 June 1911	George V and Mary of Teck	Westminster Abbey	Randall Thomas Davidson, Archbishop of Canterbury
12 May 1937	George VI and Elizabeth Bowes-Lyon	Westminster Abbey	Cosmo Gordon Lang, Archbishop of Canterbury
2 June 1953	Elizabeth II	Westminster Abbey	Geoffrey Francis Fisher, Archbishop of Canterbury

Scottish Coronations

From a very early period the Scottish kings were crowned or installed at Scone, taking their seat upon the 'Stone of Destiny' which Fergus Mor MacErc is said to have brought with him from Ireland towards the end of the fourth century. There are no detailed records of Scottish coronations before that of Malcolm III.

Date of coronation	Person crowned	Place of coronation	Prelate or other officiant
25 April 1058	Malcolm III	Scone	?
? Nov. 1093	Donald Bane	Scone	?
? May 1094	Duncan II	Scone	?
? 1097	Edgar	Scone	?
? Jan. 1107	Alexander I	Scone	?
? May 1124	David I	Scone	?
Summer 1153	Malcolm IV	Scone	?
24 Dec. 1165	William the Lion	Scone	Richard, Bishop of St Andrews
6 Dec. 1214	Alexander II	Scone	William Malvoisine, Bishop of St Andrews
13 July 1249	Alexander III	Scone	David de Bernham, Bishop of St Andrews
30 Nov. 1292	John Balliol	Scone	?
27 March 1306	Robert I	Scone	Isabella, Countess of Buchan
24 Nov. 1331	David II and Joan of England	Scone	James Bennet, Bishop of St Andrews
24 Sept. 1332	Edward Balliol	Scone	?
26 March 1371	Robert II	Scone	William de Laundels, Bishop of St Andrews
? 1372	Euphemia Ross (2nd wife of Robert II)	Scone	Alexander de Kyninmund II, Bishop of Aberdeen
14 Aug. 1390	Robert III and Annabella Drummond	Scone	Walter Trail, Bishop of St Andrews
21 May 1424	James I and Joan Beaufort	Scone	Henry Wardlaw, Bishop of St Andrews
25 March 1437	James II	Holyrood	Michael Ochiltree, Bishop of Dunblane
3 July 1449	Mary of Gueldres (wife of James II)	Holyrood	James Kennedy, Bishop of St Andrews
10 Aug. 1460	James III	Kelso Abbey	James Kennedy, Bishop of St Andrews
13 July 1469	Margaret of Denmark (wife of James III)	Holyrood	Patrick Graham, Archbishop of St Andrews
26 June 1488	James IV	Scone	William Scheves, Archbishop of St Andrews
8 Aug. 1503	Margaret Tudor (wife of James IV)	Holyrood	?
21 Sept. 1513	James V	Stirling	?
22 Feb. 1540	Mary of Guise (2nd wife of James V)	Holyrood	Cardinal Beaton, Archbishop of St Andrews
9 Sept. 1543	Mary	Stirling	Cardinal Beaton, Archbishop of St Andrews
29 July 1567	James VI	Stirling	Adam Bothwell, Bishop of Orkney
17 May 1590	Anne of Denmark (wife of James VI)	Holyrood	David Lindsay, the King's Chaplain, later Bishop of Ross, and Sir John Maitland, Lord Thirlestone, Chancellor of Scotland
18 June 1633	Charles I	Edinburgh	John Spottiswoode, Archbishop of St Andrews
1 Jan. 1651	Charles II	Scone	Archibald Campbell, Marquess of Argyll

The titular King James VIII is said to have been crowned at Scone in Sept. 1715, but no details of the ceremony have been preserved.